Fx. 3277
S87-3277
sponsor Ackild
423-4200
Curtis
279-3669

CASES AND MATERIALS ON
THE LAW OF SENTENCING, CORRECTIONS AND PRISONERS' RIGHTS

Fourth Edition

By

Sheldon Krantz
Visiting Professor of Law
American University, Washington College of Law

and

Lynn S. Branham
Associate Professor of Law
Thomas M. Cooley School of Law

AMERICAN CASEBOOK SERIES®

WEST PUBLISHING CO.
ST. PAUL, MINN., 1991

COPYRIGHT © 1973, 1981, 1986 WEST PUBLISHING CO.
COPYRIGHT © 1991 By WEST PUBLISHING CO.
            610 Opperman Drive
            P.O. Box 64526
            St. Paul, MN 55164–0526

Library of Congress Cataloging-in-Publication Data

Krantz, Sheldon, 1938–
    Cases and the materials on the law of corrections and prisoners'
rights / by Sheldon Krantz and Lynn S. Branham. — 4th ed.
        p.   cm. — (American casebook series)

    Includes index.
    ISBN 0-314-78585-X
    1. Correctional law—United States—Cases. 2. Prisoners—legal
status, laws, etc.—United States—Cases. I. Branham, Lynn S.,
1955–   . II. Law of corrections and prisoners' rights.
III. Title. IV. Series.
KF9728.A7K7 1991
345.73'077—dc20
[347.30577]   90–12923
                                                        CIP

ISBN 0-314-78585-X

 *TEXT IS PRINTED ON 10% POST CONSUMER RECYCLED PAPER*

(K. & B.) Law of Corrections, 4th Ed. ACB
1st Reprint—1995

*Dedicated
to
the memories of
Edith and Abe*

–Sheldon Krantz

————

*Dedicated
to
my husband
Bruce
with gratitude
and love*

–Lynn Branham

*

Preface

In 1973, when the First Edition of this casebook was written, the law of corrections and prisoners' rights was in an embryonic state. Courts showed little interest in the conditions of prisons or the rights of prisoners until the late 1960s. Further, sustained scholarly criticism of the nation's sentencing, plea bargaining and parole practices did not begin until the early 1970s. In addition, prior to 1973, there had been few occasions for the United States Supreme Court to define the relationship of the Federal Bill of Rights to convicted offenders or pretrial detainees.

Because the field was in such an early stage of development, the First Edition devoted as much attention to speculating on future needs as it did to then existing caselaw and legislation. Much happened between the publication of that edition and the Second Edition in 1980. Many trial judges, most of them in the federal system operating under the authority of the Federal Civil Rights Act, acted aggressively and with courage to attempt to eliminate abusive practices and conditions in many of our nation's prisons and jails. Some judges even ordered institutions to be closed down entirely. The public, during the 1970s, finally began to learn about and to understand the dangers of unbridled discretion in sentencing and parole decisions. Suddenly, corrections became an important public concern. The Uniform State Law Commissioners were commissioned to and did draft a Model Sentencing and Corrections Act. The American Bar Association created a Commission to draft standards on the legal status of prisoners. Congress and state legislatures began to focus attention on correctional issues. Substantial federal funding was made available under federal crime control legislation to improve the "correctional system."

And yet, by 1980 not much had really happened. Most prisons and jails in this country were as dreadful, if not worse, than they were before the correctional movement began in the late 1960s. The prison population was at an all-time high. Conditions within institutions continued to be degrading and inhumane despite court orders that mandated improvements. Federal and state appellate courts and the United States Supreme Court constantly reversed the more liberal constitutional interpretations of prisoners' rights rendered by many trial judges. Legislative proposals to reform sentencing and parole practices typically did not get beyond the proposal stage. The correctional reform movement at the beginning of the 1980s was in shambles and the public seemed to care little about correctional reform and about the plight of convicted offenders or those charged with crime.

That did change. There has been an explosion in legislative activity in corrections since the Second and Third Editions were published in the early and mid–1980s. During that time, for example, both Congress and many state legislatures replaced broad judicial sentencing discretion with mandatory, determinate or presumptive sentencing schemes. And with each passing year, legislative bodies have sharply increased the numbers of prison terms which qualify for mandatory minimum sentences and the length of those terms. Whereas this pattern used to apply only to violent "street crimes" and drug offenses, it has now been extended into areas such as white collar crime. New approaches have also been taken to require restitution to victims of crime by convicted offenders.

The last decade has been a period when punishment has become an accepted objective of sentencing and rehabilitation has become a more discredited one. Further, judicial decisions continue to follow the trends of the 1970s in being cautious in defining prisoners' rights and in being expansive in delegating discretionary authority to prison officials.

Even with the great reluctance of courts to interfere with the management of prisoners, a majority of state prison systems remain under federal and state court orders to alleviate shocking conditions. The escalation of the prison and jail population continues to outstrip capacity, due in part to the new "legislative reforms." Convicted offenders and detainees are being stacked like cordwood in inadequate facilities with little to do. Most informed observers acknowledge that our nation's prisons and jails are festering cesspools. Some experiments are being proposed or tried to reduce prison populations or to expand capacity. These include electronically-monitored home incarceration, boot camps, new forms of community-based corrections, day fines, and the sharing of some prison responsibility with private enterprise. This new legislative activity, the continuing deplorable nature of prison and jail facilities, the emergence of new issues such as the HIV-positive prisoner epidemic and victims' involvement in the sentencing process, and proposed new innovations in corrections have required significant changes and additions in this Edition.

This Fourth Edition was almost entirely the work of my new co-author, Professor Lynn S. Branham of the Thomas M. Cooley School of Law. Professor Branham is currently the Chair of the ABA Criminal Justice Section Committee on Prison and Jail Problems, a member of the Commission on Accreditation for Corrections, and a noted authority in the corrections field.

The underlying premise of the earlier editions remains the same for this one. There are no easy solutions for the overwhelming problems facing the correctional field, and greater interest and involvement by the legal profession alone will not guarantee constructive and basic reform. It remains unlikely, however, that essential reform and informed public policy debate can occur without a commitment to it by the legal profession. The encouragement of such a commitment is a primary goal of this casebook.

Although the organization of the Fourth Edition remains similar to that of former editions, there are notable differences. Given the significant developments in sentencing since the last edition, far more attention has been devoted to this field. Sufficient material has now been provided for the areas of sentencing and prisoners' rights to allow law teachers to deal with them as separate course areas if they choose to do so. Those wanting to teach a sentencing course only may want to supplement the casebook with the Federal Sentencing Guidelines materials published in paperback by West Publishing Company.

To a certain extent, aside from the legislative materials on sentencing, the Fourth Edition relies heavily on constitutional law materials and priority is given to the applicability of various constitutional guarantees to the correctional process. The casebook, however, goes well beyond constitutional issues in all areas, for it is obvious that there are severe limitations in using federal and state constitutions to remedy many of the deficiencies in corrections. Thus, issues relating more broadly to law reform and public policy are addressed as well. In addition, the casebook focuses upon the problem of remedies since little is gained in identifying rights and obligations unless appropriate and effective means exist to enforce them.

In view of the weaknesses of most existing remedies and of most of the current legal approaches to correctional problems, extensive notes and questions, lower court decisions and model proposals from groups such as the American Bar Association and the Uniform State Law Commissioners, have been included to stimulate discussion beyond understanding the existing state of the law. To sharpen skills training, the chapter on litigating Section 1983 suits has been updated, new simulation problems have been added, and material from sources such as actual presentence investigation reports have been incorporated.

Within the book, we have omitted footnotes of the courts and of secondary materials without so specifying. When the footnotes are included, the numbers from the original sources have been retained. All letter footnotes reflect material from the authors.

Appreciation is extended to all publishers and authors for permission to reprint from the books and articles that we have included herein. We would also like to thank librarian Marla Major for her invaluable assistance in locating materials needed to prepare this book, Roxanne Fandel and Mary Beth Peranteau for their patience and skill in typing this book, and Francis Peterson for his painstaking efforts to ensure that the citations in this book are accurate. Finally, much of the inspiration for preparing this casebook and its previous editions has come from knowing and working with those in the correctional field who labor constantly for reform, who often suffer for their efforts, but who never give up.

SHELDON KRANTZ

Washington, D.C.
August, 1990

Summary of Contents

Table of Contents

PART ONE. THE LAW OF SENTENCING

*

Table of Cases

The principal cases are in bold type. Cases cited or discussed in the text are roman type. References are to pages. Cases cited in principal cases and within other quoted materials are not included.

*

CASES AND MATERIALS ON

THE LAW OF SENTENCING, CORRECTIONS AND PRISONERS' RIGHTS

Fourth Edition

*

Part One

THE LAW OF SENTENCING

Chapter 1

INTRODUCTION TO SENTENCING

Winston Churchill once said that "[t]he mood and temper of the public with regard to the treatment of crime and criminals is one of the most unfailing tests of the civilization of any country." M. Frankel, Criminal Sentences 9 (1973). We must at times, therefore, stop and ask ourselves, "How civilized is our country's system of punishing criminals? And from a practical perspective, how effective are our efforts to punish and control crime?"

It is obvious when comparing the punishment system of today in our country with the modes of punishment employed in earlier years that punishment practices have changed. In colonial times, for example, individuals who had committed such offenses as not observing the Sabbath and being in the company of drunkards often had their legs immobilized in stocks which were then placed out in public. Pillories, wooden frames used to immobilize individuals' heads and hands, were also often used as a form of punishment, and as an added touch, offenders sometimes had their ears nailed to the wood on either side of the holes through which their heads were stuck. Members of the community then often gathered at the site of stocks and pillories to ridicule the hapless offenders and throw objects such as stale eggs, potatoes, and excrement at them.

Public humiliation was a common element of other types of punishment as well. Offenders were often required to wear letters sewn on their clothes or branded on their bodies, publicizing their malefactions. An "A" signified that an individual had committed adultery, a "B" that the individual had uttered blasphemous words, and a "D" that the individual had been drunk.

During these times, women, particularly women who scolded their husbands, were often singled out for punishment. A type of stick which pinched the tongue was sometimes placed on the tongue of a scolding wife, or the wife was sometimes placed in a ducking stool and then immersed in water. The ducking stool was used for other pur-

2

poses as well. Sometimes, for example, married couples who quarreled too much or too loudly were tied back to back and ducked together.

Whipping was also a popular form of punishment during the early years of this country, one employed for such offenses as stealing a loaf of bread, lying, and name-calling. And other forms of physical punishment were common as well. Offenders sometimes had their ears cut off, their nostrils slit, a hole bored through their tongues, or their cheeks, foreheads, or other parts of their bodies branded as punishment for an assortment of crimes. For more information on punishment in the earlier years of this country, see A. Earle, Curious Punishments of Bygone Days (1968).

Penitentiaries came into use in this country in the late 1700s as part of a reform movement designed to alleviate the harshness of some of the forms of punishment described above. Penitentiaries were viewed, as their name suggests, as places where offenders could contemplate the error of their ways, become penitent, and seek God's forgiveness for their sins. This reform process, it was felt, could be accomplished through a regimen of compulsory Bible reading and enforced silence to protect prisoners from bad influences exerted by other prisoners. American Correctional Association, The American Prison: From the Beginning 31, 44, 46 (1983).

We have now moved into another punishment phase in this country. Although prisons today are hardly characterized by pervasive silence and Bible reading, imprisonment is still a popular form of punishment in the United States. In fact, the *per capita* imprisonment rate in this country is reportedly higher than in any other industrialized country in the world except the Soviet Union and South Africa. Oversight Hearings Before the Subcomm. on Courts, Civil Liberties, and the Administration of Justice of the House Comm. on the Judiciary, 98th Cong., 1st Sess. 32 (1983) (statement of Alvin J. Bronstein). And the use of imprisonment is increasing at an astronomic rate, straining prison resources and government budgets. See, e.g., Bureau of Justice Statistics, U.S. Dep't of Justice, Prisoners in 1989 1 (1990) (reporting a 115% increase in the number of prisoners between 1980 and 1989 and a rise in the *per capita* imprisonment rate from 139 prisoners per every 100,000 residents in 1980 to 274 per every 100,000 residents in 1989).

At the same time, however, probation is widely imposed in the United States as a criminal sanction, far more frequently than imprisonment. Compare Id. 2 (710,054 prisoners incarcerated in 1989) with Bureau of Justice Statistics, U.S. Dep't of Justice, Probation and Parole 1988 1 (1989) (2,356,483 offenders on probation in 1988). In addition, other nonincarcerative sanctions, such as fines, restitution, community service, and home confinement, are being used with increasing frequency as criminal justice policymakers and participants strive to find and impose the most appropriate criminal sanctions under the circumstances, sanctions that are neither overly lenient nor overly punitive.

In assessing the soundness and efficacy of the present criminal punishment system in this country and in determining whether it is, as it purports to be, a criminal "justice" system, a number of questions must be addressed, including the following. First, for what purpose or purposes is punishment to be imposed? Second, what types of conduct should be subject to criminal sanctions? Third, what form or forms of punishment should be employed as criminal sanctions? Fourth, what constraints should be placed on the use of these sanctions in terms of amount, duration, and other conditions? And fifth, what steps should be taken to ensure that an appropriate penalty is imposed on a particular individual? After answering all of these questions, a sixth question must then be addressed: are we willing to pay the costs of the criminal justice system we are contemplating? For if we are not, then it is time to reexamine our answers concerning the direction to be taken by our nation's criminal justice system.

Set forth below is an excerpt from Criminal Law by Wayne LaFave and Austin Scott, Jr., discussing the first question described above—what are the purposes of punishment. Then follows a case, United States v. Bergman, 416 F.Supp. 496 (S.D.N.Y.1976), in which the court considered these purposes in deciding the appropriate penalty to impose on a defendant.

WAYNE R. LaFAVE & AUSTIN W. SCOTT, JR., CRIMINAL LAW 22–29 (2d ed. 1986)
Reprinted with the permission of the West Publishing Company.

PURPOSES OF THE CRIMINAL LAW—THEORIES OF PUNISHMENT

The broad purposes of the criminal law are, of course, to make people do what society regards as desirable and to prevent them from doing what society considers to be undesirable. Since criminal law is framed in terms of imposing punishment for bad conduct, rather than of granting rewards for good conduct, the emphasis is more on the prevention of the undesirable than on the encouragement of the desirable.

In determining what undesirable conduct should be punished, the criminal law properly aims more to achieve a minimum standard of conduct than to bring about ideal conduct (say, the conduct of a highly-principled, selfless, heroic person). It is a fine thing for a man, at the risk of his own life, to enter a blazing building in order to rescue a stranger trapped therein; but the law does not (and should not) punish a failure to live up to such a heroic standard of behavior. It is a virtuous thing for an engaged man and woman to refrain from engaging in sexual intercourse until they are married; but it does not follow that the law should punish a failure to adhere to such a highly moral standard of conduct.

* * *

The criminal law is not, of course, the only weapon which society uses to prevent conduct which harms or threatens to harm these important interests of the public. Education, at home and at school, as to the types of conduct that society thinks good and bad, is an important weapon; religion, with its emphasis on distinguishing between good and evil conduct, is another. The human desire to acquire and keep the affection and respect of family, friends and associates no doubt has a great influence in deterring most people from conduct which is socially unacceptable. The civil side of the law, which forces one to pay damages for the harmful results which his undesirable conduct has caused to others, or which in appropriate situations grants injunctions against bad conduct or orders the specific performance of good conduct, also plays a part in influencing behavior along desirable lines.

(a) Theories of Punishment. How does the criminal law, with its threat of punishment to violators, operate to influence human conduct away from the undesirable and toward the desirable? There are a number of theories of punishment, and each theory has or has had its enthusiastic adherents. Some of the theories are concerned primarily with the particular offender, while others focus more on the nature of the offense and the general public. These theories are:

(1) Prevention. By this theory, also called *intimidation,* or, when the deterrence theory is referred to as general deterrence, *particular deterrence,* criminal punishment aims to deter the criminal himself (rather than to deter others) from committing further crimes, by giving him an unpleasant experience he will not want to endure again. The validity of this theory has been questioned by many, who point out the high recidivism rates of those who have been punished. On the other hand, it has been observed that our attempts at prevention by punishment may enjoy an unmeasurable degree of success, in that without punishment for purposes of prevention the rate of recidivism might be much higher. This assumption is not capable of precise proof, nor is the assertion that in some instances punishment for prevention will fill the prisoner with feelings of hatred and desire for revenge against society and thus influence future criminal conduct.

(2) Restraint. The notion here, also expressed as *incapacitation, isolation,* or *disablement,* is that society may protect itself from persons deemed dangerous because of their past criminal conduct by isolating these persons from society. If the criminal is imprisoned or executed, he cannot commit further crimes against society. Some question this theory because of doubts that those who present a danger of continuing criminality can be accurately identified. It has also been noted that resort to restraint without accompanying rehabilitative efforts is unwise, as the vast majority of prisoners will ultimately be returned to society. The restraint theory is sometimes employed to justify execution or life imprisonment without chance of parole for those offenders believed to be beyond rehabilitation.

(3) Rehabilitation. Under this theory, also called *correction* or *reformation,* we "punish" the convicted criminal by giving him appropriate treatment, in order to rehabilitate him and return him to society so reformed that he will not desire or need to commit further crimes. It is perhaps not entirely correct to call this treatment "punishment," as the emphasis is away from making him suffer and in the direction of making his life better and more pleasant. The rehabilitation theory rests upon the belief that human behavior is the product of antecedent causes, that these causes can be identified, and that on this basis therapeutic measures can be employed to effect changes in the behavior of the person treated.

* * *

(4) Deterrence. Under this theory, sometimes referred to as *general prevention,* the sufferings of the criminal for the crime he has committed are supposed to deter others from committing future crimes, lest they suffer the same unfortunate fate. The extent to which punishment actually has this effect upon the general public is unclear; conclusive empirical research on the subject is lacking, and it is difficult to measure the effectiveness of fear of punishment because it is but one of several forces that restrain people from violating the law.

It does seem fair to assume, however, that the deterrent efficacy of punishment varies considerably, depending upon a number of factors. Those who commit crimes under emotional stress (such as murder in the heat of anger) or who have become expert criminals through the training and practice of many years (such as the professional safebreaker and pickpocket) are less likely than others to be deterred. Even apart from the nature of the crime, individuals undoubtedly react differently to the threat of punishment, depending upon such factors as their social class, age, intelligence, and moral training. The magnitude of the threatened punishment is clearly a factor, but perhaps not as important a consideration as the probability of discovery and punishment.

(5) Education. Under this theory, criminal punishment serves, by the publicity which attends the trial, conviction and punishment of criminals, to educate the public as to the proper distinctions between good conduct and bad—distinctions which, when known, most of society will observe. While the public may need no such education as to serious *malum in se* crimes, the educational function of punishment is important as to crimes which are not generally known, often misunderstood, or inconsistent with current morality.

(6) Retribution. This is the oldest theory of punishment, and the one which still commands considerable respect from the general public. By this theory, also called *revenge* or *retaliation,* punishment (the infliction of suffering) is imposed by society on criminals in order to obtain revenge, or perhaps (under the less emotional concept of retribution) because it is only fitting and just that one who has caused harm to

others should himself suffer for it. Typical of the criticism is that this theory "is a form of retaliation, and as such, is morally indefensible."

However, the retribution theory, when explained on somewhat different grounds, continues to draw some support. Some contend that when one commits a crime, it is important that he receive commensurate punishment in order to restore the peace of mind and repress the criminal tendencies of others. In addition, it is claimed that retributive punishment is needed to maintain respect for the law and to suppress acts of private vengeance. For this reason, even some critics of the retribution theory acknowledge that it must occupy a "minor position" in the contemporary scheme.

Although retribution was long the theory of punishment least accepted by theorists, it "is suddenly being seen by thinkers of all political persuasions as perhaps the strongest ground, after all, upon which to base a system of punishment." Today it is commonly put forward under the rubric of "deserts" or "just deserts".

> The offender may justly be subjected to certain deprivations because he deserves it; and he deserves it because he has engaged in wrongful conduct—conduct that does or threatens injury and that is prohibited by law. The penalty is thus not just a means of crime prevention but a merited response to the actor's deed, "rectifying the balance" in the Kantian sense and expressing moral reprobation of the actor for the wrong.[43]

Those who favor the theory claim it "provides an important check against tyranny, for a person is punished only when he deserves it; and the opposite is also true—that he is not punished if he does not deserve it."

* * *

(b) **Conflict Between the Theories.** For many years most of the literature on the subject of punishment was devoted to advocacy of a particular theory to the exclusion of others. Those who espoused the rehabilitation theory condemned the rest, those who favored the deterrence theory denied the validity of all others, and so on. But in recent years the "inclusive theory of punishment" has gained considerable support; there is now general agreement that all (or, at least most) of the theories described above deserve some consideration.

This has given rise to another difficult problem, namely, what the priority and relationship of these several aims should be. This problem must be confronted, as it is readily apparent that the various theories tend to conflict with one another at several points. The retribution,

43. A. von Hirsch, Doing Justice 51 (1976). It "is likely to include two princip[al] assertions. First, the primary object of criminal sanctions is to punish culpable behavior. Although punishment may result in certain utilitarian benefits, notably the reduction of criminal behavior, the justification of punishment does not require such a showing; for it is moral and just that culpable behavior be punished. Second, the severity of the sanctions visited on the offender should be proportioned to the degree of his culpability." F. Allen, The Decline of the Rehabilitative Ideal 66 (1981).

deterrence, and prevention theories call for presenting the criminal with an unpleasant experience; but the chances for rehabilitation are often defeated by harsh treatment. The rehabilitation theory would let the criminal go when (and perhaps *only* when) he had been reformed. This may be a substantially shorter period of time (or a substantially *longer* period of time) than can be justified under the deterrence and retribution theories, which would vary the punishment in accordance with the seriousness of the crime. Because of such conflicts, the legislators who enact the punishment clauses (generally with minimum and maximum provisions) for the various crimes, the judges (or, in some states as to some crimes, the juries) who must sentence the convicted defendant within the limits set forth in legislation, and the administrative officials (parole and pardoning authorities) who are empowered to release convicted criminals from imprisonment, must determine priorities.

It is undoubtedly true that the thinking of legislators, judges and juries, and administrative officers who have a part in fixing punishment, as well as the thinking of the expert criminologist and non-expert layman whose views tend to influence those officials, varies from situation to situation. Sometimes the retribution theory will predominate; most of us share the common feeling of mankind that a particularly shocking crime should be severely punished. Where, for example, a son, after thoughtfully taking out insurance on his mother's life, places a time bomb in her suitcase just before she boards a plane, which device succeeds in killing the mother and all forty-two others aboard the plane, we almost all feel that he deserves a severe punishment, and we reach this result with little reflection about influencing future conduct. Likewise, when a less serious crime is involved and it was committed by a young person who might be effectively reformed, the rehabilitation theory rightly assumes primary importance. And the deterrence theory may be most important when the crime is not inherently wrong or covered by moral prohibition. Illustrative are income tax violations, as to which deterrence is especially important because of our reliance on a system of self-assessment.

Although allowance must be made for such variables, it is fair to say, as a general proposition, that for much of the present century the pendulum has been swinging away from retribution and deterrence and in the direction of rehabilitation as the chief goal of punishment; or, to put it differently, away from the philosophy that the punishment should fit the crime toward one that the punishment should fit the criminal.

*   *   *

But skepticism regarding the rehabilitative model began developing in the mid–1960's, and about ten years later there came "an explosion of criticism *   *   * calling for restructuring of the theoretical underpinnings of the criminal sanction." This rejection of rehabilitation, usually in favor of a "just deserts" theory, was prompted by several considerations. One was the concern with the wide disparity in sentencing which resulted from giving judges broad sentencing discretion to act according to the perceived rehabilitative needs in the particular case. The "just deserts" model was seen as necessary "to counter the capricious and irresponsible uses of state power." The existing system was perceived by many as being arbitrary because rehabilitative efforts were often unsuccessful. When confidence was "lost in the rehabilitative capacities of penal programs and in the ability of parole boards and correctional officers to determine when reformation has been achieved, the rehabilitationist rationale for treatment differentials no longer serves, and the differences are seen as irrational and indefensible." Finally, the retribution or "just deserts" theory, precisely because it "operates from a consensus model of society where the community * * * is acting in the right" and "the criminal is acting in the wrong," had appeal because it seemed to reaffirm our moral values at a time when they were under frequent attack.

UNITED STATES v. BERGMAN

United States District Court, Southern District of New York, 1976.
416 F.Supp. 496.

SENTENCING MEMORANDUM

FRANKEL, DISTRICT JUDGE.

Defendant is being sentenced upon his plea of guilty to two counts of an 11–count indictment. The sentencing proceeding is unusual in some respects. It has been the subject of more extensive submissions, written and oral, than this court has ever received upon such an occasion. The court has studied some hundreds of pages of memoranda and exhibits, plus scores of volunteered letters. A broad array of issues has been addressed. Imaginative suggestions of law and penology have been tendered. A preliminary conversation with counsel, on the record, preceded the usual sentencing hearing. Having heard counsel again and the defendant speaking for himself, the court postponed the pronouncement of sentence for further reconsideration of thoughts generated during the days of studying the briefs and oral pleas. It seems fitting now to report in writing the reasons upon which the court concludes that defendant must be sentenced to a term of four months in prison.[1]

I. Defendant and His Crimes

Defendant appeared until the last couple of years to be a man of unimpeachably high character, attainments, and distinction. A doctor of divinity and an ordained rabbi, he has been acclaimed by people around the world for his works of public philanthropy, private charity,

---

1. The court considered, and finally rejected, imposing a fine in addition to the prison term. Defendant seems destined to pay hundreds of thousands of dollars in restitution. The amount is being worked out in connection with a state criminal indictment. Apart from defendant's further liabilities for federal taxes, any additional money exaction is appropriately left for the state court.

and leadership in educational enterprises. Scores of letters have come to the court from across this and other countries reporting debts of personal gratitude to him for numerous acts of extraordinary generosity. (The court has also received a kind of petition, with fifty-odd signatures, in which the signers, based upon learning acquired as newspaper readers, denounce the defendant and urge a severe sentence. Unlike the pleas for mercy, which appear to reflect unquestioned facts inviting compassion, this document should and will be disregarded.) In addition to his good works, defendant has managed to amass considerable wealth in the ownership and operation of nursing homes, in real estate ventures, and in a course of substantial investments.

Beginning about two years ago, investigations of nursing homes in this area, including questions of fraudulent claims for Medicaid funds, drew to a focus upon this defendant among several others. The results that concern us were the present indictment and two state indictments. After extensive pretrial proceedings, defendant embarked upon elaborate plea negotiations with both state and federal prosecutors. A state guilty plea and the instant plea were entered in March of this year. (Another state indictment is expected to be dismissed after defendant is sentenced on those to which he has pled guilty.) As part of the detailed plea arrangements, it is expected that the prison sentence imposed by this court will comprise the total covering the state as well as the federal convictions.

For purposes of the sentence now imposed, the precise details of the charges, and of defendant's carefully phrased admissions of guilt, are not matters of prime importance. Suffice it to say that the plea on Count One (carrying a maximum of five years in prison and a $10,000 fine) confesses defendant's knowing and wilful participation in a scheme to defraud the United States in various ways, including the presentation of wrongfully padded claims for payments under the Medicaid program to defendant's nursing homes. Count Three, for which the guilty plea carries a theoretical maximum of three more years in prison and another $5,000 fine, is a somewhat more "technical" charge. Here, defendant admits to having participated in the filing of a partnership return which was false and fraudulent in failing to list people who had bought partnership interests from him in one of his nursing homes, had paid for such interests, and had made certain capital withdrawals.

The conspiracy to defraud, as defendant has admitted it, is by no means the worst of its kind; it is by no means as flagrant or extensive as has been portrayed in the press; it is evidently less grave than other nursing-home wrongs for which others have been convicted or publicized. At the same time, the sentence, as defendant has acknowledged, is imposed for two federal felonies including, as the more important, a knowing and purposeful conspiracy to mislead and defraud the Federal Government.

II. *The Guiding Principles of Sentencing*

Proceeding through the short list of the supposed justifications for criminal sanctions, defense counsel urge that no licit purpose could be served by defendant's incarceration. Some of these arguments are plainly sound; others are not.

The court agrees that this defendant should not be sent to prison for "rehabilitation." Apart from the patent inappositeness of the concept to this individual, this court shares the growing understanding that no one should ever be sent to prison *for rehabilitation.* That is to say, nobody who would not otherwise be locked up should suffer that fate on the incongruous premise that it will be good for him or her. Imprisonment is punishment. Facing the simple reality should help us to be civilized. It is less agreeable to confine someone when we deem it an affliction rather than a benefaction. If someone must be imprisoned—for other, valid reasons—we should seek to make rehabilitative resources available to him or her. But the goal of rehabilitation cannot fairly serve in itself as grounds for the sentence to confinement.[3]

Equally clearly, this defendant should not be confined to incapacitate him. He is not dangerous. It is most improbable that he will commit similar, or any, offenses in the future. There is no need for "specific deterrence."

Contrary to counsel's submissions, however, two sentencing considerations demand a prison sentence in this case:

First, the aim of *general deterrence,* the effort to discourage similar wrongdoing by others through a reminder that the law's warnings are real and that the grim consequence of imprisonment is likely to follow from crimes of deception for gain like those defendant has admitted.

Second, the related, but not identical, concern that any lesser penalty would, in the words of the Model Penal Code, § 7.01(1)(c), "depreciate the seriousness of the defendant's crime."

Resisting the first of these propositions, defense counsel invoke Immanuel Kant's axiom that "one man ought never to be dealt with merely as a means subservient to the purposes of another."[4] In a more novel, but equally futile, effort, counsel urge that a sentence for general deterrence "would violate the Eighth Amendment proscription against cruel and unusual punishment." Treating the latter point first, because it is a short subject, it may be observed simply that if general deterrence as a sentencing purpose were now to be outlawed, as against a near unanimity of views among state and federal jurists, the bolt would have to come from a place higher than this.

As for Dr. Kant, it may well be that defense counsel mistake his meaning in the present context.[6] Whether or not that is so, and

---

3. This important point, correcting misconceptions still widely prevalent, is developed more fully by Dean Norval Morris in *The Future of Imprisonment* (1974).

4. Quoting from I. Kant, *Philosophy of Law* 1986 (Hastie Trans. 1887).

6. See H. L. A. Hart, *Punishment and Responsibility* 243–44 (1986).

without pretending to authority on that score, we take the widely accepted stance that a criminal punished in the interest of general deterrence is not being employed "*merely* as a means * * *." Reading Kant to mean that every man must be deemed *more* than the instrument of others, and must "always be treated as an end in himself," [7] the humane principle is not offended here. Each of us is served by the enforcement of the law—not least a person like the defendant in this case, whose wealth and privileges, so long enjoyed, are so much founded upon law. More broadly, we are driven regularly in our ultimate interests as members of the community to use ourselves and each other, in war and in peace, for social ends. One who has transgressed against the criminal laws is certainly among the more fitting candidates for a role of this nature. This is no arbitrary selection. Warned in advance of the prospect, the transgressor has chosen, in the law's premises, "between keeping the law required for society's protection or paying the penalty." [8]

But the whole business, defendant argues further, is guesswork; we are by no means certain that deterrence "works." The position is somewhat overstated; there is, in fact, some reasonably "scientific" evidence for the efficacy of criminal sanctions as deterrents, at least as against some kinds of crimes. Moreover, the time is not yet here when all we can "know" must be quantifiable and digestible by computers. The shared wisdom of generations teaches meaningfully, if somewhat amorphously, that the utilitarians have a point; we do, indeed, lapse often into rationality and act to seek pleasure and avoid pain. It would be better, to be sure, if we had more certainty and precision. Lacking these comforts, we continue to include among our working hypotheses a belief (with some concrete evidence in its support) that crimes like those in this case—deliberate, purposeful, continuing, non-impulsive, and committed for profit—are among those most likely to be generally deterrable by sanctions most shunned by those exposed to temptation.

The idea of avoiding depreciation of the seriousness of the offense implicates two or three thoughts, not always perfectly clear or universally agreed upon, beyond the idea of deterrence. It should be proclaimed by the court's judgment that the offenses are grave, not minor or purely technical. Some attention must be paid to the demand for equal justice; it will not do to leave the penalty of imprisonment a dead letter as against "privileged" violators while it is employed regularly, and with vigor, against others. There probably is in these conceptions an element of retributiveness, as counsel urge. And retribution, so denominated, is in some disfavor as a reason for punishment. It remains a factor, however, as Holmes perceived,[12] and as is known to anyone who talks to judges, lawyers, defendants, or people generally. It may become more palatable, and probably more humanely under-

7. Andenaes, *The Morality of Deterrence,* 37 U.Chi.L.Rev. 649 (1970). See also O. Holmes, *Common Law* 43–44, 46–47 (1881).

8. H. L. A. Hart, *supra* note 6, at 23.

12. See O. Holmes, *Common Law* 41–42, 45 (1881).

stood, under the rubric of "deserts" or "just deserts." [13] However the concept is formulated, we have not yet reached a state, supposing we ever should, in which the infliction of punishments for crime may be divorced generally from ideas of blameworthiness, recompense, and proportionality.

III. An Alternative, "Behavioral Sanction"

Resisting prison above all else, defense counsel included in their thorough memorandum on sentencing two proposals for what they call a "constructive," and therefore a "preferable" form of "behavioral sanction." One is a plan for Dr. Bergman to create and run a program of Jewish vocational and religious high school training. The other is for him to take charge of a "Committee on Holocaust Studies," again concerned with education at the secondary school level.

A third suggestion was made orally at yesterday's sentencing hearing. It was proposed that Dr. Bergman might be ordered to work as a volunteer in some established agency as a visitor and aide to the sick and the otherwise incapacitated. The proposal was that he could read, provide various forms of physical assistance, and otherwise give comfort to afflicted people.

No one can doubt either the worthiness of these proposals or Dr. Bergman's ability to make successes of them. But both of the carefully formulated "sanctions" in the memorandum involve work of an honorific nature, not unlike that done in other projects to which the defendant has devoted himself in the past. It is difficult to conceive of them as "punishments" at all. The more recent proposal is somewhat more suitable in character, but it is still an insufficient penalty. The seriousness of the crimes to which Dr. Bergman has pled guilty demands something more than "requiring" him to lend his talents and efforts to further philanthropic enterprises. It remains open to him, of course, to pursue the interesting suggestions later on as a matter of unforced personal choice.

IV. "Measuring" the Sentence

In cases like this one, the decision of greatest moment is whether to imprison or not. As reflected in the eloquent submissions for defendant, the prospect of the closing prison doors is the most appalling concern; the feeling is that the length of the sojourn is a lesser question once that threshold is passed. Nevertheless, the setting of a term remains to be accomplished. And in some respects it is a subject even more perplexing, unregulated, and unprincipled.

Days and months and years are countable with a sound of exactitude. But there can be no exactitude in the deliberations from which a number emerges. Without pretending to a nonexistent precision, the court notes at least the major factors.

13. See A. von Hirsch, *Doing Justice* 45–55 (1976); see also N. Morris, *The Future of Imprisonment* 73–77 (1974).

The criminal behavior, as has been noted, is blatant in character and unmitigated by any suggestion of necessitous circumstance or other pressures difficult to resist. However metaphysicians may conjure with issues about free will, it is a fundamental premise of our efforts to do criminal justice that competent people, possessed of their faculties, make choices and are accountable for them. In this sometimes harsh light, the case of the present defendant is among the clearest and least relieved. Viewed against the maxima Congress ordained, and against the run of sentences in other federal criminal cases, it calls for more than a token sentence.[14]

On the other side are factors that take longer to enumerate. Defendant's illustrious public life and works are in his favor, though diminished, of course, by what this case discloses. This is a first, probably a last, conviction. Defendant is 64 years old and in imperfect health, though by no means so ill, from what the court is told, that he could be expected to suffer inordinately more than many others of advanced years who go to prison.

Defendant invokes an understandable, but somewhat unworkable, notion of "disparity." He says others involved in recent nursing home fraud cases have received relatively light sentences for behavior more culpable than his. He lays special emphasis upon one defendant whose frauds appear indeed to have involved larger amounts and who was sentenced to a maximum of six months' incarceration, to be confined for that time only on week nights, not on week days or weekends. This court has examined the minutes of that sentencing proceeding and finds the case distinguishable in material respects. But even if there were a threat of such disparity as defendant warns against, it could not be a major weight on the scales.

Our sentencing system, deeply flawed, is characterized by disparity. We are to seek to "individualize" sentences, but no clear or clearly agreed standards govern the individualization. The lack of meaningful criteria does indeed leave sentencing judges far too much at large. But the result, with its nagging burdens on conscience, cannot be meaningfully alleviated by allowing any handful of sentences in a short series to fetter later judgments. The point is easy, of course, where Sentence No. 1 or Sentences 1–5 are notably harsh. It cannot be that a later judge, disposed to more leniency, should feel in any degree "bound." The converse is not identical, but it is not totally different. The net of this is that this court has considered and has given some weight to the trend of the other cited sentences (though strict logic might call for none), but without treating them as forceful "precedents" in any familiar sense.

14. Despite Biblical teachings concerning what is expected from those to whom much is given, the court has not, as his counsel feared might happen, held Dr. Bergman to a higher standard of responsibility because of his position in the community. But he has not been judged under a lower standard either.

How, then, the particular sentence adjudged in this case? As has been mentioned, the case calls for a sentence that is more than nominal. Given the other circumstances, however—including that this is a first offense, by a man no longer young and not perfectly well, where danger of recidivism is not a concern—it verges on cruelty to think of confinement for a term of years. We sit, to be sure, in a nation where prison sentences of extravagant length are more common than they are almost anywhere else. By that light, the term imposed today is not notably long. For this sentencing court, however, for a nonviolent first offense involving no direct assaults or invasions of others' security (as in bank robbery, narcotics, etc.), it is a stern sentence. For people like Dr. Bergman, who might be disposed to engage in similar wrongdoing, it should be sufficiently frightening to serve the major end of general deterrence. For all but the profoundly vengeful, it should not depreciate the seriousness of his offenses.

V. Punishment in or for the Media

Much of defendant's sentencing memorandum is devoted to the extensive barrage of hostile publicity to which he has been subjected during the years before and since his indictment. He argues, and it appears to be undisputed, that the media (and people desiring to be featured in the media) have vilified him for many kinds of evildoing of which he has in fact been innocent. Two main points are made on this score with respect to the problem of sentencing.

First, as has been mentioned, counsel express the concern that the court may be pressured toward severity by the force of the seeming public outcry. That the court should not allow itself to be affected in this way is clear beyond discussion. Nevertheless, it is not merely permissible, but entirely wholesome and responsible, for counsel to bring the expressed concern out in the open. Whatever our ideals and mixed images about judges, it would be naive to doubt that judges have sometimes been swept by a sense of popular demand toward draconian sentencing decisions. It cannot hurt for the sentencing judge to be reminded of this and cautioned about it. There can be no guarantees. The sentencer must confront and regulate himself. But it bears reaffirmance that the court must seek to discount utterly the fact of notoriety in passing its judgment upon the defendant.

* * *

Defendant's second point about his public humiliation is the frequently heard contention that he should not be incarcerated because he "has been punished enough." The thought is not without some initial appeal. If punishment were wholly or mainly retributive, it might be a weighty factor. In the end, however, it must be a matter of little or no force. Defendant's notoriety should not in the last analysis serve to lighten, any more than it may be permitted to aggravate, his sentence. The fact that he has been pilloried by journalists is essentially a consequence of the prestige and privileges he enjoyed before he was exposed as a wrongdoer. The long fall from grace was possible only because of the height he had reached. The suffering from loss of public esteem reflects a body of opinion that the esteem had been, in at least some measure, wrongly bestowed and enjoyed. It is not possible to justify the notion that this mode of nonjudicial punishment should be an occasion for leniency not given to a defendant who never basked in such an admiring light at all. The quest for both the appearance and the substance of equal justice prompts the court to discount the thought that the public humiliation serves the function of imprisonment.

Writing, as judges rarely do, about a particular sentence concentrates the mind with possibly special force upon the experience of the sentencer as well as the person sentenced. Consigning someone to prison, this defendant or any other, "is a sad necessity." There are impulses of avoidance from time to time—toward a personally gratifying leniency or toward an opposite extreme. But there is, obviously, no place for private impulse in the judgment of the court. The course of justice must be sought with such objective rationality as we can muster, tempered with mercy, but obedient to the law, which, we do well to remember, is all that empowers a judge to make other people suffer.

* * *

Questions and Points for Discussion

1. Do you agree with the sentence imposed by the court in *Bergman*? Why or why not?

2. If you were the sentencing judge, what sentence would you impose in the following four cases? Explain your conclusions in light of what you consider the appropriate purposes of criminal punishment.

a. When driving while intoxicated, the defendant ran through two red lights, hit a car, and killed two passengers in the car. Before getting into his car, the defendant had been warned by a police officer not to drive because of his apparent drunkenness. At the time of the accident, the defendant was twenty-years old and was employed as a delivery driver. He had no prior felony convictions or any convictions for reckless driving or driving while intoxicated. He had, however, received seven traffic tickets in the past three years, one of which was for leaving the scene of an accident after running into a car in a parking lot.

The defendant was willing to plead guilty to voluntary manslaughter, but refused to plead guilty to second-degree murder as the prosecutor insisted. A state statute defined second-degree murder as including "intentionally perform[ing] an act that results in the death of another person under circumstances manifesting an extreme indifference to the value of human life." A jury found the defendant guilty of two counts of second-degree murder and one count of assault. See Pears v. Alaska, 698 P.2d 1198 (Alaska 1985).

b. During a three-month period, the defendant, a former college and professional football player, a member of the state legislature, and an alcoholic, wrote seventy-six checks on a closed account to pay for $8,000 worth of goods and services. He pled guilty to one count of theft over $250. By the time of the sentencing hearing, he had paid back the money owed for the bad checks. See Minnesota v. Staten, 390 N.W.2d 914 (Minn.App.1986).

c. A jury found the defendant guilty of all counts of an indictment charging him with defrauding investors of millions of dollars. This conviction was the defendant's first, and he has never expressed any remorse for his crimes.

After the defendant's conviction, he had a stroke, which left him unable to speak and the right side of his body paralyzed. After participating in an intensive therapy program conducted both in Colorado and New York, he regained much of his ability to speak. He still, however, has curtailed use of his right arm and leg and has difficulty thinking clearly. He also continues to periodically suffer what have been described as small strokes.

At the sentencing hearing, five defense witnesses—three neurologists and two rehabilitation specialists—described the defendant's physical progress since the stroke. They also testified that this progress might be halted or undone if the defendant's physical therapy program was stopped or its quality reduced and that subsequent therapy might not be able to undo this damage. See United States v. King, 442 F.Supp. 1244 (S.D.N.Y.1978).

d. The defendant, a woman who was thirty-two-years old, a former police dispatcher, and the mother of three children ages five, three, and one, pled guilty to robbing three banks. During each of the robberies, she pointed a gun at the bank tellers. At the time of the robberies, the defendant and her family were deeply in debt. The defendant managed her family's finances, and unbeknownst to her husband, she had charged a number of expensive items for which the family did not have the money to pay.

3. The retributive theory of punishment is not new. The Bible verse importuning that "life *shall go* for life, eye for eye, tooth for tooth, hand for hand, foot for foot" is known to all. *Deuteronomy* 19:21 (King James) (emphasis in the original). Do you subscribe to the retributive theory? If so, how do we determine what punishment is "deserved" for a crime, and how can we reach a consensus on this question?

4. The American Bar Association Standards for Criminal Justice, which embrace what is known as the "least restrictive alternative principle," attempt to define the boundaries that should be placed on punishment. Standard 18–2.2(a) provides as follows:

> The sentence imposed in each case should call for the minimum sanction which is consistent with the protection of the public and the gravity of the crime. In determining the gravity of the offense and the public's need for protection, sentencing authorities best serve the public interest and the appearance of justice when they give serious consideration to the goal of sentencing equality and the need to avoid unwarranted disparities.

The commentary accompanying this Standard explains that normally the condemnatory function of punishment can be accomplished through sanctions other than imprisonment. Imprisonment should therefore normally be reserved for those cases where it is necessary for the public's protection. Do you agree with these views?

* * *

As mentioned earlier, the size of prison populations in this country has grown enormously in recent years. Prisons are now notoriously crowded, and there is undoubtedly a link between this crowding problem and prosecution and sentencing policies. For example, the declaration of a "war on drugs" has spawned the increased prosecution and confinement of drug offenders. During the 1980s, the number of federal drug prosecutions increased by 229%, culminating in federal prisons holding twice as many drug offenders in 1989 as they did ten years earlier. Fed. Bur. of Prisons, 1989 State of the Bureau 1 (1990). In addition, the length of the sentences of federal prisoners increased substantially during this time period. While 139 of every 100,000 prisoners were serving a prison sentence longer than one year in 1980, this number had increased to 260 per every 100,000 inmates by 1989. Id. But while the federal prison population grew by 30,000 inmates during the 1980s, only 8400 beds were added to the federal prison system during this time period so that the prisons are now literally bursting at the seams. Id. at 2.

Several views on what can and should be done to stem the prison crowding problem through changes in sentencing policies and policy adoption procedures are set forth below. Do you agree or disagree with the views expressed?

ALVIN J. BRONSTEIN in AMERICA'S OVERCROWDED PRISONS

The GAO Journal, Number 7 (Fall, 1989), pp. 29–31. Reprinted with the permission of The GAO Journal.

So far there have been three responses to prison overcrowding at the state and federal level.

Prison construction. Large states like California are spending billions of dollars on new prison space, and President Bush has called for $1 billion in new federal prison construction, a threefold increase in planned spending.

But in light of projected increases in prison populations, this expansion will have no impact on overcrowding in the federal system, which, according to figures from the Bureau of Justice Statistics, was 72 percent over capacity at the end of 1988. With a net national increase of 800 prisoners per week, we would have to spend $1 billion a month to build prisons just to accommodate the current increase in prison population—to say nothing of current overcrowding.

Alternatives. Various states, wary of the cost of building new prisons, are investing in alternatives to incarceration. Here too, the response has not solved the problem and has also had the effect of widening the net of social control. Kentucky has a large Intensive Community Supervision program, Florida has the greatest number of people in house arrest supervision, and both states experienced 1988 prison population increases at or above the national average.

Do nothing. A number of jurisdictions, most noticeably the District of Columbia, are bureaucratically frozen into doing nothing about prison overcrowding. This allows elected officials to brag about being tough on criminals while saving taxpayers' money—and then scapegoat federal judges who intervene when overcrowding results in unconstitutional conditions of confinement. The result is often the potential for a replay of the tragedies of Attica in 1971 or Santa Fe in 1980.

None of the current responses addresses what is causing prison overcrowding: changed sentencing practices in the last 15 years, which require longer sentences and mandatory minimum sentences, and the so-called "war on drugs." During each of the last few years, police made about 750,000 arrests for drug law violations, mostly for possession and not for manufacturing or dealing. The result has been the overwhelming of most urban criminal justice systems.

Although admittedly difficult to implement given the current mood of the country, my proposed responses have the advantage at least of directly addressing the causes of prison overcrowding.

• **Sentence as many people as we are now, perhaps more, but for shorter periods of time.** We must begin to consider prison space as a scarce resource, reserving it for short prison terms for those offenders who we feel must be punished by incarceration. Bankrupting the future of this country by building more prisons will have no significant impact on the number of crimes committed. The public is confused into thinking that locking up more criminals is the same thing as reducing crime rates. It is not, and no jurisdiction has ever successfully built its way out of overcrowding or had an impact on crime rates by an expanded incarceration policy.

Consequently, we should eliminate most mandatory minimum sentences, eliminate most repeat-offender enhanced sentences, and shorten sentences to lengths comparable to those in other industrial democracies. Faced with the decision of how to use one prison bed over a three-year period, I would rather use it to sentence 12 burglars to three months each than to sentence one burglar for all 36 months.

• **Make the drug problem a public health and social welfare problem, not a criminal justice problem.** During the last eight years, while we have conducted our national "war on drugs," so much cocaine has come into this country that the wholesale price has dropped by 80 percent even as the retail purity of a gram of cocaine has quintupled; the trend with heroin has been similar if less dramatic. We are seeing rising levels of corruption in federal, state, and local criminal justice systems largely because of the powerful allure of illicit drug dollars. We are seeing more and more drug-related crime. We are seeing the greatest benefits of our current anti-drug strategy going to drug traffickers. In other words, our absurd drug policies are proving costly, ineffective, and counterproductive—just as Prohibition did 60 years ago.

Adopting rational new drug policies would have a huge impact on prison overcrowding. We should remove drugs from the criminal justice system and, as with alcohol and tobacco, deal with drugs as a public health problem. The huge sums of money now going into ineffective law enforcement efforts should be diverted into education, treatment, and other social welfare programs.

JOHN H. KRAMER in AMERICA'S OVERCROWDED PRISONS

The GAO Journal, Number 7 (Fall, 1989), p. 34. Reprinted with the permission of The GAO Journal.

The size of prison populations has reached crisis proportions in almost all states. A few states, such as Texas and California, are trying to build themselves out of the problem. Others have established sentencing commissions to develop sentencing policy designed to reduce, eliminate, or stabilize the problem. Between these two extremes lie various proposals to develop alternatives to incarceration, such as community corrections and intensive probation.

But none of these solutions attacks the real problem in our society of an overwhelming violent crime rate. The long-term solution to the problem does not rest with any of these approaches—more prisons, sentencing guidelines, or alternatives to incarceration. Ultimately, all are stopgap measures. If there is to be a solution, it must rest in changing the social environment that spawns violent crime. Until we devote adequate and appropriate resources to the task of convincing youths to make a commitment to our social system, the crime rate will not go down. And as long as our society generates such a large number of predatory, violent offenders, the public and politicians will continue to be fearful and frustrated with crime and will support increasing penal sanctions.

Alas: The prospects for establishing a national agenda for crime prevention are slight. Political agendas are too short-term; the risk for failure is too high. We must assume that we will continue to be confronted with succeeding generations of high-rate offenders.

In my opinion, the only fair and equitable coping strategy is commission-authored sentencing guidelines such as those in Washington State and Minnesota. In these two states, prisons have not become overcrowded. Their legislatures have established sentencing commissions *and* instructed them to establish sentencing guidelines that would keep prison populations at about 95 percent of capacity. The guidelines have proved successful in ensuring fair and efficient use of available prison space. In fact, Washington and Minnesota have actually rented prison space to other states with overcrowded prisons. Moreover, neither state has suffered any noticeable increase in its crime rate.

In addition to eliminating overcrowding, the commission-based guideline model has another advantage. It allows for increases in sanction severity in conjunction with increases in capacity. This linking of sentencing policy with capacity makes possible careful and thoughtful penal policy and can also clearly identify individuals for whom alternatives to incarceration are appropriate.

Those who are skeptical of the Washington and Minnesota models might suspect that the lack of prison overcrowding in these states could be explained by lower rates of violent crime. But this does not seem to be the case. Rather, the explanation seems to be that the choice of public policy determines whether prisons will be overcrowded or not.

AMERICAN BAR ASSOCIATION, RECOMMENDATIONS ON PRISON AND JAIL IMPACT STATEMENTS

Summary of Action of the House of Delegates—
1990 Midyear Meeting 12 (1990).

BE IT RESOLVED, that the American Bar Association, recognizing the severe problem with overcrowding in the nation's prisons and jails, recommends the following:

1. The states and the federal government should adopt procedures ensuring that a prison and jail impact statement be prepared for and considered by a state legislature or Congress before the passage of laws involving the sentencing of convicted criminals, parole policies, and other issues whose resolution may directly lead to an increase in the number of persons incarcerated in correctional facilities or the length of their incarceration.

2. The prison and jail impact statement should include, at a minimum, the following information:

   (a) an estimate of the number of individuals who will annually be incarcerated in or remain incarcerated in prisons or jails as a result of the contemplated legislation being enacted;

   (b) an estimate of the amount of additional prison or jail space needed to accommodate the increase in the size of the prison or jail populations;

   (c) an estimate of the cost of building additional prisons or jails or of taking other steps to make the space available for the anticipated greater number of incarcerated persons; and

   (d) an estimate of the amount by which the expected increase in the number of persons incarcerated in prisons or jails or the duration of their confinement will increase operating expenses, which are the sums incurred when paying for staff, food, supplies, medical care, and the other costs stemming from the supervision, treatment, and care of inmates.

3. Congress and the state legislatures should not enact legislation that will increase the number of persons incarcerated in correctional facilities or the length of their confinement without taking steps to ensure that either:

    (a) the resources, including space and money for increased operating expenses, are already available to handle the increase in the size of the prison or jail populations; or

    (b) money is appropriated to cover the costs of implementing the legislation; or

    (c) other counterbalancing steps are taken to decrease the size of the prison or jail populations.

* * *

In the succeeding chapters of this book, you will learn about sentencing policies in this country, the sentencing process, and the rights of criminal offenders during and after sentencing. As you read these chapters, consider the changes which need to be made in sentencing, correctional, and other government policies to ensure that the system for controlling crime in this country is effective, humane, and affordable.

Chapter 2

GUILTY PLEAS AND PLEA BARGAINING

An individual charged with a crime can enter one of several different pleas to the charge. The individual can plead guilty or not guilty. In some jurisdictions, a third alternative exists; the individual charged with a crime can enter a plea of *nolo contendere,* which means "no contest." See, e.g., Fed.R.Crim.P. 11(a)(1). With one exception, such a plea generally has the same consequences as entering a plea of guilty. The person who pleads "no contest" can be sentenced as if he or she pled guilty to the crime, even to a period of incarceration. The principal distinction between a plea of *nolo contendere* and a guilty plea is that evidence of the former type of plea is inadmissible in civil lawsuits, which most often would be brought by victims of crimes.

The vast majority of criminal cases which result in a plea are disposed of by a plea of guilty. A study conducted by the Bureau of Justice Statistics in 1984, for example, revealed that for every one hundred felony arrests in which criminal charges were pursued, about ninety were resolved by the entry of guilty pleas. Ten cases proceeded to trial, with eight of those trials resulting in verdicts of guilty and two in acquittals. Bureau of Justice Statistics, U.S. Dep't of Justice, The Prevalence of Guilty Pleas 1 (1984). These statistics underscore the central role that guilty pleas presently play in the operation of the criminal justice system.

There are two main types of guilty pleas—what are called "blind" pleas and negotiated pleas. A "blind" plea is a plea which is uninduced by any commitment of any prosecutor or judge. The defendant simply acknowledges his or her guilt and awaits the imposition of a sentence by the court. By contrast, when a defendant enters a negotiated plea, the defendant has been promised a benefit in return for his or her guilty plea. That benefit may come in many forms. The defendant, for example, may be permitted to plead guilty to a crime which is less serious than the crime with which he or she was originally charged. Even if the defendant does not plead guilty to a reduced charge, other criminal charges may be dismissed or not filed in return for the plea of guilty. Or the defendant may plead guilty upon the condition that the prosecutor recommends or the court imposes a particular sentence.

In recent years, the practice of plea bargaining has come under attack. Chief among the criticisms of plea bargaining include the following: (1) that favorable plea offers induce innocent offenders to plead guilty; (2) that because of plea agreements, the unconstitutional actions of law enforcement officers are often concealed; (3) that plea bargaining results in more favorable dispositions for defendants who forego their constitutional right to trial, in effect punishing other defendants who invoke this constitutional right; (4) that plea bargaining results in dispositions that compromise public safety and fail to meet the objectives of criminal punishment; and (5) that behind-the-scenes negotiations invite abuse by the participants in the negotiation process. The latter criticism is prompted in part by the fact that some prosecutors are more willing to enter into a plea agreement when their case against a defendant is weak, thereby enhancing the risk of an innocent person being convicted. Alschuler, The Prosecutor's Role in Plea Bargaining, 36 U.Chi.L.Rev. 50, 58 (1968). In addition, many defense attorneys have been lambasted for simply "copping a plea" and then collecting their fee, without fully exploring whether entry of a guilty plea and the terms of a plea agreement are in their client's best interests. See e.g., Alschuler, Personal Failure, Institutional Failure, and the Sixth Amendment, 14 N.Y.U.Rev.L. & Soc.Change 149 (1986). For other criticisms of plea bargaining, see, for example, National Advisory Commission on Criminal Justice Standards and Goals, Courts, Standard 3.1 (1973) (advocates the abolition of plea bargaining) and Fine, Plea Bargaining: An Unnecessary Evil, 70 Marq.L.Rev. 615 (1987).

Plea bargaining, however, has many defenders. See e.g., American Bar Association, Standards for Criminal Justice, Standard 14–3.1 (1982); U.S. President's Commission on Law Enforcement and Administration of Justice, Task Force Report: The Courts 10 (1967). These individuals and entities candidly acknowledge the abuses that can attend plea bargaining. Yet they contend that these abuses can be limited and that the retention of plea bargaining is good for and in fact essential to the effective operation of the criminal justice system. Some of the primary argued benefits of plea bargaining include the following: (1) that without plea bargaining, the criminal justice system would simply break down, particularly in the urban areas of this country, since the system lacks the resources to provide trials for many more criminal defendants; (2) that plea bargains can relieve defendants, their families, prosecutors, and witnesses from the uncertainty and financial and psychological burdens that attend litigation; (3) that plea bargaining can facilitate law enforcement, since in exchange for leniency, defendants can be persuaded to provide officials with information needed to apprehend other criminals; and (4) that because of plea bargains, the amount of time that defendants who cannot post bail must spend in jail while awaiting trial can be reduced, to the benefit not only of the defendants, but also the public that must pay for the costs of their confinement.

The cases and materials set forth below primarily focus on the constraints placed by the Constitution on plea bargaining. While reading these materials, however, you should keep in mind that even though the Constitution may permit plea bargaining and certain plea bargaining practices, there are overarching policy questions that ultimately must be addressed concerning whether plea bargaining can and should be abolished and if not, the extent to which and way in which it should be controlled. For information and data relevant to the resolution of these questions, see U.S. Dep't of Justice, National Institute of Justice, Plea Bargaining: Critical Issues and Common Practices (1985).

A. THE DUE PROCESS REQUIREMENT OF A VOLUNTARY AND INTELLIGENT PLEA

BOYKIN v. ALABAMA

Supreme Court of the United States, 1969.
395 U.S. 238, 89 S.Ct. 1709, 23 L.Ed.2d 274.

MR. JUSTICE DOUGLAS delivered the opinion of the Court.

[In 1966, the petitioner was charged with and pled guilty to five armed robberies that had occurred in Mobile, Alabama. In Alabama at the time, these crimes were punishable by death. The record did not reflect that the judge asked the petitioner any questions when he entered his guilty pleas, nor did the petitioner apparently address the court when his pleas were entered.

The petitioner was sentenced to death for each of the robberies to which he had pled guilty. On appeal, the Alabama Supreme Court affirmed, and the United States Supreme Court then granted certiorari.]

It was error, plain on the face of the record, for the trial judge to accept petitioner's guilty plea without an affirmative showing that it was intelligent and voluntary. * * *

* * * The requirement that the prosecution spread on the record the prerequisites of a valid waiver is no constitutional innovation. In *Carnley v. Cochran,* 369 U.S. 506, 516, we dealt with a problem of waiver of the right to counsel, a Sixth Amendment right. We held: "Presuming waiver from a silent record is impermissible. The record must show, or there must be an allegation and evidence which show, that an accused was offered counsel but intelligently and understandingly rejected the offer. Anything less is not waiver."

We think that the same standard must be applied to determining whether a guilty plea is voluntarily made. For, as we have said, a plea of guilty is more than an admission of conduct; it is a conviction.[4]

* * *

Several federal constitutional rights are involved in a waiver that takes place when a plea of guilty is entered in a state criminal trial. First, is the privilege against compulsory self-incrimination guaranteed by the Fifth Amendment and applicable to the States by reason of the Fourteenth. Second, is the right to trial by jury. Third, is the right to confront one's accusers. We cannot presume a waiver of these three important federal rights from a silent record.

What is at stake for an accused facing death or imprisonment demands the utmost solicitude of which courts are capable in canvassing the matter with the accused to make sure he has a full understanding of what the plea connotes and of its consequence. When the judge discharges that function, he leaves a record adequate for any review that may be later sought and forestalls the spin-off of collateral proceedings that seek to probe murky memories.[7]

The three dissenting justices in the Alabama Supreme Court stated the law accurately when they concluded that there was reversible error "because the record does not disclose that the defendant voluntarily and understandingly entered his pleas of guilty."

Reversed.

MR. JUSTICE HARLAN, whom MR. JUSTICE BLACK joins, dissenting. [Opinion omitted.]

Questions and Points for Discussion

1. Henderson v. Morgan, 426 U.S. 637, 96 S.Ct. 2253 (1976) involved a defendant who was indicted for first-degree murder, but pled guilty to second-degree murder. He later contended that his plea was involuntary because neither the court nor his attorney apprised him that an intent to kill the victim was an element of the offense of second-degree murder. The Supreme Court agreed that his guilty plea should be set aside because the defendant was not sufficiently aware of the nature of the charge to which he was pleading guilty.

The Court took pains to note that it was not necessarily holding that defendants must always be apprised of the elements of the crimes to which they are pleading guilty in order for their pleas to be valid. In this case, however, intent to kill was "such a critical element" of the crime to which

---

4. "A plea of guilty is more than a voluntary confession made in open court. It also serves as a stipulation that no proof by the prosecution need be advanced. . . . It supplies both evidence and verdict, ending controversy." *Woodard v. State*, 42 Ala.App. 552, 558, 171 So. 2d 462, 469.

7. "A majority of criminal convictions are obtained after a plea of guilty. If these convictions are to be insulated from attack,

the trial court is best advised to conduct an on the record examination of the defendant which should include, inter alia, an attempt to satisfy itself that the defendant understands the nature of the charges, his right to a jury trial, the acts sufficient to constitute the offenses for which he is charged and the permissible range of sentences." *Commonwealth ex rel. West v. Rundle*, 428 Pa. 102, 105–106, 237 A.2d 196, 197–198 (1968).

the defendant was pleading guilty that he should have been made aware of that element before entering his plea. Id. at 647 n. 18, 96 S.Ct. at 2258 n. 18.

The Court also noted that it might generally be appropriate to assume that a defendant's attorney had adequately apprised the defendant of the nature of the charge to which the defendant was pleading guilty. In what the Court described as the "unique" circumstances of this case, however, such an assumption was unwarranted because the trial judge had specifically found that the defense attorney had not informed the defendant about the intent-to-kill element. Id. at 647, 96 S.Ct. at 2258.

In a concurring opinion, Justice White suggested another reason why this case was "unusual." The defendant in this case pled guilty to an offense with which he was not charged in the indictment. If he had been indicted for second-degree murder and the indictment had at some point been read to him, Justice White intimated that the defendant would have had sufficient notice of the charge to meet due process requirements. Id. at 649–50 n. 2, 96 S.Ct. at 2260 n. 2 (White, J. concurring).

2. When an uncounselled defendant is entering a guilty plea, the court must take steps to ensure not only that the guilty plea is otherwise voluntary and intelligent, but that the defendant is validly waiving his or her right to counsel. The government has the burden of rebutting a "strong presumption" that the defendant did not knowingly, intelligently, and voluntarily waive any right to counsel. Von Moltke v. Gillies, 332 U.S. 708, 723, 68 S.Ct. 316, 323 (1948). To meet this burden, four Justices of the Court opined in a plurality opinion written by Justice Black in the *Von Moltke* case that the government must establish that the defendant understood all of the following in order for the waiver of the right to counsel to be valid: "the nature of the charges, the statutory offenses included within them, the range of allowable punishments thereunder, possible defenses to the charges and circumstances in mitigation thereof, and all other facts essential to a broad understanding of the whole matter." Id. at 724, 68 S.Ct. at 323.

3. Apart from constitutional requirements which must be met in order for a guilty plea to be valid are the requirements which must be met under federal and state court rules and statutes. Rule 11 of the Federal Rules of Criminal Procedure, which governs the rendering and acceptance of guilty pleas in federal courts, is an example of one such court rule. That rule is set forth below:

Rule 11. Pleas

(a) Alternatives.

 (1) **In General.** A defendant may plead not guilty, guilty, or nolo contendere. If a defendant refuses to plead or if a defendant corporation fails to appear, the court shall enter a plea of not guilty.

(2) **Conditional Pleas.** With the approval of the court and the consent of the government, a defendant may enter a conditional plea of guilty or nolo contendere, reserving in writing the right,

on appeal from the judgment, to review of the adverse determination of any specified pretrial motion. A defendant who prevails on appeal shall be allowed to withdraw the plea.

(b) Nolo Contendere. A defendant may plead nolo contendere only with the consent of the court. Such a plea shall be accepted by the court only after due consideration of the views of the parties and the interest of the public in the effective administration of justice.

(c) Advice to Defendant. Before accepting a plea of guilty or nolo contendere, the court must address the defendant personally in open court and inform the defendant of, and determine that the defendant understands, the following:

(1) the nature of the charge to which the plea is offered, the mandatory minimum penalty provided by law, if any, and the maximum possible penalty provided by law, including the effect of any special parole term and, when applicable, that the court may also order the defendant to make restitution to any victim of the offense; and

(2) if the defendant is not represented by an attorney, that the defendant has the right to be represented by an attorney at every stage of the proceeding and, if necessary, one will be appointed to represent the defendant; and

(3) that the defendant has the right to plead not guilty or to persist in that plea if it has already been made, the right to be tried by a jury and at that trial the right to the assistance of counsel, the right to confront and cross-examine adverse witnesses, and the right against compelled self-incrimination; and

(4) that if a plea of guilty or nolo contendere is accepted by the court there will not be a further trial of any kind, so that by pleading guilty or nolo contendere the defendant waives the right to a trial; and

(5) if the court intends to question the defendant under oath, on the record, and in the presence of counsel about the offense to which the defendant has pleaded, that the defendant's answers may later be used against the defendant in a prosecution for perjury or false statement.

(d) Insuring That the Plea Is Voluntary. The court shall not accept a plea of guilty or nolo contendere without first, by addressing the defendant personally in open court, determining that the plea is voluntary and not the result of force or threats or of promises apart from a plea agreement. The court shall also inquire as to whether the defendant's willingness to plead guilty or nolo contendere results from prior discussions between the attorney for the government and the defendant or the defendant's attorney.

(e) Plea Agreement Procedure.

(1) In General. The attorney for the government and the attorney for the defendant or the defendant when acting pro se may engage in discussions with a view toward reaching an agreement that, upon the entering of a plea of guilty or nolo contendere to a charged offense or to a lesser or related offense, the attorney for the government will do any of the following:

(A) move for dismissal of other charges; or

(B) make a recommendation, or agree not to oppose the defendant's request, for a particular sentence, with the understanding that such recommendation or request shall not be binding upon the court; or

(C) agree that a specific sentence is the appropriate disposition of the case.

The court shall not participate in any such discussions.

(2) Notice of Such Agreement. If a plea agreement has been reached by the parties, the court shall, on the record, require the disclosure of the agreement in open court or, on a showing of good cause, in camera, at the time the plea is offered. If the agreement is of the type specified in subdivision (e)(1)(A) or (C), the court may accept or reject the agreement, or may defer its decision as to the acceptance or rejection until there has been an opportunity to consider the presentence report. If the agreement is of the type specified in subdivision (e)(1)(B), the court shall advise the defendant that if the court does not accept the recommendation or request the defendant nevertheless has no right to withdraw the plea.

(3) Acceptance of a Plea Agreement. If the court accepts the plea agreement, the court shall inform the defendant that it will embody in the judgment and sentence the disposition provided for in the plea agreement.

(4) Rejection of a Plea Agreement. If the court rejects the plea agreement, the court shall, on the record, inform the parties of this fact, advise the defendant personally in open court or, on a showing of good cause, in camera, that the court is not bound by the plea agreement, afford the defendant the opportunity to then withdraw the plea, and advise the defendant that if the defendant persists in a guilty plea or plea of nolo contendere the disposition of the case may be less favorable to the defendant than that contemplated by the plea agreement.

(5) Time of Plea Agreement Procedure. Except for good cause shown, notification to the court of the existence of a plea agreement shall be given at the arraignment or at such other time, prior to trial, as may be fixed by the court.

(6) Inadmissibility of Pleas, Plea Discussions, and Related Statements. Except as otherwise provided in this paragraph, evidence of the following is not, in any civil or criminal proceeding, admissible against the defendant who made the plea or was a participant in the plea discussions:

(A) a plea of guilty which was later withdrawn;

(B) a plea of nolo contendere;

(C) any statement made in the course of any proceedings under this rule regarding either of the foregoing pleas; or

(D) any statement made in the course of plea discussions with an attorney for the government which do not result in a plea of guilty or which result in a plea of guilty later withdrawn.

However, such a statement is admissible (i) in any proceeding wherein another statement made in the course of the same plea or plea discussions has been introduced and the statement ought in fairness be considered contemporaneously with it, or (ii) in a criminal proceeding for perjury or false statement if the statement was made by the defendant under oath, on the record, and in the presence of counsel.

(f) Determining Accuracy of Plea. Notwithstanding the acceptance of a plea of guilty, the court should not enter a judgment upon such plea without making such inquiry as shall satisfy it that there is a factual basis for the plea.

(g) Record of Proceedings. A verbatim record of the proceedings at which the defendant enters a plea shall be made and, if there is a plea of guilty or nolo contendere, the record shall include, without limitation, the court's advice to the defendant, the inquiry into the voluntariness of the plea including any plea agreement, and the inquiry into the accuracy of a guilty plea.

(h) Harmless Error. Any variance from the procedures required by this rule which does not affect substantial rights shall be disregarded.

How if at all, should Rule 11 be modified? Compare Rule 11 with the ABA Standards for Criminal Justice, Standards 14–1.1–1.8, 14–3.1–3.4 (1982).

4. Of the requirements which must be met in order for a guilty plea to be valid under Rule 11, which do you believe are also required by the Constitution? Consider the extent to which the following case has a bearing on the answer to that question.

NORTH CAROLINA v. ALFORD

Supreme Court of the United States, 1970.
400 U.S. 25, 91 S.Ct. 160, 27 L.Ed.2d 162.

MR. JUSTICE WHITE delivered the opinion of the Court.

On December 2, 1963, Alford was indicted for first-degree murder, a capital offense under North Carolina law.[1] The court appointed an attorney to represent him, and this attorney questioned all but one of the various witnesses who appellee said would substantiate his claim of innocence. The witnesses, however, did not support Alford's story but gave statements that strongly indicated his guilt. Faced with strong evidence of guilt and no substantial evidentiary support for the claim of

---

1. Under North Carolina law, first-degree murder is punished with death unless the jury recommends that the punishment shall be life imprisonment. * * *.

innocence, Alford's attorney recommended that he plead guilty, but left the ultimate decision to Alford himself. The prosecutor agreed to accept a plea of guilty to a charge of second-degree murder, and on December 10, 1963, Alford pleaded guilty to the reduced charge.

Before the plea was finally accepted by the trial court, the court heard the sworn testimony of a police officer who summarized the State's case. Two other witnesses besides Alford were also heard. Although there was no eyewitness to the crime, the testimony indicated that shortly before the killing Alford took his gun from his house, stated his intention to kill the victim, and returned home with the declaration that he had carried out the killing. After the summary presentation of the State's case, Alford took the stand and testified that he had not committed the murder but that he was pleading guilty because he faced the threat of the death penalty if he did not do so.[2] In response to the questions of his counsel, he acknowledged that his counsel had informed him of the difference between second- and first-degree murder and of his rights in case he chose to go to trial. The trial court then asked appellee if, in light of his denial of guilt, he still desired to plead guilty to second-degree murder and appellee answered, "Yes, sir. I plead guilty on—from the circumstances that he [Alford's attorney] told me." After eliciting information about Alford's prior criminal record, which was a long one, the trial court sentenced him to 30 years' imprisonment, the maximum penalty for second-degree murder.

Alford sought post-conviction relief in the state court. Among the claims raised was the claim that his plea of guilty was invalid because it was the product of fear and coercion. After a hearing, the state court in 1965 found that the plea was "willingly, knowingly, and understandingly" made on the advice of competent counsel and in the face of a strong prosecution case.

[Alford subsequently pursued his claim in habeas corpus proceedings in the federal courts. Ultimately, the Fourth Circuit Court of Appeals ruled that Alford's guilty plea, prompted by the desire to avoid the death penalty, was involuntary and hence invalid. The Supreme Court then granted certiorari.

2. After giving his version of the events of the night of the murder, Alford stated:

"I pleaded guilty on second degree murder because they said there is too much evidence, but I ain't shot no man, but I take the fault for the other man. We never had an argument in our life and I just pleaded guilty because they said if I didn't they would gas me for it, and that is all."

In response to questions from his attorney, Alford affirmed that he had consulted several times with his attorney and with members of his family and had been informed of his rights if he chose to plead not

guilty. Alford then reaffirmed his decision to plead guilty to second-degree murder:

"Q [by Alford's attorney]. And you authorized me to tender a plea of guilty to second degree murder before the court?

"A. Yes, sir.

"Q. And in doing that, that you have again affirmed your decision on that point?

"A. Well, I'm still pleading that you all got me to plead guilty. I plead the other way, circumstantial evidence; that the jury will prosecute me on—on the second. You told me to plead guilty, right. I don't—I'm not guilty but I plead guilty."

The Court began its opinion by discussing Brady v. United States, 397 U.S. 742, 90 S.Ct. 1463 (1970), see infra page 36, a case in which the Court concluded that a guilty plea was not necessarily involuntary even though entered in order to avoid the death penalty. The Court then turned to the question of the effect of Alford's protestation of innocence on the validity of his guilty plea.]

If Alford's statements were to be credited as sincere assertions of his innocence, there obviously existed a factual and legal dispute between him and the State. Without more, it might be argued that the conviction entered on his guilty plea was invalid, since his assertion of innocence negatived any admission of guilt, which, as we observed last Term in *Brady*, is normally "[c]entral to the plea and the foundation for entering judgment against the defendant . . . ."

In addition to Alford's statement, however, the court had heard an account of the events on the night of the murder, including information from Alford's acquaintances that he had departed from his home with his gun stating his intention to kill and that he had later declared that he had carried out his intention. Nor had Alford wavered in his desire to have the trial court determine his guilt without a jury trial. Although denying the charge against him, he nevertheless preferred the dispute between him and the State to be settled by the judge in the context of a guilty plea proceeding rather than by a formal trial. Thereupon, with the State's telling evidence and Alford's denial before it, the trial court proceeded to convict and sentence Alford for second-degree murder.

State and lower federal courts are divided upon whether a guilty plea can be accepted when it is accompanied by protestations of innocence and hence contains only a waiver of trial but no admission of guilt. Some courts, giving expression to the principle that "[o]ur law only authorizes a conviction where guilt is shown," *Harris v. State*, 76 Tex.Cr.R. 126, 131, 172 S.W. 975, 977 (1915), require that trial judges reject such pleas. But others have concluded that they should not "force any defense on a defendant in a criminal case," particularly when advancement of the defense might "end in disaster . . . ." *Tremblay v. Overholser*, 199 F.Supp. 569, 570 (DC 1961). They have argued that, since "guilt, or the degree of guilt, is at times uncertain and elusive," "[a]n accused, though believing in or entertaining doubts respecting his innocence, might reasonably conclude a jury would be convinced of his guilt and that he would fare better in the sentence by pleading guilty . . . ." *McCoy v. United States*, 124 U.S.App.D.C. 177, 179, 363 F.2d 306, 308 (1966). As one state court observed nearly a century ago, "[r]easons other than the fact that he is guilty may induce a defendant to so plead, . . . [and] [h]e must be permitted to judge for himself in this respect." *State v. Kaufman*, 51 Iowa 578, 580, 2 N.W. 275, 276 (1879) (dictum).[7]

7. A third approach has been to decline to rule definitively that a trial judge must either accept or reject an otherwise valid plea containing a protestation of inno-

This Court has not confronted this precise issue, but prior decisions do yield relevant principles. In *Lynch v. Overholser,* 369 U.S. 705 (1962), Lynch, who had been charged in the Municipal Court of the District of Columbia with drawing and negotiating bad checks, a misdemeanor punishable by a maximum of one year in jail, sought to enter a plea of guilty, but the trial judge refused to accept the plea since a psychiatric report in the judge's possession indicated that Lynch had been suffering from "a manic depressive psychosis, at the time of the crime charged," and hence might have been not guilty by reason of insanity. Although at the subsequent trial Lynch did not rely on the insanity defense, he was found not guilty by reason of insanity and committed for an indeterminate period to a mental institution. On habeas corpus, the Court ordered his release, construing the congressional legislation seemingly authorizing the commitment as not reaching a case where the accused preferred a guilty plea to a plea of insanity. The Court expressly refused to rule that Lynch had an absolute right to have his guilty plea accepted, but implied that there would have been no constitutional error had his plea been accepted even though evidence before the judge indicated that there was a valid defense.

The issue in *Hudson v. United States,* 272 U.S. 451 (1926), was whether a federal court has power to impose a prison sentence after accepting a plea of *nolo contendere,* a plea by which a defendant does not expressly admit his guilt, but nonetheless waives his right to a trial and authorizes the court for purposes of the case to treat him as if he were guilty. The Court held that a trial court does have such power * * *. Implicit in the *nolo contendere* cases is a recognition that the Constitution does not bar imposition of a prison sentence upon an accused who is unwilling expressly to admit his guilt but who, faced with grim alternatives, is willing to waive his trial and accept the sentence.

* * *

Nor can we perceive any material difference between a plea that refuses to admit commission of the criminal act and a plea containing a protestation of innocence when, as in the instant case, a defendant intelligently concludes that his interests require entry of a guilty plea and the record before the judge contains strong evidence of actual guilt. Here the State had a strong case of first-degree murder against Alford. Whether he realized or disbelieved his guilt, he insisted on his plea because in his view he had absolutely nothing to gain by a trial and much to gain by pleading. Because of the overwhelming evidence against him, a trial was precisely what neither Alford nor his attorney desired. Confronted with the choice between a trial for first-degree murder, on the one hand, and a plea of guilty to second-degree murder, on the other, Alford quite reasonably chose the latter and thereby limited the maximum penalty to a 30–year term. When his plea is

cence, but to leave that decision to his
sound discretion.

viewed in light of the evidence against him, which substantially negated his claim of innocence and which further provided a means by which the judge could test whether the plea was being intelligently entered,[10] its validity cannot be seriously questioned. In view of the strong factual basis for the plea demonstrated by the State and Alford's clearly expressed desire to enter it despite his professed belief in his innocence, we hold that the trial judge did not commit constitutional error in accepting it.[11]

[Justice Black, without writing a separate opinion, concurred in the Court's judgment and with most of its opinion.]

Mr. Justice Brennan, with whom Mr. Justice Douglas and Mr. Justice Marshall join, dissenting. Without reaching the question whether due process permits the entry of judgment upon a plea of guilty accompanied by a contemporaneous denial of acts constituting the crime, I believe that at the very least such a denial of guilt is also a relevant factor in determining whether the plea was voluntarily and intelligently made. With these factors in mind, it is sufficient in my view to state that the facts set out in the majority opinion demonstrate that Alford was "so gripped by fear of the death penalty" that his decision to plead guilty was not voluntary but was "the product of duress as much so as choice reflecting physical constraint." Accordingly, I would affirm the judgment of the Court of Appeals.

Questions and Points for Discussion

1. At least two purposes are served by requiring a factual basis for a guilty plea. First, determining that there is a factual basis ensures that the defendant is not unknowingly pleading guilty to a crime that he or she did not or could not have committed. McCarthy v. United States, 394 U.S. 459, 467, 89 S.Ct. 1166, 1171 (1969). Second, identifying a factual basis for the plea helps to ensure that the defendant's plea is in fact voluntary and not the result of impermissible threats, promises, or other pressures. Ames v. New York State Board of Parole, 593 F.Supp. 972, 975 (E.D.N.Y.1984), reversed 772 F.2d 13 (2d Cir.1985).

10. Because of the importance of protecting the innocent and of insuring that guilty pleas are a product of free and intelligent choice, various state and federal court decisions properly caution that pleas coupled with claims of innocence should not be accepted unless there is a factual basis for the plea, and until the judge taking the plea has inquired into and sought to resolve the conflict between the waiver of trial and the claim of innocence.

In the federal courts, Fed.Rule Crim. Proc. 11 expressly provides that a court "shall not enter a judgment upon a plea of guilty unless it is satisfied that there is a factual basis for the plea."

11. Our holding does not mean that a trial judge must accept every constitutionally valid guilty plea merely because a defendant wishes so to plead. A criminal defendant does not have an absolute right under the Constitution to have his guilty plea accepted by the court, although the States may by statute or otherwise confer such a right. Likewise, the States may bar their courts from accepting guilty pleas from any defendants who assert their innocence. Cf. Fed.Rule Crim.Proc. 11, which gives a trial judge discretion to "refuse to accept a plea of guilty . . . ." We need not now delineate the scope of that discretion.

Most courts have held that in the absence of a protestation of innocence by the defendant or some other special circumstances, due process does not require that a factual basis for a guilty plea be established before the plea is accepted. See, e.g., Rodriguez v. Ricketts, 777 F.2d 527, 528 (9th Cir.1985); Willbright v. Smith, 745 F.2d 779, 780–81 (2d Cir.1984); Banks v. McGougan, 717 F.2d 186, 188 (5th Cir.1983) (due process does not require a factual basis inquiry unless the court has been put on notice that there may be a need for such an inquiry.) Consequently, in states with no statutes or court rules requiring factual bases for guilty pleas, a court may accept a guilty plea without any evidence or information being tendered to the court which would support the conclusion that the defendant is indeed culpable of the offense to which he or she is pleading guilty.

In your opinion, when, if ever, is a factual basis for a guilty plea constitutionally required?

2. The Notes of the Advisory Committee on Rules, which drafted Rule 11 of the Federal Rules of Criminal Procedure, state that the factual basis for a guilty plea can be established in a variety of ways. Defendants themselves may, when entering their pleas, make inculpatory admissions in court which establish their guilt of the crimes charged. Or prosecutors or defense attorneys may recite details about the defendant's crime on the record as a way of establishing a factual basis. The Advisory Committee Notes also suggest that the factual basis requirement might be satisfied by presentence reports or by other undefined means.

3. Most states, like the federal system, remit the decision whether or not to accept a guilty plea to the court's discretion. Defendants sometimes challenge a trial judge's decision to reject a guilty plea on the grounds that the rejection constituted an abuse of discretion. After the rejection of their guilty pleas, these defendants have generally gone to trial, been found guilty, and received a more severe sentence than would have been imposed under a proffered plea agreement. Decisions in which no abuse of discretion was found in the trial court's rejection of a guilty plea include the following: United States v. Severino, 800 F.2d 42, 46–47 (2d Cir.1986) (no abuse of discretion where the judge thought the defendant had lied during his plea allocution); United States v. Noble, 653 F.2d 34, 36–37 (1st Cir. 1981) (no abuse of discretion where judge rejected plea to a misdemeanor so that prerogative to impose a more severe sentence upon conviction of a felony could be preserved); United States v. Adams, 634 F.2d 830, 835 (5th Cir.1981) (no abuse of discretion to reject plea agreement considered too lenient because of the defendant's criminal record); United States v. Thompson, 621 F.2d 1147, 1150–51 (1st Cir.1980) (no abuse of discretion to reject *nolo contendere* plea which would have precluded victims bringing civil actions against the defendant of the benefit of the government's prosecutorial efforts); Wilks v. Young, 586 F.Supp. 413, 416–17 (E.D.Wis. 1984) (no abuse of discretion to reject guilty plea in the absence of a factual basis).

BRADY v. UNITED STATES

Supreme Court of the United States, 1970.
397 U.S. 742, 90 S.Ct. 1463, 25 L.Ed.2d 747.

MR. JUSTICE WHITE delivered the opinion of the Court.

In 1959, petitioner was charged with kidnaping in violation of 18 U.S.C. § 1201(a).[1] Since the indictment charged that the victim of the kidnaping was not liberated unharmed, petitioner faced a maximum penalty of death if the verdict of the jury should so recommend. Petitioner, represented by competent counsel throughout, first elected to plead not guilty. * * * Upon learning that his codefendant, who had confessed to the authorities, would plead guilty and be available to testify against him, petitioner changed his plea to guilty. His plea was accepted after the trial judge twice questioned him as to the voluntariness of his plea.[2] Petitioner was sentenced to 50 years' imprisonment, later reduced to 30.

In 1967, petitioner sought relief under 28 U.S.C. § 2255, claiming that his plea of guilty was not voluntarily given because § 1201(a) operated to coerce his plea * * *.

After a hearing, the District Court for the District of New Mexico denied relief. * * * The court held that § 1201(a) was constitutional and found that petitioner decided to plead guilty when he learned that his codefendant was going to plead guilty: petitioner pleaded guilty "by reason of other matters and not by reason of the statute" or because of any acts of the trial judge. The court concluded that "the plea was voluntarily and knowingly made."

The Court of Appeals for the Tenth Circuit affirmed * * *. We granted certiorari to consider the claim that the Court of Appeals was in error in not reaching a contrary result on the authority of this

---

1. "Whoever knowingly transports in interstate or foreign commerce, any person who has been unlawfully seized, confined, inveigled, decoyed, kidnaped, abducted, or carried away and held for ransom or reward or otherwise, except, in the case of a minor, by a parent thereof, shall be punished (1) by death if the kidnaped person has not been liberated unharmed, and if the verdict of the jury shall so recommend, or (2) by imprisonment for any term of years or for life, if the death penalty is not imposed."

2. Eight days after petitioner pleaded guilty, he was brought before the court for sentencing. At that time, the court questioned petitioner for a second time about the voluntariness of his plea:

"THE COURT: . . . Having read the presentence report and the statement you made to the probation officer, I want to be certain that you know what you are doing

and you did know when you entered a plea of guilty the other day. Do you want to let that plea of guilty stand, or do you want to withdraw it and plead not guilty?

"DEFENDANT BRADY: I want to let that plea stand, sir.

"THE COURT: You understand that in doing that you are admitting and confessing the truth of the charge contained in the indictment and that that you enter a plea of guilty voluntarily, without persuasion, coercion of any kind? Is that right?

"DEFENDANT BRADY: Yes, your Honor.

"THE COURT: And you do do that?

"DEFENDANT BRADY: Yes, I do.

"THE COURT: You plead guilty to the charge?

"DEFENDANT BRADY: Yes, I do."

Court's decision in *United States v. Jackson,* 390 U.S. 570 (1968). We affirm.

I

In *United States v. Jackson,* the defendants were indicted under § 1201(a). The District Court dismissed the § 1201(a) count of the indictment, holding the statute unconstitutional because it permitted imposition of the death sentence only upon a jury's recommendation and thereby made the risk of death the price of a jury trial. This Court held the statute valid, except for the death penalty provision; with respect to the latter, the Court agreed with the trial court "that the death penalty provision . . . imposes an impermissible burden upon the exercise of a constitutional right . . . ." * * *

Since the "inevitable effect" of the death penalty provision of § 1201(a) was said by the Court to be the needless encouragement of pleas of guilty and waivers of jury trial, Brady contends that *Jackson* requires the invalidation of every plea of guilty entered under that section, at least when the fear of death is shown to have been a factor in the plea. Petitioner, however, has read far too much into the *Jackson* opinion.

* * *

Plainly, it seems to us, *Jackson* ruled neither that all pleas of guilty encouraged by the fear of a possible death sentence are involuntary pleas nor that such encouraged pleas are invalid whether involuntary or not. *Jackson* prohibits the imposition of the death penalty under § 1201(a), but that decision neither fashioned a new standard for judging the validity of guilty pleas nor mandated a new application of the test theretofore fashioned by courts and since reiterated that guilty pleas are valid if both "voluntary" and "intelligent."

II

* * *

The voluntariness of Brady's plea can be determined only by considering all of the relevant circumstances surrounding it. One of these circumstances was the possibility of a heavier sentence following a guilty verdict after a trial. It may be that Brady, faced with a strong case against him and recognizing that his chances for acquittal were slight, preferred to plead guilty and thus limit the penalty to life imprisonment rather than to elect a jury trial which could result in a death penalty. But even if we assume that Brady would not have pleaded guilty except for the death penalty provision of § 1201(a), this assumption merely identifies the penalty provision as a "but for" cause of his plea. That the statute caused the plea in this sense does not necessarily prove that the plea was coerced and invalid as an involuntary act.

* * *

Of course, the agents of the State may not produce a plea by actual or threatened physical harm or by mental coercion overbearing the will of the defendant. But nothing of the sort is claimed in this case; nor is there evidence that Brady was so gripped by fear of the death penalty or hope of leniency that he did not or could not, with the help of counsel, rationally weigh the advantages of going to trial against the advantages of pleading guilty. Brady's claim is of a different sort: that it violates the Fifth Amendment to influence or encourage a guilty plea by opportunity or promise of leniency and that a guilty plea is coerced and invalid if influenced by the fear of a possibly higher penalty for the crime charged if a conviction is obtained after the State is put to its proof.

Insofar as the voluntariness of his plea is concerned, there is little to differentiate Brady from (1) the defendant, in a jurisdiction where the judge and jury have the same range of sentencing power, who pleads guilty because his lawyer advises him that the judge will very probably be more lenient than the jury; (2) the defendant, in a jurisdiction where the judge alone has sentencing power, who is advised by counsel that the judge is normally more lenient with defendants who plead guilty than with those who go to trial; (3) the defendant who is permitted by prosecutor and judge to plead guilty to a lesser offense included in the offense charged; and (4) the defendant who pleads guilty to certain counts with the understanding that other charges will be dropped. In each of these situations,[8] as in Brady's case, the defendant might never plead guilty absent the possibility or certainty that the plea will result in a lesser penalty than the sentence that could be imposed after a trial and a verdict of guilty. We decline to hold, however, that a guilty plea is compelled and invalid under the Fifth Amendment whenever motivated by the defendant's desire to accept the certainty or probability of a lesser penalty rather than face a wider range of possibilities extending from acquittal to conviction and a higher penalty authorized by law for the crime charged.

The issue we deal with is inherent in the criminal law and its administration because guilty pleas are not constitutionally forbidden, because the criminal law characteristically extends to judge or jury a range of choice in setting the sentence in individual cases, and because both the State and the defendant often find it advantageous to preclude the possibility of the maximum penalty authorized by law. For a defendant who sees slight possibility of acquittal, the advantages of pleading guilty and limiting the probable penalty are obvious—his exposure is reduced, the correctional processes can begin immediately, and the practical burdens of a trial are eliminated. For the State there are also advantages—the more promptly imposed punishment after an admission of guilt may more effectively attain the objectives of punish-

---

8. We here make no reference to the situation where the prosecutor or judge, or both, deliberately employ their charging and sentencing powers to induce a particular defendant to tender a plea of guilty. In Brady's case there is no claim that the prosecutor threatened prosecution on a charge not justified by the evidence or that the trial judge threatened Brady with a harsher sentence if convicted after trial in order to induce him to plead guilty.

ment; and with the avoidance of trial, scarce judicial and prosecutorial resources are conserved for those cases in which there is a substantial issue of the defendant's guilt or in which there is substantial doubt that the State can sustain its burden of proof. It is this mutuality of advantage that perhaps explains the fact that at present well over three-fourths of the criminal convictions in this country rest on pleas of guilty, a great many of them no doubt motivated at least in part by the hope or assurance of a lesser penalty than might be imposed if there were a guilty verdict after a trial to judge or jury.

Of course, that the prevalence of guilty pleas is explainable does not necessarily validate those pleas or the system which produces them. But we cannot hold that it is unconstitutional for the State to extend a benefit to a defendant who in turn extends a substantial benefit to the State and who demonstrates by his plea that he is ready and willing to admit his crime and to enter the correctional system in a frame of mind that affords hope for success in rehabilitation over a shorter period of time than might otherwise be necessary.

A contrary holding would require the States and Federal Government to forbid guilty pleas altogether, to provide a single invariable penalty for each crime defined by the statutes, or to place the sentencing function in a separate authority having no knowledge of the manner in which the conviction in each case was obtained. In any event, it would be necessary to forbid prosecutors and judges to accept guilty pleas to selected counts, to lesser included offenses, or to reduced charges. The Fifth Amendment does not reach so far.

* * *

* * * Brady first pleaded not guilty; prior to changing his plea to guilty he was subjected to no threats or promises in face-to-face encounters with the authorities. He had competent counsel and full opportunity to assess the advantages and disadvantages of a trial as compared with those attending a plea of guilty; there was no hazard of an impulsive and improvident response to a seeming but unreal advantage. His plea of guilty was entered in open court and before a judge obviously sensitive to the requirements of the law with respect to guilty pleas. Brady's plea * * * was voluntary.

The standard as to the voluntariness of guilty pleas must be essentially that defined by Judge Tuttle of the Court of Appeals for the Fifth Circuit:

> " '[A] plea of guilty entered by one fully aware of the direct consequences, including the actual value of any commitments made to him by the court, prosecutor, or his own counsel, must stand unless induced by threats (or promises to discontinue improper harassment), misrepresentation (including unfulfilled or unfulfillable promises), or perhaps by promises that are by their nature improper as having no proper relationship to the prosecutor's business (e.g. bribes).' 242 F.2d at page 115."

Under this standard, a plea of guilty is not invalid merely because entered to avoid the possibility of a death penalty.

III

The record before us also supports the conclusion that Brady's plea was intelligently made. He was advised by competent counsel, he was made aware of the nature of the charge against him, and there was nothing to indicate that he was incompetent or otherwise not in control of his mental faculties; once his confederate had pleaded guilty and became available to testify, he chose to plead guilty, perhaps to ensure that he would face no more than life imprisonment or a term of years. Brady was aware of precisely what he was doing when he admitted that he had kidnaped the victim and had not released her unharmed.

It is true that Brady's counsel advised him that § 1201(a) empowered the jury to impose the death penalty and that nine years later in *United States v. Jackson,* the Court held that the jury had no such power as long as the judge could impose only a lesser penalty if trial was to the court or there was a plea of guilty. But these facts do not require us to set aside Brady's conviction.

Often the decision to plead guilty is heavily influenced by the defendant's appraisal of the prosecution's case against him and by the apparent likelihood of securing leniency should a guilty plea be offered and accepted. Considerations like these frequently present imponderable questions for which there are no certain answers; judgments may be made that in the light of later events seem improvident, although they were perfectly sensible at the time. The rule that a plea must be intelligently made to be valid does not require that a plea be vulnerable to later attack if the defendant did not correctly assess every relevant factor entering into his decision. A defendant is not entitled to withdraw his plea merely because he discovers long after the plea has been accepted that his calculus misapprehended the quality of the State's case or the likely penalties attached to alternative courses of action. More particularly, absent misrepresentation or other impermissible conduct by state agents, a voluntary plea of guilty intelligently made in the light of the then applicable law does not become vulnerable because later judicial decisions indicate that the plea rested on a faulty premise. A plea of guilty triggered by the expectations of a competently counseled defendant that the State will have a strong case against him is not subject to later attack because the defendant's lawyer correctly advised him with respect to the then existing law as to possible penalties but later pronouncements of the courts, as in this case, hold that the maximum penalty for the crime in question was less than was reasonably assumed at the time the plea was entered.

The fact that Brady did not anticipate *United States v. Jackson* does not impugn the truth or reliability of his plea. We find no requirement in the Constitution that a defendant must be permitted to disown his solemn admissions in open court that he committed the act with which he is charged simply because it later develops that the State would have had a weaker case than the defendant had thought or that the maximum penalty then assumed applicable has been held inapplicable in subsequent judicial decisions.

This is not to say that guilty plea convictions hold no hazards for the innocent or that the methods of taking guilty pleas presently employed in this country are necessarily valid in all respects. This mode of conviction is no more foolproof than full trials to the court or to the jury. Accordingly, we take great precautions against unsound results, and we should continue to do so, whether conviction is by plea or by trial. We would have serious doubts about this case if the encouragement of guilty pleas by offers of leniency substantially increased the likelihood that defendants, advised by competent counsel, would falsely condemn themselves. But our view is to the contrary and is based on our expectations that courts will satisfy themselves that pleas of guilty are voluntarily and intelligently made by competent defendants with adequate advice of counsel and that there is nothing to question the accuracy and reliability of the defendants' admissions that they committed the crimes with which they are charged. In the case before us, nothing in the record impeaches Brady's plea or suggests that his admissions in open court were anything but the truth.

Although Brady's plea of guilty may well have been motivated in part by a desire to avoid a possible death penalty, we are convinced that his plea was voluntarily and intelligently made and we have no reason to doubt that his solemn admission of guilt was truthful.

Affirmed.

[Although not writing a separate opinion, Justice Black concurred in the judgment and in substantially all of the Court's opinion.]

MR. JUSTICE BRENNAN, with whom MR. JUSTICE DOUGLAS and MR. JUSTICE MARSHALL join, concurring in the result.

In *United States v. Jackson,* 390 U.S. 570 (1968), we held that the operative effect of the capital punishment provisions of the Federal Kidnaping Act was unconstitutionally "to discourage assertion of the Fifth Amendment right not to plead guilty and to deter exercise of the Sixth Amendment right to demand a jury trial." The petitioners in these cases claim that they were the victims of the very vices we condemned in *Jackson.* Yet the Court paradoxically holds that each of the petitioners must be denied relief even if his allegations are substantiated. * * *

* * *

It has frequently been held * * * that a guilty plea induced by threats or promises by the trial judge is invalid because of the risk that the trial judge's impartiality will be compromised and because of the inherently unequal bargaining power of the judge and the accused. The assistance of counsel in this situation, of course, may improve a defendant's bargaining *ability,* but it does not alter the underlying inequality of *power.* Significantly, the Court explicitly refrains from expressing its views on this issue. This is an unfortunate omission, for judicial promises of leniency in return for a guilty plea provide a useful analogy to what has occurred in the instant cases. Here, the government has promised the accused, through the legislature, that he will receive a substantially reduced sentence if he pleads guilty. In fact, the legislature has simultaneously threatened the accused with the ultimate penalty—death—if he insists upon a jury trial and has promised a penalty no greater than life imprisonment if he pleads guilty.

It was precisely this statutorily imposed dilemma that we identified in *Jackson* as having the "inevitable effect" of discouraging assertion of the right not to plead guilty and to demand a jury trial. As recognized in *Jackson*, it is inconceivable that this sort of capital penalty scheme will not have a major impact upon the decisions of many defendants to plead guilty. In any particular case, therefore, the influence of this unconstitutional factor must necessarily be given weight in determining the voluntariness of a plea.

* * *

Of course, whether in a given case the penalty scheme has actually exercised its pernicious influence so as to make a guilty plea involuntary can be decided only by consideration of the factors that actually motivated the defendant to enter his plea. If a particular defendant can demonstrate that the death penalty scheme exercised a significant influence upon his decision to plead guilty, then, under *Jackson,* he is entitled to reversal of the conviction based upon his illicitly produced plea.

* * *

An independent examination of the record in the instant case convinces me that the conclusions of the lower courts are not clearly erroneous. Although Brady was aware that he faced a possible death sentence, there is no evidence that this factor alone played a significant role in his decision to enter a guilty plea. Rather, there is considerable evidence, which the District Court credited, that Brady's plea was triggered by the confession and plea decision of his codefendant and not by any substantial fear of the death penalty. Moreover, Brady's position is dependent in large measure upon his own assertions, years after the fact, that his plea was motivated by fear of the death penalty and thus rests largely upon his own credibility. For example, there is no indication, contemporaneous with the entry of the guilty plea, that Brady thought he was innocent and was pleading guilty merely to avoid possible execution. Furthermore, Brady's plea was accepted by a trial judge who manifested some sensitivity to the seriousness of a guilty plea and questioned Brady at length concerning his guilt and the voluntariness of the plea before it was finally accepted.

In view of the foregoing, I concur in the result reached by the Court in the *Brady* case.

Questions and Points for Discussion

1. Brady v. United States was one of three cases decided by the Supreme Court on the same day in 1970 which have come to be known as the *Brady* trilogy. The second of these cases was Parker v. North Carolina, 397 U.S. 790, 90 S.Ct. 1458 (1970). In *Parker,* the Court repeated that a defendant's guilty plea is not involuntary simply because it was entered in order to avoid imposition of the death penalty. The Court also rejected the defendant's claim that his guilty plea should be vacated because it was the "fruit" of an allegedly involuntary confession previously obtained from the defendant. The Court observed that more than a month elapsed between the defendant's confession and his guilty plea and that during that time the defendant was advised by his attorney and his family as to the advisability of pleading guilty. Consequently, the Court concluded that even if the defendant's confession was involuntary, the defendant's guilty plea was still valid because there was not a sufficient connection between the confession and the defendant's decision to plead guilty to invalidate the plea.

The defendant in *Parker* also claimed that his decision to plead guilty was not intelligent because his attorney had erred in concluding that his confession was voluntary and could be admitted in evidence against the defendant if his case proceeded to trial. The Court also rejected this claim for the same reasons set forth in McMann v. Richardson, 397 U.S. 759, 90 S.Ct. 1441 (1970). In *McMann,* the third case in the *Brady* trilogy, the Court observed as follows:

> That a guilty plea must be intelligently made is not a requirement that all advice offered by the defendant's lawyer withstand retrospective examination in a post-conviction hearing. Courts continue to have serious differences among themselves on the admissibility of evidence, both with respect to the proper standard by which the facts are to be judged and with respect to the application of that standard to particular facts. That this Court might hold a defendant's confession inadmissible in evidence, possibly by a divided vote, hardly justifies a conclusion that the defendant's attorney was incompetent or ineffective when he thought the admissibility of the confession sufficiently probable to advise a plea of guilty.

> In our view a defendant's plea of guilty based on reasonably competent advice is an intelligent plea not open to attack on the ground that counsel may have misjudged the admissibility of the defendant's confession. Whether a plea of guilty is unintelligent and therefore vulnerable when motivated by a confession erroneously thought admissible in evidence depends as an initial matter, not on whether a court would retrospectively consider counsel's advice to be right or wrong, but on whether that advice was within the range of competence demanded of attorneys in criminal cases.

Id. at 770–71, 90 S.Ct. at 1448–49.

2. In Hill v. Lockhart, 474 U.S. 52, 106 S.Ct. 366 (1985), the Supreme Court expanded upon its holding in McMann v. Richardson, ruling that even if an attorney's advice given to a defendant deciding whether or not to

plead guilty is sorely deficient, the defendant's guilty plea is not necessarily invalid. The Court in *Hill* held that a two-part test previously adopted by the Court in Strickland v. Washington, 466 U.S. 668, 104 S.Ct. 2052 (1984) should apply when determining whether defendants received ineffective assistance of counsel during the plea process, rendering a subsequent guilty plea invalid. Under the first part of this test, defendants must establish that their attorneys acted unreasonably according to "prevailing professional norms" when advising them and acting on their behalf. Id. at 688, 104 S.Ct. at 2065. To satisfy this part of the test, defendants must rebut a "strong presumption" that their attorneys acted within "the wide range of reasonable professional assistance." Id. at 689, 104 S.Ct. at 2065. Even if their attorneys acted unreasonably, however, defendants must still establish that they were prejudiced by their counsels' deficient performance. In the plea context, this means that defendants must demonstrate that there is a "reasonable probability" that had their attorneys rendered reasonable professional assistance, they would not have pled guilty and would instead have gone to trial. Hill, 474 U.S. at 59, 106 S.Ct. at 370.

In *Hill* itself, the defendant alleged that he had received ineffective assistance of counsel in violation of his sixth amendment right to counsel when he decided to plead guilty after his attorney apprised him that he would only have to serve one-third of his sentence before becoming eligible for parole. He later learned that he would actually have to serve one-half of his sentence before becoming eligible for parole. The Supreme Court held that the defendant had failed to establish that he had received ineffective assistance of counsel; he had not satisfied the second prong of the *Strickland* test because he failed to allege that he would have gone to trial had he received accurate advice about his eligibility for parole.

3. An excellent overview of the information of which a defense attorney should be aware and the steps that should be taken by a defense attorney to effectively represent a defendant who wishes to plead guilty or enter into plea negotiations can be found in A. Amsterdam, Trial Manual 5 for the Defense of Criminal Cases, vol. 1, at 339–367 (1988).

4. Tollett v. Henderson, 411 U.S. 258, 93 S.Ct. 1602 (1973) involved a defendant who sought to set aside his plea of guilty to murder on the grounds that blacks had been unconstitutionally excluded from the grand jury that had indicted him. The defendant contended that his guilty plea was not rendered intelligently because he was unaware when he pled guilty of the constitutional infirmity in the grand jury selection procedures.

The Supreme Court concluded that the principles set forth in the *Brady* trilogy foreclosed the defendant's claim that his lack of knowledge of the constitutional claim was enough to automatically invalidate his guilty plea:

> [A] guilty plea represents a break in the chain of events which has preceded it in the criminal process. When a criminal defendant has solemnly admitted in open court that he is in fact guilty of the offense with which he is charged, he may not thereafter raise independent claims relating to the deprivation of constitutional rights that occurred prior to the entry of the guilty plea. He may only attack the voluntary and intelligent character of the guilty plea by showing that the advice

> he received from counsel was not within the standards set forth in *McMann.*
>
> A guilty plea, voluntarily and intelligently entered, may not be vacated because the defendant was not advised of every conceivable constitutional plea in abatement he might have to the charge, no matter how peripheral such a plea might be to the normal focus of counsel's inquiry.

Id. at 267, 93 S.Ct. at 1608. The Court then remanded the case for consideration of the question of whether, under the facts of this case, the defendant's guilty plea was invalid because of his attorney's failure to apprise him of the unconstitutionality of the grand jury selection methods.

The Supreme Court distinguished its decision in *Tollett* in the succeeding case of Menna v. New York, 423 U.S. 61, 96 S.Ct. 241 (1975) (per curiam). In that case, the defendant was held in criminal contempt of court and sentenced to thirty days in jail after he refused to answer questions posed by a grand jury. He was then also indicted for his refusal to cooperate with the grand jury. After unsuccessfully moving to dismiss the indictment on double jeopardy grounds, the defendant pled guilty to the indictment, but then appealed, claiming his conviction was barred by the double jeopardy clause in the fifth amendment. The state responded by arguing that the defendant had waived this claim by pleading guilty.

The Supreme Court sided with the defendant, holding that "[w]here the State is precluded by the United States Constitution from haling a defendant into court on a charge, federal law requires that a conviction on that charge be set aside even if the conviction was entered pursuant to a counseled plea of guilty." Id. at 62, 96 S.Ct. at 242. In a footnote, the Court explained the distinction between the case before it and *Tollett:*

> Neither *Tollett v. Henderson* nor our earlier cases on which it relied, e.g., *Brady v. United States,* and *McMann v. Richardson* stand for the proposition that counseled guilty pleas inevitably "waive" all antecedent constitutional violations. * * * The point of these cases is that a counseled plea of guilty is an admission of factual guilt so reliable that, where voluntary and intelligent, it *quite validly* removes the issue of factual guilt from the case. In most cases, factual guilt is a sufficient basis for the State's imposition of punishment. A guilty plea, therefore, simply renders irrelevant those constitutional violations not logically inconsistent with the valid establishment of factual guilt and which do not stand in the way of conviction, if factual guilt is validly established. Here, however, the claim is that the State may not convict petitioner no matter how validly his factual guilt is established. The guilty plea, therefore, does not bar the claim.
>
> We do not hold that a double jeopardy claim may never be waived. We simply hold that a plea of guilty to a charge does not waive a claim that—judged on its face—the charge is one which the State may not constitutionally prosecute.

Id. at 62–63 n. 2, 96 S.Ct. at 242 n. 2.

In United States v. Broce, 488 U.S. 563, 109 S.Ct. 757 (1989), the Supreme Court confirmed that not all double jeopardy claims can be asserted by a defendant following entry of a guilty plea. The defendants in that case had pled guilty to two counts of conspiracy. They later sought to vacate their sentence on one of the two counts on the grounds that they had really participated in only one overarching conspiracy and that to punish them for two contravened the double jeopardy clause.

The Supreme Court responded by invoking the general rule described in *Tollett v. Henderson* under which collateral attacks on guilty pleas are barred. The exception to that rule discussed in *Menna v. New York* was inapplicable here, according to the Court, since that exception was limited to those instances where "on the face of the record the court had no power to enter the conviction or impose the sentence." 109 S.Ct. at 762. Since a reviewing court would have to go beyond the record to determine whether the defendants had been involved in one or two conspiracies and since the defendants did not allege that they had received ineffective assistance of counsel, their guilty pleas to and sentences for two separate conspiracies would remain in effect.

Do you agree with the Court's decisions in *Tollett, Menna,* and *Broce?* Under what circumstances do you believe that a defendant should be able to get a guilty plea set aside because of a constitutional violation? Can and should a defendant be able to challenge a guilty plea on the grounds that the defendant's right to a speedy trial was violated? See Tiemens v. United States, 724 F.2d 928, 929 (11th Cir.1984). What if the parties engaged in discovery before the defendant pled guilty, but the prosecutor failed to disclose exculpatory evidence to which the defendant had a right of access? Would and should the prosecutor's nondisclosure invalidate the defendant's guilty plea? See, e.g., White v. United States, 858 F.2d 416, 423–24 (8th Cir.1988); Campbell v. Marshall, 769 F.2d 314, 318–24 (6th Cir.1985).

5. Although a defendant may not have a constitutional right to assert certain constitutional claims following the entry of a guilty plea, a state retains the prerogative to permit a defendant to later assert these claims on appeal. See, e.g., N.Y.Crim.Proc.Law § 710.70(2) (defendant who has pled guilty can still challenge on appeal denials of a motion to suppress evidence).

6. In his concurring opinion in *Brady v. United States,* Justice Marshall noted that threats or promises made by a trial judge to induce a guilty plea may render that plea involuntary. See e.g., Schaffner v. Greco, 458 F.Supp. 202 (S.D.N.Y.1978). Because of the risk that judicial participation in plea bargaining will place undue pressure on a defendant to plead guilty, a number of jurisdictions have barred such participation. See, e.g., Fed.R.Crim.P. 11(e)(1). The American Bar Association Standards for Criminal Justice, however, have adopted an intermediate approach to this question, permitting judges to participate in plea discussions, but limiting where these discussions can occur and what can be said by trial judges during them:

Standard 14–3.3. Responsibilities of the judge

* * *

(c) When the parties are unable to reach a plea agreement, if the defendant's counsel and prosecutor agree, they may request to meet with the judge in order to discuss a plea agreement. If the judge agrees to meet with the parties, the judge shall serve as a moderator in listening to their respective presentations concerning appropriate charge or sentence concessions. Following the presentation of the parties, the judge may indicate what charge or sentence concessions would be acceptable or whether the judge wishes to have a preplea report before rendering a decision. The parties may thereupon decide among themselves, outside of the presence of the court, whether to accept or reject the plea agreement tendered by the court.

(d) Whenever the judge is presented with a plea agreement or consents to a conference in order to listen to the parties concerning charge or sentence concessions, the court may require or allow any person, including the defendant, the alleged victim, and others, to appear or to testify.

(e) Where the parties have neither advised the judge of a plea agreement nor requested to meet for plea discussion purposes, the judge may inquire of the parties whether disposition without trial has been explored and may allow an adjournment to enable plea discussions to occur.

(f) All discussions at which the judge is present relating to plea agreements should be recorded verbatim and preserved, except that for good cause the judge may order the transcript of proceedings to be sealed. Such discussions should be held in open court unless good cause is present for the proceedings to be held in chambers. Except as otherwise provided in this standard, the judge should never through word or demeanor, either directly or indirectly, communicate to the defendant or defense counsel that a plea agreement should be accepted or that a guilty plea should be entered.

* * *

B. BREACHES OF PLEA AGREEMENTS

SANTOBELLO v. NEW YORK

Supreme Court of the United States, 1971.
404 U.S. 257, 92 S.Ct. 495, 30 L.Ed.2d 427.

MR. CHIEF JUSTICE BURGER delivered the opinion of the Court.

We granted certiorari in this case to determine whether the State's failure to keep a commitment concerning the sentence recommendation on a guilty plea required a new trial.

The facts are not in dispute. The State of New York indicted petitioner in 1969 on two felony counts, Promoting Gambling in the First Degree, and Possession of Gambling Records in the First Degree. Petitioner first entered a plea of not guilty to both counts. After negotiations, the Assistant District Attorney in charge of the case agreed to permit petitioner to plead guilty to a lesser-included offense, Possession of Gambling Records in the Second Degree, conviction of which would carry a maximum prison sentence of one year. The prosecutor agreed to make no recommendation as to the sentence.

On June 16, 1969, petitioner accordingly withdrew his plea of not guilty and entered a plea of guilty to the lesser charge. Petitioner represented to the sentencing judge that the plea was voluntary and that the facts of the case, as described by the Assistant District Attorney, were true. The court accepted the plea and set a date for sentencing. * * *

* * *

At this appearance, another prosecutor had replaced the prosecutor who had negotiated the plea. The new prosecutor recommended the maximum one-year sentence. In making this recommendation, he cited petitioner's criminal record and alleged links with organized crime. Defense counsel immediately objected on the ground that the State had promised petitioner before the plea was entered that there would be no sentence recommendation by the prosecution. He sought to adjourn the sentence hearing in order to have time to prepare proof of the first prosecutor's promise. The second prosecutor, apparently ignorant of his colleague's commitment, argued that there was nothing in the record to support petitioner's claim of a promise, but the State, in subsequent proceedings, has not contested that such a promise was made.

The sentencing judge ended discussion, with the following statement, quoting extensively from the presentence report:

"Mr. Aronstein [Defense Counsel], I am not at all influenced by what the District Attorney says, so that there is no need to adjourn the sentence, and there is no need to have any testimony. It doesn't make a particle of difference what the District Attorney says he will do, or what he doesn't do.

"I have here, Mr. Aronstein, a probation report. I have here a history of a long, long serious criminal record. I have here a picture of the life history of this man. . . .

" 'He is unamenable to supervision in the community. He is a professional criminal.' This is in quotes. 'And a recidivist. Institutionalization—'; that means, in plain language, just putting him away, 'is the only means of halting his anti-social activities,' and protecting you, your family, me, my family, protecting society. 'Institutionalization.' Plain language, put him behind bars.

"Under the plea, I can only send him to the New York City Correctional Institution for men for one year, which I am hereby doing."

The judge then imposed the maximum sentence of one year.

[The petitioner's conviction was affirmed on appeal, and the Supreme Court then granted certiorari.]

Disposition of charges after plea discussions is not only an essential part of the process but a highly desirable part for many reasons. It leads to prompt and largely final disposition of most criminal cases; it avoids much of the corrosive impact of enforced idleness during pretrial confinement for those who are denied release pending trial; it protects the public from those accused persons who are prone to continue criminal conduct even while on pretrial release; and, by shortening the time between charge and disposition, it enhances whatever may be the rehabilitative prospects of the guilty when they are ultimately imprisoned.

However, all of these considerations presuppose fairness in securing agreement between an accused and a prosecutor. * * *

This phase of the process of criminal justice, and the adjudicative element inherent in accepting a plea of guilty, must be attended by safeguards to insure the defendant what is reasonably due in the circumstances. Those circumstances will vary, but a constant factor is that when a plea rests in any significant degree on a promise or agreement of the prosecutor, so that it can be said to be part of the inducement or consideration, such promise must be fulfilled.

On this record, petitioner "bargained" and negotiated for a particular plea in order to secure dismissal of more serious charges, but also on condition that no sentence recommendation would be made by the prosecutor. It is now conceded that the promise to abstain from a recommendation was made, and at this stage the prosecution is not in a good position to argue that its inadvertent breach of agreement is immaterial. The staff lawyers in a prosecutor's office have the burden of "letting the left hand know what the right hand is doing" or has done. That the breach of agreement was inadvertent does not lessen its impact.

We need not reach the question whether the sentencing judge would or would not have been influenced had he known all the details of the negotiations for the plea. He stated that the prosecutor's recommendation did not influence him and we have no reason to doubt that. Nevertheless, we conclude that the interests of justice and appropriate recognition of the duties of the prosecution in relation to promises made in the negotiation of pleas of guilty will be best served by remanding the case to the state courts for further consideration. The ultimate relief to which petitioner is entitled we leave to the discretion of the state court, which is in a better position to decide whether the circumstances of this case require only that there be specific performance of the agreement on the plea, in which case petitioner should be resentenced by a different judge, or whether, in the view of the state court, the circumstances require granting the relief sought by petitioner, *i.e.,* the opportunity to withdraw his plea of guilty.[2] We emphasize that this is in no sense to question the fairness of the sentencing judge; the fault here rests on the prosecutor, not on the sentencing judge.

The judgment is vacated and the case is remanded for reconsideration not inconsistent with this opinion.

2. If the state court decides to allow withdrawal of the plea, the petitioner will, of course, plead anew to the original charge on two felony counts.

MR. JUSTICE DOUGLAS, concurring.

* * *

I join the opinion of the Court and favor a constitutional rule for this as well as for other pending or oncoming cases. Where the "plea bargain" is not kept by the prosecutor, the sentence must be vacated and the state court will decide in light of the circumstances of each case whether due process requires (a) that there be specific performance of the plea bargain or (b) that the defendant be given the option to go to trial on the original charges. One alternative may do justice in one case, and the other in a different case. In choosing a remedy, however, a court ought to accord a defendant's preference considerable, if not controlling, weight inasmuch as the fundamental rights flouted by a prosecutor's breach of a plea bargain are those of the defendant, not of the State.

MR. JUSTICE MARSHALL, with whom MR. JUSTICE BRENNAN and MR. JUSTICE STEWART join, concurring in part and dissenting in part.

I agree with much of the majority's opinion, but conclude that petitioner must be permitted to withdraw his guilty plea. This is the relief petitioner requested, and, on the facts set out by the majority, it is a form of relief to which he is entitled.

* * *

Questions and Points for Discussion

1. While the prosecutor in *Santobello* had agreed as part of the plea bargain to refrain from making a sentencing recommendation, prosecutors often agree to make a particular sentencing recommendation as part of a plea bargain. In United States v. Benchimol, 471 U.S. 453, 105 S.Ct. 2103 (1985), for example, the parties had agreed that the prosecutor would recommend probation in return for the defendant's guilty plea. The court nonetheless sentenced the defendant to prison for six years.

The defendant later moved to vacate his guilty plea or to be resentenced because the prosecutor, according to the defendant, had not enthusiastically recommended a sentence of probation to the court at the sentencing hearing and had not explained the government's reasons for recommending probation. The Supreme Court held that a defendant may bargain for a commitment by the prosecutor to enthusiastically make a certain recommendation to the court or to explain the reasons for the government's recommendation. No such agreements were made between the parties in this case, however, and the Court refused to imply such terms into their agreement.

2. The Supreme Court distinguished *Santobello* in Mabry v. Johnson, 467 U.S. 504, 104 S.Ct. 2543 (1984). In *Mabry*, the defendant, who was already serving concurrent sentences of twenty-one and twelve years for burglary and assault, was facing a murder charge. The prosecutor offered to recommend a twenty-one-year sentence to be served concurrently with the defendant's other sentences if he agreed to plead guilty to being an accessory after a felony murder. The defendant's attorney then called the prosecutor, accepting the offer. The prosecutor, however, said that he had

made a mistake in making the offer to the defendant and retracted the offer. The prosecutor instead offered to recommend a twenty-one-year sentence to be served consecutively with the defendant's other sentences if he pled guilty. The defendant eventually accepted this offer and received a twenty-one-year consecutive sentence.

The defendant then filed a habeas corpus petition, contending that his due process rights were violated when the prosecutor refused to abide by the terms of his original plea offer. The Supreme Court unanimously disagreed. Noting that at the time the defendant pled guilty he knew fully well that the prosecutor would recommend a consecutive sentence, the Court concluded that the defendant's plea was simply not induced by the prosecutor's original plea offer. Consequently, the original plea offer, even though "accepted" by the defendant, was "without constitutional significance." Id. at 510, 104 S.Ct. at 2548.

3. Plea agreements may be breached, of course, not only by prosecutors, but by defendants. The Supreme Court case of Ricketts v. Adamson, 483 U.S. 1, 107 S.Ct. 2680 (1987) reveals the potentially severe consequences that can ensue from such a breach by a defendant. That case involved a defendant who was charged with first-degree murder. The prosecutor and the defendant entered into a plea agreement under which the defendant agreed to plead guilty to second-degree murder and to testify "when requested" against two other people involved in the murder. In return, the defendant would receive a prison sentence of forty-eight to forty-nine years. The trial court accepted this plea agreement.

The defendant then testified in the trials of his two co-defendants as he had agreed to do, and they were convicted of first-degree murder. Their convictions, however, were reversed on appeal and their cases remanded for retrial. At this point, the defendant, believing that he had fulfilled the terms of the plea agreement, balked at testifying again on the government's behalf unless the government agreed to release him from prison after the retrials. The state informed the defendant that he was in breach of the plea agreement and once again charged him with first-degree murder. Following a trial, the defendant was convicted of first-degree murder and sentenced to death.

The defendant contended that his right not to be subjected to double jeopardy barred his prosecution for first-degree murder, but the Supreme Court held that the terms of the plea agreement foreclosed that claim. The agreement specifically provided that " '[s]hould the defendant refuse to testify or should he at any time testify untruthfully * * * then this entire agreement is null and void and the original charge will be automatically reinstated.' " Id. at 4, 107 S.Ct. at 2682. According to the Court, when the defendant decided to unilaterally pursue his own interpretation of the meaning of the plea agreement, he assumed the risk that he would be found in breach of the agreement and subject to a first-degree murder prosecution. Even if he had acted in good faith, the defendant had taken a calculated gamble; he had lost the gamble and as a result, might now lose his life. Id. at 10–11, 107 S.Ct. at 2686.

C. CONSTRAINTS ON THE GOVERNMENT DURING AND AFTER THE PLEA PROCESS

BORDENKIRCHER v. HAYES

Supreme Court of the United States, 1978.
434 U.S. 357, 98 S.Ct. 663, 54 L.Ed.2d 604.

MR. JUSTICE STEWART delivered the opinion of the Court.

The question in this case is whether the Due Process Clause of the Fourteenth Amendment is violated when a state prosecutor carries out a threat made during plea negotiations to reindict the accused on more serious charges if he does not plead guilty to the offense with which he was originally charged.

The respondent, Paul Lewis Hayes, was indicted by a Fayette County, Ky., grand jury on a charge of uttering a forged instrument in the amount of $88.30, an offense then punishable by a term of 2 to 10 years in prison. After arraignment, Hayes, his retained counsel, and the Commonwealth's Attorney met in the presence of the Clerk of the Court to discuss a possible plea agreement. During these conferences the prosecutor offered to recommend a sentence of five years in prison if Hayes would plead guilty to the indictment. He also said that if Hayes did not plead guilty and "save the court the inconvenience and necessity of a trial," he would return to the grand jury to seek an indictment under the Kentucky Habitual Criminal Act, which would subject Hayes to a mandatory sentence of life imprisonment by reason of his two prior felony convictions. Hayes chose not to plead guilty, and the prosecutor did obtain an indictment charging him under the Habitual Criminal Act. It is not disputed that the recidivist charge was fully justified by the evidence, that the prosecutor was in possession of this evidence at the time of the original indictment, and that Hayes' refusal to plead guilty to the original charge was what led to his indictment under the habitual criminal statute.

A jury found Hayes guilty on the principal charge of uttering a forged instrument and, in a separate proceeding, further found that he had twice before been convicted of felonies. As required by the habitual offender statute, he was sentenced to a life term in the penitentiary. The Kentucky Court of Appeals rejected Hayes' constitutional objections to the enhanced sentence, holding in an unpublished opinion that imprisonment for life with the possibility of parole was constitutionally permissible in light of the previous felonies of which Hayes had been convicted, and that the prosecutor's decision to indict him as a habitual offender was a legitimate use of available leverage in the plea-bargaining process.

On Hayes' petition for a federal writ of habeas corpus, the United States District Court for the Eastern District of Kentucky agreed that there had been no constitutional violation in the sentence or the indictment procedure, and denied the writ. The Court of Appeals for the Sixth Circuit reversed the District Court's judgment. * * * We granted certiorari to consider a constitutional question of importance in the administration of criminal justice.

It may be helpful to clarify at the outset the nature of the issue in this case. While the prosecutor did not actually obtain the recidivist indictment until after the plea conferences had ended, his intention to do so was clearly expressed at the outset of the plea negotiations. Hayes was thus fully informed of the true terms of the offer when he made his decision to plead not guilty. This is not a situation, therefore, where the prosecutor without notice brought an additional and more serious charge after plea negotiations relating only to the original indictment had ended with the defendant's insistence on pleading not guilty. As a practical matter, in short, this case would be no different if the grand jury had indicted Hayes as a recidivist from the outset, and the prosecutor had offered to drop that charge as part of the plea bargain.

The Court of Appeals nonetheless drew a distinction between "concessions relating to prosecution under an existing indictment," and threats to bring more severe charges not contained in the original indictment—a line it thought necessary in order to establish a prophylactic rule to guard against the evil of prosecutorial vindictiveness.[6] Quite apart from this chronological distinction, however, the Court of Appeals found that the prosecutor had acted vindictively in the present case since he had conceded that the indictment was influenced by his desire to induce a guilty plea. The ultimate conclusion of the Court of Appeals thus seems to have been that a prosecutor acts vindictively and in violation of due process of law whenever his charging decision is influenced by what he hopes to gain in the course of plea bargaining negotiations.

* * *

This Court held in *North Carolina v. Pearce,* 395 U.S. 711, 725, that the Due Process Clause of the Fourteenth Amendment "requires that vindictiveness against a defendant for having successfully attacked his first conviction must play no part in the sentence he receives after a new trial." [a] The same principle was later applied to prohibit a

---

6. "Although a prosecutor may in the course of plea negotiations offer a defendant concessions relating to prosecution under an existing indictment . . . he may not threaten a defendant with the consequence that more severe charges may be brought if he insists on going to trial. When a prosecutor obtains an indictment less severe than the facts known to him at the time might permit, he makes a discretionary determination that the interests of the state are served by not seeking more serious charges. . . . Accordingly, if after plea negotiations fail, he then procures an indictment charging a more serious crime, a strong inference is created that

the only reason for the more serious charges is vindictiveness. Under these circumstances, the prosecutor should be required to justify his action." 547 F.2d, at 44–45.

[a. In *North Carolina v. Pearce,* the defendant successfully appealed his conviction for assault with intent to commit rape. He was then retried, convicted again, and sentenced to prison for an amount of time that exceeded his original sentence. The Court held that to impose a greater sentence on the defendant to retaliate against him for having taken an appeal violated due process of law, and under the circum-

prosecutor from reindicting a convicted misdemeanant on a felony charge after the defendant had invoked an appellate remedy, since in this situation there was also a "realistic likelihood of 'vindictiveness.' " *Blackledge v. Perry*, 417 U.S., at 27.[b]

In those cases the Court was dealing with the State's unilateral imposition of a penalty upon a defendant who had chosen to exercise a legal right to attack his original conviction—a situation "very different from the give-and-take negotiation common in plea bargaining between the prosecution and defense, which arguably possess relatively equal bargaining power." The Court has emphasized that the due process violation in cases such as *Pearce* and *Perry* lay not in the possibility that a defendant might be deterred from the exercise of a legal right, but rather in the danger that the State might be retaliating against the accused for lawfully attacking his conviction.

To punish a person because he has done what the law plainly allows him to do is a due process violation of the most basic sort, and for an agent of the State to pursue a course of action whose objective is to penalize a person's reliance on his legal rights is "patently unconstitutional." But in the "give-and-take" of plea bargaining, there is no such element of punishment or retaliation so long as the accused is free to accept or reject the prosecution's offer.

Plea bargaining flows from "the mutuality of advantage" to defendants and prosecutors, each with his own reasons for wanting to avoid trial. Defendants advised by competent counsel and protected by other procedural safeguards are presumptively capable of intelligent choice in response to prosecutorial persuasion, and unlikely to be driven to false self-condemnation. Indeed, acceptance of the basic legitimacy of plea bargaining necessarily implies rejection of any notion that a guilty plea is involuntary in a constitutional sense simply because it is the end result of the bargaining process. By hypothesis, the plea may have been induced by promises of a recommendation of a lenient sentence or a reduction of charges, and thus by fear of the possibility of a greater penalty upon conviction after a trial.

While confronting a defendant with the risk of more severe punishment clearly may have a "discouraging effect on the defendant's assertion of his trial rights, the imposition of these difficult choices [is] an inevitable"—and permissible—"attribute of any legitimate system

stances, there was a presumption that the increased sentence was due to proscribed judicial vindictiveness. This presumption could be rebutted by the prosecution, but in *Pearce,* was not.]

[b. In *Blackledge,* the defendant was charged with and convicted of the misdemeanor of assault with a deadly weapon in a district court in North Carolina. He received a six-month prison sentence. As he was entitled to do under a state statute, he then filed a notice of appeal, seeking a trial *de novo* in a superior court. Following the filing of this notice of appeal, the prosecutor obtained an indictment charging the defendant with a felony assault charge. The defendant pled guilty to this charge and was sentenced to prison for five to seven years. The Court held that, under the circumstances, there was a presumption that the enhanced charge was the product of prosecutorial vindictiveness and hence violative of the defendant's due process rights.]

which tolerates and encourages the negotiation of pleas." It follows that, by tolerating and encouraging the negotiation of pleas, this Court has necessarily accepted as constitutionally legitimate the simple reality that the prosecutor's interest at the bargaining table is to persuade the defendant to forgo his right to plead not guilty.

It is not disputed here that Hayes was properly chargeable under the recidivist statute, since he had in fact been convicted of two previous felonies. In our system, so long as the prosecutor has probable cause to believe that the accused committed an offense defined by statute, the decision whether or not to prosecute, and what charge to file or bring before a grand jury, generally rests entirely in his discretion.[8] Within the limits set by the legislature's constitutionally valid definition of chargeable offenses, "the conscious exercise of some selectivity in enforcement is not in itself a federal constitutional violation" so long as "the selection was [not] deliberately based upon an unjustifiable standard such as race, religion, or other arbitrary classification." To hold that the prosecutor's desire to induce a guilty plea is an "unjustifiable standard," which, like race or religion, may play no part in his charging decision, would contradict the very premises that underlie the concept of plea bargaining itself. Moreover, a rigid constitutional rule that would prohibit a prosecutor from acting forthrightly in his dealings with the defense could only invite unhealthy subterfuge that would drive the practice of plea bargaining back into the shadows from which it has so recently emerged.

There is no doubt that the breadth of discretion that our country's legal system vests in prosecuting attorneys carries with it the potential for both individual and institutional abuse. And broad though that discretion may be, there are undoubtedly constitutional limits upon its exercise. We hold only that the course of conduct engaged in by the prosecutor in this case, which no more than openly presented the defendant with the unpleasant alternatives of forgoing trial or facing charges on which he was plainly subject to prosecution, did not violate the Due Process Clause of the Fourteenth Amendment.

Accordingly, the judgment of the Court of Appeals is

Reversed.

MR. JUSTICE BLACKMUN, with whom MR. JUSTICE BRENNAN and MR. JUSTICE MARSHALL join, dissenting.

I feel that the Court, although purporting to rule narrowly (that is, on "the course of conduct engaged in by the prosecutor in this case"), is departing from, or at least restricting, the principles established in *North Carolina v. Pearce,* 395 U.S. 711 (1969), and in *Blackledge v. Perry,* 417 U.S. 21 (1974). If those decisions are sound and if those principles are salutary, as I must assume they are, they require, in my

8. This case does not involve the constitutional implications of a prosecutor's offer during plea bargaining of adverse or lenient treatment for some person *other* than the accused, which might pose a greater danger of inducing a false guilty plea by skewing the assessment of the risks a defendant must consider.

view, an affirmance, not a reversal, of the judgment of the Court of Appeals in the present case.

* * *

* * * In this case vindictiveness is present to the same extent as it was thought to be in *Pearce* and in *Perry;* the prosecutor here admitted that the sole reason for the new indictment was to discourage the respondent from exercising his right to a trial. Even had such an admission not been made, when plea negotiations, conducted in the face of the less serious charge under the first indictment, fail, charging by a second indictment a more serious crime for the same conduct creates "a strong inference" of vindictiveness. * * *

Prosecutorial vindictiveness, it seems to me, in the present narrow context, is the fact against which the Due Process Clause ought to protect. I perceive little difference between vindictiveness after what the Court describes as the exercise of a "legal right to attack his original conviction," and vindictiveness in the " 'give-and-take negotiation common in plea bargaining.' " Prosecutorial vindictiveness in any context is still prosecutorial vindictiveness. The Due Process Clause should protect an accused against it, however it asserts itself. The Court of Appeals rightly so held, and I would affirm the judgment.

It might be argued that it really makes little difference how this case, now that it is here, is decided. The Court's holding gives plea bargaining full sway despite vindictiveness. A contrary result, however, merely would prompt the aggressive prosecutor to bring the greater charge initially in every case, and only thereafter to bargain. The consequences to the accused would still be adverse, for then he would bargain against a greater charge, face the likelihood of increased bail, and run the risk that the court would be less inclined to accept a bargained plea. Nonetheless, it is far preferable to hold the prosecution to the charge it was originally content to bring and to justify in the eyes of its public.[2]

---

2. That prosecutors, without saying so, may sometimes bring charges more serious than they think appropriate for the ultimate disposition of a case, in order to gain bargaining leverage with a defendant, does not add support to today's decision, for this Court, in its approval of the advantages to be gained from plea negotiations, has never openly sanctioned such deliberate overcharging or taken such a cynical view of the bargaining process. Normally, of course, it is impossible to show that this is what the prosecutor is doing, and the courts necessarily have deferred to the prosecutor's exercise of discretion in initial charging decisions.

Even if overcharging is to be sanctioned, there are strong reasons of fairness why the charges should be presented at the beginning of the bargaining process, rather than as a filliped threat at the end. First,

it means that a prosecutor is required to reach a charging decision without any knowledge of the particular defendant's willingness to plead guilty; hence the defendant who truly believes himself to be innocent, and wishes for that reason to go to trial, is not likely to be subject to quite such a devastating gamble since the prosecutor has fixed the incentives for the average case.

Second, it is healthful to keep charging practices visible to the general public, so that political bodies can judge whether the policy being followed is a fair one. Visibility is enhanced if the prosecutor is required to lay his cards on the table with an indictment of public record at the beginning of the bargaining process, rather than making use of unrecorded verbal warnings of more serious indictments yet to come.

MR. JUSTICE POWELL, dissenting. [Opinion omitted.]

Questions and Points for Discussion

1. In United States v. Goodwin, 457 U.S. 368, 102 S.Ct. 2485 (1982), the Supreme Court addressed a question left open in *Bordenkircher* — whether due process is violated when unsuccessful plea negotiations are followed by the bringing, without notice, of additional and more serious charges by the prosecutor. *Goodwin* involved a defendant who, after being stopped for speeding, fled in his car after the police officer noticed a plastic bag under the armrest of the car and asked the defendant to lift up the armrest. While trying to flee, the defendant struck the police officer with his car.

The defendant was charged with multiple misdemeanor and petty offenses. Although the defendant and the prosecutor initially engaged in plea negotiations, the defendant ultimately decided that he wanted a jury trial. A few weeks later, the defendant was indicted for the felony of forcibly assaulting a federal officer and three other crimes stemming from the incident at the scene of the car stop. The defendant was convicted of the felony as well as one misdemeanor.

The defendant moved to set aside the jury's verdict on the grounds that the prosecutor had, in violation of due process of law, charged the defendant with a felony to retaliate against the defendant for having invoked his right to a jury trial. The prosecutor responded by citing a number of different reasons why he had sought the defendant's indictment, including his belief that the defendant was trafficking in drugs when his car was stopped, the number of violent crimes committed by the defendant in the past, and the fact that the defendant had fled from the jurisdiction for three years following his arrest and arraignment.

The Supreme Court focused on the question whether a presumption of vindictiveness is warranted when new and more serious charges are brought before trial following a defendant's decision to stand trial. According to the Court, for such a presumption to exist, there would have to be a "reasonable likelihood" that in such circumstances, the government's actions are due to proscribed vindictiveness. Id. at 373, 102 S.Ct. at 2488. While such a presumption may have been warranted in Blackledge v. Perry, 417 U.S. 21, 94 S.Ct. 2098 (1974), where the new charge was brought after the defendant was convicted in one court but then exercised his statutory right to a trial *de novo* in a different court, the Court distinguished the pretrial setting in which the new charges were brought in this case:

> There is good reason to be cautious before adopting an inflexible presumption of prosecutorial vindictiveness in a pretrial setting. In the course of preparing a case for trial, the prosecutor may uncover additional information that suggests a basis for further prosecution or he simply may come to realize that information possessed by the State has a broader significance. At this stage of the proceedings, the prosecutor's assessment of the proper extent of prosecution may not have crystallized. In contrast, once a trial begins—and certainly by the time a conviction has been obtained—it is much more likely that

the State has discovered and assessed all of the information against an accused and has made a determination, on the basis of that information, of the extent to which he should be prosecuted. Thus, a change in the charging decision made after an initial trial is completed is much more likely to be improperly motivated than is a pretrial decision.

* * *

Thus, the timing of the prosecutor's action in this case suggests that a presumption of vindictiveness is not warranted. A prosecutor should remain free before trial to exercise the broad discretion entrusted to him to determine the extent of the societal interest in prosecution. An initial decision should not freeze future conduct. As we made clear in *Bordenkircher,* the initial charges filed by a prosecutor may not reflect the extent to which an individual is legitimately subject to prosecution.

* * *

Moreover, unlike the trial judge in *Pearce,* no party is asked "to do over what it thought it had already done correctly." A prosecutor has no "personal stake" in a bench trial and thus no reason to engage in "self-vindication" upon a defendant's request for a jury trial. Perhaps most importantly, the institutional bias against the retrial of a decided question that supported the decisions in *Pearce* and *Blackledge* simply has no counterpart in this case.

457 U.S. at 381–83, 102 S.Ct. at 2493–94.

Although defendants charged before trial with additional and more serious charges following their insistence on going to trial cannot avail themselves of the benefits of a presumption of vindictiveness, the Supreme Court in *Goodwin* did leave open the possibility that a defendant could prevail on a due process claim by showing that the prosecutor's charging decision was actually prompted by vindictiveness. Can you reconcile this statement with the decision in *Bordenkircher,* where the Court acknowledged that the prosecutor had charged the defendant with being a habitual offender because of his decision to plead not guilty, but found no due process violation?

Concurring in the judgment in *Goodwin,* Justice Blackmun expressed his view that when a defendant elects to go to trial and the prosecutor then files additional and more serious charges, there should be a presumption of vindictiveness, whether or not the new charges are filed before or after trial. He found, however, that the prosecutor had rebutted the presumption of vindictiveness in this case. Justice Brennan, joined by Justice Marshall, dissented in this case.

2. In Alabama v. Smith, 109 S.Ct. 2201 (1989), the Supreme Court once again refused to permit a defendant to invoke a presumption of vindictiveness. In that case, the defendant pled guilty to burglary and rape in return for the state's dismissal of a sodomy charge. The trial court then sentenced the defendant to thirty years in prison for each conviction, with his sentences to be served concurrently.

The defendant successfully appealed his convictions on the grounds that his guilty pleas were invalid since he had not been sufficiently apprised of the penalties that could be imposed if he pled guilty. The government then reinstated the sodomy charge, and the case went to trial before a jury. The same judge who had initially sentenced the defendant presided at the trial.

Following the defendant's conviction on all three counts, the judge sentenced him to life imprisonment for the burglary, to a concurrent life term for the sodomy, and to 150 years in prison for the rape, with the latter sentence to be served consecutively with the other two sentences. In imposing these sentences, the trial judge noted that the trial had revealed additional facts about the defendant's crimes of which the judge was previously unaware, including the fact that the defendant had raped the victim five times, had forced her to have oral sex with him, and had threatened her with a knife.

The defendant contended that the increased sentences were imposed by the judge in order to retaliate against the defendant for having attempted to and succeeded in getting his guilty plea set aside. The question before the Supreme Court was whether the defendant could avail himself of a presumption of vindictiveness or whether he would instead have to prove actual vindictiveness to prevail on his due process claim.

Answering this question, according to the Court, required an assessment of whether there was a "reasonable likelihood" that sentences imposed after trial that are greater than those imposed following guilty pleas are the product of judicial vindictiveness. The Court answered this question in the negative:

> [W]hen a greater penalty is imposed after trial than was imposed after a prior guilty plea, the increase in sentence is not more likely than not attributable to the vindictiveness on the part of the sentencing judge. Even when the same judge imposes both sentences, the relevant sentencing information available to the judge after the plea will usually be considerably less than that available after a trial.

> * * *

> As this case demonstrates, in the course of the proof at trial the judge may gather a fuller appreciation of the nature and extent of the crimes charged. The defendant's conduct during trial may give the judge insights into his moral character and suitability for rehabilitation. See United States v. Grayson, 438 U.S. 41, 53 (1978) (sentencing authority's perception of the truthfulness of a defendant testifying on his own behalf may be considered in sentencing). Finally, after trial, the factors that may have indicated leniency as consideration for the guilty plea are no longer present. Here, too, although the same Judge who sentenced following the guilty plea also imposes sentence following trial, in conducting the trial the court is not simply "do[ing] over what it thought it had already done correctly." Each of these factors distinguishes the present case, and others like it, from cases like *Pearce*.

109 S.Ct. at 2205–06.

What might be the likely effect of the Court's decision on defendants' willingness to challenge the validity of their guilty pleas?

3. Consider the facts of the following case. The defendant was arrested and indicted for two crimes—criminal sale of a controlled sub-

stance and possession of a controlled substance. Her daughter was also arrested and indicted for a number of narcotics offenses. The prosecutor promised that if the defendant pled guilty to the distribution charge, the government would permit her daughter to plead guilty to a reduced charge, thereby avoiding a prison term. The defendant agreed to this arrangement. Was the defendant's guilty plea valid? Why or why not? See Allyn v. Commissioner of Correctional Services, 708 F.Supp. 592 (S.D.N.Y.1989) and the cases cited therein, id. at 593–94.

4. In Newton v. Rumery, 480 U.S. 386, 107 S.Ct. 1187 (1987), the Supreme Court considered the validity of what are called release-dismissal agreements. In that case, Bernard Rumery was charged with the felony of tampering with a witness. After his attorney threatened to sue certain police and other government officials for having brought unfounded charges against him, the prosecutor agreed to dismiss the criminal charge in return to Rumery's agreement not to bring a civil suit against any government officials. Rumery acquiesced, and the criminal charge was dismissed.

Ten months later, Rumery brought a § 1983 civil rights suit against the city and various local officials, claiming, among other things, that his arrest was unlawful. In a motion to dismiss, the defendants argued that the release-dismissal agreement barred this suit. Rumery responded that the agreement was contrary to public policy and consequently void.

In a 5–4 decision, the Supreme Court held that the release-dismissal agreement at issue in this case was valid and enforceable. The Court acknowledged that the prospect of such agreements might induce prosecutors to file frivolous criminal charges as a way of pressuring an individual to forego plans to sue government officials. In addition, such agreements might lead to the abandonment of criminal prosecutions when the interests of the public favored prosecution. Finally, such agreements might permit constitutional violations to go unremedied. Nonetheless, the Court concluded that such agreements are not *per se* invalid. The circumstances surrounding each agreement have to be examined to determine its validity and enforceability.

Justice O'Connor wrote a concurring opinion in *Newton* to emphasize that the burden is upon government officials sued under § 1983 to establish that a release-dismissal agreement was "voluntarily made, not the product of prosecutorial overreaching, and in the public interest." Id. at 401, 107 S.Ct. at 1197 (O'Connor, J., concurring). She went on to identify some of the facts relevant to these questions:

> Many factors may bear on whether a release was voluntary and not the product of overreaching, some of which come readily to mind. The knowledge and experience of the criminal defendant and the circumstances of the execution of the release, including, importantly, whether the defendant was counseled, are clearly relevant. The nature of the criminal charges that are pending is also important, for the greater the charge, the greater the coercive effect. The existence of a legitimate criminal justice objective for obtaining the release will support its validity. And, importantly, the possibility of abuse is

clearly mitigated if the release-dismissal agreement is executed under judicial supervision.

Id. at 401–02, 107 S.Ct. at 1197.

Even the four dissenters in this case—Justices Stevens, Brennan, Marshall, and Blackmun—acknowledged that, in certain circumstances, release-dismissal agreements might be valid. The dissenters simply felt, however, that the government officials sued under § 1983 in this case had not established the validity of the release-dismissal agreement at issue in this case. By contrast, the majority of the Court felt that the release-dismissal agreement was valid, particularly because there was evidence that the prosecutor entered into the agreement largely to avoid trauma to the witness that Rumery had allegedly tampered with and who might be called as a witness in the civil suit.

5. In your opinion, can and should a prosecutor be able to extract, as a condition of a plea agreement, a waiver by the defendant of his or her right to appeal? Compare People v. Seaberg, 74 N.Y.2d 1, 541 N.E.2d 1022, 543 N.Y.S.2d 968 (1989) (condition is enforceable) with State v. Ethington, 121 Ariz. 572, 573–74, 592 P.2d 768, 769–70 (1979) (condition is unenforceable). What about conditioning a plea agreement on the defendant's agreement to refrain from interviewing a witness, such as the victim of a sex crime with which the defendant is charged? See State v. Draper, 162 Ariz. 433, 784 P.2d 259 (1989).

6. Not only the Constitution, but statutes, court rules, and prosecution policies may limit what a prosecutor can do to induce a defendant to plead guilty. The National Advisory Commission on Criminal Justice Standards and Goals suggested in 1973 that the following limitations be placed on prosecutors during plea bargaining:

STANDARD 3.6

PROHIBITED PROSECUTORIAL INDUCEMENTS TO ENTER A PLEA OF GUILTY

No prosecutor should, in connection with plea negotiations, engage in, perform, or condone any of the following:

1. Charging or threatening to charge the defendant with offenses for which the admissible evidence available to the prosecutor is insufficient to support a guilty verdict.

2. Charging or threatening to charge the defendant with a crime not ordinarily charged in the jurisdiction for the conduct allegedly engaged in by him.

3. Threatening the defendant that if he pleads not guilty, his sentence may be more severe than that which ordinarily is imposed in the jurisdiction in similar cases on defendants who plead not guilty.

4. Failing to grant full disclosure before the disposition negotiations of all exculpatory evidence material to guilt or punishment.

Are there any other prosecutorial inducements that you would consider improper, if not unconstitutional? See e.g., Arizona v. Horning, 158 Ariz. 106, 761 P.2d 728 (App.1988) (plea involuntary when entered in return for prosecutor's agreement not to interfere with defendant's attempts to secure conjugal visits with his wife in jail).

7. The Supreme Court case of Corbitt v. New Jersey, 439 U.S. 212, 99 S.Ct. 492 (1978) dealt with the constitutionality, not of prosecutorial inducements to plead guilty, but of legislative inducements. The defendant in that case had been charged with first-degree murder. If convicted of first-degree murder following a jury trial, he faced a mandatory sentence of life imprisonment. If the jury instead found him guilty of second-degree murder, he could be sentenced to up to thirty years in prison. Although guilty pleas to murder were prohibited in New Jersey, a defendant could plead *nolo contendere* to a murder indictment. If a defendant entered such a plea, and the plea was accepted by the court, the judge could impose either a life sentence or the sentence for second-degree murder, i.e., a maximum of thirty years.

The defendant in *Corbitt* opted to go to trial and was found guilty of first-degree murder by a jury. He was then sentenced to life in prison as required by the New Jersey statute. He appealed, claiming, among other things, that the sentencing scheme in New Jersey unconstitutionally penalized defendants charged with first-degree murder who pursued their constitutional right to a jury trial.

The Supreme Court disagreed, stating as follows:

[N]ot every burden on the exercise of a constitutional right, and not every pressure or encouragement to waive such a right, is invalid. Specifically, there is no *per se* rule against encouraging guilty pleas. We have squarely held that a State may encourage a guilty plea by offering substantial benefits in return for the plea. The plea may obtain for the defendant "the possibility or certainty . . . [not only of] a lesser penalty than the sentence that could be imposed after a trial and a verdict of guilty . . . ," but also of a lesser penalty than that *required* to be imposed after a guilty verdict by a jury.

[The Court here cited and discussed *Bordenkircher v. Hayes.*]

* * *

* * * There is no doubt that those homicide defendants who are willing to plead *non vult* may be treated more leniently than those who go to trial, but withholding the possibility of leniency from the latter cannot be equated with impermissible punishment as long as our cases sustaining plea bargaining remain undisturbed. Those cases, as we have said, unequivocally recognize the constitutional propriety of extending leniency in exchange for a plea of guilty and of not extending leniency to those who have not demonstrated those attributes on which leniency is based.

Id. at 218–20, 223–24, 99 S.Ct. at 497–98, 500.

In the course of its opinion in *Corbitt*, the Court distinguished United States v. Jackson, 390 U.S. 570, 88 S.Ct. 1209 (1968), supra page 37, a case where the Court had held the sentencing scheme of the Federal Kidnapping

Act to be unconstitutional. Under that statute, a defendant found guilty by a jury of violating the Act could receive the death penalty. By contrast, the maximum penalty that could be imposed on a defendant tried in a bench trial or who pled guilty was life in prison. The Supreme Court in *Corbitt* highlighted the following distinctions between *Jackson* and the case before it:

> The principal difference is that the pressures to forgo trial and to plead to the charge in this case are not what they were in *Jackson.* First, the death penalty, which is "unique in its severity and irrevocability," is not involved here. Although we need not agree with the New Jersey court that the *Jackson* rationale is limited to those cases where a plea avoids any possibility of the death penalty's being imposed, it is a material fact that under the New Jersey law the maximum penalty for murder is life imprisonment, not death. Furthermore, in *Jackson,* any risk of suffering the maximum penalty could be avoided by pleading guilty. Here, although the punishment when a jury finds a defendant guilty of first-degree murder is life imprisonment, the risk of that punishment is not completely avoided by pleading *non vult* because the judge accepting the plea has the authority to impose a life term. New Jersey does not reserve the maximum punishment for murder for those who insist on a jury trial.

439 U.S. at 217, 99 S.Ct. at 496.

8. *Class Exercise:* Divide the class in half to debate the following question: Can and should plea bargaining be abolished? Then discuss as a group the question of what restrictions should be placed on plea bargaining in a jurisdiction which retains plea bargaining.

Chapter 3

THE SENTENCING PROCESS

A. RIGHTS DURING SENTENCING

Defendants who are charged with crimes are protected by an array of constitutional rights if their cases proceed to trial. They have the right, for example, to the assistance of an attorney, a right bestowed by the sixth amendment. Gideon v. Wainwright, 372 U.S. 335, 83 S.Ct. 792 (1963). They have the right to a jury trial when charged with a non-petty offense. Duncan v. Louisiana, 391 U.S. 145, 88 S.Ct. 1444 (1968). They have the right to present witnesses who will testify on their behalf, Washington v. Texas, 388 U.S. 14, 87 S.Ct. 1920 (1967), and to confront and cross-examine adverse witnesses. Coy v. Iowa, 487 U.S. 1012, 108 S.Ct. 2798 (1988); Smith v. Illinois, 390 U.S. 129, 88 S.Ct. 748 (1968). And they are presumed innocent unless and until the government rebuts this presumption and establishes their guilt beyond a reasonable doubt. In re Winship, 397 U.S. 358, 364, 90 S.Ct. 1068, 1072 (1970).

The procedural safeguards which must attend the guilt-innocence stage of a criminal prosecution should be contrasted with the more limited rights which the courts have recognized during the sentencing stage of criminal prosecutions. The case which follows exemplifies the courts' more restricted interpretation of the scope of the constitutional protection afforded a defendant during the sentencing process.

WILLIAMS v. NEW YORK

Supreme Court of the United States, 1949.
337 U.S. 241, 69 S.Ct. 1079, 93 L.Ed. 1337.

MR. JUSTICE BLACK delivered the opinion of the Court.

A jury in a New York state court found appellant guilty of murder in the first degree. The jury recommended life imprisonment, but the trial judge imposed sentence of death. In giving his reasons for imposing the death sentence the judge discussed in open court the evidence upon which the jury had convicted stating that this evidence had been considered in the light of additional information obtained through the court's "Probation Department, and through other sources." Consideration of this additional information was pursuant to § 482 of New York Criminal Code which provides:

> ". . . Before rendering judgment or pronouncing sentence the court shall cause the defendant's previous criminal record to be submitted to it, including any reports that may have been made as a result of a mental, phychiatric [*sic*] or physical examination of such person, and may seek any information that will aid the court in determining the proper treatment of such defendant."

The Court of Appeals of New York affirmed the conviction and sentence over the contention that as construed and applied the controlling penal statutes are in violation of the due process clause of the Fourteenth Amendment of the Constitution of the United States "in that the sentence of death was based upon information supplied by witnesses with whom the accused had not been confronted and as to whom he had no opportunity for cross-examination or rebuttal . . . ." * * *

The narrow contention here makes it unnecessary to set out the facts at length. The record shows a carefully conducted trial lasting more than two weeks in which appellant was represented by three appointed lawyers who conducted his defense with fidelity and zeal. The evidence proved a wholly indefensible murder committed by a person engaged in a burglary. The judge instructed the jury that if it returned a verdict of guilty as charged, without recommendation for life sentence, "The Court must impose the death penalty," but if such recommendation was made, "the Court may impose a life sentence." The judge went on to emphasize that "the Court is not bound to accept your recommendation."

About five weeks after the verdict of guilty with recommendation of life imprisonment, and after a statutory pre-sentence investigation report to the judge, the defendant was brought to court to be sentenced. Asked what he had to say, appellant protested his innocence. After each of his three lawyers had appealed to the court to accept the jury's recommendation of a life sentence, the judge gave reasons why he felt that the death sentence should be imposed. He narrated the shocking details of the crime as shown by the trial evidence, expressing his own complete belief in appellant's guilt. He stated that the pre-sentence investigation revealed many material facts concerning appellant's background which though relevant to the question of punishment could not properly have been brought to the attention of the jury in its consideration of the question of guilt. He referred to the experience appellant "had had on thirty other burglaries in and about the same vicinity" where the murder had been committed. The appellant had not been convicted of these burglaries although the judge had information that he had confessed to some and had been identified as the perpetrator of some of the others. The judge also referred to certain activities of appellant as shown by the probation report that indicated appellant possessed "a morbid sexuality" and classified him as a "menace to society." The accuracy of the statements made by the judge as to appellant's background and past practices was not challenged by appellant or his counsel, nor was the judge asked to disregard any of them or to afford appellant a chance to refute or discredit any of them by cross-examination or otherwise.

The case presents a serious and difficult question. The question relates to the rules of evidence applicable to the manner in which a judge may obtain information to guide him in the imposition of sentence upon an already convicted defendant. Within limits fixed by statutes, New York judges are given a broad discretion to decide the type and extent of punishment for convicted defendants. Here, for example, the judge's discretion was to sentence to life imprisonment or death. To aid a judge in exercising this discretion intelligently the New York procedural policy encourages him to consider information about the convicted person's past life, health, habits, conduct, and mental and moral propensities. The sentencing judge may consider such information even though obtained outside the courtroom from persons whom a defendant has not been permitted to confront or cross-examine. * * *

Appellant urges that the New York statutory policy is in irreconcilable conflict with the underlying philosophy of a second procedural policy grounded in the due process of law clause of the Fourteenth Amendment. That policy as stated in *In re Oliver,* 333 U.S. 257, 273, is in part that no person shall be tried and convicted of an offense unless he is given reasonable notice of the charges against him and is afforded an opportunity to examine adverse witnesses. * * *

Tribunals passing on the guilt of a defendant always have been hedged in by strict evidentiary procedural limitations. But both before and since the American colonies became a nation, courts in this country and in England practiced a policy under which a sentencing judge could exercise a wide discretion in the sources and types of evidence used to assist him in determining the kind and extent of punishment to be imposed within limits fixed by law. Out-of-court affidavits have been used frequently, and of course in the smaller communities sentencing judges naturally have in mind their knowledge of the personalities and backgrounds of convicted offenders. * * *

In addition to the historical basis for different evidentiary rules governing trial and sentencing procedures there are sound practical reasons for the distinction. In a trial before verdict the issue is whether a defendant is guilty of having engaged in certain criminal conduct of which he has been specifically accused. Rules of evidence have been fashioned for criminal trials which narrowly confine the trial contest to evidence that is strictly relevant to the particular offense charged. These rules rest in part on a necessity to prevent a time-consuming and confusing trial of collateral issues. They were also designed to prevent tribunals concerned solely with the issue of guilt of a particular offense from being influenced to convict for that offense by evidence that the defendant had habitually engaged in other misconduct. A sentencing judge, however, is not confined to the narrow issue of guilt. His task within fixed statutory or constitutional limits is to determine the type and extent of punishment after the issue of guilt has been determined. Highly relevant—if not essential—to his selection of an appropriate sentence is the possession of the fullest information possible concerning the defendant's life and characteristics.

*   *   *

*   *   *

Under the practice of individualizing punishments, investigational techniques have been given an important role. Probation workers making reports of their investigations have not been trained to prosecute but to aid offenders. Their reports have been given a high value by conscientious judges who want to sentence persons on the best available information rather than on guesswork and inadequate information. To deprive sentencing judges of this kind of information would undermine modern penological procedural policies that have been cautiously adopted throughout the nation after careful consideration and experimentation. We must recognize that most of the information now relied upon by judges to guide them in the intelligent imposition of sentences would be unavailable if information were restricted to that given in open court by witnesses subject to cross-examination. And the modern probation report draws on information concerning every aspect of a defendant's life. The type and extent of this information make totally impractical if not impossible open court testimony with cross-examination. Such a procedure could endlessly delay criminal administration in a retrial of collateral issues.

The considerations we have set out admonish us against treating the due process clause as a uniform command that courts throughout the Nation abandon their age-old practice of seeking information from out-of-court sources to guide their judgment toward a more enlightened and just sentence. New York criminal statutes set wide limits for maximum and minimum sentences. Under New York statutes a state judge cannot escape his grave responsibility of fixing sentence. In determining whether a defendant shall receive a one-year minimum or a twenty-year maximum sentence, we do not think the Federal Constitution restricts the view of the sentencing judge to the information received in open court. The due process clause should not be treated as a device for freezing the evidential procedure of sentencing in the mold of trial procedure. So to treat the due process clause would hinder if not preclude all courts—state and federal—from making progressive efforts to improve the administration of criminal justice.

*   *   *

Affirmed.

MR. JUSTICE RUTLEDGE dissents. [Opinion omitted.]

MR. JUSTICE MURPHY, dissenting. [Opinion omitted.]

* * *

Despite the more limited scope of constitutional protection afforded defendants during the sentencing stage of a criminal prosecution, defendants do retain rights during this stage as is apparent from the case which follows.

GARDNER v. FLORIDA

Supreme Court of the United States, 1977.
430 U.S. 349, 97 S.Ct. 1197, 51 L.Ed.2d 393.

MR. JUSTICE STEVENS announced the judgment of the Court and delivered an opinion, in which MR. JUSTICE STEWART and MR. JUSTICE POWELL joined.

Petitioner was convicted of first-degree murder and sentenced to death. When the trial judge imposed the death sentence he stated that he was relying in part on information in a presentence investigation report.[a] Portions of the report were not disclosed to counsel for the parties. Without reviewing the confidential portion of the presentence report, the Supreme Court of Florida, over the dissent of two justices, affirmed the death sentence. We conclude that this procedure does not satisfy the constitutional command that no person shall be deprived of life without due process of law.

* * *

* * * [W]e consider the justifications offered by the State for a capital-sentencing procedure which permits a trial judge to impose the death sentence on the basis of confidential information which is not disclosed to the defendant or his counsel.

The State first argues that an assurance of confidentiality to potential sources of information is essential to enable investigators to obtain relevant but sensitive disclosures from persons unwilling to comment publicly about a defendant's background or character. The availability of such information, it is argued, provides the person who prepares the report with greater detail on which to base a sentencing recommendation and, in turn, provides the judge with a better basis for his sentencing decision. But consideration must be given to the quality, as well as the quantity, of the information on which the sentencing judge may rely. Assurances of secrecy are conducive to the transmission of confidences which may bear no closer relation to fact than the average rumor or item of gossip, and may imply a pledge not to attempt independent verification of the information received. The risk that some of the information accepted in confidence may be erroneous, or may be misinterpreted, by the investigator or by the sentencing judge, is manifest.

[a. In imposing the death sentence, the trial judge rejected a jury recommendation that the defendant only be sentenced to life in prison. The jury had no access to the presentence investigation report which was prepared after the jury had returned its advisory verdict.]

If, as the State argues, it is important to use such information in the sentencing process, we must assume that in some cases it will be decisive in the judge's choice between a life sentence and a death sentence. If it tends to tip the scales in favor of life, presumably the information would be favorable and there would be no reason why it should not be disclosed. On the other hand, if it is the basis for a death sentence, the interest in reliability plainly outweighs the State's interest in preserving the availability of comparable information in other cases.

The State also suggests that full disclosure of the presentence report will unnecessarily delay the proceeding. We think the likelihood of significant delay is overstated because we must presume that reports prepared by professional probation officers, as the Florida procedure requires, are generally reliable.[10] In those cases in which the accuracy of a report is contested, the trial judge can avoid delay by disregarding the disputed material. Or if the disputed matter is of critical importance, the time invested in ascertaining the truth would surely be well spent if it makes the difference between life and death.

The State further urges that full disclosure of presentence reports, which often include psychiatric and psychological evaluations, will occasionally disrupt the process of rehabilitation. The argument, if valid, would hardly justify withholding the report from defense counsel. Moreover, whatever force that argument may have in noncapital cases, it has absolutely no merit in a case in which the judge has decided to sentence the defendant to death. Indeed, the extinction of all possibility of rehabilitation is one of the aspects of the death sentence that makes it different in kind from any other sentence a State may legitimately impose.

Finally, Florida argues that trial judges can be trusted to exercise their discretion in a responsible manner, even though they may base their decisions on secret information. ＊ ＊ ＊ The argument rests on the erroneous premise that the participation of counsel is superfluous to the process of evaluating the relevance and significance of aggravating and mitigating facts. Our belief that debate between adversaries is often essential to the truth-seeking function of trials requires us also to recognize the importance of giving counsel an opportunity to comment on facts which may influence the sentencing decision in capital cases.

Even if it were permissible to withhold a portion of the report from a defendant, and even from defense counsel, pursuant to an express finding of good cause for nondisclosure, it would nevertheless be necessary to make the full report a part of the record to be reviewed on appeal. Since the State must administer its capital-sentencing procedures with an even hand, it is important that the record on appeal

---

10. Our presumption that the reports are normally reliable is, of course, not inconsistent with our concern about the possibility that critical unverified information may be inaccurate and determinative in a particular case.

disclose to the reviewing court the considerations which motivated the death sentence in every case in which it is imposed. * * *

* * *

We conclude that petitioner was denied due process of law when the death sentence was imposed, at least in part, on the basis of information which he had no opportunity to deny or explain.

* * * Accordingly, the death sentence is vacated, and the case is remanded to the Florida Supreme Court with directions to order further proceedings at the trial court level not inconsistent with this opinion.

Vacated and remanded.

THE CHIEF JUSTICE concurs in the judgment.

MR. JUSTICE WHITE, concurring in the judgment.

* * *

* * * Here the sentencing judge indicated that he selected petitioner Gardner for the death penalty in part because of information contained in a presentence report which information was not disclosed to petitioner or to his counsel and to which petitioner had no opportunity to respond. A procedure for selecting people for the death penalty which permits consideration of such secret information relevant to the "character and record of the individual offender" fails to meet the "need for reliability in the determination that death is the appropriate punishment". This conclusion stems solely from the Eighth Amendment's ban on cruel and unusual punishments and my conclusion is limited to cases in which the death penalty is imposed. I thus see no reason to address in this case the possible application to sentencing proceedings—in death or other cases—of the Due Process Clause, other than as the vehicle by which the strictures of the Eighth Amendment are triggered in this case. For these reasons, I do not join the plurality opinion but concur in the judgment.

MR. JUSTICE BLACKMUN, concurring in the judgment. [Opinion omitted.]

MR. JUSTICE BRENNAN.

I agree for the reasons stated in the plurality opinion that the Due Process Clause of the Fourteenth Amendment is violated when a defendant facing a death sentence is not informed of the contents of a presentence investigation report made to the sentencing judge. However, I adhere to my view that the death penalty is in all circumstances cruel and unusual punishment prohibited by the Eighth and Fourteenth Amendments. I therefore would vacate the death sentence, and I dissent from the Court's judgment insofar as it remands for further proceedings that could lead to its imposition.

MR. JUSTICE MARSHALL, dissenting. [Opinion omitted.]

MR. JUSTICE REHNQUIST, dissenting. [Opinion omitted.]

Questions and Points for Discussion

1. *Gardner* dealt with the constitutional right of a defendant in a capital case to have access to a presentence investigation report before sentencing. In your opinion, do defendants found guilty of non-capital crimes also have this right? What other constitutional rights should apply at the sentencing stage of a criminal prosecution? Should there be a right to counsel? A right to present evidence and make statements to the court? A right to confront and cross-examine adverse witnesses? A right to a statement of reasons as to why a particular penalty was imposed? Any other rights? Do any of your answers depend on whether the defendant has been convicted of a capital or non-capital crime?

To assist you in your analysis of the rights that should be accorded a defendant during the sentencing stage of a criminal prosecution, an example of a presentence investigation report is set forth on the next few pages. The report, which concerns a defendant who pled guilty to criminal sexual conduct in the first degree, is reprinted here with the permission of the Probation Office of the Ingham County Circuit Court, Ingham County, Michigan; the names and other identifying information in the report have been deleted or changed.

MICHIGAN DEPARTMENT OF CORRECTION
PRESENTENCE INVESTIGATION REPORT

Honorable __Andrew Lopez__   County __Ingham__   Sentence Date __7-24-85__

Docket __54154__   Attorney __Ann Witt__   Appt. _____ Retained __XX__

Defendant __Fred Jones__   Age __46__   D.O.B. __9-19-38__

CURRENT CONVICTION(S) $50,000 Surety

Final Charge(s)	Max.	Jail Credit	Bond	Proposal
1. CT. II. CSC 1st Degree	LIFE	2 days	yes	yes
2.		days		
3.		days		

Convicted by: Plea _X_ Jury ___ Judge ___ Plea Under Advisement ___ Nolo Contendere ___ HYTA: Yes ___ No _XX_
Conviction Date _6-26-85_   Plea Agreement _nolle pross Cts. I, II, & IV_
Pending Charges: __none__   Where _____

PRIOR RECORD

Convictions: Felonies _1_ Misdemeanors _1_ Juvenile Record: Yes___ No _X_
Probation: Active ___ Former _yes_ Pending Violation _____
Parole: Active ___ Former _____ Pending Violation _____
Current Michigan Prisoner: Yes ___ No _X_ Number _____
Currently Under Sentence: Offense _____ Sentence _____

PERSONAL HISTORY

                        (Self employed)
Education _12th_   Employed _yes_ Where _Fred's Automotive Diagnostics, Inc._
Psychiatric History: Yes _____ No _XX_ Physical Handicaps: Yes ___ No _XX_ Marital Status _divorced_
Substance Abuse History: Yes _X_ No ___ What __alcohol__ How Long _____

RECOMMENDATION

1. 30 to 45 years with the Michigan Corrections Commission.
2. Mental Health therapy for sex offenders.

Agent _____ Deborah Keene _____ Date _7-22-85_
Signature _____ Supervisor's Approval _____

[F9760]

EVALUATION AND PLAN:

Fred Jones age 46 is before the court for his second felony conviction. His other felony conviction occurred in 1969 and it was Accosting Children for Immoral Purposes. He was given three days in jail and two years probation.

The defendant has resided in Lansing almost all of his life. After graduating from Eastern High School in 1957 he entered the United States Army. He was honorably discharged after serving three years.

The defendant is self employed. He owns and operates Fred's Automotive Diagnostics Inc., 2308 Curry Street, tx: 300–0000. He began operating this business on the date of his arrest for this offense, May 10, 1985. Respondent has worked in the automotive field four years, and he previously owned his own shop between 78 and 73. It was then located at 400 Northampton Street.

Mr. Jones is also the State Commissioner for the American Bicycle Association's BMX Racing Program. The American Bicycle Association is out of Phoenix, Arizona. As commissioner, the defendant travelled to various tracks in the state and set up promotional activities and getting tracks going as well as directing the local BMX Race Program.

Right after leaving the military the defendant was employed by Spartan Oil, and managed a station before opening his mechanic shop in 1978.

Respondent admits to a history of heavy drinking. He said that after the break up of his first marriage he, "Got into drinking constantly. I was drinking all day. I filed bankruptcy. I finally woke up and started seeing Jane (second wife)." He said he then went back to drinking heavily in 1978 or 1979 when his business was going bad. He said, "I started drinking heavy again around 1982 or 83. I had gotten into hanging out all night and running with people who were smoking pot." Mr. Jones has never participated in an alcohol or drug program. He denies selling marijuana to children in his former neighborhood, contrary to the statements given to police by some of the youngsters. Jones does admit to "occasionally" arranging for adults to purchase marijuana.

The defendant reports no physical problems. He does indicate that his left leg and foot are smaller than the right. He believes this is the result of a mild case of polio.

Since his arrest for the instant offense the defendant has gone into mental health therapy with Dr. Gilbert Riler of the Community Mental Health Program. Respondent is seeing Dr. Riler once per week. Dr. Riler said that he would provide an evaluation to the court, prior to the defendant's sentencing. When I spoke with the Doctor on July 8, 1985, he said the defendant's MMPI test shows subject is essentially a personality disorder, characterized by "Hedonistic" and "Pleasure Oriented" manifestation. Dr. Riler states the defendant['s] positive qualities are the fact that he is acknowledging his guilt in the instant offense. Also, he has been open and candid with the doctor, advising the doctor that he has been involved with 40 to 50 different boys. Also, Mr. Jones has displayed no indication of psychopathic or manipulative behavior in therapy.

Mr. Jones notes [the] following liabilities, Ingham County Friend of the Court $1500.00 in arrearages (at $40 per month), Mr. Donald Smith (Holder of defendant's land contract) $135,000 at $1700 per month, Ronald Gorman (Business associate) $9000.00 at $400 per month, Bank of Lansing $1900.00 (executive credit) at $100 per month, Master Charge/VISA $200 at $40 per month, American Express $500 at $150 per month, June Wiler (ex-wife) $2000.00, Attorney fees $1300.00.

He reports the following assets: Fred's Automotive Diagnostics Inc. $150,000 ($15000 equity), 1973 Chrysler Newport $600, 1976 Cadillac El Dorado $3000.00.

In summation, before the court is an intelligent individual with marketable skills, who has functioned as a productive member of society. He has, however, been plagued with substance abuse for many years. Also, Mr. Jones has displayed a propensity toward sexual involvement with pre-adolescent boys for well over a decade. His tendency toward Pedophillic behavior has left emotional scars not only on the instant offense victim, but the uncharged victims as well as their families. The community deserves to be protected from Mr. Jones. In the defendant's favor, he does acknowledge his guilt, but also acknowledges that his behavior is something over which he has little in the way of control.

Placement in a structured setting where he will not have access to pre-adolescent teenage boys is strongly recommended. Mr. Jones should be provided treatment in an effort to help him overcome his illness. However, the main issue in sentencing, in my opinion is protecting other potential victims from the defendant.

INVESTIGATOR'S VERSION OF OFFENSE:

According to Lansing Police Department complaint # 85–05592: On or about April 12 or 19th, 1985, the defendant Fred Jones engaged in sexual penetration with Greg Daley, dob: 3–23–72, a person under 13 years of age. Daley told investigating officers that on that occasion he had spent the night at Fred Jones's residence [in] Lansing, Michigan. Daley was asleep on a couch in the livingroom. He awoke to find Jones crawling underneath the sheet and pulling Daley's undershorts off. When asked by officers, what Jones did next, Daley said, "He gave me a blow job". Upon further questioning, Daley revealed the defendant had given him a glass of beer earlier in the evening. Daley also told officers that this same type of incident had happened, "Maybe five or six times".

Daley upon further questioning told officers that on one occasion Fred Jones was performing oral sex upon him, while two other adult males were also in the room performing fellatio on each other.

Lansing Police Officers became aware of Daley's situation as well as the assault upon numerous other early adolescent boys via an anonymous tip that was phoned into the police department on May 7, 1985. The tipster told officers that Jones was involving himself sexually with a number of children at the Jones residence. Four names were provided by the tipster. Investigating officers James Martin and Alex Finch went to the schools that the various boys attended and after getting permission from their parents, interviewed several of them. All of the boys acknowledged that they had been to Jones's home and they were aware that he was sexually involved with numerous young boys. Some of the boys interviewed said they were not sexually involved with Jones, while others admitted to [the] officers that Jones had been engaging in sexual activities with them. They also told [the] officers Jones had been providing beer, as well as marijuana to the boys, while at his home. The boys also told [the] officers that Jones had been showing them numerous pornographic movies, most of which involved homosexual activity between males. The boys had also been shown numerous items of sexual paraphernalia including magazines, pictures and various other sexual paraphernalia.

Based on the information gathered through interviewing the boys, a search warrant was requested and granted by Judge Claude R. Thomas of Lansing District Court, on May 10, 1985.

At approximately 4:15 p.m. May 10, 1985 the defendant was arrested at his place of work. He was served with a four count felony warrant for Criminal Sexual Conduct. Fifteen minutes later four officers of the Lansing Police Department Criminal Intelligence Unit executed a search warrant at the defendant's residence. A large quantity of evidence was seized and transported to the Police Department Evidence Room. Attached to this report is the list of items seized during the search. The items include numerous pictures of some of his victims in sexually provocative poses. I viewed the photographs at the Lansing Police Department. There were photographs of the victims performing and having oral sex performed upon them. There were photographs of boys sitting on the defendant's lap, kissing him on the mouth, there was a photograph of the defendant in bed with one of the victims, engaging in anal intercourse, there were a number of photographs taken at a "Birthday Party" where there were a number of joints placed on the cake so as to resemble candles.

As noted above, the defendant was arrested on May 10, 1985, and was released on bond the following day. He remains free awaiting sentence. Officers James Martin and Alex Finch who investigated this case and interviewed the victims, both recommend life imprisonment. Martin pointed out that there was a total of 19 counts against the defendant. The officers spoke with 13 different children who acknowledged they had been sexually involved with the defendant, and who were willing to press charges. Further, Martin and Finch stressed the devastating emotional effect Jones has had on the children, in arriving at their recommendation for sentencing. Daley, for instance was a straight 'A' student at Otto Junior High School, dropped out of school after the instant offense became publicized, for fear of being ridiculed by his fellow students. Another young man, Gordon Taylor, a student at Waverly West Junior High said he felt like a monster, and he also said he would commit suicide if his fellow students were to find out about his involvement with Jones. Finally, the officers said a number of the children involved had started to display acting out behavior, they had started dropping out of school and were getting involved with drinking and drugs, all of which the officers feel is related to their experiences with the defendant.

I spoke to the mother of Greg Daley (the victim that the defendant has pled guilty to assaulting), on July 12, 1985. Mrs. Daley is very bitter about the whole incident. She said that she and her family have known the defendant approximately seven years. She said he always presented himself as a "nice neighbor" who was always interested in the kids well being. She said the defendant often said, "Let's do things for the kids". She went on to say that he professed to wanting to get the kids involved in BMX Racing as a way of, "Keeping them off the street".

Mrs. Daley said her child's experience with the defendant has changed his personality. She said previously Greg, "Was usually a quiet easy going person, but now he is very closed. He just doesn't want to talk about the incident. He gets very angry. He used to be very easy going, but now he flies off the handle. I feel this has really screwed him up." Mrs. Daley said Jones had also been involved with Greg's older brother Mark, though Mark refuses to discuss his involvement with the defendant. Mark is learning disabled and has always been involved in special education.

When asked for a recommendation for sentencing, Mrs. Daley responded, "I think he should go natural life. No parole. Don't let him get to no one else. I am not a person with a lot of hate, but I know that if he were to walk and I saw him on the street, I wouldn't hesitate to run him down."

I spoke with Gordon Taylor's mother on July 18, 1985. Mrs. Taylor said, "We trusted Fred. Fred had become a real good friend of ours. He was in our home. We had him in our home for dinner. If I had a chance, I would have killed Fred. I just wanted to kill him. My husband feels the same way. My son Gordon does too. I am very hostile."

Mrs. Taylor went on to explain to me just how devastated her entire family is, as the result of learning that the defendant was engaging in sexual activity with Gordon. She said that both she and her husband are in counseling with Gordon. She also said immediately after they were told of what was going on between Fred Jones and their son, her husband went to Jones's home with a gun. He was sitting outside of Jones's home. Mrs. Taylor called Lansing Police because she was afraid there would be trouble. The police officers arrived and told Mr. Taylor to go home, and at that point he broke down and cried because he was so devastated.

Mrs. Taylor continued, "Fred bought Gordon a $160.00 bow for a birthday present. Fred was buying Gordon everything. He was going on vacation with him, going fishing and on vacation. It was like Fred was a big brother. I just don't know why I didn't see through it."

When asked how her son had been affected, Mrs. Taylor said, "Gordon is a straight 'A' student in school. When this happened he didn't go to school, see his friends, or go outside." Mrs. Taylor said during the summer of 1984, Gordon has not related to her, on one occasion Fred chased a young man out of his (Fred's) residence with a gun. Gordon was present. Fred told Gordon if Gordon told anyone about what was going on he would kill him. It was at that point that Gordon developed an ulcer. Gordon is 14 years of age.

Mrs. Taylor continued, "I blame myself for not being able to see it. I will never trust anybody again, I don't care if it is a baseball coach, or a teacher. Whenever an adult is friends with my kid I won't have it." I asked Mrs. Taylor her recommendation for sentencing. She said, "I want him to pay for what he did to my son. I want him to hurt like we hurt. I want him to think about this for a long, long time. This hurt is the most hurt we have ever had. . . . I just pray to God Fred doesn't come around us any time again. I hope the law can make us happy by putting him away and not letting him out. Fred is a sick man and he needs lots of help."

OFFENDER'S VERSION OF OFFENSE:

"Greg Daley and I have known each other for about five years. We have basically been good friends. He has stayed with me and come with me on many occasions over the five years. Greg's been a boy that always wanted fatherly attention. He has climbed in bed with me and cuddled and everything. Over the last six months he started sexually maturing and things happen."

The defendant admits to having sexual relations with Greg Daley dob: 3–23–72, Gordon Taylor dob: 9–30–71, Allen Freeman dob: 1–18–70, and Michael Cook dob: 11–16–70. Mr. Jones admits to being sexually involved with boys he has met through BMX, over the past four to five years. He went on to say he would sometimes feel "guilty" after going "all the way" with the boys. He stated, "I would discuss personal problems with the boys, when they were having them." He said he discussed the dangers of becoming involved in drugs with them.

Jones continued, "I think it started out as a kind of father/son and I let it go too far. I wouldn't always have sex with them. We spent a lot of time together fishing, bowling and time on the BMX track. But I would feel guilty afterwards. I don't feel like I took advantage of them, but I did let it go too far. But, the boys were aggressive in the sex acts and I feel they kept coming back because they enjoyed visiting."

Over the past four years Jones estimates he has worked with "about 400 youngsters", "but there has not always been the sexual activity." Finally, Jones stated, "I have gotten back involved with my own sons and I am trying to get my business back together. It was not my intention to hurt anybody. At that time I felt I was doing something I hadn't ought to be doing. I hadn't any intention of doing any harm or hurting anybody. I tried to help them, by helping with their home life and school problems. We discussed lives and I was trying to help them. I know I went too far, but what's the old saying hindsight is better than foresight. I guess sometimes when you are alone and lonely, and the aggressiveness is there and everything and especially if you are getting high you let everything go to the wind".

PREVIOUS CRIMINAL HISTORY:

Juvenile: None

Adult:

1-2-57—Lansing—Larc/Bldg.—final charge: Larc/U/$100—sentenced 1-3-57—3 months probation—$30 fine.

6-27-69—Lansing—Indecent Liberties with a Child—final charge: Accosting Children for Immoral Purposes—sentenced 9-19-69— 2 yrs. probation 3 days jail—$200 costs.

PERSONAL HISTORY:

Lorraine Jones—Mother—age 65—Daytona Beach, Florida

Willis Jones—Step-Father—age 68—Daytona Beach, Florida

Olive Cartwright—Father—deceased (defendant knows nothing about him)

Richard Jones—Brother—age 48—Lansing

Donald Jones—Brother—age 43—Daytona Beach, Florida

James Jones—Son—age 23—attends Western Michigan University.

David Jones—Son—age 20—attends MSU.

The defendant was born and raised in Lansing. Until age 11 he resided with his mother and grandparents. Subject's mother married Willis Jones when the defendant was 11 years of age.

Mr. Jones adopted the defendant and his siblings. The elder Jones was employed by the United States Postal Service while the defendant's mother was pretty much a dental office receptionist. As a teenager, respondent reports a very poor relationship with his step-father. He describes it as, "He (step-father) was a Navy man. He [would] strike first and *maybe* ask questions later." At about age 16 the defendant ran away from home and lived above a store in downtown Lansing. He said he supported himself by managing a bowling alley on South Washington. After living on his own at the apartment, and briefly at the YMCA he "begged" the principal at Eastern High School to let him return. He said he did return and graduated in 1957.

Respondent reports becoming involved in homosexual activities in his late teens.

Jones reports a good relationship with his mother, and a satisfactory relationship with his step-father. He said he and his brothers have never been close. Jones goes on to say he attempted to talk with his mother as well as his minister about his homosexual inclinations in his teens, but Jones said, "They just kind of said it would go away, they didn't want to deal with it."

MARITAL HISTORY:

The defendant married the former June Takahisha in 1960 while serving with the United States Army in Tokyo, Japan. She returned to his country with him, and two sons were born to their union. They were married 8 or 9 years, but, he said his long work hours, and the strain of having children caused the break down in their relationship. He said after a while, "It seemed like I was just a paycheck to her."

Respondent states that he and his former wife rarely communicate, however, she did loan him $2000 of the necessary money to post bond.

The defendant married the former Jane Francis in 1970. The marriage lasted five years. There were no children born to the union. This was Jones's third marriage. Respondent said, "I turned into a workaholic, alcoholic and dopeaholic, and conflicts with our children and then my gay activities started flaring up", led to the demise of this marriage.

2. Set forth below is a brief summary of some of the rights which defendants have claimed they have during the sentencing process and some courts' responses to those claims.

a. *The Right to Counsel.* In Mempa v. Rhay, 389 U.S. 128, 88 S.Ct. 254 (1967), the Supreme Court concluded that the sixth amendment right to counsel extends to sentencing hearings. Noting the "critical nature of sentencing in a criminal case," the Court observed that an attorney could assist "in marshaling the facts, introducing evidence of mitigating circumstances and in general aiding and assisting the defendant to present his case as to sentence." Id. at 134–35, 88 S.Ct. at 256–57.

The holding of the Court in *Mempa* must be read in light of the Court's subsequent decision in Scott v. Illinois, 440 U.S. 367, 99 S.Ct. 1158 (1979). In *Scott,* the Court held in a 5–4 opinion that whether an indigent defendant has the right to appointed counsel to provide assistance at trial depends on the sanction ultimately imposed on the defendant. The indigent defendant has no such right to appointed counsel unless the sanction imposed includes some period of incarceration. After *Scott,* it seems unlikely that the Court would conclude that there is a right to appointed counsel at a sentencing hearing in a case where there was no such right at trial.

The sixth amendment right to the assistance of counsel at a sentencing hearing includes the right to the effective assistance of counsel. Strickland v. Washington, 466 U.S. 668, 104 S.Ct. 2052 (1984). In *Strickland,* the Supreme Court outlined the test to be applied when determining whether a defendant at a capital sentencing hearing received the effective assistance of counsel. To prevail on an ineffectiveness claim, the defendant must prove two things: first, that his or her attorney acted unreasonably in contravention of "prevailing professional norms," and second, that the defendant was prejudiced by this deficient performance. Id. at 687–88, 104 S.Ct. at 2064–65. To establish prejudice, the defendant must prove that there is a "reasonable probability" that the death penalty would not have been imposed if the defense attorney had performed competently. Id. at 694, 104 S.Ct. at 2068. Whether the same or a different test applies when analyzing ineffectiveness claims based on defense attorneys' allegedly deficient performance during non-capital sentencing proceedings is a question that the Supreme Court specifically left open. Id. at 686, 104 S.Ct. at 2064 ("We need not consider the role of counsel in an ordinary sentencing, which may involve informal proceedings and standardless discretion in the sentencer, and hence may require a different approach to the definition of constitutionally effective assistance.").

Separate and apart from questions concerning the right to the assistance of counsel at sentencing hearings is the question whether the defendant has the sixth amendment right to the assistance of counsel at certain interviews during which information is gathered from the defendant which will be considered at the sentencing hearing. The Supreme Court addressed this question in Estelle v. Smith, 451 U.S. 454, 101 S.Ct. 1866 (1981). In that case, the defendant was charged with murder. When the state disclosed that it intended to seek imposition of the death penalty, the trial judge directed that the defendant be examined by a psychiatrist to determine his competency to stand trial.

After the defendant was convicted of murder, the state called the psychiatrist as a witness at the sentencing hearing. The psychiatrist testified that the defendant was a sociopath for whom treatment would be unavailing. This testimony bore on the question of the defendant's future dangerousness, an issue which, if resolved against the defendant, could, and in this case did, lead to the imposition of the death penalty.

The Supreme Court unanimously concluded that the interviewing of the defendant by the psychiatrist without prior notification to the defendant's attorney that the interview would cover the subject of future dangerousness as well as competency to stand trial violated the defendant's sixth amendment right to counsel. Without such notice, the defendant was deprived of the opportunity to make a knowing decision as to whether or not to participate in the interview. The Supreme Court, however added a significant caveat to its opinion, emphasizing that the defendant did not claim that he had the right to have his attorney actually present during the interview with the psychiatrist; he only claimed that his attorney should have received advance notice of the scope of topics that would be considered during the psychiatric examination. With seeming approval, the Supreme Court then quoted from the opinion of the court of appeals which had stated that " 'an attorney present during the psychiatric interview could contribute little and might seriously disrupt the examination.' " Id. at 470 n. 14, 101 S.Ct. at 1877 n. 14.

When faced with the question whether a defendant has a sixth amendment right to have counsel present when being interviewed by a probation officer conducting a presentence investigation, most lower courts have distinguished Estelle v. Smith. United States v. Jackson, 886 F.2d 838 (7th Cir.1989) is a case in point. In that case, the Seventh Circuit Court of Appeals observed as follows:

A district judge's use of a defendant's statement to a probation officer in applying the Sentencing Guidelines is markedly unlike the *prosecutor's* adversarial use of a defendant's pretrial statement to a psychiatrist to carry the state's burden of proof before a jury. A federal probation officer is an extension of the court and not an agent of the government. The probation officer does not have an adversarial role in the sentencing proceedings. In interviewing a defendant as part of the presentence investigation, the probation officer serves as a neutral information gatherer for the sentencing judge. The interview of a defendant is but one of many aspects of the presentence investigation conducted by a probation officer.

*   *   *

The pretrial statement made by the defendant in *Estelle* became a factor satisfying an element of the burden of proof borne by the prosecution in seeking the death penalty in a trial before a jury. *Estelle* is simply inapplicable on its facts and legal theory to a federal district judge's discretionary use of a defendant's postconviction statement made to a federal probation officer carrying out a nonadversarial presentence investigation.

Id. at 844–45. See also Brown v. Butler, 811 F.2d 938, 941 (5th Cir.1987).

Do you find the reasoning of the court in *Jackson* persuasive? Do you believe that a probation officer's interview with a defendant during a presentence investigation is a critical stage of the prosecution to which the sixth amendment right to counsel attaches?

b. *The Rights to Present Evidence and Make Statements.* Courts have generally assumed that defendants have a constitutional right to have their attorneys comment on the evidence and make a statement to the court at a sentencing hearing. To what extent do *Gardner v. Florida* and Mempa v. Rhay, 389 U.S. 128, 88 S.Ct. 254 (1967) support this assumption?

Defendants have claimed that they not only have a right to speak to the court through their attorneys on the subject of sentencing, but that they also have a constitutional right to address the court themselves. The right which the defendants are invoking is known as the right of allocution.

Thus far, most courts have generally refused to recognize a constitutionally-based right of allocution. See, e.g., Hill v. United States, 368 U.S. 424, 82 S.Ct. 468 (1962); United States v. Coffey, 871 F.2d 39, 40 (6th Cir. 1989); United States v. Fleming, 849 F.2d 568, 569 (11th Cir.1988). It should be noted, however, that Hill v. United States, the Supreme Court case that the lower courts have relied on in concluding that there is no constitutional right of allocution, was a case with some special facts that the Court took pains to mention. First, the Court in *Hill* noted that the sentencing court had simply failed to ask the defendant if he had anything to say before the court imposed sentence; the court had not forbidden a defendant who expressed his desire to address the court from doing so. In addition, the Court emphasized that the defendant in *Hill* was represented by an attorney at the sentencing hearing. Should this latter fact have any bearing on the question whether a defendant has a constitutional right of allocution? See Green v. United States, 365 U.S. 301, 304, 81 S.Ct. 653, 655 (1961), a case in which the Court discussed the right of allocution under

Rule 32(a) of the Federal Rules of Criminal Procedure, which is set forth on page 83, infra. ("The most persuasive counsel may not be able to speak for a defendant as the defendant might, with halting eloquence, speak for himself.").

Though a defendant may or may not have a constitutional right of allocution, it is clear that at least in some circumstances, the defendant has the right to present evidence at a sentencing hearing. For example, in Green v. Georgia, 442 U.S. 95, 99 S.Ct. 2150 (1979), the Supreme Court held that the defendant's due process rights were violated when he was not permitted to call a witness to testify at a capital sentencing hearing because the witness's testimony, under the state's evidentiary rules, would be hearsay. The witness apparently would have testified that a co-defendant had admitted to the witness that he was the one who had actually shot the victim with whose murder the defendant was charged. In concluding that the defendant's due process rights were violated when he was not allowed to call the witness to testify at the sentencing hearing, the Court emphasized both that the witness's testimony was "highly relevant" to a "critical issue" in the sentencing hearing and that there were "substantial reasons" for believing that the testimony was reliable. The reasons mentioned by the Court included the following: the co-defendant was a close friend of the witness; the co-defendant had made a declaration against penal interest; there was evidence which corroborated the co-defendant's admission; and the state had considered the admission reliable enough to use against the co-defendant during his own trial for capital murder. See also Ake v. Oklahoma, 470 U.S. 68, 105 S.Ct. 1087 (1985) (indigent defendant convicted of capital murders had a due process right to be afforded access to a psychiatrist to help the defendant prepare and present evidence on the question of his future dangerousness, a question which was a "significant factor" at his sentencing hearing).

c. *The Right to Confront and Cross–Examine Adverse Witnesses.* As is apparent from the presentence investigation report found on page 72, supra, presentence investigation reports, upon which sentencing courts frequently rely when imposing sentence, are often filled with references to the hearsay statements of witnesses. Courts have generally rejected the claims of defendants that they have a right to cross-examine these witnesses at their sentencing hearings. See, e.g., United States v. Allen, 797 F.2d 1395, 1401 (7th Cir.1986). But see Proffitt v. Wainwright, 685 F.2d 1227, 1255 (11th Cir.1982) (recognizing a general right of cross-examination in capital sentencing hearings). At the same time, however, the courts have observed that defendants do have a right protected by the due process clause to explain or rebut the hearsay evidence. See, e.g., United States v. Evans, 891 F.2d 686, 688 (8th Cir.1989); United States v. Agyemang, 876 F.2d 1264, 1272 (7th Cir.1989). What constitutes a sufficient opportunity to explain or rebut the hearsay evidence is a question which the courts have not fully answered. But see United States v. Allen, 797 F.2d 1395, 1401 (7th Cir.1986) (defendant was afforded right of rebuttal through her attorney's previous cross-examination of the witness at trial).

d. *Right to a Statement of Reasons for the Sentence Imposed.* Thus far, courts have generally refused to hold that defendants have a constitutional right to be apprised, whether orally or in writing, of the reasons why a particular sentence was imposed by a sentencer. United States v. Golomb, 754 F.2d 86, 90 (2d Cir.1985). In some exceptional circumstances, however, the courts have considered a statement of reasons constitutionally mandated. See, e.g., North Carolina v. Pearce, 395 U.S. 711, 726, 89 S.Ct. 2072, 2081 (1969) (reasons for higher sentence imposed after defendant successfully appealed his first conviction, was retried, and convicted again had to "affirmatively appear" on the record).

4. Apart from the procedural safeguards required by the United States Constitution during the sentencing process, additional rights may be bestowed by statutes, court rules, and state constitutions. An example of one such source of additional rights is Rule 32 of the Federal Rules of Criminal Procedure, which governs sentencing proceedings in the federal courts. Pertinent excerpts of Rule 32 are set forth below:

Rule 32. Sentence and Judgment

(a) Sentence.

(1) **Imposition of Sentence.** Sentence shall be imposed without unnecessary delay, but the court may, when there is a factor important to the sentencing determination that is not then capable of being resolved, postpone the imposition of sentence for a reasonable time until the factor is capable of being resolved. Prior to the sentencing hearing, the court shall provide the counsel for the defendant and the attorney for the Government with notice of the probation officer's determination, pursuant to the provisions of subdivision (c)(2)(B), of the sentencing classifications and sentencing guideline range believed to be applicable to the case. At the sentencing hearing, the court shall afford the counsel for the defendant and the attorney for the Government an opportunity to comment upon the probation officer's determination and on other matters relating to the appropriate sentence. Before imposing sentence, the court shall also—

(A) determine that the defendant and defendant's counsel have had the opportunity to read and discuss the presentence investigation report made available pursuant to subdivision (c) (3)(A) or summary thereof made available pursuant to subdivision (c)(3)(B);

(B) afford counsel for the defendant an opportunity to speak on behalf of the defendant; and

(C) address the defendant personally and determine if the defendant wishes to make a statement and to present any information in mitigation of the sentence.

The attorney for the Government shall have an equivalent opportunity to speak to the court. Upon a motion that is jointly filed by the defendant and by the attorney for the Government, the court may hear in camera such a statement by the defendant, counsel for the defendant, or the attorney for the Government.

(2) Notification of Right to Appeal. After imposing sentence in a case which has gone to trial on a plea of not guilty, the court shall advise the defendant of the defendant's right to appeal, including any right to appeal the sentence, and of the right of a person who is unable to pay the cost of an appeal to apply for leave to appeal in forma pauperis. There shall be no duty on the court to advise the defendant of any right of appeal after sentence is imposed following a plea of guilty or nolo contendere, except that the court shall advise the defendant of any right to appeal the sentence. If the defendant so requests, the clerk of the court shall prepare and file forthwith a notice of appeal on behalf of the defendant.

* * *

(c) Presentence Investigation.

(1) When Made. A probation officer shall make a presentence investigation and report to the court before the imposition of sentence unless the court finds that there is in the record information sufficient to enable the meaningful exercise of sentencing authority pursuant to 18 U.S.C. 3553, and the court explains this finding on the record.

Except with the written consent of the defendant, the report shall not be submitted to the court or its contents disclosed to anyone unless the defendant has pleaded guilty or nolo contendere or has been found guilty.

(2) Report. The report of the presentence investigation shall contain—

(A) information about the history and characteristics of the defendant, including prior criminal record, if any, financial condition, and any circumstances affecting the defendant's behavior that may be helpful in imposing sentence or in the correctional treatment of the defendant.

(B) the classification of the offense and of the defendant under the categories established by the Sentencing Commission pursuant to section 994(a) of title 28, that the probation officer believes to be applicable to the defendant's case; the kinds of sentence and the sentencing range suggested for such a category of offense committed by such a category of defendant as set forth in the guidelines issued by the Sentencing Commission pursuant to 28 U.S.C. 994(a)(1); and an explanation by the probation officer of any factors that may indicate that a sentence of a different kind or of a different length from one within the applicable guideline would be more appropriate under all the circumstances;

(C) any pertinent policy statement issued by the Sentencing Commission pursuant to 28 U.S.C. 994(a)(2);

(D) verified information stated in a nonargumentative style containing an assessment of the financial, social, psychological, and medical impact upon, and cost to, any individual against whom the offense has been committed;

(E) unless the court orders otherwise, information concerning the nature and extent of nonprison programs and resources available for the defendant; and

(F) such other information as may be required by the court.

(3) Disclosure.

(A) At least 10 days before imposing sentence, unless this minimum period is waived by the defendant, the court shall provide the defendant and the defendant's counsel with a copy of the report of the presentence investigation, including the information required by subdivision (c)(2) but not including any final recommendation as to sentence, and not to the extent that in the opinion of the court the report contains diagnostic opinions, which if disclosed, might seriously disrupt a program of rehabilitation; or sources of information obtained upon a promise of confidentiality; or any other information which, if disclosed, might result in harm, physical or otherwise, to the defendant or other persons. The court shall afford the defendant and the defendant's counsel an opportunity to comment on the report and, in the discretion of the court, to introduce testimony or other information relating to any alleged factual inaccuracy contained in it.

(B) If the court is of the view that there is information in the presentence report which should not be disclosed under subdivision (c)(3)(A) of this rule, the court in lieu of making the report or part thereof available shall state orally or in writing a summary of the factual information contained therein to be relied on in determining sentence, and shall give the defendant and the defendant's counsel an opportunity to comment thereon. The statement may be made to the parties in camera.

(C) Any material which may be disclosed to the defendant and the defendant's counsel shall be disclosed to the attorney for the government.

(D) If the comments of the defendant and the defendant's counsel or testimony or other information introduced by them allege any factual inaccuracy in the presentence investigation report or the summary of the report or part thereof, the court shall, as to each matter controverted, make (i) a finding as to the allegation, or (ii) a determination that no such finding is necessary because the matter controverted will not be taken into account in sentencing. A written record of such findings and determinations shall be appended to and accompany any copy of the presentence investigation report thereafter made available to the Bureau of Prisons.

(E) The reports of studies and recommendations contained therein made by the Director of the Bureau of Prisons pursuant to 18 U.S.C. § 3552(b) shall be considered a presentence investigation within the meaning of subdivision (c)(3) of this rule.

* * *

How, if at all, do you believe Rule 32 should be modified?

McMILLAN v. PENNSYLVANIA

Supreme Court of the United States, 1986.
477 U.S. 79, 106 S.Ct. 2411, 91 L.Ed.2d 67.

MR. JUSTICE REHNQUIST delivered the opinion of the Court.

We granted certiorari to consider the constitutionality, under the Due Process Clause of the Fourteenth Amendment and the jury trial guarantee of the Sixth Amendment, of Pennsylvania's Mandatory Minimum Sentencing Act.

I

The Act was adopted in 1982. It provides that anyone convicted of certain enumerated felonies is subject to a mandatory minimum sentence of five years' imprisonment if the sentencing judge finds, by a preponderance of the evidence, that the person "visibly possessed a firearm" during the commission of the offense. At the sentencing hearing, the judge is directed to consider the evidence introduced at trial and any additional evidence offered by either the defendant or the Commonwealth.[1] The Act operates to divest the judge of discretion to impose any sentence of less than five years for the underlying felony; it does not authorize a sentence in excess of that otherwise allowed for that offense.

1. Section 9712 provides in full:

"(a) Mandatory sentence.—Any person who is convicted in any court of this Commonwealth of murder of the third degree, voluntary manslaughter, rape, involuntary deviate sexual intercourse, robbery as defined in 18 Pa.C.S. § 3701(a)(1)(i), (ii) or (iii) (relating to robbery), aggravated assault as defined in 18 Pa.C.S. § 2702(a)(1) (relating to aggravated assault) or kidnapping, or who is convicted of attempt to commit any of these crimes, shall, if the person visibly possessed a firearm during the commission of the offense, be sentenced to a minimum sentence of at least five years of total confinement notwithstanding any other provision of this title or other statute to the contrary.

"(b) Proof at sentencing.—Provisions of this section shall not be an element of the crime and notice thereof to the defendant shall not be required prior to conviction,

but reasonable notice of the Commonwealth's intention to proceed under this section shall be provided after conviction and before sentencing. The applicability of this section shall be determined at sentencing. The court shall consider any evidence presented at trial and shall afford the Commonwealth and the defendant an opportunity to present any necessary additional evidence and shall determine, by a preponderance of the evidence, if this section is applicable.

"(c) Authority of court in sentencing.— There shall be no authority in any court to impose on an offender to which this section is applicable any lesser sentence than provided for in subsection (a) or to place such offender on probation or to suspend sentence. Nothing in this section shall prevent the sentencing court from imposing a sentence greater than that provided in this section.

Each petitioner was convicted of, among other things, one of § 9712's enumerated felonies. * * * In each case the Commonwealth gave notice that at sentencing it would seek to proceed under the Act. No § 9712 hearing was held, however, because each of the sentencing judges before whom petitioners appeared found the Act unconstitutional; each imposed a lesser sentence than that required by the Act.

The Commonwealth appealed all four cases to the Supreme Court of Pennsylvania. That court consolidated the appeals and unanimously concluded that the Act is consistent with due process. * * *

* * *

We granted certiorari and now affirm.

II

Petitioners argue that under the Due Process Clause as interpreted in [*In re*] *Winship*[, 397 U.S. 358 (1970)] and *Mullaney* [*v. Wilbur*, 421 U.S. 684 (1975)], if a state wants to punish visible possession of a firearm it must undertake the burden of proving that fact beyond a reasonable doubt. We disagree. *Winship* held that "the Due Process Clause protects the accused against conviction except upon proof beyond a reasonable doubt of every fact necessary to constitute the crime with which he is charged." In *Mullaney v. Wilbur*, we held that the Due Process Clause "requires the prosecution to prove beyond a reasonable doubt the absence of the heat of passion on sudden provocation when the issue is properly presented in a homicide case." But in *Patterson* [*v. New York*, 432 U.S. 197 (1977)], we rejected the claim that whenever a State links the "severity of punishment" to "the presence or absence of an identified fact" the State must prove that fact beyond a reasonable doubt. (State need not "prove beyond a reasonable doubt every fact, the existence or nonexistence of which it is willing to recognize as an exculpatory or mitigating circumstance affecting the degree of culpability or the severity of the punishment"). In particular, we upheld against a due process challenge New York's law placing on defendants charged with murder the burden of proving the affirmative defense of extreme emotional disturbance.

Patterson stressed that in determining what facts must be proved beyond a reasonable doubt the state legislature's definition of the elements of the offense is usually dispositive: "[T]he Due Process Clause requires the prosecution to prove beyond a reasonable doubt all of the elements *included in the definition of the offense* of which the defendant is charged." *Id.*, at 210 (emphasis added). * * *

We believe that the present case is controlled by *Patterson*, our most recent pronouncement on this subject, rather than by *Mullaney*. As the Supreme Court of Pennsylvania observed, the Pennsylvania Legislature has expressly provided that visible possession of a firearm is not an element of the crimes enumerated in the mandatory sentencing statute, but instead is a sentencing factor that comes into play only after the defendant has been found guilty of one of those crimes beyond a reasonable doubt. Indeed, the elements of the enumerated offenses, like the maximum permissible penalties for those offenses, were established long before the Mandatory Minimum Sentencing Act was passed. While visible possession might well have been included as an element of the enumerated offenses, Pennsylvania chose not to redefine those offenses in order to so include it, and *Patterson* teaches that we should hesitate to conclude that due process bars the State from pursuing its chosen course in the area of defining crimes and prescribing penalties.

As *Patterson* recognized, of course, there are constitutional limits to the State's power in this regard; in certain limited circumstances *Winship*'s reasonable-doubt requirement applies to facts not formally identified as elements of the offense charged. Petitioners argue that Pennsylvania has gone beyond those limits and that its formal provision that visible possession is not an element of the crime is therefore of no effect. We do not think so. While we have never attempted to define precisely the constitutional limits noted in *Patterson, i.e.,* the extent to which due process forbids the reallocation or reduction of burdens of proof in criminal cases, and do not do so today, we are persuaded by several factors that Pennsylvania's Mandatory Minimum Sentencing Act does not exceed those limits.

We note first that the Act plainly does not transgress the limits expressly set out in *Patterson.* Responding to the concern that its rule would permit States unbridled power to redefine crimes to the detriment of criminal defendants, the *Patterson* Court advanced the unremarkable proposition that the Due Process Clause precludes States from discarding the presumption of innocence * * *. Nor does it relieve the prosecution of its burden of proving guilt; § 9712 only becomes applicable after a defendant has been duly convicted of the crime for which he is to be punished.

The Court in *Mullaney* observed, with respect to the main criminal statute invalidated in that case, that once the State proved the elements which Maine required it to prove beyond a reasonable doubt the defendant faced "a differential in sentencing ranging from a nominal fine to a mandatory life sentence." In the present case the situation is quite different. Of the offenses enumerated in the Act, third-degree murder, robbery as defined in 18 Pa.Cons.Stat. § 3701(a)(1) (1982), kidnapping, rape, and involuntary deviate sexual intercourse are first-degree felonies subjecting the defendant to a maximum of 20 years' imprisonment. Voluntary manslaughter and aggravated assault as defined in § 2702(a)(1) are felonies of the second degree carrying a maximum sentence of 10 years. Section 9712 neither alters the maximum penalty for the crime committed nor creates a separate offense calling for a separate penalty; it operates solely to limit the sentencing court's discretion in selecting a penalty within the range already available to it without the special finding of visible possession of a firearm. Section 9712 "ups the ante" for the defendant only by raising to five years the minimum sentence which may be imposed within the

statutory plan.[4] The statute gives no impression of having been tailored to permit the visible possession finding to be a tail which wags the
dog of the substantive offense. Petitioners' claim that visible possession under the Pennsylvania statute is "really" an element of the
offenses for which they are being punished—that Pennsylvania has in
effect defined a new set of upgraded felonies—would have at least more
superficial appeal if a finding of visible possession exposed them to
greater or additional punishment, but it does not.

Finally, we note that the specter raised by petitioners of States
restructuring existing crimes in order to "evade" the commands of
Winship just does not appear in this case. As noted above, § 9712's
enumerated felonies retain the same elements they had before the
Mandatory Minimum Sentencing Act was passed. The Pennsylvania
Legislature did not change the definition of any existing offense. It
simply took one factor that has always been considered by sentencing
courts to bear on punishment—the instrumentality used in committing
a violent felony—and dictated the precise weight to be given that factor
if the instrumentality is a firearm. Pennsylvania's decision to do so
has not transformed against its will a sentencing factor into an "element" of some hypothetical "offense."

Petitioners seek support for their due process claim by observing
that many legislatures have made possession of a weapon an element of
various aggravated offenses. But the fact that the States have formulated different statutory schemes to punish armed felons is merely a
reflection of our federal system, which demands "[t]olerance for a
spectrum of state procedures dealing with a common problem of law
enforcement" * * *.

* * *

III

Having concluded that States may treat "visible possession of a
firearm" as a sentencing consideration rather than an element of a
particular offense, we now turn to petitioners' subsidiary claim that due
process nonetheless requires that visible possession be proved by at
least clear and convincing evidence. Like the court below, we have
little difficulty concluding that in this case the preponderance standard
satisfies due process. Petitioners do not and could not claim that a
sentencing court may never rely on a particular fact in passing sentence without finding that fact by "clear and convincing evidence."
Sentencing courts have traditionally heard evidence and found facts
without any prescribed burden of proof at all. Pennsylvania has
deemed a particular fact relevant and prescribed a particular burden of

4. By prescribing a mandatory minimum sentence, the Act incidentally serves
to restrict the sentencing court's discretion
in setting a maximum sentence. Pennsylvania law provides that a minimum sentence of confinement "shall not exceed one-
half of the maximum sentence imposed."
Thus, the shortest maximum term permissible under the Act is 10 years.

proof. We see nothing in Pennsylvania's scheme that would warrant constitutionalizing burdens of proof at sentencing.[8]

* * *

IV

In light of the foregoing, petitioners' final claim—that the Act denies them their Sixth Amendment right to a trial by jury—merits little discussion. Petitioners again argue that the jury must determine all ultimate facts concerning the offense committed. Having concluded that Pennsylvania may properly treat visible possession as a sentencing consideration and not an element of any offense, we need only note that there is no Sixth Amendment right to jury sentencing, even where the sentence turns on specific findings of fact. See *Spaziano v. Florida,* 468 U.S., at 459.

For the foregoing reasons, the judgment of the Supreme Court of Pennsylvania is affirmed.

* * *

JUSTICE MARSHALL, with whom JUSTICE BRENNAN and JUSTICE BLACK-MUN join, dissenting. [Opinion omitted.]

JUSTICE STEVENS, dissenting.

Petitioner Dennison, a 73–year–old man, committed an aggravated assault upon a neighborhood youth whom he suspected of stealing money from his house. After a trial at which the Commonwealth proved the elements of the offense of aggravated assault beyond a reasonable doubt, the trial judge imposed a sentence of imprisonment of 11½ to 23 months. Because he had concluded that Pennsylvania's recently enacted Mandatory Minimum Sentencing Act was unconstitutional, the trial judge refused to impose the 5–year minimum sentence mandated by that Act whenever the Commonwealth proves—by a preponderance of the evidence—that the defendant "visibly possessed a firearm during the commission of the offense."

* * *

* * * Today the Court holds that state legislatures may not only define the offense with which a criminal defendant is charged, but may also authoritatively determine that the conduct so described—*i.e.,* the prohibited activity which subjects the defendant to criminal sanctions—

---

8. *Addington v. Texas,* 441 U.S. 418 (1979), and *Santosky v. Kramer,* 455 U.S. 745 (1982), which respectively applied the "clear and convincing evidence" standard where the State sought involuntary commitment to a mental institution and involuntary termination of parental rights, are not to the contrary. Quite unlike the situation in those cases, criminal sentencing takes place only after a defendant has been adjudged guilty beyond a reasonable doubt. Once the reasonable-doubt standard has been applied to obtain a valid conviction, "the criminal defendant has been constitu-tionally deprived of his liberty to the extent that the State may confine him." *Meachum v. Fano,* 427 U.S. 215, 224 (1976). As noted in text, sentencing courts have always operated without constitutionally imposed burdens of proof; embracing petitioners' suggestion that we apply the clear-and-convincing standard here would significantly alter criminal sentencing, for we see no way to distinguish the visible possession finding at issue here from a host of other express or implied findings sentencing judges typically make on the way to passing sentence.

is *not* an element of the crime which the Due Process Clause requires to be proved by the prosecution beyond a reasonable doubt. In my view, a state legislature may not dispense with the requirement of proof beyond a reasonable doubt for conduct that it targets for severe criminal penalties. Because the Pennsylvania statute challenged in this case describes conduct that the Pennsylvania Legislature obviously intended to prohibit, and because it mandates lengthy incarceration for the same, I believe that the conduct so described is an element of the criminal offense to which the proof beyond a reasonable doubt requirement applies.

*   *   *

It would demean the importance of the reasonable-doubt standard—indeed, it would demean the Constitution itself—if the substance of the standard could be avoided by nothing more than a legislative declaration that prohibited conduct is not an "element" of a crime. A legislative definition of an offense named "assault" could be broad enough to encompass every intentional infliction of harm by one person upon another, but surely the legislature could not provide that only that fact must be proved beyond a reasonable doubt and then specify a range of increased punishments if the prosecution could show by a preponderance of the evidence that the defendant robbed, raped, or killed his victim "during the commission of the offense."

Appropriate respect for the rule of *In re Winship* requires that there be some constitutional limits on the power of a State to define the elements of criminal offenses. The high standard of proof is required because of the immense importance of the individual interest in avoiding both the loss of liberty and the stigma that results from a criminal conviction. It follows, I submit, that if a State provides that a specific component of a prohibited transaction shall give rise both to a special stigma and to a special punishment, that component must be treated as a "fact necessary to constitute the crime" within the meaning of our holding in *In re Winship*.

Pennsylvania's Mandatory Minimum Sentencing Act reflects a legislative determination that a defendant who "visibly possessed a firearm" during the commission of an aggravated assault is more blameworthy than a defendant who did not. A judicial finding that the defendant used a firearm in an aggravated assault places a greater stigma on the defendant's name than a simple finding that he committed an aggravated assault. And not to be overlooked, such a finding with respect to petitioner Dennison automatically mandates a punishment that is more than twice as severe as the *maximum* punishment that the trial judge considered appropriate for his conduct.

It is true, as the Court points out, that the enhanced punishment is within the range that was authorized for any aggravated assault. That fact does not, however, minimize the significance of a finding of visible possession of a firearm whether attention is focused on the stigmatizing or punitive consequences of that finding. The finding identifies conduct that the legislature specifically intended to prohibit and to punish by a special sanction. In my opinion the constitutional significance of the special sanction cannot be avoided by the cavalier observation that it merely "ups the ante" for the defendant. No matter how culpable petitioner Dennison may be, the difference between 11½ months and 5 years of incarceration merits a more principled justification than the luck of the draw.

I respectfully dissent.

Questions and Points for Discussion

1. What effect, if any, do you think that the Court's decision in *McMillan* might have on legislatures and the way in which they statutorily define crimes?

2. Since *McMillan*, the lower courts have split on the question of the standard of proof that must or should be applied at sentencing hearings. Compare United States v. Guerra, 888 F.2d 247, 251 (2d Cir.1989) (preponderance of the evidence standard applies to sentencing factors) with United States v. Gooden, 892 F.2d 725, 728 (8th Cir.1989) (no standard of proof constitutionally required). Even in those jurisdictions which have adopted a preponderance of the evidence standard, most have condoned placing the burden of proving the existence of mitigating circumstances on defendants. See, e.g., United States v. Harris, 882 F.2d 902, 907 (4th Cir.1989) (government has the burden of proving aggravating circumstances; defendants the burden of proving mitigating circumstances); United States v. Cuellar-Flores, 891 F.2d 92, 93 (5th Cir.1989). These courts have reasoned that it is fundamentally fair to place on a defendant the burden of proving the facts about such things as family stability, educational background, and employment history of which the defendant, but not the government, is readily aware.

3. What standard of proof, if any, must and should apply in capital sentencing hearings? For one view, see United States v. Fernandez–Vidana, 857 F.2d 673, 676 (9th Cir.1988) (Reinhardt, J., concurring) (clear and convincing evidence standard may apply in capital cases).

B. FACTORS CONSIDERED AT SENTENCING

UNITED STATES v. GRAYSON

Supreme Court of the United States, 1978.
438 U.S. 41, 98 S.Ct. 2610, 57 L.Ed.2d 582.

MR. CHIEF JUSTICE BURGER delivered the opinion of the Court.

We granted certiorari to review a holding of the Court of Appeals that it was improper for a sentencing judge, in fixing the sentence within the statutory limits, to give consideration to the defendant's false testimony observed by the judge during the trial.

I

In August 1975, respondent Grayson was confined in a federal prison camp under a conviction for distributing a controlled substance. In October, he escaped but was apprehended two days later by FBI agents in New York City. He was indicted for prison escape in violation of 18 U.S.C. § 751(a) (1976 ed.).

During its case in chief, the United States proved the essential elements of the crime, including his lawful confinement and the unlawful escape. In addition, it presented the testimony of the arresting FBI agents that Grayson, upon being apprehended, denied his true identity.

Grayson testified in his own defense. He admitted leaving the camp but asserted that he did so out of fear: "I had just been threatened with a large stick with a nail protruding through it by an inmate that was serving time at Allenwood, and I was scared, and I just ran." He testified that the threat was made in the presence of many inmates by prisoner Barnes who sought to enforce collection of a gambling debt and followed other threats and physical assaults made for the same purpose. Grayson called one inmate, who testified: "I heard [Barnes] talk to Grayson in a loud voice one day, but that's all. I never seen no harm, no hands or no shuffling whatsoever."

Grayson's version of the facts was contradicted by the Government's rebuttal evidence and by cross-examination on crucial aspects of his story. For example, Grayson stated that after crossing the prison fence he left his prison jacket by the side of the road. On recross, he stated that he also left his prison shirt but not his trousers. Government testimony showed that on the morning after the escape, a shirt marked with Grayson's number, a jacket, and a pair of prison trousers were found outside a hole in the prison fence.[1] Grayson also testified on cross-examination: "I do believe that I phrased the rhetorical question to Captain Kurd, who was in charge of [the prison], and I think I said something if an inmate was being threatened by somebody, what would . . . he do? First of all he said he would want to know who it was." On further cross-examination, however, Grayson modified his description of the conversation. Captain Kurd testified that Grayson had never mentioned in any fashion threats from other inmates. Finally, the alleged assailant, Barnes, by then no longer an inmate, testified that Grayson had never owed him any money and that he had never threatened or physically assaulted Grayson.

---

1. The testimony regarding the prison clothing was important for reasons in addition to the light it shed on quality of recollection. Grayson stated that after unpremeditatedly fleeing the prison with no possessions and crossing the fence, he hitchhiked to New York City—a difficult task for a man with no trousers. The United States suggested that by prearrangement Grayson met someone, possibly a woman friend, on the highway near the break in the fence and that this accomplice provided civilian clothes. It introduced evidence that the friend visited Grayson often en at prison, including each of the three days immediately prior to his penultimate day in the camp.

The jury returned a guilty verdict, whereupon the District Judge ordered the United States Probation Office to prepare a presentence report. At the sentencing hearing, the judge stated:

"I'm going to give my reasons for sentencing in this case with clarity, because one of the reasons may well be considered by a Court of Appeals to be impermissible; and although I could come into this Court Room and sentence this Defendant to a five-year prison term without any explanation at all, I think it is fair that I give the reasons so that if the Court of Appeals feels that one of the reasons which I am about to enunciate is an improper consideration for a trial judge, then the Court will be in a position to reverse this Court and send the case back for re-sentencing.

"In my view a prison sentence is indicated, and the sentence that the Court is going to impose is to deter you, Mr. Grayson, and others who are similarly situated. Secondly, *it is my view that your defense was a complete fabrication without the slightest merit whatsoever. I feel it is proper for me to consider that fact in the sentencing, and I will do so.*" (Emphasis added.)

He then sentenced Grayson to a term of two years' imprisonment, consecutive to his unexpired sentence.

On appeal, a divided panel of the Court of Appeals for the Third Circuit directed that Grayson's sentence be vacated and that he be resentenced by the District Court without consideration of false testimony. * * *

We granted certiorari to resolve conflicts between holdings of the Courts of Appeals. We reverse.

II

In *Williams v. New York,* 337 U.S. 241, 247 (1949), Mr. Justice Black observed that the "prevalent modern philosophy of penology [is] that the punishment should fit the offender and not merely the crime," and that, accordingly, sentences should be determined with an eye toward the "[r]eformation and rehabilitation of offenders." * * *

* * *

A defendant's truthfulness or mendacity while testifying on his own behalf, almost without exception, has been deemed probative of his attitudes toward society and prospects for rehabilitation and hence relevant to sentencing. Soon after *Williams* was decided, the Tenth Circuit concluded that "the attitude of a convicted defendant with respect to his willingness to commit a serious crime [perjury] . . . is a proper matter to consider in determining what sentence shall be imposed within the limitations fixed by statute." *Humes v. United States,* 186 F.2d 875, 878 (1951). The Second, Fourth, Fifth, Sixth, Seventh, Eighth, and Ninth Circuits have since agreed. Judge Marvin Frankel's analysis for the Second Circuit is persuasive:

"The effort to appraise 'character' is, to be sure, a parlous one, and not necessarily an enterprise for which judges are notably equipped by prior training. Yet it is in our existing scheme of sentencing one clue to the rational exercise of discretion. If the notion of 'repentance' is out of fashion today, the fact remains that a manipulative defiance of the law is not a cheerful datum for the prognosis a sentencing judge undertakes. . . . Impressions about the individual being sentenced— the likelihood that he will transgress no more, the hope that he may respond to rehabilitative efforts to assist with a lawful future career, the degree to which he does or does not deem himself at war with his society—are, for better or worse, central factors to be appraised under our theory of 'individualized' sentencing. The theory has its critics. While it lasts, however, a fact like the defendant's readiness to lie under oath before the judge who will sentence him would seem to be among the more precise and concrete of the available indicia." *United States v. Hendrix,* 505 F.2d 1233, 1236 (1974).

Only one Circuit has directly rejected the probative value of the defendant's false testimony in his own defense. In *Scott v. United States,* 135 U.S.App.D.C. 377, 382, 419 F.2d 264, 269 (1969), the court argued that

"the peculiar pressures placed upon a defendant threatened with jail and the stigma of conviction make his willingness to deny the crime an unpromising test of his prospects for rehabilitation if guilty. It is indeed unlikely that many men who commit serious offenses would balk on principle from lying in their own defense. The guilty man may quite sincerely repent his crime but yet, driven by the urge to remain free, may protest his innocence in a court of law."

The *Scott* rationale rests not only on the realism of the psychological pressures on a defendant in the dock—which we can grant—but also on a deterministic view of human conduct that is inconsistent with the underlying precepts of our criminal justice system. A "universal and persistent" foundation stone in our system of law, and particularly in our approach to punishment, sentencing, and incarceration, is the "belief in freedom of the human will and a consequent ability and duty of the normal individual to choose between good and evil." Given that long-accepted view of the "ability and duty of the normal individual to choose," we must conclude that the defendant's readiness to lie under oath—especially when, as here, the trial court finds the lie to be flagrant—may be deemed probative of his prospects for rehabilitation.

III

Against this background we evaluate Grayson's constitutional argument that the District Court's sentence constitutes punishment for the crime of perjury for which he has not been indicted, tried, or convicted by due process. A second argument is that permitting consideration of perjury will "chill" defendants from exercising their right to testify on their own behalf.

A

In his due process argument, Grayson does not contend directly that the District Court had an impermissible purpose in considering his perjury and selecting the sentence. Rather, he argues that this Court, in order to preserve due process rights, not only must prohibit the impermissible sentencing practice of incarcerating for the purpose of saving the Government the burden of bringing a separate and subsequent perjury prosecution but also must prohibit the otherwise *permissible* practice of considering a defendant's untruthfulness for the purpose of illuminating his need for rehabilitation and society's need for protection. He presents two interrelated reasons. The effect of both permissible and impermissible sentencing practices may be the same: additional time in prison. Further, it is virtually impossible, he contends, to identify and establish the impermissible practice. We find these reasons insufficient * * *.

First, the evolutionary history of sentencing * * * demonstrates that it is proper—indeed, even necessary for the rational exercise of discretion—to consider the defendant's whole person and personality, as manifested by his conduct at trial and his testimony under oath, for whatever light those may shed on the sentencing decision. The "parlous" effort to appraise "character," degenerates into a game of chance to the extent that a sentencing judge is deprived of relevant information concerning "every aspect of a defendant's life." The Government's interest, as well as the offender's, in avoiding irrationality is of the highest order. That interest more than justifies the risk that Grayson asserts is present when a sentencing judge considers a defendant's untruthfulness under oath.

Second, in our view, *Williams* fully supports consideration of such conduct in sentencing. There the Court permitted the sentencing judge to consider the offender's history of prior antisocial conduct, including burglaries for which he had not been duly convicted. This it did despite the risk that the judge might use his knowledge of the offender's prior crimes for an improper purpose.

Third, the efficacy of Grayson's suggested "exclusionary rule" is open to serious doubt. No rule of law, even one garbed in constitutional terms, can prevent improper use of firsthand observations of perjury. The integrity of the judges, and their fidelity to their oaths of office, necessarily provide the only, and in our view adequate, assurance against that.

B

Grayson's argument that judicial consideration of his conduct at trial impermissibly "chills" a defendant's statutory right, 18 U.S.C. § 3481 (1976 ed.), and perhaps a constitutional right to testify on his own behalf is without basis. The right guaranteed by law to a defendant is narrowly the right to testify truthfully in accordance with the oath—unless we are to say that the oath is mere ritual without meaning. This view of the right involved is confirmed by the unquestioned constitutionality of perjury statutes, which punish those who willfully give false testimony. Further support for this is found in an important limitation on a defendant's right to the assistance of counsel:

Counsel ethically cannot assist his client in presenting what the attorney has reason to believe is false testimony. Assuming, *arguendo,* that the sentencing judge's consideration of defendants' untruthfulness in testifying has any chilling effect on a defendant's decision to testify falsely, that effect is entirely permissible. There is no protected right to commit perjury.

Grayson's further argument that the sentencing practice challenged here will inhibit exercise of the right to testify truthfully is entirely frivolous. That argument misapprehends the nature and scope of the practice we find permissible. Nothing we say today requires a sentencing judge to enhance, in some wooden or reflex fashion, the sentences of all defendants whose testimony is deemed false. Rather, we are reaffirming the authority of a sentencing judge to evaluate carefully a defendant's testimony on the stand, determine—with a consciousness of the frailty of human judgment—whether that testimony contained willful and material falsehoods, and, if so, assess in light of all the other knowledge gained about the defendant the meaning of that conduct with respect to his prospects for rehabilitation and restoration to a useful place in society. Awareness of such a process realistically cannot be deemed to affect the decision of an accused but unconvicted defendant to testify truthfully in his own behalf.

Accordingly, we reverse the judgment of the Court of Appeals and remand for reinstatement of the sentence of the District Court.

MR. JUSTICE STEWART, with whom MR. JUSTICE BRENNAN and MR. JUSTICE MARSHALL join, dissenting.

The Court begins its consideration of this case with the assumption that the respondent gave false testimony at his trial. But there has been no determination that his testimony was false. This respondent was given a greater sentence than he would otherwise have received—how much greater we have no way of knowing—solely because a single judge *thought* that he had not testified truthfully. In essence, the Court holds today that *whenever* a defendant testifies in his own behalf and is found guilty, he opens himself to the possibility of an enhanced sentence. Such a sentence is nothing more or less than a penalty imposed on the defendant's exercise of his constitutional and statutory rights to plead not guilty and to testify in his own behalf.

It does not change matters to say that the enhanced sentence merely reflects the defendant's "prospects for rehabilitation" rather than an additional punishment for testifying falsely. The fact remains that all defendants who choose to testify, and only those who do so, face the very real prospect of a greater sentence based upon the trial judge's unreviewable perception that the testimony was untruthful. The Court prescribes no limitations or safeguards to minimize a defendant's rational fear that his truthful testimony will be perceived as false.[4]

---

4. For example, the dissenting judge in the Court of Appeals in this case suggested that a sentencing judge "should consider his independent evaluation of the testimony and behavior of the defendant only when he is convinced beyond a reasonable

Indeed, encumbrance of the sentencing process with the collateral inquiries necessary to provide such assurance would be both pragmatically unworkable and theoretically inconsistent with the assumption that the trial judge is merely considering one more piece of information in his overall evaluation of the defendant's prospects for rehabilitation. But without such safeguards I fail to see how the Court can dismiss as "frivolous" the argument that this sentencing practice will "inhibit exercise of the right to testify truthfully."

＊ ＊ ＊ Other witnesses risk punishment for perjury only upon indictment and conviction in accord with the full protections of the Constitution. Only the defendant himself, whose testimony is likely to be of critical importance to his defense, faces the additional risk that the disbelief of a single listener will itself result in time in prison.

The minimal contribution that the defendant's possibly untruthful testimony might make to an overall assessment of his potential for rehabilitation cannot justify imposing this additional burden on his right to testify in his own behalf. I do not believe that a sentencing judge's discretion to consider a wide range of information in arriving at an appropriate sentence allows him to mete out additional punishment to the defendant simply because of his personal belief that the defendant did not testify truthfully at the trial.

Accordingly, I would affirm the judgment of the Court of Appeals.

Questions and Points for Discussion

1. Statutes and sentencing guidelines often codify the factors to be considered by a judge when sentencing a defendant. The mitigating and aggravating factors outlined in Ill.Rev.Stat. ch. 38, §§ 1005–5–3.1 and 1005–5–3.2 exemplify the variety of factors which may enter into the sentencing decision:

1005–5–3.1. Factors in mitigation

§ 5–5–3.1. Factors in Mitigation. (a) The following grounds shall be accorded weight in favor of withholding or minimizing a sentence of imprisonment:

(1) the defendant's criminal conduct neither caused nor threatened serious physical harm to another;

(2) the defendant did not contemplate that his criminal conduct would cause or threaten serious physical harm to another;

(3) the defendant acted under a strong provocation;

doubt that the defendant intentionally lied on material issues of fact . . . [and] the falsity of the defendant's testimony [is] necessarily established by the finding of guilt." 550 F.2d 103, 114 (Rosenn, J., dissenting). Contrary to Judge Rosenn, I do not believe that the latter requirement was met in this case. The jury could have believed Grayson's entire story but concluded, in the words of the trial judge's instructions on the defense of duress, that "an ordinary man" would *not* "have felt it necessary to leave the Allenwood Prison Camp when faced with the same degree of compulsion, coercion or duress as the Defendant was faced with in this case."

(4) there were substantial grounds tending to excuse or justify the defendant's criminal conduct, though failing to establish a defense;

(5) the defendant's criminal conduct was induced or facilitated by someone other than the defendant;

(6) the defendant has compensated or will compensate the victim of his criminal conduct for the damage or injury that he sustained;

(7) the defendant has no history of prior delinquency or criminal activity or has led a law-abiding life for a substantial period of time before the commission of the present crime;

(8) the defendant's criminal conduct was the result of circumstances unlikely to recur;

(9) the character and attitudes of the defendant indicate that he is unlikely to commit another crime;

(10) the defendant is particularly likely to comply with the terms of a period of probation;

(11) the imprisonment of the defendant would entail excessive hardship to his dependents;

(12) the imprisonment of the defendant would endanger his or her medical condition.

(b) If the court, having due regard for the character of the offender, the nature and circumstances of the offense and the public interest finds that a sentence of imprisonment is the most appropriate disposition of the offender, or where other provisions of this Code mandate the imprisonment of the offender, the grounds listed in paragraph (a) of this subsection shall be considered as factors in mitigation of the term imposed.

1005–5–3.2. Factors in aggravation

§ 5–5–3.2. Factors in Aggravation. (a) The following factors shall be accorded weight in favor of imposing a term of imprisonment or may be considered by the court as reasons to impose a more severe sentence under Section 5–8–1:

(1) the defendant's conduct caused or threatened serious harm;

(2) the defendant received compensation for committing the offense;

(3) the defendant has a history of prior delinquency or criminal activity;

(4) the defendant, by the duties of his office or by his position, was obliged to prevent the particular offense committed or to bring the offenders committing it to justice;

(5) the defendant held public office at the time of the offense, and the offense related to the conduct of that office;

(6) the defendant utilized his professional reputation or position in the community to commit the offense, or to afford him an easier means of committing it;

(7) the sentence is necessary to deter others from committing the same crime;

(8) the defendant committed the offense against a person 60 years of age or older;

(9) the defendant committed the offense against a person who is physically handicapped;

(10) the offense took place in a place of worship or on the grounds of a place of worship, immediately prior to, during or immediately following worship services. For purposes of this subparagraph, "place of worship" shall mean any church, synagogue or other building, structure or place used primarily for religious worship;

(11) the defendant was convicted of a felony committed while he was released on bail or his own recognizance pending trial for a prior felony and was convicted of such prior felony, or the defendant was convicted of a felony committed while he was serving a period of probation or conditional discharge for a prior felony;

(12) the defendant committed or attempted to commit a felony while he was wearing a bulletproof vest. For the purposes of this paragraph (12), a bulletproof vest is any device which is designed for the purpose of protecting the wearer from bullets, shot or other lethal projectiles;

(13) the defendant held a position of trust or supervision such as, but not limited to, teacher, scout leader, baby sitter, or day care worker, in relation to a victim under 18 years of age, and the defendant committed an offense in violation of Section 11–6, 11–11, 11–15.1, 11–19.1, 11–19.2, 11–20.1, 12–13, 12–14, 12–15 or 12–16 of the Criminal Code of 1961 against that victim.[a]

(b) [T]he following factors may be considered by the court as reasons to impose an extended term sentence under Section 5–8–2 upon any offender:

(1) When a defendant is convicted of any felony, after having been previously convicted in Illinois of the same or greater class felony, when such conviction has occurred within 10 years after the previous conviction, excluding time spent in custody, and such charges are separately brought and tried and arise out of different series of acts; or

(2) When a defendant is convicted of any felony and the court finds that the offense was accompanied by exceptionally brutal or heinous behavior indicative of wanton cruelty; or

(3) When a defendant is convicted of voluntary manslaughter, second degree murder, involuntary manslaughter or reckless homicide in which the defendant has been convicted of causing the death of more than one individual; or

(4) When a defendant is convicted of any felony committed against:

(i) a person under 12 years of age at the time of the offense;

[a. These statutory provisions proscribe certain criminal sexual conduct.]

(ii) a person 60 years of age or older at the time of the offense; or

(iii) a person physically handicapped at the time of the offense.

(5) In the case of a defendant convicted of aggravated criminal sexual assault or criminal sexual assault, when the court finds that aggravated criminal sexual assault or criminal sexual assault was also committed on the same victim by one or more other individuals, and the defendant voluntarily participated in the crime with the knowledge of the participation of the others in the crime, and the commission of the crime was part of a single course of conduct during which there was no substantial change in the nature of the criminal objective.

(6) When a defendant is convicted of first degree murder, after having been previously convicted in Illinois of any offense listed under paragraph (c)(2) of Section 5–5–3, when such conviction has occurred within 10 years after the previous conviction, excluding time spent in custody, and such charges are separately brought and tried and arise out of different series of acts.

(c) The court may impose an extended term sentence under Section 5–8–2 upon any offender who was convicted of aggravated criminal sexual assault where the victim was under 18 years of age at the time of the commission of the offense.

(d) Except where the offender is sentenced to death or to a term of natural life imprisonment, the court may impose an extended term sentence under Section 5–8–2 upon any offender who is convicted of the first degree murder of a peace officer or fireman killed in the course of performing his official duties and the offender knew or should have known that the murdered individual was a peace officer or fireman.

Are there any additional aggravating or mitigating factors which should be added to the lists? Are there any that should be deleted in your opinion?

2. In Roberts v. United States, 445 U.S. 552, 100 S.Ct. 1358 (1980), the Supreme Court concluded that a defendant's failure to cooperate with authorities investigating other individuals' criminal activities of which the defendant had knowledge could appropriately be considered by a sentencing judge. The defendant in that case, both before and after being indicted for several drug distribution offenses, repeatedly refused to name his drug suppliers. The sentencing court later cited this failure to cooperate as one reason for the prison sentences imposed on the defendant.

The Supreme Court noted that a defendant's cooperation with criminal investigators suggests that the defendant is willing to abandon his or her criminal lifestyle. According to the Court, it followed that "[u]nless a different explanation is provided, a defendant's refusal to assist in the investigation of ongoing crimes gives rise to an inference that these laudable attitudes are lacking." Id. at 557, 100 S.Ct. at 1362.

The defendant in *Roberts* argued that there was indeed a "different explanation" for his refusal to name his suppliers—his fear for his safety if he betrayed his criminal associates as well as his desire not to forego his privilege against self-incrimination. The Supreme Court acknowledged that these arguments might have had merit if presented to the sentencing judge. The sentencing judge could have assessed whether the defendant's fears of retaliation and self-incrimination were well-founded. But just because there may have been legitimate reasons for the defendant's lack of cooperation was not enough to make inappropriate or unconstitutional the sentencing judge's consideration of the defendant's lack of cooperation when the defendant had failed to assert these reasons at the time of sentencing.

3. The lower courts have followed the Supreme Court's lead and condoned consideration of a wide array of factors when sentencing a criminal defendant. As in Williams v. New York, 337 U.S. 241, 69 S.Ct. 1079 (1949), supra page 64, and *United States v. Grayson,* the courts have approved consideration of criminal conduct of which the defendant has not been convicted. See, e.g., United States v. Strong, 891 F.2d 82, 85 (5th Cir. 1989) (no due process violation when defendant pled guilty to one crime, offense level under sentencing guidelines was based on more serious crime which stipulated facts revealed defendant had committed, but defendant's sentence did not exceed the maximum penalty for the offense to which she pled guilty); Coleman v. Risley, 839 F.2d 434, 459 (9th Cir.1988). The courts have also approved taking into account at sentencing a past criminal conviction presently being appealed by the defendant. See, e.g., United States v. Ochoa, 659 F.2d 547 (5th Cir.1981). And the courts have even held that the consideration of criminal conduct underlying charges of which a defendant was actually acquitted is appropriate and constitutional. See, e.g., United States v. Isom, 886 F.2d 736, 738–39 (4th Cir.1989); United States v. Mocciola, 891 F.2d 13, 16–17 (1st Cir.1989). As is demonstrated by the cases which follow, however, the Constitution does place some limits on the factors which may be taken into account at the time of sentencing.

TOWNSEND v. BURKE

Supreme Court of the United States, 1948.
334 U.S. 736, 68 S.Ct. 1252, 92 L.Ed. 1690.

MR. JUSTICE JACKSON delivered the opinion of the Court.

The Commonwealth of Pennsylvania holds petitioner prisoner under two indeterminate sentences, not exceeding 10 to 20 years, upon a plea of guilty to burglary and robbery. On review here of the State Supreme Court's denial of *habeas corpus,* the prisoner demands a discharge by this Court on federal constitutional grounds.

* * *

The proceedings as to this petitioner, following his plea of guilty, consisted of a recital by an officer of details of the crimes to which petitioner and others had pleaded guilty and of the following action by the court (italics supplied):

"By the Court (addressing Townsend):

"Q. Townsend, how old are you?

"A. 29.

"Q. You have been here before, haven't you?

"A. Yes, sir.

"Q. *1933, larceny of automobile.* 1934, larceny of produce. 1930, larceny of bicycle. 1931, entering to steal and larceny. *1938, entering to steal and larceny in Doylestown.* Were you tried up there? No, no. Arrested in Doylestown. That was up on Germantown Avenue, wasn't it? You robbed a paint store.

"A. No. That was my brother.

"Q. You were tried for it, weren't you?

"A. Yes, but I was not guilty.

"Q. And 1945, this. 1936, entering to steal and larceny, 1350 Ridge Avenue. Is that your brother too?

"A. No.

"Q. *1937, receiving stolen goods, a saxophone.* What did you want with a saxophone? Didn't hope to play in the prison band then, did you?

"The Court: Ten to twenty in the Penitentiary."

The trial court's facetiousness casts a somewhat somber reflection on the fairness of the proceeding when we learn from the record that actually the charge of receiving the stolen saxophone had been dismissed and the prisoner discharged by the magistrate. But it savors of foul play or of carelessness when we find from the record that, on two others of the charges which the court recited against the defendant, he had also been found not guilty. Both the 1933 charge of larceny of an automobile, and the 1938 charge of entry to steal and larceny, resulted in his discharge after he was adjudged not guilty. We are not at liberty to assume that items given such emphasis by the sentencing court did not influence the sentence which the prisoner is now serving.

We believe that on the record before us, it is evident that this uncounseled defendant was either overreached by the prosecution's submission of misinformation to the court or was prejudiced by the court's own misreading of the record. Counsel, had any been present, would have been under a duty to prevent the court from proceeding on such false assumptions and perhaps under a duty to seek remedy elsewhere if they persisted. Consequently, on this record we conclude that, while disadvantaged by lack of counsel, this prisoner was sentenced on the basis of assumptions concerning his criminal record which were materially untrue. Such a result, whether caused by carelessness or design, is inconsistent with due process of law, and such a conviction cannot stand.

* * * It is not the duration or severity of this sentence that renders it constitutionally invalid; it is the careless or designed pronouncement of sentence on a foundation so extensively and materially false, which the prisoner had no opportunity to correct by the services which counsel would provide, that renders the proceedings lacking in due process.

Nor do we mean that mere error in resolving a question of fact on a plea of guilty by an uncounseled defendant in a non-capital case would necessarily indicate a want of due process of law. Fair prosecutors and conscientious judges sometimes are misinformed or draw inferences from conflicting evidence with which we would not agree. But even an erroneous judgment, based on a scrupulous and diligent search for truth, may be due process of law.

In this case, counsel might not have changed the sentence, but he could have taken steps to see that the conviction and sentence were not predicated on misinformation or misreading of court records, a requirement of fair play which absence of counsel withheld from this prisoner.

Reversed.

THE CHIEF JUSTICE, MR. JUSTICE REED, and MR. JUSTICE BURTON dissent.

Questions and Points for Discussion

1. United States v. Tucker, 404 U.S. 443, 92 S.Ct. 589 (1972) is another Supreme Court case in which the Court concluded that the defendant's sentence was invalid because of misinformation upon which the sentencing judge relied at the time of sentencing. The defendant in that case had been found guilty of an armed bank robbery. Having been apprised that the defendant had three prior felony convictions, the judge imposed the maximum sentence for the armed robbery—25 years. Only later was it determined that two of the defendant's three prior convictions had been obtained unconstitutionally, in violation of the defendant's sixth amendment right to counsel.

While acknowledging the breadth of the information that can be considered by a sentencing court when imposing sentence, the Supreme Court held that the defendant's sentence in this case was invalid because it was based "at least in part upon misinformation of constitutional magnitude." Id. at 447, 92 S.Ct. at 591–92. The defendant would therefore have to be resentenced, since his original sentence "might have been different" had the sentencing judge been aware that the defendant had already spent ten years of his life unconstitutionally locked up in prison. Id. at 448, 92 S.Ct. at 592.

2. Just because evidence was obtained unconstitutionally and is inadmissible at trial does not always mean that the evidence is also inadmissible during a sentencing hearing. For example, assume that during an unconstitutional warrantless search of the home of a defendant suspected of murder, the police find a diary revealing the deliberateness with which the defendant had planned the murder. Although the diary will be inadmissible at trial because of the violation of the defendant's fourth amendment rights, if he is nonetheless convicted, many lower courts have held that such evidence obtained in violation of the defendant's fourth amendment rights can be considered by the sentencing judge. See e.g., United States v. Graves, 785 F.2d 870 (10th Cir.1986); United States v. Butler, 680 F.2d 1055 (5th Cir.1982). According to the Supreme Court, to resolve questions such as this one, concerning the scope of the fourth amendment exclusionary rule, the benefits of excluding the evidence during this stage of the criminal prosecution must be weighed against the costs

of such exclusion. United States v. Calandra, 414 U.S. 338, 349, 94 S.Ct. 613, 620 (1974). How would you assess the costs and benefits of applying the fourth amendment exclusionary rule during sentencing hearings?

3. The Federal Rules of Evidence are inapplicable in sentencing hearings. Fed.R.Evid. 1101(d)(3). Thus, although hearsay statements are generally inadmissible in federal trials, the rules do not preclude the consideration by sentencing judges of hearsay statements. An example of such a statement would be a presentence investigation report's reference to the remark of a witness that the defendant had committed a certain crime in the past for which he was neither arrested nor convicted.

The courts have concurred that consideration of hearsay statements at sentencing does not necessarily violate a defendant's due process rights. See e.g., United States v. Sciarrino, 884 F.2d 95, 97 (3d Cir.1989). At the same time, however, the courts have agreed that the sentencing judge must make some determination as to the reliability of this information, at least when the defendant claims that the information provided to the court is false. United States v. Fatico, 579 F.2d 707, 713 (2d Cir.1978). The courts have differed in their views of on whom rests the burden of proving the truth or falsity of hearsay or other types of information presented to the sentencer and as to what that burden is. Compare, e.g., United States v. Guerra, 888 F.2d 247, 251 (2d Cir.1989) (preponderance of the evidence standard must be met by the government); United States v. Fernandez–Vidana, 857 F.2d 673, 675 (9th Cir.1988) (hearsay can be considered unless " 'the factual basis for believing (it is) almost nil' "); and United States v. Rone, 743 F.2d 1169, 1171 (7th Cir.1984) (defendant must prove both that information was false and that it was relied on by the sentencing judge).

4. False information presented to the sentencing judge or the sentencing judge's misinterpretation of the facts is not enough to invalidate the sentence imposed. The mistake must first be a material one. See, e.g., United States v. Addonizio, 442 U.S. 178, 99 S.Ct. 2235 (1979) (sentencing judge's expectations about the defendant's parole release date were not enforceable against the parole board and therefore the judge's erroneous prediction as to when the defendant would be released on parole did not involve "misinformation of constitutional magnitude" that would entitle the defendant to collateral relief). See also United States v. Plain, 856 F.2d 913 (7th Cir.1988) (sentences were not "illegal" within the meaning of Rule 35 of the Federal Rules of Criminal Procedure just because the sentencing judge was misinformed by presentence investigation reports about the defendants' release dates under the parole guidelines). In addition, the sentencing judge must have relied on the material misinformation for the defendant to be entitled to resentencing. See, e.g., United States v. Talavera, 668 F.2d 625, 631 (1st Cir.1982). See also Bourgeois v. Whitley, 784 F.2d 718, 721–22 (5th Cir.1986) (although court on remand cannot consider unconstitutional convictions when sentencing the defendant, the court can consider the defendant's conduct which underlay those convictions).

5. Rule 32(c)(3)(D) of the Federal Rules of Criminal Procedure provides a judge with two options when faced with a defendant's challenge to the accuracy of information included in a presentence investigation report.

The judge must either resolve the factual dispute or confirm in writing that the disputed information was not considered when sentencing the defendant. See supra, page 85, note 4.

* * *

In the case which follows, the Supreme Court described another constitutional limitation on the information that can be considered at the time of sentencing, at least in a capital case.

BOOTH v. MARYLAND

Supreme Court of the United States, 1987.
482 U.S. 496, 107 S.Ct. 2529, 96 L.Ed.2d 440.

JUSTICE POWELL delivered the opinion of the Court.

The question presented is whether the Constitution prohibits a jury from considering a "victim impact statement" during the sentencing phase of a capital murder trial.

I

In 1983, Irvin Bronstein, 78, and his wife Rose, 75, were robbed and murdered in their West Baltimore home. The murderers, John Booth and Willie Reid, entered the victims' home for the apparent purpose of stealing money to buy heroin. Booth, a neighbor of the Bronsteins, knew that the elderly couple could identify him. The victims were bound and gagged, and then stabbed repeatedly in the chest with a kitchen knife. The bodies were discovered two days later by the Bronsteins' son.

A jury found Booth guilty of two counts of first-degree murder, two counts of robbery, and conspiracy to commit robbery. The prosecution requested the death penalty, and Booth elected to have his sentence determined by the jury instead of the judge. Before the sentencing phase began, the State Division of Parole and Probation (DPP) compiled a presentence report that described Booth's background, education and employment history, and criminal record. Under a Maryland statute, the presentence report in all felony cases also must include a victim impact statement (VIS), describing the effect of the crime on the victim and his family. Specifically, the report shall:

"(i) Identify the victim of the offense;

"(ii) Itemize any economic loss suffered by the victim as a result of the offense;

"(iii) Identify any physical injury suffered by the victim as a result of the offense along with its seriousness and permanence;

"(iv) Describe any change in the victim's personal welfare or familial relationships as a result of the offense;

"(v) Identify any request for psychological services initiated by the victim or the victim's family as a result of the offense; and "(vi) Contain any other information related to the impact of the offense upon the victim or the victim's family that the trial court requires."

Although the VIS is compiled by the DPP, the information is supplied by the victim or the victim's family. The VIS may be read to the jury during the sentencing phase, or the family members may be called to testify as to the information.

The VIS in Booth's case was based on interviews with the Bronsteins' son, daughter, son-in-law, and granddaughter. Many of their comments emphasized the victims' outstanding personal qualities, and noted how deeply the Bronsteins would be missed.[3] Other parts of the VIS described the emotional and personal problems the family members have faced as a result of the crimes. The son, for example, said that he suffers from lack of sleep and depression, and is "fearful for the first time in his life." He said that in his opinion, his parents were "butchered like animals." The daughter said she also suffers from lack of sleep, and that since the murders she has become withdrawn and distrustful. She stated that she can no longer watch violent movies or look at kitchen knives without being reminded of the murders. The daughter concluded that she could not forgive the murderer, and that such a person could "[n]ever be rehabilitated." Finally, the granddaughter described how the deaths had ruined the wedding of another close family member, that took place a few days after the bodies were discovered. Both the ceremony and the reception were sad affairs, and instead of leaving for her honeymoon, the bride attended the victims' funeral. The VIS also noted that the granddaughter had received counseling for several months after the incident, but eventually had stopped because she concluded that "no one could help her."

The DPP official who conducted the interviews concluded the VIS by writing:

"It became increasingly apparent to the writer as she talked to the family members that the murder of Mr. and Mrs. Bronstein is still such a shocking, painful, and devastating memory to them that it permeates every aspect of their daily lives. It is doubtful that they will ever be able to fully recover from this tragedy and not be haunted by the memory of the brutal manner in which their loved ones were murdered and taken from them."

3. The VIS stated:

"[T]he victims' son reports that his parents had been married for fifty-three years and enjoyed a very close relationship, spending each day together. He states that his father had worked hard all his life and had been retired for eight years. He describes his mother as a woman who was young at heart and never seemed like an old lady. She taught herself to play bridge when she was in her seventies. The victims' son relates

that his parents were amazing people who attended the senior citizens' center and made many devout friends."

"As described by their family members, the Bronsteins were loving parents and grandparents whose family was most important to them. Their funeral was the largest in the history of the Levinson Funeral Home and the family received over one thousand sympathy cards, some from total strangers."

Defense counsel moved to suppress the VIS on the ground that this information was both irrelevant and unduly inflammatory, and that therefore its use in a capital case violated the Eighth Amendment of the Federal Constitution.[5] The Maryland trial court denied the motion, ruling that the jury was entitled to consider "any and all evidence which would bear on the [sentencing decision]." Booth's lawyer then requested that the prosecutor simply read the VIS to the jury rather than call the family members to testify before the jury. Defense counsel was concerned that the use of live witnesses would increase the inflammatory effect of the information. The prosecutor agreed to this arrangement.

The jury sentenced Booth to death for the murder of Mr. Bronstein and to life imprisonment for the murder of Mrs. Bronstein. On automatic appeal, the Maryland Court of Appeals affirmed the conviction and the sentences. * * *

We granted certiorari to decide whether the Eighth Amendment prohibits a capital sentencing jury from considering victim impact evidence. We conclude that it does, and now reverse.

II

It is well settled that a jury's discretion to impose the death sentence must be "suitably directed and limited so as to minimize the risk of wholly arbitrary and capricious action." *Gregg v. Georgia,* 428 U.S. 153, 189 (1976) (joint opinion of Stewart, Powell, and Stevens, JJ.). Although this Court normally will defer to a state legislature's determination of what factors are relevant to the sentencing decision, the Constitution places some limits on this discretion. Specifically, we have said that a jury must make an "*individualized* determination" of whether the defendant in question should be executed, based on "the character of the individual and the circumstances of the crime." *Zant v. Stephens,* 462 U.S. 862, 879 (1983) (emphasis in original). And while this Court has never said that the defendant's record, characteristics, and the circumstances of the crime are the *only* permissible sentencing considerations, a state statute that requires consideration of other factors must be scrutinized to ensure that the evidence has some bearing on the defendant's "personal responsibility and moral guilt." To do otherwise would create the risk that a death sentence will be based on considerations that are "constitutionally impermissible or totally irrelevant to the sentencing process."

The VIS in this case provided the jury with two types of information. First, it described the personal characteristics of the victims and the emotional impact of the crimes on the family. Second, it set forth the family members' opinions and characterizations of the crimes and the defendant. For the reasons stated below, we find that this informa-

---

5. The Eighth Amendment provides: "Excessive bail shall not be required, nor excessive fines imposed, nor cruel and unusual punishments inflicted." The prohibitions of the Eighth Amendment apply to the States through the Due Process Clause of the Fourteenth Amendment.

tion is irrelevant to a capital sentencing decision, and that its admission creates a constitutionally unacceptable risk that the jury may impose the death penalty in an arbitrary and capricious manner.

A

The greater part of the VIS is devoted to a description of the emotional trauma suffered by the family and the personal characteristics of the victims. The State claims that this evidence should be considered a "circumstance" of the crime because it reveals the full extent of the harm caused by Booth's actions. In the State's view, there is a direct, foreseeable nexus between the murders and the harm to the family, and thus it is not "arbitrary" for the jury to consider these consequences in deciding whether to impose the death penalty.

* * *

While the full range of foreseeable consequences of a defendant's actions may be relevant in other criminal and civil contexts, we cannot agree that it is relevant in the unique circumstance of a capital sentencing hearing. In such a case, it is the function of the sentencing jury to "express the conscience of the community on the ultimate question of life or death." When carrying out this task the jury is required to focus on the defendant as a "uniquely individual human bein[g]." *Woodson v. North Carolina,* 428 U.S. 280, 304 (1976) (plurality opinion of Stewart, Powell, and Stevens, JJ.). The focus of a VIS, however, is not on the defendant, but on the character and reputation of the victim and the effect on his family. These factors may be wholly unrelated to the blameworthiness of a particular defendant. As our cases have shown, the defendant often will not know the victim, and therefore will have no knowledge about the existence or characteristics of the victim's family. Moreover, defendants rarely select their victims based on whether the murder will have an effect on anyone other than the person murdered. Allowing the jury to rely on a VIS therefore could result in imposing the death sentence because of factors about which the defendant was unaware, and that were irrelevant to the decision to kill. This evidence thus could divert the jury's attention away from the defendant's background and record, and the circumstances of the crime.

It is true that in certain cases some of the information contained in a VIS will have been known to the defendant before he committed the offense. As we have recognized, a defendant's degree of knowledge of the probable consequences of his actions may increase his moral culpability in a constitutionally significant manner. See *Tison v. Arizona,* 481 U.S. 137, 157–158 (1987). We nevertheless find that because of the nature of the information contained in a VIS, it creates an impermissible risk that the capital sentencing decision will be made in an arbitrary manner.

As evidenced by the full text of the VIS in this case, the family members were articulate and persuasive in expressing their grief and the extent of their loss. But in some cases the victim will not leave behind a family, or the family members may be less articulate in describing their feelings even though their sense of loss is equally severe. The fact that the imposition of the death sentence may turn on such distinctions illustrates the danger of allowing juries to consider this information. Certainly the degree to which a family is willing and able to express its grief is irrelevant to the decision whether a defendant, who may merit the death penalty, should live or die.

Nor is there any justification for permitting such a decision to turn on the perception that the victim was a sterling member of the community rather than someone of questionable character.[8] This type of information does not provide a "principled way to distinguish [cases] in which the death penalty was imposed, from the many cases in which it was not."

We also note that it would be difficult—if not impossible—to provide a fair opportunity to rebut such evidence without shifting the focus of the sentencing hearing away from the defendant. A threshold problem is that victim impact information is not easily susceptible to rebuttal. Presumably the defendant would have the right to cross-examine the declarants, but he rarely would be able to show that the family members have exaggerated the degree of sleeplessness, depression, or emotional trauma suffered. Moreover, if the state is permitted to introduce evidence of the victim's personal qualities, it cannot be doubted that the defendant also must be given the chance to rebut this evidence. Putting aside the strategic risks of attacking the victim's character before the jury, in appropriate cases the defendant presumably would be permitted to put on evidence that the victim was of dubious moral character, was unpopular, or was ostracized from his family. The prospect of a "mini-trial" on the victim's character is more than simply unappealing; it could well distract the sentencing jury from its constitutionally required task—determining whether the death penalty is appropriate in light of the background and record of the accused and the particular circumstances of the crime. We thus reject the contention that the presence or absence of emotional distress of the victim's family, or the victim's personal characteristics, are proper sentencing considerations in a capital case.[10]

8. We are troubled by the implication that defendants whose victims were assets to their community are more deserving of punishment than those whose victims are perceived to be less worthy. Of course, our system of justice does not tolerate such distinctions.

10. Our disapproval of victim impact statements at the sentencing phase of a capital case does not mean, however, that this type of information will never be relevant in any context. Similar types of information may well be admissible because they relate directly to the circumstances of the crime. Facts about the victim and family also may be relevant in a noncapital criminal trial. Moreover, there may be times that the victim's personal characteristics are relevant to rebut an argument offered by the defendant. See, *e.g.,* Fed. Rule Evid. 404(a)(2) (prosecution may show peaceable nature of victim to rebut charge that victim was aggressor). The trial judge, of course, continues to have the primary responsibility for deciding when this information is sufficiently relevant to some legitimate consideration to be admissible, and when its probative value outweighs any prejudicial effect. Cf. Fed.Rule Evid. 403.

B

The second type of information presented to the jury in the VIS was the family members' opinions and characterizations of the crimes. The Bronsteins' son, for example, stated that his parents were "butchered like animals," and that he "doesn't think anyone should be able to do something like that and get away with it." The VIS also noted that the Bronstein[s'] daughter:

"could never forgive anyone for killing [her parents] that way. She can't believe that anybody could do that to someone. The victims' daughter states that animals wouldn't do this. [The perpetrators] didn't have to kill because there was no one to stop them from looting . . . . The murders show the viciousness of the killers' anger. She doesn't feel that the people who did this could ever be rehabilitated and she doesn't want them to be able to do this again or put another family through this."

One can understand the grief and anger of the family caused by the brutal murders in this case, and there is no doubt that jurors generally are aware of these feelings. But the formal presentation of this information by the State can serve no other purpose than to inflame the jury and divert it from deciding the case on the relevant evidence concerning the crime and the defendant. As we have noted, any decision to impose the death sentence must "be, and appear to be, based on reason rather than caprice or emotion." The admission of these emotionally charged opinions as to what conclusions the jury should draw from the evidence clearly is inconsistent with the reasoned decisionmaking we require in capital cases.

III

We conclude that the introduction of a VIS at the sentencing phase of a capital murder trial violates the Eighth Amendment, and therefore the Maryland statute is invalid to the extent it requires consideration of this information. The decision of the Maryland Court of Appeals is vacated to the extent that it affirmed the capital sentence. The case is remanded for further proceedings not inconsistent with this opinion.

* * *

JUSTICE WHITE, with whom THE CHIEF JUSTICE, JUSTICE O'CONNOR, and JUSTICE SCALIA join, dissenting.

"[T]he decision that capital punishment may be the appropriate sanction in extreme cases is an expression of the community's belief that certain crimes are themselves so grievous an affront to humanity that the only adequate response may be the penalty of death." The affront to humanity of a brutal murder such as petitioner committed is not limited to its impact on the victim or victims; a victim's community is also injured, and in particular the victim's family suffers shock and grief of a kind difficult even to imagine for those who have not shared a similar loss. Maryland's legislature has decided that the jury should have the testimony of the victim's family in order to assist it in weighing the degree of harm that the defendant has caused and the corresponding degree of punishment that should be inflicted. This judgment is entitled to particular deference; determinations of appropriate sentencing considerations are " 'peculiarly questions of legislative policy,' " and the Court should recognize that " '[i]n a democratic society legislatures, not courts, are constituted to respond to the will and consequently the moral values of the people.' " I cannot agree that there was anything "cruel or unusual" or otherwise unconstitutional about the legislature's decision to use victim impact statements in capital sentencing hearings.

The Court's judgment is based on the premises that the harm that a murderer causes a victim's family does not in general reflect on his blameworthiness, and that only evidence going to blameworthiness is relevant to the capital sentencing decision. Many if not most jurors, however, will look less favorably on a capital defendant when they appreciate the full extent of the harm he caused, including the harm to the victim's family. There is nothing aberrant in a juror's inclination to hold a murderer accountable not only for his internal disposition in committing the crime but also for the full extent of the harm he caused; many if not most persons would also agree, for example, that someone who drove his car recklessly through a stoplight and unintentionally killed a pedestrian merits significantly more punishment than someone who drove his car recklessly through the same stoplight at a time when no pedestrian was there to be hit. I am confident that the Court would not overturn a sentence for reckless homicide by automobile merely because the punishment exceeded the maximum sentence for reckless driving; and I would hope that the Court would not overturn the sentence in such a case if a judge mentioned, as relevant to his sentencing decision, the fact that the victim was a mother or father. But if punishment can be enhanced in noncapital cases on the basis of the harm caused, irrespective of the offender's specific intention to cause such harm, I fail to see why the same approach is unconstitutional in death cases. If anything, I would think that victim impact statements are particularly appropriate evidence in capital sentencing hearings: the State has a legitimate interest in counteracting the mitigating evidence which the defendant is entitled to put in, reminding the sentencer that just as the murderer should be considered as an individual, so too the victim is an individual whose death represents a unique loss to society and in particular to his family.

The Court is "troubled by the implication that defendants whose victims were assets to their community are more deserving of punishment than those whose victims are perceived to be less worthy," and declares that "our system of justice does not tolerate such distinctions." It is no doubt true that the State may not encourage the sentencer to rely on a factor such as the victim's race in determining whether the death penalty is appropriate. But I fail to see why the State cannot, if it chooses, include as a sentencing consideration the particularized harm that an individual's murder causes to the rest of society [2] and in particular to his family. To the extent that the Court is concerned that sentencing juries might be moved by victim impact statements to rely on impermissible factors such as the race of the victim, there is no showing that the statements in this case encouraged this, nor should we lightly presume such misconduct on the jury's part.

The Court's reliance on the alleged arbitrariness that can result from the differing ability of victims' families to articulate their sense of loss is a makeweight consideration: No two prosecutors have exactly the same ability to present their arguments to the jury; no two witnesses have exactly the same ability to communicate the facts; but there is no requirement in capital cases that the evidence and argument be reduced to the lowest common denominator.

The supposed problems arising from a defendant's rebuttal of victim impact statements are speculative and unconnected to the facts of this case. No doubt a capital defendant must be allowed to introduce relevant evidence in rebuttal to a victim impact statement, but Maryland has in no wise limited the right of defendants in this regard. Petitioner introduced no such rebuttal evidence, probably because he considered, wisely, that it was not in his best interest to do so. At bottom, the Court's view seems to be that it is somehow unfair to confront a defendant with an account of the loss his deliberate act has caused the victim's family and society. I do not share that view, but even if I did I would be unwilling to impose it on States that see matters differently.

The Court's concern that the grief and anger of a victim's family will "inflame the jury" is based in large part on its view that the loss which such survivors suffer is irrelevant to the issue of punishment—a view with which I have already expressed my disagreement. To the extent that the Court determines that in this case it was inappropriate to allow the victims' family to express their opinions on, for example, whether petitioner could be rehabilitated, that is obviously not an inherent fault in all victim impact statements and no reason to declare the practice of admitting such statements at capital sentencing hearings *per se* unconstitutional. I respectfully dissent.

JUSTICE SCALIA, with whom THE CHIEF JUSTICE, JUSTICE WHITE, and JUSTICE O'CONNOR join, dissenting.

*   *   *

Recent years have seen an outpouring of popular concern for what has come to be known as "victims' rights"—a phrase that describes what its proponents feel is the failure of courts of justice to take into account in their sentencing decisions not only the factors mitigating the

---

2. I doubt that the Court means to suggest that there is any constitutional impediment, for example, to authorizing the death sentence for the assassination of the President or Vice President, see 18 U.S.C. §§ 1751, 1111, a Congressman, Cabinet official, Supreme Court Justice, or the head of an executive department, 18 U.S.C. § 351, or the murder of a policeman on active duty, see Md.Ann.Code, Art. 27, § 413(d)(1) (1982).

defendant's moral guilt, but also the amount of harm he has caused to innocent members of society. Many citizens have found one-sided and hence unjust the criminal trial in which a parade of witnesses comes forth to testify to the pressures beyond normal human experience that drove the defendant to commit his crime, with no one to lay before the sentencing authority the full reality of human suffering the defendant has produced—which (and *not* moral guilt alone) is one of the reasons society deems his act worthy of the prescribed penalty. Perhaps these sentiments do not sufficiently temper justice with mercy, but that is a question to be decided through the democratic processes of a free people, and not by the decrees of this Court. There is nothing in the Constitution that dictates the answer, no more in the field of capital punishment than elsewhere.

To require, as we have, that all mitigating factors which render capital punishment a harsh penalty in the particular case be placed before the sentencing authority, while simultaneously requiring, as we do today, that evidence of much of the human suffering the defendant has inflicted be suppressed, is in effect to prescribe a debate on the appropriateness of the capital penalty with one side muted. If that penalty is constitutional, as we have repeatedly said it is, it seems to me not remotely unconstitutional to permit both the pros and cons in the particular case to be heard.

Questions and Points for Discussion

1. In South Carolina v. Gathers, 109 S.Ct. 2207 (1989), the Supreme Court reaffirmed its decision in *Booth*. During the closing arguments to the jury in the capital sentencing hearing in *Gathers,* the prosecutor had mentioned the Bible and the voter's registration card that the victim was carrying when the defendant murdered him. The prosecutor then argued that these items revealed that the victim, a mentally ill itinerant, cared about God and the United States. The Supreme Court held that this line of argument was unconstitutional in light of *Booth*. According to the Court, the prosecutor's depiction of what the victim was like went well beyond a simple description of "the circumstances of the crime," which would be permissible under *Booth.*

When would the impact of a crime on a victim relate sufficiently to "the circumstances of the crime" that consideration of that impact would be constitutionally appropriate? See United States v. Salyer, 893 F.2d 113 (6th Cir.1989) (sentencing judge could increase the defendant's sentence under the sentencing guidelines because of "victim vulnerability" where the defendant had burned a cross in the yard of a black, elderly couple).

2. Is the introduction of a victim impact statement in a noncapital case constitutional? For example, at a sentencing hearing, could a rape victim testify about the emotional trauma which she is still experiencing because of the rape? If the woman was raped in front of her small child, could a psychologist testify that the child may have emotional problems for the rest of his life because of what he observed? Could a victim who was severely disabled when assaulted by the defendant testify about his life-

time, but now no longer realizable goal of becoming an airplane pilot or a professional athlete? Should the types of victim impact statements recounted above be treated differently than the victim impact statements deemed unconstitutional in *Booth* and *Gathers?* Why or why not?

3. In recent years, crime victims have mobilized to ensure that they are not overlooked by the criminal justice system. As a result, a number of jurisdictions have enacted legislation authorizing or requiring consideration of victim impact statements during the sentencing stage of criminal prosecutions. See, e.g., Mich.Comp.Laws § 771.14(b), (c); Va.Code § 19.2–299.1. Set forth below is one approach to the subject of victim impact statements, which is outlined in Office for Victims of Crime, U.S. Dep't of Justice, Victims of Crime: Proposed Model Legislation II–1–3 (1986) and was drafted as part of a joint project involving the National Association of Attorneys General and the Victim Witness Project of the Criminal Justice Section of the American Bar Association:

SECTION 101. FINDINGS AND PURPOSE

A. The legislature and the people of this State find and declare that:

1. Protection of the public, restitution to the crime victim and the crime victim's family, and just punishment for the harm inflicted are primary objectives of the sentencing process;

2. The financial, emotional, and physical effects of a criminal act on the victim and the victim's family are among the essential factors to be considered in the sentencing of the person responsible for the crime;

3. In order to impose a just sentence, the court must obtain and consider information about the adverse impact of the crime upon the victim and the victim's family as well as information from and about the defendant; and

4. The victim of the crime or a relative of the victim is usually in the best position to provide information to the court about the direct impact of the crime on the victim and the victim's family.

B. Therefore, the legislature and the people of this State declare that the purpose of this Act is to require the sentencing court to solicit and consider a victim impact statement prior to sentencing a convicted offender who has caused physical, emotional, or financial harm to a victim as defined herein.

SECTION 102. SHORT TITLE

This Act shall be known and may be cited as "The Victim Impact Statement Act."

SECTION 103. DEFINITIONS

As used in this Act, the following phrases have the meanings indicated, unless the context clearly indicates otherwise.

(K. & B.) Law of Corrections, 4th Ed. ACB—6

A. *Victim:*

An individual who suffers direct or threatened physical, emotional, or financial harm as the result of the commission of a crime or an immediate family member of a minor victim or a homicide victim.

B. *Victim Impact Statement:*

A statement providing information about the financial, emotional, and physical effects of the crime on the victim and the victim's family, and specific information about the victim, the circumstances surrounding the crime, and the manner in which it was perpetrated.

C. *Victim Representative:*

A spouse, parent, child, sibling, or other relative of a deceased or incapacitated victim or of a victim who is under _____ years of age, or a person who has had a close personal relationship with the victim and is designated by the court to be a victim representative.

SECTION 104. NOTICE TO VICTIM OR VICTIM REPRESENTATIVE

A. If a defendant is convicted of a felony involving one or more identifiable victims who suffered death or physical, emotional, or financial injury, the probation department (prosecuting attorney) shall notify the victim or the victim representative in writing of the date, time, and place of the sentencing hearing and advise him or her of the opportunity to present a victim impact statement.

B. A copy of any relevant rules and regulations pertaining to the victim impact statement and the hearing shall accompany the notice.

C. The notice and the copy of any relevant rules and regulations shall be sent to the last known address of the victim or the victim representative at least _____ days prior to the sentencing hearing.

SECTION 105. SUBMISSION OF VICTIM IMPACT STATEMENT TO THE COURT

A. Prior to imposition of sentence in a felony case, the probation department shall prepare a written victim impact statement and append it to the presentence report on the defendant. The statement shall include applicable information obtained during consultation with the victim or the victim representative. If the victim or victim representative cannot be located or declines to cooperate in the preparation of the statement, the probation department shall include a notation to that effect in the statement. If there are multiple victims and preparation of individual victim impact statements is not feasible, the probation department may submit one or more representative statements.

B. Prior to imposition of sentence in both felony and misdemeanor cases, the victim or victim representative may also submit a victim impact statement in one or both of the following ways:

1. By presenting an oral victim impact statement at the sentencing hearing. However, where there are multiple victims, the court may limit the number of oral victim impact statements.

2. By submitting a written statement to the probation department, which shall append such statement to the presentence report of the defendant.

SECTION 106. ACCESS TO WRITTEN VICTIM IMPACT STATEMENTS

The court shall make available copies of the statement to the defendant, defendant's counsel, and the prosecuting attorney. These parties shall return all copies of the statement to the court immediately following the imposition of sentence upon the defendant.

SECTION 107. CONSIDERATION OF THE VICTIM IMPACT STATEMENT

Any victim impact statement submitted to the court under section 105 shall be among the factors considered by the court in determining the sentence to be imposed upon the defendant.

SECTION 108. LIMITATION

This statute shall not be construed to require a victim or victim representative to submit a victim impact statement or to cooperate in the preparation of a victim impact statement.

Section 105(B) of the proposed model legislation, which leaves to the victim the decision whether or not to make an oral statement at the sentencing hearing, can be contrasted with Guideline 11 of the ABA Guidelines for the Fair Treatment of Crime Victims and Witnesses (1983). Under this guideline, the court decides whether the victim or the victim's representative will be permitted to make an oral statement at the time of sentencing, balancing "the conflicting considerations, on the one hand, of citizen participation, public confidence in law enforcement, and the victim's understandable interest; and on the other, the potentially inflammatory impact in some matters of the victim's courtroom statement and appearance." Which do you believe is the preferable approach?

Chapter 4

NONINCARCERATIVE SANCTIONS

A. MULTI-LEVEL SENTENCING STRUCTURES

In the past, the sentencing options available to judges have been limited. Generally, judges have either placed criminal offenders on probation, with very minimal supervision, or sentenced them to jail or prison. When convicted criminals have violated the conditions of their probation, judges have often felt that they had no other choice but to send the malefactors to prison or jail.

This basically two-tiered sentencing system has proven to be both ineffectual and costly, since for many criminal offenders, neither "straight probation" nor incarceration is the appropriate penalty. If simply placed on probation, many offenders will not receive the supervision or treatment that might lead them to abandon a life of crime. As a result, the public's interest in combatting crime will be thwarted and perhaps the safety of the public jeopardized. On the other hand, in many instances, incarcerating an offender may not be needed to serve the government's penological goals and in fact may undermine those goals. If incarcerated, an offender may lose his or her job, and family ties may be broken, diminishing the prospects of rehabilitation. Exposure to criminogenic influences during incarceration may further reduce the chances that the offender will in the future refrain from criminal activity. And incarceration is extremely costly, straining budgets at the local, state, and federal level.

Government decisionmakers have begun to realize that a range of sentencing options needs to be developed to respond to the wide range of criminal behavior. Set forth below is a description of one proposal for a multi-tiered sentencing structure.

PIERRE S. du PONT IV, EXPANDING SENTENCING OPTIONS: A GOVERNOR'S PERSPECTIVE *

National Institute of Justice (1985). Reprinted with the permission of the National Institute of Justice.

When I became governor in 1977, Delaware was committing about 3 percent of its State budget to corrections. * * *

This year corrections will account for more than 7 percent of the total State budget, which means that there is still more pressure on the other vital services the State must provide. Indeed, in real dollar terms, our State's corrections budget has grown over 300 percent in just 7 years. This makes it by far the most inflated budget in State government since I took office.

* * *

* * * Despite its great cost, and the promise of more increases to come, the present system might be largely acceptable if it were working properly. But it isn't. We traditionally rely on incarceration as the primary method of punishing criminals, but—as numerous studies have demonstrated—there is no evidence that higher incarceration rates have any impact on the crime rate. For one thing, prison overcrowding limits whatever chances exist for success in rehabilitative programs.

Despite the evidence that change is imperative, we seem unable to break out of our present pattern of dealing with criminals. It is as if our corrections system is a prisoner, too.

* * *

* * * In Delaware, we are beginning to consider an alternative program developed by the Delaware Sentencing Reform Commission. That alternative program stresses accountability—accountability of the offender to the victim and the State, and accountability of the corrections system to the public and other criminal justice agencies. The accountability concept could create an ordered yet flexible system of sentencing and corrections. This system would be based on the belief that an offender should be sentenced to the least restrictive (and least costly) sanction available, consistent with public safety. That is a standard, by the way, endorsed by the American Bar Association some years ago.

A system built on accountability would structure the movement of offenders into and out of the corrections system, making it fairer and more cost-efficient. It would provide incentives for offenders to work at rehabilitation, since this would permit them to move into less restrictive (and less expensive) forms of control. At the same time accountability would strengthen the safeguards against violent offenders, who could be held in prison as long as necessary, or at least as long as their sentences ran.

* This document was originally published by the National Institute of Justice, U.S. Department of Justice, Washington, D.C. in 1985. Points of view or opinions expressed in the publication are those of the author and do not necessarily represent the official position or policies of the U.S. Department of Justice.

* * *

It is not overstatement to say that the proposals of the Delaware Sentencing Reform Commission would completely overhaul our sentencing and corrections laws. They would establish a range of sanctions available to a judge over 10 "levels of accountability." The table displays these 10 levels. [See page 121.]

Level I is unsupervised probation; Level X is maximum-security imprisonment. Moving from probation, there is a full range of alternatives, each more restrictive than the last, until the judge—and the criminal—reach a sentence of maximum-security incarceration.

Within each level there are degrees of control and accountability. These involve the offender's freedom of action within the community, the amount of supervision he or she is subject to, and what privileges are to be withheld or what other special conditions are to be attached to the sentence. In addition, the system provides for a range of possible financial sanctions to be imposed, including victims' compensation. Through such flexible controls, we would be able to control the offender's choice of job, choice of residence, ability to drive, ability to drink, ability to travel, and even ability to make telephone calls.

And to all of this we would add the probation fee concept. Successfully used in Georgia and Florida, the $10– to $50–per-month fee is charged to probationers to offset the cost of their supervision. Like the sanctions, the fee could be increased depending on the level of supervision required.

What is so attractive about this idea of accountability is that it applies not only to sentencing offenders, but also to controlling them following sentencing. And the same level of flexibility available to judges would be available to corrections officials responsible for probation.

Let's look at two hypothetical cases to see how the flexible sentencing and control system might work in practice.

First, let's take a drug offender with a minimal prior record but unstable employment record. He might be sentenced in Level II to supervised probation for 2 years, with restrictions on his place of residence, his association with certain individuals, and/or his right to visit high-drug/crime locations. And we might charge him a $10–per-month fee to offset some of the costs of keeping him straight.

If he observes these conditions for the first year of his probation, he could move down the sanctions scale into Level I. This level involves unsupervised probation and levies no fees, but holds out the possibility of certain restrictions on mobility and personal associations to minimize the chance of the offender slipping back into the drug scene and its associated crime. If our hypothetical drug offender violates the terms of his probation, he could be moved on to Level III, with heightened supervision, a curfew, and an increased monthly fee. Thus, the offender has a clear incentive to comply with his sentence. And, equally

Restrictions	Level I	Level II	Level III	Level IV	Level V	Level VI	Level VII	Level VIII	Level IX	Level X
Mobility in the community[1]	100 percent (unrestricted)	100 percent (unrestricted)	90 percent (restricted 0–10 hours/week)	80 percent (restricted 10–30 hours[/] week)	60 percent (restricted 30–40 hours/ week)	30 percent (restricted 50–100 hours/ week)	20 percent (restricted 100–140 hours/week)	10 percent (90 percent of time incarcerated)	Incarcerated	Incarcerated
Amount of supervision	None	Monthly written report	1–2 face-to-face/month; 1–2 weekly phone contact	3–6 face-to-face/month; weekly phone contact	2–6 face-to-face/week; weekly written reports	Daily phone contact; daily face-to-face; weekly written reports	Daily onsite supervision 8–16 hours/day	Daily onsite supervision 24 hours/day	Daily onsite supervision 24 hours/day	Daily onsite supervision 24 hours/day
Privileges withheld or special conditions[2]	100 percent (same as prior conviction)	100 percent (same as prior conviction)	1–2 privileges withheld	1–4 privileges withheld	1–7 privileges withheld	1–10 privileges withheld	1–12 privileges withheld	5–15 privileges withheld	15–19 privileges withheld	20 or more privileges withheld
Financial obligations[3]	Fine, court costs may be applied (0– to 2-day fine)	Fine, court costs, restitution; probation (supervisory fee may be applied; 1– to 3-day fine)	Same (increase probation fee by $5–10/ month; 2– to 4-day fine)	Same (increase probation fee by $5–$10/ month; 3– to 5-day fine)	Same (pay partial cost of food/lodging/ supervision fee; 4– to 7-day fine)	Same as Level V (8– to 10-day fine)	Same as Level V (11– to 12-day fine)	Fine, court costs, restitution payable upon release to Level VII or lower (12– to 15-day fine)	Same as Level VIII	Same as Level VIII
Examples (Note: many other scenarios could be constructed meeting the requirements at each level)	$50 fine, court costs; 6 months unsupervised probation	$50 fine, court costs, restitution; 6 months supervised probation; $10 monthly fee; written report	Fine, court costs, restitution; 1 year probation; weekend community service; no drinking	Weekend community service or mandatory treatment 5 hours/day; $30 month probation fee; no drinking; no out-of-State trips	Mandatory rehabilitation skills program 8 hours/day; restitution; $40/month probation fee; no drinking; curfew	Work release; pay portion of food/lodging; restitution; no kitchen privileges outside mealtimes; no drinking; no sex; weekends home	Residential treatment program; pay portion of program costs; limited privileges	Minimum-security prison	Medium-security prison	Maximum-security prison

1. Restrictions on freedom structure an offender's time, controlling his or her schedule, whereabouts, and activities for a designated period. To the extent that monitoring is not standard or consistent or to the extent that no sanctions accrue for failure on the part of the offender, the time is *not* structured. It could consist of residential, part-time residential, community service, or other specific methods for meeting the designated hours. The judge could order that the hours be met daily (e.g., 2 hours/day) or in one period (e.g., weekend in jail).

2. Privileges/conditions; choice of job, choice of residence, mobility within setting, driving, drinking (possible use of Antabuse), out-of-State trips, phone calls, curfew, mail, urinalysis, associates, areas off limits.

3. As a more equitable guide to appropriate fines, the amount would be measured in units of equivalent daily income, such as 1 day's salary = "1-day fine."

important, the sentencing judge has available options other than prison when probation is violated. Having and using these options will increase the certainty of appropriate punishment.

The second example is near the other end of the offense spectrum. This time our hypothetical offender is a twice-convicted armed robber. He was sentenced to 20 years, with the sentence to begin at Level X, or a maximum-security prison. After serving 2 years, and adhering to all the rules, the man might be moved to Level IX, a medium-security facility, where he might be able to take advantage of expanded rehabilitative programs.

Two years later, with continued good behavior, the offender again could move down the scale, this time to a minimum-security facility with still greater opportunities for rehabilitation. By the same token, if the prisoner's action at Level IX was disruptive and uncooperative, he could be returned to Level X.

Later, at a parole hearing, some appropriate program at Level VI might be selected instead of releasing the offender to a fuller freedom in the streets or leaving him in prison.

When the Sentencing Reform Commission applied the concept of accountability levels to the present offender population in Delaware, it found that only 21 percent of that population fell within Levels IX and X. But that medium- and maximum-security population accounted for 87 percent of the total corrections budget in Delaware. The Commission also found that roughly 70 percent of the corrections population fell between Levels I and III. Less than 10 percent filled the middle ground, and most of these were in some sort of alcohol or drug abuse program. Analysis showed that many in prison could be safely released if the programs were available to restrict their activities properly and closely supervise their rehabilitation. That analysis also showed that many in probation were undersupervised. Many of these men and women clearly needed to be moved into a middle level where they would be subject to stronger, more restrictive programs.

Let me sum up by shifting the focus from corrections mechanics to corrections philosophy. In this regard, I think it reasonable to consider two important goals of sentencing reform. The first is to reverse the long-established trend of growing prison populations and skyrocketing corrections budgets. The second is to redirect the system so that it guides offenders toward a useful life within the law.

Don't expect miracles from the reform proposals I am suggesting. Even with a sophisticated accountability system, we may not be able to reverse quickly the growth of corrections populations and spending. But we reasonably can expect to slow growth in spending and, ultimately, to stabilize costs. A hallmark of the accountability concept is cost avoidance—that is, developing and using less costly alternatives in our corrections programs. And, optimally, the effect of the accountability concept, as the offender moves through the system, will be to help reduce recidivism.

* * *

B. SENTENCING OPTIONS

In the article written by Governor du Pont, he discussed the need for the development of a wide range of sentencing options to ensure that criminal sanctions are cost-effective and meet the purposes for which they are imposed. Set forth below is a discussion of some of the sanctions that can be imposed in lieu of incarceration. The way in which some of these sanctions can be applied to corporations and businesses is discussed in the next chapter on pages 186–193. As you read these materials, consider what other nonincarcerative sanctions could be developed and what can be done to make the nonincarcerative sanctions which presently exist more effective.

1. PROBATION

In the United States, probation is the classic and most common penalty imposed on criminal offenders. In 1988, 2,356,483 adults in this country were on probation. Bureau of Justice Statistics, U.S. Dep't of Justice, Probation and Parole 1988 1 (1989). When added to the 407,977 individuals who were on parole, the total number of adults being supervised while on probation or parole constituted 1.52% of all of the adults in this country. Id.

Probation is a generic term used to describe a variety of ways of controlling, treating, and supervising criminal offenders during their probationary period. In terms of the constraints placed on probationers, probation may consist of little more than a requirement that the probationers refrain from criminal activity and talk with their probation officers, either in person or on the telephone, once a month or even more infrequently. Probation supervision may, however, be much more intensive, with the probationers required to meet with their probation officers several times a week or even every day and the probationers subject to a number of other conditions and controls. Examples of some of the types of restrictions that may be placed on probationers can be found in 18 U.S.C. § 3563, which is set forth below.

§ 3563. Conditions of probation

(a) **Mandatory conditions.**—The court shall provide, as an explicit condition of a sentence of probation—

(1) for a felony, a misdemeanor, or an infraction, that the defendant not commit another Federal, State, or local crime during the term of probation;

(2) for a felony, that the defendant also abide by at least one condition set forth in subsection (b)(2), (b)(3), or (b)(13), unless the court finds on the record that extraordinary circumstances exist that would make such a condition plainly unreasonable, in which event the court shall impose one or more of the other conditions set forth under subsection (b); and

(3) for a felony, a misdemeanor, or an infraction, that the defendant not possess illegal controlled substances.

If the court has imposed and ordered execution of a fine and placed the defendant on probation, payment of the fine or adherence to the court-established installment schedule shall be a condition of the probation.

(b) Discretionary conditions.—The court may provide, as further conditions of a sentence of probation, to the extent that such conditions are reasonably related to the factors set forth in section 3553(a)(1) and (a)(2) [a] and to the extent that such conditions involve only such deprivations of liberty or property as are reasonably necessary for the purposes indicated in section 3553(a)(2), that the defendant—

(1) support his dependents and meet other family responsibilities;

(2) pay a fine imposed pursuant to the provisions of subchapter C;

(3) make restitution to a victim of the offense pursuant to the provisions of sections 3663 and 3664 (but not subject to the limitations of 3663(a));

(4) give to the victims of the offense the notice ordered pursuant to the provisions of section 3555;[b]

(5) work conscientiously at suitable employment or pursue conscientiously a course of study or vocational training that will equip him for suitable employment;

(6) refrain, in the case of an individual, from engaging in a specified occupation, business, or profession bearing a reasonably direct relationship to the conduct constituting the offense, or engage in such a specified occupation, business, or profession only to a stated degree or under stated circumstances;

(7) refrain from frequenting specified kinds of places or from associating unnecessarily with specified persons;

[**a.** Section 3553(a)(1) and (a)(2) provides as follows:

(a) Factors to be considered in imposing a sentence.—The court shall impose a sentence sufficient, but not greater than necessary, to comply with the purposes set forth in paragraph (2) of this subsection. The court, in determining the particular sentence to be imposed, shall consider—

(1) the nature and circumstances of the offense and the history and characteristics of the defendant;

(2) the need for the sentence imposed—

(A) to reflect the seriousness of the offense, to promote respect for the law, and to provide just punishment for the offense;

(B) to afford adequate deterrence to criminal conduct;

(C) to protect the public from further crimes of the defendant; and

(D) to provide the defendant with needed educational or vocational training, medical care, or other correctional treatment in the most effective manner.]

[**b.** Section 3555 authorizes a court to require a defendant convicted of fraud or "other intentionally deceptive practices" to notify the victims of the crime of his or her conviction.]

(8) refrain from excessive use of alcohol, or any use of a narcotic drug or other controlled substance, as defined in section 102 of the Controlled Substances Act (21 U.S.C. 802), without a prescription by a licensed medical practitioner;

(9) refrain from possessing a firearm, destructive device, or other dangerous weapon;

(10) undergo available medical, psychiatric, or psychological treatment, including treatment for drug or alcohol dependency, as specified by the court, and remain in a specified institution if required for that purpose;

(11) remain in the custody of the Bureau of Prisons during nights, weekends, or other intervals of time, totaling no more than the lesser of one year or the term of imprisonment authorized for the offense, during the first year of the term of probation;

(12) reside at, or participate in the program of, a community corrections facility (including a facility maintained or under contract to the Bureau of Prisons) for all or part of the term of probation;

(13) work in community service as directed by the court;

(14) reside in a specified place or area, or refrain from residing in a specified place or area;

(15) remain within the jurisdiction of the court, unless granted permission to leave by the court or a probation officer;

(16) report to a probation officer as directed by the court or the probation officer;

(17) permit a probation officer to visit him at his home or elsewhere as specified by the court;

(18) answer inquiries by a probation officer and notify the probation officer promptly of any change in address or employment;

(19) notify the probation officer promptly if arrested or questioned by a law enforcement officer;

(20) remain at his place of residence during nonworking hours and, if the court finds it appropriate, that compliance with this condition be monitored by telephonic or electronic signaling devices, except that a condition under this paragraph may be imposed only as an alternative to incarceration; or

(21) satisfy such other conditions as the court may impose.

(c) **Modifications of conditions.**—The court may modify, reduce, or enlarge the conditions of a sentence of probation at any time prior to the expiration or termination of the term of probation, pursuant to the provisions of the Federal Rules of Criminal Procedure relating to the modification of probation and the provisions applicable to the initial setting of the conditions of probation.

(d) Written statement of conditions.—The court shall direct that the probation officer provide the defendant with a written statement that sets forth all the conditions to which the sentence is subject, and that is sufficiently clear and specific to serve as a guide for the defendant's conduct and for such supervision as is required.

As 18 U.S.C. § 3563 demonstrates, many of the sanctions which are discussed subsequently in this chapter, such as fines, restitution, community service, and home confinement, can be included as conditions of an offender's probation. A rather new probation condition which is beginning to take hold in some parts of this country is to require some probationers to spend each day at what are called day reporting centers (DRCs). While there, the probationers go to classes, receive vocational training, participate in counseling sessions, and get tested for signs of drug or alcohol use. For a discussion of a DRC program instituted in Massachusetts for offenders who have been sentenced to jail, see Crime and Justice Foundation, Evaluation of the Hampden County Day Reporting Center (1989). For a discussion of other programs involving what is called intensive probation supervision, see Bureau of Justice Assistance, U.S. Dep't of Justice, Intensive Supervision Probation and Parole (ISP) 17–20 (1988); J. Petersilia, Expanding Options for Criminal Sentencing 10–31 (1987). And for a discussion of constitutional limitations on the probation conditions that can be imposed, see Chapter 16, page 529, infra.

Probation can also be combined in a variety of different ways with incarcerative sanctions when a defendant is sentenced. When what is known as a "split sentence" is imposed on a defendant, for example, the defendant is sentenced to prison or jail for a particular period of time to be followed by a period of probation.

Gaining in popularity is another sanction known as "shock incarceration." In a shock incarceration program, the most typical kind of which is boot camp, a defendant is subjected to a short but intensive incarceration program. The program generally has military-type features—a highly structured regimen, strict discipline, physical exercise, hard labor, and drills and ceremonies. Should a defendant successfully complete the program, which usually lasts three to six months, the defendant will be resentenced to probation and avoid confinement in prison. For more information on shock incarceration programs, see U.S. Dep't of Justice, National Institute of Justice, Shock Incarceration: An Overview of Existing Programs (1989).

2. HOME CONFINEMENT

In the search for intermediate sanctions falling between the extremes of straight probation and incarceration, government officials have increasingly turned to a sanction known as home confinement. As the name of the sanction suggests, offenders sentenced to home confinement must remain in their homes or apartments at certain times. The conditions of their home confinement may, however, vary.

For example, offenders may be required to be in their homes only a few designated hours a day, or they may have to stay in their homes up to twenty-four hours a day. Probation officers, police officers, and other individuals may monitor offenders' compliance with their home confinement sentences through visits or phone calls to the homes, or electronic-monitoring devices (EMDs) can be used to ensure that offenders are in their homes when they are supposed to be.

A variety of EMDs have been developed to assist in the enforcement of the home confinement sanction, and new innovations are constantly being placed on the market. There are presently two basic types of EMDs. With one type of device, involving what is called programmed contact, a computer is programmed to periodically call offenders' homes. The offenders, however, do not know when these calls will be made. When called, the offenders must confirm their presence in the home, perhaps by placing a wristlet they are required to wear in a verifier box attached to the phone, perhaps through a voice verification process, perhaps through visual confirmation if a visual telephone is being used, or through other means. The other type of EMD involves use of a radio transmitter worn by the offender. This radio transmitter continually sends a signal to a receiving device in the home which in turn apprises a central computer of the offender's presence in the home. Should an offender leave the home at a time when he or she is not authorized to do so, the central computer can alert officials who in turn can investigate the offender's whereabouts.

One concern expressed about EMDs is that offenders may be able to fool the computers used to monitor them. Perhaps, for example, a friend could be asked to place the wristlet in the verifier box if the computer calls while the offender is away from home. Or perhaps an offender could remove a radio transmitter and simply leave it in the home while he or she freely moves about the community. Technology is, however, constantly evolving to meet these concerns. For example, the EMDs are now being made so that tampering can be revealed upon inspection by a probation officer. In addition, with some of the devices, the central computer is immediately alerted if an offender attempts to remove the device.

Home confinement, particularly electronically-monitored home confinement, is still in an experimental stage as a criminal sanction. Government policymakers, judges, and others are grappling with such questions as the following as they develop standards to govern home confinement, with or without electronic monitoring:

1. What offenders should be subject to these sanctions? Should only offenders who would otherwise be sentenced to prison or jail be confined in their homes? Should only offenders convicted of nonviolent crimes be sentenced to home confinement?

2. Under what circumstances, should offenders sentenced to home confinement be permitted to leave their homes? Should the yard of an offender's home be considered part of the home

into which he or she can venture? If so, what should be done about offenders who have no homes and are to be confined in their apartments?

3. How long should home confinement sentences be?

4. Should offenders sentenced to home confinement be required to pay fees to defray the expenses of EMDs? If so, how should the fees be calculated?

How would you resolve these questions?

For more information about home confinement, both with and without electronic monitoring, see P. Hofer and B. Heierhoefer, Home Confinement: An Evolving Sanction in the Federal Criminal Justice System (1987) and J. Petersilia, Expanding Options for Criminal Sentencing 32–60 (1987).

3. FINES

One way to punish criminal offenders is to require them to pay a fine. Constitutional questions have arisen, however, when indigent defendants sentenced to pay a fine have been jailed because of their failure to do so. In Williams v. Illinois, 399 U.S. 235, 90 S.Ct. 2018 (1970), the Supreme Court addressed one of these constitutional questions. In that case, the defendant had been sentenced to one year in jail and a $500 fine for petty theft. The defendant, however, was unable to pay the fine because he was indigent and, because of his incarceration, unemployed. Under these circumstances, a state statute authorized the defendant's continued detention in jail until he had "worked off" his overdue fine at the rate of five dollars a day. The end result was that the defendant was required to remain in jail 101 days longer than the maximum jail sentence authorized for the crime of which he had been convicted.

The Supreme Court concluded that to keep an indigent unable to pay a fine in jail for a period exceeding the maximum sentence that could be imposed on a non-indigent violated the indigent defendant's right under the fourteenth amendment to be afforded equal protection of the law. At the same time, however, the Court took pains to emphasize that indigent defendants need not necessarily receive the same sentences as those who are not indigent:

> The State is not powerless to enforce judgments against those financially unable to pay a fine; indeed, a different result would amount to inverse discrimination since it would enable an indigent to avoid both the fine and imprisonment for nonpayment whereas other defendants must always suffer one or the other [penalty].

Id. at 244, 90 S.Ct. at 2024.

The Supreme Court found the *Williams* case to be controlling in the subsequent case of Tate v. Short, 401 U.S. 395, 91 S.Ct. 668 (1971). That case involved a defendant who had been fined for a series of traffic offenses, none of which were punishable by incarceration. He too was unable to pay the fines because of his indigency, and he was then sentenced to a prison farm to "work off" the fines at the rate of five dollars a day. The Court held that the defendant had been invidiously discriminated against in violation of the equal protection clause when he received a sentence which exceeded the maximum penalty for the traffic offenses and which had been imposed on the defendant "solely because of his indigency." Id. at 398, 91 S.Ct. at 670.

In Bearden v. Georgia, 461 U.S. 660, 103 S.Ct. 2064 (1983), the case which follows, the Supreme Court once again explored the effect that indigency can constitutionally have on the criminal sanction imposed on a defendant.

BEARDEN v. GEORGIA

Supreme Court of the United States, 1983.
461 U.S. 660, 103 S.Ct. 2064, 76 L.Ed.2d 221.

JUSTICE O'CONNOR delivered the opinion of the Court.

The question in this case is whether the Fourteenth Amendment prohibits a State from revoking an indigent defendant's probation for failure to pay a fine and restitution. * * * We conclude that the trial court erred in automatically revoking probation because petitioner could not pay his fine, without determining that petitioner had not made sufficient bona fide efforts to pay or that adequate alternative forms of punishment did not exist. * * *

I

In September 1980, petitioner was indicted for the felonies of burglary and theft by receiving stolen property. He pleaded guilty, and was sentenced on October 8, 1980. Pursuant to the Georgia First Offender's Act, the trial court did not enter a judgment of guilt, but deferred further proceedings and sentenced petitioner to three years on probation for the burglary charge and a concurrent one year on probation for the theft charge. As a condition of probation, the trial court ordered petitioner to pay a $500 fine and $250 in restitution. Petitioner was to pay $100 that day, $100 the next day, and the $550 balance within four months.

Petitioner borrowed money from his parents and paid the first $200. About a month later, however, petitioner was laid off from his job. Petitioner, who has only a ninth-grade education and cannot read, tried repeatedly to find other work but was unable to do so. The record indicates that petitioner had no income or assets during this period.

Shortly before the balance of the fine and restitution came due in February 1981, petitioner notified the probation office he was going to be late with his payment because he could not find a job. In May 1981, the State filed a petition in the trial court to revoke petitioner's probation because he had not paid the balance. After an evidentiary hearing, the trial court revoked probation for failure to pay the balance of the fine and restitution, entered a conviction, and sentenced petitioner to serve the remaining portion of the probationary period in prison. The Georgia Court of Appeals, relying on earlier Georgia Supreme Court cases, rejected petitioner's claim that imprisoning him for inability to pay the fine violated the Equal Protection Clause of the Fourteenth Amendment. The Georgia Supreme Court denied review. Since other courts have held that revoking the probation of indigents for failure to pay fines does violate the Equal Protection Clause, we granted certiorari to resolve this important issue in the administration of criminal justice.

II

* * *

The question presented here is whether a sentencing court can revoke a defendant's probation for failure to pay the imposed fine and restitution, absent evidence and findings that the defendant was somehow responsible for the failure or that alternative forms of punishment were inadequate. The parties, following the framework of *Williams* [*v. Illinois*] and *Tate* [*v. Short*], have argued the question primarily in terms of equal protection, and debate vigorously whether strict scrutiny or rational basis is the appropriate standard of review. There is no doubt that the State has treated the petitioner differently from a person who did not fail to pay the imposed fine and therefore did not violate probation. To determine whether this differential treatment violates the Equal Protection Clause, one must determine whether, and under what circumstances, a defendant's indigent status may be considered in the decision whether to revoke probation. This is substantially similar to asking directly the due process question of whether and when it is fundamentally unfair or arbitrary for the State to revoke probation when an indigent is unable to pay the fine. Whether analyzed in terms of equal protection or due process,[8] the issue cannot be resolved by resort to easy slogans or pigeonhole analysis, but rather requires a careful inquiry into such factors as "the nature of the individual interest affected, the extent to which it is affected, the rationality of the connection between legislative means and purpose, [and] the existence of alternative means for effectuating the purpose . . . ."

* * *

The rule of *Williams* and *Tate* is that the State cannot " 'impos[e] a fine as a sentence and then automatically conver[t] it into a jail term solely because the defendant is indigent and cannot forthwith pay the fine in full.' " In other words, if the State determines a fine or

---

8. A due process approach has the advantage in this context of directly confronting the intertwined question of the role that a defendant's financial background can play in determining an appropriate sentence. When the court is initially considering what sentence to impose, a defendant's level of financial resources is a point on a spectrum rather than a classification. Since indigency in this context is a relative term rather than a classification, fitting "the problem of this case into an equal protection framework is a task too Procrustean to be rationally accomplished." The more appropriate question is whether consideration of a defendant's financial background in setting or resetting a sentence is so arbitrary or unfair as to be a denial of due process.

restitution to be the appropriate and adequate penalty for the crime, it may not thereafter imprison a person solely because he lacked the resources to pay it. Both *Williams* and *Tate* carefully distinguished this substantive limitation on the imprisonment of indigents from the situation where a defendant was at fault in failing to pay the fine. * * *

This distinction, based on the reasons for nonpayment, is of critical importance here. If the probationer has willfully refused to pay the fine or restitution when he has the means to pay, the State is perfectly justified in using imprisonment as a sanction to enforce collection. Similarly, a probationer's failure to make sufficient bona fide efforts to seek employment or borrow money in order to pay the fine or restitution may reflect an insufficient concern for paying the debt he owes to society for his crime. In such a situation, the State is likewise justified in revoking probation and using imprisonment as an appropriate penalty for the offense. But if the probationer has made all reasonable efforts to pay the fine or restitution, and yet cannot do so through no fault of his own, it is fundamentally unfair to revoke probation automatically without considering whether adequate alternative methods of punishing the defendant are available. * * *

The State, of course, has a fundamental interest in appropriately punishing persons—rich and poor—who violate its criminal laws. A defendant's poverty in no way immunizes him from punishment. * * *

The decision to place the defendant on probation, however, reflects a determination by the sentencing court that the State's penological interests do not require imprisonment. A probationer's failure to make reasonable efforts to repay his debt to society may indicate that this original determination needs reevaluation, and imprisonment may now be required to satisfy the State's interests. But a probationer who has made sufficient bona fide efforts to pay his fine and restitution, and who has complied with the other conditions of probation, has demonstrated a willingness to pay his debt to society and an ability to conform his conduct to social norms. The State nevertheless asserts three reasons why imprisonment is required to further its penal goals.

First, the State argues that revoking probation furthers its interest in ensuring that restitution be paid to the victims of crime. A rule that imprisonment may befall the probationer who fails to make sufficient bona fide efforts to pay restitution may indeed spur probationers to try hard to pay, thereby increasing the number of probationers who make restitution. Such a goal is fully served, however, by revoking probation only for persons who have not made sufficient bona fide efforts to pay. Revoking the probation of someone who through no fault of his own is unable to make restitution will not make restitution suddenly forthcoming. Indeed, such a policy may have the perverse effect of inducing the probationer to use illegal means to acquire funds to pay in order to avoid revocation.

Second, the State asserts that its interest in rehabilitating the probationer and protecting society requires it to remove him from the temptation of committing other crimes. This is no more than a naked assertion that a probationer's poverty by itself indicates he may commit crimes in the future and thus that society needs for him to be incapacitated. * * * Given the significant interest of the individual in remaining on probation, the State cannot justify incarcerating a probationer who has demonstrated sufficient bona fide efforts to repay his debt to society, solely by lumping him together with other poor persons and thereby classifying him as dangerous. This would be little more than punishing a person for his poverty.

Third, and most plausibly, the State argues that its interests in punishing the lawbreaker and deterring others from criminal behavior require it to revoke probation for failure to pay a fine or restitution. The State clearly has an interest in punishment and deterrence, but this interest can often be served fully by alternative means. * * * For example, the sentencing court could extend the time for making payments, or reduce the fine, or direct that the probationer perform some form of labor or public service in lieu of the fine. * * *

We hold, therefore, that in revocation proceedings for failure to pay a fine or restitution, a sentencing court must inquire into the reasons for the failure to pay. If the probationer willfully refused to pay or failed to make sufficient bona fide efforts legally to acquire the resources to pay, the court may revoke probation and sentence the defendant to imprisonment within the authorized range of its sentencing authority. If the probationer could not pay despite sufficient bona fide efforts to acquire the resources to do so, the court must consider alternative measures of punishment other than imprisonment. Only if alternative measures are not adequate to meet the State's interests in punishment and deterrence may the court imprison a probationer who has made sufficient bona fide efforts to pay. To do otherwise would deprive the probationer of his conditional freedom simply because, through no fault of his own, he cannot pay the fine. Such a deprivation would be contrary to the fundamental fairness required by the Fourteenth Amendment.[12]

* * *

The judgment is reversed, and the case is remanded for further proceedings not inconsistent with this opinion.

* * *

12. As our holding makes clear, we agree with Justice White that poverty does not insulate a criminal defendant from punishment or necessarily prevent revocation of his probation for inability to pay a fine. We reject as impractical, however, the approach suggested by Justice White. He would require a "good-faith effort" by the sentencing court to impose a term of imprisonment that is "roughly equivalent" to the fine and restitution that the defendant failed to pay. Even putting to one side the question of judicial "good faith," we perceive no meaningful standard by which a sentencing or reviewing court could assess whether a given prison sentence has an equivalent sting to the original fine.

JUSTICE WHITE, with whom THE CHIEF JUSTICE, JUSTICE POWELL, and JUSTICE REHNQUIST join, concurring in the judgment.

*   *   *

Poverty does not insulate those who break the law from punishment. When probation is revoked for failure to pay a fine, I find nothing in the Constitution to prevent the trial court from revoking probation and imposing a term of imprisonment if revocation does not automatically result in the imposition of a long jail term and if the sentencing court makes a good-faith effort to impose a jail sentence that in terms of the State's sentencing objectives will be roughly equivalent to the fine and restitution that the defendant failed to pay.

The Court holds, however, that if a probationer cannot pay the fine for reasons not of his own fault, the sentencing court must at least consider alternative measures of punishment other than imprisonment, and may imprison the probationer only if the alternative measures are deemed inadequate to meet the State's interests in punishment and deterrence. There is no support in our cases or, in my view, the Constitution, for this novel requirement.

*   *   *

In this case, in view of the long prison term imposed, the state court obviously did not find that the sentence was "a rational and necessary trade-off to punish the individual who possesse[d] no accumulated assets". Accordingly, I concur in the judgment.

Questions and Points for Discussion

1. Assume that a defendant is convicted of a crime for which the maximum penalty is six months in jail and/or a $500 fine. The court sentences the defendant under this statute to either pay a $300 fine or spend 30 days in jail. If the sentence remains in effect, the defendant will have to go to jail because he has no resources with which to pay the fine. Is the sentence valid?

What if the judge, aware of the defendant's indigency and inability to pay the fine, simply imposes the 30–day jail sentence? Is there any constitutional basis for challenging this sentence?

2. In Black v. Romano, 471 U.S. 606, 105 S.Ct. 2254 (1985), the Supreme Court considered whether in all cases in which a defendant's probation is revoked, the court must state on the record that there are no sentencing alternatives other than incarceration that would meet the government's penological objectives. The Court held that although *Bearden v. Georgia* indicated that such a statement is needed when the failure to comply with the conditions of probation is due to the probationer's indigency, due process does not normally require such a statement. In explaining its conclusion, the Court stated as follows:

> We do not question the desirability of considering possible alternatives to imprisonment before probation is revoked. Nonetheless, incarceration for violation of a probation condition is not constitutionally limited to circumstances where that sanction represents the only

means of promoting the State's interest in punishment and deterrence. The decision to revoke probation is generally predictive and subjective in nature, and the fairness guaranteed by due process does not require a reviewing court to second-guess the factfinder's discretionary decision as to the appropriate sanction. * * * We believe that a general requirement that the factfinder elaborate upon the reasons for a course not taken would unduly burden the revocation proceeding without significantly advancing the interests of the probationer.

Id. at 613, 105 S.Ct. at 2258.

The Court in *Black* emphasized that one reason why probationers would not benefit that much from a specific statement that other sentencing alternatives had been found unsatisfactory is because of the number of procedural safeguards that must already attend probation revocation proceedings. See Gagnon v. Scarpelli, 411 U.S. 778, 93 S.Ct. 1756 (1973), infra page 526. When probation is revoked, for example, probationers are already entitled to a written statement outlining the evidence relied on in revoking their probation and the reasons for the revocation decision. This procedural safeguard, according to the Court, as well as others, will adequately protect probationers from unfounded probation revocations.

3. In an interesting study published by the National Institute of Justice, researchers Sally Hillsman, Joyce Sichel, and Barry Mahoney discuss the potential that fines have as a meaningful form of punishment, even for defendants who are poor. National Institute of Justice, U.S. Dep't of Justice, Fines in Sentencing: A Study of the Use of the Fine as a Criminal Sanction—Executive Summary (1984). Set forth below are some excerpts from this study, which was originally published by the National Institute of Justice. Points of view or opinions expressed in the study are those of the authors and do not necessarily represent the official position or policies of the U.S. Department of Justice.

There is a striking contrast between American and Western European theory with respect to the use of the fine as a criminal sentence. In the United States during most of the twentieth century, scholarly thought and legislative policy have tended to discourage broad use of the fine, except for minor offenses and crimes involving pecuniary gain. To a significant extent, this negative view of the fine has been based on a feeling that, as one federal commission report phrased it, "Fines do not have affirmative rehabilitative value" (National Commission on Reform of Federal Criminal Law, 1971: 296). Although rehabilitation now occupies a much less prominent place among sentencing goals than it did 10–20 years ago, fines have not become recognized as an effective form of punishment or as a potential alternative to incarceration. Sentencing statutes passed by American states in recent years have generally attempted to establish longer prison terms and provide for mandatory minimum periods of incarceration, but have seldom sought to increase fine ceilings, strengthen fine enforcement practices, or address the difficult problem of imposing meaningful (and enforceable) monetary sanctions upon offenders with limited means. Even when monetary penalties have been written into law, they have usually been intended for use as supplements to other sentences, and the emphasis has been more on restitution than on fines.

By contrast, legislators and other policymakers in Britain, Sweden, and West Germany have taken a more affirmative stance with respect to the use of fines as criminal penalties. Broad use of fines has become explicit national policy in these countries, with the express aim of reducing reliance upon short-term custodial sentences. About two-thirds of all offenders sentenced for crimes against a person in West Germany are fined, as are about half of all such offenders in England and Sweden. The fine is the sentence of choice for most criminal offenses and the primary alternative to short-term incarceration in the criminal justice systems of each of these countries. Furthermore, its use as an alternative has been increasing steadily—most dramatically in West Germany—over the past 15 years.

The emphasis upon use of the fine in Western Europe springs from a clear objective of sentencing policy: punishment of the offender. Fines are regarded as "unequivocally *punitive*" (Morgan and Bowles, 1981: 203). It is also thought that they may have some deterrent value and that they are less likely to produce harmful effects on subsequent behavior than is a jail or prison sentence (id.; also Harris, 1980: 10, McKlintock, 1963: 173; Softley, 1977: 7–9).

* * *

Most criminal court defendants are poor, but some are not. The heart of the problem, with respect to the use of the fine as a sanction, is how to set fine amounts at a level which will reflect the seriousness of an offense yet also be within the ability of the offender to pay. Courts vary widely in how they deal with this problem. One approach is to use a kind of "tariff" system. The judges who follow this approach make sentencing judgments more or less across the board for defendants convicted of particular offenses, after developing a presumption about their "typical" defendants' degree of poverty and the fine amount most are likely to be able to pay. Similar offenses result in fines of similar amounts and little or no inquiry is made into the financial situation of individual defendants. For instance, the presumption among many New York City judges seems to be that few defendants have money to pay fines and that almost no one will be able to pay a substantial fine. Therefore, they limit the amounts of most of the fines they impose in Criminal Court and seldom use fines at all in felony cases. In contrast, some courts visited in Georgia use fines extensively in felony cases. They tend to assume that defendants, however poor, will be able to pay substantial fines and to make restitution payments as well, if given the duration of a probation sentence to pay and pressure from probation officers to do so. Only when default occurs do they seem to consider seriously the offender's actual ability to pay.

At the other end of the spectrum, some judges inquire carefully into the economic situations of convicted defendants for whom a fine is a possible sentence. This approach is consistent with the ability-to-pay concept that has been incorporated into many state statutes. For example, New Jersey's statutes provide that:

> In determining the amount and method of payment of a fine, the court shall consider the financial resources of the defendant and the nature of the burden that its payment will impose (New Jersey Revised Statutes, 2C–44–2).

This statutory directive is followed by judges who ask offenders questions about the reality of their day-to-day living. For example, one judge in the Newark Municipal Court typically asks defendants such questions as: "Do you have a car? Do you buy gas? Do you smoke?"

Many of the judges interviewed during this study, when asked how they determined whether a defendant would be likely to pay a fine, tended to talk about a "feel" for the individual defendant's financial condition based on whether he was working, his age, his personal appearance, and his address of residence. Some of them would ask the defendant what he could afford (sometimes directly and sometimes through the defense attorney) and would then tailor the fine to that amount. And when court papers showed that a defendant failed to raise even a low bail, judges sometimes used this information as a basis for setting a low fine. Especially if the offense was minor and the fine set was relatively small, judges appeared to be comfortable with these "soft data." When they were contemplating a high fine or restitution in a more major case, they would be more likely to rely on presentence reports prepared by probation staffs.

The principal problem with a tariff system is that its impacts upon defendants convicted of similar offenses can be grossly inequitable. Some poverty-stricken defendants are fined more than they can possibly pay, while some relatively affluent defendants are given fines that are meaningless as punishment. Both results undermine the fine's effectiveness as a sanction. But an approach centered on the defendant's ability to pay also has conceptual and practical difficulties. If poor defendants are given very low fines (and no other punishment), there is a risk that the public will perceive such sentences as unduly lenient. On the other hand, if a judge's inquiry into the defendant's ability to pay indicates that the defendant is seriously impoverished, the sentencing decision may be jail instead of a fine.

Data from Western European countries, as well as our own findings on the rather widespread use of fines in American courts, suggest that in fact the poor *are* being fined in many courts. Moreover, there is evidence that a high proportion of these offenders—on both sides of the Atlantic—are paying their fines. It seems apparent that some degree of poverty does not necessarily preclude imposition of a fine or payment of it, but there is an obvious need to develop effective ways of tailoring fines to both the seriousness of the offense and the financial circumstances of the offender.

* * *

The "day-fine" is a Swedish innovation which is now also firmly entrenched in West German sentencing practice. It is designed to enable a sentencing judge to impose a level of punishment which is commensurate to the seriousness of the offense and the prior record of the offender, while at the same time taking account of his or her poverty or affluence.

In a day-fine system, the amount of the fine is established in two stages. The first involves setting of the number of units of punishment to be imposed, taking account of the seriousness of the offense (and perhaps the defendant's prior history, too), but without regard to the means of the offender. In the second stage, the monetary value of each unit of punishment is set in light of information about the offender's financial circumstances. Thus, at least theoretically, the degree of punishment should be in proportion to the gravity of the offense, and roughly equivalent (in terms of severity of impact on the individual) across defendants of differing means.

* * *

In West Germany, the day-fine system was adopted at about the same time that legislation was enacted providing that custodial terms of less than six months were to be replaced by fines or probation in all but exceptional cases. Together, these innovations appear to have produced significant changes in sentencing patterns. * * * [M]ore than 113,000 sentences to custodial terms of less than six months were imposed by West German courts in 1968, the year before the legislation was passed. By 1976, this number had dropped to less than 11,000 (1.8% of all sentences). During the same period, the proportion of fine sentences rose from 63% of the total to 83%.

Id. at 4–6, 14–17.

4. RESTITUTION

A restitution order, like a fine, imposes a financial burden on a criminal offender; the difference between the two sanctions is that restitution is paid to the victim of a crime, while a fine is paid to the government. Restitution is designed to compensate the victim for at least some of the losses sustained by the victim because of the crime committed by the defendant.

Restitution, like a fine, may be the sole sanction imposed on an offender. Alternatively, the offender may be placed on probation with restitution ordered as one of the conditions of that probation. Finally, restitution may be ordered in conjunction with other sanctions, such as a prison sentence, or as a condition of parole. Set forth below is one approach to the subject of restitution found in the Victim and Witness Protection Act of 1982 (the VWPA), 18 U.S.C. §§ 3663–64:

§ 3663. Order of restitution

(a) The court, when sentencing a defendant convicted of an offense under this title or under subsection (h), (i), (j), or (n) of section 902 of the Federal Aviation Act of 1958 (49 U.S.C. 1472), may order, in addition to or, in the case of a misdemeanor, in lieu of any other penalty authorized by law, that the defendant make restitution to any victim of such offense.

(b) The order may require that such defendant—

(1) in the case of an offense resulting in damage to or loss or destruction of property of a victim of the offense—

(A) return the property to the owner of the property or someone designated by the owner; or

(B) if return of the property under subparagraph (A) is impossible, impractical, or inadequate, pay an amount equal to the greater of—

(i) the value of the property on the date of the damage, loss, or destruction, or

(ii) the value of the property on the date of sentencing, less the value (as of the date the property is returned) of any part of the property that is returned;

(2) in the case of an offense resulting in bodily injury to a victim—

(A) pay an amount equal to the cost of necessary medical and related professional services and devices relating to physical, psychiatric, and psychological care, including nonmedical care and treatment rendered in accordance with a method of healing recognized by the law of the place of treatment;

(B) pay an amount equal to the cost of necessary physical and occupational therapy and rehabilitation; and

(C) reimburse the victim for income lost by such victim as a result of such offense;

(3) in the case of an offense resulting in bodily injury [that] also results in the death of a victim, pay an amount equal to the cost of necessary funeral and related services; and

(4) in any case, if the victim (or if the victim is deceased, the victim's estate) consents, make restitution in services in lieu of money, or make restitution to a person or organization designated by the victim or the estate.

(c) If the court decides to order restitution under this section, the court shall, if the victim is deceased, order that the restitution be made to the victim's estate.

(d) To the extent that the court determines that the complication and prolongation of the sentencing process resulting from the fashioning of an order of restitution under this section outweighs the need to provide restitution to any victims, the court may decline to make such an order.

(e)(1) The court shall not impose restitution with respect to a loss for which the victim has received or is to receive compensation, except that the court may, in the interest of justice, order restitution to any person who has compensated the victim for such loss to the extent that such person paid the compensation. An order of restitution shall require that all restitution to victims under such order be made before any restitution to any other person under such order is made.

(2) Any amount paid to a victim under an order of restitution shall be set off against any amount later recovered as compensatory damages by such victim in—

(A) any Federal civil proceeding; and

(B) any State civil proceeding, to the extent provided by the law of that State.

(f)(1) The court may require that such defendant make restitution under this section within a specified period or in specified installments.

(2) The end of such period or the last such installment shall not be later than—

(A) the end of the period of probation, if probation is ordered;

(B) five years after the end of the term of imprisonment imposed, if the court does not order probation; and

(C) five years after the date of sentencing in any other case.

(3) If not otherwise provided by the court under this subsection, restitution shall be made immediately.

(4) The order of restitution shall require the defendant to make restitution directly to the victim or other person eligible under this section, or to deliver the amount or property due as restitution to the Attorney General or the person designated under section 604(a)(17) of title 28 for transfer to such victim or person.

(g) If such defendant is placed on probation or sentenced to a term of supervised release under this title, any restitution ordered under this section shall be a condition of such probation or supervised release. The court may revoke probation or a term of supervised release, or modify the term or conditions of probation or a term of supervised release, or hold a defendant in contempt pursuant to section 3583(e) if the defendant fails to comply with such order. In determining whether to revoke probation or a term of supervised release, modify the term or conditions of probation or supervised release, or hold a defendant serving a term of supervised release in contempt, the court shall consider the defendant's employment status, earning ability, financial resources, the willfulness of the defendant's failure to pay, and any other special circumstances that may have a bearing on the defendant's ability to pay.

(h) An order of restitution may be enforced—

(1) by the United States—

(A) in the manner provided for the collection and payment of fines in subchapter B of chapter 229 of this title; or

(B) in the same manner as a judgment in a civil action; and

(2) by a victim named in the order to receive the restitution, in the same manner as a judgment in a civil action.

§ 3664. Procedure for issuing order of restitution

(a) The court, in determining whether to order restitution under section 3579 of this title and the amount of such restitution, shall consider the amount of the loss sustained by any victim as a result of the offense, the financial resources of the defendant, the financial needs and earning ability of the defendant and the defendant's dependents, and such other factors as the court deems appropriate.

(b) The court may order the probation service of the court to obtain information pertaining to the factors set forth in subsection (a) of this section. The probation service of the court shall include the information collected in the report of presentence investigation or in a separate report, as the court directs.

(c) The court shall disclose to both the defendant and the attorney for the Government all portions of the presentence or other report pertaining to the matters described in subsection (a) of this section.

(d) Any dispute as to the proper amount or type of restitution shall be resolved by the court by the preponderance of the evidence. The burden of demonstrating the amount of the loss sustained by a victim as a result of the offense shall be on the attorney for the Government. The burden of demonstrating the financial resources of the defendant and the financial needs of the defendant and such defendant's dependents shall be on the defendant. The burden of demonstrating such other matters as the court deems appropriate shall be upon the party designated by the court as justice requires.

(e) A conviction of a defendant for an offense involving the act giving rise to restitution under this section shall estop the defendant from denying the essential allegations of that offense in any subsequent Federal civil proceeding or State civil proceeding, to the extent consistent with State law, brought by the victim.

Questions and Points for Discussion

1. The seventh amendment to the Constitution provides in part that "[i]n suits at common law, where the value in controversy shall exceed twenty dollars, the right of trial by jury shall be preserved. * * *"

Some defendants have challenged the constitutionality of the VWPA on the grounds that it violates this seventh amendment right to a jury trial. The lower courts have generally rejected these claims, holding that the VWPA exacts a criminal penalty and not a civil one, even though the penalty is paid to the victim. See the cases cited in United States v. Palma, 760 F.2d 475, 479 (3d Cir.1985). See also Kelly v. Robinson, 479 U.S. 36, 52–53, 107 S.Ct. 353, 362–63 (1986).

In support of their conclusion that the seventh amendment does not proscribe restitution orders under the VWPA, the courts have noted several important distinctions between the VWPA and civil actions for damages brought by victims of crimes. Under the VWPA, a victim at most will only recover for certain specified losses. In addition, the victim may not recover at all under the VWPA or the recovery may be diminished because of limitations on the defendant's ability to pay; by contrast, in a civil proceeding, the defendant's financial resources would not normally affect the amount of compensatory damages awarded to the victim. Id., 107 S.Ct. at 362.

2. Assume that a defendant is convicted of "childnapping" under a state statute because she fled out of the state with her child in violation of a court order awarding custody to her former husband. A probation officer states in the presentence investigation report that the husband incurred $20,000 in expenses to locate the child. This statement is based on remarks of the husband made during an interview with the probation officer. The court then places the defendant on probation for five years and orders her, as a condition of probation, to pay restitution in the amount of $20,000 to her ex-husband. Is there any constitutional basis for challenging this restitution order?

3. Under the VWPA, the defendant's financial resources and financial obligations to others may reduce or forestall a restitution award. This limitation on the amount of restitution ordered is due to a concern that unduly high restitution awards may impede offenders' rehabilitation and literally cause them to "rob Peter to pay Paul."

An alternative approach to this problem can be found in the American Bar Association Guidelines Governing Restitution to Victims of Criminal Conduct (1988). Under these guidelines, a court can order restitution in the full amount, but then stay payment of all or part of the restitution awarded. Guideline 1.5(a). If the offender's financial situation should later change, making it feasible for the offender to pay more of the restitution award, the victim can then file a motion to remove the stay. Guideline 1.11(a).

5. COMMUNITY SERVICE

Sentencing criminal offenders to perform certain services for the community without pay is another sanction that has increasingly gained favor in recent years. In a sense, community service is a form of restitution. Instead of paying their debts to crime victims, however, offenders pay society as a whole for their crimes.

The advantages of community service sentences are many. Rather than sitting around in a prison or jail as so many inmates do, offenders sentenced to community service programs are involved in productive work—planting trees, picking up litter in parks and next to roads, refurbishing public buildings, and so on. Community service programs also cost much less than incarceration, and if offenders are sentenced to perform community service, they can avoid the criminogenic influences that prevail in prisons and jails. In addition, they can maintain ties with family members.

At present, however, there are substantial impediments which curb the widespread use of this criminal sanction. In many jurisdictions, for example, there is no central agency that is responsible for ensuring both that community service programs are in place and readily available as a sentencing option and that they are meeting their objectives. In any event, even when a sentence to community service could feasibly be imposed on an offender, presentence investigators and defense attorneys very often fail to apprise judges of the availability of this sentencing option. The community service sentencing option also raises concerns about its possible misuse. Without carefully defined restrictions, such programs could, for example, take on some of the characteristics of the "chain gangs" of the not so distant past.

For a discussion of one highly regarded community service sentencing program established by the Vera Institute of Justice in New York City, see J. Petersilia, Expanding Options for Criminal Sentencing 74–76 (1987).

6. IMPOSITION OF THE APPROPRIATE SENTENCE

United States District Judge John Kane expressed the views of many trial judges when he said, "I know of no more excruciating decision for a judge to make than whether to confine and, if so, for how long and under what terms and conditions." United States v. O'Driscoll, 586 F.Supp. 1486, 1486 (D.Colo.1984). Having reviewed information about some of the many sentencing options that may be available to a sentencing judge, what sentence would you impose in the two cases set forth below if you were the sentencing judge and all penalty options were available to you? In addition, reconsider what the appropriate penalty would be in the cases described on pages 16–17, supra.

1. Samuel E. Cole has pled guilty to two counts of Distribution of a Controlled Substance—Cocaine. Cole is 26. His father is former Marine who is presently self-employed as an insurance agent. His mother is a homemaker.

Cole has been described as having been hyperactive when growing up, but he never received medication or counseling for his hyperactivity. His academic skills were above average, but he was not interested in school and eventually dropped out of high school six months before graduation. Over the next six years, Cole worked at a variety of different jobs—as a horse groomer, salesman, construction carpenter apprentice, van and moving assistant, aluminum siding installer, and a waiter. Few of these jobs, however, appealed to him, but he did receive his G.E.D. by attending night classes during this time period.

Six years ago, Cole was involved in a car accident. According to Cole, the occupants of the car came up to him after the accident and began hitting him. In self-defense, he struck back, slapping one of his assailants. He was later charged with assault and battery. Though he insisted he was not guilty, Cole followed his attorney's advice and pled guilty. The court then placed Cole on what is called "Probation Before Judgment."

Three years ago, Cole began working at a restaurant, where he met people who regularly used cocaine. Cole too began to use the drug two to three times a week. Eventually, his cocaine use escalated, and he began losing weight and working only sporadically. Within a few months, he was in financial trouble, and about this time, he was also arrested for D.W.I.—driving while under the influence of intoxicating liquor.

When a police informant contacted Cole and asked Cole if he knew of a cocaine dealer from whom the informant could buy cocaine, Cole bought some cocaine from a dealer and sold it to the informant three different times. One sale involved a half-ounce of cocaine, one involved one ounce, and one involved two ounces. Cole was arrested for these three drug transactions and released on his own recognizance. Since Cole's arrest ten months ago, he has worked full time as a restaurant employee. His manager has described Cole as "one of the restaurant's best employees."

2. Nathan Forester is a 32–year–old dentist who was raised by religious and hardworking parents. His father has worked for Ford Motor Company for the last twenty-seven years, but sometimes worked two or three jobs at a time to support his family. His mother is a salesclerk in a men's clothing store.

Nathan was an above-average student and extremely athletic. He lettered in basketball, baseball, and football while in high school and played on the college baseball team.

After taking graduate courses in biology for several years, Nathan decided to become a dentist, and he acquired his D.D.S. in three years. He then entered two post-doctoral programs, one of which was in orthodontics. He also began working in two dental health care clinics five days a week for half-days.

The consequences of Nathan's extensive commitments soon became evident. His grades dropped, he fell behind in his research, and he could not meet deadlines. He began to feel desperate, incompetent, and depressed. It was during this time that Nathan attended the annual convention of the American Association of Orthodontists. On the first day of the convention, he felt "inexplainable anxiety" and skipped the meetings. Instead, he went and sat on a knoll near a bank. When he saw a woman enter the bank to use the automatic teller machine, he went in after her, threatened her, and then sexually assaulted her. During the assault, which was recorded on film by the bank's security camera, he was unable to have an erection.

After the assault, Nathan, who was extremely distraught, went to find one of his professors, and she accompanied him to his room. She described him as disoriented, incoherent, and suicidal. While she was in the room, he was crying and tried several times to jump out of the tenth-floor window.

Nathan was eventually convicted of second-degree forcible rape. His dental license has been suspended, and it appears as though it will soon be revoked.

Information about the two cases described above was drawn from sentencing proposals prepared by the National Center on Institutions and Alternatives (NCIA), which is located in Alexandria, Virginia. NCIA, a private, non-profit agency, was founded in 1978 by Dr. Jerome Miller and Herbert J. Hoeltner, for the purpose of promoting the use of safe and effective alternative sanctions to prisons and jails.

C. NON–IMPRISONMENT GUIDELINES

The need for the development of a wide range of sentencing sanctions of differing severity was discussed in the beginning of this chapter. But with nonincarcerative sanctions, as with penalties involving incarceration, there is a concern about disparity in the treatment of criminal offenders—a concern that the ad hoc exercise of discretion by sentencing judges will lead to the imposition of much more onerous nonincarcerative sanctions on some criminal offenders than on others who are similarly situated. The article set forth below discusses one way of allaying this concern and limiting disparity in the imposition of nonincarcerative sanctions.

KAY A. KNAPP, NEXT STEP: NON–IMPRISONMENT GUIDELINES

American Probation and Parole Association, Perspectives 8–10 (Winter, 1988).
Reprinted with the permission of the American Probation
and Parole Association.

* * *

There has been significant innovation in the development of intermediate sanctions in recent years. In addition to the traditional use of short jail terms, other options like community service, residential treatment, non-residential treatment, fines, restitution, home detention, electronic monitoring and drug testing, and various levels and forms of probation supervision are commonly used as sentencing options by a judge or as administrative tools by a corrections agency. These options have yet to be structured into a comprehensive sentencing system.

Their unstructured use has raised three types of concerns. One area of concern is disparity and lack of proportionality in the use of sentencing options. The wide discretion given judges in the use of non-imprisonment sanctions inevitably results in different judges using the same sanction for very different types of offenders; or alternatively stated, using very different levels of sanctions for similar kinds of offender. Another area of concern involves the effectiveness of sentencing options in achieving rehabilitation and specific deterrence, in-so-far as they are goals of the programs. The wide discretion awarded judges does not ensure that programs are used for the targeted offenders. A third area of concern is resource planning. It is difficult to determine non-imprisonment resource needs and to obtain funding for them absent detailed policy prescribing their use.

* * *

* * * The object of those concerned with structured sentencing and non-imprisonment sanctions is to conceptualize a structured sentencing policy which deals with community and intermediate sanctions [in] a way that: 1) allows for sensitivity in individualizing sanctions for the non-prison-bound offender; 2) articulates general policy guidance; 3) enables the coordination of structured sentencing policy with correctional resources; and 4) provides for efficient and effective use of non-imprisonment sanctions.

Such an approach rests on the development of two concepts: 1) sanctioning levels; and 2) exchange rates. The first concept, sanctioning level, is substituted in the guidelines system for the more traditional sanction. Thus, instead of defining six months imprisonment as the proper presumptive sentence for a particular category of offenders, the policy would prescribe a sanctioning level of six units (or eight or ten or twelve). The concept of exchange rates would be used to translate units into specific sanctions, such that one unit translates into 40 community service hours, or a month in jail, or two months on probation, or two weeks in residential treatment. Essentially the court would be provided with a menu of sanctions from which to fashion a sentence to meet the sanctioning level prescribed by policy.

This approach establishes general policy regarding sanctioning levels and defines level of resource use for the intermediate range of offenses and offenders. It has several advantages. First, it has the advantage of providing for the complexities of sanctioning given the array of purposes (rehabilitation, deterrence and punishment) pursued in imposing various non-imprisonment sanctions. Judges can choose the specific sanctions most appropriate to the individual offender. At the same time, the disparity and lack of proportionality of a highly discretionary system is alleviated by means of uniform sanctioning levels.

A second advantage of this approach is that resource variability across a jurisdiction's regions is less problematic than a more rigid policy approach. By including a broad array of sanctions in the menu, judges can choose from those available in the geographical area, while still sentencing according to state-wide policy prescriptions. Since the cost of specific non-imprisonment sanctions vary substantially, local jurisdictions retain significant control over their correctional expenditures.

The utility of a comprehensive structured sentencing system such as that sketched above can only be tested through actual experience. Each of the jurisdictions currently developing sentencing guidelines has the need and opportunity to explore the development of such a system. * * * A more comprehensive approach to structured sentencing may well emerge from these efforts.

Chapter 5

SENTENCING STATUTES AND GUIDELINES

A. "PURE" SENTENCING MODELS

Two critical decisions must be made in the course of sentencing a criminal defendant. First, what is known as the in-out decision must be made—a decision as to whether or not the defendant will be incarcerated. Once this decision has been made, the duration or amount of the defendant's sentence must then be determined—in other words, the length of any nonincarcerative or incarcerative sentence and the amount of any fine or restitution to be paid by the defendant. Set forth below is a description of three different ways of allocating the authority to make these very important sentencing decisions.

ALAN M. DERSHOWITZ, Background Paper From FAIR AND CERTAIN PUNISHMENT: REPORT OF THE TWENTI-ETH CENTURY FUND TASK FORCE ON CRIMINAL SEN-TENCING 79–80 (1976)

Reprinted with the permission of The Twentieth Century Fund, Inc., © by The Twentieth Century Fund, New York.

The history of criminal sentencing in the United States has been a history of shift in institutional power and in the theories that have guided the exercise of such power. In each period, one of three sentencing models has predominated, either the legislative, judicial, or administrative model. These are so called in recognition of the institution or the group of policy makers [that] exercises the power to imprison and to determine the length of imprisonment. Although incarcerative powers usually are shared by several persons or agencies, it is nevertheless possible to postulate pure sentencing models.

In the *legislatively fixed model,* the legislature determines that conviction for a given crime warrants a given term of imprisonment. For example, a first offender convicted of armed robbery must be sentenced to five years' imprisonment. There is no judicial or administrative discretion under this model; the legislature has authorized but one sentence.

* * *

In the *judicially fixed model,* the legislature determines the general range of imprisonment for a given crime. For example, a first offender convicted of armed robbery shall be sentenced to no less than 1 and no more than 10 years' imprisonment. The sentencing judge must fix a determinate sentence within that range: "I sentence the defendant to five years' imprisonment." Once this sentence is fixed, it cannot be increased or reduced by any parole board or adult authority; the defendant must serve for five years. (This model does not consider good-time provisions or other relatively automatic reductions, nor does it consider commutation or pardon.)

Under this model, discretion is vested in the sentencing judge; how much is vested depends on the range of imprisonment authorized by the legislature. On the day he is sentenced, however, the defendant knows precisely how long he will serve; there is no discretion vested in the parole board or prison authorities.

In the *administratively fixed model,* the legislature sets an extremely wide permissible range of imprisonment for a given crime. A first-offense armed robber, for example, shall be sentenced to a term of one day to life. The sentencing judge must—or may—impose the legislatively determined sentence: "You are sentenced to one day to life." The actual duration of the sentence is decided by an administrative agency while the prisoner is serving his sentence. For example, after five years of imprisonment, the adult authority decides that the prisoner is ready for release.

Under this model, vast discretion is vested in the administrative agency and in the prison authorities. On the day he is sentenced, the defendant does not know how long he will have to serve, although he probably can make an educated guess based on past practices.

Questions and Points for Discussion

1. What are the advantages and disadvantages of each of the three sentencing models described above? Can you construct a sentencing model that incorporates most or many of the advantages of the three "pure" sentencing models, but not their disadvantages?

2. The "pure" legislative sentencing model purports to eliminate judicial and administrative discretion in the sentencing process. Are there any reasons why this aim of eliminating the exercise of discretion as to the sentence to be served by a defendant might still be frustrated in a jurisdiction adopting this model? See note 3, supra page 157.

B. SENTENCING STATUTES

1. INDETERMINATE SENTENCING STATUTES

Most of the sentencing systems in this country are hybrids of the "pure" legislative, judicial, and administrative sentencing models described earlier. Sentencing statutes are generally divided into two categories: indeterminate and determinate. When an indeterminate sentence is imposed, as its name suggests, the offender does not know how much time he or she will actually spend in prison. The legislature alone, or the legislature in conjunction with the sentencing judge, will define the minimum period of incarceration, if there is one, and the maximum term of confinement. A parole board, however, will actually decide when the inmate should be released from prison.

In practice, here is how an indeterminate sentencing scheme might work. Assume that the legislature authorizes a sentence of from one to thirty years for a particular crime. The judge then imposes a sentence falling within this range, sentencing the defendant to a minimum of ten years in prison and a maximum of thirty. The parole board then decides when to actually release the defendant from prison, whether after ten years, thirty years, or some time in between.

The Iowa statutory provisions set forth below, Iowa Code Ann. §§ 902.3, 902.7, 902.8, and 902.9, further exemplify the way in which an indeterminate sentencing system can operate:

902.3 Indeterminate sentence

When a judgment of conviction of a felony other than a class "A" felony is entered against a person, the court, in imposing a sentence of confinement, shall commit the person into the custody of the director of the Iowa department of corrections for an indeterminate term, the maximum length of which shall not exceed the limits as fixed by section 707.3 or section 902.9 nor shall the term be less than the minimum term imposed by law, if a minimum sentence is provided.

902.7 Minimum sentence—use of a firearm

At the trial of a person charged with participating in a forcible felony, if the trier of fact finds beyond a reasonable doubt that the person is guilty of a forcible felony and that the person represented that the person was in the immediate possession and control of a firearm, displayed a firearm in a threatening manner, or was armed with a firearm while participating in the forcible felony the convicted person shall serve a minimum of five years of the sentence imposed by law. A person sentenced pursuant to this section shall not be eligible for parole until the person has served the minimum sentence of confinement imposed by this section.

902.8 Minimum sentence—habitual offender

An habitual offender is any person convicted of a class "C" or a class "D" felony, who has twice before been convicted of any felony in a court of this or any other state, or of the United States. An offense is a felony if, by the law under which the person is convicted, it is so classified at the time of his or her conviction. A person sentenced as an habitual offender shall not be eligible for parole until he or she has served the minimum sentence of confinement of three years.

902.9 Maximum sentence for felons

The maximum sentence for any person convicted of a felony shall be that prescribed by statute or, if not prescribed by statute, if other than a class "A" felony [a] shall be determined as follows:

1. A class "B" felon shall be confined for no more than twenty-five years.

2. An habitual offender shall be confined for no more than fifteen years.

3. A class "C" felon, not an habitual offender, shall be confined for no more than ten years, and in addition may be sentenced to a fine of not more than ten thousand dollars.

4. A class "D" felon, not an habitual offender, shall be confined for no more than five years, and in addition may be sentenced to a fine of not more than seven thousand five hundred dollars.

Questions and Points for Discussion

1. The provisions of indeterminate sentencing statutes vary widely from state to state. For example, statutes may differ as to whether a minimum period of incarceration is prescribed, what that minimum is, and what the maximum penalty is.

There are several different ways in which a legislature can define the minimum prison sentence that can be imposed for a particular crime. A state may, for example, do what Iowa does with habitual offenders, specifying a certain amount of time that such offenders must spend in prison before they can be considered for release on parole. Alternatively or in addition, a state can require that the minimum sentence be no more or no less than a certain percentage of the maximum sentence imposed on a defendant. See, e.g., N.Y.Penal Law § 70.00(3)(b) (McKinney) (minimum prison sentence for most class "B," "C," "D," and "E" felonies shall be no less than one year, but no more than one-third of the maximum sentence imposed); Wyo.Stat. § 7–13–201 (minimum should be no greater than 90% of the maximum sentence). Why would a legislature limit a minimum sentence to a certain percentage of the maximum sentence?

2. One of the chief criticisms of indeterminate sentencing statutes is that they lead to disparity in sentencing. This problem with sentencing disparity was highlighted by statistics gathered when indeterminate sentences were imposed by the federal district courts before adoption of the federal sentencing guidelines. These statistics, gathered during a study of the federal district courts, revealed gross differences in the sentencing decisions of the various district courts. For example, while 84% of the individuals convicted in the District of Minnesota of larceny or theft during the year before June 30, 1977 were sentenced to prison, only 8% of those convicted of these crimes in the District of Colorado were imprisoned. Legislation to Revise and Recodify Federal Criminal Laws: Hearings Before the Subcomm. on Criminal Justice of the House Comm. on the

[a. Under Iowa Code Ann. § 902.1, a defendant convicted of a class "A" felony must be sentenced to life in prison and cannot be released on parole unless the governor commutes the sentence to a term of years.]

Judiciary, 95th Cong., 1st & 2d Sess. 2459 (1978) (statement of William J. Anderson). In addition to such differences in the percentage of offenders incarcerated, the study revealed stark contrasts in the average length of prison sentences imposed by the courts. For example, in the Southern District of New York, the average sentence for bank robbery was seven years during the time of the study; in the District of South Carolina, by contrast, the average sentence was eighteen years. Id.

Judges working within the same court or judicial district also treat offenders differently. The report of the President's Commission on Law Enforcement and the Administration of Justice, for example, discussed the results of a study of the Detroit Recorder's Court that revealed considerable differences in the sentencing decisions of judges who worked in that court. One of the ten judges studied sentenced 75 to 90% of the offenders who appeared before him to prison, while another judge imposed a prison sentence in only 35% of the cases. The President's Commission on Law Enforcement and the Administration of Justice, Task Force Report: The Courts 23 (1967).

Such disparity in sentencing not only contravenes basic notions of fairness, but also creates practical problems as well. Offenders who have received much more severe sentences than other offenders who have similar backgrounds and who committed similar crimes are naturally resentful. This resentment can breed hostility and contempt for the law which in turn makes the offenders more difficult for correctional officials to control and less amenable to rehabilitative efforts. In addition, the different sentencing practices of judges can lead to logjams in the courts as defense attorneys, whose cases are scheduled before more punitive judges, try to stall the cases in hopes of getting them transferred to a more lenient judge.

2. DETERMINATE SENTENCING STATUTES

In recent years, more and more states have abandoned their indeterminate sentencing systems, supplanting them with determinate sentencing laws. Determinate sentencing statutes differ from indeterminate sentencing statutes in that offenders, after they are sentenced, generally know how much time they will spend in prison; they will be incarcerated for the amount of time designated in the sentencing order minus any good-time credits to which they are entitled for their good behavior while in prison.

Determinate sentencing statutes can take many different forms. Set forth below are examples of three different types of determinate sentencing statutes. The Illinois statutory provisions depict what is called determinate-discretionary sentencing; the California and Indiana laws exemplify what is known as presumptive sentencing; and the Michigan felony-firearm statute is an example of a mandatory sentencing statute.

a. Determinate–Discretionary Sentencing

ILL.REV.STAT. ch. 38, § 1005–8–1

Sentence of Imprisonment for Felony. (a) Except as otherwise provided in the statute defining the offense, a sentence of imprisonment for a felony shall be a determinate sentence set by the court under this Section, according to the following limitations:

(1) for first degree murder, (a) a term shall be not less than 20 years and not more than 60 years, or (b) if the court finds that the murder was accompanied by exceptionally brutal or heinous behavior indicative of wanton cruelty or that any of the aggravating factors listed in subsection (b) of Section 9–1 of the Criminal Code of 1961 are present, the court may sentence the defendant to a term of natural life imprisonment, or (c) if the defendant has previously been convicted of first degree murder under any state or federal law or is found guilty of murdering more than one victim, the court shall sentence the defendant to a term of natural life imprisonment;

(2) for a person adjudged a habitual criminal under Article 33B of the Criminal Code of 1961, as amended, the sentence shall be a term of natural life imprisonment;

(3) except as otherwise provided in the statute defining the offense, for a Class X felony, the sentence shall be not less than 6 years and not more than 30 years;

(4) for a Class 1 felony, the sentence shall be not less than 4 years and not more than 15 years;

(5) for a Class 2 felony, the sentence shall be not less than 3 years and not more than 7 years;

(6) for a Class 3 felony, the sentence shall be not less than 2 years and not more than 5 years;

(7) for a Class 4 felony, the sentence shall be not less than 1 year and not more than 3 years.

(b) The sentencing judge in each felony conviction shall set forth his reasons for imposing the particular sentence he enters in the case, as provided in Section 5–4–1 of this Code. Those reasons may include any mitigating or aggravating factors [b] specified in this Code, or the lack of any such circumstances, as well as any other such factors as the judge shall set forth on the record that are consistent with the purposes and principles of sentencing set out in this Code.

* * *

(d) Except where a term of natural life is imposed, every sentence shall include as though written therein a term in addition to the term of imprisonment. For those sentenced under the law in effect prior to February 1, 1978, such term shall be identified as a parole term. For

[b]. A list of these mitigating and aggravating factors can be found on pages 98–101, supra.

those sentenced on or after February 1, 1978, such term shall be identified as a mandatory supervised release term. Subject to earlier termination under Section 3–3–8, the parole or mandatory supervised release term shall be as follows:

(1) for first degree murder or a Class X felony, 3 years;

(2) for a Class 1 felony or a Class 2 felony, 2 years;

(3) for a Class 3 felony or a Class 4 felony, 1 year. * * *

b. Presumptive Sentencing

CAL.PENAL CODE § 1170 (West)

(a)(1) The Legislature finds and declares that the purpose of imprisonment for crime is punishment. This purpose is best served by terms proportionate to the seriousness of the offense with provision for uniformity in the sentences of offenders committing the same offense under similar circumstances. The Legislature further finds and declares that the elimination of disparity and the provision of uniformity of sentences can best be achieved by determinate sentences fixed by statute in proportion to the seriousness of the offense as determined by the Legislature to be imposed by the court with specified discretion.

(2) In any case in which the punishment prescribed by statute for a person convicted of a public offense is a term of imprisonment in the state prison of 16 months, two or three years; two, three, or four years; two, three, or five years; three, four, or five years; two, four, or six years; three, four, or six years; three, five, or seven years; three, six, or eight years; five, seven, or nine years; five, seven, or 11 years, or any other specification of three time periods, the court shall sentence the defendant to one of the terms of imprisonment specified unless such convicted person is given any other disposition provided by law, including a fine, jail, probation, or the suspension of imposition or execution of sentence or is sentenced pursuant to subdivision (b) of Section 1168 because he or she had committed his or her crime prior to July 1, 1977. In sentencing the convicted person, the court shall apply the sentencing rules of the Judicial Council.[c] The court, unless it determines that there are circumstances in mitigation of the punishment prescribed, shall also impose any other term which it is required by law to impose as an additional term. * * *

(b) When a judgment of imprisonment is to be imposed and the statute specifies three possible terms, the court shall order imposition of the middle term, unless there are circumstances in aggravation or mitigation of the crime. At least four days prior to the time set for imposition of judgment, either party or the victim, or the family of the victim if the victim is deceased, may submit a statement in aggravation

[c. Cal.Penal Code § 1170.3 directs the Judicial Council to establish rules which will guide sentencing courts when making such decisions as whether or not to place a defendant on probation, whether or not to impose other than the middle imprisonment term, and whether to impose consecutive or concurrent sentences.]

or mitigation to dispute facts in the record or the probation officer's report, or to present additional facts. In determining whether there are circumstances that justify imposition of the upper or lower term, the court may consider the record in the case, the probation officer's report, other reports including reports received pursuant to Section 1203.03 and statements in aggravation or mitigation submitted by the prosecution, the defendant, or the victim, or the family of the victim if the victim is deceased, and any further evidence introduced at the sentencing hearing. The court shall set forth on the record the facts and reasons for imposing the upper or lower term. * * *

(c) The court shall state the reasons for its sentence choice on the record at the time of sentencing. The court shall also inform the defendant that as part of the sentence after expiration of the term he or she may be on parole for a period as provided in Section 3000.

* * *

(f)(1) Within one year after the commencement of the term of imprisonment, the Board of Prison Terms shall review the sentence to determine whether the sentence is disparate in comparison with the sentences imposed in similar cases. If the Board of Prison Terms determines that the sentence is disparate, the board shall notify the judge, the district attorney, the defense attorney, the defendant, and the Judicial Council. The notification shall include a statement of the reasons for finding the sentence disparate.

Within 120 days of receipt of this information, the sentencing court shall schedule a hearing and may recall the sentence and commitment previously ordered and resentence the defendant in the same manner as if the defendant had not been sentenced previously, provided the new sentence is no greater than the initial sentence. In resentencing under this subdivision the court shall apply the sentencing rules of the Judicial Council and shall consider the information provided by the Board of Prison Terms.

(2) The review under this section shall concern the decision to deny probation and the sentencing decisions enumerated in paragraphs (2), (3), and (4) * * * of subdivision (a) of Section 1170.3 and apply the sentencing rules of the Judicial Council and the information regarding the sentences in this state of other persons convicted of similar crimes so as to eliminate disparity of sentences and to promote uniformity of sentencing.

(g) Prior to sentencing pursuant to this chapter, the court may request information from the Board of Prison Terms concerning the sentences in this state of other persons convicted of similar crimes under similar circumstances.

IND.CODE ANN. § 35–50–2–3

Murder.—(a) A person who commits murder shall be imprisoned for a fixed term of forty (40) years, with not more than twenty (20) years added for aggravating circumstances or not more than ten (10) years subtracted for mitigating circumstances; in addition, the person may be fined not more than ten thousand dollars ($10,000).

(b) Notwithstanding subsection (a), a person who was at least sixteen (16) years of age at the time the murder was committed may be sentenced to death under section 9 [IC 35–50–2–9] of this chapter.

IND.CODE ANN. § 35–50–2–4

Class A felony.—A person who commits a class A felony shall be imprisoned for a fixed term of thirty (30) years, with not more than twenty (20) years added for aggravating circumstances or not more than ten (10) years subtracted for mitigating circumstances; in addition, he may be fined not more than ten thousand dollars ($10,000).

IND.CODE ANN. § 35–50–2–5

Class B felony.—A person who commits a class B felony shall be imprisoned for a fixed term of ten (10) years, with not more than ten (10) years added for aggravating circumstances or not more than four (4) years subtracted for mitigating circumstances; in addition, he may be fined not more than ten thousand dollars ($10,000).

IND.CODE ANN. § 35–50–2–6

Class C felony.—A person who commits a class C felony shall be imprisoned for a fixed term of five (5) years, with not more than three (3) years added for aggravating circumstances or not more than three (3) years subtracted for mitigating circumstances; in addition, he may be fined not more than ten thousand dollars ($10,000).

IND.CODE ANN. § 35–50–2–7(a)

Class D felony.—(a) A person who commits a class D felony shall be imprisoned for a fixed term of two (2) years, with not more than two (2) years added for aggravating circumstances or not more than one (1) year subtracted for mitigating circumstances; in addition, he may be fined not more than ten thousand dollars ($10,000).

c. *Mandatory Sentences*

MICH. COMP. LAWS § 750.227B

(1) A person who carries or has in his possession a firearm at the time he commits or attempts to commit a felony, except the violation of section 227 or section 227a,[d] is guilty of a felony, and shall be imprisoned for 2 years. Upon a second conviction under this section, the person shall be imprisoned for 5 years. Upon a third or subsequent

[**d.** Sections 227 and 227a prohibit the unlawful concealment, carrying, and possession of firearms.]

conviction under this section, the person shall be imprisoned for 10 years.

(2) The term of imprisonment prescribed by this section shall be in addition to the sentence imposed for the conviction of the felony or the attempt to commit the felony, and shall be served consecutively with and preceding any term of imprisonment imposed for the conviction of the felony or attempt to commit the felony.

(3) The term of imprisonment imposed under this section shall not be suspended. The person subject to the sentence mandated by this section shall not be eligible for parole or probation during the mandatory term imposed pursuant to subsection (1).

Questions and Points for Discussion

1. Determinate sentencing statutes, as well as indeterminate ones, that outline the possible prison sentences that can be imposed on convicted felons must be considered in conjunction with other statutes that generally provide judges with the option of sentencing offenders to probation or imposing some other nonincarcerative sanction. An example of one such statute is Ill.Rev.Stat. ch. 38, § 1005–6–1, portions of which are set forth below:

1005–6–1. Sentences of probation and of conditional discharge and disposition of supervision

§ 5–6–1. Sentences of Probation and of Conditional Discharge and Disposition of Supervision. (a) Except where specifically prohibited by other provisions of this Code,[e] the court shall impose a sentence of probation or conditional discharge [f] upon an offender unless, having regard to the nature and circumstance of the offense, and to the history, character and condition of the offender, the court is of the opinion that:

(1) his imprisonment or periodic imprisonment is necessary for the protection of the public; or

(2) probation or conditional discharge would deprecate the seriousness of the offender's conduct and would be inconsistent with the ends of justice.

(b) The court may impose a sentence of conditional discharge for an offense if the court is of the opinion that neither a sentence of imprisonment nor of periodic imprisonment nor of probation supervision is appropriate.

(c) The court may, upon a plea of guilty or a stipulation by the defendant of the facts supporting the charge or a finding of guilt, defer further proceedings and the imposition of a sentence, and enter an

[e. Examples of some of the crimes for which a sentence to probation or conditional discharge cannot be imposed include first-degree murder, rape, some drug offenses, and residential burglary. § 1005–5–3(c)(2).]

[f. Ill.Rev.Stat. ch. 38, § 1005–1–4 defines conditional discharge as "a sentence or disposition of conditional and revocable release without probationary supervision but under such conditions as may be imposed by the court."]

order for supervision [g] of the defendant if the defendant is not charged with a felony and having regard for the circumstances of the offense, and the history, character and condition of the offender, the court is of the opinion that:

(1) the offender is not likely to commit further crimes;

(2) the defendant and the public would be best served if the defendant were not to receive a criminal record; and

(3) in the best interests of justice an order of supervision is more appropriate than a sentence otherwise permitted under this Code. * * *

For other examples of statutes according judges the general discretion to impose a probationary sentence in lieu of a determinate or indeterminate prison sentence, see Iowa Code Ann. § 907.3, Cal.Penal Code § 1203(e) (West), and Ind.Code Ann. § 35–50–2–2.

2. As was mentioned earlier, even when an offender receives a determinate prison sentence, the amount of time that the offender spends in prison may be reduced if the offender is awarded good-time credits for good behavior while in prison. An example of a good-time-credit statute is Ill. Rev.Stat. § 1003–6–3, which provides for what is called day-for-day good time; for every day of good behavior while in prison, the offender's sentence is reduced by one day. An Illinois prisoner who is sentenced to prison for six years may therefore be released in three years if the prisoner, while incarcerated, complies with all institutional rules and regulations.

3. In response to public demands to "get tough on crime," legislatures across the country have enacted mandatory sentencing statutes, requiring that a designated prison or jail sentence be imposed for certain crimes. Mandatory sentencing statutes often apply to such crimes as murder, drunk driving, drug offenses, and felonies in which firearms were used as well as to persons found to be habitual offenders. M. Tonry, Sentencing Reform Impacts 25 (National Institute of Justice 1987). Researchers have found, however, that the purpose of mandatory sentencing laws—to ensure that a particular sentence is imposed for a particular crime—is often thwarted by police officers, prosecutors, and judges. Id. at 26–35. Police officers may, for example, not arrest an individual for a crime for which the offender, if convicted, will have to be incarcerated. Or prosecutors may, for the same reason, refrain from filing charges or file charges for a related offense for which there is not a mandatory penalty. Even judges may attempt to circumvent what they consider unduly harsh mandatory sentencing statutes by dismissing charges or finding defendants not guilty in order to avoid imposing a mandatory incarcerative sentence. In cases where a mandatory sentence is imposed because of particular conduct of the defendant during the course of a felony, such as using a firearm, a

[g. In many ways, a sentence to court supervision is like a conditional discharge sentence; the defendant is not subject to probationary supervision, but the court may impose various restrictions as conditions of the court supervision sentence. The difference between the two types of sentences is that following successful completion of the period of court supervision, the charges against a defendant will be dismissed, which means that the defendant can avoid the onus of a criminal conviction. Ill.Rev.Stat. ch. 38, § 1005–1–21.]

judge may also in effect nullify the mandatory penalty by decreasing the sentence for the underlying felony by the amount by which the sentence will then be increased under the mandatory sentencing statute.

C. SENTENCING GUIDELINES

Sentencing guidelines differ from sentencing statutes in that they are generally developed by judges or by a sentencing commission established by the legislature, rather than by the legislature itself. Sentencing guideline systems have been held constitutional despite arguments that they are the product of an excessive delegation of legislative power and violate separation-of-power principles. See, e.g., Mistretta v. United States, 488 U.S. 361, 109 S.Ct. 647 (1989). In part, this is because the legislature still plays a role in a sentencing process governed by guidelines by defining the ranges of punishment within which the guidelines will operate and often by approving the guidelines formulated by a sentencing commission. For example, a state statute might state that a convicted burglar can be sentenced to probation or anywhere from one to ten years in prison. Sentencing guidelines can then provide further guidance as to whether or not a convicted burglar should be imprisoned and, if imprisoned, the length of the term of imprisonment.

Sentencing guidelines may be purely voluntary, giving judges the prerogative of departing from them without explanation. Or guidelines can be presumptive, which means that the sentence outlined in the guidelines must be imposed unless the judge explains on the record why a departure from the guidelines is warranted. Minnesota was the first state to establish a sentencing commission to draft presumptive sentencing guidelines. These guidelines were approved by the legislature in 1980 and have served as a model since then for other jurisdictions contemplating the adoption of sentencing guidelines. Portions of these guidelines and the commentary explaining them are set forth below.

MINNESOTA SENTENCING GUIDELINES AND COMMENTARY
Revised August 1, 1989.

I.   STATEMENT OF PURPOSE AND PRINCIPLES

The purpose of the sentencing guidelines is to establish rational and consistent sentencing standards which reduce sentencing disparity and ensure that sanctions following conviction of a felony are proportional to the severity of the offense of conviction and the extent of the offender's criminal history. Equity in sentencing requires (a) that convicted felons similar with respect to relevant sentencing criteria ought to receive similar sanctions, and (b) that convicted felons substantially different from a typical case with respect to relevant criteria ought to receive different sanctions.

The sentencing guidelines embody the following principles:

1. Sentencing should be neutral with respect to the race, gender, social, or economic status of convicted felons.

2. While commitment to the Commissioner of Corrections is the most severe sanction that can follow conviction of a felony, it is not the only significant sanction available to the sentencing judge. Development of a rational and consistent sentencing policy requires that the severity of sanctions increase in direct proportion to increases in the severity of criminal offenses and the severity of criminal histories of convicted felons.

3. Because the capacities of state and local correctional facilities are finite, use of incarcerative sanctions should be limited to those convicted of more serious offenses or those who have longer criminal histories. To ensure such usage of finite resources, sanctions used in sentencing convicted felons should be the least restrictive necessary to achieve the purposes of the sentence.

4. While the sentencing guidelines are advisory to the sentencing judge, departures from the presumptive sentences established in the guidelines should be made only when substantial and compelling circumstances exist.

II. DETERMINING PRESUMPTIVE SENTENCES

The presumptive sentence for any offender convicted of a felony committed on or after May 1, 1980, is determined by locating the appropriate cell of the Sentencing Guidelines Grid.[h] The grid represents the two dimensions most important in current sentencing and releasing decisions—offense severity and criminal history.

A. Offense Severity: The offense severity level is determined by the offense of conviction. When an offender is convicted of two or more felonies, the severity level is determined by the most severe offense of conviction. Felony offenses are arrayed into ten levels of severity, ranging from low (Severity Level I) to high (Severity Level X). First degree murder is excluded from the sentencing guidelines, because by law the sentence is mandatory imprisonment for life. Offenses listed within each level of severity are deemed to be generally equivalent in severity. The most frequently occurring offenses within each severity level are listed on the vertical axis of the Sentencing Guidelines Grid. The severity level for infrequently occurring offenses can be determined by consulting Section V, entitled "Offense Severity Reference Table."

Comment

II.A.01. Offense severity is determined by the offense of conviction. The Commission thought that serious legal and ethical questions would be raised if punishment were to be determined on the basis of alleged, but unproven, behavior, and prosecutors and defenders would

[h. A copy of the grid can be found on page 174, *infra.*]

be less accountable in plea negotiation. It follows that if the offense of conviction is the standard from which to determine severity, departures from the guidelines should not be permitted for elements of offender behavior not within the statutory definition of the offense of conviction. Thus, if an offender is convicted of simple robbery, a departure from the guidelines to increase the severity of the sentence should not be permitted because the offender possessed a firearm or used another dangerous weapon.

* * *

B. Criminal History: A criminal history index constitutes the horizontal axis of the Sentencing Guidelines Grid. The criminal history index is comprised of the following items: (1) prior felony record; (2) custody status at the time of the offense; (3) prior misdemeanor and gross misdemeanor record; and (4) prior juvenile record for young adult felons.

Comment

II.B.01. The sentencing guidelines reduce the emphasis given to criminal history in sentencing decisions. Under past judicial practice, criminal history was the primary factor in dispositional decisions. Under sentencing guidelines, the offense of conviction is the primary factor, and criminal history is a secondary factor in dispositional decisions. In the past there were no uniform standards regarding what should be included in an offender's criminal history, no weighting format for different types of offenses, and no systematic process to check the accuracy of the information on criminal history.

II.B.02. The guidelines provide uniform standards for the inclusion and weighting of criminal history information. The sentencing hearing provides a process to assure the accuracy of the information in individual cases. These improvements will increase fairness and equity in the consideration of criminal history.

* * *

The offender's criminal history index score is computed in the following manner:

1. Subject to the conditions listed below, the offender is assigned a particular weight for every felony conviction for which a felony sentence was stayed or imposed before the current sentencing or for which a stay of imposition [i] of sentence was given before the current sentencing.

[i. In Minnesota, there is a distinction between what is called a stay of imposition and a stay of execution. The distinction is explained in the definitional section of the guidelines as follows:

Stay of Imposition/Stay of Execution— There are two steps in sentencing—the imposition of a sentence, and the execution of the sentence which was imposed. The imposition of sentence consists of pronouncing the sentence to be served in

prison (for example, three years imprisonment). The execution of an imposed sentence consists of transferring the felon to the custody of the Commissioner of Corrections to serve the prison sentence. A stayed sentence may be accomplished by either a stay of imposition or a stay of execution.

If a stay of imposition is granted, the imposition (or pronouncement) of a prison sentence is delayed to some future

a. The weight assigned to each prior felony sentence is determined according to its severity level, as follows:

Severity Level I–II = ½ point;

Severity Level III–V = 1 point;

Severity Level VI–VII = 1½ point;

Severity Level VIII–X = 2 points; and

Murder 1st Degree = 2 points.

b. When multiple sentences for a single course of conduct were imposed pursuant to Minn.Stats. §§ 609.585 or 609.251,[i] only the offense at the highest severity level is considered;

c. Only the two offenses at the highest severity levels are considered for prior multiple sentences arising out of a single course of conduct in which there were multiple victims;

* * *

e. Prior felony sentences or stays of imposition following felony convictions will not be used in computing the criminal history score if a period of fifteen years has elapsed since the date of discharge from or expiration of the sentence, to the date of the current offense.

Comment

II.B.101. The basic rule for computing the number of prior felony points in the criminal history score is that the offender is assigned a particular weight for every felony conviction for which a felony sentence was stayed or imposed before the current sentencing or for which a stay of imposition of sentence was given before the current sentencing. The felony point total is the sum of these weights. No partial points are given—thus, a person with less than a full point is not given that point. For example, an offender with a total weight of 2½ would have 2 felony points. The Commission determined that it was important to establish a weighting scheme for prior felony sentences to assure a greater degree of proportionality in the current sentencing. Offenders who have a history of serious felonies are considered more culpable than those offenders whose prior felonies consist primarily of low severity, nonviolent offenses.

* * *

date, provided that until that date the offender comply with conditions established by the court. If the offender does comply with those conditions until that date, the case is discharged, and for civil purposes (employment applications, etc.) the offender has a record of a misdemeanor rather than a felony conviction.

If a stay of execution is granted, a prison sentence is pronounced, but the execution (transfer to the custody of the Commissioner of Corrections) is delayed to some future date, provided that until that date the offender comply with conditions established by the court. If the offender does comply with those conditions, the case is discharged, but the offender continues to have a record of a felony conviction.]

[j. Section 609.585 permits a conviction for both a burglary and a crime committed in the course of the burglary, while § 609.251 authorizes a conviction for both the crime of kidnapping and any other crime committed during the kidnapping.]

2. The offender is assigned one point if he or she was on probation or parole or confined in a jail, workhouse, or prison following conviction of a felony or gross misdemeanor, or released pending sentencing at the time the felony was committed for which he or she is being sentenced.

*   *   *

3. Subject to the conditions listed below, the offender is assigned one unit for each misdemeanor conviction and for each gross misdemeanor conviction (excluding traffic offenses with the exception of DWI and aggravated DWI offenses, which are assigned two units each, when the current conviction offense is criminal vehicular operation) for which a sentence was stayed or imposed before the current sentencing. Four such units shall equal one point on the criminal history score, and no offender shall receive more than one point for prior misdemeanor or gross misdemeanor convictions.

a. Only convictions of statutory misdemeanors and gross misdemeanors listed in the *Misdemeanor and Gross Misdemeanor Offense List* (see Section V.) shall be used to compute units. All felony convictions resulting in a misdemeanor or gross misdemeanor sentence shall also be used to compute units.

*   *   *

c. A prior misdemeanor or gross misdemeanor sentence shall not be used in computing the criminal history score if a period of ten years has elapsed since the offender was adjudicated guilty for that offense, to the sentencing date for the current offense. However, this does not apply to misdemeanor sentences that result from successful completion of a stay of imposition for a felony conviction.

Comment

II.B.301. The Commission established a measurement procedure based on units for misdemeanor and gross misdemeanor sentences which are totaled and then converted to a point value. The purpose of this procedure is to provide different weightings for convictions of felonies, gross misdemeanors, and misdemeanors. Under this procedure, misdemeanors and gross misdemeanors are assigned one unit. An offender must have a total of four units to receive one point on the criminal history score. No partial points are given—thus, a person with three units is assigned no point value. As a general rule, the Commission eliminated traffic misdemeanors and gross misdemeanors from consideration. However, the traffic offenses of driving while intoxicated and aggravated driving while intoxicated have particular relevance to the offense of criminal vehicular operation. Therefore, prior misdemeanor and gross misdemeanor sentences for DWI and aggravated DWI shall be used in the computation of the misdemeanor/ gross misdemeanor point when the current conviction offense is criminal vehicular operation.

*   *   *

II.B.302. The Commission placed a limit of one point on the consideration of misdemeanors or gross misdemeanors in the criminal history score. This was done because with no limit on point accrual, persons with lengthy, but relatively minor, misdemeanor records could accrue high criminal history scores and, thus, be subject to inappropriately severe sentences upon their first felony conviction. The Commission limited consideration of misdemeanors to particularly relevant misdemeanors under existing state statute. The Commission believes that only certain misdemeanors and gross misdemeanors are particularly relevant in determining the appropriate sentence for the offender's current felony conviction(s). Offenders whose criminal record includes at least four prior sentences for misdemeanors and gross misdemeanors contained in the *Misdemeanor and Gross Misdemeanor Offense List,* are considered more culpable and are given an additional criminal history point under the guidelines.

* * *

4. The offender is assigned one point for every two offenses committed and prosecuted as a juvenile that would have been felonies if committed by an adult, provided that:

a. Findings were made by the juvenile court pursuant to an admission in court or after trial;

b. Each offense represented a separate behavioral incident or involved separate victims in a single behavioral incident;

c. The juvenile offenses occurred after the offender's sixteenth birthday;

d. The offender had not attained the age of twenty-one at the time the felony was committed for which he or she is being currently sentenced; and

e. No offender may receive more than one point for offenses committed and prosecuted as a juvenile unless at least one of the offenses is Murder, Assault in the 1st or 2nd Degree, Criminal Sexual Conduct in the First, Second, or Third Degree or Aggravated Robbery involving a dangerous weapon. No offender may receive more than two points for offenses committed and prosecuted as a juvenile.

Comment

* * *

II.B.405. [T]he Commission decided that, provided the above conditions are met, it would take two juvenile offenses to equal one point on the criminal history score, and that no offender may receive more than one point on the basis of prior juvenile offenses, unless at least one of the prior offenses was a serious violent offense, subject to provision II.B.4.e., upon which the offender may receive no more than two points. Again, no partial points are allowed, so an offender with only one juvenile offense meeting the above criteria would receive no point on the criminal history score. The two point limit was deemed consistent with the purpose of including the juvenile record in the criminal history—to distinguish the young adult felon with no juvenile record in felony-type behavior from the young adult offender who has a prior juvenile record of repeated felony-type behavior. The two point limit also was deemed advisable to limit the impact of findings obtained under a juvenile court procedure that does not afford the full procedural rights available in adult courts. The former one point limit was expanded to two points to differentiate the youthful violent offender.

* * *

5. The designation of out-of-state convictions as felonies, gross misdemeanors, or misdemeanors shall be governed by the offense definitions and sentences provided in Minnesota law.

* * *

6. The criminal history score is the sum of points accrued under items one through four above.

C. Presumptive Sentence: The offense of conviction determines the appropriate severity level on the vertical axis. The offender's criminal history score, computed according to section B above, determines the appropriate location on the horizontal axis. The presumptive fixed sentence for a felony conviction is found in the Sentencing Guidelines Grid cell at the intersection of the column defined by the criminal history score and the row defined by the offense severity level. The offenses within the Sentencing Guidelines Grid are presumptive with respect to the duration of the sentence and whether imposition or execution of the felony sentence should be stayed.

The line of the Sentencing Guidelines Grid demarcates those cases for whom the presumptive sentence is executed from those for whom the presumptive sentence is stayed. For cases contained in cells below and to the right of the line, the sentence should be executed. For cases contained in cells above and to the left of the line, the sentence should be stayed, unless the conviction offense carries a mandatory minimum sentence.

* * *

Every cell in the Sentencing Guidelines Grid provides a fixed duration of sentence. For cells below the solid line, the guidelines provide both a presumptive prison sentence and a range of time for that sentence. Any prison sentence duration pronounced by the sentencing judge which is outside the range of the presumptive duration is a departure from the guidelines, regardless of whether the sentence is executed or stayed, and requires written reasons from the judge pursuant to Minn.Stat. § 244.10, subd. 2, and section E of these guidelines.

Comment

II.C.01. The guidelines provide sentences which are presumptive with respect to (a) disposition—whether or not the sentence should be executed, and (b) duration—the length of the sentence. For cases below and to the right of the dispositional line, the guidelines create a presumption in favor of execution of the sentence. For cases in cells above and to the left of the dispositional line, the guidelines create a presumption against execution of the sentence, unless the conviction offense carries a mandatory minimum sentence.

The dispositional policy adopted by the Commission was designed so that scarce prison resources would primarily be used for serious person offenders and community resources would be used for most property offenders. The Commission believes that a rational sentencing policy requires such trade-offs, to ensure the availability of correctional resources for the most serious offenders.

* * *

D. Departures From the Guidelines: The sentences provided in the Sentencing Guidelines Grid are presumed to be appropriate for every case. The judge shall utilize the presumptive sentence provided in the sentencing guidelines unless the individual case involves substantial and compelling circumstances. When such circumstances are present, the judge may depart from the presumptive sentence and stay or impose any sentence authorized by law. When departing from the presumptive sentence, the court should pronounce a sentence which is proportional to the severity of the offense of conviction and the extent of the offender's prior criminal history, and should take into substantial consideration the statement of purpose and principles in Section I, above. When departing from the presumptive sentence, a judge must provide written reasons which specify the substantial and compelling nature of the circumstances, and which demonstrate why the sentence selected in the departure is more appropriate, reasonable, or equitable than the presumptive sentence.

Comment

II.D.01. The guideline sentences are presumed to be appropriate for every case. However, there will be a small number of cases where substantial and compelling aggravating or mitigating factors are present. When such factors are present, the judge may depart from the presumptive disposition or duration provided in the guidelines, and stay or impose a sentence that is deemed to be more appropriate, reasonable, or equitable than the presumptive sentence.

II.D.02. Decisions with respect to disposition and duration are logically separate. Departures with respect to disposition and duration also are logically separate decisions. A judge may depart from the presumptive disposition without departing from the presumptive duration, and vice-versa. A judge who departs from the presumptive disposition as well as the presumptive duration has made two separate departure decisions, each requiring written reasons.

II.D.03. The aggravating or mitigating factors and the written reasons supporting the departure must be substantial and compelling to overcome the presumption in favor of the guideline sentence. The purposes of the sentencing guidelines cannot be achieved unless the presumptive sentences are applied with a high degree of regularity. Sentencing disparity cannot be reduced if judges depart from the guidelines frequently. Certainty in sentencing cannot be attained if departure rates are high. Prison populations will exceed capacity if departures increase imprisonment rates significantly above past practice.

1. *Factors that should not be used as reasons for departure:* The following factors should not be used as reasons for departing from the presumptive sentences provided in the Sentencing Guidelines Grid:

    a. Race

    b. Sex

    c. Employment factors, including:

        (1) occupation or impact of sentence on profession or occupation;

        (2) employment history;

        (3) employment at time of offense;

        (4) employment at time of sentencing.

    d. Social factors, including:

        (1) educational attainment;

        (2) living arrangements at time of offense or sentencing;

        (3) length of residence;

        (4) marital status.

    e. The exercise of constitutional rights by the defendant during the adjudication process.

Comment

II.D.101. The Commission believes that sentencing should be neutral with respect to offenders' race, sex, and income levels. Accordingly, the Commission has listed several factors which should not be used as reasons for departure from the presumptive sentence, because these factors are highly correlated with sex, race, or income levels. Employment is excluded as a reason for departure not only because of its correlation with race and income levels, but also because this factor is manipulable—offenders could lessen the severity of the sentence by obtaining employment between arrest and sentencing. While it may be desirable for offenders to obtain employment between arrest and sentencing, some groups (those with low income levels, low education levels, and racial minorities generally) find it more difficult to obtain employment than others. It is impossible to reward those employed without, in fact, penalizing those not employed at time of sentencing. The use of the factors "amenable to probation (or treatment)" or "unamenable to probation" to justify a dispositional departure, could be closely related to social and economic factors. The use of these factors, alone, to explain the reason for departure is insufficient and the trial court shall demonstrate that the departure is not based on any of the excluded factors.

* * *

2. *Factors that may be used as reasons for departure:* The following is a *nonexclusive* list of factors which may be used as reasons for departure:

a. *Mitigating Factors:*

(1) The victim was an aggressor in the incident.

(2) The offender played a minor or passive role in the crime or participated under circumstances of coercion or duress.

(3) The offender, because of physical or mental impairment, lacked substantial capacity for judgment when the offense was committed. The voluntary use of intoxicants (drugs or alcohol) does not fall within the purview of this factor.

(4) The offender's presumptive sentence is a commitment to the commissioner but not a mandatory minimum sentence, and either of the following exist:

(a) The current conviction offense is at severity level I or II and the offender received all of his or her prior felony sentences during less than three separate court appearances; or

(b) The current conviction offense is at severity level III or IV and the offender received all of his or her prior felony sentences during one court appearance.

(5) Other substantial grounds exist which tend to excuse or mitigate the offender's culpability, although not amounting to a defense.

b. *Aggravating Factors:*

(1) The victim was particularly vulnerable due to age, infirmity, or reduced physical or mental capacity, which was known or should have been known to the offender.

(2) The victim was treated with particular cruelty for which the individual offender should be held responsible.

(3) The current conviction is for a Criminal Sexual Conduct offense or an offense in which the victim was otherwise injured and there is a prior felony conviction for a Criminal Sexual Conduct offense or an offense in which the victim was otherwise injured.

(4) The offense was a major economic offense, identified as an illegal act or series of illegal acts committed by other than physical means and by concealment or guile to obtain money or property, to avoid payment or loss of money or property, or to obtain business or professional advantage. The presence of

two or more of the circumstances listed below are aggravating factors with respect to the offense:

(a) the offense involved multiple victims or multiple incidents per victim;

(b) the offense involved an attempted or actual monetary loss substantially greater than the usual offense or substantially greater than the minimum loss specified in the statutes;

(c) the offense involved a high degree of sophistication or planning or occurred over a lengthy period of time;

(d) the defendant used his or her position or status to facilitate the commission of the offense, including positions of trust, confidence, or fiduciary relationships; or

(e) the defendant has been involved in other conduct similar to the current offense as evidenced by the findings of civil or administrative law proceedings or the imposition of professional sanctions.

(5) The offense was a major controlled substance offense, identified as an offense or series of offenses related to trafficking in controlled substances under circumstances more onerous than the usual offense. The presence of two or more of the circumstances listed below are aggravating factors with respect to the offense:

(a) the offense involved at least three separate transactions wherein controlled substances were sold, transferred, or possessed with intent to do so; or

(b) the offense involved an attempted or actual sale or transfer of controlled substances in quantities substantially larger than for personal use; or

(c) the offense involved the manufacture of controlled substances for use by other parties; or

(d) the offender knowingly possessed a firearm during the commission of the offense; or

(e) the circumstances of the offense reveal the offender to have occupied a high position in the drug distribution hierarchy; or

(f) the offense involved a high degree of sophistication or planning or occurred over a lengthy period of time or involved a broad geographic area of disbursement; or

(g) the offender used his or her position or status to facilitate the commission of the offense, including positions of trust, confidence or fiduciary relationships (e.g., pharmacist, physician or other medical professional).

(6) The offender committed, for hire, a crime against the person.

(7) The offender committed a crime against the person in furtherance of criminal activity by an organized gang. An "organized gang" is defined as an association of five or more persons, with an established hierarchy, formed to encourage gang members to perpetrate crimes or to provide support to gang members who do commit crimes.

(8) The offender was convicted of a controlled substance offense in violation of chapter 152 and the offense was committed in a park zone or in a school zone as defined in chapter 152.01.

* * *

(9) Offender is a "patterned sex offender" (See Minn.Stat. § 609.1352).

Comment

II.D.201. The Commission provided a non-exclusive list of reasons which may be used as reasons for departure. The factors are intended to describe specific situations involving a small number of cases. * * * Some of these factors may be considered in establishing conditions of stayed sentences, even though they may not be used as reasons for departure. For example, whether or not a person is employed at time of sentencing may be an important factor in deciding whether restitution should be used as a condition of probation, or in deciding on the terms of restitution payment.

II.D.202. The Commission recognizes that the criminal history score does not differentiate between the crime spree offender who has been convicted of several offenses but has not been previously sanctioned by the criminal justice system and the repeat offender who continues to commit new crimes despite receiving previous consequences from the criminal justice system. The Commission believes the nonviolent crime spree offender should perhaps be sanctioned in the community at least once or twice before a prison sentence is appropriate. At this time, the Commission believes that the judge is best able to distinguish these offenders and can depart from the guidelines accordingly.

* * *

F. Concurrent/Consecutive Sentences:[k] When an offender is convicted of multiple current offenses, or when there is a prior felony sentence which has not expired or been discharged, concurrent sentences shall be given in all cases not covered below. The most severe offense among multiple current offenses determines the appro-

[k. With concurrent sentences, an offender serves several sentences at the same time. When consecutive sentences are imposed, the offender first serves one sentence and then the other. Thus, if a defendant was convicted of two armed robberies and sentenced to two years in prison for each robbery with the sentences to run concurrently, the defendant would spend two years in prison minus good time. By contrast, if the sentences imposed were to run consecutively, the defendant would spend four years in prison minus good time.]

priate offense severity level for purposes of determining the presumptive guideline sentence.

Consecutive sentences may be given only in the following cases:

1. When a prior felony sentence for a crime against a person has not expired or been discharged and one or more of the current felony convictions is for a crime against a person, and when the sentence for the most severe current conviction is executed according to the guidelines; *or*

2. When the offender is convicted of multiple current felony convictions for crimes against different persons, and when the sentence for the most severe current conviction is executed according to the guidelines; *or*

3. When the conviction is for escape from lawful custody, as defined in Minn.Stat. § 609.485. The presumptive disposition for escapes from executed sentences shall be execution of the escape sentence. If the executed escape sentence is to be served concurrently with other sentences, the presumptive duration shall be that indicated by the appropriate cell of the Sentencing Guidelines Grid. If the executed escape sentence is to be served consecutively to other sentences, the presumptive duration shall be that indicated by the aggregation process set forth below.

The use of consecutive sentences in any other case constitutes a departure from the guidelines and requires written reasons pursuant to Minn.Stat. § 244.10, subd. 2 and section E of these guidelines.

For persons given consecutive sentences, the sentence durations for each separate offense sentenced consecutively shall be aggregated into a single presumptive sentence. The presumptive duration for offenses sentenced consecutively is determined by locating the Sentencing Guidelines Grid cell defined by the most severe offense and the offender's criminal history score and by adding to the duration shown therein the duration indicated for every other offense sentenced consecutively at their respective levels of severity but at the zero criminal history column on the Grid. The purpose of this procedure is to count an individual's criminal history score only one time in the computation of consecutive sentence durations.

* * *

Comment

* * *

II.F.06. The criterion that crimes must be against different persons for permissive consecutive sentencing is designed to exclude consecutive sentences in two types of situations. One type involves multiple offenses against a victim in a single behavioral incident such as burglary with a dangerous weapon and aggravated robbery with bodily harm. The requirement of different victims is also intended to exclude consecutive sentences in domestic abuse and child abuse situations when there are multiple incidents perpetrated against a victim over time. Assault, criminal sexual conduct, and incest are the conviction offenses most frequently found in domestic abuse and child abuse cases. Multiple incidents against a victim typifies these types of situations. In fact, one criminal sexual conduct provision delineates multiple incidents as an element of the offense. The high severity rankings assigned to offenses that tend to involve very young victims reflect the understanding that multiple incidents generally occur in these kinds of situations. The Commission believes that a uniform policy reflected in high severity rankings provides the best approach in sentencing these cases. Permissive consecutive sentences would result in enormous disparity based on varying charging practices of prosecutors and discretionary judicial decisions.

*   *   *

III. RELATED POLICIES

A. Establishing Conditions of Stayed Sentences:

1. *Method of Granting Stayed Sentences:* When the appropriate cell of the Sentencing Guidelines Grid provides a stayed sentence, and when the judge chooses to grant that stay by means of a stay of execution, the duration of prison sentence shown in the appropriate cell is pronounced, but its execution is stayed. When the judge chooses to grant the stay by means of a stay of imposition, the duration of the prison sentence in the appropriate cell is not pronounced and the imposition of the sentence is stayed. The judge would then establish conditions which are deemed appropriate for the stayed sentence, including establishing a length of probation, which may exceed the duration of the presumptive prison sentence.

The Commission recommends that stays of imposition be used as the means of granting a stayed sentence for felons convicted of lower severity offenses with low criminal history scores. The Commission further recommends that convicted felons be given one stay of imposition, although for very low severity offenses, a second stay of imposition may be appropriate.

Comment

III.A.101. When the presumptive sentence is a stay, the judge may grant the stay by means of either a stay of imposition or a stay of execution. The use of either a stay of imposition or stay of execution is at the discretion of the judge. The Commission has provided a non-presumptive recommendation regarding which categories of offenders should receive stays of imposition, and has recommended that convicted felons generally should receive only one stay of imposition. The Commission believes that stays of imposition are a less severe sanction, and ought to be used for those convicted of less serious offenses and those with short criminal histories. Under current sentencing practices, judges use stays of imposition most frequently for these types of offenders.

*   *   *

2. *Conditions of Stayed Sentences:* The Commission has chosen not to develop specific guidelines relating to the conditions of stayed sentences. The Commission recognizes that there are several penal objectives to be considered in establishing conditions of stayed sentences, including, but not limited to, retribution, rehabilitation, public protection, restitution, deterrence, and public condemnation of criminal conduct. The Commission also recognizes that the relative importance of these objectives may vary with both offense and offender characteristics and that multiple objectives may be present in any given sentence. The development of principled standards for establishing conditions of stayed sentences requires that judges first consider the objectives to be served by a stayed sentence and, second, consider the resources available to achieve those objectives. When retribution is an important objective of a stayed sentence, the severity of the retributive sanction should be proportional to the severity of the offense and the prior criminal record of the offender, and judges should consider the availability and adequacy of local jail or correctional facilities in establishing such sentences. The Commission urges judges to utilize the least restrictive conditions of stayed sentences that are consistent with the objectives of the sanction. When rehabilitation is an important objective of a stayed sentence, judges are urged to make full use of local programs and resources available to accomplish the rehabilitative objectives. The absence of a rehabilitative resource, in general, should not be a basis for enhancing the retributive objective in sentencing and, in particular, should not be a basis for more extensive use of incarceration than is justified on other grounds. The Commission urges judges to make expanded use of restitution and community work orders as conditions of a stayed sentence, especially for persons with short criminal histories who are convicted of property crimes, although the use of such conditions in other cases may be appropriate. Supervised probation should continue as a primary condition of stayed sentences. To the extent that fines are used, the Commission urges the expanded use of day fines, which standardizes the financial impact of the sanction among offenders with different income levels.

Comment

III.A.201. The judge may attach any conditions to a stayed sentence which are permitted by law and which he or she deems appropriate. The guidelines neither enlarge nor restrict the conditions that judges may attach to a stayed sentence. Laws 1978, Chapter 723 permits, but does not require, the Commission to establish guidelines covering conditions of stayed sentences. The Commission chose not to develop such guidelines during their initial guideline development effort. The Commission has provided some language in the above section of the guidelines which provides general direction in the use of conditions of stayed sentences.

* * *

B. Revocation of Stayed Sentences: The decision to imprison an offender following a revocation of a stayed sentence should not be undertaken lightly and, in particular, should not be a reflexive reaction to technical violations of the conditions of the stay. Great restraint should be exercised in imprisoning those violating conditions of a stayed sentence who were convicted originally of low severity offenses or who have short prior criminal histories. Rather the Commission urges the use of more restrictive and onerous conditions of a stayed sentence, such as periods of local confinement. Less judicial forbearance is urged for persons violating conditions of a stayed sentence who were convicted of a more severe offense or who had a longer criminal history. Even in these cases, however, imprisonment upon a technical violation of the conditions of a stayed sentence should not be reflexive.

The Commission would view commitment to the Commissioner of Corrections following revocation of a stayed sentence to be justified when:

    1. The offender has been convicted of a new felony for which the guidelines would recommend imprisonment; or

    2. Despite prior use of expanded and more onerous conditions of a stayed sentence, the offender persists in violating conditions of the stay.

* * *

C. Jail Credit: Pursuant to Minn.Stat. § 609.145, subd. 2, and Minn.R.Crim.P. 27.03, subd. 4(b), when a convicted felon is committed to the custody of the Commissioner of Corrections, the court shall assure that the record accurately reflects all time spent in custody between arrest and sentencing, including examinations under Minn.R. Crim.P. 20 or 27.03, subd. 1(A), for the offense or behavioral incident for which the person is sentenced, which time shall be deducted by the Commissioner of Corrections from the sentence imposed. Time spent in confinement as a condition of a stayed sentence when the stay is later revoked and the offender committed to the custody of the Commissioner of Corrections shall be included in the above record, and shall be deducted from the sentence imposed. * * *

Comment

III.C.01. The Commission believes that offenders should receive jail credit for time spent in custody between arrest and sentencing. During that time, the defendant is presumed innocent. There is evidence that the poor and members of racial minorities are more likely to be subject to pre-trial detention than others. Granting such jail credit for those receiving executed sentences makes the total periods of incarceration more equitable.

* * *

F. Modifications: Modifications to the Minnesota Sentencing Guidelines will be applied to offenders whose date of offense is on or after the specified modification effective date. Modifications to the

Commentary will be applied to offenders sentenced on or after the specified effective date.

IV. SENTENCING GUIDELINES GRID

Presumptive Sentence Lengths in Months

Italicized numbers within the grid denote the range within which a judge may sentence without the sentence being deemed a departure.

Offenders with nonimprisonment felony sentences are subject to jail time according to law.

SEVERITY LEVELS OF CONVICTION OFFENSE		CRIMINAL HISTORY SCORE						
		0	1	2	3	4	5	6 or more
Sale of a Simulated Controlled Substance	I	12*	12*	12*	13	15	17	19 18-20
Theft Related Crimes ($2500 or less) Check Forgery ($200-$2500)	II	12*	12*	13	15	17	19	21 20-22
Theft Crimes ($2500 or less)	III	12*	13	15	17	19 18-20	22 21-23	25 24-26
Nonresidential Burglary Theft Crimes (over $2500)	IV	12*	15	18	21	25 24-26	32 30-34	41 37-45
Residential Burglary Simple Robbery	V	18	23	27	30 29-31	38 36-40	46 43-49	54 50-58
Criminal Sexual Conduct 2nd Degree (a) & (b)	VI	21	26	30	34 33-35	44 42-46	54 50-58	65 60-70
Aggravated Robbery	VII	48 44-52	58 54-62	68 64-72	78 74-82	88 84-92	98 94-102	108 104-112
Criminal Sexual Conduct, 1st Degree Assault, 1st Degree	VIII	86 81-91	98 93-103	110 105-115	122 117-127	134 129-139	146 141-151	158 153-163
Murder, 3rd Degree Murder, 2nd Degree (felony murder)	IX	150 144-156	165 159-171	180 174-186	195 189-201	210 204-216	225 219-231	240 234-246
Murder, 2nd Degree (with intent)	X	306 299-313	326 319-333	346 339-353	366 359-373	386 379-393	406 399-413	426 419-433

1st Degree Murder is excluded from the guidelines by law and continues to have a mandatory life sentence. See section **II.E. Mandatory Sentences** for policy regarding those sentences controlled by law.

At the discretion of the judge, up to a year in jail and/or other non-jail sanctions can be imposed as conditions of probation.

Presumptive commitment to state imprisonment.   * one year and one day

35

V. OFFENSE SEVERITY REFERENCE TABLE

First Degree Murder is excluded from the guidelines by law, and continues to have a mandatory life sentence.

X
Adulteration—609.687, subd. 3(1)
Murder 2—609.19(1)
Murder 2 of an Unborn Child—609.2662(1)

IX
Murder 2—609.19(2)
Murder 2 of an Unborn Child—609.2662(2)
Murder 3—609.195(a)
Murder 3 of an Unborn Child—609.2663

VIII
Assault 1—609.221
Assault 1 of an Unborn Child—609.267
Controlled Substance Crime in the First Degree—152.021
Criminal Sexual Conduct 1—609.342
Death of an Unborn Child in Commission of Crime—609.268, subd. 1
Kidnapping (w/great bodily harm)—609.25, subd. 2(2)
Manslaughter 1—609.20(1) & (2)
Manslaughter 1 of an Unborn Child—609.2664(1) & (2)
Murder 3—609.195(b)
Prostitution (Patron)—609.324, subd. 1(a)
Receiving Profit Derived from Prostitution—609.323, subd. 1
Solicitation of Prostitution—609.322, subd. 1

VII
Aggravated Robbery—609.245
Arson 1—609.561
Burglary 1—609.582, subd. 1(b) & (c)
Controlled Substance Crime in the Second Degree—152.022
Controlled Substance Crime in the Third Degree—152.023, subd. 2(1) & (2)
Criminal Sexual Conduct 2—609.343, subd. 1(c), (d), (e), (f), & (h)
Criminal Sexual Conduct 3—609.344, subd. 1(c), (d), (g), (h), (i), (j), & (k)
Fleeing Peace Officer (resulting in death)—609.487, subd. 4(a)
Great Bodily Harm Caused by Distribution of Drugs—609.228
Kidnapping (not in safe place)—609.25, subd. 2(2)
Manslaughter 1—609.20(3) & (4)
Manslaughter 1 of an Unborn Child—609.2664(3)
Manslaughter 2—609.205(1)
Manslaughter 2 of an Unborn Child—609.2665(1)

Arson 2—609.562
Assault 2—609.222
Bringing Stolen Goods into State (over $2,500)—609.525
Burglary 1—609.582, subd. 1(a)
Controlled Substance Crime in the Third Degree—152.023, subd.
 1 and subd. 2(3), (4), & (5)
Criminal Sexual Conduct 2—609.343, subd. 1(a), (b) & (g)
Criminal Sexual Conduct 4—609.345, subd. 1(c), (d), (g), (h), (i),
 (j), & (k)
Criminal Vehicular Operation—609.21, subd. 1 & 3
Escape from Custody—609.485, subd. 4(5)

VI Failure to Affix Stamp on Cocaine—297D.09, subd. 1
Failure to Affix Stamp on Hallucinogens or PCP—297D.09,
 subd. 1
Failure to Affix Stamp on Heroin—297D.09, subd. 1
Failure to Affix Stamp on Remaining Schedule I & II Narcot-
 ics—297D.09, subd. 1
Fleeing Peace Officer (great bodily harm)—609.487, subd. 4(b)
Kidnapping—609.25, subd. 2(1)
Precious Metal Dealers, Receiving Stolen Goods (over $2,500)—
 609.526, (1)
Precious Metal Dealers, Receiving Stolen Goods (over $300)—
 609.526, second or subsequent violations
Price Fixing/Collusive Bidding—325D.53, subd. 1(2)(a)
Theft over $35,000—609.52, subd. 3(1)

Bringing Stolen Goods into State ($1,000–$2,500)—609.525
Burglary—609.582, subd. 2(a) & (b)
Check Forgery over $35,000—609.631, subd. 4(1)
Criminal Sexual Conduct 3—609.344, subd. 1(b), (e), & (f)
Criminal Vehicular Operation—609.21, subd. 2 and 4
Financial Transaction Card Fraud over $35,000—609.821, subd.
 3(1)(i)
Manslaughter 2—609.205(2), (3), & (4)
V Manslaughter 2 of an Unborn Child—609.2665(2), (3), & (4)
Perjury—609.48, subd. 4(1)
Possession of Incendiary Device—299F.79; 299F.80, subd. 1;
 299F.811; 299F.815; 299F.82, subd. 1
Price Fixing/Collusive Bidding—325D.53, subd. 1(1), and subd.
 1(2)(b) & (c)
Prostitution (Patron)—609.324, subd. 1(b)
Receiving Profit Derived from Prostitution—609.323, subd. 1a
Simple Robbery—609.24
Solicitation of Prostitution—609.322, subd. 1a
Tampering w/Witness—609.498, subd. 1

Accidents—169.09, subd. 14(a)(1)

Adulteration—609.687, subd. 3(2)

Assault 2 of an Unborn Child—609.2671

Assault 3—609.223

Bribery—609.42; 90.41; 609.86

Bring Contraband into State Prison—243.55

Bring Dangerous Weapon into County Jail—641.165. subd. 2(b)

Bring Stolen Goods into State ($301–$999)—609.525

Burglary 2—609.582, subd. 2(c) & (d)

Burglary 3—609.582, subd. 3

Controlled Substance Crime in the Fourth Degree—152.024

Criminal Sexual Conduct 4—609.345, subd. 1(b), (e), & (f)

False Imprisonment—609.255, subd. 3

Fleeing Peace Officer (substantial bodily harm)—609.487, subd. 4(c)

Injury of an Unborn Child in Commission of Crime—609.268, subd. 2

Malicious Punishment of Child—609.377

Negligent Fires—609.576, subd. 1(a)

IV   Perjury—290.53, subd. 4; 300.61; & 609.48, subd. 4(2)

Precious Metal Dealers, Receiving Stolen Goods ($301–$2,500)—609.526(1) & (2)

Receiving Stolen Goods (over $2,500)—609.53

Receiving Stolen Property (firearm)—609.53

Security Violations (over $2,500)—80A.22, subd. 1; 80B.10, subd. 1; 80C.16, subd. 3(a) & (b)

Sports Bookmaking—609.75, subd. 7

Tax Evasion—290.53, subd. 4 & 8

Tax Withheld at Source; Fraud (over $2,500)—290.92, subd. 15(5) & (12), 290A.11, subd. 2

Terroristic Threats—609.713, subd. 1

Theft Crimes—Over $2,500 (*See Theft Offense List*)

Theft from Person—609.52

Theft of Controlled Substances—609.52, subd. 3(2)

Theft of Motor Vehicle—609.52, subd. 3(3)(d)(vi)

Use of Drugs to Injure or Facilitate Crime—609.235

Accidents—169.09, subd. 14(a)(2)

Arson 3—609.563

Check Forgery (over $2,500)—609.631, subd. 4(2)

Coercion—609.27, subd. 1(1)

Coercion (over $2,500)—609.27. subd. 1(2), (3), (4), & (5)

Damage to Property—609.595, subd. 1(1)

Dangerous Smoking—609.576, subd. 2

Dangerous Trespass, Railroad Tracks—609.85(1)

Dangerous Weapons—609.67. subd. 2; 624.713, subd. 1(b)

Depriving Another of Custodial or Parental Rights—609.26, subd. 6(2)

Escape from Custody—609.485, subd. 4(1)

False Imprisonment—609.255, subd. 2

False Traffic Signal—609.851, subd. 2

Intentional Release of Harmful Substance—624.732, subd. 2

Motor Vehicle Use without Consent—609.52, subd. 2(17)

III Negligent Discharge of Explosive—299F.83

Possession of Burglary Tools—609.59

Possession of Shoplifting Gear—609.521

Prostitution (Patron)—609.324, subd. 1(c)

Receiving Profit Derived from Prostitution—609.323, subd. 2

Receiving Stolen Goods ($2,500 or less)—609.53

Security Violations (under $2,500)—80A.22, subd. 1; 80B.10, subd. 1; 80C.16, subd. 3(a) & (b)

Solicitation of Children to Engage in Sexual Conduct—609.352, subd. 2

Solicitation of Prostitution—609.322, subd. 2

Tax Withheld at Source; Fraud ($301–$2,500)—290.92, subd. 25(5) & (12); 290A.11, subd. 2

Tear Gas & Tear Gas Compounds—624.731, subd. 3(b)

Theft Crimes—$2,500 or less (See Theft Offense List)

Theft of Controlled Substances—609.52, subd. 3(3)(b)

Theft of a Firearm—609.52, subd. 3(3)(d)(v)

Theft of Public Records—609.52

Theft Related Crimes—Over $2,500 (See Theft Related Offense List)

Unauthorized Presence at Camp Ripley—609.396, subd. 2

Accidents—169.09, subd. 14(a)(3) & (b)(1)

Aggravated Forgery (misc.) (non-check)—609.625; 609.635, 609.64

Check Forgery ($200–$2,500)—609.631, subd. 4(3)(a)

Coercion ($300–$2,500)—609.27, subd. 1(2), (3), (4), & (5)

Controlled Substance in the Fifth Degree—152.025

Damage to Property—609.595, subd. 1(2), (3), & (4)

II Failure to Affix Stamp on Remaining Schedule I, II, & III Non-Narcotics—297D.09, subd. 1

Negligent Fires (damage greater than $10,000)—609.576, subd. 1(b)(3)

Precious Metal Dealers, Regulatory Provisions—325F.743

Riot—609.71

Terroristic Threats—609.713, subd. 2

Theft-Looting—609.52

Theft Related Crimes—$2,500 or less (See Theft Related Offense List)

Accidents—169.09, subd. 14(b)(2)

Aiding Offender to Avoid Arrest—609.495

Assault 4—609.2231, subd. 1

Assaults Motivated by Bias—609.2231, subd. 4(b)

Cable Communication Systems Interference—609.80, subd. 2

Check Forgery (less than $200)—609.631, subd. 4(3)(b)

Criminal Damage to Property Motivated by Bias—609.595, subd. 1a, (a)

Depriving Another of Custodial or Parental Rights—609.26, subd. 6(1)

Escape from Custody—609.485, subd. 4(2)

Failure to Affix Stamp on Marijuana/Hashish/Tetrahydrocannabinols—297D.09, subd. 1

Failure to Affix Stamp on Schedule IV Substances—297D.09, subd. 1

Financial Transaction Card Fraud—609.821, subd. 2(3) & (4)

Fleeing a Police Officer—609.487, subd. 3

Forgery—609.63; and Forgery Related Crimes (*See Forgery Related Offense List*)

Leaving State to Evade Establishment of Paternity—609.31

Nonsupport of Wife or Child—609.375, subd. 2, 3, & 4

Sale of Simulated Controlled Substance—152.097

Solicitation of Prostitution—609.322, subd. 3

Terroristic Threats—609.713, subd. 3(a)

Unlawful Acts Involving Liquor—340A.701

Voting Violations—201.014; 201.016; 201.054

Theft Offense List

It is recommended that the following property crimes be treated similarly. This is the list cited for the two THEFT CRIMES ($2,500 or less and over $2,500) in the Offense Severity Reference Table.

Altering Serial Number
609.52, subd. 2(10) & (11)

Computer Damage
609.88

Computer Theft
609.89

Diversion of Corporate Property
609.52, subd. 2(15) & (16)

Embezzlement of Public Funds
609.54

Failure to Pay Over State Funds
609.445

False Declaration of Claim
471.392

Permitting False Claims Against Government
609.455

Rustling and Livestock Theft
609.551

Theft
609.52, subd. 2(1)

Theft by Soldier of Military Goods
192.36

Theft by Trick
609.52, subd. 2(4)

Theft of Public Funds
609.52

Theft of Trade Secret
609.52, subd. 2(8)

Theft Related Offense List

It is recommended that the following property crimes be treated similarly. This is the list cited for the two THEFT RELATED CRIMES ($2,500 or less and over $2,500) in the Offense Severity Reference Table.

Defeating Security on Personalty
609.62

Defeating Security on Realty
609.615

Defrauding Insurer
609.611

Federal Food Stamp Program
393.07, subd. 10

Financial Transaction Card Fraud
609.821, subd. 2(1), (2), (5), (6), (7), & (8)

Fraud in Obtaining Credit
609.82

Fraudulent Long Distance Telephone Calls
609.785

Medical Assistance Fraud
609.466

Presenting False Claims to Public Officer or Body
609.465

Refusing to Return Lost Property
609.52, subd. 2(6)

Taking Pledged Property
609.52, subd. 2(2)

Temporary Theft
609.52, subd. 2(5)

Theft by Check
609.52, subd. 2(3)

Theft of Cable TV Services
609.52, subd. 2(12)

Theft of Leased Property
609.52, subd. 2(9)

Theft of Services
609.52, subd. 2(13)

Theft of Telecommunications Services
609.52, subd. 2(14)

Wrongfully Obtaining Assistance
256.98

Forgery Related Offense List

It is recommended that the following property crimes be treated similarly. This is the list cited for the FORGERY and FORGERY RELATED CRIMES in the Offense Severity Reference Table.

Altering Livestock Certificate
35.824

Altering Packing House Certificate
226.05

Destroy or Falsify Private Business Record
609.63, subd. 1(5)

Destroy or Falsify Public Record
609.63, subd. 1(6)

Destroy Writing to Prevent Use at Trial
609.63, subd. 1(7)

False Bill of Lading
228.45; 228.47; 228.49; 228.50; 228.51

False Certification by Notary Public
609.65

False Information—Certificate of Title Application
168A.30

False Membership Card
609.63, subd. 1(3)

False Merchandise Stamp
609.63, subd. 1(2)

Fraudulent Statements
609.645

Obtaining Signature by False Pretense
609.635

Offer Forged Writing at Trial
609.63, subd. 2

Use False Identification
609.63, subd. 1(1)

Misdemeanor and Gross Misdemeanor Offense List

The following misdemeanors and gross misdemeanors will be used to compute units in the criminal history score. All felony convictions resulting in a misdemeanor or gross misdemeanor sentence shall also be used to compute units.

Arson 3rd Degree
609.563, subd. 2

Assault
609.224

Burglary 4th Degree
609.582

Carrying Pistol
624.714

Check Forgery
609.631

Contributing to Delinquency of Minor
260.315

Criminal Sexual Conduct 5th Degree
609.3451

Damage to Property
609.595

Dangerous Weapons
609.66

Fleeing a Police Officer
609.487

Furnishing Liquor to Persons Under 21
340A.503

Indecent Exposure
617.23

Interference with Privacy
609.746

Possession of Small Amount of Marijuana in Motor Vehicle
152.15

Possession of Stolen Property
609.53

Theft
609.52, subd. 2(1)

Trespass (gross misdemeanor)
609.605

Violating an Order for Protection
518B.01, subd. 14

* * *

Questions and Points for Discussion

1. How, if at all, would you modify the Minnesota sentencing guidelines? Assume that the Minnesota sentencing guidelines apply in each of the following cases. Before referring to the guidelines, consider what sentence you believe would be appropriate in each case and why. Is there any additional information which you would want to know in arriving at an appropriate sentence?

Now apply the guidelines to these cases. How did the presumptive sentences under the guidelines differ from your initial views about the appropriate penalty? Upon reflection, which penalty is most appropriate?

Case # 1

Defendant is convicted of aggravated robbery. In Minnesota, aggravated robbery is defined as a robbery committed while armed with a dangerous weapon or during which the perpetrator inflicts bodily harm upon another. The defendant is 21–years–old. He has no immediate family, limited work skills, and a bad employment record. He also has a severe drug problem. Defendant has three prior convictions, two for burglary and one for robbery. He served 18 months on the last conviction and received probation on each of the first two. Defendant was a juvenile when he committed the burglaries. In the robbery for which the defendant is awaiting sentencing, the victim was assaulted and received a laceration on his skull which required surgical care.

Case # 2

Defendant Patty Hearst is convicted of aggravated robbery. She is in her early 20's, comes from a wealthy family, is well-educated, and has no prior convictions. Ms. Hearst was kidnapped by a group of revolutionaries and later participated with them in the bank robbery for which she was convicted. Her defense was that she committed the crime out of fear for her safety since she was under the control of the kidnappers. The jury did not believe her.

Case # 3

Defendant is convicted of embezzlement of $2,500 from a bank where he is employed. Defendant took the money to pay off gambling and loansharking debts. He is in his late 20's, is married, and has two young children. He is also a college graduate, has been employed at the bank for eight years, is reasonably well-paid, and has no prior criminal record.

2. The Minnesota sentencing guidelines have to some extent succeeded in achieving two of their objectives—reducing sentencing disparity and ensuring that the punishment meted out in a particular case is proportionate to the severity of the crime committed. During the first three years after the guidelines were adopted, judges adhered to the dispositional prescriptions of the guidelines, which govern the "in-out decision," in over

90% of the cases covered by the guidelines. M. Tonry, Sentencing Reform Impacts 61 (National Institute of Justice 1987). Compliance with the durational prescriptions of the guidelines was also quite high. Id. at 61–62. In addition, the use of the imprisonment sanction for non-violent offenders was drastically decreased as prison resources were directed more towards punishing violent offenders. During the first year in which the guidelines were in effect, for example, only 15% of offenders convicted of minor property crimes were sentenced to prison, 72% less than were imprisoned before the guidelines were adopted. Id. at 68. On the other hand, 78% of the offenders with no criminal history or low criminal history scores who were convicted of serious, violent crimes were imprisoned, 73% more than before implementation of the guidelines. Id.

3. The initial success of the Minnesota sentencing guidelines was somewhat tempered in later years by attempts to circumvent the guidelines through charging decisions and negotiations. Displeasure with what many prosecutors consider the too lenient treatment of property offenders under the guidelines led them to file more charges against such offenders and to require guilty pleas to more such charges than in the past. Id. at 71–73. For example, while in pre-guidelines days, prosecutors might agree to entry of a plea of guilty to one count of burglary by a defendant charged with several burglaries, after adoption of the guidelines, prosecutors often insisted on a plea of guilty to several of the burglaries to increase an offender's criminal history score. On the other hand, since the offense severity level is based on the offense of conviction, what was considered too severe a penalty could be avoided through charge reductions.

Other jurisdictions have taken steps to avoid similar circumvention of sentencing guidelines. The state of Washington, for example, has, in conjunction with sentencing guidelines, adopted guidelines to govern prosecutorial charging and bargaining practices. Wash.Rev.Code §§ 9.94A.430–.460. The federal sentencing guidelines, on the other hand, take a different approach to limit to a certain extent the effects of plea bargaining on the operation of the guidelines, adopting a modified version of what is called "real offense" sentencing. As is apparent from § 1B1.2(a) of the guidelines, which is set forth below, the offense severity level under the guidelines is not exclusively or always determined by the offense of conviction.

> The court shall apply the guideline in Chapter Two (Offense Conduct) most applicable to the offense of conviction. *Provided,* however, in the case of conviction by a plea of guilty or *nolo contendere* containing a stipulation that specifically establishes a more serious offense than the offense of conviction, the court shall apply the guideline in such chapter most applicable to the stipulated offense.

See also § 3–206(d) of the Uniform Law Commissioners' Model Sentencing and Corrections Act, which provides that when sentencing, a court "shall consider the nature and characteristics of the criminal conduct involved without regard to the offense charged," except that the sentence can be no higher than that authorized for the offense of conviction.

What do you believe, is the appropriate focus when determining offense severity level under sentencing guidelines—the offense of conviction or the "real offense?" For one view on the advisability of "real offense" sentencing, see Tonry, Real Offense Sentencing: The Model Sentencing and Corrections Act, 72 J.Crim.L. & Criminology 1550 (1981).

4. The federal sentencing guidelines differ from the Minnesota sentencing guidelines in a number of different ways. The federal sentencing guidelines, for example, contain forty-three offense levels as compared to the ten offense levels in Minnesota.

Many of the differences between the two sets of guidelines are attributable to differences in the views of the sentencing commissions about the appropriate kinds and amount of punishment for particular types of crimes. Of particular importance are the different opinions as to what constitutes a proportionate penalty for nonviolent criminals and what is an appropriate use of prison resources. The Minnesota Sentencing Commission believed that most nonviolent offenders can and should be effectively punished in the community and that prisons should generally be reserved for violent offenders. In addition, the Commission believed that the guidelines should not lead to a substantial increase in the size of the state's prison population. The guidelines reflect these beliefs. The vast majority of felony offenders in Minnesota are presumptively subject to community sanctions under the guidelines, with judges having the option of imposing or not imposing a jail term as one of these sanctions. M. Tonry, Sentencing Reform Impacts 62 (National Institute of Justice 1987) (nonimprisonment is the presumptive sentence in 80 to 85% of the felony cases).

By contrast, the United States Sentencing Commission did not consider itself bound to avoid an increase in the number of federal prisoners due to operation of the guidelines. In addition, the Commission disagreed with the past practice of generally imposing nonincarcerative sanctions for such economic crimes as theft, tax evasion, antitrust offenses, insider trading, fraud, and embezzlement. Federal Sentencing Guidelines, 18 U.S.C.App. ch. 1, Policy Statement 4(d). The Commission believed that these crimes are usually "serious," therefore warranting some mandatory period of confinement. Id. As a result, under the federal sentencing guidelines, the vast majority of offenders are now subject to some period of confinement, either in prison or elsewhere. Only under the first six offense levels is a first offender eligible for probation without any attending confinement. Id. at § 5B1.1(a)(1). See U.S. Sentencing Commission Ann.Rep.1988, at 27 (1989) (77.8% of the guideline cases studied by the Commission as of February, 1989 had resulted in a prison sentence).

To what extent do your views correspond with those of the United States Sentencing Commission? To what extent do they correspond with the views of the Minnesota Sentencing Commission? For more information about the federal sentencing guidelines and practical tips for litigating under the guidelines, see Practice Under the New Federal Sentencing Guidelines (P. Bamberger ed. 1989).

5. In recent years, there has been an increasing focus, particularly at the federal level, on crimes committed by corporations. These crimes include money laundering offenses by financial institutions, fraud committed by defense contractors and health providers, and environmental crimes committed by entities whose products or services are potentially harmful to the public or to their own employees. While there is now general accept-

ance of the notion that corporations and other organizations should be subject to the criminal law, there has been considerable debate over the purposes and nature of the sanctions to be imposed.

As this book was going to press, the United States Sentencing Commission had begun the process of drafting sentencing guidelines to govern organizational sanctions. The Commission's initial proposals sparked such strong objection from the business community that they were subsequently withdrawn during the spring of 1990. Some of these proposals are set forth below as an example of one approach to the subject of organizational sanctions. What issues are raised by these proposals, and how should they be resolved?

§ 8B1.3. Community Service–Organizations (Policy Statement)

An organization may be ordered to perform community service where such community service provides an expeditious way of repairing the harm caused by the offense.

Commentary

An organization can perform community service only by paying its employees or others to do so. Thus, the effect of an order to perform community service on an organization is equivalent to an indirect monetary sanction, and therefore is generally less desirable than a direct monetary sanction such as restitution. In some instances, however, the convicted organization may possess knowledge, facilities, or skills that uniquely qualify it to repair damage caused by the offense. Community service directed at repairing damage may provide an efficient means of remedying the harm caused.

In the past some forms of community service imposed on organizations have not been related to the purposes of sentencing. Requiring a defendant to endow a chair at a university or to contribute to a local charity would not be authorized by this section unless such community service provided a means for preventive or corrective action directly related to the offense and served one of the purposes of sentencing set forth in 18 U.S.C. § 3553(a)(2).[1] For example, a condition of probation requiring an organization to make its laboratory facilities available to a university would be authorized if it were subject to the limitation that the facilities be used for research to develop new anti-pollution or clean-up techniques related to the instant offense.

§ 8C2.1. Determining the Fine Guideline Range—Organizations

(a) The guideline fine range shall be determined under subsections (b)–(d) below * * *.

[1. 18 U.S.C. § 3553(a)(2) can be found on page 124 in n. [a].]

(b) Adjust the offense level determined pursuant to § 8A1.2 (Application Instructions—Organizations) for each aggravating and mitigating factor set forth below:

(1) Aggravating Factors.

(A) If high-level management aided or abetted, knowingly encouraged, or condoned the offense, add 1 level.

(B) If the defendant within 15 years of the commencement of the current offense has one or more prior convictions (other than a conviction for a petty offense) or within 10 years of the commencement of the current offense engaged in similar misconduct, as determined by a prior civil or administrative adjudication, add 1 level.

(C) If the commission of the offense constituted a violation of a judicial order or injunction, or of a condition of probation, add 1 level.

(D) If high-level management aided or abetted, or encouraged obstruction of the investigation or prosecution of the offense or, with knowledge thereof, failed to take reasonable steps to prevent such obstruction, add 1 level.

(E) If the defendant, in connection with the offense, bribed or unlawfully gave a gratuity to a public official, or attempted or conspired to bribe or unlawfully give a gratuity to a public official, add 1 level.

(F) If the offense targeted a vulnerable victim as defined in § 3A1.1, add 1 level.

(G) If the offense presented a substantial risk to the continued existence of a financial or consumer market, add 1 level.

(H) If the offense constituted a substantial risk to national security, add 2 levels.

(3) [sic] Mitigating Factors.

(A) If the organization, promptly upon discovering the offense, and prior to the commencement of a government investigation, the imminent threat of a government investigation, or the imminent threat of disclosure of the wrongdoing, reported the offense to government authorities, subtract 1 level.

(B) If high-level management did not have knowledge of the offense and the lack of knowledge was reasonable, subtract 1 level.

(C) If the offense represented an isolated incident of criminal activity that was committed notwithstanding bona fide policies and programs of the organization reflecting a substantial effort to prevent conduct of the type that constituted the offense, subtract 1 level.

(D) If the organization has taken substantial steps to prevent a recurrence of similar offenses, such as, implementing appropriate monitoring procedures and disciplining any officer, director, employee, or agent of the organization responsible for the offense, subtract 1 level.

(c) The fine guideline range is (1) the amount set forth in the Fine Table below corresponding to the adjusted offense level determined above; plus (2) the amount, if any, from subsection (d) below.

Fine Table

Offense Level	Guideline Range	
1	$250 –	$500
2	$500 –	$1,000
3	$850 –	$2,000
4	$1,500 –	$3,500
5	$2,500 –	$6,000
6	$3,200 –	$8,000
7	$4,000 –	$10,000
8	$7,500 –	$18,000
9	$14,000 –	$34,000
10	$25,000 –	$64,000
11	$45,000 –	$103,000
12	$70,000 –	$160,000
13	$90,000 –	$206,000
14	$108,000 –	$240,000
15	$180,000 –	$400,000
16	$300,000 –	$700,000
17	$525,000 –	$1,000,000
18	$700,000 –	$1,520,000
19	$1,100,000 –	$2,850,000
20	$2,100,000 –	$4,750,000
21	$3,250,000 –	$9,000,000
22	$6,500,000 –	$18,000,000
23	$13,000,000 –	$36,000,000
24	$24,000,000 –	$68,000,000
25	$48,000,000 –	$136,000,000
26	$80,000,000 –	$170,000,000
27	$100,000,000 –	$204,000,000
28	$120,000,000 –	$238,000,000
29	$140,000,000 –	$272,000,000
30	$160,000,000 –	$306,000,000
31	$180,000,000 –	$340,000,000
32 & above	$200,000,000 –	$374,000,000

(d) Loss or Gain not Subject to Restitution or Disgorgement. Determine the greater of—

(1) any pecuniary loss caused by the offense for which restitution has not been made or ordered, or

(2) any pecuniary gain to the defendant from the offense that will otherwise not be disgorged by the defendant.

§ 8C2.2. Determination of the Fine Within the Guideline Range (Policy Statement)

(a) Under 18 U.S.C. §§ 3553(a) and 3572(a), the court, in determining the amount of the fine within the applicable guideline range, is required to consider:

(1) the nature and circumstances of the offense and the history and characteristics of the defendant;

(2) the need for the sentence to reflect the seriousness of the offense, promote respect for the law, provide just punishment, afford adequate deterrence, and protect the public from further crimes of the defendant;

(3) the defendant's income, earning capacity, size, and financial resources;

(4) the burden that the fine will impose upon the defendant or any person who is financially dependent on the defendant;

(5) any pecuniary loss inflicted upon others as a result of the offense;

(6) whether restitution is ordered or made and the amount of such restitution;

(7) the need to deprive the defendant of illegally obtained gains from the offense;

(8) whether the defendant can pass on to consumers or other persons the expense of the fine; and

(9) any measure taken by the defendant to discipline any officer, director, employee, or agent of the organization responsible for the offense and to prevent a recurrence of such an offense.

(b) In addition, the court, in determining the amount of the fine within the guideline range, should consider:

(1) the degree of difficulty of detecting the violation;

(2) the reasonable costs of investigating and prosecuting the organization's offense;

(3) any collateral consequences of conviction, including civil obligations arising from the defendant's conduct; and

(4) any other pertinent equitable considerations, including the aggravating and mitigating factors set forth in § 8C2.1.

(c) The amount of the fine should always be sufficient to ensure that the fine, taken together with other sanctions imposed, is punitive.

Commentary

* * *

Subsection (b)(1) provides that the court should consider, among other factors, the degree of difficulty of detecting the violation due either to the defendant's efforts to conceal the offense or to the inherent difficulty of detecting that particular type of offense. For purposes of general deterrence, offenses that are particularly difficult to detect should receive greater punishment.

5. DEPARTURES

§ 8C5.1. Substantial Assistance to Authorities (Policy Statement)

(a) Upon motion of the government stating that the defendant has provided substantial assistance in the investigation or prosecution of the individuals responsible for the offense for which the organization is sentenced, the court may depart from the guidelines.

(b) The appropriate reduction shall be determined by the court for reasons it states that may include, but are not limited to, consideration of the following:

(1) the court's evaluation of the significance and usefulness of the defendant's assistance, taking into consideration the government's evaluation of the assistance rendered;

(2) the nature and extent of the defendant's assistance; and

(3) the timeliness of the defendant's assistance.

§ 8C5.2. Risk of Death or Serious Bodily Injury (Policy Statement)

If the offense resulted in a foreseeable and substantial risk of death or serious bodily injury and the kind or degree of that risk was not adequately taken into consideration in setting the fine guideline range, an upward departure may be warranted. In making this determination, the court should take into account both the seriousness of the potential injury and the probability of its occurring.

PART D—ORGANIZATIONAL PROBATION

§ 8D1.1. Imposition of Probation

An organization shall be sentenced to probation:

(a) if such sentence is necessary as a mechanism to impose restitution, a remedial order, or community service;

(b) if the organization is sentenced to pay a monetary penalty, whether restitution, fine, or special assessment, and the penalty is not paid in full at the time of sentencing; or

(c) in the following circumstances:

(1) the court finds that the organization or a member of its high-level management had a criminal conviction within the previous five years for conduct similar to that involved in the instant offense and any part of the instant offense occurred after that conviction; or

(2) the court finds that the offense indicated a significant problem with the organization's policies or procedures for preventing crimes, as evidenced, for example, by (A) high-level manage-

ment involvement in, or encouragement or countenance of, the offense; (B) inadequate internal accounting or monitoring controls; or (C) a sustained or pervasive pattern of criminal behavior, unless the court finds that the problem has already been remedied, or that there is clear assurance that the problem will be remedied (e.g., where the defendant will be under intensive supervision by a regulatory agency); or

(3) the court finds that probation will significantly increase the likelihood of future compliance with the law.

§ 8D1.2. Term of Probation

When a sentence of probation is imposed, the term of probation shall be sufficient to accomplish the purposes for which probation is imposed but in no event more than five years, and in the case of a felony, at least one year.

§ 8D1.3. Conditions of Probation (Policy Statement)

(a) Any sentence of probation shall include the condition that the organization not commit, or attempt to commit, another Federal, state, or local crime during the term of probation.

(b) The court may impose other conditions that (1) are reasonably related to the nature and circumstances of the offense, the history and characteristics of the defendant, and the purposes of sentencing; and (2) involve only such deprivations of liberty or property as are necessary to effect the purposes of sentencing.

(c) If probation is imposed under § 8D1.1(b), it is recommended that the following conditions be imposed to the extent that they appear necessary to secure the defendant's obligation to pay any deferred portion of an order of restitution or fine:

(1) The organization shall make periodic submissions to the court or probation officer, at intervals specified by the court, reporting on the organization's financial condition and results of business operations and accounting for the disposition of all funds received.

(2) The organization shall submit: (A) to a reasonable number of regular or unannounced examinations of its books and records by the probation officer or auditors engaged by the court; and (B) interrogation of knowledgeable individuals within the organization.

(3) The organization shall be prohibited from engaging in any of the following transactions or activities without prior notice to and approval by the court: (A) paying dividends or making any other distribution to its equity holders; (B) issuing new debt or equity securities or commercial paper, or otherwise obtaining substantial new financing outside the ordinary course of business; or (C) entering into any merger, consolidation, sale of substantially all assets, reorganization, refinancing, dissolution, liquidation, bankruptcy, or other major transaction. In addition, all employ-

ment compensation or other payments or property transfers by the organization to any equity holder, director, officer, or managing agent shall be subject to prior review and approval by the court.

(4) The organization shall be required to notify the court or probation officer immediately upon learning of any (A) material adverse change in its business or financial condition or prospects, or (B) the commencement of any bankruptcy proceeding, major civil litigation, criminal prosecution, or administrative proceeding against the organization, or any investigation or formal inquiry by government authorities regarding the organization.

(5) The organization shall be required to make periodic payments, as specified by the court, in the following priority: (1) the unpaid amount of the organization's restitution; (2) any fine; or (3) any other monetary sanction.

(d) If probation is ordered under § 8D1.1(c), it is recommended that the following conditions be imposed:

(1) The organization shall be required to develop and submit for approval by the court a compliance plan for avoiding a recurrence of the criminal behavior for which it was convicted. The court may employ appropriate experts to assess the efficacy of a submitted plan, if necessary, and shall approve any plan that appears reasonably calculated to avoid recurrence of the criminal behavior. The organization shall not be required to adopt any compliance measure unless such measure is reasonably necessary to avoid a recurrence of the type of criminal behavior involved in the offense.

(2) Upon approval of a compliance plan by the court, the organization shall notify its employees and shareholders of the criminal behavior and the compliance plan. Such notice shall be in a form to be prescribed by the court.

(3) The organization shall be required to make periodic reports to the court or probation officer, at intervals specified by the court, regarding the organization's progress in (A) implementing any compliance plan required and approved by the court under subsection (d) and (B) avoiding the commission of future criminal offenses. Such reports shall be in a form to be prescribed by the court, and (A) shall disclose any criminal prosecution, civil litigation, or administrative proceeding commenced against the organization, or any investigations or formal inquiries by government authorities of which the organization learned since its last report, and (B) shall not require disclosure of any trade secrets or other confidential business information, including future business plans.

Commentary

Subsection (b) authorizes the court to impose other conditions that (1) are reasonabl[y] related to the nature and circumstances of the offense, the history and characteristics of the defendant, and the purposes of sentencing; and (2) involve only such deprivations of liberty or property as are necessary to effect the purposes of sentencing. In meeting these requirements, the court should tailor such conditions of probation to the circumstances of the case. For example, the court may determine that a condition of probation is necessary to assure that a defendant not avoid the impact of a fine by inappropriately passing the costs of such on to consumers or other persons.

In addition, 18 U.S.C. § 3563(a) [m] provides that if a sentence of probation is imposed for a felony, the court shall impose at least one of the following as a condition of probation: a fine, restitution, or community service, unless the court finds on the record that extraordinary circumstances exist that would make such a condition plainly unreasonable, in which event the court shall impose one or more other conditions set forth in 18 U.S.C. § 3563(b).

6. Guideline III.F. of the Minnesota sentencing guidelines, which limits the application of guideline modifications to offenders who commit their crimes on or after the date a modification goes into effect, is designed to avoid *ex post facto* problems with the guidelines. Article I, § 10 of the United States Constitution prohibits the states from enacting any *ex post facto* laws. A law which increases the punishment for a crime after the crime has been committed falls within this *ex post facto* prohibition. Lindsey v. Washington, 301 U.S. 397, 57 S.Ct. 797 (1937). The Supreme Court has interpreted the *ex post facto* clause as proscribing a presumptive sentence imposed on a defendant under sentencing guidelines in effect at the time of sentencing that was higher than the presumptive sentence under the guidelines in effect at the time of his crime. Miller v. Florida, 482 U.S. 423, 107 S.Ct. 2446 (1987). See also Weaver v. Graham, 450 U.S. 24, 101 S.Ct. 960 (1981) (law enacted after the date of the defendant's crime and sentencing, which decreased the rate that good-time credits accumulate, is an unconstitutional *ex post facto* law).

[m. 18 U.S.C. § 3563 can be found on pages 123–126, supra.]

Chapter 6

THE DEATH PENALTY

Few criminal justice issues have engendered as much controversy as the question of whether the death penalty can and should be imposed on certain criminal offenders. The array of opinions on this subject has manifested itself in the decisions of the Supreme Court, which are often characterized by 5–4 holdings and a confusing mix of plurality, concurring, and dissenting opinions.

Since 1972, when the Supreme Court decided the seminal case of Furman v. Georgia, 408 U.S. 238, 92 S.Ct. 2726 (1972), the Court has constantly been grappling with questions concerning the constitutionality of the death penalty. In *Furman*, the Court held that two death penalty statutes that left the decision whether or not to impose the death penalty to the unconfined discretion of the judge or jury violated the eighth amendment's prohibition of cruel and unusual punishment. These statutes had resulted in such arbitrary and haphazard imposition of the death penalty that, in the words of Justice White, there was "no meaningful basis for distinguishing the few cases in which it is imposed from the many cases in which it is not." Id. at 313, 92 S.Ct. at 2764 (White, J., concurring).

It was evident from *Furman* that other death penalty statutes across the country were also unconstitutional. A number of state legislatures responded by enacting new death penalty statutes that they hoped would pass constitutional muster. In several cases decided in 1976, one of which is set forth below, and another of which can be found on page 214, the Supreme Court considered the constitutionality of some of these statutes.

GREGG v. GEORGIA

Supreme Court of the United States, 1976.
428 U.S. 153, 96 S.Ct. 2909, 49 L.Ed.2d 859.

Judgment of the Court, and opinion of MR. JUSTICE STEWART, MR. JUSTICE POWELL, and MR. JUSTICE STEVENS, announced by MR. JUSTICE STEWART.

The issue in this case is whether the imposition of the sentence of death for the crime of murder under the law of Georgia violates the Eighth and Fourteenth Amendments.

I

The petitioner, Troy Gregg, was charged with committing armed robbery and murder. In accordance with Georgia procedure in capital cases, the trial was in two stages, a guilt stage and a sentencing stage. The evidence at the guilt trial established that on November 21, 1973, the petitioner and a traveling companion, Floyd Allen, while hitchhiking north in Florida were picked up by Fred Simmons and Bob Moore. * * * A short time later the four men interrupted their journey for a rest stop along the highway. The next morning the bodies of Simmons and Moore were discovered in a ditch nearby.

* * * The next afternoon, the petitioner and Allen, while in Simmons' car, were arrested in Asheville, N.C. * * * [W]hile being transferred to Lawrenceville, Ga., the petitioner and Allen were taken to the scene of the shootings. Upon arriving there, Allen recounted the events leading to the slayings. His version of these events was as follows: After Simmons and Moore left the car, the petitioner stated that he intended to rob them. The petitioner then took his pistol in hand and positioned himself on the car to improve his aim. As Simmons and Moore came up an embankment toward the car, the petitioner fired three shots and the two men fell near a ditch. The petitioner, at close range, then fired a shot into the head of each. He robbed them of valuables and drove away with Allen.

A medical examiner testified that Simmons died from a bullet wound in the eye and that Moore died from bullet wounds in the cheek and in the back of the head. He further testified that both men had several bruises and abrasions about the face and head which probably were sustained either from the fall into the ditch or from being dragged or pushed along the embankment. Although Allen did not testify, a police detective recounted the substance of Allen's statements about the slayings and indicated that directly after Allen had made these statements the petitioner had admitted that Allen's account was accurate. The petitioner testified in his own defense. He confirmed that Allen had made the statements described by the detective, but denied their truth or ever having admitted to their accuracy. He indicated that he had shot Simmons and Moore because of fear and in self-defense, testifying they had attacked Allen and him, one wielding a pipe and the other a knife.[1]

* * * The jury found the petitioner guilty of two counts of armed robbery and two counts of murder.

1. On cross-examination the State introduced a letter written by the petitioner to Allen entitled, "[a] statement for you," with the instructions that Allen memorize and then burn it. The statement was consistent with the petitioner's testimony at trial.

At the penalty stage, which took place before the same jury, neither the prosecutor nor the petitioner's lawyer offered any additional evidence. Both counsel, however, made lengthy arguments dealing generally with the propriety of capital punishment under the circumstances and with the weight of the evidence of guilt. The trial judge instructed the jury that it could recommend either a death sentence or a life prison sentence on each count. The judge further charged the jury that in determining what sentence was appropriate the jury was free to consider the facts and circumstances, if any, presented by the parties in mitigation or aggravation.

Finally, the judge instructed the jury that it "would not be authorized to consider [imposing] the penalty of death" unless it first found beyond a reasonable doubt one of these aggravating circumstances:

"One—That the offense of murder was committed while the offender was engaged in the commission of two other capital felonies, to-wit the armed robbery of [Simmons and Moore].

"Two—That the offender committed the offense of murder for the purpose of receiving money and the automobile described in the indictment.

"Three—The offense of murder was outrageously and wantonly vile, horrible and inhuman, in that they [*sic*] involved the depravity of [the] mind of the defendant."

Finding the first and second of these circumstances, the jury returned verdicts of death on each count.

The Supreme Court of Georgia affirmed the convictions and the imposition of the death sentences for murder. * * *

* * *

II

Before considering the issues presented it is necessary to understand the Georgia statutory scheme for the imposition of the death penalty. * * *

* * * After a verdict, finding, or plea of guilty to a capital crime, a presentence hearing is conducted before whoever made the determination of guilt. The sentencing procedures are essentially the same in both bench and jury trials. At the hearing:

"[T]he judge [or jury] shall hear additional evidence in extenuation, mitigation, and aggravation of punishment, including the record of any prior criminal convictions and pleas of guilty or pleas of nolo contendere of the defendant, or the absence of any prior conviction and pleas: Provided, however, that only such evidence in aggravation as the State has made known to the defendant prior to his trial shall be admissible. The judge [or jury] shall also hear argument by the defendant or his counsel and the prosecuting attorney . . . regarding the punishment to be imposed." § 27–2503 (Supp.1975). * * *

In the assessment of the appropriate sentence to be imposed the judge is also required to consider or to include in his instructions to the jury "any mitigating circumstances or aggravating circumstances otherwise authorized by law and any of [10] statutory aggravating circumstances which may be supported by the evidence. . . ." § 27–2534.1(b) (Supp.1975). The scope of the non-statutory aggravating or mitigating circumstances is not delineated in the statute. Before a convicted defendant may be sentenced to death, however, except in cases of treason or aircraft hijacking, the jury, or the trial judge in cases tried without a jury, must find beyond a reasonable doubt one of the 10 aggravating circumstances specified in the statute. The sentence of death may be imposed only if the jury (or judge) finds one of the statutory aggravating circumstances and then elects to impose that sentence. If the verdict is death, the jury or judge must specify the aggravating circumstance(s) found. In jury cases, the trial judge is bound by the jury's recommended sentence.

In addition to the conventional appellate process available in all criminal cases, provision is made for special expedited direct review by the Supreme Court of Georgia of the appropriateness of imposing the sentence of death in the particular case. The court is directed to consider "the punishment as well as any errors enumerated by way of appeal," and to determine:

"(1) Whether the sentence of death was imposed under the influence of passion, prejudice, or any other arbitrary factor, and

"(2) Whether, in cases other than treason or aircraft hijacking, the evidence supports the jury's or judge's finding of a statutory aggravating circumstance as enumerated in section 27.2534.1(b), and

"(3) Whether the sentence of death is excessive or disproportionate to the penalty imposed in similar cases, considering both the crime and the defendant." § 27–2537 (Supp.1975).

If the court affirms a death sentence, it is required to include in its decision reference to similar cases that it has taken into consideration.

A transcript and complete record of the trial, as well as a separate report by the trial judge, are transmitted to the court for its use in reviewing the sentence. The report is in the form of a 6½–page questionnaire, designed to elicit information about the defendant, the crime, and the circumstances of the trial. It requires the trial judge to characterize the trial in several ways designed to test for arbitrariness and disproportionality of sentence. Included in the report are responses to detailed questions concerning the quality of the defendant's representation, whether race played a role in the trial, and, whether, in the trial court's judgment, there was any doubt about the defendant's guilt or the appropriateness of the sentence. A copy of the report is served upon defense counsel. Under its special review authority, the court may either affirm the death sentence or remand the case for resentencing. In cases in which the death sentence is affirmed there remains the possibility of executive clemency.

III

We address initially the basic contention that the punishment of death for the crime of murder is, under all circumstances, "cruel and unusual" in violation of the Eighth and Fourteenth Amendments of the Constitution.   *   *   *

*   *   *

A

*   *   *

In the earliest cases raising Eighth Amendment claims, the Court focused on particular methods of execution to determine whether they were too cruel to pass constitutional muster. The constitutionality of the sentence of death itself was not at issue, and the criterion used to evaluate the mode of execution was its similarity to "torture" and other "barbarous" methods.   *   *   *

But the Court has not confined the prohibition embodied in the Eighth Amendment to "barbarous" methods that were generally outlawed in the 18th century. Instead, the Amendment has been interpreted in a flexible and dynamic manner. The Court early recognized that "a principle to be vital must be capable of wider application than the mischief which gave it birth." *Weems v. United States,* 217 U.S. 349, 373 (1910). Thus the Clause forbidding "cruel and unusual" punishments "is not fastened to the obsolete but may acquire meaning as public opinion becomes enlightened by a humane justice."

*   *   *

*   *   * As Mr. Chief Justice Warren said, in an oft-quoted phrase, "[t]he Amendment must draw its meaning from the evolving standards of decency that mark the progress of a maturing society." *Trop v. Dulles,* [356 U.S.] at 101 [(1958)]. Thus, an assessment of contemporary values concerning the infliction of a challenged sanction is relevant to the application of the Eighth Amendment. As we develop below more fully, this assessment does not call for a subjective judgment. It requires, rather, that we look to objective indicia that reflect the public attitude toward a given sanction.

But our cases also make clear that public perceptions of standards of decency with respect to criminal sanctions are not conclusive. A penalty also must accord with "the dignity of man," which is the "basic concept underlying the Eighth Amendment." This means, at least, that the punishment not be "excessive." When a form of punishment in the abstract (in this case, whether capital punishment may ever be imposed as a sanction for murder) rather than in the particular (the propriety of death as a penalty to be applied to a specific defendant for a specific crime) is under consideration, the inquiry into "excessiveness" has two aspects. First, the punishment must not involve the unnecessary and wanton infliction of pain. Second, the punishment must not be grossly out of proportion to the severity of the crime.

B

Of course, the requirements of the Eighth Amendment must be applied with an awareness of the limited role to be played by the courts. This does not mean that judges have no role to play, for the Eighth Amendment is a restraint upon the exercise of legislative power. * * *[19]

But, while we have an obligation to insure that constitutional bounds are not overreached, we may not act as judges as we might as legislators. * * *

Therefore, in assessing a punishment selected by a democratically elected legislature against the constitutional measure, we presume its validity. We may not require the legislature to select the least severe penalty possible so long as the penalty selected is not cruelly inhumane or disproportionate to the crime involved. And a heavy burden rests on those who would attack the judgment of the representatives of the people.

This is true in part because the constitutional test is intertwined with an assessment of contemporary standards and the legislative judgment weighs heavily in ascertaining such standards. "[I]n a democratic society legislatures, not courts, are constituted to respond to the will and consequently the moral values of the people." The deference we owe to the decisions of the state legislatures under our federal system is enhanced where the specification of punishments is concerned, for "these are peculiarly questions of legislative policy." * * *

C

In the discussion to this point we have sought to identify the principles and considerations that guide a court in addressing an Eighth Amendment claim. We now consider specifically whether the sentence of death for the crime of murder is a *per se* violation of the Eighth and Fourteenth Amendments to the Constitution. * * *

The imposition of the death penalty for the crime of murder has a long history of acceptance both in the United States and in England. The common-law rule imposed a mandatory death sentence on all convicted murderers. And the penalty continued to be used into the 20th century by most American States, although the breadth of the common-law rule was diminished, initially by narrowing the class of murders to be punished by death and subsequently by widespread adoption of laws expressly granting juries the discretion to recommend mercy.

19. Although legislative measures adopted by the people's chosen representatives provide one important means of ascertaining contemporary values, it is evident that legislative judgments alone cannot be determinative of Eighth Amendment standards since that Amendment was intended to safeguard individuals from the abuse of legislative power. * * *

It is apparent from the text of the Constitution itself that the existence of capital punishment was accepted by the Framers. At the time the Eighth Amendment was ratified, capital punishment was a common sanction in every State. Indeed, the First Congress of the United States enacted legislation providing death as the penalty for specified crimes. The Fifth Amendment, adopted at the same time as the Eighth, contemplated the continued existence of the capital sanction by imposing certain limits on the prosecution of capital cases:

> "No person shall be held to answer for a capital, or otherwise infamous crime, unless on a presentment or indictment of a Grand Jury . . .; nor shall any person be subject for the same offense to be twice put in jeopardy of life or limb; . . . nor be deprived of life, liberty, or property, without due process of law . . .."

And the Fourteenth Amendment, adopted over three-quarters of a century later, similarly contemplates the existence of the capital sanction in providing that no State shall deprive any person of "life, liberty, or property" without due process of law.

* * *

* * * Despite the continuing debate, dating back to the 19th century, over the morality and utility of capital punishment, it is now evident that a large proportion of American society continues to regard it as an appropriate and necessary criminal sanction.

The most marked indication of society's endorsement of the death penalty for murder is the legislative response to *Furman.* The legislatures of at least 35 States have enacted new statutes that provide for the death penalty for at least some crimes that result in the death of another person. And the Congress of the United States, in 1974, enacted a statute providing the death penalty for aircraft piracy that results in death. These recently adopted statutes have attempted to address the concerns expressed by the Court in *Furman* primarily (i) by specifying the factors to be weighed and the procedures to be followed in deciding when to impose a capital sentence, or (ii) by making the death penalty mandatory for specified crimes. But all of the post–*Furman* statutes make clear that capital punishment itself has not been rejected by the elected representatives of the people.

In the only statewide referendum occurring since *Furman* and brought to our attention, the people of California adopted a constitutional amendment that authorized capital punishment, in effect negating a prior ruling by the Supreme Court of California in *People v. Anderson,* 6 Cal.3d 628, 493 P.2d 880 (1972), that the death penalty violated the California Constitution.[25]

The jury also is a significant and reliable objective index of contemporary values because it is so directly involved. The Court has said

---

25. * * * A December 1972 Gallup poll indicated that 57% of the people favored the death penalty, while a June 1973 Harris survey showed support of 59%.

Vidmar & Ellsworth, Public Opinion and the Death Penalty, 26 Stan.L.Rev. 1245, 1249 n. 22 (1974).

that "one of the most important functions any jury can perform in making . . . a selection [between life imprisonment and death for a defendant convicted in a capital case] is to maintain a link between contemporary community values and the penal system." It may be true that evolving standards have influenced juries in recent decades to be more discriminating in imposing the sentence of death. But the relative infrequency of jury verdicts imposing the death sentence does not indicate rejection of capital punishment *per se*. Rather, the reluctance of juries in many cases to impose the sentence may well reflect the humane feeling that this most irrevocable of sanctions should be reserved for a small number of extreme cases. Indeed, the actions of juries in many States since *Furman* are fully compatible with the legislative judgments, reflected in the new statutes, as to the continued utility and necessity of capital punishment in appropriate cases. At the close of 1974 at least 254 persons had been sentenced to death since *Furman*, and by the end of March 1976, more than 460 persons were subject to death sentences.

As we have seen, however, the Eighth Amendment demands more than that a challenged punishment be acceptable to contemporary society. The Court also must ask whether it comports with the basic concept of human dignity at the core of the Amendment. Although we cannot "invalidate a category of penalties because we deem less severe penalties adequate to serve the ends of penology," the sanction imposed cannot be so totally without penological justification that it results in the gratuitous infliction of suffering.

The death penalty is said to serve two principal social purposes: retribution and deterrence of capital crimes by prospective offenders.[28]

In part, capital punishment is an expression of society's moral outrage at particularly offensive conduct. This function may be unappealing to many, but it is essential in an ordered society that asks its citizens to rely on legal processes rather than self-help to vindicate their wrongs. * * * "Retribution is no longer the dominant objective of the criminal law," but neither is it a forbidden objective nor one inconsistent with our respect for the dignity of men. Indeed, the decision that capital punishment may be the appropriate sanction in extreme cases is an expression of the community's belief that certain crimes are themselves so grievous an affront to humanity that the only adequate response may be the penalty of death.[30]

28. Another purpose that has been discussed is the incapacitation of dangerous criminals and the consequent prevention of crimes that they may otherwise commit in the future.

30. Lord Justice Denning, Master of the Rolls of the Court of Appeal in England, spoke to this effect before the British Royal Commission on Capital Punishment:

"Punishment is the way in which society expresses its denunciation of wrong do-

ing: and, in order to maintain respect for law, it is essential that the punishment inflicted for grave crimes should adequately reflect the revulsion felt by the great majority of citizens for them. It is a mistake to consider the objects of punishment as being deterrent or reformative or preventive and nothing else. . . . The truth is that some crimes are so outrageous that society insists on adequate punishment, because

Statistical attempts to evaluate the worth of the death penalty as a deterrent to crimes by potential offenders have occasioned a great deal of debate. The results simply have been inconclusive. As one opponent of capital punishment has said:

"[A]fter all possible inquiry, including the probing of all possible methods of inquiry, we do not know, and for systematic and easily visible reasons cannot know, what the truth about this 'deterrent' effect may be . . . .

"The inescapable flaw is . . . that social conditions in any state are not constant through time, and that social conditions are not the same in any two states. If an effect were observed (and the observed effects, one way or another, are not large) then one could not at all tell whether any of this effect is attributable to the presence or absence of capital punishment. A 'scientific'—that is to say, a soundly based— conclusion is simply impossible, and no methodological path out of this tangle suggests itself." C. Black, Capital Punishment: The Inevitability of Caprice and Mistake 25–26 (1974).

Although some of the studies suggest that the death penalty may not function as a significantly greater deterrent than lesser penalties, there is no convincing empirical evidence either supporting or refuting this view. We may nevertheless assume safely that there are murderers, such as those who act in passion, for whom the threat of death has little or no deterrent effect. But for many others, the death penalty undoubtedly is a significant deterrent. There are carefully contemplated murders, such as murder for hire, where the possible penalty of death may well enter into the cold calculus that precedes the decision to act. And there are some categories of murder, such as murder by a life prisoner, where other sanctions may not be adequate.

The value of capital punishment as a deterrent of crime is a complex factual issue the resolution of which properly rests with the legislatures, which can evaluate the results of statistical studies in terms of their own local conditions and with a flexibility of approach that is not available to the courts. * * *

In sum, we cannot say that the judgment of the Georgia Legislature that capital punishment may be necessary in some cases is clearly wrong. Considerations of federalism, as well as respect for the ability of a legislature to evaluate, in terms of its particular State, the moral consensus concerning the death penalty and its social utility as a sanction, require us to conclude, in the absence of more convincing evidence, that the infliction of death as a punishment for murder is not without justification and thus is not unconstitutionally severe.

Finally, we must consider whether the punishment of death is disproportionate in relation to the crime for which it is imposed. There is no question that death as a punishment is unique in its severity and

the wrong-doer deserves it, irrespective of whether it is a deterrent or not." Royal Commission on Capital Punish-ment, Minutes of Evidence, Dec. 1, 1949, p. 207 (1950).

irrevocability. When a defendant's life is at stake, the Court has been particularly sensitive to insure that every safeguard is observed. But we are concerned here only with the imposition of capital punishment for the crime of murder, and when a life has been taken deliberately by the offender, we cannot say that the punishment is invariably disproportionate to the crime. It is an extreme sanction, suitable to the most extreme of crimes.

We hold that the death penalty is not a form of punishment that may never be imposed, regardless of the circumstances of the offense, regardless of the character of the offender, and regardless of the procedure followed in reaching the decision to impose it.

IV

We now consider whether Georgia may impose the death penalty on the petitioner in this case.

A

*   *   *

Furman mandates that where discretion is afforded a sentencing body on a matter so grave as the determination of whether a human life should be taken or spared, that discretion must be suitably directed and limited so as to minimize the risk of wholly arbitrary and capricious action.

*   *   *

While some have suggested that standards to guide a capital jury's sentencing deliberations are impossible to formulate, the fact is that such standards have been developed. When the drafters of the Model Penal Code faced this problem, they concluded "that it is within the realm of possibility to point to the main circumstances of aggravation and of mitigation that should be weighed *and weighed against each other* when they are presented in a concrete case." ALI, Model Penal Code § 201.6, Comment 3, p. 71 (Tent. Draft No. 9, 1959) (emphasis in original).[44] While such standards are by necessity somewhat general,

---

44. The Model Penal Code proposes the following standards:

"(3) Aggravating Circumstances.

"(a) The murder was committed by a convict under sentence of imprisonment.

"(b) The defendant was previously convicted of another murder or of a felony involving the use or threat of violence to the person.

"(c) At the time the murder was committed the defendant also committed another murder.

"(d) The defendant knowingly created a great risk of death to many persons.

"(e) The murder was committed while the defendant was engaged or was an accomplice in the commission of, or an attempt to commit, or flight after committing or attempting to commit robbery, rape or deviate sexual intercourse by force or threat of force, arson, burglary or kidnapping.

"(f) The murder was committed for the purpose of avoiding or preventing a lawful arrest or effecting an escape from lawful custody.

"(g) The murder was committed for pecuniary gain.

"(h) The murder was especially heinous, atrocious or cruel, manifesting exceptional depravity.

"(4) Mitigating Circumstances.

"(a) The defendant has no significant history of prior criminal activity.

"(b) The murder was committed while the defendant was under the influence of

they do provide guidance to the sentencing authority and thereby reduce the likelihood that it will impose a sentence that fairly can be called capricious or arbitrary. Where the sentencing authority is required to specify the factors it relied upon in reaching its decision, the further safeguard of meaningful appellate review is available to ensure that death sentences are not imposed capriciously or in a freakish manner.

In summary, the concerns expressed in *Furman* that the penalty of death not be imposed in an arbitrary or capricious manner can be met by a carefully drafted statute that ensures that the sentencing authority is given adequate information and guidance. As a general proposition these concerns are best met by a system that provides for a bifurcated proceeding at which the sentencing authority is apprised of the information relevant to the imposition of sentence and provided with standards to guide its use of the information.

We do not intend to suggest that only the above-described procedures would be permissible under *Furman* or that any sentencing system constructed along these general lines would inevitably satisfy the concerns of *Furman*,[46] for each distinct system must be examined on an individual basis. Rather, we have embarked upon this general exposition to make clear that it is possible to construct capital-sentencing systems capable of meeting *Furman's* constitutional concerns.

B

We now turn to consideration of the constitutionality of Georgia's capital-sentencing procedures. In the wake of *Furman*, Georgia amended its capital punishment statute, but chose not to narrow the scope of its murder provisions. * * *

Georgia did act, however, to narrow the class of murderers subject to capital punishment by specifying 10 statutory aggravating circumstances, one of which must be found by the jury to exist beyond a reasonable doubt before a death sentence can ever be imposed. In

extreme mental or emotional disturbance.

"(c) The victim was a participant in the defendant's homicidal conduct or consented to the homicidal act.

"(d) The murder was committed under circumstances which the defendant believed to provide a moral justification or extenuation for his conduct.

"(e) The defendant was an accomplice in a murder committed by another person and his participation in the homicidal act was relatively minor.

"(f) The defendant acted under duress or under the domination of another person.

"(g) At the time of the murder, the capacity of the defendant to appreciate

the criminality [wrongfulness] of his conduct or to conform his conduct to the requirements of law was impaired as a result of mental disease or defect or intoxication.

"(h) The youth of the defendant at the time of the crime." ALI Model Penal Code § 210.6 (Proposed Official Draft 1962).

46. A system could have standards so vague that they would fail adequately to channel the sentencing decision patterns of juries with the result that a pattern of arbitrary and capricious sentencing like that found unconstitutional in *Furman* could occur.

addition, the jury is authorized to consider any other appropriate aggravating or mitigating circumstances. The jury is not required to find any mitigating circumstance in order to make a recommendation of mercy that is binding on the trial court, but it must find a *statutory* aggravating circumstance before recommending a sentence of death.

These procedures require the jury to consider the circumstances of the crime and the criminal before it recommends sentence. No longer can a Georgia jury do as Furman's jury did: reach a finding of the defendant's guilt and then, without guidance or direction, decide whether he should live or die. Instead, the jury's attention is directed to the specific circumstances of the crime: Was it committed in the course of another capital felony? Was it committed for money? Was it committed upon a peace officer or judicial officer? Was it committed in a particularly heinous way or in a manner that endangered the lives of many persons? In addition, the jury's attention is focused on the characteristics of the person who committed the crime: Does he have a record of prior convictions for capital offenses? Are there any special facts about this defendant that mitigate against imposing capital punishment (*e.g.,* his youth, the extent of his cooperation with the police, his emotional state at the time of the crime). As a result, while some jury discretion still exists, "the discretion to be exercised is controlled by clear and objective standards so as to produce non-discriminatory application."

As an important additional safeguard against arbitrariness and caprice, the Georgia statutory scheme provides for automatic appeal of all death sentences to the State's Supreme Court. That court is required by statute to review each sentence of death and determine whether it was imposed under the influence of passion or prejudice, whether the evidence supports the jury's finding of a statutory aggravating circumstance, and whether the sentence is disproportionate compared to those sentences imposed in similar cases.

In short, Georgia's new sentencing procedures require as a prerequisite to the imposition of the death penalty, specific jury findings as to the circumstances of the crime or the character of the defendant. Moreover, to guard further against a situation comparable to that presented in *Furman,* the Supreme Court of Georgia compares each death sentence with the sentences imposed on similarly situated defendants to ensure that the sentence of death in a particular case is not disproportionate. On their face these procedures seem to satisfy the concerns of *Furman.* No longer should there be "no meaningful basis for distinguishing the few cases in which [the death penalty] is imposed from the many cases in which it is not."

The petitioner contends, however, that the changes in the Georgia sentencing procedures are only cosmetic, that the arbitrariness and capriciousness condemned by *Furman* continue to exist in Georgia—both in traditional practices that still remain and in the new sentencing procedures adopted in response to *Furman.*

1

First, the petitioner focuses on the opportunities for discretionary action that are inherent in the processing of any murder case under Georgia law. He notes that the state prosecutor has unfettered authority to select those persons whom he wishes to prosecute for a capital offense and to plea bargain with them. Further, at the trial the jury may choose to convict a defendant of a lesser included offense rather than find him guilty of a crime punishable by death, even if the evidence would support a capital verdict. And finally, a defendant who is convicted and sentenced to die may have his sentence commuted by the Governor of the State and the Georgia Board of Pardons and Paroles.

The existence of these discretionary stages is not determinative of the issues before us. At each of these stages an actor in the criminal justice system makes a decision which may remove a defendant from consideration as a candidate for the death penalty. *Furman,* in contrast, dealt with the decision to impose the death sentence on a specific individual who had been convicted of a capital offense. Nothing in any of our cases suggests that the decision to afford an individual defendant mercy violates the Constitution. *Furman* held only that, in order to minimize the risk that the death penalty would be imposed on a capriciously selected group of offenders, the decision to impose it had to be guided by standards so that the sentencing authority would focus on the particularized circumstances of the crime and the defendant.[50]

2

*   *   *

The petitioner next argues that the requirements of *Furman* are not met here because the jury has the power to decline to impose the death penalty even if it finds that one or more statutory aggravating circumstances are present in the case. This contention misinterprets *Furman.* Moreover, it ignores the role of the Supreme Court of Georgia which reviews each death sentence to determine whether it is proportional to other sentences imposed for similar crimes. Since the proportionality requirement on review is intended to prevent caprice in the decision to inflict the penalty, the isolated decision of a jury to afford mercy does not render unconstitutional death sentences imposed on

---

50. The petitioner's argument is nothing more than a veiled contention that *Furman* indirectly outlawed capital punishment by placing totally unrealistic conditions on its use. In order to repair the alleged defects pointed to by the petitioner, it would be necessary to require that prosecuting authorities charge a capital offense whenever arguably there had been a capital murder and that they refuse to plea bargain with the defendant. If a jury refused to convict even though the evidence supported the charge, its verdict would have to be reversed and a verdict of guilty entered or a new trial ordered, since the discretionary act of jury nullification would not be permitted. Finally, acts of executive clemency would have to be prohibited. Such a system, of course, would be totally alien to our notions of criminal justice.

*   *   *

defendants who were sentenced under a system that does not create a substantial risk of arbitrariness or caprice.

* * *

V

The basic concern of *Furman* centered on those defendants who were being condemned to death capriciously and arbitrarily. Under the procedures before the Court in that case, sentencing authorities were not directed to give attention to the nature or circumstances of the crime committed or to the character or record of the defendant. Left unguided, juries imposed the death sentence in a way that could only be called freakish. The new Georgia sentencing procedures, by contrast, focus the jury's attention on the particularized nature of the crime and the particularized characteristics of the individual defendant. While the jury is permitted to consider any aggravating or mitigating circumstances, it must find and identify at least one statutory aggravating factor before it may impose a penalty of death. In this way the jury's discretion is channeled. No longer can a jury wantonly and freakishly impose the death sentence; it is always circumscribed by the legislative guidelines. In addition, the review function of the Supreme Court of Georgia affords additional assurance that the concerns that prompted our decision in *Furman* are not present to any significant degree in the Georgia procedure applied here.

For the reasons expressed in this opinion, we hold that the statutory system under which Gregg was sentenced to death does not violate the Constitution. Accordingly, the judgment of the Georgia Supreme Court is affirmed.

* * *

MR. JUSTICE WHITE, with whom THE CHIEF JUSTICE and MR. JUSTICE REHNQUIST join, concurring in the judgment.

* * *

* * * As the types of murders for which the death penalty may be imposed become more narrowly defined and are limited to those which are particularly serious or for which the death penalty is peculiarly appropriate as they are in Georgia by reason of the aggravating-circumstance requirement, it becomes reasonable to expect that juries—even given discretion *not* to impose the death penalty—will impose the death penalty in a substantial portion of the cases so defined. If they do, it can no longer be said that the penalty is being imposed wantonly and freakishly or so infrequently that it loses its usefulness as a sentencing device. There is, therefore, reason to expect that Georgia's current system would escape the infirmities which invalidated its previous system under *Furman*. However, the Georgia Legislature was not satisfied with a system which might, but also might not, turn out in practice to result in death sentences being imposed with reasonable consistency for certain serious murders. Instead, it gave the Georgia Supreme Court the power and the obligation to perform * * * the task of deciding whether *in fact* the death penalty

was being administered for any given class of crime in a discriminatory, standardless, or rare fashion.

* * *

Petitioner * * * argues that decisions made by the prosecutor—either in negotiating a plea to some lesser offense than capital murder or in simply declining to charge capital murder—are standardless and will inexorably result in the wanton and freakish imposition of the penalty condemned by the judgment in *Furman.* I address this point separately because the cases in which no capital offense is charged escape the view of the Georgia Supreme Court and are not considered by it in determining whether a particular sentence is excessive or disproportionate.

Petitioner's argument that prosecutor's behave in a standardless fashion in deciding which cases to try as capital felonies is unsupported by any facts. Petitioner simply asserts that since prosecutors have the power not to charge capital felonies they will exercise that power in a standardless fashion. This is untenable. Absent facts to the contrary, it cannot be assumed that prosecutors will be motivated in their charging decision by factors other than the strength of their case and the likelihood that a jury would impose the death penalty if it convicts. Unless prosecutors are incompetent in their judgments, the standards by which they decide whether to charge a capital felony will be the same as those by which the jury will decide the questions of guilt and sentence. Thus defendants will escape the death penalty through prosecutorial charging decisions only because the offense is not sufficiently serious; or because the proof is insufficiently strong. This does not cause the system to be standardless any more than the jury's decision to impose life imprisonment on a defendant whose crime is deemed insufficiently serious or its decision to acquit someone who is probably guilty but whose guilt is not established beyond a reasonable doubt. Thus the prosecutor's charging decisions are unlikely to have removed from the sample of cases considered by the Georgia Supreme Court any which are truly "similar." If the cases really were "similar" in relevant respects, it is unlikely that prosecutors would fail to prosecute them as capital cases; and I am unwilling to assume the contrary.

Petitioner's argument that there is an unconstitutional amount of discretion in the system which separates those suspects who receive the death penalty from those who receive life imprisonment, a lesser penalty, or are acquitted or never charged, seems to be in final analysis an indictment of our entire system of justice. Petitioner has argued, in effect, that no matter how effective the death penalty may be as a punishment, government, created and run as it must be by humans, is inevitably incompetent to administer it. This cannot be accepted as a proposition of constitutional law. Imposition of the death penalty is surely an awesome responsibility for any system of justice and those who participate in it. Mistakes will be made and discriminations will occur which will be difficult to explain. However, one of society's most basic tasks is that of protecting the lives of its citizens and one of the most basic ways in which it achieves the task is through criminal laws against murder. I decline to interfere with the manner in which Georgia has chosen to enforce such laws on what is simply an assertion of lack of faith in the ability of the system of justice to operate in a fundamentally fair manner.

* * *

I therefore concur in the judgment of affirmance.

* * *

MR. JUSTICE BLACKMUN, concurring in the judgment. [Opinion omitted.]

MR. JUSTICE BRENNAN, dissenting.

The Cruel and Unusual Punishments Clause "must draw its meaning from the evolving standards of decency that mark the progress of a maturing society." The opinions of Mr. Justice Stewart, Mr. Justice Powell, and Mr. Justice Stevens today hold that "evolving standards of decency" require focus not on the essence of the death penalty itself but primarily upon the procedures employed by the State to single out persons to suffer the penalty of death. * * *

In *Furman v. Georgia,* 408 U.S. 238, 257 (1972) (concurring opinion), I read "evolving standards of decency" as requiring focus upon the essence of the death penalty itself and not primarily or solely upon the procedures under which the determination to inflict the penalty upon a particular person was made. * * *

* * *

* * * Death for whatever crime and under all circumstances "is truly an awesome punishment. The calculated killing of a human being by the State involves, by its very nature, a denial of the executed person's humanity. . . . An executed person has indeed 'lost the right to have rights.' " Death is not only an unusually severe punishment, unusual in its pain, in its finality, and in its enormity, but it serves no penal purpose more effectively than a less severe punishment; therefore the principle inherent in the Clause that prohibits pointless infliction of excessive punishment when less severe punishment can adequately achieve the same purposes invalidates the punishment.

The fatal constitutional infirmity in the punishment of death is that it treats "members of the human race as nonhumans, as objects to be toyed with and discarded. [It is] thus inconsistent with the fundamental premise of the Clause that even the vilest criminal remains a human being possessed of common human dignity." As such it is a penalty that "subjects the individual to a fate forbidden by the principle of civilized treatment guaranteed by the [Clause]." I therefore would hold, on that ground alone, that death is today a cruel and unusual punishment prohibited by the Clause. "Justice of this kind is obviously no less shocking than the crime itself, and the new 'official' murder, far from offering redress for the offense committed against society, adds instead a second defilement to the first."

* * *

MR. JUSTICE MARSHALL, dissenting.

* * *

In *Furman* I concluded that the death penalty is constitutionally invalid for two reasons. First, the death penalty is excessive. And second, the American people, fully informed as to the purposes of the death penalty and its liabilities, would in my view reject it as morally unacceptable.

Since the decision in *Furman,* the legislatures of 35 States have enacted new statutes authorizing the imposition of the death sentence for certain crimes, and Congress has enacted a law providing the death penalty for air piracy resulting in death. I would be less than candid if I did not acknowledge that these developments have a significant bearing on a realistic assessment of the moral acceptability of the death penalty to the American people. But if the constitutionality of the death penalty turns, as I have urged, on the opinion of an *informed* citizenry, then even the enactment of new death statutes cannot be viewed as conclusive. In *Furman,* I observed that the American people are largely unaware of the information critical to a judgment on the morality of the death penalty, and concluded that if they were better informed they would consider it shocking, unjust, and unacceptable. A recent study, conducted after the enactment of the post-*Furman* statutes, has confirmed that the American people know little about the death penalty, and that the opinions of an informed public would differ significantly from those of a public unaware of the consequences and effects of the death penalty.[1]

Even assuming, however, that the post-*Furman* enactment of statutes authorizing the death penalty renders the prediction of the views of an informed citizenry an uncertain basis for a constitutional decision, the enactment of those statutes has no bearing whatsoever on the conclusion that the death penalty is unconstitutional because it is excessive. An excessive penalty is invalid under the Cruel and Unusual Punishments Clause "even though popular sentiment may favor" it. The inquiry here, then, is simply whether the death penalty is necessary to accomplish the legitimate legislative purposes in punishment, or whether a less severe penalty—life imprisonment—would do as well.

The two purposes that sustain the death penalty as nonexcessive in the Court's view are general deterrence and retribution. In *Furman,* I canvassed the relevant data on the deterrent effect of capital punishment. The state of knowledge at that point, after literally centuries of debate, was summarized as follows by a United Nations Committee:

1. Sarat & Vidmar, Public Opinion, The Death Penalty, and the Eighth Amend- ment: Testing the Marshall Hypothesis, 1976 Wis.L.Rev. 171.

"It is generally agreed between the retentionists and abolitionists, whatever their opinions about the validity of comparative studies of deterrence, that the data which now exist show no correlation between the existence of capital punishment and lower rates of capital crime." [3]

The available evidence, I concluded in *Furman,* was convincing that "capital punishment is not necessary as a deterrent to crime in our society."

*   *   *

There remains for consideration, however, what might be termed the purely retributive justification for the death penalty—that the death penalty is appropriate, not because of its beneficial effect on society, but because the taking of the murderer's life is itself morally good. *   *   *

*   *   * It is this latter notion, in particular, that I consider to be fundamentally at odds with the Eighth Amendment. The mere fact that the community demands the murderer's life in return for the evil he has done cannot sustain the death penalty, for as Justices Stewart, Powell, and Stevens remind us, "the Eighth Amendment demands more than that a challenged punishment be acceptable to contemporary society." To be sustained under the Eighth Amendment, the death penalty must "compor[t] with the basic concept of human dignity at the core of the Amendment."; the objective in imposing it must be "[consistent] with our respect for the dignity of [other] men." Under these standards, the taking of life "because the wrongdoer deserves it" surely must fall, for such a punishment has as its very basis the total denial of the wrongdoer's dignity and worth.

The death penalty, unnecessary to promote the goal of deterrence or to further any legitimate notion of retribution, is an excessive penalty forbidden by the Eighth and Fourteenth Amendments. I respectfully dissent from the Court's judgment *   *   *.

Questions and Points for Discussion

1. As of December 31, 1989, 36 states and the federal government authorized the death penalty in some circumstances. Bureau of Justice Statistics, U.S. Dep't of Justice, Capital Punishment 1989, at 3 (1989). Between 1976, when it became apparent from *Gregg v. Georgia* that the Court considered the death penalty constitutional in some cases, and the end of 1989, 120 people sentenced to death were executed. Id. at 1. The execution rate each year was as follows:

3. United Nations, Department of Economic and Social Affairs, Capital Punishment, pt. II, ¶ 159, p. 123 (1968).

1977–1	1984–21
1978–0	1985–18
1979–2	1986–18
1980–0	1987–25
1981–1	1987–25
1982–2	1988–11
1983–5	1989–16

Id. There were an additional 2,250 prisoners awaiting execution at the end of December, 1989.

2. In *Gregg v. Georgia,* the Supreme Court emphasized the critical role that the proportionality review conducted by the Supreme Court of Georgia played in reducing the risk that the death penalty had been arbitrarily imposed. Since *Gregg* was decided, however, the Court has held that such proportionality review, under which the death penalty imposed in the case before an appellate court is compared with the sanction imposed in other similar cases, is not necessarily required in order for a capital punishment system to be constitutional. Pulley v. Harris, 465 U.S. 37, 104 S.Ct. 871 (1984). Whether such proportionality review would ever be constitutionally mandated would depend on what other checks against arbitrariness are included in the system adopted by a jurisdiction for imposing capital punishment. Id. at 51, 104 S.Ct. at 879. In *Pulley,* those checks included review by the trial judge and the state supreme court of a jury's verdict of death.

3. In *Gregg v. Georgia,* the Supreme Court also emphasized the role that the jury plays as an indicator of "contemporary community values" when deciding whether or not to impose the death penalty. Yet there is no constitutional requirement, according to the Court, that a death sentence be imposed by a jury. Spaziano v. Florida, 468 U.S. 447, 104 S.Ct. 3154 (1984). In *Spaziano,* the Supreme Court therefore upheld the death sentence imposed on the defendant by a judge despite an advisory jury's recommendation that the defendant be sentenced to life in prison.

4. To guard against arbitrariness in the imposition of the death penalty, the courts have scrutinized the language of death penalty statutes to ensure that they are not unconstitutionally vague. In Maynard v. Cartwright, 486 U.S. 356, 108 S.Ct. 1853 (1988), for example, the Supreme Court struck down, on eighth amendment grounds, a provision of a death penalty statute under which the fact that a murder was "especially heinous, atrocious, or cruel" was treated as an aggravating circumstance. In concluding that this language was unconstitutionally vague, the Court noted that "an ordinary person could honestly believe that every unjustified, intentional taking of human life is 'especially heinous.'" Id. at 364, 108 S.Ct. at 1859. How might the statute be redrafted to pass constitutional muster? See, e.g., Walton v. Arizona, 110 S.Ct. 3047, 3057–58 (1990).

5. Despite the Supreme Court's holding in *Gregg v. Georgia* that the Georgia death penalty scheme on its face provided enough procedural safeguards to sufficiently avert arbitrariness and irrationality in the imposition of the death penalty, the Supreme Court was later confronted in McCleskey v. Kemp, 481 U.S. 279, 107 S.Ct. 1756 (1987) with the claim that the statutory framework as applied did not meet constitutional standards—

that the system was actually suffused with arbitrariness. The defendant in *McCleskey,* a black man sentenced to death for the killing of a white police officer, produced statistics demonstrating that defendants in Georgia charged with killing white victims were 4.3 times more likely to be sentenced to death than defendants whose victims were black. In addition, a black defendant who killed a white victim was much more likely to receive the death penalty than a white defendant who killed a white victim. While 22% of the murder cases studied involving black defendants and white victims resulted in imposition of the death penalty, the death penalty was imposed in only 8% of the cases in which both the defendant and the victim were white. In cases involving black victims, 3% of the white defendants were sentenced to death, while only 1% of the black defendants received the death penalty.

The Supreme Court assumed that these statistics were reliable, but nonetheless, in a 5–4 decision, upheld the constitutionality of the capital punishment system in Georgia. To the defendant's argument that the system violated his fourteenth amendment right to be afforded the equal protection of the law, the Court responded that the defendant had failed to prove, as required by the equal protection clause, that he had been intentionally discriminated against. The Court refused to assume that the jury which had actually sentenced the defendant to death had done so because of his race or the race of his victim. In addition, the Court noted that there was no evidence that the Georgia legislature had enacted the death penalty statute in order to discriminate against blacks.

The Supreme Court also rejected the defendant's cruel and unusual punishment claim, emphasizing once again that the statistical evidence adduced by the defendant did not demonstrate that race was actually a factor in the imposition of the death penalty in his case. Nor was the Court willing to conclude that the capital punishment system in Georgia was arbitrarily applied in violation of the eighth amendment because of the risk that racial bias entered into capital sentencing decisions. The Court observed:

> At most, the Baldus study indicates a discrepancy that appears to correlate with race. Apparent disparities in sentencing are an inevitable part of our criminal justice system. The discrepancy indicated by the Baldus study is "a far cry from the major systemic defects identified in *Furman.*" As this Court has recognized, any mode for determining guilt or punishment "has its weaknesses and the potential for misuse." Specifically, "there can be 'no perfect procedure for deciding in which cases governmental authority should be used to impose death.'" Despite these imperfections, our consistent rule has been that constitutional guarantees are met when "the mode [for determining guilt or punishment] itself has been surrounded with safeguards to make it as fair as possible." Where the discretion that is fundamental to our criminal process is involved, we decline to assume that what is unexplained is invidious. In light of the safeguards designed to minimize racial bias in the process, the fundamental value of jury trial in our criminal justice system, and the benefits that discretion provides to criminal defendants, we hold that the Baldus study does not demon-

strate a constitutionally significant risk of racial bias affecting the Georgia capital sentencing process.

Id. at 312–13, 107 S.Ct. at 1777–78.

In a dissenting opinion, Justice Brennan, joined by Justices Marshall, Blackmun, and Stevens, objected to the majority's observation that the risk of racial bias when defendants in Georgia are sentenced to death is not "constitutionally significant." Justice Brennan noted that for every eleven defendants sentenced to death in Georgia for killing a white person, six would not have received the death penalty if their victims had been black. "Surely," Justice Brennan observed, "we would not be willing to take a person's life if the chance that his death was irrationally imposed is *more* likely than not." Id. at 328, 107 S.Ct. at 1786 (Brennan, J., dissenting) (emphasis in the original).

6. Could a state substantially reduce the risk of racial prejudice affecting capital sentencing decisions without abandoning the death penalty? In a separate dissenting opinion in *McCleskey v. Kemp,* Justice Stevens answered this question in the affirmative. Justice Stevens pointed to the results of the statistical study cited by the defendant, known as the Baldus study, which revealed that there is a class of extremely egregious murders which result in the imposition of the death penalty regardless of the race of the victim or of the defendant. Justice Stevens suggested that constitutional problems could be averted if the death penalty was reserved for this limited category of murders.

What about mandating imposition of the death penalty in certain circumstances? Would such a system eliminate the problem of racial bias in the application of death penalty statutes? Would such a system be constitutional? This latter question was addressed by the Court in Woodson v. North Carolina, 428 U.S. 280, 96 S.Ct. 2978 (1976), the case which follows.

WOODSON v. NORTH CAROLINA
Supreme Court of the United States, 1976.
428 U.S. 280, 96 S.Ct. 2978, 49 L.Ed.2d 944.

Judgment of the Court, and opinion of MR. JUSTICE STEWART, MR. JUSTICE POWELL, and MR. JUSTICE STEVENS, announced by MR. JUSTICE STEWART.

The question in this case is whether the imposition of a death sentence for the crime of first-degree murder under the law of North Carolina violates the Eighth and Fourteenth Amendments.

The petitioners were convicted of first-degree murder as the result of their participation in an armed robbery of a convenience food store, in the course of which the cashier was killed and a customer was seriously wounded. There were four participants in the robbery: the petitioners James Tyrone Woodson and Luby Waxton and two others, Leonard Tucker and Johnnie Lee Carroll. At the petitioners' trial Tucker and Carroll testified for the prosecution after having been permitted to plead guilty to lesser offenses; the petitioners testified in their own defense.

The evidence for the prosecution established that the four men had been discussing a possible robbery for some time. On the fatal day Woodson had been drinking heavily. About 9:30 p.m., Waxton and Tucker came to the trailer where Woodson was staying. When Woodson came out of the trailer, Waxton struck him in the face and threatened to kill him in an effort to make him sober up and come along on the robbery. The three proceeded to Waxton's trailer where they met Carroll. Waxton armed himself with a nickel-plated derringer, and Tucker handed Woodson a rifle. The four then set out by automobile to rob the store. Upon arriving at their destination Tucker and Waxton went into the store while Carroll and Woodson remained in the car as lookouts. Once inside the store, Tucker purchased a package of cigarettes from the woman cashier. Waxton then also asked for a package of cigarettes, but as the cashier approached him he pulled the derringer out of his hip pocket and fatally shot her at point-blank range. Waxton then took the money tray from the cash register and gave it to Tucker, who carried it out of the store, pushing past an entering customer as he reached the door. After he was outside, Tucker heard a second shot from inside the store, and shortly thereafter Waxton emerged, carrying a handful of paper money. Tucker and Waxton got in the car and the four drove away.

The petitioners' testimony agreed in large part with this version of the circumstances of the robbery. It differed diametrically in one important respect: Waxton claimed that he never had a gun, and that Tucker had shot both the cashier and the customer.

* * *

The petitioners were found guilty on all charges, and, as was required by statute, sentenced to death. The Supreme Court of North Carolina affirmed. * * *

The North Carolina General Assembly in 1974 * * * enacted a new statute that was essentially unchanged from the old one except that it made the death penalty mandatory. The statute now reads as follows:

> "*Murder in the first and second degree defined; punishment.*—A murder which shall be perpetrated by means of poison, lying in wait, imprisonment, starving, torture, or by any other kind of willful, deliberate and premeditated killing, or which shall be committed in the perpetration or attempt to perpetrate any arson, rape, robbery, kidnapping, burglary or other felony, shall be deemed to be murder in the first degree and shall be punished with death. All other kinds of murder shall be deemed murder in the second degree, and shall be punished by imprisonment for a term of not less than two years nor more than life imprisonment in the State's prison."

It was under this statute that the petitioners, who committed their crime on June 3, 1974, were tried, convicted, and sentenced to death.

* * * In ruling on the constitutionality of the sentences imposed on the petitioners under this North Carolina statute, the Court now addresses for the first time the question whether a death sentence returned pursuant to a law imposing a mandatory death penalty for a broad category of homicidal offenses [7] constitutes cruel and unusual punishment within the meaning of the Eighth and Fourteenth Amendments. * * *

A

The Eighth Amendment stands to assure that the State's power to punish is "exercised within the limits of civilized standards." Central to the application of the Amendment is a determination of contemporary standards regarding the infliction of punishment. As discussed in *Gregg v. Georgia,* indicia of societal values identified in prior opinions include history and traditional usage, legislative enactments, and jury determinations.

In order to provide a frame for assessing the relevancy of these factors in this case we begin by sketching the history of mandatory death penalty statutes in the United States. At the time the Eighth Amendment was adopted in 1791, the States uniformly followed the common-law practice of making death the exclusive and mandatory sentence for certain specified offenses. Although the range of capital offenses in the American Colonies was quite limited in comparison to the more than 200 offenses then punishable by death in England, the Colonies at the time of the Revolution imposed death sentences on all persons convicted of any of a considerable number of crimes, typically including at a minimum, murder, treason, piracy, arson, rape, robbery, burglary, and sodomy. As at common law, all homicides that were not involuntary, provoked, justified, or excused constituted murder and were automatically punished by death. Almost from the outset jurors reacted unfavorably to the harshness of mandatory death sentences. The States initially responded to this expression of public dissatisfaction with mandatory statutes by limiting the classes of capital offenses.

This reform, however, left unresolved the problem posed by the not infrequent refusal of juries to convict murderers rather than subject them to automatic death sentences. In 1794, Pennsylvania attempted to alleviate the undue severity of the law by confining the mandatory death penalty to "murder of the first degree" encompassing all "wilful, deliberate and premeditated" killings. Other jurisdictions, including Virginia and Ohio, soon enacted similar measures, and within a generation the practice spread to most of the States.

Despite the broad acceptance of the division of murder into degrees, the reform proved to be an unsatisfactory means of identifying persons appropriately punishable by death. Although its failure was due in

7. This case does not involve a mandatory death penalty statute limited to an extremely narrow category of homicide, such as murder by a prisoner serving a life sentence, defined in large part in terms of the character or record of the offender. We thus express no opinion regarding the constitutionality of such a statute.

part to the amorphous nature of the controlling concepts of willfulness, deliberateness, and premeditation, a more fundamental weakness of the reform soon became apparent. Juries continued to find the death penalty inappropriate in a significant number of first-degree murder cases and refused to return guilty verdicts for that crime.

The inadequacy of distinguishing between murderers solely on the basis of legislative criteria narrowing the definition of the capital offense led the States to grant juries sentencing discretion in capital cases. Tennessee in 1838, followed by Alabama in 1841, and Louisiana in 1846, were the first States to abandon mandatory death sentences in favor of discretionary death penalty statutes. This flexibility remedied the harshness of mandatory statutes by permitting the jury to respond to mitigating factors by withholding the death penalty. By the turn of the century, 23 States and the Federal Government had made death sentences discretionary for first-degree murder and other capital offenses. During the next two decades 14 additional States replaced their mandatory death penalty statutes. Thus, by the end of World War I, all but eight States, Hawaii, and the District of Columbia either had adopted discretionary death penalty schemes or abolished the death penalty altogether. By 1963, all of these remaining jurisdictions had replaced their automatic death penalty statutes with discretionary jury sentencing.

The history of mandatory death penalty statutes in the United States thus reveals that the practice of sentencing to death all persons convicted of a particular offense has been rejected as unduly harsh and unworkably rigid. The two crucial indicators of evolving standards of decency respecting the imposition of punishment in our society—jury determinations and legislative enactments—both point conclusively to the repudiation of automatic death sentences. * * *[29]

* * *

Still further evidence of the incompatibility of mandatory death penalties with contemporary values is provided by the results of jury sentencing under discretionary statutes. * * * Various studies indicate that even in first-degree murder cases juries with sentencing discretion do not impose the death penalty "with any great frequency." H. Kalven & H. Zeisel, The American Jury 436 (1966).[31] The actions of sentencing juries suggest that under contemporary standards of decen-

29. See unpublished Hearings on S. 138 before the Subcommittee on the Judiciary of the Senate Committee on the District of Columbia 19–20 (May 17, 1961) (testimony of Sen. Keating). Data compiled by a former United States Attorney for the District of Columbia indicated that juries convicted defendants of first-degree murder in only 12 of the 60 jury trials for first-degree murder held in the District of Columbia between July 1, 1953, and February 1960. The conviction rate was "substantially below the general average in prosecuting oth-er crimes." The lower conviction rate was attributed to the reluctance of jurors to impose the harsh consequences of a first-degree murder conviction in cases where the record might justify a lesser punishment.

* * *

31. Data compiled on discretionary jury sentencing of persons convicted of capital murder reveal that the penalty of death is generally imposed in less than 20% of the cases.

cy death is viewed as an inappropriate punishment for a substantial portion of convicted first-degree murderers.

* * *

Although it seems beyond dispute that, at the time of the *Furman* decision in 1972, mandatory death penalty statutes had been renounced by American juries and legislatures, there remains the question whether the mandatory statutes adopted by North Carolina and a number of other States following *Furman* evince a sudden reversal of societal values regarding the imposition of capital punishment. In view of the persistent and unswerving legislative rejection of mandatory death penalty statutes beginning in 1838 and continuing for more than 130 years until *Furman*, it seems evident that the post-*Furman* enactments reflect attempts by the States to retain the death penalty in a form consistent with the Constitution, rather than a renewed societal acceptance of mandatory death sentencing. The fact that some States have adopted mandatory measures following *Furman* while others have legislated standards to guide jury discretion appears attributable to diverse readings of this Court's multi-opinioned decision in that case.

* * *

It is now well established that the Eighth Amendment draws much of its meaning from "the evolving standards of decency that mark the progress of a maturing society." As the above discussion makes clear, one of the most significant developments in our society's treatment of capital punishment has been the rejection of the common-law practice of inexorably imposing a death sentence upon every person convicted of a specified offense. North Carolina's mandatory death penalty statute for first-degree murder departs markedly from contemporary standards respecting the imposition of the punishment of death and thus cannot be applied consistently with the Eighth and Fourteenth Amendments' requirement that the State's power to punish "be exercised within the limits of civilized standards."

B

A separate deficiency of North Carolina's mandatory death sentence statute is its failure to provide a constitutionally tolerable response to *Furman*'s rejection of unbridled jury discretion in the imposition of capital sentences. Central to the limited holding in *Furman* was the conviction that the vesting of standardless sentencing power in the jury violated the Eighth and Fourteenth Amendments. It is argued that North Carolina has remedied the inadequacies of the death penalty statutes held unconstitutional in *Furman* by withdrawing all sentencing discretion from juries in capital cases. But when one considers the long and consistent American experience with the death penalty in first-degree murder cases, it becomes evident that mandatory statutes enacted in response to *Furman* have simply papered over the problem of unguided and unchecked jury discretion.

As we have noted * * *, there is general agreement that American juries have persistently refused to convict a significant portion of persons charged with first-degree murder of that offense under mandatory death penalty statutes. * * * North Carolina's mandatory death penalty statute provides no standards to guide the jury in its inevitable exercise of the power to determine which first-degree murderers shall live and which shall die. And there is no way under the North Carolina law for the judiciary to check arbitrary and capricious exercise of that power through a review of death sentences. Instead of rationalizing the sentencing process, a mandatory scheme may well exacerbate the problem identified in *Furman* by resting the penalty determination on the particular jury's willingness to act lawlessly. While a mandatory death penalty statute may reasonably be expected to increase the number of persons sentenced to death, it does not fulfill *Furman*'s basic requirement by replacing arbitrary and wanton jury discretion with objective standards to guide, regularize, and make rationally reviewable the process for imposing a sentence of death.

C

A third constitutional shortcoming of the North Carolina statute is its failure to allow the particularized consideration of relevant aspects of the character and record of each convicted defendant before the imposition upon him of a sentence of death. * * * A process that accords no significance to relevant facets of the character and record of the individual offender or the circumstances of the particular offense excludes from consideration in fixing the ultimate punishment of death the possibility of compassionate or mitigating factors stemming from the diverse frailties of humankind. It treats all persons convicted of a designated offense not as uniquely individual human beings, but as members of a faceless, undifferentiated mass to be subjected to the blind infliction of the penalty of death.

* * * Consideration of both the offender and the offense in order to arrive at a just and appropriate sentence has been viewed as a progressive and humanizing development. While the prevailing practice of individualizing sentencing determinations generally reflects simply enlightened policy rather than a constitutional imperative, we believe that in capital cases the fundamental respect for humanity underlying the Eighth Amendment requires consideration of the character and record of the individual offender and the circumstances of the particular offense as a constitutionally indispensable part of the process of inflicting the penalty of death.

This conclusion rests squarely on the predicate that the penalty of death is qualitatively different from a sentence of imprisonment, however long. Death, in its finality, differs more from life imprisonment than a 100–year prison term differs from one of only a year or two. Because of that qualitative difference, there is a corresponding difference in the need for reliability in the determination that death is the appropriate punishment in a specific case.

For the reasons stated, we conclude that the death sentences imposed upon the petitioners under North Carolina's mandatory death sentence statute violated the Eighth and Fourteenth Amendments and therefore must be set aside. The judgment of the Supreme Court of North Carolina is reversed insofar as it upheld the death sentences imposed upon the petitioners, and the case is remanded for further proceedings not inconsistent with this opinion.

* * *

MR. JUSTICE BRENNAN, concurring in the judgment. [Opinion omitted.]

MR. JUSTICE MARSHALL, concurring in the judgment. [Opinion omitted.]

MR. JUSTICE WHITE, with whom THE CHIEF JUSTICE and MR. JUSTICE REHNQUIST join, dissenting. [Opinion omitted.]

MR. JUSTICE BLACKMUN, dissenting. [Opinion omitted.]

MR. JUSTICE REHNQUIST, dissenting.

* * *

The plurality is simply mistaken in its assertion that "[t]he history of mandatory death penalty statutes in the United States thus reveals that the practice of sentencing to death all persons convicted of a particular offense has been rejected as unduly harsh and unworkably rigid." This conclusion is purportedly based on two historic developments: the first a series of legislative decisions during the 19th century narrowing the class of offenses punishable by death; the second a series of legislative decisions during both the 19th and 20th centuries, through which mandatory imposition of the death penalty largely gave way to jury discretion in deciding whether or not to impose this ultimate sanction. * * *

There can be no question that the legislative and other materials discussed in the plurality's opinion show a widespread conclusion on the part of state legislatures during the 19th century that the penalty of death was being required for too broad a range of crimes, and that these legislatures proceeded to narrow the range of crimes for which such penalty could be imposed. If this case involved the imposition of the death penalty for an offense such as burglary or sodomy, the virtually unanimous trend in the legislatures of the States to exclude such offenders from liability for capital punishment might bear on the plurality's Eighth Amendment argument. But petitioners were convicted of first-degree murder, and there is not the slightest suggestion in the material relied upon by the plurality that there had been any turning away at all, much less any such unanimous turning away, from the death penalty as a punishment for those guilty of first-degree murder. * * *

The second string to the plurality's analytical bow is that legislative change from mandatory to discretionary imposition of the death sentence likewise evidences societal rejection of mandatory death penalties. The plurality simply does not make out this part of its case, however, in large part because it treats as being of equal dignity with legislative judgments the judgments of particular juries and of individual jurors.

There was undoubted dissatisfaction, from more than one sector of 19th century society, with the operation of mandatory death sentences. One segment of that society was totally opposed to capital punishment, and was apparently willing to accept the substitution of discretionary imposition of that penalty for its mandatory imposition as a halfway house on the road to total abolition. Another segment was equally unhappy with the operation of the mandatory system, but for an entirely different reason. As the plurality recognizes, this second segment of society was unhappy with the operation of the mandatory system, not because of the death sentences imposed under it, but because people obviously guilty of criminal offenses were *not* being convicted under it. Change to a discretionary system was accepted by these persons not because they thought mandatory imposition of the death penalty was cruel and unusual, but because they thought that if jurors were permitted to return a sentence other than death upon the conviction of a capital crime, fewer guilty defendants would be acquitted.

So far as the action of juries is concerned, the fact that in some cases juries operating under the mandatory system refused to convict obviously guilty defendants does not reflect any "turning away" from the death penalty, or the mandatory death penalty, supporting the proposition that it is "cruel and unusual." Given the requirement of unanimity with respect to jury verdicts in capital cases, * * * it is apparent that a single juror could prevent a jury from returning a verdict of conviction. Occasional refusals to convict, therefore, may just as easily have represented the intransigence of only a small minority of 12 jurors as well as the unanimous judgment of all 12. The fact that the presence of such jurors could prevent conviction in a given case, even though the majority of society, speaking through legislatures, had decreed that it should be imposed, certainly does not indicate that society as a whole rejected mandatory punishment for such offenders; it does not even indicate that those few members of society who serve on juries, as a whole, had done so.

* * *

The second constitutional flaw which the plurality finds in North Carolina's mandatory system is that it has simply "papered over" the problem of unchecked jury discretion. * * *

* * *

In Georgia juries are entitled to return a sentence of life, rather than death, for no reason whatever, simply based upon their own subjective notions of what is right and what is wrong. In Florida the judge and jury are required to weigh legislatively enacted aggravating factors against legislatively enacted mitigating factors, and then base their choice between life or death on an estimate of the result of that weighing. Substantial discretion exists here, too, though it is somewhat more canalized than it is in Georgia. Why these types of discretion are regarded by the plurality as constitutionally permissible,[a] while that which may occur in the North Carolina system is not, is not readily apparent. The freakish and arbitrary nature of the death penalty described in the separate concurring opinions of Justices Stewart and White in *Furman* arose not from the perception that so *many* capital sentences were being imposed but from the perception that so *few* were being imposed. To conclude that the North Carolina system is bad because juror nullification may permit jury discretion while concluding that the Georgia and Florida systems are sound because they *require* this same discretion, is, as the plurality opinion demonstrates, inexplicable.

* * *

The plurality opinion's insistence, in Part III–C, that if the death penalty is to be imposed there must be "particularized consideration of relevant aspects of the character and record of each convicted defendant" is buttressed by neither case authority nor reason. * * *

* * *

The plurality * * * relies upon the indisputable proposition that "death is different" for the result which it reaches in Part III–C. But the respects in which death is "different" from other punishment which may be imposed upon convicted criminals do not seem to me to establish the proposition that the Constitution requires individualized sentencing.

One of the principal reasons why death is different is because it is irreversible; an executed defendant cannot be brought back to life. This aspect of the difference between death and other penalties would undoubtedly support statutory provisions for especially careful review of the fairness of the trial, the accuracy of the factfinding process, and the fairness of the sentencing procedure where the death penalty is imposed. But none of those aspects of the death sentence is at issue here. Petitioners were found guilty of the crime of first-degree murder in a trial the constitutional validity of which is unquestioned here. And since the punishment of death is conceded by the plurality not to be a cruel and unusual punishment for such a crime, the irreversible aspect of the death penalty has no connection whatever with any requirement for individualized consideration of the sentence.

The second aspect of the death penalty which makes it "different" from other penalties is the fact that it is indeed an ultimate penalty, which ends a human life rather than simply requiring that a living human being be confined for a given period of time in a penal institution. This aspect of the difference may enter into the decision of whether or not it is a "cruel and unusual" penalty for a given offense.

[a. The Supreme Court upheld the Georgia death penalty scheme alluded to in Gregg v. Georgia, 428 U.S. 153, 96 S.Ct. 2909 (1976), supra page 194, while the Florida death penalty statute was held to be constitutional in Proffitt v. Florida, 428 U.S. 242, 96 S.Ct. 2960 (1976).]

But since in this case the offense was first-degree murder, that particular inquiry need proceed no further.

The plurality's insistence on individualized consideration of the sentencing, therefore, does not depend upon any traditional application of the prohibition against cruel and unusual punishment contained in the Eighth Amendment. The punishment here is concededly not cruel and unusual, and that determination has traditionally ended judicial inquiry in our cases construing the Cruel and Unusual Punishments Clause. * * *

* * *

Questions and Points for Discussion

1. In Sumner v. Shuman, 483 U.S. 66, 107 S.Ct. 2716 (1987), the Supreme Court answered a question left open in *Woodson*—whether a statute which requires imposition of the death penalty when an inmate commits a murder while serving a life sentence without possibility of parole is constitutional. The Court held that such a mandatory death sentence violates the eighth amendment. The Court noted that even when an inmate serving a life sentence without possibility of parole commits a murder, there might be mitigating circumstances which contraindicate imposition of the death penalty. Circumstances surrounding the murder itself, for example, might diminish the inmate's culpability, even though those circumstances did not rise to the level of a legal defense to the charge of murder. Or there might have been circumstances surrounding the conduct underlying the conviction for which the defendant is serving a life sentence that might suggest to the sentencer that imposition of the death penalty is unwarranted. And there might be other factors, such as the defendant's age, which point against imposition of a death sentence.

To the argument that a mandatory death sentence is necessary in order to deter murders by inmates serving life sentences with no possibility of parole and to provide a means of punishing such inmates, the Court responded that these purposes could be effectuated by retaining the death penalty, though not a mandatory one. As for such inmates who are not sentenced to die, they could be punished for the murders, according to the Court, by withdrawing privileges from them that they would otherwise enjoy in the prison environment. See also Roberts v. Louisiana, 431 U.S. 633, 97 S.Ct. 1993 (1977) (mandatory death sentence for murdering a police officer violates the eighth amendment).

2. According to the Supreme Court, not every death penalty statute which has a mandatory component in it violates constitutional strictures. In Blystone v. Pennsylvania, 110 S.Ct. 1078 (1990), the Court upheld the constitutionality of a death penalty statute which required the jury to sentence a defendant to death if it found that aggravating circumstances in the case outweighed any mitigating circumstances. The Supreme Court distinguished *Woodson*, noting that in the case before it "[d]eath is not automatically imposed upon conviction for certain types of murder. It is imposed only after a determination that the aggravating circumstances outweigh the mitigating circumstances present in the particular crime

committed by the particular defendant, or that there are no such mitigating circumstances." 110 S.Ct. at 1082–83.

3.   The eighth amendment requirement adverted to in *Woodson* that a defendant in a death penalty case be afforded an individualized sentencing determination has led the Court to conclude that a sentencer must not be precluded from considering any relevant mitigating circumstances when deciding whether or not to sentence a defendant to death.   See, e.g., Hitchcock v. Dugger, 481 U.S. 393, 107 S.Ct. 1821 (1987) (defendant has a right to introduce and have the sentencer consider evidence of mitigating circumstances not mentioned in the death penalty statute); Skipper v. South Carolina, 476 U.S. 1, 106 S.Ct. 1669 (1986) (defendant should have been permitted to introduce evidence about how well he had adjusted to jail while awaiting trial); Eddings v. Oklahoma, 455 U.S. 104, 102 S.Ct. 869 (1982) (sentencing judge acted unconstitutionally in refusing to consider evidence of defendant's troubled childhood and his emotional problems). According to the Court, this eighth amendment requirement is consistent with the eighth amendment requirement discussed in Gregg v. Georgia, 428 U.S. 153, 96 S.Ct. 2909 (1976), supra page 194, that the decision whether or not to impose the death penalty not be remitted to the unconfined discretion of the sentencer.   What the eighth amendment seeks to ensure, according to the Court is that any system developed for imposing the death penalty is "at once consistent and principled but also humane and sensible to the uniqueness of the individual."   Eddings v. Oklahoma, 455 U.S. at 110, 102 S.Ct. at 874.

Have these two goals been met and the appropriate balance between these goals reached as the Court has applied the eighth amendment in specific death penalty cases?   In answering this question, consider the Supreme Court death penalty cases about which you have already read as well as the cases and materials which follow.

COKER v. GEORGIA

Supreme Court of the United States, 1977.
433 U.S. 584, 97 S.Ct. 2861, 53 L.Ed.2d 982.

MR. JUSTICE WHITE announced the judgment of the Court and filed an opinion in which MR. JUSTICE STEWART, MR. JUSTICE BLACKMUN, and MR. JUSTICE STEVENS, joined.

* * * Petitioner Coker was convicted of rape and sentenced to death.   Both the conviction and the sentence were affirmed by the Georgia Supreme Court.   Coker was granted a writ of certiorari, limited to the single claim, rejected by the Georgia court, that the punishment of death for rape violates the Eighth Amendment, which proscribes "cruel and unusual punishments" and which must be observed by the States as well as the Federal Government.

I

While serving various sentences for murder, rape, kidnaping, and aggravated assault, petitioner escaped from the Ware Correctional Institution near Waycross, Ga., on September 2, 1974.   At approximately 11 o'clock that night, petitioner entered the house of Allen and Elnita Carver through an unlocked kitchen door. Threatening the couple with a "board," he tied up Mr. Carver in the bathroom, obtained a knife from the kitchen, and took Mr. Carver's money and the keys to the family car. Brandishing the knife and saying "you know what's going to happen to you if you try anything, don't you," Coker then raped Mrs. Carver. Soon thereafter, petitioner drove away in the Carver car, taking Mrs. Carver with him. Mr. Carver, freeing himself, notified the police; and not long thereafter petitioner was apprehended. Mrs. Carver was unharmed.

Petitioner was charged with escape, armed robbery, motor vehicle theft, kidnaping, and rape. * * * The jury returned a verdict of guilty, rejecting his general plea of insanity. A sentencing hearing was then conducted in accordance with the procedures dealt with at length in *Gregg v. Georgia,* 428 U.S. 153 (1976), where this Court sustained the death penalty for murder when imposed pursuant to the statutory procedures. The jury was instructed that it could consider as aggravating circumstances whether the rape had been committed by a person with a prior record of conviction for a capital felony and whether the rape had been committed in the course of committing another capital felony, namely, the armed robbery of Allen Carver. The court also instructed, pursuant to statute, that even if aggravating circumstances were present, the death penalty need not be imposed if the jury found they were outweighed by mitigating circumstances, that is, circumstances not constituting justification or excuse for the offense in question, "but which, in fairness and mercy, may be considered as extenuating or reducing the degree" of moral culpability or punishment. The jury's verdict on the rape count was death by electrocution. Both aggravating circumstances on which the court instructed were found to be present by the jury.

II

* * *

In sustaining the imposition of the death penalty in *Gregg,* * * * the Court firmly embraced the holdings and dicta from prior cases to the effect that the Eighth Amendment bars not only those punishments that are "barbaric" but also those that are "excessive" in relation to the crime committed. Under *Gregg,* a punishment is "excessive" and unconstitutional if it (1) makes no measurable contribution to acceptable goals of punishment and hence is nothing more than the purposeless and needless imposition of pain and suffering; or (2) is grossly out of proportion to the severity of the crime. A punishment might fail the test on either ground. * * * In *Gregg,* * * * the Court's judgment was that the death penalty for deliberate murder was neither the purposeless imposition of severe punishment nor a punishment grossly disproportionate to the crime. But the Court reserved the question of the constitutionality of the death penalty when imposed for other crimes.

III

That question, with respect to rape of an adult woman, is now before us. We have concluded that a sentence of death is grossly disproportionate and excessive punishment for the crime of rape and is therefore forbidden by the Eighth Amendment as cruel and unusual punishment.[4]

A

As advised by recent cases, we seek guidance in history and from the objective evidence of the country's present judgment concerning the acceptability of death as a penalty for rape of an adult woman. At no time in the last 50 years have a majority of the States authorized death as a punishment for rape. In 1925, 18 States, the District of Columbia, and the Federal Government authorized capital punishment for the rape of an adult female. By 1971 just prior to the decision in *Furman v. Georgia,* that number had declined, but not substantially, to 16 States plus the Federal Government. *Furman* then invalidated most of the capital punishment statutes in this country, including the rape statutes, because, among other reasons, of the manner in which the death penalty was imposed and utilized under those laws.

With their death penalty statutes for the most part invalidated, the States were faced with the choice of enacting modified capital punishment laws in an attempt to satisfy the requirements of *Furman* or of being satisfied with life imprisonment as the ultimate punishment for *any* offense. Thirty-five States immediately reinstituted the death penalty for at least limited kinds of crime. * * *

* * * In reviving death penalty laws to satisfy *Furman*'s mandate, none of the States that had not previously authorized death for rape chose to include rape among capital felonies. Of the 16 States in which rape had been a capital offense, only three provided the death penalty for rape of an adult woman in their revised statutes—Georgia, North Carolina, and Louisiana. In the latter two States, the death penalty was mandatory for those found guilty, and those laws were invalidated by *Woodson* and *Roberts*. When Louisiana and North Carolina, responding to those decisions, again revised their capital punishment laws, they re-enacted the death penalty for murder but not for rape * * *.

* * *

It should be noted that Florida, Mississippi, and Tennessee also authorized the death penalty in some rape cases, but only where the victim was a child and the rapist an adult. The Tennessee statute has since been invalidated because the death sentence was mandatory. The upshot is that Georgia is the sole jurisdiction in the United States at the present time that authorizes a sentence of death when the rape

---

4. Because the death sentence is a disproportionate punishment for rape, it is cruel and unusual punishment within the meaning of the Eighth Amendment even though it may measurably serve the legitimate end of punishment and therefore is not invalid for its failure to do so. * * *

victim is an adult woman, and only two other jurisdictions provide capital punishment when the victim is a child.

The current judgment with respect to the death penalty for rape is not wholly unanimous among state legislatures, but it obviously weighs very heavily on the side of rejecting capital punishment as a suitable penalty for raping an adult woman.[10]

B

It was also observed in *Gregg* that "[t]he jury . . . is a significant and reliable objective index of contemporary values because it is so directly involved" and that it is thus important to look to the sentencing decisions that juries have made in the course of assessing whether capital punishment is an appropriate penalty for the crime being tried.

*   *   *

According to the factual submissions in this Court, out of all rape convictions in Georgia since 1973—and that total number has not been tendered—63 cases had been reviewed by the Georgia Supreme Court as of the time of oral argument; and of these, 6 involved a death sentence, 1 of which was set aside, leaving 5 convicted rapists now under sentence of death in the State of Georgia. Georgia juries have thus sentenced rapists to death six times since 1973. This obviously is not a negligible number; and the State argues that as a practical matter juries simply reserve the extreme sanction for extreme cases of rape and that recent experience surely does not prove that jurors consider the death penalty to be a disproportionate punishment for every conceivable instance of rape, no matter how aggravated. Nevertheless, it is true that in the vast majority of cases, at least 9 out of 10, juries have not imposed the death sentence.

IV

These recent events evidencing the attitude of state legislatures and sentencing juries do not wholly determine this controversy, for the Constitution contemplates that in the end our own judgment will be brought to bear on the question of the acceptability of the death penalty under the Eighth Amendment. Nevertheless, the legislative rejection of capital punishment for rape strongly confirms our own judgment, which is that death is indeed a disproportionate penalty for the crime of raping an adult woman.

We do not discount the seriousness of rape as a crime. It is highly reprehensible, both in a moral sense and in its almost total contempt for the personal integrity and autonomy of the female victim and for the latter's privilege of choosing those with whom intimate relationships are to be established. Short of homicide, it is the "ultimate

---

10. In *Trop v. Dulles,* 356 U.S. 86, 102 (1958), the plurality took pains to note the climate of international opinion concerning the acceptability of a particular punishment. It is thus not irrelevant here that out of 60 major nations in the world surveyed in 1965, only 3 retained the death penalty for rape where death did not ensue. United Nations, Department of Economic and Social Affairs, Capital Punishment 40, 86 (1968).

violation of self." It is also a violent crime because it normally involves force, or the threat of force or intimidation, to overcome the will and the capacity of the victim to resist. Rape is very often accompanied by physical injury to the female and can also inflict mental and psychological damage. Because it undermines the community's sense of security, there is public injury as well.

Rape is without doubt deserving of serious punishment; but in terms of moral depravity and of the injury to the person and to the public, it does not compare with murder, which does involve the unjustified taking of human life. Although it may be accompanied by another crime, rape by definition does not include the death of or even the serious injury to another person. The murderer kills; the rapist, if no more than that, does not. Life is over for the victim of the murderer; for the rape victim, life may not be nearly so happy as it was, but it is not over and normally is not beyond repair. We have the abiding conviction that the death penalty, which "is unique in its severity and irrevocability" is an excessive penalty for the rapist who, as such, does not take human life.

This does not end the matter; for under Georgia law, death may not be imposed for any capital offense, including rape, unless the jury or judge finds one of the statutory aggravating circumstances and then elects to impose that sentence. For the rapist to be executed in Georgia, it must therefore be found not only that he committed rape but also that one or more of the following aggravating circumstances were present: (1) that the rape was committed by a person with a prior record of conviction for a capital felony; (2) that the rape was committed while the offender was engaged in the commission of another capital felony, or aggravated battery; or (3) the rape "was outrageously or wantonly vile, horrible or inhuman in that it involved torture, depravity of mind, or aggravated battery to the victim." Here, the first two of these aggravating circumstances were alleged and found by the jury.

Neither of these circumstances, nor both of them together, change our conclusion that the death sentence imposed on Coker is a disproportionate punishment for rape. Coker had prior convictions for capital felonies—rape, murder, and kidnaping—but these prior convictions do not change the fact that the instant crime being punished is a rape not involving the taking of life.

It is also true that the present rape occurred while Coker was committing armed robbery, a felony for which the Georgia statutes authorize the death penalty. But Coker was tried for the robbery offense as well as for rape and received a separate life sentence for this crime; the jury did not deem the robbery itself deserving of the death penalty, even though accompanied by the aggravating circumstance, which was stipulated, that Coker had been convicted of a prior capital crime.[16]

* * * The judgment of the Georgia Supreme Court upholding the death sentence is reversed, and the case is remanded to that court for further proceedings not inconsistent with this opinion.

* * *

MR. JUSTICE BRENNAN, concurring in the judgment. [Opinion omitted.]

MR. JUSTICE MARSHALL, concurring in the judgment. [Opinion omitted.]

* * *

MR. JUSTICE POWELL, concurring in the judgment in part and dissenting in part.

I concur in the judgment of the Court on the facts of this case, and also in the plurality's reasoning supporting the view that ordinarily death is disproportionate punishment for the crime of raping an adult woman. Although rape invariably is a reprehensible crime, there is no indication that petitioner's offense was committed with excessive brutality or that the victim sustained serious or lasting injury. The plurality, however, does not limit its holding to the case before us or to similar cases. Rather, in an opinion that ranges well beyond what is necessary, it holds that capital punishment *always*—regardless of the circumstances—is a disproportionate penalty for the crime of rape.

* * *

Today, in a case that does not require such an expansive pronouncement, the plurality draws a bright line between murder and all rapes—regardless of the degree of brutality of the rape or the effect upon the victim. I dissent because I am not persuaded that such a bright line is appropriate. As noted in *Snider v. Peyton*, 356 F.2d 626, 627 (CA4 1966), "[t]here is extreme variation in the degree of culpability of rapists." The deliberate viciousness of the rapist may be greater than that of the murderer. Rape is never an act committed accidentally. Rarely can it be said to be unpremeditated. There also is wide variation in the effect on the victim. The plurality opinion says that "[l]ife is over for the victim of the murderer; for the rape victim, life may not be nearly so happy as it was, but it is not over and normally is not beyond repair." But there is indeed "extreme variation" in the crime of rape. Some victims are so grievously injured physically or psychologically that life *is* beyond repair.

Thus, it may be that the death penalty is not disproportionate punishment for the crime of aggravated rape. Final resolution of the question must await careful inquiry into objective indicators of society's

16. * * * Where the third aggravating circumstance mentioned in the text is present—that the rape is particularly vile or involves torture or aggravated battery— it would seem that the defendant could very likely be convicted, tried, and appropriately punished for this additional conduct.

"evolving standards of decency," particularly legislative enactments and the responses of juries in capital cases.[2] * * *

MR. CHIEF JUSTICE BURGER, with whom MR. JUSTICE REHNQUIST joins, dissenting.

* * *

(1)

On December 5, 1971, the petitioner, Ehrlich Anthony Coker, raped and then stabbed to death a young woman. Less than eight months later Coker kidnaped and raped a second young woman. After twice raping this 16–year–old victim, he stripped her, severely beat her with a club, and dragged her into a wooded area where he left her for dead. He was apprehended and pleaded guilty to offenses stemming from these incidents. He was sentenced by three separate courts to three life terms, two 20–year terms, and one 8–year term of imprisonment. Each judgment specified that the sentences it imposed were to run consecutively rather than concurrently. Approximately 1½ years later, on September 2, 1974, petitioner escaped from the state prison where he was serving these sentences. He promptly raped another 16–year–old woman in the presence of her husband, abducted her from her home, and threatened her with death and serious bodily harm. It is this crime for which the sentence now under review was imposed.

The Court today holds that the State of Georgia may not impose the death penalty on Coker. In so doing, it prevents the State from imposing any effective punishment upon Coker for his latest rape. The Court's holding, moreover, bars Georgia from guaranteeing its citizens that they will suffer no further attacks by this habitual rapist. In fact, given the lengthy sentences Coker must serve for the crimes he has already committed, the Court's holding assures that petitioner—as well as others in his position—will henceforth feel no compunction whatsoever about committing further rapes as frequently as he may be able to escape from confinement and indeed even within the walls of the prison itself. * * *

(2)

* * *

Unlike the plurality, I would narrow the inquiry in this case to the question actually presented: Does the Eighth Amendment's ban against cruel and unusual punishment prohibit the State of Georgia from executing a person who has, within the space of three years, raped three separate women, killing one and attempting to kill another, who is serving prison terms exceeding his probable lifetime and who has not hesitated to escape confinement at the first available opportunity? Whatever one's view may be as to the State's constitutional power to impose the death penalty upon a rapist who stands before a court

2. These objective indicators are highly relevant, but the ultimate decision as to the appropriateness of the death penalty under the Eighth Amendment—as the plu-rality notes—must be decided on the basis of our own judgment in light of the precedents of this Court.

convicted for the first time, this case reveals a chronic rapist whose continuing danger to the community is abundantly clear.

Mr. Justice Powell would hold the death sentence inappropriate in *this* case because "there is no indication that petitioner's offense was committed with excessive brutality or that the victim sustained serious or lasting injury." Apart from the reality that rape is inherently one of the most egregiously brutal acts one human being can inflict upon another, there is nothing in the Eighth Amendment that so narrowly limits the factors which may be considered by a state legislature in determining whether a particular punishment is grossly excessive. Surely recidivism, especially the repeated commission of heinous crimes, is a factor which may properly be weighed as an aggravating circumstance, permitting the imposition of a punishment more severe than for one isolated offense. * * *

* * *

In sum, once the Court has held that "the punishment of death does not invariably violate the Constitution," it seriously impinges upon the State's legislative judgment to hold that it may not impose such sentence upon an individual who has shown total and repeated disregard for the welfare, safety, personal integrity, and human worth of others, and who seemingly cannot be deterred from continuing such conduct. I therefore would hold that the death sentence here imposed is within the power reserved to the State and leave for another day the question of whether such sanction would be proper under other circumstances. * * * Since the Court now invalidates the death penalty as a sanction for all rapes of adults at all times under all circumstances, I reluctantly turn to what I see as the broader issues raised by this holding.

(3)

* * *

The analysis of the plurality opinion is divided into two parts: (a) an "objective" determination that most American jurisdictions do not presently make rape a capital offense, and (b) a subjective judgment that death is an excessive punishment for rape because the crime does not, in and of itself, cause the death of the victim. I take issue with each of these points.

(a)

The plurality opinion bases its analysis, in part, on the fact that "Georgia is the sole jurisdiction in the United States at the present time that authorizes a sentence of death when the rape victim is an adult woman." Surely, however, this statistic cannot be deemed determinative, or even particularly relevant. * * *

* * * [I]t is myopic to base sweeping constitutional principles upon the narrow experience of the past five years. Considerable uncertainty was introduced into this area of the law by this Court's *Furman* decision. A large number of States found their death penalty

statutes invalidated; legislatures were left in serious doubt by the expressions vacillating between discretionary and mandatory death penalties, as to whether this Court would sustain *any* statute imposing death as a criminal sanction.   Failure of more States to enact statutes imposing death for rape of an adult woman may thus reflect hasty legislative compromise occasioned by time pressures following *Furman,* a desire to wait on the experience of those States which did enact such statutes, or simply an accurate forecast of today's holding.

In any case, when considered in light of the experience since the turn of this century, where more than one-third of American jurisdictions have consistently provided the death penalty for rape, the plurality's focus on the experience of the immediate past must be viewed as truly disingenuous. * * * Far more representative of societal mores of the 20th century is the accepted practice in a substantial number of jurisdictions preceding the *Furman* decision. * * *

However, even were one to give the most charitable acceptance to the plurality's statistical analysis, it still does not, to my mind, support its conclusion. * * * Even if these figures could be read as indicating that no other States view the death penalty as an appropriate punishment for the rape of an adult woman, it would not necessarily follow that Georgia's imposition of such sanction violates the Eighth Amendment.

The Court has repeatedly pointed to the reserve strength of our federal system which allows state legislatures, within broad limits, to experiment with laws, both criminal and civil, in the effort to achieve socially desirable results. * * *

Statutory provisions in criminal justice applied in one part of the country can be carefully watched by other state legislatures, so that the experience of one State becomes available to all.   Although human lives are in the balance, it must be remembered that failure to allow flexibility may also jeopardize human lives—those of the victims of undeterred criminal conduct.   Our concern for the accused ought not foreclose legislative judgments showing a modicum of consideration for the potential victims.

Three state legislatures have, in the past five years, determined that the taking of human life and the devastating consequences of rape will be minimized if rapists may, in a limited class of cases, be executed for their offenses.   That these States are presently a minority does not, in my view, make their judgment less worthy of deference. * * *

                              *   *   *

* * * Social change on great issues generally reveals itself in small increments, and the "current judgment" of many States could well be altered on the basis of Georgia's experience, were we to allow its statute to stand.

(b)

The subjective judgment that the death penalty is simply disproportionate to the crime of rape is even more disturbing than the
"objective" analysis discussed *supra*. The plurality's conclusion on this
point is based upon the bare fact that murder necessarily results in the
physical death of the victim, while rape does not. * * * Until now,
the issue under the Eighth Amendment has not been the state of any
particular victim after the crime, but rather whether the punishment
imposed is grossly disproportionate to the evil committed by the perpetrator. As a matter of constitutional principle, that test cannot have
the primitive simplicity of "life for life, eye for eye, tooth for tooth."
Rather States must be permitted to engage in a more sophisticated
weighing of values in dealing with criminal activity which consistently
poses serious danger of death or grave bodily harm. If innocent life
and limb are to be preserved I see no constitutional barrier in punishing by death all who engage in such activity, regardless of whether the
risk comes to fruition in any particular instance. * * *

* * *

Whatever our individual views as to the wisdom of capital punishment, I cannot agree that it is constitutionally impermissible for a state
legislature to make the "solemn judgment" to impose such penalty for
the crime of rape. Accordingly, I would leave to the States the task of
legislating in this area of the law.

Questions and Points for Discussion

1. In Thompson v. Oklahoma, 487 U.S. 815, 108 S.Ct. 2687 (1988), the
Supreme Court addressed the question whether the execution of defendants
for crimes committed while they were fifteen or younger would invariably
constitute cruel and unusual punishment. Four of the Justices, in an
opinion written by Justice Stevens, concluded that it would. Justice
Stevens mentioned two reasons why such executions violate the eighth
amendment. First, they contravene societal standards of decency, both
because none of the states that have designated a minimum age for
imposition of the death penalty permit the infliction of the penalty on
individuals who were fifteen or younger at the time of their crimes and
because of the rarity with which such young defendants have been sentenced to death. Second, executing defendants for crimes committed while
they were younger than sixteen represents " 'nothing more than the
purposeless and needless imposition of pain and suffering.' " Id. at 838,
108 S.Ct. at 2700 (quoting Coker v. Georgia, 433 U.S. at 592, 97 S.Ct. at
2866). In explaining this latter conclusion, the plurality expressed its view
that the retributive purpose of the death penalty would be ill-served under
such circumstances because juveniles, due to their immaturity, are not as
culpable as adults when they commit crimes. Nor, according to the
plurality, would the death penalty likely have a deterrent effect on young
people who are known for their rash and impulsive actions.

Justice O'Connor wrote a separate concurring opinion in *Thompson*,
noting that it was not sufficiently clear in her mind whether or not there

was a national consensus against the death penalty for those who had committed crimes when they were fifteen-years-old or younger. Under such circumstances, she considered imposition of the death penalty to be unconstitutional where a state, such as Oklahoma, had not set a minimum age for imposition of the death penalty and specifically authorized the execution of individuals who were younger than sixteen at the time of their crimes. In a dissenting opinion, Justice Scalia lambasted this point of view, contending that the concurrence was basically saying, "We cannot really say that what you are doing is contrary to national consensus and therefore unconstitutional, but since we are not entirely sure you must in the future legislate in the manner that we say." Id. at 877, 108 S.Ct. at 2721 (Scalia, J., dissenting).

2. A year after *Thompson* was decided, the Supreme Court, in a 5–4 decision, upheld the constitutionality of death sentences imposed on defendants who were sixteen and seventeen at the time of their crimes. Stanford v. Kentucky, 109 S.Ct. 2969 (1989). While acknowledging that such individuals are infrequently sentenced to death, the Court, in an opinion written by Justice Scalia, observed that "it is not only possible but overwhelmingly probable that the very considerations which induce petitioners and their supporters to believe that death should *never* be imposed on offenders under 18 cause prosecutors and juries to believe that it should *rarely* be imposed." Id. at 2977 (emphasis in the original).

In a potentially portentous section of his opinion, a section which did not garner a majority but in which three other Justices joined, Justice Scalia wrote as follows:

Having failed to establish a consensus against capital punishment for 16- and 17-year-old offenders through state and federal statutes and the behavior of prosecutors and juries, petitioners seek to demonstrate it through other indicia, including public opinion polls, the views of interest groups and the positions adopted by various professional associations. We decline the invitation to rest constitutional law upon such uncertain foundations. A revised national consensus so broad, so clear and so enduring as to justify a permanent prohibition upon all units of democratic government must appear in the operative acts (laws and the application of laws) that the people have approved.

We also reject petitioners' argument that we should invalidate capital punishment of 16- and 17-year-old offenders on the ground that it fails to serve the legitimate goals of penology. According to petitioners, it fails to deter because juveniles, possessing less developed cognitive skills than adults, are less likely to fear death; and it fails to exact just retribution because juveniles, being less mature and responsible, are also less morally blameworthy. In support of these claims, petitioners and their supporting *amici* marshall an array of socioscientific evidence concerning the psychological and emotional development of 16- and 17-year-olds.

If such evidence could conclusively establish the entire lack of deterrent effect and moral responsibility, resort to the Cruel and Unusual Punishments Clause would be unnecessary; the Equal Protection Clause of the Fourteenth Amendment would invalidate these laws for lack of rational basis. But as the adjective "socioscientific" suggests (and insofar as evaluation of moral responsibility is concerned perhaps the adjective "ethicoscientific" would be more apt), it is not demonstrable that no 16–year–old is "adequately responsible" or significantly deterred. It is rational, even if mistaken, to think the contrary. The battle must be fought, then, on the field of the Eighth Amendment; and in that struggle socioscientific, ethicoscientific, or even purely scientific evidence is not an available weapon. The punishment is either "cruel *and* unusual" (i.e., society has set its face against it) or it is not. The audience for these arguments, in other words, is not this Court but the citizenry of the United States. It is they, not we, who must be persuaded. For as we stated earlier, our job is to *identify* the "evolving standards of decency"; to determine, not what they *should* be, but what they *are*. We have no power under the Eighth Amendment to substitute our belief in the scientific evidence for the society's apparent skepticism. In short, we emphatically reject petitioner's suggestion that the issues in this case permit us to apply our "own informed judgment" regarding the desirability of permitting the death penalty for crimes by 16– and 17–year–olds.

We reject the dissent's contention that our approach, by "largely return[ing] the task of defining the contours of Eighth Amendment protection to political majorities," leaves " '[c]onstitutional doctrine [to] be formulated by the acts of those institutions which the Constitution is supposed to limit' ". When this Court cast loose from the historical moorings consisting of the original application of the Eighth Amendment, it did not embark rudderless upon a wide-open sea. Rather, it limited the Amendment's extension to those practices contrary to the "evolving *standards* of decency that mark the progress of a maturing *society*." Trop v. Dulles, 356 U.S. 86, 101 (1958) (plurality opinion) (emphasis added). It has never been thought that this was a shorthand reference to the preferences of a majority of this Court. By reaching a decision supported neither by constitutional text nor by the demonstrable current standards of our citizens, the dissent displays a failure to appreciate that "those institutions which the Constitution is supposed to limit" include the Court itself. To say, as the dissent says, that "it is for *us* ultimately to judge whether the Eighth Amendment permits imposition of the death penalty" and to mean that as the dissent means it, i.e., that it is for *us* to judge, not on the basis of what we perceive the Eighth Amendment originally prohibited, or on the basis of what we perceive the society through its democratic processes now overwhelmingly disapproves, but on the basis of what we think "proportionate" and "measurably contributory to acceptable goals of punishment"—to say and mean that, is to replace judges of the law with a committee of philosopher-kings.

Id. at 2979–80.

Do you agree with the views of Justice Scalia? In your opinion, of what significance, if any, are the following factors to the question of whether the death penalty in certain circumstances or all circumstances constitutes cruel and unusual punishment: public opinion polls, the views of professional organizations, the practices of other countries, and the results of studies that bear on the question of whether the death penalty effectuates penological goals.

3. In Penry v. Lynaugh, 109 S.Ct. 2934 (1989) the Supreme Court held that executing a person who is mentally retarded does not necessarily constitute cruel and unusual punishment. The defendant in that case, who was 22 at the time he raped and murdered a woman, had the mental capacity of a six-year-old; with an IQ of between 50 and 63, he was considered somewhere between mildly and moderately retarded. The Court held that the defendant's mental retardation was a mitigating circumstance that should be considered by the sentencer when deciding whether or not to sentence the defendant to death, but that his mental limitations did not automatically preclude imposition of the death penalty.

A prisoner who has been convicted of a capital crime and sentenced to death, but who is now insane, however, cannot be executed unless and until his or her sanity is restored. In explaining why execution of an insane person would be cruel and unusual punishment, the Court in Ford v. Wainwright, 477 U.S. 399, 106 S.Ct. 2595 (1986) noted that for a number of different reasons, not one state in the country permits an insane person to be executed. One of these reasons is that many people doubt that the death penalty could serve its retributive aim when the person being executed is incapable of understanding why he or she is being put to death. The Court also mentioned the religious roots of such execution bans—the belief that it would be unconscionable to kill individuals who are incapable of first seeking forgiveness for their sins.

4. In Tison v. Arizona, 481 U.S. 137, 107 S.Ct. 1676 (1987), the Supreme Court concluded that it is not necessarily cruel and unusual punishment to impose the death penalty on a defendant who did not kill a murder victim and did not intend that the victim be killed. In that case, the defendants, who were brothers, smuggled guns into a prison and then used them to help their father and another prisoner escape. When they later had car trouble, one of the defendants flagged down a passing car whose passengers included a mother and father, their two-year-old son, and their fifteen-year-old niece. The defendants' father and the other escaped prisoner eventually shot and killed all four passengers. The defendants were then convicted of four counts of capital murder under the state's felony-murder statute and another statute holding certain felons responsible for crimes committed by their accomplices.

The Supreme Court, in a 5–4 decision, held that there is nothing cruel and unusual about sentencing to death a defendant whose participation in "the felony" was "major" and who had acted with "reckless indifference to human life." Id. at 158, 107 S.Ct. at 1691. The Court observed that a defendant's reckless disregard for human life can be inferred when a defendant "knowingly engag[es] in criminal activities known to carry a grave risk of death." Id. at 157, 107 S.Ct. at 1688. In the course of its opinion in Tison, the Court distinguished Enmund v. Florida, 458 U.S. 782, 102 S.Ct. 3368 (1982), a case where the Court had ruled unconstitutional imposition of the death penalty on a defendant who had driven the getaway car in an armed robbery, but had not killed the two murder victims. As the Court explained in *Tison*, the defendant's role in the armed robbery and murders in *Enmund* was "minor," and there was no finding that he either had the intent to kill the victims or had acted with reckless indifference to human life.

What if there had been a finding in *Enmund* that the defendant had acted with reckless disregard of the risk that the armed robbery could culminate in the death of the victims? Would imposition of the death penalty have been constitutional in those circumstances?

5. *Class Exercise:* Discuss and debate the following two questions:

1. Is the death penalty, in your opinion, constitutional?

2. Assuming that, as the Supreme Court has concluded, the death penalty is not invariably unconstitutional, in what circumstances can and should the death penalty be authorized by a state or the federal government?

Chapter 7

CRUEL AND UNUSUAL PUNISHMENT AND NONCAPITAL CASES

The previous chapter dealt with limitations placed by the cruel and unusual punishment clause on the imposition of the death sentence as a penalty for a crime. We turn now to a discussion of the application of the cruel and unusual punishment clause in cases where some sentence other than the death penalty was imposed.

RUMMEL v. ESTELLE

Supreme Court of the United States, 1980.
445 U.S. 263, 100 S.Ct. 1133, 63 L.Ed.2d 382.

MR. JUSTICE REHNQUIST delivered the opinion of the Court.

Petitioner William James Rummel is presently serving a life sentence imposed by the State of Texas in 1973 under its "recidivist statute," formerly Art. 63 of its Penal Code, which provided that "[w]hoever shall have been three times convicted of a felony less than capital shall on such third conviction be imprisoned for life in the penitentiary." On January 19, 1976, Rummel sought a writ of habeas corpus in the United States District Court for the Western District of Texas, arguing that life imprisonment was "grossly disproportionate" to the three felonies that formed the predicate for his sentence and that therefore the sentence violated the ban on cruel and unusual punishments of the Eighth and Fourteenth Amendments. The District Court and the United States Court of Appeals for the Fifth Circuit rejected Rummel's claim, finding no unconstitutional disproportionality. We granted certiorari and now affirm.

I

In 1964 the State of Texas charged Rummel with fraudulent use of a credit card to obtain $80 worth of goods or services. Because the amount in question was greater than $50, the charged offense was a felony punishable by a minimum of 2 years and a maximum of 10 years in the Texas Department of Corrections. Rummel eventually pleaded guilty to the charge and was sentenced to three years' confinement in a state penitentiary.

In 1969 the State of Texas charged Rummel with passing a forged check in the amount of $28.36, a crime punishable by imprisonment in a penitentiary for not less than two nor more than five years. Rummel pleaded guilty to this offense and was sentenced to four years' imprisonment.

In 1973 Rummel was charged with obtaining $120.75 by false pretenses. Because the amount obtained was greater than $50, the charged offense was designated "felony theft," which, by itself, was punishable by confinement in a penitentiary for not less than 2 nor more than 10 years. The prosecution chose, however, to proceed against Rummel under Texas' recidivist statute, and cited in the indictment his 1964 and 1969 convictions as requiring imposition of a life sentence if Rummel were convicted of the charged offense. A jury convicted Rummel of felony theft and also found as true the allegation that he had been convicted of two prior felonies. As a result, on April 26, 1973, the trial court imposed upon Rummel the life sentence mandated by Art. 63.

* * *

II

Initially, we believe it important to set forth two propositions that Rummel does not contest. First, Rummel does not challenge the constitutionality of Texas' recidivist statute as a general proposition. * * * Here, Rummel attacks only the result of applying this concededly valid statute to the facts of his case.

Second, Rummel does not challenge Texas' authority to punish each of his offenses as felonies, that is, by imprisoning him in a state penitentiary. Under Texas law Rummel concededly could have received sentences totaling 25 years in prison for what he refers to as his "petty property offenses." Indeed, when Rummel obtained $120.75 by false pretenses he committed a crime punishable as a felony in at least 35 States and the District of Columbia. Similarly, a large number of States authorized significant terms of imprisonment for each of Rummel's other offenses at the times he committed them. Rummel's challenge thus focuses only on the State's authority to impose a sentence of life imprisonment, as opposed to a substantial term of years, for his third felony.

This Court has on occasion stated that the Eighth Amendment prohibits imposition of a sentence that is grossly disproportionate to the severity of the crime. In recent years this proposition has appeared most frequently in opinions dealing with the death penalty. Rummel cites these latter opinions dealing with capital punishment as compelling the conclusion that his sentence is disproportionate to his offenses. But as Mr. Justice Stewart noted in *Furman:*

"The penalty of death differs from all other forms of criminal punishment, not in degree but in kind. It is unique in its total irrevocability. It is unique in its rejection of rehabilitation of the convict as a basic purpose of criminal justice. And it is unique, finally, in its absolute renunciation of all that is embodied in our concept of humanity."

This theme, the unique nature of the death penalty for purposes of Eighth Amendment analysis, has been repeated time and time again in our opinions. Because a sentence of death differs in kind from any sentence of imprisonment, no matter how long, our decisions applying the prohibition of cruel and unusual punishments to capital cases are of limited assistance in deciding the constitutionality of the punishment meted out to Rummel.

Outside the context of capital punishment, successful challenges to the proportionality of particular sentences have been exceedingly rare. In *Weems v. United States,* [217 U.S. 349 (1910)], coming to this Court from the Supreme Court of the Philippine Islands, petitioner successfully attacked the imposition of a punishment known as *"cadena temporal"* for the crime of falsifying a public record. Although the Court in *Weems* invalidated the sentence after weighing "the mischief and the remedy," its finding of disproportionality cannot be wrenched from the extreme facts of that case. As for the "mischief," Weems was convicted of falsifying a public document, a crime apparently complete upon the knowing entry of a single item of false information in a public record, "though there be no one injured, though there be no fraud or purpose of it, no gain or desire of it." The mandatory "remedy" for this offense was *cadena temporal,* a punishment described graphically by the Court:

"Its minimum degree is confinement in a penal institution for twelve years and one day, a chain at the ankle and wrist of the offender, hard and painful labor, no assistance from friend or relative, no marital authority or parental rights or rights of property, no participation even in the family council. These parts of his penalty endure for the term of imprisonment. From other parts there is no intermission. His prison bars and chains are removed, it is true, after twelve years, but he goes from them to a perpetual limitation of his liberty. He is forever kept under the shadow of his crime, forever kept within voice and view of the criminal magistrate, not being able to change his domicil without giving notice to the 'authority immediately in charge of his surveillance,' and without permission in writing."

Although Rummel argues that the length of Weems' imprisonment was, by itself, a basis for the Court's decision, the Court's opinion does not support such a simple conclusion. The opinion consistently referred jointly to the length of imprisonment and its "accessories" or "accompaniments." * * * Thus, we do not believe that *Weems* can be applied without regard to its peculiar facts: the triviality of the charged offense, the impressive length of the minimum term of imprisonment, and the extraordinary nature of the "accessories" included within the punishment of *cadena temporal.*

Given the unique nature of the punishments considered in *Weems* and in the death penalty cases, one could argue without fear of contradiction by any decision of this Court that for crimes concededly classified and classifiable as felonies, that is, as punishable by significant terms of imprisonment in a state penitentiary, the length of the sentence actually imposed is purely a matter of legislative prerogative.[11]   *   *   *

*   *   *

*   *   * [I]n *Weems* the Court could differentiate in an objective fashion between the highly unusual *cadena temporal* and more traditional forms of imprisonment imposed under the Anglo–Saxon system. But a more extensive intrusion into the basic line-drawing process that is pre-eminently the province of the legislature when it makes an act criminal would be difficult to square with the view expressed in *Coker* [*v. Georgia,* 433 U.S. 584 (1977)] that the Court's Eighth Amendment judgments should neither be nor appear to be merely the subjective views of individual Justices.

In an attempt to provide us with objective criteria against which we might measure the proportionality of his life sentence, Rummel points to certain characteristics of his offenses that allegedly render them "petty." He cites, for example, the absence of violence in his crimes. But the presence or absence of violence does not always affect the strength of society's interest in deterring a particular crime or in punishing a particular criminal. A high official in a large corporation can commit undeniably serious crimes in the area of antitrust, bribery, or clean air or water standards without coming close to engaging in any "violent" or short-term "life-threatening" behavior. Additionally, Rummel cites the "small" amount of money taken in each of his crimes. But to recognize that the State of Texas could have imprisoned Rummel for life if he had stolen $5,000, $50,000, or $500,000, rather than the $120.75 that a jury convicted him of stealing, is virtually to concede that the lines to be drawn are indeed "subjective," and therefore properly within the province of legislatures, not courts. Moreover, if Rummel had attempted to defraud his victim of $50,000, but had failed, no money whatsoever would have changed hands; yet Rummel would be no less blameworthy, only less skillful, than if he had succeeded.

In this case, however, we need not decide whether Texas could impose a life sentence upon Rummel merely for obtaining $120.75 by false pretenses. Had Rummel only committed that crime, under the law enacted by the Texas Legislature he could have been imprisoned for no more than 10 years. In fact, at the time that he obtained the $120.75 by false pretenses, he already had committed and had been imprisoned for two other felonies, crimes that Texas and other States felt were serious enough to warrant significant terms of imprisonment even in the absence of prior offenses. Thus the interest of the State of

11. This is not to say that a proportionality principle would not come into play in the extreme example mentioned by the dissent, if a legislature made overtime parking a felony punishable by life imprisonment.

Texas here is not simply that of making criminal the unlawful acquisition of another person's property; it is in addition the interest, expressed in all recidivist statutes, in dealing in a harsher manner with those who by repeated criminal acts have shown that they are simply incapable of conforming to the norms of society as established by its criminal law. By conceding the validity of recidivist statutes generally, Rummel himself concedes that the State of Texas, or any other State, has a valid interest in so dealing with that class of persons.

* * *

* * * Rummel attempts to ground his proportionality attack on an alleged "nationwide" trend away from mandatory life sentences and toward "lighter, discretionary sentences." According to Rummel, "[n]o jurisdiction in the United States or the Free World punishes habitual offenders as harshly as Texas." In support of this proposition, Rummel offers detailed charts and tables documenting the history of recidivist statutes in the United States since 1776.

Before evaluating this evidence, we believe it important to examine the exact operation of Art. 63 as interpreted by the Texas courts. In order to qualify for a mandatory life sentence under that statute, Rummel had to satisfy a number of requirements. First, he had to be convicted of a felony and actually sentenced to prison. Second, at some time subsequent to his first conviction, Rummel had to be convicted of another felony and again sentenced to imprisonment. Finally, after having been sent to prison a second time, Rummel had to be convicted of a third felony. Thus, under Art. 63, a three-time felon receives a mandatory life sentence, with possibility of parole, only if commission and conviction of each succeeding felony followed conviction for the preceding one, and only if each prior conviction was followed by actual imprisonment. Given this necessary sequence, a recidivist must twice demonstrate that conviction and actual imprisonment do not deter him from returning to crime once he is released. One in Rummel's position has been both graphically informed of the consequences of lawlessness and given an opportunity to reform, all to no avail. Article 63 thus is nothing more than a societal decision that when such a person commits yet another felony, he should be subjected to the admittedly serious penalty of incarceration for life, subject only to the State's judgment as to whether to grant him parole.

In comparing this recidivist program with those presently employed in other States, Rummel creates a complex hierarchy of statutes and places Texas' recidivist scheme alone on the top rung. This isolation is not entirely convincing. Both West Virginia and Washington, for example, impose mandatory life sentences upon the commission of a third felony. * * *

Rummel's charts and tables do appear to indicate that he might have received more lenient treatment in almost any State other than Texas, West Virginia, or Washington. The distinctions, however, are subtle rather than gross. A number of States impose a mandatory life sentence upon conviction of four felonies rather than three. Other States require one or more of the felonies to be "violent" to support a life sentence. Still other States leave the imposition of a life sentence after three felonies within the discretion of a judge or jury. * * *

Nor do Rummel's extensive charts even begin to reflect the complexity of the comparison he asks this Court to make. Texas, we are told, has a relatively liberal policy of granting "good time" credits to its prisoners, a policy that historically has allowed a prisoner serving a life sentence to become eligible for parole in as little as 12 years. We agree with Rummel that his inability to enforce any "right" to parole precludes us from treating his life sentence as if it were equivalent to a sentence of 12 years. Nevertheless, because parole is "an established variation on imprisonment of convicted criminals," a proper assessment of Texas' treatment of Rummel could hardly ignore the possibility that he will not actually be imprisoned for the rest of his life. * * *

* * *

We offer these additional considerations not as inherent flaws in Rummel's suggested interjurisdictional analysis but as illustrations of the complexities confronting any court that would attempt such a comparison. Even were we to assume that the statute employed against Rummel was the most stringent found in the 50 States, that severity hardly would render Rummel's punishment "grossly disproportionate" to his offenses or to the punishment he would have received in the other States. As Mr. Justice Holmes noted in his dissenting opinion in *Lochner v. New York,* 198 U.S. 45, 76 (1905), our Constitution "is made for people of fundamentally differing views. . . . " Until quite recently, Arizona punished as a felony the theft of any "neat or horned animal," regardless of its value; California considers the theft of "avocados, olives, citrus or deciduous fruits, nuts and artichokes" particularly reprehensible. In one State theft of $100 will earn the offender a fine or a short term in jail; in another State it could earn him a sentence of 10 years' imprisonment. Absent a constitutionally imposed uniformity inimical to traditional notions of federalism, some State will always bear the distinction of treating particular offenders more severely than any other State.[27]

27. The dissent draws some support for its belief that Rummel's sentence is unconstitutional by comparing it with punishments imposed by Texas for crimes other than those committed by Rummel. Other crimes, of course, implicate other societal interests, making any such comparison inherently speculative. Embezzlement, dealing in "hard" drugs, and forgery, to name only three offenses, could be denominated "property related" offenses, and yet each can be viewed as an assault on a unique set of societal values as defined by the political process. The notions embodied in the dissent that if the crime involved "violence," a more severe penalty is warranted under objective standards simply will not wash, whether it be taken as a matter of morals, history, or law. * * * The highly placed executive who embezzles huge sums from a state savings and loan association, causing many shareholders of limited means to lose substantial parts of their savings, has committed a crime very different from a man who takes a smaller amount of money from the same savings and loan at the point of a gun. Yet rational people could disagree as to which criminal merits harsher punishment. By the same token, a State cannot be required to treat persons who have committed three "minor" offenses less severely than persons

Perhaps, as asserted in *Weems,* "time works changes" upon the Eighth Amendment, bringing into existence "new conditions and purposes." We all, of course, would like to think that we are "moving down the road toward human decency." Within the confines of this judicial proceeding, however, we have no way of knowing in which direction that road lies. Penologists themselves have been unable to agree whether sentences should be light or heavy, discretionary or determinate. This uncertainty reinforces our conviction that any "nationwide trend" toward lighter, discretionary sentences must find its source and its sustaining force in the legislatures, not in the federal courts.

III

* * *

The purpose of a recidivist statute such as that involved here is not to simplify the task of prosecutors, judges, or juries. Its primary goals are to deter repeat offenders and, at some point in the life of one who repeatedly commits criminal offenses serious enough to be punished as felonies, to segregate that person from the rest of society for an extended period of time. This segregation and its duration are based not merely on that person's most recent offense but also on the propensities he has demonstrated over a period of time during which he has been convicted of and sentenced for other crimes. Like the line dividing felony theft from petty larceny, the point at which a recidivist will be deemed to have demonstrated the necessary propensities and the amount of time that the recidivist will be isolated from society are matters largely within the discretion of the punishing jurisdiction.

We therefore hold that the mandatory life sentence imposed upon this petitioner does not constitute cruel and unusual punishment under the Eighth and Fourteenth Amendments. The judgment of the Court of Appeals is

Affirmed.

MR. JUSTICE STEWART, concurring.

I am moved to repeat the substance of what I had to say on another occasion about the recidivist legislation of Texas:

"If the Constitution gave me a roving commission to impose upon the criminal courts of Texas my own notions of enlightened policy, I would not join the Court's opinion. For it is clear to me that the recidivist procedures adopted in recent years by many other States

who have committed one or two "more serious" offenses. If nothing else, the three-time offender's conduct supports inferences about his ability to conform with social norms that are quite different from possible inferences about first- or second-time offenders.

In short, the "seriousness" of an offense or a pattern of offenses in modern society is not a line, but a plane. Once the death penalty and other punishments different in kind from fine or imprisonment have been put to one side, there remains little in the way of objective standards for judging whether or not a life sentence imposed under a recidivist statute for several separate felony convictions not involving "violence" violates the cruel-and-unusual-punishment prohibition of the Eighth Amendment. * * *

. . . are far superior to those utilized [here]. But the question for decision is not whether we applaud or even whether we personally approve the procedures followed in [this case]. The question is whether those procedures fall below the minimum level the [Constitution] will tolerate. Upon that question I am constrained to join the opinion and judgment of the Court." *Spencer v. Texas,* 385 U.S. 554, 569 (concurring opinion).

MR. JUSTICE POWELL, with whom MR. JUSTICE BRENNAN, MR. JUSTICE MARSHALL, and MR. JUSTICE STEVENS join, dissenting.

* * *

The scope of the Cruel and Unusual Punishments Clause extends not only to barbarous methods of punishment, but also to punishments that are grossly disproportionate. Disproportionality analysis measures the relationship between the nature and number of offenses committed and the severity of the punishment inflicted upon the offender. The inquiry focuses on whether a person deserves such punishment, not simply on whether punishment would serve a utilitarian goal. A statute that levied a mandatory life sentence for overtime parking might well deter vehicular lawlessness, but it would offend our felt sense of justice. * * *

* * *

Under Texas law, petitioner has been sentenced to a mandatory life sentence. Even so, the Court of Appeals rejected the petitioner's Eighth Amendment claim primarily because it concluded that the petitioner probably would not serve a life sentence. * * *

It is true that imposition in Texas of a mandatory life sentence does not necessarily mean that petitioner will spend the rest of his life behind prison walls. If petitioner attains sufficient good-time credits, he may be eligible for parole within 10 or 12 years after he begins serving his life sentence. But petitioner will have no right to early release; he will merely be eligible for parole. And parole is simply an act of executive grace.

* * *

Recent events in Texas demonstrate that parole remains a matter of executive grace. In June 1979, the Governor of Texas refused to grant parole to 79% of the state prisoners whom the parole board recommended for release.[11] The State's chief executive acted well within his rights in declining to follow the board, but his actions emphasize the speculative nature of the Court of Appeals' reasoning. As this case comes to us, petitioner has been deprived by operation of state law of his right to freedom from imprisonment for the rest of his life. We should judge the case accordingly.

The Eighth Amendment commands this Court to enforce the constitutional limitation of the Cruel and Unusual Punishments Clause. In

11. Austin American–Statesman, Sept. 23, 1979, p. A1, col. 4. The newspaper reported that in a 6–month period including June 1979, the Governor rejected 33% of the parole board recommendations that prisoners be released. *Ibid.*

discharging this responsibility, we should minimize the risk of constitutionalizing the personal predilections of federal judges by relying upon certain objective factors. Among these are (i) the nature of the offense, (ii) the sentence imposed for commission of the same crime in other jurisdictions, and (iii) the sentence imposed upon other criminals in the same jurisdiction.

A

Each of the crimes that underlies the petitioner's conviction as a habitual offender involves the use of fraud to obtain small sums of money ranging from $28.36 to $120.75. In total, the three crimes involved slightly less than $230. None of the crimes involved injury to one's person, threat of injury to one's person, violence, the threat of violence, or the use of a weapon. Nor does the commission of any such crimes ordinarily involve a threat of violent action against another person or his property. It is difficult to imagine felonies that pose less danger to the peace and good order of a civilized society than the three crimes committed by the petitioner. Indeed, the state legislature's recodification of its criminal law supports this conclusion. Since the petitioner was convicted as a habitual offender, the State has reclassified his third offense, theft by false pretext, as a misdemeanor.[12]

B

Apparently, only 12 States have ever enacted habitual offender statutes imposing a mandatory life sentence for the commission of two or three nonviolent felonies and only 3, Texas, Washington, and West Virginia, have retained such a statute. Thus, three-fourths of the States that experimented with the Texas scheme appear to have decided that the imposition of a mandatory life sentence upon some persons who have committed three felonies represents excess punishment.
* * *

More than three-quarters of American jurisdictions have never adopted a habitual offender statute that would commit the petitioner to mandatory life imprisonment. The jurisdictions that currently employ habitual offender statutes either (i) require the commission of more than three offenses, (ii) require the commission of at least one violent crime, (iii) limit a mandatory penalty to less than life, or (iv) grant discretion to the sentencing authority. In none of the jurisdictions could the petitioner have received a mandatory life sentence merely

---

12. The Court suggests that an inquiry into the nature of the offense at issue in this case inevitably involves identifying subjective distinctions beyond the province of the judiciary. Yet the distinction between forging a check for $28 and committing a violent crime or one that threatens violence is surely no more difficult for the judiciary to perceive than the distinction between the gravity of murder and rape. See *Coker v. Georgia*, 433 U.S. 584, 598 (1977). I do not suggest that all criminal acts may be separated into precisely identifiable compartments. A professional seller of addictive drugs may inflict greater bodily harm upon members of society than the person who commits a single assault. But the difficulties of line-drawing that might be presented in other cases need not obscure our vision here.

upon the showing that he committed three nonviolent property-related offenses.[19]

* * * These legislative decisions lend credence to the view that a mandatory life sentence for the commission of three nonviolent felonies is unconstitutionally disproportionate.

C

Finally, it is necessary to examine the punishment that Texas provides for other criminals. First and second offenders who commit more serious crimes than the petitioner may receive markedly less severe sentences. The only first-time offender subject to a mandatory life sentence is a person convicted of capital murder. A person who commits a first-degree felony, including murder, aggravated kidnaping, or aggravated rape, may be imprisoned from 5 to 99 years. Persons who commit a second-degree felony, including voluntary manslaughter, rape, or robbery, may be punished with a sentence of between 2 and 20 years. A person who commits a second felony is punished as if he had committed a felony of the next higher degree. Thus, a person who rapes twice may receive a 5–year sentence. He also may, but need not, receive a sentence functionally equivalent to life imprisonment.

The State argues that these comparisons are not illuminating because a three-time recidivist may be sentenced more harshly than a first-time offender. Of course, the State may mandate extra punishment for a recidivist. In Texas a person convicted twice of the unauthorized use of a vehicle receives a greater sentence than a person once convicted for that crime, but he does not receive a sentence as great as a person who rapes twice. * * *

Texas recognizes when it sentences two-time offenders that the amount of punishment should vary with the severity of the offenses committed. But all three-time felons receive the same sentence. In my view, imposition of the same punishment upon persons who have committed completely different types of crimes raises serious doubts about the proportionality of the sentence applied to the least harmful offender. Of course, the Constitution does not bar mandatory sentences. I merely note that the operation of the Texas habitual offender system raises a further question about the extent to which a mandatory life sentence, no doubt a suitable sentence for a person who has committed three violent crimes, also is a proportionate punishment for a person who has committed the three crimes involved in this case.

* * *

19. A State's choice of a sentence will, of course, never be unconstitutional simply because the penalty is harsher than the sentence imposed by other States for the same crime. Such a rule would be inconsistent with principles of federalism. The Eighth Amendment prohibits grossly disproportionate punishment, but it does not require local sentencing decisions to be controlled by majority vote of the States. Nevertheless, a comparison of the Texas standard with the sentencing statutes of other States is one method of "assess[ing] contemporary values concerning the infliction of a challenged sanction." The relevant objective factors should be considered together and, although the weight assigned to each may vary, no single factor will ever be controlling.

I recognize that the difference between the petitioner's grossly disproportionate sentence and other prisoners' constitutionally valid sentences is not separated by the clear distinction that separates capital from noncapital punishment. "But the fact that a line has to be drawn somewhere does not justify its being drawn anywhere." The Court has, in my view, chosen the easiest line rather than the best.

* * *

We are construing a living Constitution. The sentence imposed upon the petitioner would be viewed as grossly unjust by virtually every layman and lawyer. In my view, objective criteria clearly establish that a mandatory life sentence for defrauding persons of about $230 crosses any rationally drawn line separating punishment that lawfully may be imposed from that which is proscribed by the Eighth Amendment. I would reverse the decision of the Court of Appeals.

In Hutto v. Davis, 454 U.S. 370, 102 S.Ct. 703 (1982) (per curiam), the Supreme Court held, in a 5–4 decision, that a 40–year prison sentence for possessing and distributing approximately nine ounces of marijuana that had a street value of about $200 did not constitute cruel and unusual punishment. Justice Powell, in his words, "reluctantly" concurred in the Court's judgment because in his opinion, *Rummel* was controlling. He noted that the defendant in *Rummel* had committed crimes "far less serious" than the crimes committed by this defendant and yet had suffered a much greater penalty than the 40–year sentence imposed on the defendant in this case. *Id.* at 380, 102 S.Ct. at 708 (Powell, J., concurring).

Two years later, the Court revisited the question whether a sentence was unconstitutionally disproportionate in Solem v. Helm, 463 U.S. 277, 103 S.Ct. 3001 (1983), the case which follows. This time, Justice Powell wrote the majority opinion for the Court.

SOLEM v. HELM

Supreme Court of the United States, 1983.
463 U.S. 277, 103 S.Ct. 3001, 77 L.Ed.2d 637.

JUSTICE POWELL delivered the opinion of the Court.

* * *

The issue presented is whether the Eighth Amendment proscribes a life sentence without possibility of parole for a seventh nonviolent felony.

I

By 1975 the State of South Dakota had convicted respondent Jerry Helm of six nonviolent felonies. In 1964, 1966, and 1969 Helm was convicted of third-degree burglary. In 1972 he was convicted of obtaining money under false pretenses. In 1973 he was convicted of grand larceny. And in 1975 he was convicted of third-offense driving while intoxicated. The record contains no details about the circumstances of any of these offenses, except that they were all nonviolent, none was a crime against a person, and alcohol was a contributing factor in each case.

In 1979 Helm was charged with uttering a "no account" check for $100. * * * Helm pleaded guilty.

Ordinarily the maximum punishment for uttering a "no account" check would have been five years' imprisonment in the state penitentiary and a $5,000 fine. As a result of his criminal record, however, Helm was subject to South Dakota's recidivist statute:

> "When a defendant has been convicted of at least three prior convictions *[sic]* in addition to the principal felony, the sentence for the principal felony shall be enhanced to the sentence for a Class 1 felony." S.D. Codified Laws § 22–7–8 (1979) (amended 1981).

The maximum penalty for a "Class 1 felony" was life imprisonment in the state penitentiary and a $25,000 fine. Moreover, South Dakota law explicitly provides that parole is unavailable: "A person sentenced to life imprisonment is not eligible for parole by the board of pardons and paroles." The Governor is authorized to pardon prisoners, or to commute their sentences, but no other relief from sentence is available even to a rehabilitated prisoner.

Immediately after accepting Helm's guilty plea, the South Dakota Circuit Court sentenced Helm to life imprisonment under § 22–7–8. * * * The South Dakota Supreme Court, in a 3–2 decision, affirmed the sentence despite Helm's argument that it violated the Eighth Amendment.

After Helm had served two years in the state penitentiary, he requested the Governor to commute his sentence to a fixed term of years. Such a commutation would have had the effect of making Helm eligible to be considered for parole when he had served three-fourths of his new sentence. The Governor denied Helm's request in May 1981.

[Helm then filed a petition for a writ of habeas corpus in the United States District Court for the District of South Dakota, contending that his sentence constituted cruel and unusual punishment. The district court rejected this claim, but on appeal, the Eighth Circuit Court of Appeals reversed. The Supreme Court then granted certiorari.]

II

The Eighth Amendment declares: "Excessive bail shall not be required, nor excessive fines imposed, nor cruel and unusual punishments inflicted." The final clause prohibits not only barbaric punishments, but also sentences that are disproportionate to the crime committed.

* * *

There is no basis for the State's assertion that the general principle of proportionality does not apply to felony prison sentences.[14] The constitutional language itself suggests no exception for imprisonment. We have recognized that the Eighth Amendment imposes "parallel limitations" on bail, fines, and other punishments, and the text is explicit that bail and fines may not be excessive. It would be anomalous indeed if the lesser punishment of a fine and the greater punishment of death were both subject to proportionality analysis, but the intermediate punishment of imprisonment were not. There is also no historical support for such an exception. * * *

* * * We agree * * * that, "[o]utside the context of capital punishment, *successful* challenges to the proportionality of particular sentences [will be] exceedingly rare." This does not mean, however, that proportionality analysis is entirely inapplicable in noncapital cases.

In sum, we hold as a matter of principle that a criminal sentence must be proportionate to the crime for which the defendant has been convicted. Reviewing courts, of course, should grant substantial deference to the broad authority that legislatures necessarily possess in determining the types and limits of punishments for crimes, as well as to the discretion that trial courts possess in sentencing convicted criminals.[16] But no penalty is *per se* constitutional. * * *

III

A

When sentences are reviewed under the Eighth Amendment, courts should be guided by objective factors that our cases have recognized. First, we look to the gravity of the offense and the harshness of the penalty. * * *

Second, it may be helpful to compare the sentences imposed on other criminals in the same jurisdiction. If more serious crimes are subject to the same penalty, or to less serious penalties, that is some indication that the punishment at issue may be excessive. * * *

14. According to *Rummel v. Estelle,* "*one could argue* without fear of contradiction by any decision of this Court that for crimes concededly classified and classifiable as felonies, that is, as punishable by significant terms of imprisonment in a state penitentiary, the length of sentence actually imposed is purely a matter of legislative prerogative." The Court did not adopt the standard proposed, but merely recognized that the argument was possible. To the extent that the State—or the dissent—makes this argument here, we find it meritless.

16. Contrary to the dissent's suggestions, we do not adopt or imply approval of a general rule of appellate review of sentences. Absent specific authority, it is not the role of an appellate court to substitute its judgment for that of the sentencing court as to the appropriateness of a particular sentence; rather, in applying the Eighth Amendment the appellate court decides only whether the sentence under review is within constitutional limits. In view of the substantial deference that must be accorded legislatures and sentencing courts, a reviewing court rarely will be required to engage in extended analysis to determine that a sentence is not constitutionally disproportionate.

Third, courts may find it useful to compare the sentences imposed for commission of the same crime in other jurisdictions. * * *

* * *

B

Application of these factors assumes that courts are competent to judge the gravity of an offense, at least on a relative scale. In a broad sense this assumption is justified, and courts traditionally have made these judgments—just as legislatures must make them in the first instance. Comparisons can be made in light of the harm caused or threatened to the victim or society, and the culpability of the offender. * * * For example, as the criminal laws make clear, nonviolent crimes are less serious than crimes marked by violence or the threat of violence.

There are other accepted principles that courts may apply in measuring the harm caused or threatened to the victim or society. The absolute magnitude of the crime may be relevant. Stealing a million dollars is viewed as more serious than stealing a hundred dollars—a point recognized in statutes distinguishing petty theft from grand theft. Few would dispute that a lesser included offense should not be punished more severely than the greater offense. Thus a court is justified in viewing assault with intent to murder as more serious than simple assault. It also is generally recognized that attempts are less serious than completed crimes. Similarly, an accessory after the fact should not be subject to a higher penalty than the principal.

Turning to the culpability of the offender, there are again clear distinctions that courts may recognize and apply. * * * Most would agree that negligent conduct is less serious than intentional conduct. South Dakota, for example, ranks criminal acts in ascending order of seriousness as follows: negligent acts, reckless acts, knowing acts, intentional acts, and malicious acts. A court, of course, is entitled to look at a defendant's motive in committing a crime. Thus a murder may be viewed as more serious when committed pursuant to a contract.

This list is by no means exhaustive. It simply illustrates that there are generally accepted criteria for comparing the severity of different crimes on a broad scale, despite the difficulties courts face in attempting to draw distinctions between similar crimes.

C

Application of the factors that we identify also assumes that courts are able to compare different sentences. This assumption, too, is justified. The easiest comparison, of course, is between capital punishment and noncapital punishments, for the death penalty is different from other punishments in kind rather than degree. For sentences of imprisonment, the problem is not so much one of ordering, but one of line-drawing. It is clear that a 25–year sentence generally is more severe than a 15–year sentence, but in most cases it would be difficult to decide that the former violates the Eighth Amendment while the latter does not. Decisions of this kind, although troubling, are not unique to this area. The courts are constantly called upon to draw similar lines in a variety of contexts.

* * *

IV

It remains to apply the analytical framework established by our prior decisions to the case before us. * * *

A

Helm's crime was "one of the most passive felonies a person could commit." It involved neither violence nor threat of violence to any person. The $100 face value of Helm's "no account" check was not trivial, but neither was it a large amount. One hundred dollars was less than half the amount South Dakota required for a felonious theft. It is easy to see why such a crime is viewed by society as among the less serious offenses.

Helm, of course, was not charged simply with uttering a "no account" check, but also with being a habitual offender. And a State is justified in punishing a recidivist more severely than it punishes a first offender. Helm's status, however, cannot be considered in the abstract. His prior offenses, although classified as felonies, were all relatively minor. All were nonviolent and none was a crime against a person. Indeed, there was no minimum amount in either the burglary or the false pretenses statutes, and the minimum amount covered by the grand larceny statute was fairly small.

Helm's present sentence is life imprisonment without possibility of parole. Barring executive clemency, Helm will spend the rest of his life in the state penitentiary. This sentence is far more severe than the life sentence we considered in *Rummel v. Estelle.* Rummel was likely to have been eligible for parole within 12 years of his initial confinement,[25] a fact on which the Court relied heavily. Helm's sentence is the most severe punishment that the State could have imposed on any criminal for any crime. Only capital punishment, a penalty not authorized in South Dakota when Helm was sentenced, exceeds it.

We next consider the sentences that could be imposed on other criminals in the same jurisdiction. When Helm was sentenced, a South Dakota court was required to impose a life sentence for murder and was authorized to impose a life sentence for treason, first-degree manslaughter, first-degree arson, and kidnaping. No other crime was punishable so severely on the first offense. Attempted murder, placing an explosive device on an aircraft, and first-degree rape were only Class 2 felonies. Aggravated riot was only a Class 3 felony. Distribution of heroin and aggravated assault were only Class 4 felonies.

---

25. We note that Rummel was, in fact, released within eight months of the Court's decision in his case.

Helm's habitual offender status complicates our analysis, but relevant comparisons are still possible. Under [S.D.Codified Laws] § 22–7–7, the penalty for a second or third felony is increased by one class. Thus a life sentence was mandatory when a second or third conviction was for treason, first-degree manslaughter, first-degree arson, or kidnaping, and a life sentence would have been authorized when a second or third conviction was for such crimes as attempted murder, placing an explosive device on an aircraft, or first-degree rape. Finally, § 22–7–8, under which Helm was sentenced, authorized life imprisonment after three prior convictions, regardless of the crimes.

In sum, there were a handful of crimes that were necessarily punished by life imprisonment: murder, and, on a second or third offense, treason, first-degree manslaughter, first-degree arson, and kidnaping. There was a larger group for which life imprisonment was authorized in the discretion of the sentencing judge, including: treason, first-degree manslaughter, first-degree arson, and kidnaping; attempted murder, placing an explosive device on an aircraft, and first-degree rape on a second or third offense; and any felony after three prior offenses. Finally, there was a large group of very serious offenses for which life imprisonment was not authorized, including a third offense of heroin dealing or aggravated assault.

Criminals committing any of these offenses ordinarily would be thought more deserving of punishment than one uttering a "no account" check—even when the bad-check writer had already committed six minor felonies. * * *[26] In any event, Helm has been treated in the same manner as, or more severely than, criminals who have committed far more serious crimes.

Finally, we compare the sentences imposed for commission of the same crime in other jurisdictions. The Court of Appeals found that "Helm could have received a life sentence without parole for his offense in only one other state, Nevada," and we have no reason to doubt this finding. At the very least, therefore, it is clear that Helm could not have received such a severe sentence in 48 of the 50 States. But even under Nevada law, a life sentence without possibility of parole is merely authorized in these circumstances. We are not advised that any defendant such as Helm, whose prior offenses were so minor, actually has received the maximum penalty in Nevada. It appears that Helm was treated more severely than he would have been in any other State.

B

The State argues that the present case is essentially the same as *Rummel v. Estelle,* for the possibility of parole in that case is matched by the possibility of executive clemency here. The State reasons that

---

26. The State contends that § 22–7–8 is more lenient than the Texas habitual offender statute in *Rummel,* for life imprisonment under § 22–7–8 is discretionary rather than mandatory. Helm, however, has challenged only his own sentence. No one suggests that § 22–7–8 may not be applied constitutionally to fourth-time heroin dealers or other violent criminals. * * *

the Governor could commute Helm's sentence to a term of years. We conclude, however, that the South Dakota commutation system is fundamentally different from the parole system that was before us in *Rummel.*

As a matter of law, parole and commutation are different concepts, despite some surface similarities. Parole is a regular part of the rehabilitative process. Assuming good behavior, it is the normal expectation in the vast majority of cases. The law generally specifies when a prisoner will be eligible to be considered for parole, and details the standards and procedures applicable at that time. Thus it is possible to predict, at least to some extent, when parole might be granted. Commutation, on the other hand, is an ad hoc exercise of executive clemency. A Governor may commute a sentence at any time for any reason without reference to any standards.

* * *

The Texas and South Dakota systems in particular are very different. * * * A Texas prisoner became eligible for parole when his calendar time served plus "good conduct" time equaled one-third of the maximum sentence imposed or 20 years, whichever is less. An entering prisoner earned 20 days good-time per 30 days served, and this could be increased to 30 days good-time per 30 days served. Thus Rummel could have been eligible for parole in as few as 10 years, and could have expected to become eligible, in the normal course of events, in only 12 years.

In South Dakota commutation is more difficult to obtain than parole. For example, the Board of Pardons and Paroles is authorized to make commutation recommendations to the Governor, but § 24–13–4 provides that "no recommendation for the commutation of . . . a life sentence, or for a pardon . . ., shall be made by less than the unanimous vote of all members of the board." In fact, no life sentence has been commuted in over eight years, while parole—where authorized—has been granted regularly during that period. Furthermore, even if Helm's sentence were commuted, he merely would be eligible to be considered for parole. Not only is there no guarantee that he would be paroled, but the South Dakota parole system is far more stringent than the one before us in *Rummel.* Helm would have to serve three-fourths of his revised sentence before he would be eligible for parole, and the provision for good-time credits is less generous.

The possibility of commutation is nothing more than a hope for "an *ad hoc* exercise of clemency." It is little different from the possibility of executive clemency that exists in every case in which a defendant challenges his sentence under the Eighth Amendment. Recognition of such a bare possibility would make judicial review under the Eighth Amendment meaningless.

V

The Constitution requires us to examine Helm's sentence to determine if it is proportionate to his crime. Applying objective criteria, we find that Helm has received the penultimate sentence for relatively minor criminal conduct. He has been treated more harshly than other criminals in the State who have committed more serious crimes. He has been treated more harshly than he would have been in any other jurisdiction, with the possible exception of a single State. We conclude that his sentence is significantly disproportionate to his crime, and is therefore prohibited by the Eighth Amendment.[32] The judgment of the Court of Appeals is accordingly

Affirmed.

CHIEF JUSTICE BURGER, with whom JUSTICE WHITE, JUSTICE REHN-QUIST, and JUSTICE O'CONNOR join, dissenting.

The controlling law governing this case is crystal clear, but today the Court blithely discards any concept of *stare decisis*, trespasses gravely on the authority of the states, and distorts the concept of proportionality of punishment by tearing it from its moorings in capital cases. Only three Terms ago, we held in *Rummel v. Estelle* that a life sentence imposed after only a *third* nonviolent felony conviction did not constitute cruel and unusual punishment under the Eighth Amendment. Today, the Court ignores its recent precedent and holds that a life sentence imposed after a *seventh* felony conviction constitutes cruel and unusual punishment under the Eighth Amendment.[3] Moreover, I reject the fiction that all Helm's crimes were innocuous or nonviolent. Among his felonies were three burglaries and a third conviction for drunken driving. By comparison Rummel was a relatively "model citizen." Although today's holding cannot rationally be reconciled with *Rummel,* the Court does not purport to overrule *Rummel.* I therefore dissent.

*   *   *

Questions and Points for Discussion

1. Many of the lower courts have narrowly construed *Solem,* holding that the disproportionality analysis described in that case need be under-

---

32. Contrary to the suggestion in the dissent, our conclusion today is not inconsistent with *Rummel v. Estelle.* The *Rummel* Court recognized—as does the dissent—that some sentences of imprisonment are so disproportionate that they violate the Eighth Amendment. * * * *Rummel* did reject a proportionality challenge to a particular sentence. But since the *Rummel* Court—like the dissent today—offered no standards for determining when an Eighth Amendment violation has occurred, it is controlling only in a similar factual situation. Here the facts are clearly distinguishable. Whereas Rummel was eligible for a reasonably early parole, Helm, at age 36, was sentenced to life with no possibility of parole.

[3. I agree that the Cruel and Unusual Punishments Clause might apply to those rare cases where reasonable men cannot differ as to the inappropriateness of a punishment. In all other cases, we should defer to the legislature's line-drawing. However, the Court does not contend that this is such an extraordinary case that reasonable men could not differ about the appropriateness of this punishment.]

taken only when a defendant has been sentenced to life in prison with no possibility of parole. See, e.g., Young v. Miller, 883 F.2d 1276, 1283 (6th Cir.1989); United States v. Rosenberg, 806 F.2d 1169, 1175 (3d Cir.1986). What if a fifty-year-old defendant is sentenced to prison for one hundred years without possibility of parole? Should the *Solem* disproportionality test apply? For one court's approach to this question, see United States v. Rhodes, 779 F.2d 1019, 1028 (4th Cir.1985) where a defendant sentenced to prison for seventy-five years would, at the earliest, have been eligible for release when he was eighty-eight.

Even when courts have applied the *Solem* disproportionality test, they have often found the sentences before them, unlike the sentence at issue in *Solem,* to be constitutional. See, e.g., Cocio v. Bramlett, 872 F.2d 889 (9th Cir.1989) (life sentence for felon who, while on probation for conspiracy to commit burglary, killed someone while driving recklessly under the influence of alcohol, but who would become eligible for parole release after serving twenty-five years); Chandler v. Jones, 813 F.2d 773, 779–80 (6th Cir.1987) (defendant, sentenced to life in prison as a habitual offender following his third felony conviction, with the last one being for burglary, would become eligible for parole release in thirty years, if not earlier); United States v. Ray, 828 F.2d 399, 424–25 (7th Cir.1987) (25–year sentence imposed on a defendant who, while in prison, spearheaded a scheme to bilk victims of a total of $1,800 by fraudulently altering postal money orders).

2. The sentencing decisions of courts have spawned other types of cruel and usual punishment claims. Assume that a convicted rapist is sentenced to thirty years in prison. The sentencing judge, however, announces that this sentence will be suspended and the defendant placed on probation for five years if he agrees to be surgically castrated. Does the condition of probation inflict cruel and unusual punishment? See State v. Brown, 284 S.C. 407, 411, 326 S.E.2d 410, 412 (1985) (analyzing this question under the state constitution). What if the defendant is not surgically castrated, but given a drug which would make him temporarily impotent? See People v. Gauntlett, 134 Mich.App. 737, 746–52, 352 N.W.2d 310, 314–17 (1984), modified 419 Mich. 909, 353 N.W.2d 463 (1984), another decision resting on state law grounds. What if, as a condition of the defendant's probation, he is required to place signs outside his home and on his car that read, "Dangerous Sex Offender—No Children Allowed." Compare the concurring and dissenting opinions in State v. Bateman, 95 Or.App. 456, 771 P.2d 314 (Or.App.1989) (Riggs, J., concurring) and (Warden, J., dissenting).

3. If a sentence is not disproportionate in the constitutional sense, appellate courts have traditionally been extremely reluctant to set aside a sentence on the grounds that it is excessive. Dorszynski v. United States, 418 U.S. 424, 440, 94 S.Ct. 3042, 3051 (1974). A standard commonly applied when appellate courts are reviewing sentencing decisions is whether the sentence was the product of a "manifest abuse of discretion." United States v. Ray, 828 F.2d 399, 425 (7th Cir.1987). If a sentence falls within statutory limits, such abuse will generally only occur when the " 'sentencing judge relied upon improper considerations or unreliable information in exercising his discretion or failed to exercise any discretion at all in

imposing the sentence.' " United States v. George, 891 F.2d 140, 143 (7th Cir.1989) (quoting United States v. Harris, 761 F.2d 394, 402–03 (7th Cir. 1985)).

Assume that a federal statute authorizes "imprisonment for any term of years or for life" for the crime of kidnapping. If a life sentence is imposed under this statute, a prisoner becomes eligible for parole release no later than ten years after he or she is incarcerated. On the other hand, a prisoner serving a sentence for a term of years must serve at least one-third of this sentence before becoming eligible for parole. A judge sentences a defendant convicted of kidnapping to three hundred years in prison. Has the judge abused his or her sentencing discretion? Compare United States v. O'Driscoll, 761 F.2d 589 (10th Cir.1985) with People v. Moore, 432 Mich. 311, 439 N.W.2d 684 (1989).

4. Defendants are not the only parties concerned about disproportionate sentences. Prosecutors too may be concerned that a sentence does not adequately reflect the seriousness of the crime committed or the culpability of the offender. Some legislatures have responded to this concern by enacting statutes under which prosecutors can, in limited circumstances, contest the lenity of a sentence on appeal. See, e.g., 18 U.S.C. § 3742(b) (providing for government appeals of sentences that (1) are imposed "in violation of law," (2) are the product of an "incorrect application of the sentencing guidelines," (3) are less than the guideline range, or, (4) where no guidelines apply, are "plainly unreasonable").

In United States v. DiFrancesco, 449 U.S. 117, 101 S.Ct. 426 (1980), the Supreme Court held that the imposition of a greater sentence by an appellate court authorized to do so by statute does not violate the double jeopardy clause of the fifth amendment. The Court reasoned that in effect, the government had simply established a permissible "two-stage sentencing procedure." Id. at 140 n. 16, 101 S.Ct. at 439 n. 16.

5. The American Bar Association is opposed to permitting prosecutors to appeal sentences considered too lenient. This opposition is grounded in part on the concern that prosecutors might in effect force defendants to forego certain rights, such as the right to trial, by threatening to seek higher sentences on appeal if the defendants are convicted. Pertinent excerpts from the ABA Standards for Criminal Justice governing appellate review of sentences are set forth below:

Standard 20–1.1. Principles of review; appeal by the defendant

(a) In principle, judicial review should be available for all sentences imposed in cases where provision is made for review of the conviction. This is specifically meant to include:

    (i) review of a sentence imposed after a guilty plea or the equivalent, if the case is one in which review of the conviction would be available had the case gone to trial;

    (ii) review of a sentence imposed by a trial judge, a trial jury, or the two in combination; and

    (iii) review of a resentence in the same class of cases.

(b) Appeal should be available on the initiative of the defendant.

(c) During an initial period of appellate review in a state, reasonable controls should be applied to the length and kind of sentence subject to review. Thus, with respect to sentences to confinement, the availability of a set of presumptively correct sentence ranges for offenses could provide a basis for restricting or limiting appeals from sentences within the prescribed range; likewise, official data concerning terms of confinement actually imposed or served for comparable offenses by comparable offenders can be utilized to set statistical parameters for restricting or limiting appeals from sentences.

(d) The prosecution should not be permitted to appeal a sentence on the grounds that it is too lenient.

Standard 20-1.2. Purposes of review

The general objectives of sentence review are:

(a) to correct the sentence which is excessive in length, having regard to the nature of the offense, the character of the offender, and the protection of the public interest;

(b) to promote respect for law by correcting abuses of the sentencing power and by increasing the fairness of the sentencing process;

(c) to facilitate the possible rehabilitation of an offender by reducing manifest and unwarranted inequalities among the sentences of comparable offenders; and

(d) to promote the development and application of criteria for sentencing which are both rational and just.

Standard 20-2.3. Record on appeal; statement explaining sentence

* * *

(c) The sentencing judge should be required in every case to state the reasons for selecting the particular sentence imposed. This should be done for the record in the presence of the defendant at the time of sentence.

Standard 20-3.1. Duties of reviewing court

(a) It should be the obligation of the reviewing court to establish procedures to implement a system of appellate review of sentences. Such procedures should be simple and flexible in nature so as to expedite consideration of sentence appeals. The procedures for sentence appeals should be consistent with the procedures for criminal appeals generally.

(b) Having received and considered the contentions of the parties and having examined the record compiled in the sentencing court, the reviewing court should seek to make effective the goals of sentence review. The reviewing court should set forth the basis for its decision in a reasoned opinion.

Standard 20–3.2. Powers of reviewing court: scope of review

The authority of the reviewing court with respect to the sentence should specifically extend to review of:

(a) the propriety of the sentence, having regard to the nature of the offense, the character of the offender, and the protection of the public interest; and

(b) the manner in which the sentence was imposed, including the sufficiency and accuracy of the information on which it was based.

Standard 20–3.3. Powers of reviewing court: available dispositions

(a) Every reviewing court should be specifically empowered to:

(i) affirm the sentence under review;

(ii) with the exception stated in paragraph (b), substitute for the sentence under review any other disposition that was open to the sentencing court; or

(iii) remand the case for any further proceedings that could have been conducted prior to the imposition of the sentence under review and, with the exception stated in paragraph (b), for resentencing on the basis of such further proceedings.

(b) When an appellate court reviews a sentence on appeal by a defendant, the reviewing court should be precluded from imposing a sentence more severe than the sentence appealed from. Likewise, if a reviewing court remands such a case for purposes of resentencing, the trial court should be precluded from imposing a sentence more severe than the sentence originally imposed.

*

Part Two

THE LAW OF CORRECTIONS AND PRISONERS' RIGHTS

Chapter 8

PRISONERS' RIGHTS: AN INTRODUCTION

A. CONSTITUTIONAL RIGHTS FOR PRISONERS?

To many people, the phrase, "prisoners' rights" is an oxymoron, a combination of incongruent words. The United States Supreme Court, thus far, has disagreed. According to the Court, "[t]here is no iron curtain drawn between the Constitution and the prisons of this country." Wolff v. McDonnell, 418 U.S. 539, 555–56, 94 S.Ct. 2963, 2974–75 (1974). Prisoners, no matter how incorrigible, no matter how despicable their crimes, do have rights. They have rights derived from the United States Constitution; they have rights under many state constitutions; and they have rights under certain statutes and regulations.

The basic premise that prisoners have rights under the United States Constitution is one, however, which should be explored, since the force or lack of force of the reasons for concluding that prisoners have rights may affect the scope of these rights and the extent to which the rights of prisoners are vigilantly protected by the courts and prison officials themselves. This section of the book focuses on the rights, both in legal and real terms, of prisoners and pretrial detainees (persons awaiting trial). Although the starting point for analyzing the rights of pretrial detainees is different because detainees retain a presumption of innocence on the charges filed against them, as will be seen in the materials that follow, the differences are mostly illusory ones.

Before reading the materials in this section of the book, consider these fundamental questions: (1) Do and should prisoners have rights under the Constitution? (2) Why or why not? (3) Assuming that prisoners do retain rights under the Constitution, what should be the scope of those rights? Do you agree with the way in which Standard 23–1.1 of the American Bar Association Standards Relating to the Legal

Status of Prisoners (1981), which is set forth below, has responded to questions concerning the existence and scope of prisoners' rights?

PART I. GENERAL PRINCIPLE

Standard 23–1.1

Prisoners retain the rights of free citizens except:

(a) As specifically provided to the contrary in these standards; or

(b) When restrictions are necessary to assure their orderly confinement and interaction; or

(c) When restrictions are necessary to provide reasonable protection for the rights and physical safety of all members of the prison system and the general public.

B. HISTORY OF PRISONERS' RIGHTS—A GENERAL OVERVIEW

1. SLAVES OF THE STATE—THE 1800s

RUFFIN v. THE COMMONWEALTH

Court of Appeals of Virginia, 1871.
62 Va. 790.

CHRISTIAN, J., delivered the opinion of the court.

[Woody Ruffin, an inmate in a Virginia penitentiary, killed a correctional officer while in Bath County, Virginia. Charged with murder, he was tried by a jury in Richmond, Virginia under a state statute directing that all criminal trials of inmates confined in a state penitentiary be held in Richmond. After being found guilty and sentenced to hang, Ruffin appealed. He contended that the failure to have his guilt adjudicated by a jury comprised of people from Bath County violated his state constitutional right to be tried by "an impartial jury of his vicinage."]

We have said that a reasonable and not a literal construction must be given to the clause under consideration, and a construction that is consistent with the other declarations of general principles in the same instrument. One of these declarations is, "that government is instituted for the common benefit, protection and security of the people". Now one of the most effectual means of promoting the common benefit and ensuring the protection and security of the people, is the certain punishment and prevention of crime. It is essential to the safety of society, that those who violate its criminal laws should suffer punishment. A convicted felon, whom the law in its humanity punishes by confinement in the penitentiary instead of with death, is subject while undergoing that punishment, to all the laws which the Legislature in its wisdom may enact for the government of that institution and the control of its inmates. For the time being, during his term of service in the penitentiary, he is in a state of penal servitude to the State. He has, as a consequence of his crime, not only forfeited his liberty, but all his personal rights except those which the law in its humanity accords to him. He is for the time being the slave of the State. He is *civiliter mortuus;* and his estate, if he has any, is administered like that of a dead man.

The bill of rights is a declaration of general principles to govern a society of freemen, and not of convicted felons and men civilly dead. Such men have some rights it is true, such as the law in its benignity accords to them, but not the rights of free men. They are the slaves of the State undergoing punishment for heinous crimes committed against the laws of the land. While in this state of penal servitude, they must be subject to the regulations of the institution of which they are inmates, and the laws of the State to whom their service is due in expiation of their crimes.

When a convict in the penitentiary, while undergoing punishment for the crime of which he stands convicted, commits other offen[s]es, it is unquestionably in the power of the State, to which his penal servitude is due, to prescribe, through its Legislature, the mode of punishment as well as the manner of his trial. * * *

* * * If he has forfeited this right, which every freeman may claim, "a trial by a jury of his vicinage," that forfeiture is a consequence of his crime, and is one of the penalties which the law denounces against a convicted felon, as much one of the penalties attached to his crime, as the whipping post, the iron mask, the gag, or the dungeon, which is provided for offen[s]es other than felonies. He is for the time being a slave, in a condition of penal servitude to the State, and is subject to such laws and regulations as the State may choose to prescribe.

We are therefore of opinion, that there was no error in the refusal of the Circuit [C]ourt of Richmond either to remand the prisoner to the county of Bath for trial, or to send to said county for a jury to try him.

Ruffin v. The Commonwealth reflected the general notion prevailing in the United States in the 1800's that prisoners have no rights. As part of the penalty suffered for having committed a crime, a convict sentenced to prison forewent constitutional protection.

2. THE "HANDS-OFF DOCTRINE"—THE EARLY TO MID-1900s

The notion that prisoners have no rights was gradually displaced in the 1900s by a different approach to claims of prisoners asserting violations of constitutional rights. The courts adopted what has become known as the "hands-off doctrine." Under this doctrine, the courts refused to adjudicate prisoners' constitutional claims, not necessarily because prisoners have no constitutional rights, but because, whatever their rights, the courts felt that they generally had neither the duty nor the power to define and protect those rights.

Although the opinions of the courts dismissing the prisoners' suits during this time were often cursory, some reasons for the "hands-off" approach can be gleaned from the cases. The reasons, some of which seem interrelated, include the following:

1. *Separation of Powers*—Some courts expressed the concern that judicial review of prisoners' complaints would usurp the authority of the legislative and executive branches of the government to supervise and operate prisons. See, e.g., Tabor v. Hardwick, 224 F.2d 526, 529 (5th Cir.1955) ("The control of federal penitentiaries is entrusted to the Attorney General of the United States and the Bureau of Prisons who, no doubt, exercise a wise and humane discretion in safeguarding the rights and privileges of prisoners so far as consistent with effective prison discipline. Unless perhaps in extreme cases, the courts should not interfere with the conduct of a prison or its discipline."); Banning v. Looney, 213 F.2d 771, 771 (10th Cir.1954) ("Courts are without power to supervise prison administration or to interfere with the ordinary prison rules or regulations.").

2. *Federalism*—Many courts believed that consideration of the claims of state prisoners by the federal courts would encroach on an area falling within the states' domain—the punishment of criminals who have violated state criminal laws. See, e.g., U.S. ex rel. Morris v. Radio Station WENR, 209 F.2d 105, 107 (7th Cir.1953) ("Inmates of State penitentiaries should realize that prison officials are vested with wide discretion in safeguarding prisoners committed to their custody. Discipline reasonably maintained in State prisons is not under the supervisory discretion of federal courts."); Cullum v. California Dep't of Corrections, 267 F.Supp. 524, 525 (N.D.Cal.1967) ("[I]nternal matters in state penitentiaries are the sole concern of the state except under exceptional circumstances.").

3. *Maintenance of Institutional Security and Furtherance of Correctional Goals*—The courts were also concerned that judicial interference in the operation of prisons would cause security and discipline problems and frustrate the purposes of incarceration. Underlying this concern was the belief that judges untrained in the complexities of prison administration might not fully understand the need for certain prison rules and practices and might, as a result, render decisions adversely affecting prison security and/or the goals of incarceration. In addition some courts were concerned that if prison officials knew that their actions were subject to judicial oversight, they might be dissuaded from taking the steps necessary to main-

[Handwritten margin notes: "injured party is entitled to comp.", "a civil wrong", "no breach of contract"]

tain order in the prisons out of fear that their actions would lead to lawsuits and possibly liability. See, e.g., Cullum v. California Dep't of Corrections, 267 F.Supp. 524, 525 (N.D.Cal. 1967) ("[I]f every time a guard were called upon to maintain order he had to consider his possible tort liabilities it might unduly limit his actions. Such limitation may jeopardize his safety as well as the safety of other prisoners."). Finally, some courts were troubled by the complications and security problems that would attend the transporting of prisoners, whether parties or witnesses, to court. See, e.g., Tabor v. Hardwick, 224 F.2d 526, 529 (5th Cir.1955) ("[P]enitentiary wardens and the courts might be swamped with an endless number of unnecessary and even spurious law suits filed by inmates in remote jurisdictions in the hope of obtaining leave to appear at the hearing of any such case, with the consequent disruption of prison routine and concomitant hazard of escape from custody.").

4. *Dislike of Prisoners' Lawsuits*—This reason for dismissing prisoners' suits was generally camouflaged in the courts' opinions. At most, some courts were willing to acknowledge a concern about being overrun by frivolous lawsuits filed by prisoners if the courts took cognizance of prisoners' suits. See, e.g., Stroud v. Swope, 187 F.2d 850, 852 (9th Cir.1951) ("Aside from the purely legal aspects of this case very practical considerations militate against granting to appellant the relief for which he prays for to do so would open the door to a flood of applications from federal prisoners which would seriously hamper the administration of our prison system.").

3. THE PRISONERS' RIGHTS ERA—THE 1960s AND 70s

Even before the 1960s, a few courts were troubled by and refused to apply the "hands-off doctrine." See, e.g., Coffin v. Reichard, 143 F.2d 443 (6th Cir.1944). The idea that prisoners have rights which the courts are bound to protect, however, was not generally accepted by most courts until the 1960s and 1970s. During those decades, the "hands-off doctrine" was implicitly and sometimes expressly repudiated as courts, with increasing frequency, agreed to review claims of prisoners alleging violations of their constitutional rights. The movement to discard the "hands-off doctrine" reached its pinnacle when the Supreme Court, in a series of opinions, acknowledged that prisoners have constitutional rights for whose protection the courts have responsibility. See, e.g., Cruz v. Beto, 405 U.S. 319, 92 S.Ct. 1079 (1972) (freedom of religion); Wolff v. McDonnell, 418 U.S. 539, 94 S.Ct. 2963 (1974) (procedural due process); Pell v. Procunier, 417 U.S. 817, 94 S.Ct. 2800 (1974) (freedom of speech).

a. Reasons for the Abandonment of the "Hands–Off Doctrine"

Several explanations have been offered for the courts' turnabout in the 1960s and 1970s. First, prisoners during this time became more assertive, and even militant, as they clamored for recognition of their constitutional rights. During this time of civil rights demonstrations, school integrations, Vietnam war protests, and ghetto riots, the nation's prisons, like the rest of the country, were filled with turmoil and ferment. *agitation & unrest*

Second, in the 1960s and 1970s, more lawyers became concerned about civil rights and receptive to the idea of helping prisoners bring suits to vindicate their constitutional rights. With the development of a civil liberties bar and the more effective presentation of prisoners' claims, it became more and more difficult for the courts to ignore some of the allegations about what was transpiring in the nation's prisons.

Third, a number of prison disturbances and several bloody riots, particularly the riot at the Attica State Prison in Attica, New York in 1971, which resulted in forty-three deaths, jolted the nation, alerting the public, including judges, to the problems plaguing the nation's prisons. As knowledge about prison conditions and practices became more widespread, the courts' confidence that the executive and legislative branches would not abuse their authority to operate and supervise prisons became shaken, and it became more difficult for judges to say that the complaints of prisoners, even those making forceful claims of constitutional impingements, were none of the courts' business.

Finally, with the advent of the "Warren Court" in 1953 came a commitment to protect the constitutional rights of disfavored minorities. The Warren Court, for example, expansively interpreted the rights of individuals accused of committing crimes, rendering such seminal decisions as Miranda v. Arizona, 384 U.S. 436, 86 S.Ct. 1602 (1966) (*Miranda* warnings and valid waiver must precede custodial interrogation), Mapp v. Ohio, 367 U.S. 643, 81 S.Ct. 1684 (1961) (fourth amendment exclusionary rule applicable to states through the due process clause), and Katz v. United States, 389 U.S. 347, 88 S.Ct. 507 (1967) (fourth amendment protections not limited to physical intrusions). The same libertarian philosophy underlying the Supreme Court's opinions concerning the rights of the criminally accused also made the Court amenable to recognizing and protecting rights of individuals incarcerated following their convictions.

For a discussion of the way in which the above events contributed to the abandonment of the "hands-off doctrine," see J. Gobert & N. Cohen, Rights of Prisoners 1–3 (1981).

b. The Role of Legal Developments in the Discarding of the "Hands–Off Doctrine"

Several developments in the law in the 1960s contributed to the abandonment of the "hands-off doctrine." Of central importance was the Supreme Court's decision in Monroe v. Pape, 365 U.S. 167, 81 S.Ct. 473 (1961). In that case, the plaintiffs brought suit after thirteen Chicago police officers allegedly entered the plaintiffs' home without a warrant and forced the plaintiffs to stand nude in the living room while their home was searched. The civil rights statute under which the lawsuit was brought, 42 U.S.C. § 1983, provides as follows:

> Every person who, under color of any statute, ordinance, regulation, custom, or usage, of any State or Territory or the District of Columbia, subjects or causes to be subjected, any citizen of the United States or other person within the jurisdiction thereof to the deprivation of any rights, privileges, or immunities secured by the Constitution and laws, shall be liable to the party injured in an action at law, suit in equity, or other proper proceeding for redress.

At issue in *Monroe v. Pape* was the meaning of the requirement in § 1983 that the person sued, to be liable, must have acted "under color of" a state "statute, ordinance, regulation, custom, or usage" to be liable. The defendants in *Monroe* argued that this state action requirement had not been met, since the actions of the police officers were not authorized by any state laws or customs and in fact were contrary to certain provisions of the Illinois Constitution and state statutes. In an opinion written by Justice Douglas, the Supreme Court responded that § 1983 was enacted in large part because of the failure of state governments in the south to control the lawlessness sparked by activities of the Ku Klux Klan following the Civil War. To Congress, it did not matter whether this failure was due to the reluctance of the state governments to rein in the Ku Klux Klan or simply to their inability to do so; what mattered was that, without this legislation providing a federal remedy for the violation of constitutional rights, the rights of citizens would remain unvindicated. Section 1983 was therefore directed against state officials whose "prejudice, passion, neglect, intolerance, or otherwise" caused the violation or unenforcement of others' constitutional rights. Id. at 180, 81 S.Ct. at 480.

Congress's recognition that the availability of a state remedy in theory did not necessarily mean that a state remedy was available in practice influenced the Supreme Court's interpretation in Monroe v. Pape of § 1983's "under-color-of"-state-law requirement. The Court held that for activities to have been taken "under-color-of" state law, it was not necessary that the activities be authorized by state law. The "under-color-of"-state-law requirement would be satisfied as long as there was "'[m]isuse of power, possessed by virtue of state law and made possible only because the wrongdoer is clothed with the authority of state law.'" Id. at 184, 81 S.Ct. at 482 (quoting United States v. Classic, 313 U.S. 299, 326, 61 S.Ct. 1031, 1043 (1941)).

Monroe v. Pape, therefore, put to rest the notion that the state action requirement of § 1983 was not met if state governmental officials had violated state law at the same time federal constitutional rights were allegedly violated. That notion had lent support to courts previously opting to stay away from the task of adjudicating prisoners' constitutional claims. See, e.g., U.S. ex rel. Atterbury v. Ragen, 237 F.2d 953, 954–55 (7th Cir.1956).

A further development in the case law facilitating review by the courts of constitutional claims filed by prisoners occurred when the Supreme Court in the 1960s held that a number of constitutional protections found in the Bill of Rights operated, through the due process clause of the fourteenth amendment, as constraints on the states. Although there were numerous decisions during that decade in which the Court found that restrictions in the first ten amendments had been selectively incorporated into the due process clause, the most important decision for prisoners wanting to challenge the conditions of their confinement or their treatment in state prisons was Robinson v. California, 370 U.S. 660, 82 S.Ct. 1417 (1962). In *Robinson*, the Court held that the eighth amendment right not to be subjected to cruel and unusual punishment was a right not to be infringed upon by the states as well as the federal government.

In previous years, the Court had also directly or indirectly indicated that other rights of which prisoners frequently try to avail themselves, such as the first amendment rights to freedom of speech and religious freedom and the fourth amendment right to be free from unreasonable searches and seizures, were applicable to the states through the due process clause. See, e.g., Fiske v. Kansas, 274 U.S. 380, 47 S.Ct. 655 (1927) (freedom of speech); Stromberg v. California, 283 U.S. 359, 51 S.Ct. 532 (1931) (freedom of speech); Cantwell v. Connecticut, 310 U.S. 296, 60 S.Ct. 900 (1940) (freedom of religion); Wolf v. Colorado, 338 U.S. 25, 69 S.Ct. 1359 (1949) (fourth amendment).

4. PRISONERS' RIGHTS TODAY

The courts have now held that prisoners do have constitutional rights and that those rights are to be protected by the courts. For example, according to the Supreme Court, prisoners have first amendment free speech rights, the right to religious freedom, the right to marry, a right of access to the courts, the right to equal protection of the law, some procedural due process rights, and the right to be free from cruel and unusual punishment.

At the same time, however, as will be seen in subsequent chapters, vestiges of the "hands-off doctrine" remain. In a number of cases, the Supreme Court, in rejecting prisoners' claims, has underscored the deference with which the courts should treat the judgments of prison officials as to what is needed to protect institutional security and further correctional goals. The reasons given for this deference are many of the same reasons which underlay the "hands-off doctrine"—separation of powers, federalism, judges' lack of expertise in correctional matters, and a concern that judicial intervention will undermine institutional security and the purposes of incarceration.

In addition, the Supreme Court has begun excluding areas of constitutional protection from the reach of prisoners. For example, the Court held in Hudson v. Palmer, 468 U.S. 517, 104 S.Ct. 3194 (1984), infra page 409, that courts should not consider claims of prisoners asserting that searches of their cells were unreasonable searches in contravention of the fourth amendment. According to the Court, the interest of prisoners in their cells is not one which is protected by the fourth amendment.

Some observers of the Supreme Court, and even members of the Court, see the "hands-off doctrine" rearing its hoary head in the background of these recent Supreme Court cases spurning prisoners' constitutional claims. These observers fear that the notion of prisoners' rights is on its way to becoming a legal and historical anachronism.

Others only see the Court giving effect to the common-sense proposition that the Constitution cannot fully apply in the prison setting. Under this view, the Court is simply struggling to balance the imperatives of institutional security and the purposes of incarceration, on the one hand, against the interest of prisoners as well as the public in ensuring that all people in this country, including prisoners, receive the basic protection from arbitrary and oppressive government actions that the Constitution was designed to afford. As the Court attempts to reach the appropriate balance, some constitutional rights will be excluded from the prison domain while others, although affording some protection to prisoners, will be applied in a diluted fashion.

C. THE PURPOSES OF INCARCERATION

In cases analyzing prisoners' constitutional claims, the courts have repeatedly evinced and emphasized their concern that their decisions not unduly interfere with the objectives purportedly served by incarcerating criminal offenders. The courts have obviously taken these objectives, as well as the governmental interests in maintaining prison security, order, and discipline, into account when defining the parameters of the rights of prisoners. A brief review of the primary purposes of imprisonment therefore seems in order. For further discussion of the purposes of punishment, see chapter 1, supra pages 4–17.

When touting the benefits of imprisonment, commentators and governmental officials customarily point to at least four purposes which may be served by incarceration:

1. *Incapacitation*—What this purported benefit means is that while individuals are in prison, they will be physically "incapacitated" or unable to commit many crimes which might otherwise be committed during the period of confinement. In the past, the focus of this penological objective has been on protecting members of the public in the free world by limiting the physical freedom of convicts. On the other hand, it is common knowledge that the criminal activities of many prisoners persist while in prison; pris-

oners, with disturbing frequency, steal from each other, sell drugs to each other, rape each other, and kill each other. Prisoners also assault, rape, maim, and kill correctional officers and other prison officials. To the extent that the purpose of confining convicted criminals is viewed to be the prevention of *any* crimes during the time of confinement and the protection of *all* persons from victimization, regardless of employment status or criminal record, the courts may condone greater restrictions on claimed rights of prisoners.

2. *Deterrence*—Incarceration is said to further two types of deterrence—specific and general. Specific deterrence refers to the effect that imprisonment is hoped to have on the particular individual imprisoned. This objective of incarceration is realized if the offender, upon release from prison, commits no further crimes because of the desire to avoid returning to prison.

General deterrence, as the name suggests, concerns the broader impact that the imprisonment sanction may have on society in general. This purpose of incarceration is served when members of the public refrain from criminal activity because of the fear of imprisonment.

3. *Rehabilitation*—The rehabilitative objective is somewhat similar to the goal of specific deterrence, at least in terms of the end result following the realization of either goal. Both penological objectives, when achieved, result in prisoners refraining from criminal activity after release from prison. One difference between the two objectives, however, is in the reason why the released prisoners refrain from further crimes. Prisoners who spurn further criminal activity because they have been deterred by what they experienced when previously imprisoned are motivated by an aversion to incarceration; on the other hand, prisoners who abide by the law after release from prison because they are rehabilitated are reacting to an aversion, though newfound, to crime itself.

4. *Retribution*—What retribution basically means is that the individuals convicted of crimes are being incarcerated to punish them for their crimes. In other words, through incarceration, society is retaliating against or exacting vengeance on the prisoners for the crimes they have committed.

Questions and Points for Discussion

1. As noted above, to the extent that courts take into account penological goals when defining prisoners' rights, a broader interpretation of what the goal of incapacitation means may lead to a more restrictive interpretation of the scope of prisoners' rights. Would the other penological goals of deterrence, both specific and general, rehabilitation, and retribution support a more expansive or contracted definition of the rights of prisoners?

2.   At least some of the goals of incarceration may be conflicting. For example, steps taken to make imprisonment a sufficiently onerous and unpleasant experience to satisfy retributive aims may thwart attempts to rehabilitate the offender.

Any tension between the goals of retribution and rehabilitation would be of no concern if either goal was abandoned as a purpose of incarceration. Some commentators have urged that rehabilitation not be considered a reason for imprisonment. They have argued that to believe that criminals can be forced to become penitent and regard with disdain a further life of crime is to engage in fantasy. See, e.g., N. Morris, The Future of Imprisonment 14 (1974). Under this view, prisons are not and cannot be rehabilitative; prisoners are either incorrigible or will reform themselves because of internal forces rather than external pressures.

3.   Even if the rehabilitation of prisoners, in the sense of forcing them to become "better," were an unrealistic goal, should one penological objective be to ensure that prisoners do not become "worse" or more criminally inclined because of their prison experiences? How would this goal of preventing any criminal propensities of an individual from being nurtured while the individual was in prison affect the balance for or against the recognition of prisoner's rights?

4.   Retribution as an object of punishment has been attacked over the years. Opponents of retribution argue that for society to act out of revenge when imposing a criminal sanction is unseemly, lowly, and uncivilized. See, e.g., K. Menninger, The Crime of Punishment 190–218 (1968). Others respond that to deny that one purpose of punishment is to punish is absurd and delusive. See, e.g., N. Morris, The Future of Imprisonment 58–60 (1974) (approving a retributive aim to punishment, but underscoring that the punishment imposed should be no more severe than what the offender deserves); Armstrong, The Retributivist Hits Back, Theories of Punishment 19–40 (S. Grupp ed. 1971).

5.   The deterrent objective of incarceration has also met with controversy in recent years. Of particular concern has been the failure of the prison experience to deter many prisoners from committing further crimes after they have been released from prison. One study about the recidivism rates of prisoners, for example, revealed that 61% of the inmates surveyed had previously been incarcerated. Bureau of Justice Statistics, U.S. Dep't of Justice, Examining Recidivism 1 (1985). See also Bureau of Justice Statistics, U.S. Dep't of Justice, Recidivism of Young Parolees 1 (1987) (69% of young parolees studied were rearrested for a serious crime within six years after their release from prison, 53% were convicted, and 49% were sent to prison again).

6.   Imprisonment is not the only punishment facing a convicted felon. Offenders can lose voting and other civil rights. The loss of such rights and issues surrounding their restoration upon release are addressed in Chapter 17.

Chapter 9

FIRST AMENDMENT RIGHTS

A. FREEDOM OF SPEECH

The first amendment to the United States Constitution provides in part that "Congress shall make no law * * * abridging the freedom of speech." This constitutional provision serves as a restraint on the states as well, through operation of the due process clause of the fourteenth amendment. Rankin v. McPherson, 483 U.S. 378, 386, 107 S.Ct. 2891, 2897 (1987).

In a number of cases, the Supreme Court has considered the application of the first amendment in the correctional setting. One of these cases is set forth below.

PROCUNIER v. MARTINEZ
Supreme Court of the United States, 1974.
416 U.S. 396, 94 S.Ct. 1800, 40 L.Ed.2d 224.

MR. JUSTICE POWELL delivered the opinion of the Court.

This case concerns the constitutionality of certain regulations promulgated by appellant Procunier in his capacity as Director of the California Department of Corrections. Appellees brought a class action on behalf of themselves and all other inmates of penal institutions under the Department's jurisdiction to challenge the rules relating to censorship of prisoner mail * * *.

* * *

* * * Under these regulations, correspondence between inmates of California penal institutions and persons other than licensed attorneys and holders of public office was censored for nonconformity to certain standards. Rule 2401 stated the Department's general premise that personal correspondence by prisoners is "a privilege, not a right . . . ." More detailed regulations implemented the Department's policy. Rule 1201 directed inmates not to write letters in which they "unduly complain" or "magnify grievances." Rule 1205(d) defined as contraband writings "expressing inflammatory political, racial, reli-

gious or other views or beliefs . . . ." Finally, Rule 2402(8) provided that inmates "may not send or receive letters that pertain to criminal activity; are lewd, obscene, or defamatory; contain foreign matter, or are otherwise inappropriate."

Prison employees screened both incoming and outgoing personal mail for violations of these regulations. No further criteria were provided to help members of the mailroom staff decide whether a particular letter contravened any prison rule or policy. When a prison employee found a letter objectionable, he could take one or more of the following actions: (1) refuse to mail or deliver the letter and return it to the author; (2) submit a disciplinary report, which could lead to suspension of mail privileges or other sanctions; or (3) place a copy of the letter or a summary of its contents in the prisoner's file, where it might be a factor in determining the inmate's work and housing assignments and in setting a date for parole eligibility.

The District Court held that the regulations relating to prisoner mail authorized censorship of protected expression without adequate justification in violation of the First Amendment and that they were void for vagueness. The court also noted that the regulations failed to provide minimum procedural safeguards against error and arbitrariness in the censorship of inmate correspondence. Consequently, it enjoined their continued enforcement.

* * *

A

Traditionally, federal courts have adopted a broad hands-off attitude toward problems of prison administration. * * * Prison administrators are responsible for maintaining internal order and discipline, for securing their institutions against unauthorized access or escape, and for rehabilitating, to the extent that human nature and inadequate resources allow, the inmates placed in their custody. The Herculean obstacles to effective discharge of these duties are too apparent to warrant explication. Suffice it to say that the problems of prisons in America are complex and intractable, and, more to the point, they are not readily susceptible of resolution by decree. Most require expertise, comprehensive planning, and the commitment of resources, all of which are peculiarly within the province of the legislative and executive branches of government. For all of those reasons, courts are ill equipped to deal with the increasingly urgent problems of prison administration and reform.[9] Judicial recognition of that fact reflects no more than a healthy sense of realism. Moreover, where state penal institutions are involved, federal courts have a further reason for deference to the appropriate prison authorities.

But a policy of judicial restraint cannot encompass any failure to take cognizance of valid constitutional claims whether arising in a

9. * * * Moreover, the capacity of our criminal justice system to deal fairly and fully with legitimate claims will be impaired by a burgeoning increase of frivolous prisoner complaints. * * *

federal or state institution. When a prison regulation or practice offends a fundamental constitutional guarantee, federal courts will discharge their duty to protect constitutional rights. * * *

* * *

* * * [T]he arguments of the parties reflect the assumption that the resolution of this case requires an assessment of the extent to which prisoners may claim First Amendment freedoms. In our view this inquiry is unnecessary. In determining the proper standard of review for prison restrictions on inmate correspondence, we have no occasion to consider the extent to which an individual's right to free speech survives incarceration, for a narrower basis of decision is at hand. In the case of direct personal correspondence between inmates and those who have a particularized interest in communicating with them,[11] mail censorship implicates more than the right of prisoners.

* * * Whatever the status of a prisoner's claim to uncensored correspondence with an outsider, it is plain that the latter's interest is grounded in the First Amendment's guarantee of freedom of speech. And this does not depend on whether the nonprisoner correspondent is the author or intended recipient of a particular letter, for the addressee as well as the sender of direct personal correspondence derives from the First and Fourteenth Amendments a protection against unjustified governmental interference with the intended communication. * * * The wife of a prison inmate who is not permitted to read all that her husband wanted to say to her has suffered an abridgment of her interest in communicating with him as plain as that which results from censorship of her letter to him. In either event, censorship of prisoner mail works a consequential restriction on the First and Fourteenth Amendment rights of those who are not prisoners.

* * * We therefore turn for guidance, not to cases involving questions of "prisoners' rights," but to decisions of this Court dealing with the general problem of incidental restrictions on First Amendment liberties imposed in furtherance of legitimate governmental activities.

* * *

In *United States v. O'Brien,* 391 U.S. 367 (1968), the Court dealt with incidental restrictions on free speech occasioned by the exercise of the governmental power to conscript men for military service. O'Brien had burned his Selective Service registration certificate on the steps of a courthouse in order to dramatize his opposition to the draft and to our country's involvement in Vietnam. He was convicted of violating a provision of the Selective Service law that had recently been amended to prohibit knowing destruction or mutilation of registration certificates. O'Brien argued that the purpose and effect of the amendment were to abridge free expression and that the statutory provision was therefore unconstitutional, both as enacted and as applied to him.

---

11. Different considerations may come into play in the case of mass mailings. No such issue is raised on these facts, and we intimate no view as to its proper resolution.

Although O'Brien's activity involved "conduct" rather than pure "speech," the Court did not define away the First Amendment concern, and neither did it rule that the presence of a communicative intent necessarily rendered O'Brien's actions immune to governmental regulation. Instead, it enunciated the following four-part test:

"[A] government regulation is sufficiently justified if it is within the constitutional power of the Government; if it furthers an important or substantial governmental interest; if the governmental interest is unrelated to the suppression of free expression; and if the incidental restriction on alleged First Amendment freedoms is no greater than is essential to the furtherance of that interest."

* * *

The case at hand arises in the context of prisons. One of the primary functions of government is the preservation of societal order through enforcement of the criminal law, and the maintenance of penal institutions is an essential part of that task. The identifiable governmental interests at stake in this task are the preservation of internal order and discipline,[12] the maintenance of institutional security against escape or unauthorized entry, and the rehabilitation of the prisoners. While the weight of professional opinion seems to be that inmate freedom to correspond with outsiders advances rather than retards the goal of rehabilitation, the legitimate governmental interest in the order and security of penal institutions justifies the imposition of certain restraints on inmate correspondence. Perhaps the most obvious example of justifiable censorship of prisoner mail would be refusal to send or deliver letters concerning escape plans or containing other information concerning proposed criminal activity, whether within or without the prison. Similarly, prison officials may properly refuse to transmit encoded messages. * * *

Applying the teachings of our prior decisions to the instant context, we hold that censorship of prisoner mail is justified if the following criteria are met. First, the regulation or practice in question must further an important or substantial governmental interest unrelated to the suppression of expression. Prison officials may not censor inmate correspondence simply to eliminate unflattering or unwelcome opinions or factually inaccurate statements. Rather, they must show that a regulation authorizing mail censorship furthers one or more of the substantial governmental interests of security, order, and rehabilitation. Second, the limitation of First Amendment freedoms must be no greater than is necessary or essential to the protection of the particular governmental interest involved. Thus a restriction on inmate correspondence that furthers an important or substantial interest of penal administration will nevertheless be invalid if its sweep is unnecessarily broad. This does not mean, of course, that prison administrators may be required to show with certainty that adverse consequences would

---

12. We need not and do not address in this case the validity of a temporary prohibition of an inmate's personal correspon- dence as a disciplinary sanction (usually as part of the regimen of solitary confinement) for violation of prison rules.

flow from the failure to censor a particular letter. Some latitude in anticipating the probable consequences of allowing certain speech in a prison environment is essential to the proper discharge of an administrator's duty. But any regulation or practice that restricts inmate correspondence must be generally necessary to protect one or more of the legitimate governmental interests identified above.[14]

C

On the basis of this standard, we affirm the judgment of the District Court. The regulations invalidated by that court authorized, *inter alia,* censorship of statements that "unduly complain" or "magnify grievances," expression of "inflammatory political, racial, religious or other views," and matter deemed "defamatory" or "otherwise inappropriate." These regulations fairly invited prison officials and employees to apply their own personal prejudices and opinions as standards for prisoner mail censorship. Not surprisingly, some prison officials used the extraordinary latitude for discretion authorized by the regulations to suppress unwelcome criticism. For example, at one institution under the Department's jurisdiction, the checklist used by the mailroom staff authorized rejection of letters "criticizing policy, rules or officials," and the mailroom sergeant stated in a deposition that he would reject as "defamatory" letters "belittling staff or our judicial system or anything connected with Department of Corrections." Correspondence was also censored for "disrespectful comments," "derogatory remarks," and the like.

Appellants have failed to show that these broad restrictions on prisoner mail were in any way necessary to the furtherance of a governmental interest unrelated to the suppression of expression. * * * Appellants contend that statements that "magnify grievances" or "unduly complain" are censored "as a precaution against flash riots and in the furtherance of inmate rehabilitation." But they do not suggest how the magnification of grievances or undue complaining, which presumably occurs in outgoing letters, could possibly lead to flash riots, nor do they specify what contribution the suppression of complaints makes to the rehabilitation of criminals. And appellants defend the ban against "inflammatory political, racial, religious or other views" on the ground that "[s]uch matter clearly presents a danger to prison security . . . ." The regulation, however, is not narrowly drawn to reach only material that might be thought to encourage violence nor is its application limited to incoming letters. In short, the Department's regulations authorized censorship of prisoner mail far broader than any legitimate interest of penal administration demands and were properly found invalid by the District Court.

---

14. While not necessarily controlling, the policies followed at other well-run institutions would be relevant to a determination of the need for a particular type of restriction. * * *

D

We also agree with the District Court that the decision to censor or withhold delivery of a particular letter must be accompanied by minimum procedural safeguards. The interest of prisoners and their correspondents in uncensored communication by letter, grounded as it is in the First Amendment, is plainly a "liberty" interest within the meaning of the Fourteenth Amendment even though qualified of necessity by the circumstance of imprisonment. As such, it is protected from arbitrary governmental invasion. The District Court required that an inmate be notified of the rejection of a letter written by or addressed to him, that the author of that letter be given a reasonable opportunity to protest that decision, and that complaints be referred to a prison official other than the person who originally disapproved the correspondence. These requirements do not appear to be unduly burdensome, nor do appellants so contend. Accordingly, we affirm the judgment of the District Court with respect to the Department's regulations relating to prisoner mail.

[Justice Marshall, joined by Justice Brennan, concurred in the Court's judgment. Justice Douglas also wrote a concurring opinion. Both opinions are omitted here.]

Questions and Points for Discussion

1. Left unresolved by the Supreme Court in *Procunier v. Martinez* were the questions whether inmates retain free speech rights while in prison and if so, to what extent. The Court addressed these questions in Pell v. Procunier, 417 U.S. 817, 94 S.Ct. 2800 (1974). The plaintiffs in that case, four California prison inmates and three journalists, had filed a § 1983 suit challenging the constitutionality of a regulation promulgated by the California Department of Corrections that prohibited media members from conducting face-to-face interviews with individual inmates of their choice. The inmate plaintiffs contended that the regulation violated their free speech rights, while the media plaintiffs contended that the regulation violated the right to freedom of the press protected by the first and fourteenth amendments.

In addressing the inmates' claim, the Court, in an opinion written by Justice Stewart, observed that "a prison inmate retains those First Amendment rights that are not inconsistent with his status as a prisoner or with the legitimate penological objectives of the corrections system." Id. at 822, 94 S.Ct. at 2804. The penological objectives mentioned by the Court against which the constitutionality of a restriction on inmates' first amendment interests would be measured were deterrence, incapacitation, rehabilitation, and the maintenance of institutional security within the prison.

The Court then concluded that the restriction on the inmates' first amendment interests in this case was constitutional. In arriving at this conclusion, the Court balanced the burden that this restriction placed on the inmates' communicative interests against the governmental interests purportedly justifying the restriction. The Court found the burden on the inmates diminished by the fact that the inmates had alternative ways of communicating with the media—through the mail and through messages sent via family members, attorneys, clergy, and friends who had permission to visit the inmates. Although the Court acknowledged that for illiterate inmates, communicating through the mail might not be a viable alternative unless the inmate received some assistance from someone who was literate, the Court was untroubled by this fact since, in this particular case, there was no indication that inmates who needed assistance had been deprived of such assistance. The Court also emphasized that the regulation was content-neutral.

To the extent that the restriction on press interviews did burden the first amendment interests of inmates, the Court found this burden outweighed by the interest in institutional security furthered by the restriction. If members of the press could designate inmates for interviews, the designated inmates might become power figures within the institution, exerting a disproportionate influence on other inmates. Availing themselves of this influence, the inmate power figures might then challenge the authority of prison officials and provoke disturbances. The regulation at issue in this case forestalled that threat and also preserved institutional security by keeping the number of visits at a "manageable level." Id. at 827, 94 S.Ct. at 2806.

The Court rejected the media plaintiffs' freedom of press claim as well, noting that the press has no broader right of access to prisons than does the general public. Four Justices dissented from this portion of the Court's opinion—Justices Powell, Brennan, Marshall, and Douglas. The dissenters' principal contention was that since the public is dependent on the press for information about prisons, the press has a right of access to prisons even when members of the public are not afforded the same access. In his dissenting opinion, Justice Powell also emphasized that there were less drastic means of achieving the government's objective of preserving institutional security. For example, to control what was denominated the "big wheel phenomenon," the number of interviews that any one inmate could have with members of the press during a certain time period could be limited. Justice Powell, incidentally, unlike the other three dissenters, concurred in the majority's disposition of the inmates' claim.

2. Should the interest in retribution be considered a "legitimate penological objective" which would justify the abridgement of inmates' first amendment rights? See Hudson v. Palmer, 468 U.S. 517, 524, 104 S.Ct. 3194, 3199 (1984), infra page 409.

3. The next case in which the Supreme Court addressed the first amendment rights of prisoners was Jones v. North Carolina Prisoners' Labor Union, 433 U.S. 119, 97 S.Ct. 2532 (1977). The plaintiff in that case was a prisoners' labor union whose designated purpose was to improve, through collective bargaining, the working conditions of inmate laborers. A North Carolina statute, however, proscribed collective bargaining on behalf of inmates.

The plaintiff brought suit challenging the constitutionality of three rules promulgated by the North Carolina Department of Correction, which inhibited the activities of the labor union in North Carolina prisons. The first rule prohibited inmates from trying to persuade other inmates to join the union. The second barred union meetings in the prison, and the third prohibited the bulk mailing of union materials into the prison. Despite these rules, authorities permitted inmates to be members of the union. In addition, the mailing of union materials to individual inmates was permitted, since individual mailings did not pose the same risk of contraband being smuggled into a prison as did bulk mailings.

The prisoners' labor union contended that these three rules impinged upon its constitutional rights and those of its members. Specifically, the union claimed that all of the rules violated the first amendment guarantee of freedom of speech and that the no-solicitation and no-meeting rules contravened both the right to freedom of association protected by the first amendment and the fourteenth amendment right to equal protection of the law. The latter claim was grounded on the fact that other organizations—the Jaycees and Alcoholics Anonymous—were permitted to hold meetings in the prisons and distribute bulk mailings within the prisons.

State correctional officials defended the regulations, arguing that a prisoners' labor union posed dangers to institutional security. They contended that in furthering the goals of the union, certain union spokesmen could become power figures within the prison, commanding undue influence over other inmates. This influence might be misused, leading to general chaos within the institution, work stoppages, and even riots.

The district court credited this testimony, but noted that there was absolutely no evidence that the union had interfered in the past with the operations of the state prisons. The court furthermore observed that since correctional officials permitted inmates to join the union, the ban on inmate-to-inmate solicitation to join the union made no sense and therefore violated the first amendment. The district court also struck down the no-meeting and bulk-mailing rules on equal protection grounds.

· In an opinion written by Justice (now Chief Justice) Rehnquist, the Supreme Court reversed:

> State correctional officials uniformly testified that the concept of a prisoners' labor union was itself fraught with potential dangers, whether or not such a union intended, illegally, to press for collective-bargaining recognition. * * * The District Court did not reject these beliefs as fanciful or erroneous. It, instead, noted that they were held "sincerely," and were arguably correct. Without a showing that these beliefs were unreasonable, it was error for the District Court to conclude that appellants needed to show more. In particular, the burden was not on appellants to show affirmatively that the Union would be "detrimental to proper penological objectives" or would constitute a "present danger to security and order." Rather, "[s]uch considerations are peculiarly within the province and professional expertise of corrections officials, and, in the absence of substantial evidence in the record to indicate that the officials have exaggerated their response to these considerations, courts should ordinarily defer to their expert judgment in such matters."

Id. at 126–28, 97 S.Ct. at 2538.

The Court disagreed that the no-solicitation and no-meeting rules were unreasonable because inmate membership in the union was permissible. The Court opined: "It is clearly not irrational to conclude that individuals may believe what they want, but that concerted group activity, or solicitation therefor, would pose additional and unwarranted problems and frictions in the State's penal institutions." Id. at 129, 97 S.Ct. at 2539. The Court further observed:

> Appellant prison officials concluded that the presence, perhaps even the objectives, of a prisoners' labor union would be detrimental to order and security in the prisons. It is enough to say that they have not been conclusively shown to be wrong in this view. The interest in preserving order and authority in the prisons is self-evident. Prison life, and relations between the inmates themselves and between the inmates and prison officials or staff, contain the ever-present potential for violent confrontation and conflagration. Responsible prison officials must be permitted to take reasonable steps to forestall such a threat, and they must be permitted to act before the time when they can compile a dossier on the eve of a riot.

Id. at 132–133, 97 S.Ct. at 2541–42.

The Court therefore concluded that as far as the first amendment was concerned, the rules were "reasonable" and "consistent with the inmates' status as prisoners and with the legitimate operational considerations of the institution." Id. at 130, 97 S.Ct. at 2540. At the same time, the Court emphasized that an internal grievance mechanism provided inmates with an alternative way of voicing complaints and that inmates could still receive individual mailings of union materials.

The Supreme Court also rejected the union's argument that the proscription of bulk mailings of union materials and union meetings violated the right to equal protection of the law. To withstand scrutiny under the equal protection clause, according to the Court, there only had to be a "rational basis" for treating the union differently than the Jaycees and Alcoholics Anonymous. The Court found such a rational basis here, both because participation by inmates in the Jaycees and Alcoholics Anonymous was considered rehabilitative and because a central goal of the union, unlike the Jaycees and Alcoholics Anonymous, was to engage in an activity—collective bargaining—which was illegal under state law.

Justice Marshall, joined by Justice Brennan, dissented. The dissenters strongly objected to the reasonableness standard propounded by the majority, particularly to that portion of the Court's opinion condoning the curtailment of prisoners' associational activities whenever prison officials "reasonably conclude" that such activities pose the "likelihood" of a disruption within the prison or of other adverse effects on the institution's legitimate penological objectives. Justice Marshall observed as follows:

> The central lesson of over a half century of First Amendment adjudication is that freedom is sometimes a hazardous enterprise, and that the Constitution requires the State to bear certain risks to preserve our liberty. See, e.g., Tinker v. Des Moines School Dist., 393 U.S. 503 (1969). To my mind, therefore, the fact that appellants have not acted wholly irrationally in banning Union meetings is not disposi-

tive. Rather, I believe that where, as here, meetings would not pose an immediate and substantial threat to the security or rehabilitative functions of the prisons, the First Amendment guarantees Union members the right to associate freely, and the Fourteenth Amendment guarantees them the right to be treated as favorably as members of other inmate organizations. The State can surely regulate the time, place, and manner of the meetings, and perhaps can monitor them to assure that disruptions are not planned, but the State cannot outlaw such assemblies altogether.

Id. at 146, 97 S.Ct. at 2548.

4. Is the Court's approach to prisoners' rights in *Jones* fully consistent with its approach in *Pell v. Procunier,* supra page 278, note 1?

5. An interesting contrast results when the Supreme Court's discussion in *Jones* is compared to decisions of the Court involving the first amendment rights of nonprisoners. One such decision is Tinker v. Des Moines Independent School District, 393 U.S. 503, 89 S.Ct. 733 (1969), which was cited by Justice Marshall in his dissenting opinion in *Jones.* In that case, in which the Court held unconstitutional the disciplining of students who wore black armbands to protest the Vietnam War, the Court stated:

The District Court concluded that the action of the school authorities was reasonable because it was based upon their fear of a disturbance from the wearing of the armbands. But, in our system, undifferentiated fear or apprehension of disturbance is not enough to overcome the right to freedom of expression. Any departure from absolute regimentation may cause trouble. Any variation from the majority's opinion may inspire fear. Any word spoken, in class, in the lunchroom, or on the campus, that deviates from the views of another person may start an argument or cause a disturbance. But our Constitution says we must take this risk.

Id. at 508, 89 S.Ct. at 737.

Would the outcome of *Tinker* have been the same if the persons wearing the black armbands to protest the war had been prisoners? What if prisoners wore black armbands to protest the failure of prison officials to provide adequate protection from assaults by other inmates? Or to protest the food? Or to protest the refusal of prison officials to provide each inmate with a television?

6. Bell v. Wolfish, 441 U.S. 520, 99 S.Ct. 1861 (1979) was the next in a series of Supreme Court cases discussing the first amendment rights of prisoners. In *Bell,* the Court addressed the constitutionality of what it called the "publisher-only" rule, a rule in force at the Metropolitan Correctional Center, a federal custodial facility in New York City. Under this rule, prisoners and pretrial detainees, who are individuals incarcerated while awaiting trial on criminal charges, could only receive books and magazines mailed to them by publishers, bookstores, and book clubs.

While the case was pending before the Supreme Court, the Bureau of Prisons informed the Court of its plans to amend its rules to permit inmates to receive paperback books and magazines from any source. The restriction with regard to the source of hardbound books, however, would remain in force, since drugs, money, and other contraband could so easily be hidden in the book bindings and smuggled into the institution. To manually inspect the pages and bindings of each hardbound book for contraband would, according to the MCC warden, be too time-consuming for the MCC staff.

Once again writing for the majority, Justice Rehnquist concluded that only permitting inmates to receive hardcover books from publishers, bookstores, and book clubs was a "rational response" to "an obvious security problem." Id. at 550, 99 S.Ct. at 1880. The Court then said that there were several other factors contributing to its conclusion that the "publisher-only" rule did not violate the first amendment:

> The rule operates in a neutral fashion, without regard to the content of the expression. And there are alternative means of obtaining reading material that have not been shown to be burdensome or insufficient. "[W]e regard the available 'alternative means of [communication as] a relevant factor' in a case such as this where 'we [are] called upon to balance First Amendment rights against [legitimate] governmental . . . interests.'" The restriction, as it is now before us, allows soft-bound books and magazines to be received from any source and hardback books to be received from publishers, bookstores, and book clubs. In addition, the MCC has a "relatively large" library for use by inmates. We are also influenced in our decision by the fact that the rule's impact on pretrial detainees is limited to a maximum period of approximately 60 days. See n. 3, supra.[a] In sum, considering all the circumstances, we view the rule, as we now find it, to be a "reasonable 'time, place and manner' regulatio[n that is] necessary to further significant governmental interests . . . ."

Id. at 551–52, 99 S.Ct. at 1880–81.

It is noteworthy that in conducting its first amendment analysis, the Court did not distinguish between pretrial detainees and convicted inmates. The Court said:

> Neither the Court of Appeals nor the District Court distinguished between pretrial detainees and convicted inmates in reviewing the challenged security practices, and we see no reason to do so. There is no basis for concluding that pretrial detainees pose any lesser security risk than convicted inmates. Indeed, it may be that in certain circumstances they present a greater risk to jail security and order. In the federal system, a detainee is committed to the detention facility only because no other less drastic means can reasonably assure his presence at trial. As a result, those who are detained prior to trial may in many cases be individuals who are charged with serious crimes or who

[a. Footnote 3 to which the Court alluded stated:

This group of nondetainees may comprise, on a daily basis, between 40% and 60% of the MCC population. Prior to the District Court's order, 50% of *all* MCC inmates spent less than 30 days at the facility and 73% less than 60 days. However, of the unsentenced detainees, over half spent less than 10 days at the MCC, three-quarters were released within a month and more than 85% were released within 60 days.]

have prior records. They also may pose a greater risk of escape than convicted inmates. This may be particularly true at facilities like the MCC, where the resident convicted inmates have been sentenced to only short terms of incarceration and many of the detainees face the possibility of lengthy imprisonment if convicted.

Id. at 547 n. 28, 99 S.Ct. at 1878 n. 28.

In a dissenting opinion, Justice Marshall objected to what he considered the Court's blunderbuss approach to the first amendment. Emphasizing that pretrial detainees are presumed to be innocent and are often incarcerated only because they are too poor to post bail, he advocated the following approach to the first amendment claims of pretrial detainees:

> When assessing the restrictions on detainees, * * * I believe the Government must bear a more rigorous burden of justification than the rational-basis standard mandates. At a minimum, I would require a showing that a restriction is substantially necessary to jail administration. Where the imposition is of particular gravity, that is, where it implicates interests of fundamental importance or inflicts significant harms, the Government should demonstrate that the restriction serves a compelling necessity of jail administration.
>
> *   *   *
>
> Simply stated, the approach I advocate here weighs the detainees' interests implicated by a particular restriction against the governmental interests the restriction serves. As the substantiality of the intrusion on detainees' rights increases, so must the significance of the countervailing governmental objectives.

Id. at 570–71, 99 S.Ct. at 1890–91.

Justice Marshall then concluded that the compelling necessity test had to be applied in this case to the "publisher-only" rule, since the rule interfered with the "fundamental" right under the first amendment to receive information. Applying this test to the facts of the case before the Court, Justice Marshall opined that the test was not met. Although the "publisher-only" rule might be one rational way of curtailing the flow of contraband into a prison, less restrictive ways of achieving this objective existed. The number of hardbound books that any prisoner could receive, for example, could be limited, and books could be fluoroscoped for contraband.

Justice Stevens, joined by Justice Brennan, also dissented from the Court's opinion. Analyzing the constitutionality of the "publisher only" rule under the due process clause, Justice Stevens concluded that the rule was unconstitutional.

*   *   *

TURNER v. SAFLEY

Supreme Court of the United States, 1987.
482 U.S. 78, 107 S.Ct. 2254, 96 L.Ed.2d 64.

JUSTICE O'CONNOR delivered the opinion of the Court.

*   *   *

I

Respondents brought this class action for injunctive relief and damages in the United States District Court for the Western District of Missouri. The regulations challenged in the complaint were in effect at all prisons within the jurisdiction of the Missouri Division of Corrections. This litigation focused, however, on practices at the Renz Correctional Institution (Renz), located in Cedar City, Missouri. The Renz prison population includes both male and female prisoners of varying security levels. Most of the female prisoners at Renz are classified as medium or maximum security inmates, while most of the male prisoners are classified as minimum security offenders. Renz is used on occasion to provide protective custody for inmates from other prisons in the Missouri system. * * *

Two regulations are at issue here. The first of the challenged regulations relates to correspondence between inmates at different institutions. It permits such correspondence "with immediate family members who are inmates in other correctional institutions," and it permits correspondence between inmates "concerning legal matters." Other correspondence between inmates, however, is permitted only if "the classification/treatment team of each inmate deems it in the best interest of the parties involved." * * * At Renz, the District Court found that the rule "as practiced is that inmates may not write non-family inmates."

The challenged marriage regulation, which was promulgated while this litigation was pending, permits an inmate to marry only with the permission of the superintendent of the prison, and provides that such approval should be given only "when there are compelling reasons to do so." The term "compelling" is not defined, but prison officials testified at trial that generally only a pregnancy or the birth of an illegitimate child would be considered a compelling reason. * * *

* * *

The District Court issued a memorandum opinion and order finding both the correspondence and marriage regulations unconstitutional. The court, relying on *Procunier v. Martinez,* applied a strict scrutiny standard. * * *

The Court of Appeals for the Eighth Circuit affirmed. * * *

* * *

II

* * *

Our task * * * is to formulate a standard of review for prisoners' constitutional claims that is responsive both to the "policy of judicial restraint regarding prisoner complaints and [to] the need to protect constitutional rights." As the Court of Appeals acknowledged, *Martinez* did not itself resolve the question that it framed. * * * The *Martinez* Court based its ruling striking down the content-based regulation on the First Amendment rights of those who are not prisoners

* * *. We expressly reserved the question of the proper standard of review to apply in cases "involving questions of 'prisoners' rights.'"

In four cases following *Martinez*, this Court has addressed such "questions of 'prisoners' rights.'" * * *

[The Court's opinion then discusses *Pell v. Procunier*, *Jones v. North Carolina Prisoners' Union*, *Bell v. Wolfish*, and *Block v. Rutherford*, infra page 299.]

In none of these four "prisoners' rights" cases did the Court apply a standard of heightened scrutiny, but instead inquired whether a prison regulation that burdens fundamental rights is "reasonably related" to legitimate penological objectives, or whether it represents an "exaggerated response" to those concerns. The Court of Appeals in this case nevertheless concluded that *Martinez* provided the closest analogy for determining the appropriate standard of review for resolving respondents' constitutional complaints. The Court of Appeals distinguished this Court's decisions in *Pell*, *Jones*, *Bell*, and *Block* as variously involving "time, place, or manner" regulations, or regulations that restrict "presumptively dangerous" inmate activities. * * *

We disagree with the Court of Appeals that the reasoning in our cases subsequent to *Martinez* can be so narrowly cabined. In *Pell*, for example, it was found "relevant" to the reasonableness of a restriction on face-to-face visits between prisoners and news reporters that prisoners had other means of communicating with members of the general public. These alternative means of communication did not, however, make the prison regulation a "time, place, or manner" restriction in any ordinary sense of the term. As *Pell* acknowledged, the alternative methods of personal communication still available to prisoners would have been "unimpressive" if offered to justify a restriction on personal communication among members of the general public. Nevertheless, they were relevant in determining the scope of the burden placed by the regulation on inmates' First Amendment rights. *Pell* thus simply teaches that it is appropriate to consider the extent of this burden when "we [are] called upon to balance First Amendment rights against [legitimate] governmental interests."

Nor, in our view, can the reasonableness standard adopted in *Jones* and *Bell* be construed as applying only to "presumptively dangerous" inmate activities. To begin with, the Court of Appeals did not indicate how it would identify such "presumptively dangerous" conduct, other than to conclude that the group meetings in *Jones*, and the receipt of hardback books in *Bell*, both fall into that category. The Court of Appeals found that correspondence between inmates did not come within this grouping because the court did "not think a letter presents the same sort of 'obvious security problem' as does a hardback book." It is not readily apparent, however, why hardback books, which can be scanned for contraband by electronic devices and fluoroscopes are qualitatively different in this respect from inmate correspondence, which can be written in codes not readily subject to detection; or why coordinated inmate activity within the same prison is categorically different from inmate activity coordinated by mail among different prison institutions. ＊ ＊ ＊

If *Pell, Jones,* and *Bell* have not already resolved the question posed in *Martinez,* we resolve it now: when a prison regulation impinges on inmates' constitutional rights, the regulation is valid if it is reasonably related to legitimate penological interests. In our view, such a standard is necessary if "prison administrators . . ., and not the courts, [are] to make the difficult judgments concerning institutional operations." Subjecting the day-to-day judgments of prison officials to an inflexible strict scrutiny analysis would seriously hamper their ability to anticipate security problems and to adopt innovative solutions to the intractable problems of prison administration. The rule would also distort the decisionmaking process, for every administrative judgment would be subject to the possibility that some court somewhere would conclude that it had a less restrictive way of solving the problem at hand. Courts inevitably would become the primary arbiters of what constitutes the best solution to every administrative problem, thereby "unnecessarily perpetuat[ing] the involvement of the federal courts in affairs of prison administration."

As our opinions in *Pell, Bell,* and *Jones* show, several factors are relevant in determining the reasonableness of the regulation at issue. First, there must be a "valid, rational connection" between the prison regulation and the legitimate governmental interest put forward to justify it. Thus, a regulation cannot be sustained where the logical connection between the regulation and the asserted goal is so remote as to render the policy arbitrary or irrational. Moreover, the governmental objective must be a legitimate and neutral one. We have found it important to inquire whether prison regulations restricting inmates' First Amendment rights operated in a neutral fashion, without regard to the content of the expression.

A second factor relevant in determining the reasonableness of a prison restriction, as *Pell* shows, is whether there are alternative means of exercising the right that remain open to prison inmates. Where "other avenues" remain available for the exercise of the asserted right, courts should be particularly conscious of the "measure of judicial deference owed to corrections officials . . . in gauging the validity of the regulation."

A third consideration is the impact accommodation of the asserted constitutional right will have on guards and other inmates, and on the allocation of prison resources generally. In the necessarily closed environment of the correctional institution, few changes will have no ramifications on the liberty of others or on the use of the prison's limited resources for preserving institutional order. When accommodation of an asserted right will have a significant "ripple effect" on fellow inmates or on prison staff, courts should be particularly deferential to the informed discretion of corrections officials.

Finally, the absence of ready alternatives is evidence of the reasonableness of a prison regulation. By the same token, the existence of obvious, easy alternatives may be evidence that the regulation is not reasonable, but is an "exaggerated response" to prison concerns. This is not a "least restrictive alternative" test: prison officials do not have to set up and then shoot down every conceivable alternative method of accommodating the claimant's constitutional complaint. But if an inmate claimant can point to an alternative that fully accommodates the prisoner's rights at *de minimis* cost to valid penological interests, a court may consider that as evidence that the regulation does not satisfy the reasonable relationship standard.

III

Applying our analysis to the Missouri rule barring inmate-to-inmate correspondence, we conclude that the record clearly demonstrates that the regulation was reasonably related to legitimate security interests. We find that the marriage restriction, however, does not satisfy the reasonable relationship standard, but rather constitutes an exaggerated response to petitioners' rehabilitation and security concerns.

A

According to the testimony at trial, the Missouri correspondence provision was promulgated primarily for security reasons. Prison officials testified that mail between institutions can be used to communicate escape plans and to arrange assaults and other violent acts. Witnesses stated that the Missouri Division of Corrections had a growing problem with prison gangs, and that restricting communications among gang members, both by transferring gang members to different institutions and by restricting their correspondence, was an important element in combating this problem. Officials also testified that the use of Renz as a facility to provide protective custody for certain inmates could be compromised by permitting correspondence between inmates at Renz and inmates at other correctional institutions.

The prohibition on correspondence between institutions is logically connected to these legitimate security concerns. Undoubtedly, communication with other felons is a potential spur to criminal behavior: this sort of contact frequently is prohibited even after an inmate has been released on parole. See, *e.g.*, 28 CFR § 2.40(a)(10) (1986) (federal parole conditioned on nonassociation with known criminals, unless permission is granted by the parole officer). In Missouri prisons, the danger of such coordinated criminal activity is exacerbated by the presence of prison gangs. The Missouri policy of separating and isolating gang members—a strategy that has been frequently used to control gang activity—logically is furthered by the restriction on prisoner-to-prisoner correspondence. Moreover, the correspondence regulation does not deprive prisoners of all means of expression. Rather, it bars communication only with a limited class of other people with whom prison officials have particular cause to be concerned—inmates at other institutions within the Missouri prison system.

We also think that the Court of Appeals' analysis overlooks the impact of respondents' asserted right on other inmates and prison personnel. Prison officials have stated that in their expert opinion, correspondence between prison institutions facilitates the development of informal organizations that threaten the core functions of prison administration, maintaining safety and internal security. As a result, the correspondence rights asserted by respondents, like the organizational activities at issue in *Jones v. North Carolina Prisoners' Union,* can be exercised only at the cost of significantly less liberty and safety for everyone else, guards and other prisoners alike. Indeed, the potential "ripple effect" is even broader here than in *Jones,* because exercise of the right affects the inmates and staff of more than one institution. Where exercise of a right requires this kind of tradeoff, we think that the choice made by corrections officials—which is, after all, a judgment "peculiarly within [their] province and professional expertise"—should not be lightly set aside by the courts.

Finally, there are no obvious, easy alternatives to the policy adopted by petitioners. Other well-run prison systems, including the Federal Bureau of Prisons, have concluded that substantially similar restrictions on inmate correspondence were necessary to protect institutional order and security. As petitioners have shown, the only alternative proffered by the claimant prisoners, the monitoring of inmate correspondence, clearly would impose more than a *de minimis* cost on the pursuit of legitimate corrections goals. Prison officials testified that it would be impossible to read every piece of inmate-to-inmate correspondence, and consequently there would be an appreciable risk of missing dangerous messages. In any event, prisoners could easily write in jargon or codes to prevent detection of their real messages. The risk of missing dangerous communications, taken together with the sheer burden on staff resources required to conduct item-by-item censorship, supports the judgment of prison officials that this alternative is not an adequate alternative to restricting correspondence.

The prohibition on correspondence is reasonably related to valid corrections goals. The rule is content neutral, it logically advances the goals of institutional security and safety identified by Missouri prison officials, and it is not an exaggerated response to those objectives. On that basis, we conclude that the regulation does not unconstitutionally abridge the First Amendment rights of prison inmates.

B

In support of the marriage regulation, petitioners first suggest that the rule does not deprive prisoners of a constitutionally protected right. They concede that the decision to marry is a fundamental right under *Zablocki v. Redhail,* 434 U.S. 374 (1976), and *Loving v. Virginia,* 388 U.S. 1 (1967), but they imply that a different rule should obtain "in . . . a prison forum." * * *

We disagree with petitioners that *Zablocki* does not apply to prison inmates. It is settled that a prison inmate "retains those [constitutional] rights that are not inconsistent with his status as a prisoner or with the legitimate penological objectives of the corrections system." The right to marry, like many other rights, is subject to substantial restrictions as a result of incarceration. Many important attributes of marriage remain, however, after taking into account the limitations imposed by prison life. First, inmate marriages, like others, are expressions of emotional support and public commitment. These elements are an important and significant aspect of the marital relationship. In addition, many religions recognize marriage as having spiritual significance; for some inmates and their spouses, therefore, the commitment of marriage may be an exercise of religious faith as well as an expression of personal dedication. Third, most inmates eventually will be released by parole or commutation, and therefore most inmate marriages are formed in the expectation that they ultimately will be fully consummated. Finally, marital status often is a precondition to the receipt of government benefits (*e.g.,* Social Security benefits), property rights (*e.g.,* tenancy by the entirety, inheritance rights), and other, less tangible benefits (*e.g.,* legitimation of children born out of wedlock). These incidents of marriage, like the religious and personal aspects of the marriage commitment, are unaffected by the fact of confinement or the pursuit of legitimate corrections goals.

Taken together, we conclude that these remaining elements are sufficient to form a constitutionally protected marital relationship in the prison context. * * *

The Missouri marriage regulation prohibits inmates from marrying unless the prison superintendent has approved the marriage after finding that there are compelling reasons for doing so. As noted previously, generally only pregnancy or birth of a child is considered a "compelling reason" to approve a marriage. In determining whether this regulation impermissibly burdens the right to marry, we note initially that the regulation prohibits marriages between inmates and civilians, as well as marriages between inmates. Although not urged by respondents, this implication of the interests of nonprisoners may support application of the *Martinez* standard, because the regulation may entail a "consequential restriction on the [constitutional] rights of those who are not prisoners." We need not reach this question, however, because even under the reasonable relationship test, the marriage regulation does not withstand scrutiny.

Petitioners have identified both security and rehabilitation concerns in support of the marriage prohibition. The security concern emphasized by petitioners is that "love triangles" might lead to violent confrontations between inmates. With respect to rehabilitation, prison officials testified that female prisoners often were subject to abuse at home or were overly dependent on male figures, and that this dependence or abuse was connected to the crimes they had committed. The superintendent at Renz, petitioner William Turner, testified that in his view, these women prisoners needed to concentrate on developing skills of self-reliance and that the prohibition on marriage furthered this rehabilitative goal. * * *

We conclude that on this record, the Missouri prison regulation, as written, is not reasonably related to these penological interests. No doubt legitimate security concerns may require placing reasonable restrictions upon an inmate's right to marry, and may justify requiring approval of the superintendent. The Missouri regulation, however, represents an exaggerated response to such security objectives. There are obvious, easy alternatives to the Missouri regulation that accommodate the right to marry while imposing a *de minimis* burden on the pursuit of security objectives. See, *e.g.,* 28 CFR § 551.10 (1986) (marriage by inmates in federal prison generally permitted, but not if warden finds that it presents a threat to security or order of institution, or to public safety). We are aware of no place in the record where prison officials testified that such ready alternatives would not fully satisfy their security concerns. Moreover, with respect to the security concern emphasized in petitioners' brief—the creation of "love triangles"—petitioners have pointed to nothing in the record suggesting that the marriage regulation was viewed as preventing such entanglements. Common sense likewise suggests that there is no logical connection between the marriage restriction and the formation of love triangles: surely in prisons housing both male and female prisoners, inmate rivalries are as likely to develop without a formal marriage ceremony as with one. Finally, this is not an instance where the "ripple effect" on the security of fellow inmates and prison staff justifies a broad restriction on inmates' rights * * *.

Nor, on this record, is the marriage restriction reasonably related to the articulated rehabilitation goal. First, in requiring refusal of permission absent a finding of a compelling reason to allow the marriage, the rule sweeps much more broadly than can be explained by petitioners' penological objectives. Missouri prison officials testified that generally they had experienced no problem with the marriage of male inmates, and the District Court found that such marriages had routinely been allowed as a matter of practice at Missouri correctional institutions prior to adoption of the rule. The proffered justification thus does not explain the adoption of a rule banning marriages by these inmates. Nor does it account for the prohibition on inmate marriages to civilians. Missouri prison officials testified that generally they had no objection to inmate-civilian marriages, and Superintendent Turner testified that he usually did not object to the marriage of either male or female prisoners to civilians. The rehabilitation concern appears from the record to have been centered almost exclusively on female inmates marrying other inmates or ex-felons; it does not account for the ban on inmate-civilian marriages.

* * *

It is undisputed that Missouri prison officials may regulate the time and circumstances under which the marriage ceremony itself takes place. On this record, however, the almost complete ban on the decision to marry is not reasonably related to legitimate penological objectives. We conclude, therefore, that the Missouri marriage regulation is facially invalid.

IV

We uphold the facial validity of the correspondence regulation, but we conclude that the marriage rule is constitutionally infirm. * * *

Accordingly, the judgment of the Court of Appeals striking down the Missouri marriage regulation is affirmed; its judgment invalidating the correspondence rule is reversed; and the case is remanded to the Court of Appeals for further proceedings consistent with this opinion.

* * *

JUSTICE STEVENS, with whom JUSTICE BRENNAN, JUSTICE MARSHALL, and JUSTICE BLACKMUN join, concurring in part and dissenting in part.

How a court describes its standard of review when a prison regulation infringes fundamental constitutional rights often has far less consequence for the inmates than the actual showing that the court demands of the State in order to uphold the regulation. This case provides a prime example.

There would not appear to be much difference between the question whether a prison regulation that burdens fundamental rights in the quest for security is "needlessly broad"—the standard applied by the District Court and the Court of Appeals—and this Court's requirement that the regulation must be "reasonably related to legitimate penological interests" and may not represent "an 'exaggerated response' to those concerns." But if the standard can be satisfied by nothing more than a "logical connection" between the regulation and any legitimate penological concern perceived by a cautious warden, it is virtually meaningless. Application of the standard would seem to permit disregard for inmates' constitutional rights whenever the imagination of the warden produces a plausible security concern and a deferential trial court is able to discern a logical connection between that concern and the challenged regulation. Indeed, there is a logical connection between prison discipline and the use of bullwhips on prisoners; and security is logically furthered by a total ban on inmate communication, not only with other inmates but also with outsiders who conceivably might be interested in arranging an attack within the prison or an escape from it. Thus, I dissent from Part II of the Court's opinion.

I am able to join Part III–B because the Court's invalidation of the marriage regulation does not rely on a rejection of a standard of review more stringent than the one announced in Part II. The Court in Part III–B concludes after careful examination that, even applying a "reasonableness" standard, the marriage regulation must fail because the justifications asserted on its behalf lack record support.[15] * * *

Questions and Points for Discussion

1. In Thornburgh v. Abbott, 109 S.Ct. 1874 (1989), the Supreme Court considered the constitutionality of certain regulations promulgated by the Federal Bureau of Prisons. According to these regulations, prisoners could receive publications from outside the prison, but the power of a warden to withhold a publication deemed "detrimental to the security, good order, or discipline of the institution" or which might "facilitate criminal activity" was reserved. In the language set forth below, the regulations then delineated some of the instances when censorship would be appropriate, taking care to note that the list was not exhaustive:

* * * Publications which may be rejected by a Warden include but are not limited to publications which meet one of the following criteria:

(1) It depicts or describes procedures for the construction or use of weapons, ammunition, bombs or incendiary devices;

(2) It depicts, encourages, or describes methods of escape from correctional facilities, or contains blueprints, drawings or similar descriptions of Bureau of Prisons institutions;

(3) It depicts or describes procedures for the brewing of alcoholic beverages, or the manufacture of drugs;

(4) It is written in code;

(5) It depicts, describes or encourages activities which may lead to the use of physical violence or group disruption;

(6) It encourages or instructs in the commission of criminal activity;

(7) It is sexually explicit material which by its nature or content poses a threat to the security, good order, or discipline of the institution, or facilitates criminal activity.

The regulations also placed certain restrictions on a warden's power to limit a prisoner's receipt of a publication. The warden could not, for example, reject a publication "solely because its content is religious, philosophical, political, social or sexual, or because its content is unpopular or repugnant." Nor could the warden set up a "hit list" of publications absolutely barred from distribution within the prison. Instead, the warden had to review each issue of a publication to determine whether some portion of that particular issue posed a threat to institutional security or would facilitate a crime. If any part of the issue was censorable, the practice within the Bureau of Prisons was to bar the entire publication from the prison.

[15. The Court's bifurcated treatment of the mail and marriage regulations leads to the absurd result that an inmate at Renz may marry another inmate, but may not carry on the courtship leading to the marriage by corresponding with him or her beforehand because he or she would not then be an "immediate family member."]

The federal prisoners and publishers who were the plaintiffs in this case contended that the Bureau of Prison regulations governing incoming publications violated the first amendment on their face. The plaintiffs additionally challenged, on first amendment grounds, the way in which these regulations had actually been applied to a number of incoming publications.

Applying a deferential reasonableness standard, the United States District Court for the District of Columbia upheld all of the challenged regulations. The Court of Appeals for the District of Columbia, however, reversed. Since the case involved not just the first amendment rights of prisoners, but also of nonprisoners—the publishers who wish to circulate their publications within a prison—the court of appeals concluded that the constitutionality of the regulations had to be analyzed under the more stringent standard of Procunier v. Martinez, 416 U.S. 396, 94 S.Ct. 1800 (1974), supra page 273.

In an opinion written by Justice Blackmun, the Supreme Court reversed. Distinguishing *Martinez,* the majority opinion stated as follows:

> [A] careful reading of *Martinez* suggests that our rejection of the regulation at issue resulted not from a least restrictive means requirement, but from our recognition that the regulated activity centrally at issue in that case—outgoing personal correspondence from prisoners— did not, by its very nature, pose a serious threat to prison order and security. * * * We deal here with incoming publications, material requested by an individual inmate but targeted to a general audience. Once in the prison, material of this kind reasonably may be expected to circulate among prisoners, with the concomitant potential for coordinated disruptive conduct. Furthermore, prisoners may observe particular material in the possession of a fellow prisoner, draw inferences about their fellow's [sic] beliefs, sexual orientation, or gang affiliations from that material, and cause disorder by acting accordingly.

109 S.Ct. at 1880–81.

The Court then concluded that when assessing the constitutionality of prison regulations which concern incoming publications, the standard to be applied is the standard which was described in *Turner v. Safley.* Under this standard, the regulations would be valid as long as they were "reasonably related to legitimate penological interests." To the extent that *Martinez* suggested that a different standard should apply, it was overruled. The *Martinez* standard was only to be applied to "outgoing correspondence." Id. at 1881.

In the course of its opinion, the Supreme Court said that it was confident that the *Turner* reasonableness test was not a "toothless" one. Id. at 1882. After applying this test to the censorship regulations before it, however, the Court concluded that the regulations, on their face, were constitutional.

The Court's application of the four *Turner* factors to the facts of the case is instructive. Pertinent excerpts from this portion of the Court's opinion are set forth below:

The first *Turner* factor is multifold: we must determine whether the governmental objective underlying the regulations at issue is legitimate and neutral, and that the regulations are rationally related to that objective. We agree with the District Court that this requirement has been met.

The legitimacy of the Government's purpose in promulgating these regulations is beyond question. The regulations are expressly aimed at protecting prison security, a purpose this Court has said is "central to all other correctional goals."

As to neutrality, "[w]e have found it important to inquire whether prison regulations restricting inmates' First Amendment rights operated in a neutral fashion, without regard to the content of the expression." The ban on *all* correspondence between certain classes of inmates at issue in *Turner* clearly met this "neutrality" criterion, as did the restrictions at issue in *Pell* and *Wolfish*. The issue, however, in this case is closer.

On their face, the regulations distinguish between rejection of a publication "solely because its content is religious, philosophical, political, social or sexual, or because its content is unpopular or repugnant" (prohibited) and rejection because the publication is detrimental to security (permitted). Both determinations turn, to some extent, on content. But the Court's reference to "neutrality" in *Turner* was intended to go no further than its requirement in *Martinez* that "the regulation or practice in question must further an important or substantial governmental interest unrelated to the suppression of expression." Where, as here, prison administrators draw distinctions between publications solely on the basis of their potential implications for prison security, the regulations are "neutral" in the technical sense in which we meant and used that term in *Turner*.

We also conclude that the broad discretion accorded prison wardens by the regulations here at issue is rationally related to security interests. We reach this conclusion for two reasons. The first has to do with the kind of security risk presented by incoming publications.

* * *

Second, we are comforted by the individualized nature of the determinations required by the regulation. Under the regulations, no publication may be excluded unless the warden himself makes the determination that it is "detrimental to the security, good order, or discipline of the institution or . . . might facilitate criminal activity." This is the controlling standard. A publication which fits within one of the "criteria" for exclusion *may* be rejected, but only if it is determined to meet that standard under the conditions prevailing at the institution at the time. Indeed, the regulations expressly reject certain shortcuts that would lead to needless exclusions. See [28 CFR] § 540.70(b) (non-delegability of power to reject publications); § 540.71(c) (prohibition against establishing an excluded list of publications). We agree that it is rational for the Bureau to exclude materials that, although not necessarily "likely" to lead to violence, are determined by the warden to create an intolerable risk of disorder under the conditions of a particular prison at a particular time.

A second factor the Court in *Turner* held to be "relevant in determining the reasonableness of a prison restriction . . . is whether there are alternative means of exercising the right that remain open to prison inmates." As has already been made clear in *Turner* and *O'Lone* [infra page 311], "the right" in question must be viewed sensibly and expansively. * * * As the regulations at issue in the present case permit a broad range of publications to be sent, received, and read, this factor is clearly satisfied.

The third factor to be addressed under the *Turner* analysis is the impact that accommodation of the asserted constitutional right will have on others (guards and inmates) in the prison. * * * Where, as here, the right in question "can be exercised only at the cost of significantly less liberty and safety for everyone else, guards and other prisoners alike," the courts should defer to the "informed discretion of corrections officials."

Finally, *Turner* held that "the existence of obvious, easy alternatives may be evidence that the regulation is not reasonable, but is an 'exaggerated response' to prison concerns." * * * We agree with the District Court that these regulations, on their face, are not an "exaggerated response" to the problem at hand: no obvious, easy alternative has been established.

Regarding the all-or-nothing rule, we analyze respondents' proposed alternatives to that rule as alternative means of accommodating respondents' asserted rights. The District Court discussed the evidence and found, on the basis of testimony in the record, that petitioners' fear that tearing out the rejected portions and admitting the rest of the publication would create more discontent than the current practice was "reasonably founded." * * *

* * * In our view, when prison officials are able to demonstrate that they have rejected a less restrictive alternative because of reasonably founded fears that it will lead to greater harm, they succeed in demonstrating that the alternative they in fact selected was not an "exaggerated response" under *Turner*. Furthermore, the administrative inconvenience of this proposed alternative is also a factor to be considered, and adds additional support to the District Court's conclusion that petitioners were not obligated to adopt it.

109 S.Ct. at 1882–84.

In a significant footnote in the midst of its opinion, the Supreme Court indicated that just because a publication is admitted in one prison does not mean that its exclusion from another prison is irrational and hence in contravention of the first *Turner* factor. The Court said:

[W]hat may appear to be inconsistent results are not necessarily signs of arbitrariness or irrationality. Given the likely variability within and between institutions over time, greater consistency might be attainable only at the cost of a more broadly restrictive rule against admission of incoming publications. Any attempt to achieve greater consistency by broader exclusions might itself run afoul of the second *Turner* factor, i.e., the presence or absence of "alternative means of exercising the right" in question.

Id. at 1883, n. 15.

After holding that the Bureau of Prison regulations were constitutional on their face, the Court then remanded the case back to the lower courts for application of the reasonableness test to each of the publications whose withholding from a federal prison had been challenged by the plaintiffs. In an opinion joined by Justices Brennan and Marshall, Justice Stevens concurred in part and dissented in part. Justice Stevens agreed with the Court's decision to send the case back for consideration of the constitutionality of the actions of prison officials in rejecting particular publications. On the broader question of the standard to be applied when assessing the constitutionality of prison censorship regulations on their face and as applied, however, Justice Stevens disagreed with the majority. The majority's limitation of the holding of *Martinez* to outgoing correspondence was, in his opinion, disingenuous; the language of *Martinez* did not suggest, nor its reasoning support, such a constrained interpretation of its scope.

Justice Stevens also disagreed with the majority's conclusion that the Bureau of Prison regulations were constitutional on their face. In Justice Stevens's opinion, the regulations were unconstitutional, whatever the test applied to them—the *Procunier* standard or the *Turner* reasonableness test. Justice Stevens first disputed the contention that the regulations were content-neutral. Words like "detrimental to the security, good order, or discipline" of the prison and references to publications that "might facilitate criminal activity" were content-oriented, and they were also so vague that they encouraged censorship based on the personal biases of the censor.

Justice Stevens then lambasted the majority for contending that prisoners had alternative means of exercising the first amendment right in question since they had a number of other publications to which they could gain access. To this argument, Justice Stevens responded: "Some of the rejected publications may represent the sole medium for conveying and receiving a particular unconventional message; thus it is irrelevant that the regulations permit many other publications to be delivered to prisoners." Id. at 1890.

Finally, Justice Stevens attacked the Bureau of Prison's "all-or-nothing rule" under which a publication was either distributed in its entirety to a prisoner or toally banned from the institution. Justice Stevens described this rule as "a meat-ax abridgement of the First Amendment rights of either a free citizen or a prison inmate." Id. at 1892. Since the evidence, in Justice Stevens's opinion, did not support the conclusion that admitting part of a publication into the prison would threaten institutional security, the justification for the rule was really administrative convenience. But this purported justification for the "all-or-nothing rule" was unconvincing to Justice Stevens. Assuming that the prison officials individually scrutinized the publications as they were supposed to do, the additional time needed to rip one article out of the publication was infinitesimal—certainly of no "constitutional significance." Id.

2. *Pell v. Procunier, Bell v. Wolfish,* and *Jones v. North Carolina Prisoners' Labor Union* also involved the constitutionality, under the first amendment, of prison regulations restricting communications of non-prisoners with prisoners. Did these cases necessitate the Court's refusal to apply the *Martinez* standard in *Thornburgh?* Can the regulations at issue in *Thornburgh* be distinguished from those reviewed by the Court in *Pell, Bell,* and *Jones?*

3. Is *Thornburgh* consistent with the Supreme Court's rejection of the "presumptively dangerous" test in *Turner v. Safley?*

4. Could an article in a magazine describing deficiencies in the medical care afforded federal prisoners and charging that one federal prisoner was "murdered by neglect" because his medical needs were not attended to be constitutionally excluded from a federal prison? Could a letter written by a prisoner to an outsider containing such allegations be censored? Could a prisoner be disciplined for making such a statement to another prisoner or to a correctional officer?

What if the article, letter, or statement described the criminal justice system as racist? What if it described correctional officers as "racist pigs?"

B. FREEDOM OF ASSOCIATION

Subsumed within the first amendment and the due process clauses of the fifth and fourteenth amendments is what has come to be known as the freedom of association. Despite the generality of the term "association," the Constitution does not extend its protection to all contemplated encounters between individuals. See, e.g., Dallas v. Stanglin, 490 U.S. 19, 109 S.Ct. 1591 (1989) (restriction on the ages of the people who can be admitted to certain recreational dances does not implicate the first amendment). The constitutionally protected freedom of association is rather a more narrow concept.

As described by the Supreme Court in Roberts v. United States Jaycees, 468 U.S. 609, 104 S.Ct. 3244 (1984), the right to freedom of association has two dimensions. First, the right prevents the government from unduly encroaching on "choices to enter into and maintain certain intimate human relationships." Id. at 617, 104 S.Ct. at 3249. Family relationships, for example, are protected by this right to "intimate association," according to the Supreme Court, because they are marked by such characteristics as "relative smallness, a high degree of selectivity in decisions to begin and maintain the affiliation, and seclusion from others in critical aspects of the relationship." Id. at 620, 104 S.Ct. at 3250.

The Court in *Roberts* explained its reasoning for affording constitutional protection to certain intimate associations:

> The Court has long recognized that, because the Bill of Rights is designed to secure individual liberty, it must afford the formation and preservation of certain kinds of highly personal relationships a substantial measure of sanctuary from unjustified interference by the State. Without precisely identifying every consideration that may

underlie this type of constitutional protection, we have noted certain kinds of personal bonds have played a critical role in t.. culture and traditions of the Nation by cultivating and transmitting shared ideals and beliefs; they thereby foster diversity and act as critical buffers between the individual and the power of the State. Moreover, the constitutional shelter afforded such relationships reflects the realization that individuals draw much of their emotional enrichment from close ties with others. Protecting these relationships from unwarranted state interference therefore safeguards the ability independently to define one's identity that is central to any concept of liberty.

Id. at 618–19, 104 S.Ct. at 3249–50.

In addition to protecting the freedom of "intimate association," the Constitution, through the first amendment, protects what the Supreme Court has described as "expressive association." What "expressive association" encompasses is the right to gather together with others in order to engage in the activities protected by the first amendment, such as speaking, worshipping, and petitioning the government for a redress of grievances. Id. at 618, 104 S.Ct. at 3249. The Court has been careful to note, however, that not all encounters during which words or ideas are exchanged are considered "associational" within the meaning of the first amendment. Nowhere in the Constitution, said the Court in *Dallas v. Stanglin,* is there "a generalized right of 'social association.'" 109 S.Ct. at 1595.

In the prison context, two questions arise concerning the freedom of association. First, do prisoners retain any associational rights under either the first amendment or other constitutional provisions, and second, assuming that they do, to what extent can those associational rights be curbed? As you read the case below, which concerns the associational rights of pretrial detainees, consider these two questions.

BLOCK v. RUTHERFORD

Supreme Court of the United States, 1984.
468 U.S. 576, 104 S.Ct. 3227, 82 L.Ed.2d 438.

CHIEF JUSTICE BURGER delivered the opinion of the Court.

We granted certiorari to decide whether pretrial detainees have a right guaranteed by the United States Constitution to contact visits * * *.

I

Los Angeles County Central Jail is one of seven principal facilities operated by the Sheriff of Los Angeles County. The three-story jail complex, located in downtown Los Angeles, is the largest jail in the country, with a capacity of over 5,000 inmates. It is the primary facility in Los Angeles County for male pretrial detainees, the vast majority of whom remain at the facility at most a few days or weeks while they await trial.

In 1975, respondents, pretrial detainees at Central Jail, brought a class action under 42 U.S.C. §§ 1983, 1985, against the County Sheriff, certain administrators of Central Jail, and the County Board of Supervisors, challenging * * * the policy of the jail denying pretrial detainees contact visits with their spouses, relatives, children, and friends * * *.[1]

The District Court agreed with respondents that "the ability of a man to embrace his wife and his children from time to time during the weeks or months while he is awaiting trial is a matter of great importance to him," yet it recognized that "unrestricted contact visitation would add greatly" to security problems at the jail. * * *

* * *

The court found that the "hardship" on detainees of being unable to "embrace their loved ones" for only a few days or a few weeks could not justify imposition of these substantial burdens. However, the court believed, the factors rendering contact visitation impracticable for detainees incarcerated for short periods are considerably less compelling when detention is prolonged.

The court reasoned that "the scope, burden and dangers of [a] program [of contact visitation] would be substantially diminished" were contact visitation limited to detainees "who have been in uninterrupted custody for a month or more *and who are not determined to be drug oriented or escape risks,*" and a ceiling imposed on the total number of contact visits that the jail must provide.[2] With these limitations, the court suggested, a contact visitation program would require only "[m]odest alteration" of the existing facility. Alternatively, the court said, the Sheriff could build or occupy a new facility for contact visits and transport inmates back and forth, as necessary.

* * *

* * * [T]he [Ninth Circuit] Court of Appeals affirmed the District Court's orders requiring that certain of the detainees be allowed contact visits * * *. It suggested that a blanket prohibition of contact visits for all detainees would be an "unreasonable, exaggerated response to security concerns."

* * *

1. When respondents instituted this suit, contact visits were not generally allowed. However, all detainees at Central Jail were allowed unmonitored noncontact visits each day between the hours of 8:30 a.m. and 8:30 p.m. It is estimated that there were over 63,000 such visits each month in an air-conditioned visiting area that accommodates 228 visitors at once. Privacy partitions separated each individual visiting location from the others, and clear glass panels separated the inmates from the visitors, who visit over telephones.

[2]. The District Court ordered that petitioners

"make available a contact visit once each week to each pretrial detainee that has been held in the jail for one month or more, and concerning whom there is no indication or drug or escape propensities; provided, however, that no more than fifteen hundred such visits need be allowed in any one week." * * *

We granted certiorari because of both the importance of the issue to the administration of detention facilities and the conflict among the Federal Courts of Appeals. We reverse.

II

The administration of seven separate jail facilities for a metropolitan area of more than seven million people is a task of monumental proportions. Housed in these facilities annually are 200,000 persons awaiting trial and confined because they are unable to meet the requirements for release on bail. Generalizations are of little value, but no one familiar with even the barest outline of the problems of the administration of a prison or jail, or with the administration of criminal justice, could fail to be aware of the ease with which one can obtain release on bail or personal recognizance. The very fact of nonrelease pending trial thus is a significant factor bearing on the security measures that are imperative to proper administration of a detention facility.

Four Terms ago, in *Bell v. Wolfish,* 441 U.S. 520 (1979), we considered for the first time, in light of these security concerns, the scope of constitutional protection that must be accorded pretrial detainees. * * * We held that, where it is alleged that a pretrial detainee has been deprived of liberty without due process, the dispositive inquiry is whether the challenged condition, practice, or policy constitutes punishment, "[f]or under the Due Process Clause, a detainee must not be punished prior to an adjudication of guilt in accordance with due process of law."

In addressing the particular challenges in *Wolfish,* we carefully outlined the principles to be applied in evaluating the constitutionality of conditions of pretrial detention. Specifically, we observed that "[a] court must decide whether the disability is imposed for the purpose of punishment or whether it is but an incident of some other legitimate governmental purpose." Absent proof of intent to punish, we noted, this determination "generally will turn on 'whether an alternative purpose to which [the restriction] may rationally be connected is assignable for it, and whether it appears excessive in relation to the alternative purpose assigned [to it].'" We concluded:

> "[I]f a particular condition or restriction of pretrial detention is reasonably related to a legitimate governmental objective, it does not, without more, amount to 'punishment.' Conversely, if a restriction or condition is not reasonably related to a legitimate goal—if it is arbitrary or purposeless—a court permissibly may infer that the purpose of the governmental action is punishment that may not constitutionally be inflicted upon detainees *qua* detainees."

In setting forth these guidelines, we reaffirmed the very limited role that courts should play in the administration of detention facilities. In assessing whether a specific restriction is "reasonably related" to security interests, we said, courts should "heed our warning that '[s]uch considerations are peculiarly within the province and professional expertise of corrections officials, and, in the absence of substantial evidence in the record to indicate that the officials have exaggerated their response to these considerations courts should ordinarily defer to their expert judgment in such matters.'" *Id.*, at 540–541, n. 23 (quoting *Pell v. Procunier,* 417 U.S. 817, 827 (1974)).

* * * The principles articulated in *Wolfish* govern resolution of this case.

III

A

Petitioners' first contention is that it was error to conclude that even low risk detainees incarcerated for more than a month are constitutionally entitled to contact visits from friends and relatives. Petitioners maintain, as they have throughout these proceedings that, in the interest of institutional and public security, it is within their discretion as officials of a detention facility to impose an absolute prohibition on contact visits. The District Court did not find, nor did the Court of Appeals suggest, that the purpose of petitioners' policy of denying contact visitation is to punish the inmates. To the contrary, the District Court found that petitioners are fully cognizant of the possible value of contact visitation, and it commended petitioners for their conscientious efforts to accommodate the large numbers of inmates at Central Jail.

The question before us, therefore, is narrow: whether the prohibition of contact visits is reasonably related to legitimate governmental objectives. More particularly, because there is no dispute that internal security of detention facilities is a legitimate governmental interest, our inquiry is simply whether petitioners' blanket prohibition on contact visits at Central Jail is reasonably related to the security of that facility.

That there is a valid, rational connection between a ban on contact visits and internal security of a detention facility is too obvious to warrant extended discussion. The District Court acknowledged as much. Contact visits invite a host of security problems. They open the institution to the introduction of drugs, weapons, and other contraband. Visitors can easily conceal guns, knives, drugs, or other contraband in countless ways and pass them to an inmate unnoticed by even the most vigilant observers. And these items can readily be slipped from the clothing of an innocent child, or transferred by other visitors permitted close contact with inmates.

Contact visitation poses other dangers for a detention facility, as well. Detainees—by definition persons unable to meet bail—often are awaiting trial for serious, violent offenses, and many have prior criminal convictions. Exposure of this type person to others, whether family, friends, or jail administrators, necessarily carries with it risks that the safety of innocent individuals will be jeopardized in various ways. They may, for example, be taken as hostages or become innocent pawns in escape attempts. It is no answer, of course, that we deal here with restrictions on pretrial detainees rather than convicted criminals. For, as we observed in *Wolfish,* in this context, "[t]here is no basis for concluding that pretrial detainees pose any lesser security risk than convicted inmates." Indeed, we said, "it may be that in certain circumstances [detainees] present a greater risk to jail security and order."

The District Court and Court of Appeals held that totally disallowing contact visits is excessive in relation to the security and other interests at stake. We reject this characterization. There are many justifications for denying contact visits entirely, rather than attempting the difficult task of establishing a program of limited visitation such as that imposed here. It is not unreasonable to assume, for instance, that low security risk detainees would be enlisted to help obtain contraband or weapons by their fellow inmates who are denied contact visits. Additionally, identification of those inmates who have propensities for violence, escape, or drug smuggling is a difficult if not impossible task, and the chances of mistaken identification are substantial. The burdens of identifying candidates for contact visitation—glossed over by the District Court—are made even more difficult by the brevity of detention and the constantly changing nature of the inmate population. Or a complete prohibition could reasonably be thought necessary because selectively allowing contact visits to some—even if feasible— could well create tension between those allowed contact visits and those not.[9]

*   *   *

On this record, we must conclude that the District Court simply misperceived the limited scope of judicial inquiry under *Wolfish.* When the District Court found that many factors counseled against contact visits, its inquiry should have ended. The court's further "balancing" resulted in an impermissible substitution of its view on the proper administration of Central Jail for that of the experienced administrators of that facility. Here, as in *Wolfish,* "[i]t is plain from [the] opinions that the lower courts simply disagreed with the judgment of [the jail] officials about the extent of the security interests affected and the means required to further those interests."

In rejecting the District Court's order, we do not in any sense denigrate the importance of visits from family or friends to the detain-

---

[9]. The reasonableness of petitioners' blanket prohibition is underscored by the costs—financial and otherwise—of the alternative response ordered by the District Court. Jail personnel, whom the District Court recognized are now free from the "complicated, expensive, and time-consuming process[es]" of interviewing, searching, and processing visitors, would have to be reassigned to perform these tasks, perhaps requiring the hiring of additional personnel. Intrusive strip searches after contact visits would be necessary. Finally, as the District Court noted, at the very least, "modest" improvements of existing facilities would be required to accommodate a contact visitation program if the county did not purchase or build a new facility elsewhere. These are substantial costs that a facility's administrators might reasonably attempt to avoid.

ee. Nor do we intend to suggest that contact visits might not be a factor contributing to the ultimate reintegration of the detainee into society. We hold only that the Constitution does not require that detainees be allowed contact visits when responsible, experienced administrators have determined, in their sound discretion, that such visits will jeopardize the security of the facility.

[Justice Blackmun concurred in the Court's judgment. His opinion is omitted.]

JUSTICE MARSHALL, with whom JUSTICE BRENNAN and JUSTICE STEVENS join, dissenting.

* * * Guided by an unwarranted confidence in the good faith and "expertise" of prison administrators and by a pinched conception of the meaning of the Due Process Clauses and the Eighth Amendment, a majority of the Court increasingly appears willing to sanction any prison condition for which the majority can imagine a colorable rationale, no matter how oppressive or ill-justified that condition is in fact. So, here, the Court upholds two policies in force at the Los Angeles County Central Jail. Under one, a pretrial detainee is not permitted any physical contact with members of his family, regardless of how long he is incarcerated pending his trial or how slight is the risk that he will abuse a visitation privilege.[a] * * *

* * *

* * * [R]espondents can and do point to a fundamental right abridged by the jail's policy—namely, their freedom to engage in and prevent the deterioration of their relationships with their families.

The importance of the right asserted by respondents was acknowledged by the District Court. * * *[2] Denial of contact visitation, the court concluded, is "very traumatic treatment." Substantial evidence in the record supports the District Court's findings. William Nagel, an expert in the field of corrections, testified that contact visitation was crucial in allowing prisoners to maintain their familial bonds. Similarly, Dr. Terry Kupers, a psychiatrist, testified that denial of contact visitation contributes to the breakup of prisoners' marriages and generally threatens their mental health. The secondary literature buttresses these assertions, as do the conclusions reached by other courts.[4]

The significant injury to familial relations wrought by the jail's policy of denying contact visitation means that that policy must be tested against a legal standard more constraining than the rule an-

[a. The other policy to which Justice Marshall alludes, under which pretrial detainees were not permitted to watch searches of their cells, is discussed *infra* on page 417.]

2. It should be stressed that, while most of the jail inmates are detained for only brief periods of time (and thus are not covered by the District Court's order), some are detained for very substantial periods.

For example, plaintiffs Rutherford and Taylor were held in the jail pending their trials for 38 months and 32 months, respectively.

4. See *Boudin v. Thomas,* 533 F.Supp. 786, 792–793 (SDNY 1982) (pointing out, *inter alia,* that, when an inmate's child is too young to talk, denial of contact visitation is the equivalent of denial of any visitation whatsoever).

nounced in *Wolfish*. Our cases leave no doubt that persons' freedom to enter into, maintain, and cultivate familial relations is entitled to constitutional protection. Among the relationships that we have expressly shielded from state interference are bonds between spouses, see *Zablocki v. Redhail*, 434 U.S. 374 (1978), and between parents and their children, see *Wisconsin v. Yoder*, 406 U.S. 205 (1972). The special status of these relationships in our constitutional scheme derives from several considerations: the fact that traditionally they have been regarded as sacrosanct, the important role they have played in fostering diversity and pluralism in our culture, and their centrality to the emotional life of many persons.

Determination of exactly how the doctrine established in the aforementioned cases bears upon a ban on contact visitation by pretrial detainees would be difficult. On the one hand, it could be argued that the "withdrawal or limitation of many privileges and rights" that necessarily accompanies incarceration, combined with the fact that the inmates' familial bonds are not altogether severed by such a ban, means that something less than a "compelling" government interest would suffice to legitimate the impairment of the inmates' rights.[8] On the other hand, two factors suggest that only a very important public purpose could sustain the policy. First, even persons lawfully incarcerated after being convicted of crimes retain important constitutional rights; presumptively innocent persons surely are entitled to no less. Second, we have previously insisted upon very persuasive justifications for government regulations that significantly, but not prohibitively, interfered with the exercise of familial rights; arguably, a similarly stringent test should control here. However, a sensitive balancing of these competing considerations is unnecessary to resolve the case before us. At a minimum, petitioners, to prevail, should be required to show that the jail's policy materially advances a substantial government interest. Petitioners have not made and, on this record, could not make such a demonstration.

It should be emphasized that what petitioners must defend is not their reluctance to allow *unlimited* contact visitation, but rather their refusal to adopt the specific reforms ordered by the lower courts.

* * *

* * * [P]etitioners contend that a ban on contact visitation is necessary to prevent the introduction into the jail of drugs and weapons. It must be admitted that this is a legitimate and important goal. However, petitioners fail to show that its realization would be materially impaired by adoption of the reforms ordered by the District Court. Indeed, evidence adduced at trial establishes the contrary. Several witnesses testified that security procedures could be implemented that would make importation of contraband very difficult. Among the

8. Cf. *Schall v. Martin*, 467 U.S. 253, 291, n. 15 (1984) (Marshall, J., dissenting) (suggesting a test under which "the strength of the state interest needed to legitimate a statute [would depend] upon the *degree* to which the statute encroaches upon fundamental rights") (emphasis in original).

precautions effectively used at other institutions are: searches of prisoners before and after visits; dressing of prisoners in special clothes for visitation; examination of prisoners and visitors with metal detectors and fluoroscopes; exclusion of parcels from the visiting area; rejection of visitors who do not comply with visiting rules; and continuous observation of the visiting area by guards.[13] * * * Further protection against the transmission of contraband from visitors to inmates is provided by the District Court's restriction of its order to inmates who have been classified as low risk. In short, there is no reason to think that compliance with the lower courts' directive would result in more than a negligible increase in the flow of drugs or weapons into the jail.[14]

Second, petitioners contend that allowance of contact visitation would endanger innocent visitors who are placed in near proximity to dangerous detainees. Again, though the importance of the objective is apparent, the nexus between it and the jail's current policy is not. As indicated above, the District Court's order applies only to detainees who are unlikely to try to escape. And security measures could be employed by petitioners that would make it very difficult for inmates to hurt or take advantage of visitors. Finally, the administrators of other institutions that have long permitted contact visits between inmates and their families testified at trial that violent incidents resulting from such visitation are rare, apparently because inmates value their visitation privileges so highly.

The majority seeks to shore up petitioners' two arguments with miscellaneous subsidiary claims. In an effort to discredit the limitations on the District Court's order, the majority argues that determination of which inmates have a sufficiently low propensity to misbehave would be difficult and time-consuming, especially in light of "the brevity of detention and the constantly changing nature of the inmate population." This contention is rebutted by the District Court's finding that, after an inmate has been incarcerated for a month, jail officials have considerable information regarding his background and behavior patterns, and by evidence in the record that the jail already has a classification system that, with some modification and improvement, could be used to evaluate detainees' propensities for escape and drug abuse. Next, the majority contends that compliance with the District Court's order would be expensive. Again, the District Court's findings are decisive; the court found that only "modest" changes in the jail facilities would be required. More fundamentally, a desire to run a jail as cheaply as possible is not a legitimate reason for abridging the constitutional rights of its occupants. Finally, the majority suggests

13. The majority implies that the intrusiveness of some of these measures provides an additional justification for petitioners' refusal to allow any contact visitation. It is possible that some inmates or visitors might decide to forgo visitation rather than submit to such procedures, but surely the choice should be left to them.

14. It should be pointed out that drugs and weapons enter the jail in significant quantities through several other routes. It would thus be a mistake to think that the jail is currently free of contraband, and that the small amounts that might enter the facility through contact visitation would infect the facility for the first time.

that the District Court's order might cause some dissension in the jail, because inmates denied visitation privileges would resent those granted such privileges. There is no evidence whatsoever in the record to support this speculative observation.

In sum, neither petitioners nor the majority have shown that permitting low-risk pretrial detainees who have been incarcerated for more than a month occasionally to have contact visits with their spouses and children would frustrate the achievement of any substantial state interest.[17] Because such visitation would significantly alleviate the adverse impact of the jail's current policies upon respondents' familial rights, its deprivation violates the Due Process Clause.

*   *   *

Questions and Points for Discussion

1. Was the Supreme Court's repudiation of "balancing" in *Block v. Rutherford* consistent with its decisions you have read thus far? Without such balancing, how is a court to determine whether officials "have exaggerated their response" to security concerns? Without such balancing, what happens to the protection supposedly afforded prisoners by the Constitution? See Valentine v. Englehardt, 474 F.Supp. 294, 300–01 (D.N.J.1979) ("A naked man in chains poses no risk. From that point on, every increase in freedom brings at least some decrease in security.")

2. Assume that jail officials banned not only contact visits but all non-contact visits with pretrial detainees and convicted inmates. Would such a total ban on visitation be constitutional? In answering this question, of what significance are the following remarks about associational rights made by the Supreme Court in Jones v. North Carolina Prisoners' Labor Union, 433 U.S. 119, 97 S.Ct. 2532 (1977), supra page 279, note 3:

> [N]umerous associational rights are necessarily curtailed by the realities of confinement. They may be curtailed whenever the institution's officials, in the exercise of their informed discretion, reasonably conclude that such associations, whether through group meetings or otherwise, possess the likelihood of disruption to prison order or stability, or otherwise interfere with the legitimate penological objectives of the prison environment.

Id. at 132, 97 S.Ct. at 2541.

3. Many courts have ducked the ultimate question of whether inmates retain associational rights protected by the first amendment, holding that, in any event, the particular restriction before the court was reasonable and constitutional. See e.g., Smith v. Coughlin, 748 F.2d 783, 788 (2d Cir.1984) (permitting inmate on death row to only visit with family members, but not friends was constitutional); Robinson v. Palmer, 619 F.Supp.

---

17. The feasibility of the limited contact visitation program ordered by the District Court is further suggested by the number of other institutions that have similar programs. Approximately 80% of the inmates in the California prison system are permitted contact visitation. It appears that the current policy of the Federal Bureau of Prisons is to allow visitation privileges to both convicted inmates and pretrial detainees. In New York City, all except identifiably dangerous pretrial detainees are permitted contact visits with their families. *   *   *

344 (D.D.C.1985) (permanently suspending visiting privileges of inmate's wife after she attempted to smuggle marijuana into the prison did not violate any first amendment rights of either the inmate or his wife).

4. Regardless of whether or not restrictions on visiting privileges can violate the first amendment rights of inmates or constitute proscribed punishment of pretrial detainees in violation of due process, can such restrictions violate the Constitution in other ways? In Kentucky Dept. of Corrections v. Thompson, 109 S.Ct. 1904 (1989), infra page 391, the Supreme Court held that inmates do not generally have a liberty interest within the meaning of the due process clause to visit with a particular person. The existence of such a liberty interest would be necessary for the inmate to be constitutionally entitled to certain procedural safeguards before the privilege to meet with that person was withdrawn.

Some courts have held that although inmates may not have a constitutional right to visitation, restrictions on visiting privileges are one factor which may support a finding that the inmates are being subjected to cruel and unusual punishment under the eighth amendment. See, e.g., Hardwick v. Ault, 447 F.Supp. 116, 131 (M.D.Ga.1978) (limiting visits to weekdays and only with family members contributed to court's finding of an eighth amendment violation).

5. The importance to inmates and their family and friends of having personal contact with each other has prompted proposals that liberal visitation policies be adopted in all jurisdictions. The Model Sentencing and Corrections Act (1978), for example, proposes the following:

§ 4–115. [Visitation.]

(a) A confined person has a protected interest in receiving visitors from the free community.

(b) The director shall:

(1) establish a visiting schedule for each facility which provides opportunity for confined persons to meet with visitors and includes hours on holidays and weekends and in the evenings;

(2) permit each confined person to have at least [5] hours of visitation weekly and to accumulate unused visiting hours within a [2–month] period for extended visits within the established visiting schedule; and

(3) permit each confined person, other than a person classified as dangerous, to have monthly a private visit for a substantial period of time. Private visits need not be given to a confined person who has been permitted a furlough to visit his family or friends within the preceding 3 months.

(c) The director shall adopt measures to prevent the introduction of contraband or prohibited material into the facility by visitors. The director shall:

(1) assure that each visitor is given reasonable notice of what constitutes contraband and prohibited materials;

(2) utilize procedures, such as subjecting visitors to scanners or requiring thorough searches of confined persons both before and after visits, that minimize the need for more intrusive searches of visitors themselves;

(3) prohibit any search of a visitor unless he consents to be searched; and

(4) permit the exclusion from the facility of any visitor who refuses to consent to a search or causes a scanner to react or there is reliable information that he is carrying contraband or prohibited material.

(d) The director may not restrict the persons a confined person may receive as visitors except pursuant to § 4–118.

§ 4–118. [Limiting Visitors and Correspondents.]

(a) The director may issue an order that:

(1) prevents a specific person from communicating with a confined person if,

(i) the person seeking to communicate with a confined person knowingly has violated the rules relating to communication with confined persons, and

(ii) less restrictive measures, such as intercepting communications between the person and confined persons, are not feasible.

(2) prevents a specific person from entering facilities or visiting confined persons if,

(i) the person has in the past knowingly violated the rules of a facility relating to visitation; or

(ii) the director has reliable information that if admitted to the facility, the person is likely to advocate unlawful acts or rule violations that jeopardize the safety of the public or security or safety within a facility.

(b) A person against whom an order is issued is entitled to a written statement of the basis for the order, an opportunity to contest the order at a hearing before the director or his delegate, and judicial review.

(c) A confined person affected by an order issued pursuant to this section must be informed in writing of the order, the person against whom it is issued, and the specific reason for the order.

(d) An order pursuant to this section may not continue for more than 180 days without further evaluation.

Do you agree with the above provisions? Why or why not? If you do agree with these provisions, should "private visits" include conjugal privileges? If so, should conjugal visits be restricted to spouses? For other proposals on visitation rights, see Standards 23–6.2–6.4 of the American Bar Association Standards Relating to the Legal Status of Prisoners (1981).

7. *Drafting Exercise:* Draft a prison regulation outlining the organizational rights of prisoners. Be sure to include in that regulation any constraints governing the formation of inmate organizations, their activities, and participation in them by outsiders. In addition, include in the regulation standards governing the circulation by inmate organizations as well as individual prisoners of petitions and other written materials.

C. FREEDOM OF RELIGION

The first amendment provides in part that "Congress shall make no law respecting an establishment of religion, or prohibiting the free exercise thereof." The Supreme Court confirmed in Cruz v. Beto, 405 U.S. 319, 92 S.Ct. 1079 (1972) that inmates retain rights to religious freedom. In that case, a Buddhist had filed a § 1983 suit, claiming that he was not afforded the same opportunities to practice his religion as were prisoners of other faiths. His complaint alleged, for example, that while other prisoners were allowed to use the prison chapel, he was not. The plaintiff also contended that the state encouraged prisoners to join orthodox religions, and not his own; he alleged, for example, that the state funded Catholic, Jewish, and Protestant chaplains in the prison and provided inmates free-of-charge with Jewish and Christian Bibles.

In the course of holding that the district court had erred in dismissing the plaintiff's complaint, the Supreme Court made the following observation: "If Cruz was a Buddhist and if he was denied a reasonable opportunity of pursuing his faith comparable to the opportunity afforded fellow prisoners who adhere to conventional religious precepts, then there was palpable discrimination by the State against the Buddhist religion. . . . " Id. at 322, 92 S.Ct. at 1081. In an important footnote, the Court added:

> We do not suggest, of course, that every religious sect or group within a prison—however few in number—must have identical facilities or personnel. A special chapel or place of worship need not be provided for every faith regardless of size; nor must a chaplain, priest, or minister be provided without regard to the extent of the demand. But reasonable oportunities must be afforded to all prisoners to exercise the religious freedom guaranteed by the First and Fourteenth Amendments without fear of penalty.

Id. at 322 n. 2, 92 S.Ct. at 322 n. 2.

Fifteen years later, in the case set forth below, the Supreme Court returned to the subject of the scope of inmates' right to religious freedom.

O'LONE v. ESTATE OF SHABAZZ

Supreme Court of the United States, 1987.
482 U.S. 342, 107 S.Ct. 2400, 96 L.Ed.2d 282.

CHIEF JUSTICE REHNQUIST delivered the opinion of the Court.

* * * Respondents, members of the Islamic faith, were prisoners in New Jersey's Leesburg State Prison. They challenged policies adopted by prison officials which resulted in their inability to attend Jumu'ah, a weekly Muslim congregational service regularly held in the main prison building and in a separate facility known as "the Farm." Jumu'ah is commanded by the Koran and must be held every Friday after the sun reaches its zenith and before the Asr, or afternoon prayer.

* * *

Inmates at Leesburg are placed in one of three custody classifications. Maximum security and "gang minimum" security inmates are housed in the main prison building, and those with the lowest classification—full minimum—live in "the Farm." * * *

Several changes in prison policy prompted this litigation. In April 1983, the New Jersey Department of Corrections issued Standard 853, which provided that inmates could no longer move directly from maximum security to full minimum status, but were instead required to first spend a period of time in the intermediate gang minimum status. This change was designed to redress problems that had arisen when inmates were transferred directly from the restrictive maximum security status to full minimum status, with its markedly higher level of freedom. Because of serious overcrowding in the main building, Standard 853 further mandated that gang minimum inmates ordinarily be assigned jobs outside the main building. These inmates work in details of 8 to 15 persons, supervised by one guard. Standard 853 also required that full minimum inmates work outside the main institution, whether on or off prison grounds, or in a satellite building such as the Farm.

* * *

Significant problems arose with those inmates assigned to outside work details. Some avoided reporting for their assignments, while others found reasons for returning to the main building during the course of the workday (including their desire to attend religious services). Evidence showed that the return of prisoners during the day resulted in security risks and administrative burdens that prison officials found unacceptable. Because details of inmates were supervised by only one guard, the whole detail was forced to return to the main gate when one prisoner desired to return to the facility. The gate was the site of all incoming foot and vehicle traffic during the day, and prison officials viewed it as a high security risk area. When an inmate returned, vehicle traffic was delayed while the inmate was logged in and searched.

In response to these burdens, Leesburg officials took steps to ensure that those assigned to outside details remained there for the whole day.

Thus, arrangements were made to have lunch and required medications brought out to the prisoners, and appointments with doctors and social workers were scheduled for the late afternoon. These changes proved insufficient, however, and prison officials began to study alternatives. After consulting with the director of social services, the director of professional services, and the prison's imam and chaplain, prison officials in March 1984 issued a policy memorandum which prohibited inmates assigned to outside work details from returning to the prison during the day except in the case of emergency.

The prohibition of returns prevented Muslims assigned to outside work details from attending Jumu'ah. Respondents filed suit under 42 U.S.C. § 1983, alleging that the prison policies unconstitutionally denied them their Free Exercise rights under the First Amendment, as applied to the States through the Fourteenth Amendment. The District Court, applying the standards announced in an earlier decision of the Court of Appeals for the Third Circuit, concluded that no constitutional violation had occurred. * * *

The Court of Appeals, *sua sponte* hearing the case en banc, decided that its earlier decision relied upon by the District Court was not sufficiently protective of prisoners' free exercise rights, and went on to state that prison policies could be sustained only if:

"the state . . . show[s] that the challenged regulations were intended to serve, and do serve, the important penological goal of security, and that no reasonable method exists by which [prisoners'] religious rights can be accommodated without creating bona fide security problems.
* * *

In considering whether a potential method of accommodation is reasonable, the court added, relevant factors include cost, the effects of overcrowding, understaffing, and inmates' demonstrated proclivity to unruly conduct. The case was remanded to the District Court for reconsideration under the standards enumerated in the opinion. We granted certiorari * * *.

* * *

* * * To ensure that courts afford appropriate deference to prison officials, we have determined that prison regulations alleged to infringe constitutional rights are judged under a "reasonableness" test less restrictive than that ordinarily applied to alleged infringements of fundamental constitutional rights. We recently restated the proper standard: "[W]hen a prison regulation impinges on inmates' constitutional rights, the regulation is valid if it is reasonably related to legitimate penological interests." *Turner v. Safley.* * * *

We think the Court of Appeals decision in this case was wrong when it established a separate burden on prison officials to prove "that no reasonable method exists by which [prisoners'] religious rights can be accommodated without creating bona fide security problems." * * * Though the availability of accommodations is relevant to the reasonableness inquiry, we have rejected the notion that "prison officials . . . have to set up and then shoot down every conceivable alternative method of accommodating the claimant's constitutional complaint." By placing the burden on prison officials to disprove the availability of alternatives, the approach articulated by the Court of Appeals fails to reflect the respect and deference that the United States Constitution allows for the judgment of prison administrators.

Turning to consideration of the policies challenged in this case, we think the findings of the District Court establish clearly that prison officials have acted in a reasonable manner. *Turner v. Safley* drew upon our previous decisions to identify several factors relevant to this reasonableness determination. First, a regulation must have a logical connection to legitimate governmental interests invoked to justify it. The policies at issue here clearly meet that standard. The requirement that full minimum and gang minimum prisoners work outside the main facility was justified by concerns of institutional order and security, for the District Court found that it was "at least in part a response to a critical overcrowding in the state's prisons, and . . . at least in part designed to ease tension and drain on the facilities during that part of the day when the inmates were outside the confines of the main buildings." We think it beyond doubt that the standard is related to this legitimate concern.

The subsequent policy prohibiting returns to the institution during the day also passes muster under this standard. Prison officials testified that the returns from outside work details generated congestion and delays at the main gate, a high risk area in any event. Return requests also placed pressure on guards supervising outside details, who previously were required to "evaluate each reason possibly justifying a return to the facilities and either accept or reject that reason." Rehabilitative concerns further supported the policy; corrections officials sought a simulation of working conditions and responsibilities in society. Chief Deputy Ucci testified: "One of the things that society demands or expects is that when you have a job, you show up on time, you put in your eight hours, or whatever hours you are supposed to put in, and you don't get off. . . . If we can show inmates that they're supposed to show up for work and work a full day, then when they get out at least we've done something." These legitimate goals were advanced by the prohibition on returns; it cannot seriously be maintained that "the logical connection between the regulation and the asserted goal is so remote as to render the policy arbitrary or irrational."

Our decision in *Turner* also found it relevant that "alternative means of exercising the right . . . remain open to prison inmates." There are, of course, no alternative means of attending Jumu'ah; respondents' religious beliefs insist that it occur at a particular time. But the very stringent requirements as to the time at which Jumu'ah may be held may make it extraordinarily difficult for prison officials to assure that every Muslim prisoner is able to attend that service. While we in no way minimize the central importance of Jumu'ah to respondents, we are unwilling to hold that prison officials are required by the Constitution to sacrifice legitimate penological objectives to that end. In *Turner,* we did not look to see whether prisoners had other means of communicating with fellow inmates, but instead examined whether the inmates were deprived of "all means of expression." Here, similarly, we think it appropriate to see whether under these regulations respondents retain the ability to participate in other Muslim religious ceremonies. The record establishes that respondents are not deprived of all forms of religious exercise, but instead freely observe a number of their religious obligations. The right to congregate for prayer or discussion is "virtually unlimited except during working hours," and the state-provided imam has free access to the prison. Muslim prisoners are given different meals whenever pork is served in the prison cafeteria. Special arrangements are also made during the month-long observance of Ramadan, a period of fasting and prayer. During Ramadan, Muslim prisoners are awakened at 4 a.m. for an early breakfast, and receive dinner at 8:30 p.m. each evening. We think this ability on the part of respondents to participate in other religious observances of their faith supports the conclusion that the restrictions at issue here were reasonable.

Finally, the case for the validity of these regulations is strengthened by examination of the impact that accommodation of respondents' asserted right would have on other inmates, on prison personnel, and on allocation of prison resources generally. Respondents suggest several accommodations of their practices, including placing all Muslim inmates in one or two inside work details or providing weekend labor for Muslim inmates. As noted by the District Court, however, each of respondents' suggested accommodations would, in the judgment of prison officials, have adverse effects on the institution. Inside work details for gang minimum inmates would be inconsistent with the legitimate concerns underlying Standard 853, and the District Court found that the extra supervision necessary to establish weekend details for Muslim prisoners "would be a drain on scarce human resources" at the prison. Prison officials determined that the alternatives would also threaten prison security by allowing "affinity groups" in the prison to flourish. Administrator O'Lone testified that "we have found out and think almost every prison administrator knows that any time you put a group of individuals together with one particular affinity interest . . . you wind up with . . . a leadership role and an organizational structure that will almost invariably challenge the institutional authority." Finally, the officials determined that special arrangements for one group would create problems as "other inmates [see] that a certain segment is escaping a rigorous work detail" and perceive favoritism. These concerns of prison administrators provide adequate support for the conclusion that accommodations of respondents' request to attend Jumu'ah would have undesirable results in the institution. These difficulties also make clear that there are no "obvious, easy alternatives to the policy adopted by petitioners."

* * * Here the District Court decided that the regulations alleged to infringe constitutional rights were reasonably related to legitimate penological objectives. We agree with the District Court, and it necessarily follows that the regulations in question do not offend the Free Exercise Clause of the First Amendment to the United States Constitution. The judgment of the Court of Appeals is therefore

Reversed.

JUSTICE BRENNAN, with whom JUSTICE MARSHALL, JUSTICE BLACKMUN, and JUSTICE STEVENS join, dissenting.

* * *

I

Prisoners are persons whom most of us would rather not think about. Banished from everyday sight, they exist in a shadow world that only dimly enters our awareness. They are members of a "total institution"[1] that controls their daily existence in a way that few of us can imagine * * *.

It is thus easy to think of prisoners as members of a separate netherworld, driven by its own demands, ordered by its own customs, ruled by those whose claim to power rests on raw necessity. Nothing can change the fact, however, that the society that these prisoners inhabit is our own. Prisons may exist on the margins of that society, but no act of will can sever them from the body politic. When prisoners emerge from the shadows to press a constitutional claim, they invoke no alien set of principles drawn from a distant culture. Rather, they speak the language of the charter upon which all of us rely to hold official power accountable. They ask us to acknowledge that power exercised in the shadows must be restrained at least as diligently as power that acts in the sunlight.

* * *

In my view, adoption of "reasonableness" as a standard of review for *all* constitutional challenges by inmates is inadequate to this task. Such a standard is categorically deferential, and does not discriminate among degrees of deprivation. From this perspective, restricting use of the prison library to certain hours warrants the same level of scrutiny as preventing inmates from reading at all. * * *

It is true that the degree of deprivation is one of the factors in the Court's reasonableness determination. This by itself does not make the standard of review appropriate, however. If it did, we would need but a single standard for evaluating all constitutional claims, as long as every relevant factor were considered under its rubric. Clearly, we have never followed such an approach. * * * The use of differing levels of

1. See E. Goffman, Asylums: Essays on the Social Situation of Mental Patients and Other Inmates 1–125 (1961).

scrutiny proclaims that on some occasions official power must justify itself in a way that otherwise it need not. A relatively strict standard of review is a signal that a decree prohibiting a political demonstration on the basis of the participants' political beliefs is of more serious concern, and therefore will be scrutinized more closely, than a rule limiting the number of demonstrations that may take place downtown at noon.

* * *

An approach better suited to the sensitive task of protecting the constitutional rights of inmates is laid out by Judge Kaufman in *Abdul Wali v. Coughlin,* 754 F.2d 1015 (CA2 1985). That approach maintains that the degree of scrutiny of prison regulations should depend on "the nature of the right being asserted by prisoners, the type of activity in which they seek to engage, and whether the challenged restriction works a total deprivation (as opposed to a mere limitation) on the exercise of that right." Essentially, if the activity in which inmates seek to engage is presumptively dangerous, or if a regulation merely restricts the time, place, or manner in which prisoners may exercise a right, a prison regulation will be invalidated only if there is no reasonable justification for official action. Where exercise of the asserted right is not presumptively dangerous, however, and where the prison has completely deprived an inmate of that right, then prison officials must show that "a particular restriction is necessary to further an important governmental interest, and that the limitations on freedoms occasioned by the restrictions are no greater than necessary to effectuate the governmental objective involved."

The court's analytical framework in *Abdul Wali* recognizes that in many instances it is inappropriate for courts "to substitute our judgments for those of trained professionals with years of firsthand experience." *Ibid.* It would thus apply a standard of review identical to the Court's "reasonableness" standard in a significant percentage of cases. At the same time, the *Abdul Wali* approach takes seriously the Constitution's function of requiring that official power be called to account when it completely deprives a person of a right that society regards as basic. In this limited number of cases, it would require more than a demonstration of "reasonableness" to justify such infringement. To the extent that prison is meant to inculcate a respect for social and legal norms, a requirement that prison officials persuasively demonstrate the need for the absolute deprivation of inmate rights is consistent with that end. Furthermore, prison officials are in control of the evidence that is essential to establish the superiority of such deprivation over other alternatives. It is thus only fair for these officials to be held to a stringent standard of review in such extreme cases.

The prison in this case has completely prevented respondent inmates from attending the central religious service of their Muslim faith. I would therefore hold prison officials to the standard articulated in *Abdul Wali,* and would find their proffered justifications wanting.

The State has neither demonstrated that the restriction is necessary to further an important objective nor proved that less extreme measures may not serve its purpose. Even if I accepted the Court's standard of review, however, I could not conclude on this record that prison officials have proved that it is reasonable to preclude respondents from attending Jumu'ah. * * *

II

* * * The Court in this case acknowledges that "respondents' sincerely held religious beliefs compe[l] attendance at Jumu'ah" and concedes that there are "no alternative means of attending Jumu'ah." Nonetheless, the Court finds that prison policy does not work a complete deprivation of respondents' asserted religious right, because respondents have the opportunity to participate in other religious activities. This analysis ignores the fact that, as the District Court found, Jumu'ah is the central religious ceremony of Muslims, "comparable to the Saturday service of the Jewish faith and the Sunday service of the various Christian sects." * * *

Jumu'ah therefore cannot be regarded as one of several essentially fungible religious practices. The ability to engage in other religious activities cannot obscure the fact that the denial at issue in this case is absolute: respondents are completely foreclosed from participating in the core ceremony that reflects their membership in a particular religious community. If a Catholic prisoner were prevented from attending Mass on Sunday, few would regard that deprivation as anything but absolute, even if the prisoner were afforded other opportunities to pray, to discuss the Catholic faith with others, and even to avoid eating meat on Friday if that were a preference. Prison officials in this case therefore cannot show that " 'other avenues' remain available for the exercise of the asserted right."

Under the Court's approach, as enunciated in *Turner*, the availability of other means of exercising the right in question counsels considerable deference to prison officials. By the same token, the infliction of an absolute deprivation should require more than mere assertion that such a deprivation is necessary. * * *

* * *

* * * [A] reasonableness test in this case demands at least minimal substantiation by prison officials that alternatives that would permit participation in Jumu'ah are infeasible. Under the standard articulated by the Court in *Turner*, this does not mean that petitioners are responsible for identifying and discrediting these alternatives; "prison officials do not have to set up and then shoot down every conceivable alternative method of accommodating the claimant's constitutional complaint." When prisoners themselves present alternatives, however, and when they fairly call into question official claims that these alternatives are infeasible, we must demand at least some evidence beyond mere assertion that the religious practice at issue cannot be accommodated. Examination of the alternatives proposed in this

case indicates that prison officials have not provided such substantiation.

III

Respondents' first proposal is that gang minimum prisoners be assigned to an alternative inside work detail on Friday, as they had been before the recent change in policy. Prison officials testified that the alternative work detail is now restricted to maximum security prisoners, and that they did not wish maximum and minimum security prisoners to mingle. Even the District Court had difficulty with this assertion, as it commented that "[t]he defendants did not explain why inmates of different security levels are not mixed on work assignments when otherwise they are mixed." The court found, nonetheless, that this alternative would be inconsistent with Standard 853's mandate to move gang minimum inmates to outside work details. This conclusion, however, neglects the fact that the very issue is whether the prison's policy, of which Standard 853 is a part, should be administered so as to accommodate Muslim inmates. The policy itself cannot serve as a justification for its failure to provide reasonable accommodation. The record as it now stands thus does not establish that the Friday alternative work detail would create a problem for the institution.

Respondents' second proposal is that gang minimum inmates be assigned to work details inside the main building on a regular basis. While admitting that the prison used inside details in the kitchen, bakery, and tailor shop, officials stated that these jobs are reserved for the riskiest gang minimum inmates, for whom an outside job might be unwise. Thus, concluded officials, it would be a bad idea to move these inmates outside to make room for Muslim gang minimum inmates. Respondents contend, however, that the prison's own records indicate that there are a significant number of jobs inside the institution that could be performed by inmates posing a lesser security risk. This suggests that it might not be necessary for the riskier gang minimum inmates to be moved outside to make room for the less risky inmates. Officials provided no data on the number of inside jobs available, the number of high-risk gang minimum inmates performing them, the number of Muslim inmates that might seek inside positions, or the number of staff that would be necessary to monitor such an arrangement. Given the plausibility of respondents' claim, prison officials should present at least this information in substantiating their contention that inside assignments are infeasible.

Third, respondents suggested that gang minimum inmates be assigned to Saturday or Sunday work details, which would allow them to make up any time lost by attending Jumu'ah on Friday. While prison officials admitted the existence of weekend work details, they stated that "[s]ince prison personnel are needed for other programs on weekends, the creation of additional weekend details would be a drain on scarce human resources." The record provides no indication, however, of the number of Muslims that would seek such a work detail, the current number of weekend details, or why it would be infeasible simply to reassign current Saturday or Sunday workers to Friday, rather than create additional details. The prison is able to arrange work schedules so that Jewish inmates may attend services on Saturday and Christian inmates may attend services on Sunday. Despite the fact that virtually all inmates are housed in the main building over the weekend, so that the demand on the facility is greater than at any other time, the prison is able to provide sufficient staff coverage to permit Jewish and Christian inmates to participate in their central religious ceremonies. Given the prison's duty to provide Muslims a "reasonable opportunity of pursuing [their] faith comparable to the opportunity afforded fellow prisoners who adhere to conventional religious precepts," *Cruz v. Beto,* 405 U.S. 319, 322 (1972), prison officials should be required to provide more than mere assertions of the infeasibility of weekend details for Muslim inmates.

Finally, respondents proposed that minimum security inmates living at the Farm be assigned to jobs either in the Farm building or in its immediate vicinity. Since Standard 853 permits such assignments for full minimum inmates, and since such inmates need not return to prison facilities through the main entrance, this would interfere neither with Standard 853 nor the concern underlying the no-return policy. Nonetheless, prison officials stated that such an arrangement might create an "affinity group" of Muslims representing a threat to prison authority. Officials pointed to no such problem in the five years in which Muslim inmates were permitted to assemble for Jumu'ah, and in which the alternative Friday work detail was in existence. Nor could they identify any threat resulting from the fact that during the month of Ramadan all Muslim prisoners participate in both breakfast and dinner at special times. Furthermore, there was no testimony that the concentration of Jewish or Christian inmates on work details or in religious services posed any type of "affinity group" threat. As the record now stands, prison officials have declared that a security risk is created by a grouping of Muslim inmates in the least dangerous security classification, but not by a grouping of maximum security inmates who are concentrated in a work detail inside the main building, and who are the only Muslims assured of participating in Jumu'ah. Surely, prison officials should be required to provide at least some substantiation for this facially implausible contention.

Petitioners also maintained that the assignment of full minimum Muslim inmates to the Farm or its near vicinity might provoke resentment because of other inmates' perception that Muslims were receiving special treatment. Officials pointed to no such perception during the period in which the alternative Friday detail was in existence, nor to any resentment of the fact that Muslims' dietary preferences are accommodated and that Muslims are permitted to operate on a special schedule during the month of Ramadan. Nor do they identify any such problems created by the accommodation of the religious preferences of inmates of other faiths. Once again, prison officials should be required at a minimum to identify the basis for their assertions.

*   *   *

IV

* * * *Turner* directed attention to two factors of particular relevance to this case: the degree of constitutional deprivation and the availability of reasonable alternatives. The respondents in this case have been absolutely foreclosed from participating in the central religious ceremony of their Muslim faith. At least a colorable claim that such a drastic policy is not necessary can be made * * *. If the Court's standard of review is to represent anything more than reflexive deference to prison officials, any finding of reasonableness must rest on firmer ground than the record now presents.

Incarceration by its nature denies a prisoner participation in the larger human community. To deny the opportunity to affirm membership in a spiritual community, however, may extinguish an inmate's last source of hope for dignity and redemption. Such a denial requires more justification than mere assertion that any other course of action is infeasible. While I would prefer that this case be analyzed under the approach set out in Part I, I would at a minimum remand to the District Court for an analysis of respondents' claims in accordance with the standard enunciated by the Court in *Turner* and in this case. I therefore dissent.

Questions and Points for Discussion

1. Is the Supreme Court's approach to prisoners' free exercise claims in *O'Lone* consistent with the standard set forth in *Cruz v. Beto*?

2. As in other cases where individuals assert free exercise claims, a court may have to determine both whether the protection sought by the prisoner is for "religious" beliefs or practices and whether these religious beliefs are sincerely held by the prisoner. The care with which courts must embark on these inquiries is underscored by the fact that prison gangs have been known to invoke the free exercise clause in seeking protection for their activities. See, e.g., Faheem–El v. Lane, 657 F.Supp. 638 (C.D.Ill. 1986).

3. The lower courts have struggled with questions concerning the extent to which prison officials must accommodate the religious practices of inmates. Frequently litigated questions include whether, when an inmate's faith so dictates, the inmate has a first amendment right to grow a beard, to grow long hair, or to be provided with a special diet. See, e.g., Fromer v. Scully, 874 F.2d 69 (2d Cir.1989) (challenge by orthodox Jewish inmate to a prison regulation limiting the length of inmates' beards); Pollock v. Marshall, 845 F.2d 656 (6th Cir.1988) (challenge by American Indian to prison regulation requiring him to cut his hair in violation of his religious beliefs); and Udey v. Kastner, 805 F.2d 1218 (5th Cir.1986) (inmate's sincerely held religious beliefs required him to eat only organical-

ly grown produce washed in distilled water). Consider these questions under the *O'Lone* standard.

4. Would a ban on group worship services in prison be constitutional? Why or why not?

5. Consider the following problem:

The plaintiff, an inmate at a maximum-security prison in Illinois, has filed a § 1983 suit in a federal district court against various prison officials claiming that his right to religious freedom under the first and fourteenth amendments has been unconstitutionally abridged. According to the plaintiff, he is a Muslim and therefore has a religious duty to make charitable contributions. To meet that duty, he has asked that money be withdrawn from his prison trust fund account and sent to "Sister" Zubaydah Maydun, the trustee of what is called the "Fellowship Trust Fund." The defendants have refused to transfer the funds as requested.

Since being sued, the defendants have filed a motion for summary judgment. The defendants contend that they are entitled to summary judgment because, as required by Rule 56(c) of the Federal Rules of Civil Procedure, there is no "genuine issue" of "material fact" and they are entitled to judgment as a matter of law.

In support of their motion, the defendants have submitted the affidavit of an assistant warden recounting the prison's policy regarding the withdrawal of funds from inmates' trust accounts. Under this policy, a prisoner's request to have money withdrawn from his account can be denied for three reasons: (1) if the request is involuntary due to pressure exerted on the prisoner by another inmate; (2) if the designated recipient of the money is not "authentic, legitimate, and accountable;" and (3) if the designated recipient is related to some other prisoner in the prison. The purpose of this policy, according to the affidavit, is to ward off disputes and tension between inmates. The policy applies to all inmates, regardless of their religious affiliation.

The assistant warden has further stated in her affidavit that the plaintiff's disbursement request was denied for two reasons: one, because "Sister" Maydun is the wife of another inmate and two, because the "Fellowship Trust Fund" is not connected with an "authentic" religion since the American Muslim Mission exercises no authority over the fund. The plaintiff has filed an affidavit attempting to demonstrate the authenticity of the fund.

Should the defendants' motion for summary judgment be granted?

Chapter 10

RIGHT OF ACCESS TO THE COURTS

Prisoners file lawsuits for a variety of reasons. Prisoners who file petitions for habeas corpus and other types of post-conviction complaints are seeking release from what they contend is illegal confinement. Habeas corpus petitions, for example, quite frequently allege that prisoners' constitutional rights were violated at trial, nullifying the convictions subsequently obtained. Other prisoners file suits for damages and/or equitable relief under one or more of the civil rights statutes, most commonly 42 U.S.C. § 1983. In these suits, the prisoners generally challenge, on constitutional grounds, the way in which they have been treated by prison officials or the conditions of their confinement. Finally, prisoners, like ordinary citizens, may turn to the courts to resolve everyday civil disputes; prisoners, for example, may be involved in divorce proceedings, custody disputes, or personal injury suits.

Some prisoners also file lawsuits for less laudable reasons. The filing of a frivolous lawsuit, for example, may offer a welcome diversion from the boredom of prison life, the opportunity to harass prison officials, or the chance to leave the institution for an appearance in court. But there are other prisoners, on the other hand, who have valid claims to pursue but never file them because they are too intimidated to do so or do not know how and have no access to effective legal services.

When analyzing prisoners' claims that their right to seek redress in the courts has been unconstitutionally impinged by prison officials, the courts are fully aware of the fundamental importance of court access to many inmates. For example, habeas corpus relief is the vehicle through which innocent persons wrongfully convicted of a crime may ultimately obtain their release from prison. On the other hand, the courts are cognizant of the many illegitimate reasons for which some, or perhaps many, prisoner lawsuits are filed—lawsuits which threaten institutional security, hassle prison officials, and encumber the courts. Mindful of the fundamental importance of court access to prisoners on the one hand, but the abusive use of litigation by some prisoners on the other, the courts wrestle with questions concerning the extent to which a prisoner's access to the courts may constitutionally be restricted.

A. COMMUNICATIONS WITH AND APPEARANCES IN COURTS

EX PARTE HULL

Supreme Court of the United States, 1941.
312 U.S. 546, 61 S.Ct. 640, 85 L.Ed. 1034.

MR. JUSTICE MURPHY delivered the opinion of the Court.

* * *

In November, 1940, petitioner prepared a petition for writ of habeas corpus and exhibits to file in this Court. He took the papers to a prison official and requested him to notarize them. The official refused and informed petitioner that the papers and a registered letter to the clerk of this Court concerning them would not be accepted for mailing. Although the papers were not notarized, petitioner then delivered them to his father for mailing outside the prison but guards confiscated them. Several days later, petitioner again attempted to mail a letter concerning his case to the clerk of this Court. It was intercepted and sent to the legal investigator for the state parole board.[1] Apparently neither of the letters was returned to the petitioner, and the papers taken from his father were not returned until late in December.

Petitioner then prepared another document which he somehow managed to have his father, as "agent," file with the clerk of this Court on December 26, 1940. In this document petitioner detailed his efforts to file the papers confiscated by prison officials, contended that he was therefore unlawfully restrained, and prayed that he be released.

On January 6, 1941, we issued a rule to show cause why leave to file a petition for writ of habeas corpus should not be granted. The warden filed a return to the rule * * *. In justification of the action preventing petitioner from filing his papers or communicating with this Court, the warden alleged that in November, 1940, he had published a regulation providing that: "All legal documents, briefs, petitions, motions, habeas corpus proceedings and appeals will first have to be submitted to the institutional welfare office and if favorably acted upon be then referred to Perry A. Maynard, legal investigator to the Parole

---

1. About a week later petitioner received the following reply from the legal investigator: "Your letter of November 18, 1940, addressed to the Clerk of the United States Supreme Court, has been referred to the writer for reply. In the first place your application in its present form would not be acceptable to that court. You must file a petition for whatever relief you are seeking and state your reasons therefor, together with a memorandum brief. Your petition must be verified under oath and supported by proper affidavits, if any you have. Your letter was, no doubt, intercepted for the reason that it was deemed to be inadequate and which undoubtedly accounts for the fact that it found its way to my desk."

* * *

Board, Lansing, Michigan. Documents submitted to Perry A. Maynard, if in his opinion are properly drawn, will be directed to the court designated or will be referred back to the inmate."

* * *

The first question concerns the effect of the regulation quoted in the warden's return.

The regulation is invalid. The considerations that prompted its formulation are not without merit, but the state and its officers may not abridge or impair petitioner's right to apply to a federal court for a writ of habeas corpus. Whether a petition for writ of habeas corpus addressed to a federal court is properly drawn and what allegations it must contain are questions for that court alone to determine.

[The Court then turned to the substantive issues raised by the habeas corpus petition, rejecting the petitioner's argument that he was unconstitutionally confined.]

Questions and Points for Discussion

1. Ex Parte Hull, as it was later described by Justice (now Chief Justice) Rehnquist, was a "bare-bones holding." Bounds v. Smith, 430 U.S. 817, 838, 97 S.Ct. 1491, 1503 (1977) (Rehnquist, J., dissenting). The Court in *Hull* never identified the source of the right not to have a habeas corpus petition screened and approved by prison officials prior to transmittal to a court. Only in subsequent cases did the Supreme Court identify what it considered the source of the constitutional right of access to the courts; that right, according to the Court, is embodied in the due process clauses of the fifth and fourteenth amendments. See, e.g., Procunier v. Martinez, 416 U.S. 396, 419, 94 S.Ct. 1800, 1814 (1974) on page 325, infra.

2. When prison officials refuse to forward a prisoner's legal documents to a court, other rights may arguably be infringed. See, e.g., Cochran v. Kansas, 316 U.S. 255, 62 S.Ct. 1068 (1942) (if state prison officials prevented prisoner from filing documents necessary to appeal his conviction, the prisoner was denied the equal protection of the law guaranteed by the fourteenth amendment).

3. Can correctional officials at least read inmate correspondence addressed to courts before mailing the correspondence? Why or why not? For the opinion of one court on this issue, see Guajardo v. Estelle, 580 F.2d 748, 758 (5th Cir.1978) (such mail cannot be opened or read).

4. Some lower courts have held that the right of prison inmates to have access to and to communicate with the courts does not always include the right to have particular witnesses appear at trial or even the right to personally appear themselves at a hearing or trial. For example, in Holt v. Pitts, 619 F.2d 558 (6th Cir.1980), the Sixth Circuit Court of Appeals held that the district court had properly exercised its discretion under 28 U.S.C. § 2241(a), which authorizes the issuance of writs of habeas corpus, when it refused to issue a writ of habeas corpus ordering federal prison officials in California to bring the plaintiff to Tennessee for a pretrial hearing in a § 1983 suit challenging the treatment of the plaintiff while previously incarcerated in a Tennessee jail. Two facts were central to the court's

decision: one, the distance between the place where the plaintiff was incarcerated and the place where the pretrial hearing was to be held, and two, that the writ was sought for a pretrial stage of the proceeding.

How would you resolve whether and when an inmate has a constitutional right to appear in court or, in any event, a right under 28 U.S.C. § 2241(a)?

5. Many of the lower court cases in which the courts have either refused to grant or approved the refusal to grant a prisoner's petition for a writ of habeas corpus directing the bringing of the prisoner to court for trial or for a pretrial hearing have relied on Price v. Johnston, 334 U.S. 266, 68 S.Ct. 1049 (1948). In *Price,* the Supreme Court held that prisoners have no "absolute right" to either argue their own appeals or to be present during oral arguments before the appellate court. The Court observed that the decision whether or not to issue a writ of habeas corpus directing prison officials to bring a prisoner before the appellate court is one falling within the appellate court's discretion. As long as there was a "reasonable necessity" for not issuing the writ, the appellate court's exercise of its discretion would be sustained.

B. COMMUNICATIONS WITH ATTORNEYS

PROCUNIER v. MARTINEZ

Supreme Court of the United States, 1974.
416 U.S. 396, 94 S.Ct. 1800, 40 L.Ed.2d 224.

Mr. Justice Powell delivered the opinion of the Court.

This case concerns the constitutionality of certain regulations promulgated by appellant Procunier in his capacity as Director of the California Department of Corrections. Appellees brought a class action on behalf of themselves and all other inmates of penal institutions under the Department's jurisdiction to challenge * * * the ban against the use of law students and legal paraprofessionals to conduct attorney-client interviews with inmates. Pursuant to 28 U.S.C. § 2281 a three-judge United States District Court was convened to hear appellees' request for declaratory and injunctive relief. * * *

* * *

The District Court * * * enjoined continued enforcement of Administrative Rule MV–IV–02, which provides in pertinent part:

"Investigators for an attorney-of-record will be confined to not more than two. Such investigators must be licensed by the State or must be members of the State Bar. Designation must be made in writing by the Attorney."

By restricting access to prisoners to members of the bar and licensed private investigators, this regulation imposed an absolute ban on the use by attorneys of law students and legal paraprofessionals to interview inmate clients. In fact, attorneys could not even delegate to such persons the task of obtaining prisoners' signatures on legal documents.

The District Court reasoned that this rule constituted an unjustifiable restriction on the right of access to the courts. We agree.

The constitutional guarantee of due process of law has as a corollary the requirement that prisoners be afforded access to the courts in order to challenge unlawful convictions and to seek redress for violations of their constitutional rights. This means that inmates must have a reasonable opportunity to seek and receive the assistance of attorneys. Regulations and practices that unjustifiably obstruct the availability of professional representation or other aspects of the right of access to the courts are invalid.

The District Court found that the rule restricting attorney-client interviews to members of the bar and licensed private investigators inhibited adequate professional representation of indigent inmates. The remoteness of many California penal institutions makes a personal visit to an inmate client a time-consuming undertaking. The court reasoned that the ban against the use of law students or other paraprofessionals for attorney-client interviews would deter some lawyers from representing prisoners who could not afford to pay for their traveling time or that of licensed private investigators. And those lawyers who agreed to do so would waste time that might be employed more efficaciously in working on the inmates' legal problems. Allowing law students and paraprofessionals to interview inmates might well reduce the cost of legal representation for prisoners. The District Court therefore concluded that the regulation imposed a substantial burden on the right of access to the courts.

As the District Court recognized, this conclusion does not end the inquiry, for prison administrators are not required to adopt every proposal that may be thought to facilitate prisoner access to the courts. The extent to which that right is burdened by a particular regulation or practice must be weighed against the legitimate interests of penal administration and the proper regard that judges should give to the expertise and discretionary authority of correctional officials. In this case the ban against the use of law students and other paraprofessional personnel was absolute. Its prohibition was not limited to prospective interviewers who posed some colorable threat to security or to those inmates thought to be especially dangerous. Nor was it shown that a less restrictive regulation would unduly burden the administrative task of screening and monitoring visitors.

Appellants' enforcement of the regulation in question also created an arbitrary distinction between law students employed by practicing attorneys and those associated with law school programs providing legal assistance to prisoners. While the Department flatly prohibited interviews of any sort by law students working for attorneys, it freely allowed participants of a number of law school programs to enter the prisons and meet with inmates. These largely unsupervised students were admitted without any security check other than verification of their enrollment in a school program. Of course, the fact that appellants have allowed some persons to conduct attorney-client interviews with prisoners does not mean that they are required to admit others, but the arbitrariness of the distinction between the two categories of law students does reveal the absence of any real justification for the sweeping prohibition of Administrative Rule MV–IV–02. We cannot say that the District Court erred in invalidating this regulation.

* * *

Questions and Points for Discussion

1. Courts have periodically had to consider whether prison officials can constitutionally open, inspect, read, censor, and withhold mail to and from inmates and their attorneys. In Wolff v. McDonnell, 418 U.S. 539, 94 S.Ct. 2963 (1974), the Court addressed the constitutionality of opening and inspecting mail from an attorney to an inmate. Such mail was opened in the inmate's presence. In upholding the constitutionality of the inspection scheme, which was designed to thwart the entry of contraband into the prison, the Court, in an opinion written by Justice White, observed as follows:

> As to the ability to open the mail in the presence of inmates, this could in no way constitute censorship, since the mail would not be read. Neither could it chill such communications, since the inmate's presence insures that prison officials will not read the mail. * * * [W]e think that petitioners, by acceding to a rule whereby the inmate is present when mail from attorneys is inspected, have done all, and perhaps even more, than the Constitution requires.

Id. at 577, 94 S.Ct. at 2985.

Although the Supreme Court in *Wolff* intimated that the prison officials might have exceeded the requirements of the Constitution by deciding to refrain from opening and inspecting mail from an attorney to an inmate unless the inmate was present, the lower courts have generally required the inmate to be present before mail from an attorney can be opened and inspected for contraband. See, e.g., Jensen v. Klecker, 648 F.2d 1179, 1182 (8th Cir.1981); Jones v. Diamond, 594 F.2d 997, 1014 (5th Cir. 1979).

2. Can correctional authorities open and inspect outgoing mail to an attorney? Compare *Jensen v. Klecker*, supra note 1 (outgoing mail to an attorney may be inspected for contraband if the inmate is present) with *Jones v. Diamond*, supra note 1 (mail to attorneys cannot be opened).

3. Can prison officials read correspondence between attorneys and inmates? The lower courts have divided on this question in the past. Compare Taylor v. Sterrett, 532 F.2d 462, 475 (5th Cir.1976) (although mail from attorneys can be inspected in the inmate's presence, neither mail from nor mail to attorneys can be read); with Wright v. McMann, 460 F.2d 126, 132 (2d Cir.1972) (prison officials can read attorney/inmate mail) and Collins v. Schoonfield, 344 F.Supp. 257, 276 (D.Md.1972) (security concerns may justify reading of mail to or from attorneys and persons confined in jail, including pretrial detainees).

4. If prison officials could read an inmate's mail to or from an attorney, presumably they could, in some instances, refuse to forward the mail to the addressee. See, e.g., Wright v. McMann, 460 F.2d 126, 131–32 (2d Cir.1972) (censorship or withholding of attorney/inmate mail justified when attorney or inmate has used access privilege to the other to transmit contraband or communicate plans for engaging in illegal activities). Procedural safeguards, however, would have to attend this censorship process. See Procunier v. Martinez, 416 U.S. 396, 94 S.Ct. 1800 (1974), supra page 273.

5. Individuals charged with a crime generally have a sixth amendment right to the assistance of an attorney at their trial and during certain "critical stages" preceding the trial. Reading the mail of pretrial detainees to or from their attorneys may pose special constitutional problems by interfering with this right to counsel.

Maine v. Moulton, 474 U.S. 159, 106 S.Ct. 477 (1985) arguably supports the proposition that potential sixth amendment problems would not be obviated by the security interests arguably furthered by the reading of mail between attorneys and pretrial detainees. In *Moulton,* the Supreme Court considered whether the police violated a defendant's sixth amendment right to counsel when, after he had been indicted, they electronically monitored a conversation which he had with a co-defendant. The police monitored this conversation for two reasons—to protect the co-defendant should the defendant discover that the co-defendant was cooperating with the police and to discover whether the defendant was going to follow up on a threat to kill a witness. Despite these legitimate reasons for monitoring the defendant's conversation with his co-defendant, the Supreme Court concluded that the police had abridged the defendant's sixth amendment right to "rely on counsel as a 'medium' between him and the State." Id. at 176, 106 S.Ct. at 487.

If the sixth amendment right to counsel may be violated even though government officials had legitimate and important reasons for circumventing or interfering with the criminal defendant's right to consult with his attorney, are not jail officials, who reasonably believe that communications between a pretrial detainee charged with a crime and his attorney will threaten the jail's security or result in the planning of another crime, faced with a "Hobson's-choice"—either read the mail between the detainee and the attorney, exposing themselves to liability under § 1983, or refrain from reading the mail, possibly jeopardizing the jail's security or facilitating the commission of a crime?

C. JAILHOUSE LAWYERS AND OTHER LEGAL ASSISTANCE

JOHNSON v. AVERY

Supreme Court of the United State, 1969.
393 U.S. 483, 89 S.Ct. 747, 21 L.Ed.2d 718.

MR. JUSTICE FORTAS delivered the opinion of the Court.

I.

Petitioner is serving a life sentence in the Tennessee State Penitentiary. In February 1965 he was transferred to the maximum security building in the prison for violation of a prison regulation which provides:

"No inmate will advise, assist or otherwise contract to aid another, either with or without a fee, to prepare Writs or other legal matters. It is not intended that an innocent man be punished. When a man believes he is unlawfully held or illegally convicted, he should prepare a brief or state his complaint in letter form and address it to his lawyer or a judge. A formal Writ is not necessary to receive a hearing. False charges or untrue complaints may be punished. Inmates are forbidden to set themselves up as practitioners for the purpose of promoting a business of writing Writs."

In July 1965 petitioner filed in the United States District Court for the Middle District of Tennessee a "motion for law books and a typewriter," in which he sought relief from his confinement in the maximum security building. The District Court treated this motion as a petition for a writ of habeas corpus and, after a hearing, ordered him released from disciplinary confinement and restored to the status of an ordinary prisoner. The District Court held that the regulation was void because it in effect barred illiterate prisoners from access to federal habeas corpus and conflicted with 28 U.S.C. § 2242.[1]

* * *

The State appealed. The Court of Appeals for the Sixth Circuit reversed, concluding that the regulation did not unlawfully conflict with the federal right of habeas corpus. According to the Sixth Circuit, the interest of the State in preserving prison discipline and in limiting the practice of law to licensed attorneys justified whatever burden the regulation might place on access to federal habeas corpus.

II.

This Court has constantly emphasized the fundamental importance of the writ of habeas corpus in our constitutional scheme, and the Congress has demonstrated its solicitude for the vigor of the Great Writ. The Court has steadfastly insisted that "there is no higher duty than to maintain it unimpaired."

Since the basic purpose of the writ is to enable those unlawfully incarcerated to obtain their freedom, it is fundamental that access of prisoners to the courts for the purpose of presenting their complaints may not be denied or obstructed. For example, the Court has held that a State may not validly make the writ available only to prisoners who could pay a $4 filing fee. *Smith v. Bennett,* 365 U.S. 708 (1961).

* * *

---

1. 28 U.S.C. § 2242 provides in part: "Application for a writ of habeas corpus shall be in writing signed and verified by the person for whose relief it is intended or by someone acting in his behalf."

Tennessee urges, however, that the contested regulation in this case is justified as a part of the State's disciplinary administration of the prisons. There is no doubt that discipline and administration of state detention facilities are state functions. They are subject to federal authority only where paramount federal constitutional or statutory rights supervene. It is clear, however, that in instances where state regulations applicable to inmates of prison facilities conflict with such rights, the regulations may be invalidated.

* * *

There can be no doubt that Tennessee could not constitutionally adopt and enforce a rule forbidding illiterate or poorly educated prisoners to file habeas corpus petitions. Here Tennessee has adopted a rule which, in the absence of any other source of assistance for such prisoners, effectively does just that. The District Court concluded that "[f]or all practical purposes, if such prisoners cannot have the assistance of a 'jail-house lawyer,' their possibly valid constitutional claims will never be heard in any court." The record supports this conclusion.

Jails and penitentiaries include among their inmates a high percentage of persons who are totally or functionally illiterate, whose educational attainments are slight, and whose intelligence is limited. This appears to be equally true of Tennessee's prison facilities.

In most federal courts, it is the practice to appoint counsel in post-conviction proceedings only after a petition for post-conviction relief passes initial judicial evaluation and the court has determined that issues are presented calling for an evidentiary hearing.

It has not been held that there is any general obligation of the courts, state or federal, to appoint counsel for prisoners who indicate, without more, that they wish to seek post-conviction relief. Accordingly, the initial burden of presenting a claim to post-conviction relief usually rests upon the indigent prisoner himself with such help as he can obtain within the prison walls or the prison system. In the case of all except those who are able to help themselves—usually a few old hands or exceptionally gifted prisoners—the prisoner is, in effect, denied access to the courts unless such help is available.

It is indisputable that prison "writ writers" like petitioner are sometimes a menace to prison discipline and that their petitions are often so unskillful as to be a burden on the courts which receive them. But, as this Court held in *Ex parte Hull,* in declaring invalid a state prison regulation which required that prisoners' legal pleadings be screened by state officials:

"The considerations that prompted [the regulation's] formulation are not without merit, but the state and its officers may not abridge or impair petitioner's right to apply to a federal court for a writ of habeas corpus."

Tennessee does not provide an available alternative to the assistance provided by other inmates. The warden of the prison in which petitioner was confined stated that the prison provided free notarization of prisoners' petitions. That obviously meets only a formal requirement. He also indicated that he sometimes allowed prisoners to examine the listing of attorneys in the Nashville telephone directory so they could select one to write to in an effort to interest him in taking the case, and that "on several occasions" he had contacted the public defender at the request of an inmate. There is no contention, however, that there is any regular system of assistance by public defenders. In its brief the State contends that "[t]here is absolutely no reason to believe that prison officials would fail to notify the court should an inmate advise them of a complete inability, either mental or physical, to prepare a habeas application on his own behalf," but there is no contention that they have in fact ever done so.

This is obviously far short of the showing required to demonstrate that, in depriving prisoners of the assistance of fellow inmates, Tennessee has not, in substance, deprived those unable themselves, with reasonable adequacy, to prepare their petitions, of access to the constitutionally and statutorily protected availability of the writ of habeas corpus. By contrast, in several States, the public defender system supplies trained attorneys, paid from public funds, who are available to consult with prisoners regarding their habeas corpus petitions. At least one State employs senior law students to interview and advise inmates in state prisons. Another State has a voluntary program whereby members of the local bar association make periodic visits to the prison to consult with prisoners concerning their cases.[10] We express no judgment concerning these plans, but their existence indicates that techniques are available to provide alternatives if the State elects to prohibit mutual assistance among inmates.

Even in the absence of such alternatives, the State may impose reasonable restrictions and restraints upon the acknowledged propensity of prisoners to abuse both the giving and the seeking of assistance in the preparation of applications for relief: for example, by limitations on the time and location of such activities and the imposition of punishment for the giving or receipt of consideration in connection with such activities. But unless and until the State provides some reasonable alternative to assist inmates in the preparation of petitions for post-conviction relief, it may not validly enforce a regulation such as that here in issue, barring inmates from furnishing such assistance to other prisoners.[11]

10. One State has designated an inmate as the official prison writ-writer.

11. In reversing the District Court, the Court of Appeals relied on the power of the State to restrict the practice of law to licensed attorneys as a source of authority for the prison regulation. The power of the States to control the practice of law cannot be exercised so as to abrogate federally protected rights. In any event, the type of activity involved here—preparation of petitions for post-conviction relief—though historically and traditionally one which may benefit from the services of a trained and dedicated lawyer, is a function often, perhaps generally, performed by laymen. Title 28 U.S.C. § 2242 apparently contemplates that in many situations petitions for federal habeas corpus relief will be prepared by laymen.

The judgment of the Court of Appeals is reversed and the case is remanded for further proceedings consistent with this opinion.

[The concurring opinion of Justice Douglas is omitted.]

MR. JUSTICE WHITE, with whom MR. JUSTICE BLACK joins, dissenting.

*   *   *

The majority admits that it "is indisputable" that jailhouse lawyers like petitioner "are sometimes a menace to prison discipline and that their petitions are often so unskillful as to be a burden on the courts which receive them." That is putting it mildly. The disciplinary problems are severe, the burden on the courts serious, and the disadvantages to prisoner clients of the jailhouse lawyer are unacceptable.

Although some jailhouse lawyers are no doubt very capable, it is not necessarily the best amateur legal minds which are devoted to jailhouse lawyering. Rather, the most aggressive and domineering personalities may predominate. And it may not be those with the best claims to relief who are served as clients, but those who are weaker and more gullible. Many assert that the aim of the jailhouse lawyer is not the service of truth and justice, but rather self-aggrandizement, profit, and power. According to prison officials, whose expertise in such matters should be given some consideration, the jailhouse lawyer often succeeds in establishing his own power structure, quite apart from the formal system of warden, guards, and trusties which the prison seeks to maintain. Those whom the jailhouse lawyer serves may come morally under his sway as the one hope of their release, and repay him not only with obedience but with what minor gifts and other favors are available to them. When a client refuses to pay, violence may result, in which the jailhouse lawyer may be aided by his other clients.

*   *   *

*   *   * [S]ome jailhouse clients are illiterate; and whether illiterate or not, there are others who are unable to prepare their own petitions. They need help, but I doubt that the problem of the indigent convict will be solved by subjecting him to the false hopes, dominance, and inept representation of the average unsupervised jailhouse lawyer.

I cannot say, therefore, that petitioner Johnson, who is a convicted rapist serving a life sentence and whose prison conduct the State has wide discretion in regulating, cannot be disciplined for violating a prison rule against aiding other prisoners in seeking post-conviction relief, particularly when there is no showing that any prisoner in the Tennessee State Penitentiary has been denied access to the courts, that Johnson has confined his services to those who need it, or that Johnson is himself competent to give the advice which he offers. *   *   *

*   *   *

Questions and Points for Discussion

1. In Wolff v. McDonnell, 418 U.S. 539, 94 S.Ct. 2963 (1974), the Supreme Court extended its holding in *Johnson v. Avery* when it concluded that the right to assistance from a jailhouse lawyer or to some other

"reasonable alternative" assistance is not limited to assistance in preparing habeas corpus petitions; in *Wolff,* the Court held that the right to assistance also extends to prisoners preparing civil rights complaints.

The litigation in *Wolff* was prompted by a prison regulation authorizing the warden to appoint one prisoner purportedly versed in the law to advise other prisoners on legal matters. Under the regulation, prisoners were barred from obtaining assistance in preparing legal documents from inmates other than the inmate designated by the warden unless the warden gave his or her written approval. Since the warden had denied permission to seek advice from inmates other than the appointed legal advisor, the question was raised whether a single inmate advisor for all the prisoners in the prison constituted "reasonable alternative" assistance within the meaning of *Johnson v. Avery.*

In resolving that question, the Eighth Circuit Court of Appeals directed the district court to consider the inmates' need for assistance not only in preparing habeas corpus petitions, but civil rights complaints as well. When the case reached the Supreme Court, the prison officials argued that the court of appeals had erred—that the adequacy of the available assistance is to be evaluated only in light of the need for assistance in preparing habeas corpus petitions. The Supreme Court, in an opinion written by Justice White, rejected the prison officials' narrow construction of *Johnson v. Avery:*

> [W]hile it is true that only in habeas actions may relief be granted which will shorten the term of confinement, it is more pertinent that both actions serve to protect basic constitutional rights. The right of access to the courts, upon which *Avery* was premised, is founded in the Due Process Clause and assures that no person will be denied the opportunity to present to the judiciary allegations concerning violations of fundamental constitutional rights. It is futile to contend that the Civil Rights Act of 1871 has less importance in our constitutional scheme than does the Great Writ. The recognition by this Court that prisoners have certain constitutional rights which can be protected by civil rights actions would be diluted if inmates, often "totally or functionally illiterate," were unable to articulate their complaints to the courts.

Id. at 579, 94 S.Ct. at 2984.

2. An illiterate inmate might seek the assistance of a jailhouse lawyer for a variety of reasons having nothing to do with filing a constitutional claim. The inmate, for example, might want help with a divorce proceeding or a tort suit for personal injuries occurring before or during confinement. Does the illiterate inmate have a constitutional right to consult a jailhouse lawyer about such ordinary civil matters if no "reasonable alternative assistance" has been made available to the inmate? Why or why not?

3. In determining whether inmates of a particular prison have available to them the assistance needed to prepare court documents with "reasonable adequacy," not only are the types of claims for which there is a constitutional right of assistance relevant, but also the number of inmates entitled to assistance and the number of persons rendering assistance. See,

e.g., Walters v. Thompson, 615 F.Supp. 330, 336 (N.D.Ill.1985) (two inmate clerks and two inmate trainees insufficient for prison population of over 1,200); Taylor v. Perini, 413 F.Supp. 189, 203 (N.D.Ohio 1976) (two designated inmate advisors for 1,321 prisoners constitutionally inadequate).

Some lower courts have spurned the suggestion that only illiterate inmates have the right to the assistance expounded in *Johnson v. Avery,* noting that *Johnson* also evinced a concern for "poorly educated" prisoners. See, e.g., Wainwright v. Coonts, 409 F.2d 1337 (5th Cir.1969). If the right to assistance extends to uneducated inmates, when, if ever, does an inmate lose that right because of his or her educational attainments?

4. If entitlement to assistance is predicated on the inability to competently perform legal research and writing, the vast majority of prison inmates are probably entitled to some form of assistance, at least when litigating cases involving constitutional claims. In Battle v. Anderson, 457 F.Supp. 719, 731 (E.D.Okl.1978), the court observed that 70% of the inmates at one prison lacked the intelligence and/or education to do legal research, while in Walters v. Thompson, 615 F.Supp. 330, 336 (N.D.Ill.1985), the court said that fully 90% of the inmates at another prison were incapable of doing their own legal research or writing.

5. The ban on inmate-to-inmate correspondence at issue in Turner v. Safley, 482 U.S. 78, 107 S.Ct. 2254 (1987), supra page 284, exempted correspondence "concerning legal matters." In an amicus brief filed with the Supreme Court in *Turner,* the state of Texas recounted prison gangs' use of what purported to be legal correspondence to transmit messages, including directives to kill other inmates:

> Throughout the document legal terms such as "plaintiff" and "plaintiff-class" are used to refer to the gang and its members. Investigation has revealed that other legal phrases, as well as all types of other innocuous words and phrases, have been added to the underground vocabulary of the AB and other gangs. "File a brief," "file an affidavit," "file a writ," "file a suit," in AB parlance, are all instructions to kill another inmate. Depending on how it is used in a sentence and what is already known about an individual, "give our regards to John Doe" could mean that the inmate is to be killed, or that the inmate has been approved for AB membership. TDC's list of gang phraseology now includes in excess of 100 phrases, and of course many have not been uncovered.

Brief for the State of Texas at 13.

What limitations could constitutionally be placed on correspondence between inmates concerning legal matters? Is the standard to be applied when assessing the constitutionality of such limitations the same as the standard set forth in *Turner?* Should it be? Would the ban on jailhouse lawyers deemed unconstitutional in *Johnson v. Avery* have survived the Court's scrutiny under the *Turner* test?

6. To retaliate against a prisoner for pursuing litigation is unconstitutional, violating the due process right of access to the courts. Cases abound with prisoners' allegations that they have been taunted, threatened, transferred to other prisons, transferred from coveted work assignments, beaten,

and otherwise hassled because of lawsuits they brought against prison officials. Such retaliatory measures have been directed against both the inmates bringing suit and the jailhouse lawyers willing to assist with the litigation. Examples of cases containing allegations of retaliation include: Adams v. Wainwright, 875 F.2d 1536 (11th Cir.1989) (transfer to another prison); Harris v. Fleming, 839 F.2d 1232 (7th Cir.1988) (firing from prison job and transfer to cellblock where two of inmate's known enemies lived); Hall v. Sutton, 755 F.2d 786 (11th Cir.1985) (destruction of tennis shoes); Jones v. Coughlin, 696 F.Supp. 916 (S.D.N.Y.1988) (denial of work release and furlough privileges).

7. Prison officials are not the only ones who have not looked too kindly on the activities of jailhouse lawyers. In an acerbic dissent in Cruz v. Beto, 405 U.S. 319, 92 S.Ct. 1079 (1972), Justice (now Chief Justice) Rehnquist argued that a different standard should be applied to prisoner complaints when determining whether they state a claim upon which relief can be granted because of what Justice Rehnquist considered prisoners' abuse of the right of access. To support his argument, Justice Rehnquist quoted from a Law Review article discussing jailhouse lawyers:

> When decisions do not help a writ-writer, he may employ a handful of tricks which damage his image in the state courts. Some of the not too subtle subterfuges used by a small minority of writ-writers would tax the credulity of any lawyer. One writ-writer simply made up his own legal citations when he ran short of actual ones. In one action against the California Adult Authority involving the application of administrative law, one writ-writer used the following citations: Aesop v. Fables, First Baptist Church v. Sally Stanford, Doda v. One Forty-four Inch Chest, and Dogood v. The Planet Earth. The references to the volumes and page numbers of the nonexistent publications were equally fantastic, such as 901 Penal Review, page 17,240. To accompany each case, he composed an eloquent decision which, if good law, would make selected acts of the Adult Authority unconstitutional. In time the 'decisions' freely circulated among other writ-writers, and several gullible ones began citing them also.

Id. at 327 n. 7 (quoting Larsen, A Prisoner Looks at Writ–Writing, 56 Cal.L. Rev. 343, 355 (1968)).

Has an illiterate or uneducated inmate whose jailhouse lawyer is citing *Doda v. One Forty-four Inch Chest* received the "meaningful access" to the courts to which he or she is supposedly entitled? Can an inmate who has had the assistance of a jailhouse lawyer still assert a violation of the right of access to the courts on the grounds that the jailhouse lawyer or lawyers in the prison are not sufficiently competent? Why or why not?

8. When analyzing the scope of inmates' right to legal assistance, two of the Supreme Court cases which should be considered are Pennsylvania v. Finley, 481 U.S. 551, 107 S.Ct. 1990 (1987) and Murray v. Giarratano, 109 S.Ct. 2765 (1989). In both cases, the Court discussed whether indigent inmates have the constitutional right to have an attorney appointed to assist them when challenging the validity of their convictions in a state postconviction proceeding. Relying on Ross v. Moffitt, 417 U.S. 600, 94 S.Ct. 2437 (1974), the Court rejected this notion in *Finley*. In *Ross,* the

Court had held that while indigent inmates challenging their convictions may have the right to an appointed attorney when first appealing their convictions, they have no right to appointed counsel when seeking the discretionary review of their convictions by a state supreme court or the United States Supreme Court.

The inmate in *Finley* was serving time for a noncapital crime, so the question still remained after *Finley* whether inmates sentenced to death have the right to appointed counsel to assist them during postconviction proceedings. In *Murray v. Giarratano,* the Supreme Court, in a 5–4 decision, answered this question in the negative. In a plurality opinion, Chief Justice Rehnquist, joined by Justices White, O'Connor, and Scalia, observed that *Finley* was controlling. That the prisoner from Virginia in this case was faced with the ultimate sanction—death—was considered inconsequential, since safeguards surrounding capital cases at the trial stage, according to the plurality, provide sufficient assurance that the death penalty is imposed only in appropriate cases. Consequently, the failure to appoint counsel to assist death-row inmates in collaterally attacking their convictions violated neither the due process clause of the fourteenth amendment nor the prohibition of cruel and unusual punishment found in the eighth amendment.

Justice Kennedy's concurring opinion, in which he was joined by Justice O'Connor, provided the fifth vote for the Court, so his opinion is of especial significance. In the course of his opinion, Justice Kennedy emphasized that there was no evidence that any Virginia inmate on death row had ever been unable to procure the assistance of an attorney during postconviction proceedings. Justice Kennedy also noted that in Virginia, lawyers were assigned to the prisons who could assist inmates in drafting petitions for postconviction relief even though they might not actually represent inmates throughout the postconviction review process. The emphasis placed on these facts by Justice Kennedy suggests that in a case with different facts, a majority of the Court might find that the failure to afford an indigent inmate on death row with an appointed attorney, both to help in preparing a petition for postconviction relief and to represent the inmate during the postconviction proceeding, violates the inmate's constitutional rights.

Justice Stevens wrote a dissenting opinion in *Murray v. Giarrataro* in which Justices Brennan, Marshall, and Blackmun joined. Justice Stevens noted the Court's prior emphasis in Bounds v. Smith, 430 U.S. 817, 97 S.Ct. 1491 (1977), infra page 337 that a prisoner's access to the courts be "meaningful." By no means, said Justice Stevens could the access of an indigent death-row inmate to the postconviction review process be considered "meaningful" when that inmate was not provided with an attorney to draft the petition for postconviction relief and represent the inmate throughout the postconviction proceeding. In support of his conclusion, Justice Stevens cited a number of factors, including the following: (1) the limited time that an inmate will often have to file a postconviction petition; (2) the inordinate complexity of the issues in capital cases; (3) the difficulty of preparing legal documents when faced with the pressures of an impending death; and (4) the large number of capital cases in which a collateral attack has been successful.

9. Apart from the question of the assistance to which an inmate is constitutionally entitled when litigating a court case is the question of the right to assistance, if any, which should be accorded by statute. Rule 8(c) of the Rules Governing Section 2254 Cases in the United States District Courts (federal habeas corpus actions involving state prisoners), 28 foll. § 2254, for example, requires that counsel be appointed to represent an indigent inmate once the decision is made to hold an evidentiary hearing on the merits of the inmate's habeas corpus petition.

The decision whether or not to appoint an attorney to represent an indigent prisoner bringing a § 1983 suit in federal court presently falls within the court's discretion. 28 U.S.C. § 1915(d). Most inmate civil rights suits, however, proceed without the inmates being assisted by lawyers. On the other hand, the prison officials being sued are usually represented by an attorney. The prison officials normally do not have to pay fees to their attorneys, since the attorneys are usually employees of and paid by the government.

Should Congress and the states pass laws under which at least some inmates would be entitled to representation by an attorney? If so, when should an inmate have a statutory right to such representation?

D. LAW LIBRARIES AND OTHER LITIGATION TOOLS

BOUNDS v. SMITH

Supreme Court of the United States, 1977.
430 U.S. 817, 97 S.Ct. 1491, 52 L.Ed.2d 72.

MR. JUSTICE MARSHALL delivered the opinion of the Court.

* * *

I

Respondents are inmates incarcerated in correctional facilities of the Division of Prisons of the North Carolina Department of Correction. They filed three separate actions under 42 U.S.C. § 1983, all eventually consolidated in the District Court for the Eastern District of North Carolina. Respondents alleged, in pertinent part, that they were denied access to the courts in violation of their Fourteenth Amendment rights by the State's failure to provide legal research facilities.

The District Court granted respondents' motion for summary judgment on this claim, finding that the sole prison library in the State was "severely inadequate" and that there was no other legal assistance available to inmates. It held * * * that respondents' rights to access to the courts and equal protection of the laws had been violated because there was "no indication of any assistance at the initial stage of preparation of writs and petitions." The court recognized, however, that determining the "appropriate relief to be ordered . . . presents a difficult problem," in view of North Carolina's decentralized prison system.[3] Rather than attempting "to dictate precisely what course the State should follow," the court "charge[d] the Department of Correction with the task of devising a Constitutionally sound program" to assure inmate access to the courts. It left to the State the choice of what alternative would "most easily and economically" fulfill this duty, suggesting that a program to make available lawyers, law students, or public defenders might serve the purpose at least as well as the provision of law libraries.

The State responded by proposing the establishment of seven libraries in institutions located across the State chosen so as to serve best all prison units. In addition, the State planned to set up smaller libraries in the Central Prison segregation unit and the Women's Prison. Under the plan, inmates desiring to use a library would request appointments. They would be given transportation and housing, if necessary, for a full day's library work. In addition to its collection of lawbooks, each library would stock legal forms and writing paper and have typewriters and use of copying machines. The State proposed to train inmates as research assistants and typists to aid fellow prisoners. It was estimated that ultimately some 350 inmates per week could use the libraries, although inmates not facing court deadlines might have to wait three or four weeks for their turn at a library. Respondents protested that the plan was totally inadequate and sought establishment of a library at every prison.

*   *   *

In its final decision, the District Court * * * found that the library plan was sufficient to give inmates reasonable access to the courts * * *.

*   *   *

Both sides appealed from those portions of the District Court orders adverse to them. The Court of Appeals for the Fourth Circuit affirmed in all respects save one. It found that the library plan denied women prisoners the same access rights as men to research facilities. Since there was no justification for this discrimination, the Court of Appeals ordered it eliminated. The State petitioned for review and we granted certiorari.[7] We affirm.

II

A. It is now established beyond doubt that prisoners have a constitutional right of access to the courts. * * *

* * * States must "assure the indigent defendant an adequate opportunity to present his claims fairly." *Ross v. Moffitt*, 417 U.S., at 616. "[M]eaningful access" to the courts is the touchstone.

Petitioners contend, however, that this constitutional duty merely obliges States to allow inmate "writ writers" to function. They argue

3. North Carolina's 13,000 inmates are housed in 77 prison units located in 67 counties. Sixty-five of these units hold fewer than 200 inmates.

7. Respondents filed no cross-appeal and do not now question the library plan, nor do petitioners challenge the sex discrimination ruling.

that under *Johnson v. Avery,* as long as inmate communications on legal problems are not restricted, there is no further obligation to expend state funds to implement affirmatively the right of access. This argument misreads the cases.

In *Johnson* and *Wolff v. McDonnell,* the issue was whether the access rights of ignorant and illiterate inmates were violated without adequate justification. Since these inmates were unable to present their own claims in writing to the courts, we held that their "constitutional right to help" required at least allowing assistance from their literate fellows. But in so holding, we did not attempt to set forth the full breadth of the right of access. * * *

Moreover, our decisions have consistently required States to shoulder affirmative obligations to assure all prisoners meaningful access to the courts. It is indisputable that indigent inmates must be provided at state expense with paper and pen to draft legal documents, with notarial services to authenticate them, and with stamps to mail them. States must forgo collection of docket fees otherwise payable to the treasury and expend funds for transcripts. State expenditures are necessary to pay lawyers for indigent defendants at trial and in appeals as of right.[12] This is not to say that economic factors may not be considered, for example, in choosing the methods used to provide meaningful access. But the cost of protecting a constitutional right cannot justify its total denial. Thus, neither the availability of jailhouse lawyers nor the necessity for affirmative state action is dispositive of respondents' claims. The inquiry is rather whether law libraries or other forms of legal assistance are needed to give prisoners a reasonably adequate opportunity to present claimed violations of fundamental constitutional rights to the courts.

B. Although it is essentially true, as petitioners argue, that a habeas corpus petition or civil rights complaint need only set forth facts giving rise to the cause of action, it hardly follows that a law library or other legal assistance is not essential to frame such documents. It would verge on incompetence for a lawyer to file an initial pleading without researching such issues as jurisdiction, venue, standing, exhaustion of remedies, proper parties plaintiff and defendant, and types of relief available. Most importantly, of course, a lawyer must know what the law is in order to determine whether a colorable claim exists, and if so, what facts are necessary to state a cause of action.

If a lawyer must perform such preliminary research, it is no less vital for a *pro se* prisoner. Indeed, despite the "less stringent standards" by which a *pro se* pleading is judged, *Haines v. Kerner,* 404 U.S. 519, 520 (1972), it is often more important that a prisoner complaint set forth a nonfrivolous claim meeting all procedural prerequisites, since the court may pass on the complaint's sufficiency before allowing filing

12. Cf. *Estelle v. Gamble,* 429 U.S. 97 (1976), holding that States must treat prisoners' serious medical needs, a constitutional duty obviously requiring outlays for personnel and facilities.

in forma pauperis and may dismiss the case if it is deemed frivolous. See 28 U.S.C. § 1915. Moreover, if the State files a response to a *pro se* pleading, it will undoubtedly contain seemingly authoritative citations. Without a library, an inmate will be unable to rebut the State's argument. It is not enough to answer that the court will evaluate the facts pleaded in light of the relevant law. Even the most dedicated trial judges are bound to overlook meritorious cases without the benefit of an adversary presentation. * * *

We reject the State's claim that inmates are "ill-equipped to use" "the tools of the trade of the legal profession," making libraries useless in assuring meaningful access. In the first place, the claim is inconsistent with the State's * * * argument that access is adequately protected by allowing inmates to help each other with legal problems. More importantly, this Court's experience indicates that *pro se* petitioners are capable of using lawbooks to file cases raising claims that are serious and legitimate even if ultimately unsuccessful. Finally, we note that if petitioners had any doubts about the efficacy of libraries, the District Court's initial decision left them free to choose another means of assuring access.

* * *

We hold, therefore, that the fundamental constitutional right of access to the courts requires prison authorities to assist inmates in the preparation and filing of meaningful legal papers by providing prisoners with adequate law libraries or adequate assistance from persons trained in the law.[17]

* * *

It should be noted that while adequate law libraries are one constitutionally acceptable method to assure meaningful access to the courts, our decision here * * * does not foreclose alternative means to achieve that goal. Nearly half the States and the District of Columbia provide some degree of professional or quasi-professional legal assistance to prisoners. Such programs take many imaginative forms and may have a number of advantages over libraries alone. Among the alternatives are the training of inmates as paralegal assistants to work under lawyers' supervision, the use of paraprofessionals and law students, either as volunteers or in formal clinical programs, the organization of volunteer attorneys through bar associations or other groups, the hiring of lawyers on a part-time consultant basis, and the use of full-time staff attorneys, working either in new prison legal assistance organizations or as part of public defender or legal services offices. Legal services plans not only result in more efficient and

---

17. Since our main concern here is "protecting the ability of an inmate to prepare a petition or complaint," it is irrelevant that North Carolina authorizes the expenditure of funds for appointment of counsel in some state post-conviction proceedings for prisoners whose claims survive initial review by the courts. Moreover, this statute does not cover appointment of counsel in federal habeas corpus or state or federal civil rights actions, all of which are encompassed by the right of access.

* * *

skillful handling of prisoner cases, but also avoid the disciplinary problems associated with writ writers. * * *

* * *

* * * The District Court initially held only that petitioners had violated the "fundamental constitutional guarantee" of access to the courts. It did not thereupon thrust itself into prison administration. Rather, it ordered petitioners themselves to devise a remedy for the violation, strongly suggesting that it would prefer a plan providing trained legal advisors. Petitioners chose to establish law libraries, however, and their plan was approved with only minimal changes over the strong objections of respondents. Prison administrators thus exercised wide discretion within the bounds of constitutional requirements in this case.

The judgment is

Affirmed.

MR. JUSTICE POWELL, concurring. [Opinion omitted.]

MR. CHIEF JUSTICE BURGER, dissenting. [Opinion omitted.]

* * *

MR. JUSTICE STEWART, with whom THE CHIEF JUSTICE joins, dissenting.

* * *

If, as the Court says, there is a constitutional duty upon a State to provide its prisoners with "meaningful access" to the federal courts, * * * "meaningful access" to the federal courts can seldom be realistically advanced by the device of making law libraries available to prison inmates untutored in their use. In the vast majority of cases, access to a law library will, I am convinced, simply result in the filing of pleadings heavily larded with irrelevant legalisms—possessing the veneer but lacking the substance of professional competence.

If, on the other hand, Mr. Justice Rehnquist is correct in his belief that a convict in a state prison pursuant to a final judgment of a court of competent jurisdiction has no constitutional right of "meaningful access" to the federal courts in order to attack his sentence, then a State can be under no constitutional duty to make that access "meaningful." If the extent of the constitutional duty of a State is simply not to deny or obstruct a prisoner's access to the courts, then it cannot have, even arguably, any affirmative constitutional obligation to provide law libraries for its prison inmates.

I respectfully dissent.

MR. JUSTICE REHNQUIST, with whom THE CHIEF JUSTICE joins, dissenting.

* * *

* * * [T]he Court's opinion today does not appear to proceed upon the guarantee of equal protection of the laws, a guarantee which at least has the merit of being found in the Fourteenth Amendment to the Constitution. It proceeds instead to enunciate a "fundamental

constitutional right of access to the courts," which is found nowhere in the Constitution. But if a prisoner incarcerated pursuant to a final judgment of conviction is not prevented from physical access to the federal courts in order that he may file therein petitions for relief which Congress has authorized those courts to grant, he has been accorded the only constitutional right of access to the courts that our cases have articulated in a reasoned way. Respondents here make no additional claims that prison regulations invidiously deny them access to those with knowledge of the law so that such regulations would be inconsistent with *Johnson, Procunier,* and *Wolff.* Since none of these reasons is present here, the "fundamental constitutional right of access to the courts" which the Court announces today is created virtually out of whole cloth with little or no reference to the Constitution from which it is supposed to be derived.

* * *

Questions and Points for Discussion

1. In Johnson v. Avery, 393 U.S. 483, 89 S.Ct. 747 (1969) supra page 328, and Wolff v. McDonnell, 418 U.S. 539, 94 S.Ct. 2963 (1974), supra page 332, the Supreme Court said that prison officials must permit jailhouse lawyers to assist at least some inmates in preparing habeas corpus petitions and civil rights complaints unless some "reasonable alternative" to jailhouse lawyers is made available to the inmates. If a prison contains an "adequate" law library to which prisoners have ready access, can prison officials prohibit jailhouse lawyers from doing legal work for other prisoners? See, e.g., Cruz v. Hauck, 627 F.2d 710, 721 (5th Cir.1980); Wetmore v. Fields, 458 F.Supp. 1131, 1143 (W.D.Wis.1978). On the other hand, if prison officials permit jailhouse lawyers "trained in the law" to render legal assistance to other inmates, can prison officials forego the expense of setting up and maintaining a prison law library?

2. Setting up a prison law library will not alone satisfy the requirements set forth in *Bounds v. Smith.* The law library must, in the Court's words, be "adequate." A number of courts have held prison law libraries constitutionally deficient because of books not included in the library collection. See, e.g., Gilmore v. Lynch, 319 F.Supp. 105, 110–11 (N.D.Cal. 1970), affirmed sub nom. Younger v. Gilmore, 404 U.S. 15, 92 S.Ct. 250 (1971) (regulation listing books to be included in state prison law libraries, which omits *U.S. Supreme Court Reports,* other federal reporters, the *United States Code,* annotated copies of the state's codes, many local federal district court rules, and U.S. Law Week, violates right of access to the courts); Ramos v. Lamm, 639 F.2d 559, 584 (10th Cir.1980) (prison law library lacking most volumes of the Federal Reporter Second and the Federal Supplement is inadequate); Wade v. Kane, 448 F.Supp. 678, 684 (E.D.Pa.1978), affirmed, 591 F.2d 1338 (3d Cir.1979) (library not containing the *U.S. Supreme Court Reports,* the Federal Reporter Second, Federal Rules Decisions, the annotated version of 28 U.S.C. §§ 2254 and 2255 dealing with habeas corpus relief, the annotated state statutes on criminal procedure, the Atlantic Reporter Second, many state reporters, the Federal

Rules of Criminal Procedure, the Federal Rules of Civil Procedure, and the local rules of the federal district courts located in the state is inadequate).

3. Even if a prison law library is "adequate" as far as the books found in that library, constitutional problems may remain if prisoners are not provided with sufficient access to those books. Challenges to the adequacy of library access may be mounted from several fronts. Prisoners may, for example, complain about the small size of some prison law libraries. See, e.g., Harrell v. Keohane, 621 F.2d 1059, 1061 (10th Cir.1980) (rejecting prisoner's complaint about small size of law library, which accommodated only five inmates, since litigation had not been adversely affected by any delay in using the law library). Or they may more directly contest restrictions that have been placed on the number of inmates that can use the law library at any one time or the number of hours that an inmate can use the library during a particular visit. See, e.g., Ramos v. Lamm, 639 F.2d 559, 582, 586 (10th Cir.1980) (regulation confining use of library to thirteen inmates a day for three-hour sessions, which may result in inmates having access to the law library only three hours every thirteen weeks, violates right of access to the courts). Inmates may instead or in addition challenge limits placed on the total amount of time that the law library is open. See e.g., Taylor v. Perini, 413 F.Supp. 189, 203, 205 (N.D. Ohio 1976) (law library hours extending from 6 to 8:30 p.m. Mondays through Fridays and 9 a.m. to 3 p.m. on Saturdays are constitutionally inadequate). Or they may focus on the specific times that the library is open, since some inmates may effectively be denied access to a prison law library because of the library's hours. For example, prisoners who have work and school assignments during the day may be unable to use the law library and hence have a constitutional claim if the law library is only open during the day and the inmates are unable to leave their assignments to use the library.

4. Implementing the right of access to the courts poses special problems for county or city jails or similar short-term detention facilities. Many jails are small and cannot afford the costs of a law library. In addition, because of the transient nature of jail populations, jailhouse lawyers may not be available to render assistance to other persons incarcerated in the jail.

Effectuating an inmate's right of access to the courts may also be difficult when the inmate has been placed in disciplinary segregation, protective custody, or some type of administrative segregation designed to protect correctional officers and other inmates from a particularly disruptive or violent prisoner. Releasing the prisoner from restrictive confinement for a visit to the prison law library may not be feasible. Release may precipitate the security problems that the restrictive confinement was designed to avert or may undermine the punitive and deterrent purposes of disciplinary confinement.

An inmate's right of access to the courts, however, is not vitiated by restrictive confinement. In fact, an inmate isolated from the general prison population may have a particularly pressing reason for pursuing a court action. Conditions of confinement in segregation units may be especially onerous, not meeting basic needs as to food, space, or sanitation.

Or a prisoner may be seeking relief from a long sentence to disciplinary segregation imposed after proceedings not conforming to the requirements of due process of law.

What options might a warden pursue to ensure that segregation inmates' right of access to the courts is preserved? What are the drawbacks, if any, of each option?

5. In his dissenting opinion in *Bounds,* former Chief Justice Burger distinguished between interfering with inmates' access to the courts and subsidizing that access. According to the former Chief Justice, while prison officials may be prohibited from unduly obstructing court access, they need not, as a constitutional matter, provide "affirmative assistance" to facilitate that access.

Do you subscribe to this viewpoint? If so, do indigent inmates then have no right to free paper and pens needed to communicate with a court? Do they have a right to free photocopies of documents which they file with a court? To free stamps needed to mail the documents to the court? Where would you draw the line on the scope of the right of access and why?

6. The courts, many of whom have probably seen inmate complaints written on sacks, toilet paper, and other artifacts, have been hospitable to claims that prison officials must provide indigent inmates with free paper and pens to prepare legal documents. The district court in Wade v. Kane, 448 F.Supp. 678, 685 (E.D.Pa.1978), affirmed, 591 F.2d 1338 (3d Cir.1979), for example, held that the failure to provide indigent inmates with free paper and pens abridges not only their due process right of access to the courts, but also their right to equal protection of the law. According to the court in *Wade,* this latter right is infringed if poor inmates are not given free paper and pens, since inmates with money have available to them these basic litigation tools.

7. Although "typed papers may leap more vividly than handwritten ones to the watery judicial eye," United States ex rel. Wolfish v. Levi, 439 F.Supp. 114, 131 (S.D.N.Y.1977), most courts have held that inmates have no right to be provided with typewriters to prepare court documents. Id.; Ramos v. Lamm, 485 F.Supp. 122, 166 (D.Colo.1979). Although prison officials may not have to provide inmates with typewriters, can they, in your opinion, prohibit inmates from acquiring or possessing their own typewriters? See Wolfish v. Levi, 573 F.2d 118, 132 (2d Cir.1978).

8. An inmate who is preparing or litigating a court case may want to use a photocopying machine to duplicate documents to be filed with the court or to duplicate cases, statutes, and other materials that may be relevant to the litigation. The extent to which an inmate has a right to have access to a photocopier may depend on the extent to which the inmate has access to a typewriter as well as other supplies such as carbon paper and paper for writing or typing. The amount of time that inmates are permitted to stay in the law library and the permissibility of taking law books to cells may also affect whether an inmate has a right of access to photocopying equipment. In addition, the feasibility of sending papers to family members and friends for photocopying will be considered when determining the extent to which there is a constitutional right to have

access to a photocopier. See Harrell v. Keohane, 621 F.2d 1059 (10th Cir. 1980).

9. If inmates are afforded access to a photocopying machine, are indigent inmates entitled to free photocopies? When, if ever? If they have such a right, to how many free photocopies are they entitled? In Walters v. Thompson, 615 F.Supp. 330, 340 (N.D.Ill.1985), the court concluded that under the circumstances of that case, including the fact that the inmates housed in segregation were not given direct access to law books, a limit on free photocopies to three hundred a year unconstitutionally impinged on the segregated inmates' right of access to the courts.

10. Even if prison officials may satisfy *Bounds* by providing inmates with access to an "adequate" law library, as a policy matter, should prison officials opt instead to provide inmates with one of the forms of "adequate" assistance from persons "trained in the law" described by the Court in *Bounds?* Why or why not?

Chapter 11

PRISON DISCIPLINARY
PROCEEDINGS

A. PROCEDURAL DUE PROCESS

To correctional officials, the disciplining of inmates for their misconduct while in prison is critical to the maintenance of security and order within the institution. And to prisoners, the disciplinary system is of inordinate importance. In a place where privileges are few and freedom is curtailed, prisoners have a heightened interest in retaining the privileges with which they are allotted in the prison environment.

To penalize inmates for having violated a prison rule or regulation, one or more of a variety of different sanctions might be imposed. The inmates, for example, might simply not be permitted to use the commissary or watch television for a certain number of days. Alternatively, the inmates might be placed in the disciplinary segregation unit where privileges are drastically curtailed and the prisoners spend most of the day in their cells. Or prisoners might lose accumulated good-time credits as a result of a disciplinary infraction, thereby prolonging their confinement in prison.

As is true when a person is charged with a crime, there is always the possibility that a prisoner charged with violating a prison rule or regulation is innocent of wrongdoing. The question then arises as to what steps, if any, must be taken by prison officials to minimize the risk of punishing an inerrant prisoner. The Supreme Court addressed this question in the case which follows.

WOLFF v. McDONNELL

Supreme Court of the United States, 1974.
418 U.S. 539, 94 S.Ct. 2963, 41 L.Ed.2d 935.

MR. JUSTICE WHITE delivered the opinion of the Court.

[The respondent, an inmate incarcerated in the Nebraska Penal and Correctional Complex in Lincoln, Nebraska, filed a class action suit under § 1983 claiming, among other things, that the disciplinary proceedings at the prison failed to conform to the requirements of due process of law. The district court rejected this claim, but on appeal, the Eighth Circuit Court of Appeals reversed. The Supreme Court then agreed to review the case.]

I

* * *

Section 16 of the Nebraska Treatment and Corrections Act provides that the chief executive officer of each penal facility is responsible for the discipline of inmates in a particular institution. The statute provides for a range of possible disciplinary action. "Except in flagrant or serious cases, punishment for misconduct shall consist of deprivation of privileges. In cases of flagrant or serious misconduct, the chief executive officer may order that a person's reduction of term as provided in section 83–1,107 [good-time credit] be forfeited or withheld and also that the person be confined in a disciplinary cell." Each breach of discipline is to be entered in the person's file together with the disposition or punishment therefor.

* * *

The only statutory provision establishing procedures for the imposition of disciplinary sanctions which pertains to good time merely requires that an inmate be "consulted regarding the charges of misconduct" in connection with the forfeiture, withholding, or restoration of credit. But prison authorities have framed written regulations dealing with procedures and policies for controlling inmate misconduct. By regulation, misconduct is classified into two categories: major misconduct is a "serious violation" and must be formally reported to an Adjustment Committee, composed of the Associate Warden Custody, the Correctional Industries Superintendent, and the Reception Center Director. This Committee is directed to "review and evaluate all misconduct reports" and, among other things, to "conduct investigations, make findings, [and] impose disciplinary actions." If only minor misconduct, "a less serious violation," is involved, the problem may either be resolved informally by the inmate's supervisor or it can be formally reported for action to the Adjustment Committee. Repeated minor misconduct must be reported. The Adjustment Committee has available a wide range of sanctions. "Disciplinary action taken and recommended may include but not necessarily be limited to the following: reprimand, restrictions of various kinds, extra duty, confinement in the Adjustment Center [the disciplinary cell], withholding of statutory good time and/or extra earned good time, or a combination of the elements listed herein."

Additional procedures have been devised by the Complex governing the actions of the Adjustment Committee. Based on the testimony, the District Court found that the following procedures were in effect when an inmate is written up or charged with a prison violation:

"(a) [t]he chief correction supervisor reviews the 'write-ups' on the inmates by the officers of the Complex daily;

"(b) the convict is called to a conference with the chief correction supervisor and the charging party;

"(c) following the conference, a conduct report is sent to the Adjustment Committee;

"(d) there follows a hearing before the Adjustment Committee and the report is read to the inmate and discussed;

"(e) if the inmate denies charge he may ask questions of the party writing him up;

"(f) the Adjustment Committee can conduct additional investigations if it desires;

"(g) punishment is imposed."

* * *

Petitioners assert that the procedure for disciplining prison inmates for serious misconduct is a matter of policy raising no constitutional issue. If the position implies that prisoners in state institutions are wholly without the protections of the Constitution and the Due Process Clause, it is plainly untenable. Lawful imprisonment necessarily makes unavailable many rights and privileges of the ordinary citizen, a "retraction justified by the considerations underlying our penal system." *Price v. Johnston,* 334 U.S. 266, 285 (1948). But though his rights may be diminished by the needs and exigencies of the institutional environment, a prisoner is not wholly stripped of constitutional protections when he is imprisoned for crime. There is no iron curtain drawn between the Constitution and the prisons of this country.

* * *

Of course, as we have indicated, the fact that prisoners retain rights under the Due Process Clause in no way implies that these rights are not subject to restrictions imposed by the nature of the regime to which they have been lawfully committed. Prison disciplinary proceedings are not part of a criminal prosecution, and the full panoply of rights due a defendant in such proceedings does not apply. In sum, there must be mutual accommodation between institutional needs and objectives and the provisions of the Constitution that are of general application.

We also reject the assertion of the State that whatever may be true of the Due Process Clause in general or of other rights protected by that Clause against state infringement, the interest of prisoners in disciplinary procedures is not included in that "liberty" protected by the Fourteenth Amendment. It is true that the Constitution itself does not guarantee good-time credit for satisfactory behavior while in prison. But here the State itself has not only provided a statutory right to good time but also specifies that it is to be forfeited only for serious misbehavior. * * *

* * *

We think a person's liberty is equally protected, even when the liberty itself is a statutory creation of the State. The touchstone of due process is protection of the individual against arbitrary action of government. Since prisoners in Nebraska can only lose good-time credits if they are guilty of serious misconduct, the determination of whether such behavior has occurred becomes critical, and the minimum requirements of procedural due process appropriate for the circumstances must be observed.

As found by the District Court, the procedures employed are: (1) a preliminary conference with the Chief Corrections Supervisor and the charging party, where the prisoner is informed of the misconduct charge and engages in preliminary discussion on its merits; (2) the preparation of a conduct report and a hearing held before the Adjustment Committee, the disciplinary body of the prison, where the report is read to the inmate; and (3) the opportunity at the hearing to ask questions of the charging party. The State contends that the procedures already provided are adequate. The Court of Appeals held them insufficient and ordered that the due process requirements outlined in *Morrissey* [*v. Brewer,* 408 U.S. 471 (1972)] and [*Gagnon v.*] *Scarpelli,* [411 U.S. 778 (1973)] be satisfied in serious disciplinary cases at the prison.

Morrissey held that due process imposed certain minimum procedural requirements which must be satisfied before parole could finally be revoked. These procedures were:

> "(a) written notice of the claimed violations of parole; (b) disclosure to the parolee of evidence against him; (c) opportunity to be heard in person and to present witnesses and documentary evidence; (d) the right to confront and cross-examine adverse witnesses (unless the hearing officer specifically finds good cause for not allowing confrontation); (e) a 'neutral and detached' hearing body such as a traditional parole board, members of which need not be judicial officers or lawyers; and (f) a written statement by the factfinders as to the evidence relied on and reasons for revoking parole."

The Court did not reach the question as to whether the parolee is entitled to the assistance of retained counsel or to appointed counsel, if he is indigent. Following the decision in *Morrissey,* in *Gagnon v. Scarpelli,* the Court held the requirements of due process established for parole revocation were applicable to probation revocation proceedings. The Court added to the required minimum procedures of *Morrissey* the right to counsel, where a probationer makes a request, "based on a timely and colorable claim (i) that he has not committed the alleged violation of the conditions upon which he is at liberty; or (ii) that, even if the violation is a matter of public record or is uncontested, there are substantial reasons which justified or mitigated the violation and make revocation inappropriate, and that the reasons are complex or otherwise difficult to develop or present." In doubtful cases, the agency was to consider whether the probationer appeared to be capable of speaking effectively for himself, and a record was to be made of the grounds for refusing to appoint counsel.

We agree with neither petitioners nor the Court of Appeals: the Nebraska procedures are in some respects constitutionally deficient but the *Morrissey–Scarpelli* procedures need not in all respects be followed in disciplinary cases in state prisons.

We have often repeated that "[t]he very nature of due process negates any concept of inflexible procedures universally applicable to every imaginable situation." "[C]onsideration of what procedures due process may require under any given set of circumstances must begin with a determination of the precise nature of the government function involved as well as of the private interest that has been affected by governmental action." Viewed in this light it is immediately apparent that one cannot automatically apply procedural rules designed for free citizens in an open society, or for parolees or probationers under only limited restraints, to the very different situation presented by a disciplinary proceeding in a state prison.

Revocation of parole may deprive the parolee of only conditional liberty, but it nevertheless "inflicts a 'grievous loss' on the parolee and often on others." Simply put, revocation proceedings determine whether the parolee will be free or in prison, a matter of obvious great moment to him. For the prison inmate, the deprivation of good time is not the same immediate disaster that the revocation of parole is for the parolee. The deprivation, very likely, does not then and there work any change in the conditions of his liberty. It can postpone the date of eligibility for parole and extend the maximum term to be served, but it is not certain to do so, for good time may be restored. Even if not restored, it cannot be said with certainty that the actual date of parole will be affected; and if parole occurs, the extension of the maximum term resulting from loss of good time may affect only the termination of parole, and it may not even do that. The deprivation of good time is unquestionably a matter of considerable importance. The State reserves it as a sanction for serious misconduct, and we should not unrealistically discount its significance. But it is qualitatively and quantitatively different from the revocation of parole or probation.

In striking the balance that the Due Process Clause demands, however, we think the major consideration militating against adopting the full range of procedures suggested by *Morrissey* for alleged parole violators is the very different stake the State has in the structure and content of the prison disciplinary hearing. That the revocation of parole be justified and based on an accurate assessment of the facts is a critical matter to the State as well as the parolee; but the procedures by which it is determined whether the conditions of parole have been breached do not themselves threaten other important state interests, parole officers, the police, or witnesses—at least no more so than in the case of the ordinary criminal trial. Prison disciplinary proceedings, on the other hand, take place in a closed, tightly controlled environment peopled by those who have chosen to violate the criminal law and who have been lawfully incarcerated for doing so. Some are first offenders, but many are recidivists who have repeatedly employed illegal and often very violent means to attain their ends. They may have little regard for the safety of others or their property or for the rules designed to provide an orderly and reasonably safe prison life. Although there are very many varieties of prisons with different degrees of security, we must realize that in many of them the inmates are closely supervised and their activities controlled around the clock. Guards and inmates co-exist in direct and intimate contact. Tension between them is unremitting. Frustration, resentment, and despair are commonplace. Relationships among the inmates are varied and complex and perhaps subject to the unwritten code that exhorts inmates not to inform on a fellow prisoner.

It is against this background that disciplinary proceedings must be structured by prison authorities; and it is against this background that we must make our constitutional judgments, realizing that we are dealing with the maximum security institution as well as those where security considerations are not paramount. The reality is that disciplinary hearings and the imposition of disagreeable sanctions necessarily involve confrontations between inmates and authority and between inmates who are being disciplined and those who would charge or furnish evidence against them. Retaliation is much more than a theoretical possibility; and the basic and unavoidable task of providing reasonable personal safety for guards and inmates may be at stake, to say nothing of the impact of disciplinary confrontations and the resulting escalation of personal antagonisms on the important aims of the correctional process.

Indeed, it is pressed upon us that the proceedings to ascertain and sanction misconduct themselves play a major role in furthering the institutional goal of modifying the behavior and value systems of prison inmates sufficiently to permit them to live within the law when they are released. Inevitably there is a great range of personality and character among those who have transgressed the criminal law. Some are more amenable to suggestion and persuasion than others. Some may be incorrigible and would merely disrupt and exploit the disciplinary process for their own ends. With some, rehabilitation may be best achieved by simulating procedures of a free society to the maximum possible extent; but with others, it may be essential that discipline be swift and sure. In any event, it is argued, there would be great unwisdom in encasing the disciplinary procedures in an inflexible constitutional straitjacket that would necessarily call for adversary proceedings typical of the criminal trial, very likely raise the level of confrontation between staff and inmate, and make more difficult the utilization of the disciplinary process as a tool to advance the rehabilitative goals of the institution. This consideration, along with the necessity to maintain an acceptable level of personal security in the institution, must be taken into account as we now examine in more detail the Nebraska procedures that the Court of Appeals found wanting.

Two of the procedures that the Court held should be extended to parolees facing revocation proceedings are not, but must be, provided to prisoners in the Nebraska Complex if the minimum requirements of procedural due process are to be satisfied. These are advance written notice of the claimed violation and a written statement of the factfinders as to the evidence relied upon and the reasons for the disciplinary action taken. * * *

Part of the function of notice is to give the charged party a chance to marshal the facts in his defense and to clarify what the charges are, in fact. Neither of these functions was performed by the notice described by the Warden. Although the charges are discussed orally with the inmate somewhat in advance of the hearing, the inmate is sometimes brought before the Adjustment Committee shortly after he is orally informed of the charges. Other times, after this initial discussion, further investigation takes place which may reshape the nature of the charges or the evidence relied upon. In those instances, under procedures in effect at the time of trial, it would appear that the inmate first receives notice of the actual charges at the time of the hearing before the Adjustment Committee. We hold that written notice of the charges must be given to the disciplinary-action defendant in order to inform him of the charges and to enable him to marshal the facts and prepare a defense. At least a brief period of time after the notice, no less than 24 hours, should be allowed to the inmate to prepare for the appearance before the Adjustment Committee.

We also hold that there must be a "written statement by the factfinders as to the evidence relied on and reasons" for the disciplinary action. Although Nebraska does not seem to provide administrative review of the action taken by the Adjustment Committee, the actions taken at such proceedings may involve review by other bodies. They might furnish the basis of a decision by the Director of Corrections to transfer an inmate to another institution because he is considered "to be incorrigible by reason of frequent intentional breaches of discipline" and are certainly likely to be considered by the state parole authorities in making parole decisions. Written records of proceedings will thus protect the inmate against collateral consequences based on a misunderstanding of the nature of the original proceeding. Further, as to the disciplinary action itself, the provision for a written record helps to insure that administrators, faced with possible scrutiny by state officials and the public, and perhaps even the courts, where fundamental constitutional rights may have been abridged, will act fairly. Without written records, the inmate will be at a severe disadvantage in propounding his own cause to or defending himself from others. It may be that there will be occasions when personal or institutional safety is so implicated that the statement may properly exclude certain items of evidence, but in that event the statement should indicate the fact of the omission. Otherwise, we perceive no conceivable rehabilitative objective or prospect of prison disruption that can flow from the requirement of these statements.

We are also of the opinion that the inmate facing disciplinary proceedings should be allowed to call witnesses and present documentary evidence in his defense when permitting him to do so will not be unduly hazardous to institutional safety or correctional goals. Ordinarily, the right to present evidence is basic to a fair hearing; but the unrestricted right to call witnesses from the prison population carries obvious potential for disruption and for interference with the swift punishment that in individual cases may be essential to carrying out the correctional program of the institution. We should not be too ready to exercise oversight and put aside the judgment of prison administrators. It may be that an individual threatened with serious sanctions would normally be entitled to present witnesses and relevant documentary evidence; but here we must balance the inmate's interest in avoiding loss of good time against the needs of the prison, and some amount of flexibility and accommodation is required. Prison officials must have the necessary discretion to keep the hearing within reasonable limits and to refuse to call witnesses that may create a risk of reprisal or undermine authority, as well as to limit access to other inmates to collect statements or to compile other documentary evidence. Although we do not prescribe it, it would be useful for the Committee to state its reason for refusing to call a witness, whether it be for irrelevance, lack of necessity, or the hazards presented in individual cases. Any less flexible rule appears untenable as a constitutional matter, at least on the record made in this case. The operation of a correctional institution is at best an extraordinarily difficult undertaking. Many prison officials, on the spot and with the responsibility for the safety of inmates and staff, are reluctant to extend the unqualified right to call witnesses; and in our view, they must have the necessary discretion without being subject to unduly crippling constitutional impediments. There is this much play in the joints of the Due Process Clause, and we stop short of imposing a more demanding rule with respect to witnesses and documents.

Confrontation and cross-examination present greater hazards to institutional interests. If confrontation and cross-examination of those furnishing evidence against the inmate were to be allowed as a matter of course, as in criminal trials, there would be considerable potential for havoc inside the prison walls. Proceedings would inevitably be longer and tend to unmanageability. These procedures are essential in criminal trials where the accused, if found guilty, may be subjected to the most serious deprivations, or where a person may lose his job in society. But they are not rights universally applicable to all hearings. Rules of procedure may be shaped by consideration of the risks of error and should also be shaped by the consequences which will follow their adoption. Although some States do seem to allow cross-examination in disciplinary hearings, we are not apprised of the conditions under which the procedure may be curtailed; and it does not appear that confrontation and cross-examination are generally required in this context. We think that the Constitution should not be read to impose the procedure at the present time and that adequate bases for decision in prison disciplinary cases can be arrived at without cross-examination.

Perhaps as the problems of penal institutions change and correctional goals are reshaped, the balance of interests involved will require otherwise. But in the current environment, where prison disruption remains a serious concern to administrators, we cannot ignore the desire and effort of many States, including Nebraska, and the Federal Government to avoid situations that may trigger deep emotions and that may scuttle the disciplinary process as a rehabilitation vehicle. To some extent, the American adversary trial presumes contestants who are able to cope with the pressures and aftermath of the battle, and such may not generally be the case of those in the prisons of this country. At least, the Constitution, as we interpret it today, does not require the contrary assumption. Within the limits set forth in this opinion we are content for now to leave the continuing development of measures to review adverse actions affecting inmates to the sound discretion of corrections officials administering the scope of such inquiries.

We recognize that the problems of potential disruption may differ depending on whom the inmate proposes to cross-examine. If he proposes to examine an unknown fellow inmate, the danger may be the greatest, since the disclosure of the identity of the accuser, and the cross-examination which will follow, may pose a high risk of reprisal within the institution. Conversely, the inmate accuser, who might freely tell his story privately to prison officials, may refuse to testify or admit any knowledge of the situation in question. Although the dangers posed by cross-examination of known inmate accusers, or guards, may be less, the resentment which may persist after confrontation may still be substantial. Also, even where the accuser or adverse witness is known, the disclosure of third parties may pose a problem. There may be a class of cases where the facts are closely disputed, and the character of the parties minimizes the dangers involved. However, any constitutional rule tailored to meet these situations would undoubtedly produce great litigation and attendant costs in a much wider range of cases. Further, in the last analysis, even within the narrow range of cases where interest balancing may well dictate cross-examination, courts will be faced with the assessment of prison officials as to the dangers involved, and there would be a limited basis for upsetting such judgments. The better course at this time, in a period where prison practices are diverse and somewhat experimental, is to leave these matters to the sound discretion of the officials of state prisons.

As to the right to counsel, the problem as outlined in *Scarpelli* with respect to parole and probation revocation proceedings is even more pertinent here:

> "The introduction of counsel into a revocation proceeding will alter significantly the nature of the proceeding. If counsel is provided for

the probationer or parolee, the State in turn will normally provide its own counsel; lawyers, by training and disposition, are advocates and bound by professional duty to present all available evidence and arguments in support of their clients' positions and to contest with vigor all adverse evidence and views. The role of the hearing body itself, aptly described in *Morrissey* as being 'predictive and discretionary' as well as factfinding, may become more akin to that of a judge at a trial, and less attuned to the rehabilitative needs of the individual probationer or parolee. In the greater self-consciousness of its quasi-judicial role, the hearing body may be less tolerant of marginal deviant behavior and feel more pressure to reincarcerate than to continue nonpunitive rehabilitation. Certainly, the decisionmaking process will be prolonged, and the financial cost to the State—for appointed counsel, counsel for the State, a longer record, and the possibility of judicial review—will not be insubstantial."

The insertion of counsel into the disciplinary process would inevitably give the proceedings a more adversary cast and tend to reduce their utility as a means to further correctional goals. There would also be delay and very practical problems in providing counsel in sufficient numbers at the time and place where hearings are to be held. At this stage of the development of these procedures we are not prepared to hold that inmates have a right to either retained or appointed counsel in disciplinary proceedings.

Where an illiterate inmate is involved, however, or where the complexity of the issue makes it unlikely that the inmate will be able to collect and present the evidence necessary for an adequate comprehension of the case, he should be free to seek the aid of a fellow inmate, or if that is forbidden, to have adequate substitute aid in the form of help from the staff or from a sufficiently competent inmate designated by the staff. We need not pursue the matter further here, however, for there is no claim that respondent, McDonnell, is within the class of inmates entitled to advice or help from others in the course of a prison disciplinary hearing.

Finally, we decline to rule that the Adjustment Committee which conducts the required hearings at the Nebraska Prison Complex and determines whether to revoke good time is not sufficiently impartial to satisfy the Due Process Clause. The Committee is made up of the Associate Warden Custody as chairman, the Correctional Industries Superintendent, and the Reception Center Director. The Chief Corrections Supervisor refers cases to the Committee after investigation and an initial interview with the inmate involved. The Committee is not left at large with unlimited discretion. It is directed to meet daily and to operate within the principles stated in the controlling regulations, among which is the command that "[f]ull consideration must be given to the causes for the adverse behavior, the setting and circumstances in which it occurred, the man's accountability, and the correctional treatment goals," as well as the direction that "disciplinary measures will be taken only at such times and to such degrees as are necessary to regulate and control a man's behavior within acceptable limits and will never be rendered capriciously or in the nature of retaliation or revenge." We find no warrant in the record presented here for concluding that the Adjustment Committee presents such a hazard of arbitrary decisionmaking that it should be held violative of due process of law.

Our conclusion that some, but not all, of the procedures specified in *Morrissey* and *Scarpelli* must accompany the deprivation of good time by state prison authorities [19] is not graven in stone. As the nature of the prison disciplinary process changes in future years, circumstances may then exist which will require further consideration and reflection of this Court. It is our view, however, that the procedures we have now required in prison disciplinary proceedings represent a reasonable accommodation between the interests of the inmates and the needs of the institution.

MR. JUSTICE MARSHALL, with whom MR. JUSTICE BRENNEN joins, concurring in part and dissenting in part.

* * *

My disagreement with the majority is over its disposition of the primary issue presented by this case, the extent of the procedural protections required by the Due Process Clause of the Fourteenth Amendment in prison disciplinary proceedings. I have previously stated my view that a prisoner does not shed his basic constitutional rights at the prison gate, and I fully support the Court's holding that the interest of inmates in freedom from imposition of serious discipline is a "liberty" entitled to due process protection. But, in my view, the content which the Court gives to this due process protection leaves these noble holdings as little more than empty promises. To be sure, the Court holds that inmates are constitutionally entitled to advance written notice of the charges against them and a statement of the evidence relied on, the facts found, and the reasons supporting the disciplinary board's decision. Apparently, an inmate is also constitutionally entitled to a hearing and an opportunity to speak in his own defense. These are valuable procedural safeguards, and I do not mean for a moment to denigrate their importance.

19. Although the complaint put at issue the procedures employed with respect to the deprivation of good time, under the Nebraska system, the same procedures are employed where disciplinary confinement is imposed. The deprivation of good time and imposition of "solitary" confinement are reserved for instances where serious misbehavior has occurred. This appears a realistic approach, for it would be difficult for the purposes of procedural due process to distinguish between the procedures that are required where good time is forfeited and those that must be extended when solitary confinement is at issue. The latter represents a major change in the conditions of confinement and is normally imposed only when it is claimed and proved that there has been a major act of misconduct. Here, as in the case of good time, there should be minimum procedural safeguards as a hedge against arbitrary determination of the factual predicate for imposition of the sanction. We do not suggest, however, that the procedures required by today's decision for the deprivation of good time would also be required for the imposition of lesser penalties such as the loss of privileges.

But the purpose of notice is to give the accused the opportunity to prepare a defense, and the purpose of a hearing is to afford him the chance to present that defense. Today's decision deprives an accused inmate of any enforceable constitutional right to the procedural tools essential to the presentation of any meaningful defense, and makes the required notice and hearing formalities of little utility. * * *

* * *

* * * Our decisions flatly reject the Court's view of the dispensability of confrontation and cross-examination. We have held that "[i]n almost every setting where important decisions turn on questions of fact, due process requires an opportunity to confront and cross-examine adverse witnesses." * * * Surely confrontation and cross-examination are as crucial in the prison disciplinary context as in any other, if not more so. Prison disciplinary proceedings will invariably turn on disputed questions of fact, and, in addition to the usual need for cross-examination to reveal mistakes of identity, faulty perceptions, or cloudy memories, there is a significant potential for abuse of the disciplinary process by "persons motivated by malice, vindictiveness, intolerance, prejudice, or jealousy," whether these be other inmates seeking revenge or prison guards seeking to vindicate their otherwise absolute power over the men under their control. I can see no rational means for resolving these disputed questions of fact without providing confrontation and cross-examination.

The majority, however, denies accused prisoners these basic constitutional rights, and leaves these matters for now to the "sound discretion" of prison officials. * * * I see no persuasive justification for this result. The Court cites concern for administrative efficiency in support of its holding: "Proceedings would inevitably be longer and tend to unmanageability." I can only assume that these are makeweights, for I refuse to believe that the Court would deny fundamental rights in reliance on such trivial and easily handled concerns.

A more substantial problem with permitting the accused inmate to demand confrontation with adverse witnesses is the need to preserve the secrecy of the identity of inmate informers and protect them from the danger of reprisal. I am well aware of the seriousness of this problem, and I agree that in some circumstances this confidentiality must prevail over the accused's right of confrontation. "But this concern for the safety of inmates does not justify a wholesale denial of the right to confront and cross-examine adverse witnesses." *Clutchette v. Procunier,* 497 F.2d, at 819. The need to keep the identity of informants confidential will exist in only a small percentage of disciplinary cases. Whether because of the "inmates' code" or otherwise, the disciplinary process is rarely initiated by a fellow inmate and almost invariably by a correctional officer. I see no legitimate need to keep confidential the identity of a prison guard who files charges against an inmate; indeed, Nebraska, like most States, routinely informs accused prisoners of the identity of the correctional officer who is the charging party, if he does not already know. In the relatively few instances where inmates press disciplinary charges, the accused inmate often knows the identity of his accuser, as, for example, where the accuser was the victim of a physical assault.

Thus, the Court refuses to enforce prisoners' fundamental procedural rights because of a legitimate concern for secrecy which must affect only a tiny fraction of disciplinary cases. This is surely permitting the tail to wag the constitutional dog. When faced with a similar problem in *Morrissey v. Brewer*, we nonetheless held that the parolee had the constitutional right to confront and cross-examine adverse witnesses, and permitted an exception to be made "if the hearing officer determines that an informant would be subjected to risk of harm if his identity were disclosed." In my view, the same approach would be appropriate here.

* * * The Court apparently accepts petitioners' arguments that there is a danger that such cross-examination will produce hostility between inmate and guard, or inmate and inmate, which will eventually lead to prison disruption; or that cross-examination of a guard by an inmate would threaten the guard's traditional role of absolute authority; or that cross-examination would somehow weaken the disciplinary process as a vehicle for rehabilitation.

I do not believe that these generalized, speculative, and unsupported theories provide anything close to an adequate basis for denying the accused inmate the right to cross-examine his accusers. The State's arguments immediately lose most of their potential force when it is observed that Nebraska already permits inmates to question the correctional officer who is the charging party with respect to the charges. Moreover, by far the greater weight of correctional authority is that greater procedural fairness in disciplinary proceedings, including permitting confrontation and cross-examination, would enhance rather than impair the disciplinary process as a rehabilitative tool.

> "Time has proved . . . that blind deference to correctional officials does no real service to them. Judicial concern with procedural regularity has a direct bearing upon the maintenance of institutional order; the orderly care with which decisions are made by the prison authority is intimately related to the level of respect with which prisoners regard that authority. There is nothing more corrosive to the fabric of a public institution such as a prison than a feeling among those whom it contains that they are being treated unfairly." *Palmigiano v. Baxter,* 487 F.2d 1280, 1283 (CA1 1973).

As The Chief Justice noted in *Morrissey v. Brewer,* 408 U.S., at 484, "fair treatment . . . will enhance the chance of rehabilitation by avoiding reactions to arbitrariness."

Significantly, a substantial majority of the States do permit confrontation and cross-examination in prison disciplinary proceedings, and their experience simply does not bear out the speculative fears of Nebraska authorities. The vast majority of these States have observed "no noticeable effect on prison security or safety. Furthermore, there was general agreement that the quality of the hearings had been 'upgraded' and that some of the inmate feelings of powerlessness and frustration had been relieved." The only reported complaints have been, not the theoretical problems suggested by petitioners, but that these procedures are time consuming and have slowed down the disciplinary process to some extent. These are small costs to bear to achieve significant gains in procedural fairness.

Thus, in my view, we should recognize that the accused prisoner has a constitutional right to confront and cross-examine adverse witnesses, subject to a limited exception when necessary to protect the identity of a confidential inmate informant. This does not mean that I would not permit the disciplinary board to rely on written reports concerning the charges against a prisoner. Rather, I would think this constitutional right sufficiently protected if the accused had the power to compel the attendance of an adverse witness so that his story can be tested by cross-examination. Again, whenever the right to confront an adverse witness is denied an accused, I would require that this denial and the reasons for it be noted in writing in the record of the proceeding. I would also hold that where it is found necessary to restrict the inmate's right of confrontation, the disciplinary board has the constitutional obligation to call the witness before it *in camera* and itself probe his credibility, rather than accepting the unchallenged and otherwise unchallengeable word of the informer. * * *

The Court next turns to the question of an accused inmate's right to counsel, and quotes a long passage from our decision last Term in *Gagnon v. Scarpelli,* 411 U.S. 778 (1973), in support of its conclusion that appointed counsel need not be provided and retained counsel need not be permitted in prison disciplinary proceedings at this time. The Court seemingly forgets that the holding of *Scarpelli* was that fundamental fairness requires the appointment of counsel in some probation revocation or parole revocation proceedings * * *.

* * * I think it is clear that, at least in those serious disciplinary cases meeting the *Scarpelli* requirements, any inmate who seeks assistance in the preparation of his defense must be constitutionally entitled to have it. But, although for me the question is fraught with great difficulty, I agree with the Court that it would be inappropriate at this time to hold that this assistance must be provided by an appointed member of the bar.[2] There is considerable force to the argument that counsel on either side would be out of place in these disciplinary proceedings, and the practical problems of providing appointed counsel in these proceedings may well be insurmountable. But the controlling consideration for me is my belief that, in light of the types of questions likely to arise in prison discipline cases, counsel substitutes should be

---

2. * * * I would reserve for another day the questions whether the Constitution requires that an inmate able to afford counsel be permitted to bring counsel into the disciplinary hearing, or whether the Constitution allows a State to permit the presence of retained counsel when counsel is not appointed for indigents.

able to provide sufficiently effective assistance to satisfy due process. At least 41 States already provide such counsel substitutes, reflecting the nearly universal recognition that for most inmates, this assistance with the preparation of a defense, particularly as disciplinary hearings become more complex, is absolutely essential. Thus, I would hold that any prisoner is constitutionally entitled to the assistance of a competent fellow inmate or correctional staff member—or, if the institution chooses, such other alternatives as the assistance of law students—to aid in the preparation of his defense.

Finally, the Court addresses the question of the need for an impartial tribunal to hear these prison disciplinary cases. We have recognized that an impartial decisionmaker is a fundamental requirement of due process in a variety of relevant situations, and I would hold this requirement fully applicable here. But in my view there is no constitutional impediment to a disciplinary board composed of responsible prison officials like those on the Adjustment Committee here. While it might well be desirable to have persons from outside the prison system sitting on disciplinary panels, so as to eliminate any possibility that subtle institutional pressures may affect the outcome of disciplinary cases and to avoid any appearance of unfairness, in my view due process is satisfied as long as no member of the disciplinary board has been involved in the investigation or prosecution of the particular case, or has had any other form of personal involvement in the case. * * *

Thus, it is my conclusion that the Court of Appeals was substantially correct in its holding that the minimum due process procedural requirements of *Morrissey v. Brewer* are applicable in the context of prison disciplinary proceedings. To the extent that the Court is willing to tolerate reduced procedural safeguards for accused inmates facing serious punishment which do not meet the standards set out in this opinion, I respectfully dissent.

MR. JUSTICE DOUGLAS, dissenting in part, concurring in the result in part.

* * *

I would start with the presumption that cross-examination of adverse witnesses and confrontation of one's accusers are essential rights which ought always to be available absent any special overriding considerations. * * * The decision as to whether an inmate should be allowed to confront his accusers should not be left to the unchecked and unreviewable discretion of the prison disciplinary board. The argument offered for that result is that the danger of violent response by the inmate against his accusers is great, and that only the prison administrators are in a position to weigh the necessity of secrecy in each case. But it is precisely this unchecked power of prison administrators which is the problem that due process safeguards are required to cure. "Not only the principle of judicial review, but the whole scheme of American government, reflects an institutionalized mistrust of any such unchecked and unbalanced power over essential liberties. That mistrust does not depend on an assumption of inveterate venality or incompetence on the part of men in power . . . ." *Covington v. Harris,* 136 U.S.App.D.C. 35, 39, 419 F.2d 617, 621. Likewise the prisoner should have the right to cross-examine adverse witnesses who testify at the hearing.   *   *   *

* * *

* * * In some circumstances it may be that an informer's identity should be shielded. Yet in criminal trials the rule has been that if the informer's information is crucial to the defense, then the government must choose between revealing his identity and allowing confrontation, or dismissing the charges. *Roviaro v. United States,* 353 U.S. 53. And it is the court, not the prosecutor, who determines the defendant's need for the information. We should no more place the inmate's constitutional rights in the hands of the prison administration's discretion than we should place the defendant's right in the hands of the prosecutor.

* * *

Questions and Points for Discussion

1. Since *Wolff* was decided, a recurring question before the lower courts has been what is a constitutionally adequate statement of the evidence relied on and reasons for the disciplinary action taken. Seeming vacillations in the decisions of the Seventh Circuit Court of Appeals reflect the difficulty which courts have had in resolving this question.

In a series of decisions, different panels of the Seventh Circuit deemed the following statements of the disciplinary decisionmaker to be constitutionally inadequate:

1. "Based on our review of the violation report and the report by the special investigator it is our motion that we find Mr. Hayes guilty as charged. We find that Mr. Hayes is guilty of conspiracy to incite to riot and commit mutinous acts." (Hayes v. Walker, 555 F.2d 625, 631–33 (7th Cir.1977)).

2. "We recognize and consider the resident(')s statement(,) however(,) we accept the reporting officer(')s charges." (Chavis v. Rowe, 643 F.2d 1281, 1286–87 (7th Cir.1981)).

3. "All evidence presented has convinced the committee the resident is guilty of forging a pass or altering a pass, giving false information to a [*sic*] employee and disobeying a prison rule." (Redding v. Fairman, 717 F.2d 1105, 1115–16 (7th Cir.1983)).

According to these decisions, simply referring to unspecified "evidence" as the basis for a guilty finding or, without elaboration, to the charge filed by the reporting officer or to an investigator's report does not adequately fulfill the purposes of the written statement described in *Wolff.*

Subsequent decisions rendered by panels comprised of different Seventh Circuit judges, however, held that the following statements satisfied due process:

1. "Officer Fabry's written statement supports the finding of guilt that an attempt was made by Inmate Saenz to commit battery upon the (other) inmate." (Saenz v. Young, 811 F.2d 1172, 1173–74 (7th Cir.1987)).

2. [Guilty finding based] "on statements in C.R. (conduct report) by Staff in guilt finding that inmate was disrespectful" and "caused disruption by his actions." (Culbert v. Young, 834 F.2d 624, 630–31 (7th Cir.1987)).

In *Culbert,* the court said that "the kind of statements that will satisfy the constitutional minimum will vary from case to case depending on the severity of the charges and the complexity of the factual circumstances and proof offered by both sides." Id. at 631. In that case, since the inmate was found guilty of charges that were not complex and since the only evidence pointing to his innocence was his own protestation of innocence, the Adjustment Committee's statement, according to the court, met the requirements of due process.

In *Saenz,* the court proffered another rationale for its conclusion that the Adjustment Committee's statement comported with due process. The court said as follows:

> A statement of reasons has no particular value in itself. It is instrumental to the goal of making sure that prisoners are not subjected through sloppy procedures to an undue risk of being disciplined for things they have not actually done. As that risk did not materialize here, we find no denial of due process * * *.

Id. at 1174.

Do you agree with the results and reasoning of the court in the *Culbert* and *Saenz* cases? If not, how should the decision of the disciplinary decisionmaker be written in order to comply with the requirements of due process?

2. In *Wolff v. McDonnell,* the Supreme Court observed that prisoners found guilty of a disciplinary infraction are entitled to a " 'written statement by the factfinders as to the evidence relied on *and* reasons' for the disciplinary action." 418 U.S. at 564 (quoting Morrissey v. Brewer, 408 U.S. 471, 489, 92 S.Ct. 2593, 2604 (1972) (emphasis added). The lower courts have differing views on the significance of the Court's reference to the reasons for the disciplinary action taken. Some courts have suggested that the disciplinary decisionmaker must explain why the particular penalty imposed is considered appropriate and warranted. See, e.g., Redding v. Fairman, 717 F.2d 1105, 1115 n. 4 (7th Cir.1983) (statement must reveal reasons for type as well as amount of punishment imposed). Other courts have required such an explanation only when the sanction imposed on the prisoner is much more severe than the penalty imposed on other prisoners found guilty of committing the same offense. See, e.g., Ivey v. Wilson, 577 F.Supp. 169, 173 (W.D.Ky.1983). Still other courts do not require the disciplinary decisionmaker to explain and defend the actual penalty imposed. These courts consider the constitutional requirement that the disciplinary decisionmaker explain in writing why the disciplinary action was taken satisfied as long as the written decision recounts the factual

basis for the guilty finding, i.e., what it is that the prisoner actually did that constituted a violation of the prison's rules or regulations. See, e.g., Harmon v. Auger, 768 F.2d 270, 276 (8th Cir.1985).

3. Is a prison policy under which an inmate's requested witnesses are generally barred from appearing at a disciplinary hearing, but written statements obtained from the witnesses are admitted in evidence constitutional? What if the policy only applies to witnesses confined in the prison's segregation unit? See Devaney v. Hall, 509 F.Supp. 497 (D.Mass.1981) (across-the-board policy barring live testimony from witnesses confined in segregation unit is constitutional).

4. In Pino v. Dalsheim, 605 F.Supp. 1305 (S.D.N.Y.1984), the inmate-plaintiff challenged on due process grounds a hearing officer's refusal to permit several inmates to testify on the plaintiff's behalf at a disciplinary hearing. The plaintiff had been charged with a number of disciplinary offenses after yelling at and threatening a correctional officer. According to the plaintiff, his witnesses would have testified that he was provoked by the correctional officer, who had been taunting and hassling him. Written statements recounting this provocation were obtained from the witnesses and admitted at the disciplinary hearing.

The district court found no due process violation. After noting that the witnesses' expected testimony concerned the question whether there were mitigating circumstances surrounding the plaintiff's commission of the disciplinary offense, the court observed that the right to call witnesses at disciplinary hearings is confined to witnesses who can testify on the issue of the inmate's guilt or innocence of the disciplinary infraction. The right does not encompass witnesses whose testimony only bears on the question of the appropriate penalty to be imposed. Obtaining a written statement from the latter type of witness will, according to the court, normally satisfy due process.

5. In Ponte v. Real, 471 U.S. 491, 105 S.Ct. 2192 (1985), the Supreme Court revisited an issue which had been at least partially addressed in *Wolff*. The issue was whether due process required support or reasons for a disciplinary committee's decision not to permit a witness to testify before it to appear in the administrative record. The Court, in an opinion written by Justice Rehnquist, reaffirmed its conclusion in *Wolff* that a disciplinary committee does not, at the time of the disciplinary hearing, have to explain its reason for not calling a witness. Nor need the administrative record otherwise contain support for the disciplinary committee's decision. If a prisoner, however, later contests in court the decision not to permit a witness to testify at the disciplinary hearing, due process requires that the committee then explain, at least "in a limited manner," the basis for its decision. Id. at 497, 105 S.Ct. at 2196. If necessary to protect institutional security or other "paramount interests," however, the reasons for not calling a witness before the disciplinary committee can be presented to the court *in camera*.

The Court in *Ponte* made the following observation in the course of its opinion:

> The requirement that contemporaneous reasons for denying witnesses and evidence be given admittedly has some appeal, and it may

commend itself to prison officials as a matter of choice: recollections of the event will be fresher at the moment, and it seems a more lawyer-like way to do things. But the primary business of prisons is the supervision of inmates, and it may well be that those charged with this responsibility feel that the additional administrative burdens which would be occasioned by such a requirement detract from the ability to perform the principal mission of the institution.

Id. at 497–98, 105 S.Ct. at 2196–97.

Justice Marshall, joined by Justice Brennan in a dissenting opinion, disagreed that due process permitted the decision whether or not to give contemporaneous reasons for refusing to call a witness to be remitted to the discretion of the disciplinary committee. Concluding that "*post hoc* court-room rationalizations" could not possibly satisfy due process, Justice Marshall emphasized the ease with which a disciplinary committee could record its reasons for not calling a witness at the time the decision was made. And if institutional security would be imperilled by divulging this reason to the inmate charged with a disciplinary infraction, that part of the record could simply be kept confidential.

With whose views do you agree—the majority's or the dissenters'?

6. How specific must a disciplinary committee's explanation of its reasons for barring a witness from testifying at a disciplinary hearing be in order to satisfy due process? Would a statement that calling the witness would jeopardize institutional security suffice?

7. In *Wolff,* the Supreme Court outlined two instances when an inmate has a right to assistance in preparing and presenting a defense to a disciplinary charge: (1) when the inmate is illiterate, and (2) when the case is sufficiently complex that it is unlikely that the inmate could adequately mount a defense without such assistance. Are there any other circumstances which would, in your opinion, give rise to a constitutional right to assistance?

8. In Redding v. Fairman, 717 F.2d 1105 (7th Cir.1983), the Seventh Circuit Court of Appeals discussed prisoners' due process right to have their guilt or innocence of a disciplinary infraction adjudicated by a "sufficiently impartial" decisionmaker. The prisoner-plaintiff in that case contended that this right was automatically violated when an Adjustment Committee found him guilty of a number of disciplinary offenses, since one member of that committee was a defendant in a civil rights suit filed by the plaintiff and pending in court at the time the Adjustment Committee rendered its guilty findings. The court of appeals disagreed:

> Although the requirement of a "neutral and detached" decisionmaker must not be impaired, disqualification is not necessary in every case. * * * A prisoners' rights lawsuit often includes several defendants, some of whom may not know the plaintiff. Moreover, if an Adjustment Committee member is a defendant in the unrelated action named in her or his administrative capacity for performing ministerial duties, then the Committee member may have little personal involvement in the case. Under these circumstances, the Committee member's ability to serve as a neutral and detached decisionmaker at a hearing involving the plaintiff-prisoner may not be impaired, and

disqualification may not be necessary. From a practical standpoint, requiring each staff member who is the subject of a separate lawsuit to disqualify himself from sitting in judgment of that inmate would heavily tax the working capacity of the prison staff. Additionally, prisoners may file many lawsuits naming multiple defendants. If every named defendant in a prisoners' rights lawsuit must be disqualified from sitting on the Adjustment Committee, such a litigation strategy would vest too much control in a prisoner to determine the Committee make-up. For these reasons, the disqualification issue should be decided on a case-by-case basis.

Id. at 1112–13.

The following remarks of Judge George Fagg rendered in the midst of a concurring and dissenting opinion in the case of Malek v. Camp, 822 F.2d 812 (8th Cir.1987) reflect a different approach to the problem discussed in *Redding:*

> Malek's discipline was upheld by an appeals board. While such a circumstance would be irrelevant in a case involving a court adjudication, I do not believe the same conclusion should follow in the case of prison disciplinary proceedings. The Supreme Court has recognized that "one cannot automatically apply procedural rules designed for free citizens in an open society * * * to the very different situation presented by a [prison] disciplinary proceeding."
>
> I believe a prison disciplinary hearing and the accompanying administrative review should be considered a unitary proceeding. Due process would then depend not on the internal integrity of distinct trial and appellate tiers but on the fairness of prison disciplinary procedures taken as a whole. Specifically, there would be no prejudice from a biased decisionmaker, and no constitutional violation, if a neutral appeals board found in the record the minimal "some evidence" needed to sustain the prison disciplinary action.

Id. at 817 (Fagg, J., concurring and dissenting).

How would you reconcile the due process right to a relatively unbiased disciplinary decisionmaker with the reality of litigious prisoners, many of whom appear with regularity before disciplinary decisionmakers whom they subsequently sue?

Eleven years after the Supreme Court decided *Wolff v. McDonnell,* the Court recognized another procedural due process right that prisoners have during at least some prison disciplinary proceedings. In *Walpole v. Hill,* the case which follows, the Court discussed that right.

SUPERINTENDENT, MASSACHUSETTS CORRECTIONAL INSTITUTION, WALPOLE v. HILL

Supreme Court of the United States, 1985.
472 U.S. 445, 105 S.Ct. 2768, 86 L.Ed.2d 356.

JUSTICE O'CONNOR delivered the opinion of the Court.

* * *

Respondents Gerald Hill and Joseph Crawford are inmates at a state prison in Walpole, Mass. In May 1982, they each received prison disciplinary reports charging them with assaulting another inmate. At separate hearings for each inmate, a prison disciplinary board heard testimony from a prison guard, Sergeant Maguire, and received his written disciplinary report. According to the testimony and report, Maguire heard an inmate twice say loudly, "What's going on?" The voice came from a walkway that Maguire could partially observe through a window. Maguire immediately opened the door to the walkway and found an inmate named Stephens bleeding from the mouth and suffering from a swollen eye. Dirt was strewn about the walkway, and Maguire viewed this to be further evidence of a scuffle. He saw three inmates, including respondents, jogging away together down the walkway. There were no other inmates in the area, which was enclosed by a chain link fence. Maguire concluded that one or more of the three inmates had assaulted Stephens and that they had acted as a group. Maguire also testified at Hill's hearing that a prison "medic" had told him that Stephens had been beaten. Hill and Crawford each declared their innocence before the disciplinary board, and Stephens gave written statements that the other inmates had not caused his injuries.

After hearing the evidence in each case, the disciplinary board found respondents guilty of violating prison regulations based on their involvement in the assault. The board recommended that Hill and Romano each lose 100 days of good time and be confined in isolation for 15 days. Respondents unsuccessfully appealed the board's action to the superintendent of the prison. They then filed a complaint in the Superior Court, State of Massachusetts, alleging that the decisions of the board violated their constitutional rights because "there was no evidence to confirm that the incident took place nor was there any evidence to state that if the incident did take place the [respondents] were involved." After reviewing the record, the Superior Court concluded that "the Board's finding of guilty rested, in each case, on no evidence constitutionally adequate to support that finding." The Superior Court granted summary judgment for respondents and ordered that the findings of the disciplinary board be voided and the lost good time restored.

The Massachusetts Supreme Judicial Court affirmed. * * *

* * *

The issue we address is whether findings of a prison disciplinary board that result in the loss of good time credits must be supported by a certain amount of evidence in order to satisfy due process. * * *

* * *

The requirements of due process are flexible and depend on a balancing of the interests affected by the relevant government action. Where a prisoner has a liberty interest in good time credits, the loss of such credits threatens his prospective freedom from confinement by extending the length of imprisonment. Thus the inmate has a strong interest in assuring that the loss of good time credits is not imposed arbitrarily. This interest, however, must be accommodated in the distinctive setting of a prison, where disciplinary proceedings "take place in a closed, tightly controlled environment peopled by those who have chosen to violate the criminal law and who have been lawfully incarcerated for doing so." Consequently, in identifying the safeguards required by due process, the Court has recognized the legitimate institutional needs of assuring the safety of inmates and prisoners, avoiding burdensome administrative requirements that might be susceptible to manipulation, and preserving the disciplinary process as a means of rehabilitation.

Requiring a modicum of evidence to support a decision to revoke good time credits will help to prevent arbitrary deprivations without threatening institutional interests or imposing undue administrative burdens. * * * Because the written statement mandated by *Wolff* requires a disciplinary board to explain the evidence relied upon, recognizing that due process requires some evidentiary basis for a decision to revoke good time credits will not impose significant new burdens on proceedings within the prison. Nor does it imply that a disciplinary board's factual findings or decisions with respect to appropriate punishment are subject to second-guessing upon review.

We hold that the requirements of due process are satisfied if some evidence supports the decision by the prison disciplinary board to revoke good time credits. This standard is met if "there was some evidence from which the conclusion of the administrative tribunal could be deduced . . . ." Ascertaining whether this standard is satisfied does not require examination of the entire record, independent assessment of the credibility of witnesses, or weighing of the evidence. Instead, the relevant question is whether there is any evidence in the record that could support the conclusion reached by the disciplinary board. We decline to adopt a more stringent evidentiary standard as a constitutional requirement. Prison disciplinary proceedings take place in a highly charged atmosphere, and prison administrators must often act swiftly on the basis of evidence that might be insufficient in less exigent circumstances. The fundamental fairness guaranteed by the Due Process Clause does not require courts to set aside decisions of prison administrators that have some basis in fact. Revocation of good time credits is not comparable to a criminal conviction, and neither the amount of evidence necessary to support such a conviction nor any other standard greater than some evidence applies in this context.

Turning to the facts of this case, we conclude that the evidence before the disciplinary board was sufficient to meet the requirements imposed by the Due Process Clause. The disciplinary board received evidence in the form of testimony from the prison guard and copies of his written report. That evidence indicated that the guard heard some commotion and, upon investigating, discovered an inmate who evidently had just been assaulted. The guard saw three other inmates fleeing together down an enclosed walkway. No other inmates were in the area. The Supreme Judicial Court found that this evidence was constitutionally insufficient because it did not support an inference that more than one person had struck the victim or that either of the respondents was the assailant or otherwise participated in the assault. This conclusion, however, misperceives the nature of the evidence required by the Due Process Clause.

The Federal Constitution does not require evidence that logically precludes any conclusion but the one reached by the disciplinary board. Instead, due process in this context requires only that there be some evidence to support the findings made in the disciplinary hearing. Although the evidence in this case might be characterized as meager, and there was no direct evidence identifying any one of three inmates as the assailant, the record is not so devoid of evidence that the findings of the disciplinary board were without support or otherwise arbitrary. Respondents relied only upon the Federal Constitution, and did not claim that the disciplinary board's findings failed to meet evidentiary standards imposed by state law. Because the determination of the disciplinary board was not so lacking in evidentiary support as to violate due process, the judgment of the Supreme Judicial Court is reversed, and the case is remanded for further proceedings not inconsistent with this opinion.

* * *

[Justice Stevens, joined by Justices Brennan and Marshall, wrote an opinion concurring in part and dissenting in part. Believing that the Massachusetts Attorney General had improperly petitioned for certiorari, Justice Stevens disagreed with the Court's decision to review this case, but agreed that the "some evidence" standard adopted by the Court was the appropriate one.]

Questions and Points for Discussion

1. Assume that an inmate was charged with a number of disciplinary infractions, including extortion. The notice apprising the inmate of the charges stated as follows: "Information has been received from various confidential sources, that during the months of June, July and August, 1980, while confined in [Marion] you pressured other inmates to pay you commissary and perform homosexual acts with you. You applied this pressure by threat of harm to their person or their friends." The inmate was not provided with any additional details about the alleged offense on the grounds that to do so would jeopardize the lives and safety of the informants.

A prison investigator spoke with the informants and submitted an unsworn report to the disciplinary committee summarizing their statements to the investigator. The informants themselves did not appear before the committee.

Relying on the investigator's report, the disciplinary committee found the inmate guilty of the offense charged. After basically repeating the contents of the notice previously given to the inmate, the committee added in its report finding the inmate guilty: "Information received from confidential sources has proven reliable in the past."

Was the inmate afforded due process of law? Why or why not? See McCollum v. Miller, 695 F.2d 1044 (7th Cir.1982) (*McCollum I*) and McCollum v. Williford, 793 F.2d 903 (7th Cir.1986) (*McCollum II*). For other cases discussing the interplay between the use of confidential information in prison disciplinary proceedings and due process, see Hensley v. Wilson, 850 F.2d 269 (6th Cir.1988) and Wells v. Israel, 854 F.2d 995 (7th Cir.1988).

2. Under a state statute or regulation, the standard of proof which must be met before an inmate can be found guilty of a disciplinary infraction may be greater than the minimum constitutional threshold set forth in *Hill*. See, e.g., Mich.Comp.Laws § 791.255(4) ("substantial evidence"). A state prisoner might also be able to argue that the state constitution imposes a heavier burden of proof in prison disciplinary proceedings.

3. There are other state-created rights which inmates have during prison disciplinary proceedings which go beyond the constitutional baseline. See, e.g., Mich.Comp.Laws § 791.251(4) (hearings officer must be an attorney); 28 C.F.R. § 541.15(i) (all inmates have the right to assistance from a staff representative at disciplinary hearings). Other than the rights set forth in *Wolff*, what additional rights, if any, do you believe should be accorded inmates during prison disciplinary proceedings?

The American Bar Association Standards Relating to the Legal Status of Prisoners (1981) suggest that the following procedural safeguards attend prison disciplinary proceedings:

STANDARD 23–3.1.

RULES OF CONDUCT

(a) Correctional authorities should promulgate clear written rules for prisoner conduct. These rules and implementing criteria should include:

(i) a specific definition of offenses, the differentiation of offenses into "minor" and "major" categories, a statement that the least severe punishment appropriate to each offense should be imposed, and a schedule indicating the minimum and maximum possible punishment for each offense, proportionate to the offense; and

(ii) specific criteria and procedures for prison discipline and classification decisions, including decisions involving security status and work and housing assignments.

(b) A personal copy of the rules for each prisoner and an oral summary of their substance, in all languages spoken by a significant number of prisoners, should be provided upon entry to the institution.

STANDARD 23–3.2.

DISCIPLINARY HEARING PROCEDURES

(a) *Minor Rule Violation.* At a hearing concerning violation of a "minor" rule, the prisoner should be entitled to:

(i) written notice of the charge, in a language he or she understands, within [72] hours of the time he or she is suspected of having committed an offense; within another [24] hours the prisoner should be given copies of any written information which the tribunal may consider;

(ii) a hearing within [72] hours of the time the written notice of the charge was received;

(iii) be present and speak on his or her own behalf;

(iv) a written decision based upon a preponderance of the evidence, with specified reasons. The decision should be rendered promptly and in all cases within [5] days after conclusion of the hearing; and

(v) appeal, within [5] days, to the chief executive officer of the institution, and the right to a written decision by that officer within [30] days, based upon a written summary of the hearing, any documentary evidence considered at the hearing, and the prisoner's written reason for appealing. The chief executive officer should either affirm or reverse the determination of misconduct and decrease or approve the punishment imposed. Execution of the punishment should be suspended during the appeal.

(b) *Major Rule Violation.* At a hearing concerning violation of a "major" rule, in addition to the requirements of subsection (a), the prisoner should be entitled to:

(i) compel the attendance of any person within the prison community who has relevant information; and

(ii) examine or cross-examine witnesses except when the hearing officer(s):

(A) exclude testimony as unduly cumulative; or

(B) receive testimony outside the presence of the prisoner pursuant to a written finding that the physical safety of a person would be endangered by disclosure of his or her identity.

(c) Disciplinary hearings should be conducted by one or more impartial persons.

(d) Unless the prisoner is found guilty, no record relating to the charge should be retained in the prisoner's file or used against him or her in any way.

(e) Where necessary as an emergency matter, pending the hearing required by subsection (b), correctional authorities may confine separately a prisoner alleged to have committed a "major" rule violation. This emergency pre-hearing confinement should not extend more than

[48] hours unless necessitated by the prisoner's request for a continuance, in which case another [24] hours delay is permissible.

(f) In the event of a situation requiring the chief executive officer to declare all, or a part, of an institution to be in a state of emergency, the rights provided in this section may be temporarily suspended for up to [24] hours after the emergency has terminated.

STANDARD 23–3.3.

CRIMINAL MISCONDUCT

(a) Where a prisoner is alleged to have engaged in conduct which would be a criminal offense under state or federal law, the prosecutor should be notified and, in consultation with the chief executive officer, should determine promptly whether to charge the prisoner. Institutional proceedings arising from the same conduct need not be suspended while the decision to charge is being made, nor while resolution of the charge is pending. However, correctional authorities should exercise caution in conducting institutional proceedings so that the right of the public and of the prisoner to a fair criminal trial is not infringed.

(b) If required by institutional order and security, the prisoner to be charged criminally may be confined in his or her assigned quarters or in a more secure housing unit for no more than [90] days, unless during that time an indictment or information is brought against him or her. If a charge is made he or she may be so confined until the criminal proceeding is resolved.

(c) After disposition of the criminal charge, the prisoner may be reclassified. He or she also may be subjected to disciplinary proceedings if they were suspended during the prosecution.

4. Even with respect to rights derived from the United States Constitution, some lower courts have held that prisoners have rights during prison disciplinary proceedings in addition to those delineated in *Wolff*. Several courts, for example, have noted that prisoners have a constitutional right to be apprised of the rules or regulations whose violation will lead to the imposition of punishment. See, e.g., Noren v. Straw, 578 F.Supp. 1, 6 (D.Mont.1982); Duckett v. Ward, 458 F.Supp. 624, 626 (S.D.N.Y.1978). Others have recognized an inmate's due process right to be informed by the disciplinary committee of exculpatory information of which it is aware. See, e.g., Chavis v. Rowe, 643 F.2d 1281, 1285–86 (7th Cir.1981) (Adjustment Committee should have disclosed to plaintiff-inmate, who was charged with stabbing a correctional officer, the results of a polygraph test administered to an inmate who was apparently telling the truth when he identified someone other than the plaintiff as the assailant).

What other constitutional rights in your opinion, if any, extend to prisoners during disciplinary proceedings?

B. MIRANDA, THE PRIVILEGE AGAINST SELF-INCRIMINATION, AND THE SIXTH AMENDMENT RIGHT TO COUNSEL IN THE PRISON CONTEXT

Questions and Points for Discussion

DOES NOT HAVE TO SPEAK

1. In Miranda v. Arizona, 384 U.S. 436, 86 S.Ct. 1602 (1966), the Supreme Court held that for statements obtained during custodial interrogation to be admissible in a criminal prosecution, individuals questioned by a government official must have been apprised of the following before they were interrogated: that they had the right to remain silent, that anything they said could subsequently be used against them in a court of law, that they had the right to consult an attorney and to have the attorney present during the interrogation, and that if they could not afford an attorney, one would be appointed to represent them.

The question arises whether an inmate must be given these *Miranda* warnings before being questioned about a disciplinary offense which is also a crime, such as an assault or a theft, that the inmate is suspected of having committed. In Baxter v. Palmigiano, 425 U.S. 308, 96 S.Ct. 1551 (1976), the Supreme Court noted that the failure to comply with the dictates of *Miranda* only affects the admissibility of statements in criminal cases. If an inmate is therefore questioned by a correctional officer or disciplinary committee about the circumstances surrounding the inmate's suspected or alleged commission of a disciplinary offense, the inmate's responses can properly be considered during a disciplinary hearing, regardless of whether the inmate was given *Miranda* warnings before the questioning occurred.

More difficult is the question whether the inmate's answers are admissible in court to prove that the inmate is guilty of a crime with which he or she is charged. In answering this question, the Supreme Court's decision in Mathis v. United States, 391 U.S. 1, 88 S.Ct. 1503 (1968) must be considered. *Mathis* concerned an inmate who, while incarcerated in a state prison for a state crime, was questioned by an IRS agent about suspected criminal tax violations. The IRS agent did not apprise the inmate of his *Miranda* rights before questioning him, and the inmate made incriminating statements to the agent. His statements were later admitted in evidence to help secure his conviction for criminal tax fraud.

The Supreme Court held that since the inmate was in custody when he was questioned by the IRS agent, the interrogation should have been preceded by the giving of *Miranda* warnings. Consequently, the inmate's statement should not have been admitted during his criminal trial.

The Supreme Court distinguished *Mathis* in Illinois v. Perkins, 110 S.Ct. 2394 (1990). In *Perkins,* an undercover police officer was placed in the same jail cell with the defendant, who was awaiting trial for aggravated battery. The undercover agent then questioned the defendant about a murder that the defendant was suspected of having committed, and the defendant made some incriminating statements. The Supreme Court held that the defendant's statements could be used against him in his subsequent trial for murder even though the undercover agent did not give the defendant the *Miranda* warnings before questioning him. The Court held that the concerns that prompted the Court's ruling in *Miranda* —that a defendant's will might be overborne by the coercive influences exerted on him in a "police-dominated atmosphere"—simply were not present when the defendant was being asked questions by someone that he believed to be just an inmate.

In the course of its opinion in *Perkins,* the Supreme Court made the following potentially telling observation: "The bare fact of custody may not in every instance require a warning even when the suspect is aware that he is speaking to an official, but we do not have occasion to explore that issue here." Id. at 2398. Some lower courts have agreed with this observation, holding that inmates need not invariably be given *Miranda* warnings when prison staff members question them about criminal conduct. See e.g., United States v. Conley, 779 F.2d 970 (4th Cir.1985); Cervantes v. Walker, 589 F.2d 424 (9th Cir.1978). These courts have distinguished *Mathis* on the grounds that the inmate in *Mathis* was subjected to coercive pressures sufficient to trigger the protections of *Miranda* because he was questioned by an outside government investigator.

2. The Supreme Court has held that a disciplinary committee can constitutionally consider an inmate's silence during a disciplinary hearing as evidence of the inmate's guilt of the alleged disciplinary infraction. Baxter v. Palmigiano, 425 U.S. 308, 96 S.Ct. 1551 (1976). In *Baxter,* the disciplinary committee had informed the inmate that his silence could be used against him.

The Supreme Court noted that not all pressures placed by the government upon an individual to speak violate the privilege against self-incrimination. At the same time, however, the Court emphasized that under the law of the state in which the inmate was incarcerated, an inmate's silence was not enough evidence by itself to support a guilty finding.

Do you agree with the Court's ruling in *Baxter?* How will it affect inmates confronted with disciplinary charges?

3. Separate and apart from the right to have counsel present during custodial interrogation, which was discussed in *Miranda,* is the sixth amendment right to counsel. The sixth amendment provides in part that "[i]n all criminal prosecutions, the accused shall enjoy the right * * * to have the assistance of Counsel for his defense."

In United States v. Gouveia, 467 U.S. 180, 104 S.Ct. 2292 (1984), the Supreme Court discussed the relationship between the sixth amendment right to counsel and actions taken by prison officials to maintain security and punish inmate misconduct. In that case, six inmates were suspected of the murders of fellow inmates. Each was placed in administrative detention and remained there for an extended period of time, approximately nineteen months, before they were eventually indicted on criminal charges. While the inmates were segregated, disciplinary hearings were held, and all of the inmates were found guilty of participating in the murders.

All of the inmates were eventually also convicted on murder charges. On appeal, the defendants argued that because they were confined in administrative segregation, the extended delay between the commission of the crimes and their indictments without appointment of counsel violated their sixth amendment right to counsel.

The Ninth Circuit Court of Appeals agreed, reasoning that an inmate segregated for more than ninety days while a felony is being investigated has been effectively "accused" of a crime, thereby triggering the protections of the sixth amendment right to counsel. Consequently, according to the court of appeals, indigent inmates isolated in administrative detention while the subject of felony investigations must be afforded counsel after ninety days or else be released back into the prison population, in order to ensure that they or their lawyers will be able to take the investigatory steps necessary to preserve their defense at trial.

The Supreme Court, in a majority opinion by Justice Rehnquist, reversed. The Court emphasized that the purpose of the sixth amendment right to counsel is to protect the defendant once the government has committed itself to prosecute the defendant. Not until the government has made this commitment—one manifested through the filing of a formal charge or information, the return of an indictment, or the holding of an arraignment or a preliminary hearing—is the defendant "faced with the prosecutorial forces of organized society, and immersed in the intricacies of substantive and procedural criminal law." Id. at 189, 104 S.Ct. at 2298 (quoting Kirby v. Illinois, 406 U.S. 682, 689, 92 S.Ct. 1877, 1882 (1972)).

To the inmates' arguments that while in segregation, they needed the assistance of counsel to avert prejudice which they might otherwise suffer because of the prosecutor's delay in bringing charges against them, the Court responded

> that the concern is that because an inmate suspected of a crime is already in prison, the prosecution may have little incentive promptly to bring formal charges against him, and that the resulting preindictment delay may be particularly prejudicial to the inmate, given the problems inherent in investigating prison crimes, such as the transient nature of the prison population and the general reluctance of inmates to cooperate. But applicable statutes of limitations protect against the prosecution's bringing stale criminal charges against any defendant, and, beyond that protection, the Fifth Amendment requires the dismissal of an indictment, even if it is brought within the statute of limitations, if the defendant can prove that the Government's delay in bringing the indictment was a deliberate device to gain an advantage over him and that it caused him actual prejudice in presenting his defense. Those protections apply to criminal defendants within and without the prison walls, and we decline to depart from our traditional interpretation of the Sixth Amendment right to counsel in order to provide additional protections for respondents here.

Id. at 192, 104 S.Ct. at 2299–2300. Justice Marshall dissented.

Chapter 12

CLASSIFICATION, TRANSFER,
AND WITHHOLDING OF
PRIVILEGES

A. PROCEDURAL DUE PROCESS

After an individual is sentenced to prison, correctional officers must then make a number of decisions concerning that individual. To what prison should the individual be sent? In what section of that prison should the individual be housed? To what work or school programs, if any, should the individual be assigned? And the list goes on.

Throughout a person's incarceration in prison, decisions will continue to be made which may affect both the location and the conditions of the inmate's confinement. The inmate may, for example, be transferred from one prison to another, perhaps to a prison which is more dilapidated and has fewer amenities than the prison in which the inmate was initially confined. Or the inmate may be placed in an administrative segregation unit where privileges are few and confinement in one's cell for almost twenty-four hours a day is the norm. Or the inmate may be removed from a work assignment or lose other privileges because of a concern that the inmate will abuse the privileges, causing disruption within the institution.

As with all decisions, there is the risk that correctional officials will mistakenly make decisions adversely affecting a prisoner. Perhaps a decision will be grounded on misinformation or even no information; or perhaps a decision will stem from personal animosity directed against a particular prisoner. One question which therefore arises is whether prison officials are constitutionally obliged to take steps to reduce the risk of error when making decisions having an immediate and negative impact on individual prisoners. This question was addressed by the Supreme Court in the case which follows.

MEACHUM v. FANO

Supreme Court of the United States, 1976.
427 U.S. 215, 96 S.Ct. 2532, 49 L.Ed.2d 451.

[After a number of fires were started at the Massachusetts Correctional Institution at Norfolk, a medium-security prison, several prisoners were transferred to Bridgewater, a prison with both maximum and medium-security units, and Walpole, a maximum-security prison with much more onerous conditions of confinement than those at Norfolk. The prisoners then filed a § 1983 suit, contending that their transfers were effected without due process of law. The district court agreed, holding that the prisoners were entitled to the procedural safeguards set forth in *Wolff v. McDonnell,* 418 U.S. 539, 94 S.Ct. 2963 (1974), *supra* page 346, before their transfers. The First Circuit Court of Appeals affirmed.]

MR. JUSTICE WHITE delivered the opinion of the Court.

* * *

The Fourteenth Amendment prohibits any State from depriving a person of life, liberty, or property without due process of law. The initial inquiry is whether the transfer of respondents from Norfolk to Walpole and Bridgewater infringed or implicated a "liberty" interest of respondents within the meaning of the Due Process Clause. Contrary to the Court of Appeals, we hold that it did not. We reject at the outset the notion that *any* grievous loss visited upon a person by the State is sufficient to invoke the procedural protections of the Due Process Clause. In *Board of Regents v. Roth,* 408 U.S. 564 (1972), a university professor was deprived of his job, a loss which was surely a matter of great substance, but because the professor had no property interest in his position, due process procedures were not required in connection with his dismissal. We there held that the determining factor is the nature of the interest involved rather than its weight.

Similarly, we cannot agree that *any* change in the conditions of confinement having a substantial adverse impact on the prisoner involved is sufficient to invoke the protections of the Due Process Clause. The Due Process Clause by its own force forbids the State from convicting any person of [a] crime and depriving him of his liberty without complying fully with the requirements of the Clause. But given a valid conviction, the criminal defendant has been constitutionally deprived of his liberty to the extent that the State may confine him and subject him to the rules of its prison system so long as the conditions of confinement do not otherwise violate the Constitution. The Constitution does not require that the State have more than one prison for convicted felons; nor does it guarantee that the convicted prisoner will be placed in any particular prison if, as is likely, the State has more than one correctional institution. The initial decision to assign the convict to a particular institution is not subject to audit under the Due Process Clause, although the degree of confinement in one prison may be quite different from that in another. The conviction has sufficiently extinguished the defendant's liberty interest to empower the State to confine him in *any* of its prisons.

Neither, in our view, does the Due Process Clause in and of itself protect a duly convicted prisoner against transfer from one institution to another within the state prison system. Confinement in any of the State's institutions is within the normal limits or range of custody which the conviction has authorized the State to impose. That life in one prison is much more disagreeable than in another does not in itself signify that a Fourteenth Amendment liberty interest is implicated when a prisoner is transferred to the institution with the more severe rules.

* * * [T]o hold as we are urged to do that *any* substantial deprivation imposed by prison authorities triggers the procedural protections of the Due Process Clause would subject to judicial review a wide spectrum of discretionary actions that traditionally have been the business of prison administrators rather than of the federal courts.

Transfers between institutions, for example, are made for a variety of reasons and often involve no more than informed predictions as to what would best serve institutional security or the safety and welfare of the inmate. Yet under the approach urged here, any transfer, for whatever reason, would require a hearing as long as it could be said that the transfer would place the prisoner in substantially more burdensome conditions tha[n] he had been experiencing. We are unwilling to go so far.

Wolff v. McDonnell, on which the Court of Appeals heavily relied, is not to the contrary. Under that case, the Due Process Clause entitles a state prisoner to certain procedural protections when he is deprived of good-time credits because of serious misconduct. But the liberty interest there identified did not originate in the Constitution, which "itself does not guarantee good-time credit for satisfactory behavior while in prison." The State itself, not the Constitution, had "not only provided a statutory right to good time but also specifies that it is to be forfeited only for serious misbehavior." * * *

Here, Massachusetts law conferred no right on the prisoner to remain in the prison to which he was initially assigned, defeasible only upon proof of specific acts of misconduct. Insofar as we are advised, transfers between Massachusetts prisons are not conditioned upon the occurrence of specified events.[7] On the contrary, transfer in a wide

---

7. At the time the transfers in this case occurred, Massachusetts General Laws Annotated, c. 127, § 97 (1974) provided as follows:

* * *

"§ 97. Transfers from and to correctional institutions; approval

"The commissioner may transfer any sentenced prisoner from one correctional institution of the commonwealth to another, and with the approval of the sheriff of the county from any such institution except a prisoner serving a life sentence to any jail or house of correction or a sentenced prisoner from any jail or house of correction, to any such institution except the state prison, or from any jail or house of correction to any other jail or house of

variety of circumstances is vested in prison officials. The predicate for invoking the protection of the Fourteenth Amendment as construed and applied in *Wolff v. McDonnell* is totally nonexistent in this case.

Even if Massachusetts has not represented that transfers will occur only on the occurrence of certain events, it is argued that charges of serious misbehavior, as in this case, often initiate and heavily influence the transfer decision and that because allegations of misconduct may be erroneous, hearings should be held before transfer to a more confining institution is to be suffered by the prisoner. That an inmate's conduct, in general or in specific instances, may often be a major factor in the decision of prison officials to transfer him is to be expected unless it be assumed that transfers are mindless events. A prisoner's past and anticipated future behavior will very likely be taken into account in selecting a prison in which he will be initially incarcerated or to which he will be transferred to best serve the State's penological goals.

A prisoner's behavior may precipitate a transfer; and absent such behavior, perhaps transfer would not take place at all. But, as we have said, Massachusetts prison officials have the discretion to transfer prisoners for any number of reasons. Their discretion is not limited to instances of serious misconduct. As we understand it no legal interest or right of these respondents under Massachusetts law would have been violated by their transfer whether or not their misconduct had been proved in accordance with procedures that might be required by the Due Process Clause in other circumstances. Whatever expectation the prisoner may have in remaining at a particular prison so long as he behaves himself, it is too ephemeral and insubstantial to trigger procedural due process protections as long as prison officials have discretion to transfer him for whatever reason or for no reason at all.

Holding that arrangements like this are within reach of the procedural protections of the Due Process Clause would place the Clause astride the day-to-day functioning of state prisons and involve the judiciary in issues and discretionary decisions that are not the business of federal judges. We decline to so interpret and apply the Due Process Clause. The federal courts do not sit to supervise state prisons, the administration of which is of acute interest to the States. The individual States, of course, are free to follow another course, whether by statute, by rule or regulation, or by interpretation of their own constitutions. They may thus decide that prudent prison administration requires pretransfer hearings. Our holding is that the Due Process Clause does not impose a nationwide rule mandating transfer hearings.

The judgment of the Court of Appeals accordingly is

Reversed.

MR. JUSTICE STEVENS, with whom MR. JUSTICE BRENNAN and MR. JUSTICE MARSHALL join, dissenting.

correction. Prisoners so removed shall be subject to the terms of their original sentences and to the provisions of law governing parole from the correctional institutions of the commonwealth."

The Court's rationale is more disturbing than its narrow holding. If the Court had merely held that the transfer of a prisoner from one penal institution to another does not cause a sufficiently grievous loss to amount to a deprivation of liberty within the meaning of the Due Process Clause of the Fourteenth Amendment, I would disagree with the conclusion but not with the constitutional analysis. The Court's holding today, however, appears to rest on a conception of "liberty" which I consider fundamentally incorrect.

The Court indicates that a "liberty interest" may have either of two sources. According to the Court, a liberty interest may "originate in the Constitution," or it may have "its roots in state law." Apart from those two possible origins, the Court is unable to find that a person has a constitutionally protected interest in liberty.

If man were a creature of the State, the analysis would be correct. But neither the Bill of Rights nor the laws of sovereign States create the liberty which the Due Process Clause protects. The relevant constitutional provisions are limitations on the power of the sovereign to infringe on the liberty of the citizen. The relevant state laws either create property rights, or they curtail the freedom of the citizen who must live in an ordered society. Of course, law is essential to the exercise and enjoyment of individual liberty in a complex society. But it is not the source of liberty, and surely not the exclusive source.

I had thought it self-evident that all men were endowed by their Creator with liberty as one of the cardinal unalienable rights. It is that basic freedom which the Due Process Clause protects, rather than the particular rights or privileges conferred by specific laws or regulations.

A correct description of the source of the liberty protected by the Constitution does not, of course, decide this case. For, by hypothesis, we are dealing with persons who may be deprived of their liberty because they have been convicted of criminal conduct after a fair trial. We should therefore first ask whether the deprivation of liberty which follows conviction is total or partial.

At one time the prevailing view was that the deprivation was essentially total. The penitentiary inmate was considered "the slave of the State."   *   *   *

*   *   *

*   *   * [I]f the inmate's protected liberty interests are no greater than the State chooses to allow, he is really little more than the slave described in the 19th century cases. I think it clear that even the inmate retains an unalienable interest in liberty—at the very minimum the right to be treated with dignity—which the Constitution may never ignore.

*   *   *

Imprisonment is intended to accomplish more than the temporary removal of the offender from society in order to prevent him from committing like offenses during the period of his incarceration. While custody denies the inmate the opportunity to offend, it also gives him an opportunity to improve himself and to acquire skills and habits that will help him to participate in an open society after his release. Within the prison community, if my basic hypothesis is correct, he has a protected right to pursue his limited rehabilitative goals, or at the minimum, to maintain whatever attributes of dignity are associated with his status in a tightly controlled society. It is unquestionably within the power of the State to change that status, abruptly and adversely; but if the change is sufficiently grievous, it may not be imposed arbitrarily. In such case due process must be afforded.

That does not mean, of course, that every adversity amounts to a deprivation within the meaning of the Fourteenth Amendment.[7] There must be grievous loss, and that term itself is somewhat flexible. I would certainly not consider every transfer within a prison system, even to more onerous conditions of confinement, such a loss. On the other hand, I am unable to identify a principled basis for differentiating between a transfer from the general prison population to solitary confinement and a transfer involving equally disparate conditions between one physical facility and another.

In view of the Court's basic holding, I merely note that I agree with the Court of Appeals that the transfer involved in this case was sufficiently serious to invoke the protection of the Constitution.[8]

I respectfully dissent.

Questions and Points for Discussion

1. The Supreme Court reiterated its holding in Meachum v. Fano in the companion case of Montanye v. Haymes, 427 U.S. 236, 96 S.Ct. 2543 (1976). In *Montanye,* the plaintiff, a prisoner incarcerated in a New York prison, contended that his due process rights were violated when he was transferred from one prison to another. Noting that transfers of inmates from one prison to another fell, under New York law, within the unconfined discretion of the Commissioner of Corrections, the Court concluded that the plaintiff had not been deprived of the liberty interest needed to trigger due process. To the Supreme Court, unlike the Second Circuit Court of Appeals, it was immaterial that the transfer could be characterized as "disciplinary" instead of purely "administrative."

7. * * * "Moreover, in determining whether to require due process, we need not choose between the 'full panoply' of rights accorded a defendant in a criminal prosecution, on the one hand, and no safeguards whatsoever, on the other. Rather, the requirements of due process may be shaped to fit the needs of a particular situation." *United States ex rel. Miller v. Twomey,* 479 F.2d, at 713.

8. There is no question that respondents in this case suffered loss because of the transfer. Hathaway lost his laundry business—a source of income—which he had been running at Norfolk; Dussault lost his job as a plumber, in which he had been performing "a difficult job especially well"; Royce was separated from counselors with whom he had a "good relationship" which had helped him in his effort "to get himself together." These losses were in addition to the generally more restrictive conditions inherent in a maximum-security institution as compared to a medium-security institution.

2. In Olim v. Wakinekona, 461 U.S. 238, 103 S.Ct. 1741 (1983), the prisoner-plaintiff also challenged, on due process grounds, his transfer to another prison. In *Olim*, however, the prisoner was transferred from his home state of Hawaii to a prison over 2500 miles away in California. Nonetheless, the Supreme Court, in a decision written by Justice Blackmun, concluded that scrutiny of the transfer under the due process clause was foreclosed, since the transfer did not deprive the plaintiff of any protected liberty interest.

In explaining why it found no constitutionally derived liberty interest at stake, the Court said:

> Just as an inmate has no justifiable expectation that he will be incarcerated in any particular prison within a State, he has no justifiable expectation that he will be incarcerated in any particular State. Often, confinement in the inmate's home State will not be possible. A person convicted of a federal crime in a State without a federal correctional facility usually will serve his sentence in another State. Overcrowding and the need to separate particular prisoners may necessitate interstate transfers. For any number of reasons, a State may lack prison facilities capable of providing appropriate correctional programs for all offenders.
>
>   *   *   *
>
> In short, it is neither unreasonable nor unusual for an inmate to serve practically his entire sentence in a State other than the one in which he was convicted and sentenced, or to be transferred to an out-of-state prison after serving a portion of his sentence in his home State. Confinement in another State, unlike confinement in a mental institution, is "within the normal limits or range of custody which the conviction has authorized the State to impose." Even when, as here, the transfer involves long distances and an ocean crossing, the confinement remains within constitutional limits. The difference between such a transfer and an intrastate or interstate transfer of shorter distance is a matter of degree, not of kind, and *Meachum* instructs that "the determining factor is the nature of the interest involved rather than its weight." The reasoning of *Meachum* and *Montanye* compels the conclusion that an interstate prison transfer, including one from Hawaii to California, does not deprive an inmate of any liberty interest protected by the Due Process Clause in and of itself.

Id. at 245–48, 103 S.Ct. at 1745–47.

Furthermore, the Court observed, no state-created liberty interest was implicated by the plaintiff's transfer. The Court acknowledged that the state had set up an elaborate procedural mechanism to govern such interstate transfers. A Program Committee had to hold a hearing on the question of an inmate's prospective transfer, and the inmate had the right to attend the hearing, present his own views, and confront and cross-examine witnesses. The inmate could also retain an attorney to represent him if he wanted, and the inmate was entitled to be apprised of the Program Committee's findings.

According to the Supreme Court, however, these procedural safeguards, though mandated by administrative regulations, did not give rise to a liberty interest. For a state-created liberty interest to exist, the state must have placed "substantive limitations on official discretion." Id. at 249, 103 S.Ct. at 1747. Here there were no such limitations, since the decision whether or not to transfer a prisoner out-of-state fell within the unlimited discretion of the warden, who could accept, reject, or modify the recommendations of the Program Committee.

3.   Although the absence of a protected liberty interest might preclude a prisoner from challenging a transfer to another prison on procedural due process grounds, could there be any other possible constitutional bases for such a challenge?

HEWITT v. HELMS

Supreme Court of the United States, 1983.
459 U.S. 460, 103 S.Ct. 864, 74 L.Ed.2d 675.

JUSTICE REHNQUIST delivered the opinion of the Court.

[Because prison officials suspected that he had participated in a prison riot, respondent Aaron Helms was transferred to the administrative segregation unit of the State Correctional Institution at Huntington, Pennsylvania to await the completion of an investigation by prison officials and state police and the adjudication of disciplinary charges. Helms later filed a § 1983 suit against certain prison officials contending that his transfer had been effected without due process of law. After the case had progressed through the lower courts, the Supreme Court granted certiorari to decide two questions: first, whether Helms had been deprived of a liberty interest falling within the scope of the due process clause, and second, if so, the procedural safeguards to which he was entitled under the due process clause when being transferred to administrative segregation.]

While no State may "deprive any person of life, liberty, or property, without due process of law," it is well settled that only a limited range of interests fall within this provision. Liberty interests protected by the Fourteenth Amendment may arise from two sources—the Due Process Clause itself and the laws of the States. Respondent argues, rather weakly, that the Due Process Clause implicitly creates an interest in being confined to a general population cell, rather than the more austere and restrictive administrative segregation quarters. While there is little question on the record before us that respondent's confinement added to the restraints on his freedom, we think his argument seeks to draw from the Due Process Clause more than it can provide.

We have repeatedly said both that prison officials have broad administrative and discretionary authority over the institutions they manage and that lawfully incarcerated persons retain only a narrow range of protected liberty interests. * * *

It is plain that the transfer of an inmate to less amenable and more restrictive quarters for nonpunitive reasons is well within the terms of confinement ordinarily contemplated by a prison sentence. The phrase "administrative segregation," as used by the state authorities here, appears to be something of a catchall: it may be used to protect the prisoner's safety, to protect other inmates from a particular prisoner, to break up potentially disruptive groups of inmates, or simply to await later classification or transfer. Accordingly, administrative segregation is the sort of confinement that inmates should reasonably anticipate receiving at some point in their incarceration. This conclusion finds ample support in our decisions regarding parole and good-time credits. Both these subjects involve release from institutional life altogether, which is a far more significant change in a prisoner's freedoms than that at issue here, yet in *Greenholtz* [*v. Nebraska Penal Inmates*, 442 U.S. 1 (1979)] and *Wolff* [*v. McDonnell*, 418 U.S. 539 (1974)], we held that neither situation involved an interest independently protected by the Due Process Clause. These decisions compel an identical result here.

Despite this, respondent points out that the Court has held that a State may create a liberty interest protected by the Due Process Clause through its enactment of certain statutory or regulatory measures. Thus, in *Wolff,* where we rejected any notion of an interest in good-time credits inherent in the Constitution, we also found that Nebraska had created a right to such credits. * * *

* * *

* * * The deprivations imposed in the course of the daily operations of an institution are likely to be minor when compared to the release from custody at issue in parole decisions and good-time credits. Moreover, the safe and efficient operation of a prison on a day-to-day basis has traditionally been entrusted to the expertise of prison officials. These facts suggest that regulations structuring the authority of prison administrators may warrant treatment, for purposes of creation of entitlements to "liberty," different from statutes and regulations in other areas. Nonetheless, we conclude in the light of the Pennsylvania statutes and regulations here in question, the relevant provisions of which are set forth in full in the margin,[6] that respondent did acquire a protected liberty interest in remaining in the general prison population.

---

6. Title 37 Pa.Code § 95.104(b)(1) (1978) provides:

"An inmate who has allegedly committed a Class I Misconduct may be placed in Close or Maximum Administrative Custody upon approval of the officer in charge of the institution, not routinely but based upon his assessment of the situation and the need for control pending application of procedures under § 95.103 of this title."

Section 95.104(b)(3) of the same Title provides:

"An inmate may be temporarily confined to Close or Maximum Administrative Custody in an investigative status upon approval of the officer in charge of the institution where it has been deter-

mined that there is a threat of a serious disturbance, or a serious threat to the individual or others. The inmate shall be notified in writing as soon as possible that he is under investigation and that he will receive a hearing if any disciplinary action is being considered after the investigation is completed. An investigation shall begin immediately to determine whether or not a behavior violation has occurred. If no behavior violation has occurred, the inmate must be released as soon as the reason for the security concern has abated but in all cases within ten days."

Finally, a State Bureau of Correction Administrative Directive states that when the

Respondent seems to suggest that the mere fact that Pennsylvania has created a careful procedural structure to regulate the use of administrative segregation indicates the existence of a protected liberty interest. We cannot agree. The creation of procedural guidelines to channel the decision-making of prison officials is, in the view of many experts in the field, a salutary development. It would be ironic to hold that when a State embarks on such desirable experimentation it thereby opens the door to scrutiny by the federal courts, while States that choose not to adopt such procedural provisions entirely avoid the strictures of the Due Process Clause. The adoption of such procedural guidelines, without more, suggests that it is these restrictions alone, and not those federal courts might also impose under the Fourteenth Amendment, that the State chose to require.

Nonetheless, in this case the Commonwealth has gone beyond simple procedural guidelines. It has used language of an unmistakably mandatory character, requiring that certain procedures "shall," "will," or "must" be employed and that administrative segregation will not occur absent specified substantive predicates—viz., "the need for control," or "the threat of a serious disturbance." Petitioners argue, with considerable force, that these terms must be read in light of the fact that the decision whether to confine an inmate to administrative segregation is largely predictive, and therefore that it is not likely that the State meant to create binding requirements. But on balance we are persuaded that the repeated use of explicitly mandatory language in connection with requiring specific substantive predicates demands a conclusion that the State has created a protected liberty interest.

That being the case, we must then decide whether the process afforded respondent satisfied the minimum requirements of the Due Process Clause. We think that it did. * * *

Under *Mathews v. Eldridge,* 424 U.S. 319, 335 (1976), we consider the private interests at stake in a governmental decision, the governmental interests involved, and the value of procedural requirements in determining what process is due under the Fourteenth Amendment. Respondent's private interest is not one of great consequence. He was merely transferred from one extremely restricted environment to an even more confined situation. Unlike disciplinary confinement the stigma of wrongdoing or misconduct does not attach to administrative segregation under Pennsylvania's prison regulations. Finally, there is no indication that administrative segregation will have any significant effect on parole opportunities.

State Police have been summoned to an institution:

"Pending arrival of the State Police, the institutional representative shall:

"1. Place all suspects and resident witnesses or complainants in such custody, protective or otherwise, as may be necessary to maintain security. A hearing complying with [37 Pa.Code § 95.103 (1972)] will be carried out after the investigation period. Such hearing shall be held within four (4) days unless the investigation warrants delay and in that case as soon as possible."

Petitioners had two closely related reasons for confining Helms to administrative segregation prior to conducting a hearing on the disciplinary charges against him. First, they concluded that if housed in the general population, Helms would pose a threat to the safety of other inmates and prison officials and to the security of the institution. Second, the prison officials believed that it was wiser to separate respondent from the general population until completion of state and institutional investigations of his role in the December 3 riot and the hearing on the charges against him. Plainly, these governmental interests are of great importance. The safety of the institution's guards and inmates is perhaps the most fundamental responsibility of the prison administration. Likewise, the isolation of a prisoner pending investigation of misconduct charges against him serves important institutional interests relating to the insulating of possible witnesses from coercion or harm.

Neither of these grounds for confining Helms to administrative segregation involved decisions or judgments that would have been materially assisted by a detailed adversary proceeding. * * * In assessing the seriousness of a threat to institutional security, prison administrators necessarily draw on more than the specific facts surrounding a particular incident; instead, they must consider the character of the inmates confined in the institution, recent and longstanding relations between prisoners and guards, prisoners *inter se,* and the like. In the volatile atmosphere of a prison, an inmate easily may constitute an unacceptable threat to the safety of other prisoners and guards even if he himself has committed no misconduct; rumor, reputation, and even more imponderable factors may suffice to spark potentially disastrous incidents. The judgment of prison officials in this context, like that of those making parole decisions, turns largely on "purely subjective evaluations and on predictions of future behavior;" indeed, the administrators must predict not just one inmate's future actions, as in parole, but those of an entire institution. Owing to the central role of these types of intuitive judgments, a decision that an inmate or group of inmates represents a threat to the institution's security would not be appreciably fostered by the trial-type procedural safeguards suggested by respondent.[7] This, and the balance of public and private interests, lead us to conclude that the Due Process Clause requires only an informal nonadversary review of evidence, discussed more fully below, in order to confine an inmate feared to be a threat to institutional security to administrative segregation.

Likewise, confining respondent to administrative segregation pending completion of the investigation of the disciplinary charges against him is not based on an inquiry requiring any elaborate procedural safeguards. * * *

7. Indeed, we think an administrator's judgment probably would be hindered. Prison officials, wary of potential legal liability, might well spend their time mechanically complying with cumbersome, marginally helpful procedural requirements, rather than managing their institution wisely.

* * *

We think an informal, nonadversary evidentiary review is sufficient both for the decision that an inmate represents a security threat
and the decision to confine an inmate to administrative segregation
pending completion of an investigation into misconduct charges
against him.   An inmate must merely receive some notice of the
charges against him and an opportunity to present his views to the
prison official charged with deciding whether to transfer him to
administrative segregation.   Ordinarily a written statement by the
inmate will accomplish this purpose, although prison administrators
may find it more useful to permit oral presentations in cases where
they believe a written statement would be ineffective.   So long as this
occurs, and the decisionmaker reviews the charges and then-available
evidence against the prisoner, the Due Process Clause is satisfied.[8]
This informal procedure permits a reasonably accurate assessment of
probable cause to believe that misconduct occurred, and the "value [of
additional 'formalities and safeguards'] would be too slight to justify
holding, as a matter of constitutional principle" that they must be
adopted.

Measured against these standards we are satisfied that respondent
received all the process that was due after being confined to administrative segregation.   *   *   *[9]

JUSTICE BLACKMUN, concurring in part and dissenting in part.

*   *   * In *Meachum* and *Montanye*, we held that certain prison
transfers were "within the normal limits or range of custody" even
though conditions of confinement were more severe in the prisons to
which the inmates were transferred.   Because I believe that a transfer
to administrative segregation within a prison likewise is within the
normal range of custody, I agree with the Court that respondent has

8.   The proceeding must occur within a
reasonable time following an inmate's
transfer, taking into account the relatively insubstantial private interest at stake
and the traditionally broad discretion of
prison officials.

9.   Of course, administrative segregation
may not be used as a pretext for indefinite
confinement of an inmate.   Prison officials
must engage in some sort of periodic review of the confinement of such inmates.
This review will not necessarily require
that prison officials permit the submission
of any additional evidence or statements.
The decision whether a prisoner remains a
security risk will be based on facts relating
to a particular prisoner—which will have
been ascertained when determining to confine the inmate to administrative segregation—and on the officials' general knowledge of prison conditions and tensions,
which are singularly unsuited for "proof"

in any highly structured manner.   Likewise, the decision to continue confinement
of an inmate pending investigation of misconduct charges depends upon circumstances that prison officials will be well
aware of—most typically, the progress of
the investigation.   In both situations, the
ongoing task of operating the institution
will require the prison officials to consider
a wide range of administrative considerations; here, for example, petitioners had to
consider prison tensions in the aftermath
of the December 3 riot, the ongoing state
criminal investigation, and so forth.   The
record plainly shows that on January 2 a
Program Review Committee considered
whether Helms' confinement should be
continued.   This review, occurring less
than a month after the initial decision to
confine Helms to administrative segregation, is sufficient to dispel any notions that
the confinement was a pretext.

not been deprived of "an interest independently protected by the Due Process Clause."

I also agree that the Pennsylvania statutes and prison regulations at issue in this case created an entitlement not to be placed in administrative segregation without due process. * * *

Having found a state-created liberty interest, I cannot agree with the Court that the procedures used here comported with due process. Accordingly, I join Parts II and III of Justice Stevens' dissenting opinion.

JUSTICE STEVENS, with whom JUSTICE BRENNAN and JUSTICE MARSHALL join, and with whom JUSTICE BLACKMUN joins as to Parts II and III, dissenting.

When respondent Helms was transferred to "administrative segregation," he was placed in solitary confinement in B–Block at the State Correctional Institution at Huntingdon, Pennsylvania. The conditions in B–Block are significantly more restrictive than those experienced by inmates in the general prison population.[1] Indeed, in all material respects conditions in administrative custody are the same as those in disciplinary segregation. The reasons for placing one inmate in administrative and another in punitive segregation may be different, and the periods of confinement may vary, but the Court properly assumes for purposes of this case that "the conditions in the two types of confinement are substantially identical."

* * * Despite the severity of conditions in solitary confinement, and the admitted differences between segregated custody and the general prison population, petitioners urge us to hold that the transfer of an inmate into administrative segregation does not deprive him of any interest in liberty protected by the Due Process Clause. The Court correctly rejects this contention today. It does so, however, for reasons that do not withstand analysis. It then concludes that the procedures afforded by prison authorities in this case "plainly satisfied the due process requirements for continued confinement of Helms pending the outcome of the investigation." I cannot agree.

1. In an uncontroverted affidavit, respondent Helms described those conditions as follows:

"While confined in segregation I had no access to vocational, educational, recreational, and rehabilitative programs as I would have had while out in the general population. Exercise was limited to between five and ten minutes a day and was often only three or four days a week. Showers were virtually nonexistent in segregation in December and January. The changing of clothes was also only once or twice a week while I could have changed more often in population. Had I been in general population I would have had access to various exercise facilities such as the gym and the yard and would have been able to do this for most of the time out of my cell which would have been approximately 14 hours a day. While in segregation I only got out of my cell a few minutes for exercise, showers and an occasional visit. I was virtually confined there 24 hours a day otherwise."

The State has not challenged the factual accuracy of this description.

I

* * *

The Court properly rejects the contention that the Due Process Clause is simply inapplicable to transfers of inmates into administrative segregation. It holds that respondent's transfer from the general population into administrative confinement was a deprivation of liberty that must be accompanied by due process of law. The majority's reasoning in support of this conclusion suffers, however, from a fundamental flaw. In its view, a "liberty interest" exists only because Pennsylvania's written prison regulations display a magical combination of "substantive predicates" and "explicitly mandatory language." This analysis attaches no significance either to the character of the conditions of confinement or to actual administrative practices in the institution. Moreover, the Court seems to assume that after his conviction a prisoner has, in essence, no liberty save that created, in writing, by the State which imprisons him. Under this view a prisoner crosses into limbo when he enters into penal confinement. He might have some minimal freedoms if the State chooses to bestow them; but such freedom as he has today may be taken away tomorrow.

* * *

* * * [T]he relevant question in this case is whether transfer into administrative segregation constitutes a "sufficiently grievous" change in a prisoner's status to require the protection of "due process."

* * *

Ordinarily the mere fact that the existence of a general regulation may significantly impair individual liberty raises no question under the Due Process Clause.[8] But the Clause is implicated when the State singles out one person for adverse treatment significantly different from that imposed on the community at large. For an essential attribute of the liberty protected by the Constitution is the right to the same kind of treatment as the State provides to other similarly situated persons. A convicted felon, though he is properly placed in a disfavored class, retains this essential right.

Thus, for a prisoner as for other persons, the grievousness of any claimed deprivation of liberty is, in part, a relative matter: one must compare the treatment of the particular prisoner with the customary, habitual treatment of the population of the prison as a whole. In general, if a prisoner complains of an adverse change in conditions which he shares with an entire class of his fellow prisoners as part of the day-to-day operations of the prison, there would be no reason to find that he has been deprived of his constitutionally protected liberty.[11]

8. * * * There are, of course, particular liberties that have constitutional status in their own right, such as freedom of speech and the free exercise of religion, whose deprivation by a State on a classwide as well as an individual basis may violate the Due Process Clause of the Fourteenth Amendment.

11. * * * When an entire class is affected by a change, individual prisoners are neither more acutely affected by it than other members of their class nor uniquely able to bring personal knowledge to bear on the appropriateness of its implementation. Therefore the reasons for the

But if a prisoner is singled out for disparate treatment and if the disparity is sufficiently severe, his liberty is at stake.

In this case, by definition, the institutional norm is confinement in the "general prison population." The deprivation of which respondent complains is transfer to "administrative segregation"—that is, solitary confinement—which by its nature singles out individual prisoners. That confinement was not specified by the terms of his initial criminal sentence. Not only is there a disparity, the disparity is drastic. It is concededly as serious as the difference between confinement in the general prison population and "disciplinary segregation." * * *[15]

In this case, the Court's exclusive focus on written regulations happens to lead it to the conclusion that there is a "liberty interest." I agree that the regulations are relevant: by limiting the substantive reasons for a transfer to administrative segregation and by establishing prescribed procedures, these regulations indicate that the State recognizes the substantiality of the deprivation. They therefore provide evidentiary support for the conclusion that the transfer affects a constitutionally protected interest in liberty. But the regulations do not *create* that interest. Even in their absence due process safeguards would be required when an inmate's liberty is further curtailed by a transfer into administrative custody that is the functional equivalent of punitive isolation.

II

The "touchstone of due process," as we pointed out in *Wolff v. McDonnell,* is "protection of the individual against arbitrary action of government." Pennsylvania may not arbitrarily place a prisoner in administrative segregation. The majority agrees with this general proposition, but I believe its standards guarding against arbitrariness fall short of what the Constitution requires.

First, the majority declares that the Constitution is satisfied by an initial proceeding [16] with minimal participation by the inmate who is being transferred into administrative custody. * * *

I agree with the Court that the Constitution does not require a hearing with all of the procedural safeguards set forth in *Wolff v.*

due process requirement of some kind of hearing are absent. * * *

15. See *Wolff,* [418 U.S.] at 571–572, n. 19 (due process applies to transfer to solitary confinement for major misconduct because it "represents a major change in the conditions of confinement").

16. The Court of Appeals recognized that, in the emergency conditions on December 3, 1978, prison officials were justified in placing respondent in administrative segregation without a hearing. Respondent does not contend otherwise. The Due Process Clause allows prison officials flexibility to cope with emergencies.

But petitioners acknowledge that the disturbance was "quelled" the same day and that, within a day or two after the December 3, 1978, prison riot, conditions had returned completely to normal. At that point the emergency rationale for administrative segregation without a hearing had expired. The Due Process Clause then required a prompt proceeding to determine whether continued administrative segregation was justified. Yet Helms was not accorded any procedural safeguards whatsoever until five days after the riot—another violation of his due process rights.

McDonnell when prison officials initially decide to segregate an inmate to safeguard institutional security or to conduct an investigation of an unresolved misconduct charge. But unlike the majority, I believe that due process does require that the inmate be given the opportunity to present his views in person to the reviewing officials. As many prisoners have little education, limiting an inmate to a written statement is unlikely to provide a "meaningful opportunity to be heard" in accordance with due process principles.

Of greater importance, the majority's due process analysis fails to provide adequate protection against arbitrary continuation of an inmate's solitary confinement.[18] The opinion recognizes that "[p]rison officials must engage in some sort of periodic review of the confinement of such inmates." It thus recognizes that the deprivation of liberty in the prison setting is a continuous process rather than an isolated event. But the Court requires only minimal review procedures; prison officials need not permit the submission of any additional evidence or statements and need not give the inmate a chance to present his position. It is constitutionally sufficient, according to the majority, that administrative segregation not be a pretext for indefinite confinement. In my view, the Due Process Clause requires a more searching review of the justifiability of continued confinement.

* * *

At each periodic review, I believe due process requires that the prisoner be allowed to make an oral statement about the need for and the consequences of continued confinement. Concededly some of the information relevant to a decision whether to continue confinement will be beyond the reach of a prisoner who has been held in segregated custody, including conditions in the general prison population and the progress of an ongoing investigation. But the prisoner should have the right to be present in order to explain his current attitude toward his past activities and his present circumstances, and the impact of solitary confinement on his rehabilitation program and training. These factors may change as the period of confinement continues.

Further, if the decisionmaker decides to retain the prisoner in segregation, I believe he should be required to explain his reasons in a brief written statement which is retained in the file and given to the prisoner. As Justice Marshall has written in a related prison context, this requirement would direct the decisionmaker's focus "to the relevant . . . criteria and promote more careful consideration of the evidence. It would also enable inmates to detect and correct inaccuracies that could have a decisive impact. And the obligation to justify a decision publicly would provide the assurance, critical to the appear-

18. Unlike disciplinary custody, which is imposed for a fixed term, in practice administrative custody sometimes continues for lengthy or indefinite periods. See *Ruiz v. Estelle,* 503 F.Supp. 1265, 1365, 1367 (SD Tex.1980) ("months or even years"); *Mims v. Shapp,* 457 F.Supp. 247, 249 (WD Pa.1978) (five years); *United States ex rel. Hoss v. Cuyler,* 452 F.Supp. 256 (ED Pa.1978) (more than five years); *Wright v. Enomoto,* 462 F.Supp. 397, 403–404 (ND Cal.1976) (various instances up to a year).

ance of fairness, that the Board's decision is not capricious." A written statement of reasons would facilitate administrative and judicial review and might give the prisoner an opportunity to improve his conduct.

Neither a right to personal appearance by the prisoner nor a requirement of written reasons would impose an undue burden on prison officials. It is noteworthy that these procedural safeguards are provided in regulations governing both the Pennsylvania and federal prison systems. Given the importance of the prisoner's interest in returning to the general prison population, the benefits of additional procedural safeguards, and the minimal burden on prison officials, I am convinced that the Due Process Clause requires more substantial periodic reviews than the majority acknowledges.

III

[In this portion of his opinion, Justice Stevens concluded that the procedures in Pennsylvania governing transfers to and continued confinement in prison administrative segregation units did not satisfy the requirements of due process.]

Questions and Points for Discussion

1. In Kentucky Department of Corrections v. Thompson, 109 S.Ct. 1904 (1989), the Supreme Court once again addressed the subject of state-created liberty interests in the prison context. The question before the Court in *Thompson* was whether certain Kentucky prison regulations gave prisoners a liberty interest in visiting with people from outside the prison.

One of these regulations, which was promulgated by the Kentucky Department of Corrections, provided as follows:

Certain visitors who are either a threat to the security or order of the institution or nonconducive to the successful re-entry of the inmate to the community may be excluded. These are, but [are] not restricted to:

A. The visitor's presence in the institution would constitute a clear and probable danger to the institution's security or interfere with the orderly operation of the institution.

B. The visitor has a past record of disruptive conduct.

C. The visitor is under the influence of alcohol or drugs.

D. The visitor refuses to submit to search, if requested to do so, or show proper identification.

E. The visitor is directly related to the inmate's criminal behavior.

F. The visitor is currently on probation or parole and does not have special written permission from both his or her Probation or Parole Office and the institutional Superintendent.

A written policy governing visiting privileges at the Kentucky State Penitentiary, the prison where the inmates who instituted this litigation were housed, similarly set forth a nonexhaustive list of reasons for excluding visitors from the prison.

The instant litigation was commenced after the visiting privileges of several prisoners at the Kentucky State Penitentiary were curtailed without a hearing. One inmate was not permitted to see his mother for six months because she brought someone to the prison who had previously been involved in smuggling contraband into the prison. The mother and girlfriend of another prisoner were forbidden from visiting at the prison for awhile after the inmate was found with contraband after one of their visits.

The United States District Court for the Western District of Kentucky held that before a visitor could be excluded from the Kentucky State Penitentiary, a prisoner had to be provided with notice of and the reasons for the exclusion and afforded the opportunity to present his views as to why the exclusion order was unwarranted. The Sixth Circuit Court of Appeals affirmed.

The Supreme Court, however, reversed, finding that the necessary predicate to a successful due process claim was absent. According to the Court, curtailment of an individual prisoner's visiting privileges at the Kentucky State Penitentiary did not effect a deprivation of liberty within the meaning of the due process clause. In an opinion written by Justice Blackmun, the Court explained its conclusion:

> Respondents do not argue—nor can it seriously be contended, in light of our prior cases—that an inmate's interest in unfettered visitation is guaranteed directly by the Due Process Clause. * * * The denial of prison access to a particular visitor "is well within the terms of confinement ordinarily contemplated by a prison sentence" and therefore is not independently protected by the Due Process Clause.

> We have held, however, that state law may create enforceable liberty interests in the prison setting. * * *

> Stated simply, "a State creates a protected liberty interest by placing substantive limitations on official discretion." A State may do this in a number of ways. Neither the drafting of regulations nor their interpretation can be reduced to an exact science. Our past decisions suggest, however, that the most common manner in which a State creates a liberty interest is by establishing "substantive predicates" to govern official decisionmaking and, further, by mandating the outcome to be reached upon a finding that the relevant criteria have been met.

> Most of our procedural due process cases in the prison context have turned on the presence or absence of language creating "substantive predicates" to guide discretion. * * *

> We have also articulated a requirement, implicit in our earlier decisions, that the regulations contain "explicitly mandatory language," i.e., specific directives to the decisionmaker that if the regulations' substantive predicates are present, a particular outcome must follow, in order to create a liberty interest. The regulations at issue in *Hewitt* mandated that certain procedures be followed, and "that administrative segregation will not occur absent specified substantive predicates." * * * In sum, the use of "explicitly mandatory lan-

guage," in connection with the establishment of "specific substantive predicates" to limit discretion, forces a conclusion that the State has created a liberty interest.

The regulations and procedures at issue in this case do provide certain "substantive predicates" to guide the decisionmaker. The state procedures provide that a visitor "may be excluded" when, *inter alia,* officials find reasonable grounds to believe that the "visitor's presence in the institution would constitute a clear and probable danger to the institution's security or interfere with [its] orderly operation." Among the more specific reasons listed for denying visitation are the visitor's connection to the inmate's criminal behavior, the visitor's past disruptive behavior or refusal to submit to a search or show proper identification, and the visitor's being under the influence of alcohol or drugs.

* * *

The regulations at issue here, however, lack the requisite relevant mandatory language. They stop short of requiring that a particular result is to be reached upon a finding that the substantive predicates are met. * * * Visitors *may* be excluded if they fall within one of the described categories, but they need not be. Nor need visitors fall within one of the described categories in order to be excluded. The overall effect of the regulations is not such that an inmate can reasonably form an objective expectation that a visit would necessarily be allowed absent the occurrence of one of the listed conditions. Or, to state it differently, the regulations are not worded in such a way that an inmate could reasonably expect to enforce them against the prison officials.

Because the regulations at issue here do not establish a liberty interest entitled to the protections of the Due Process Clause, the judgment of the Court of Appeals is reversed.

Id. at 1908–11.

Justice Kennedy wrote a brief concurring opinion emphasizing that the case did not involve a general ban on prison visitors.

Justices Marshall, Brennan, and Stevens dissented. First, they disagreed with the Court's summary rejection of the notion that a prisoner could have a constitutionally derived liberty interest in retained visiting privileges. "[T]he 'within the sentence' test," they observed, "knows few rivals for vagueness and pliability, not the least because a typical prison sentence says little more than that the defendant must spend a specified period of time behind bars." Id. at 1912.

The dissenters also disagreed with the Court's approach to state-created liberty interests. Justice Marshall observed:

I fail to see why mandatory language always is an essential element of a state-created liberty interest. Once it is clear that the State has imposed substantive criteria in statutes or regulations to guide or limit official discretion, there is no reason to assume—as the majority does—that officials applying the statutes or regulations are likely to ignore the criteria if there is not some undefined quantity of the words "shall" or "must." * * * Common sense suggests that expectations stem from practice as well as from the language of statutes or regulations.

Id. at 1914.

The dissenters finally noted that even if certain mandatory language was a prerequisite to a finding of a state-created liberty interest, such mandatory language could be found in the Kentucky prison regulations governing prison visitation. They cited such provisions as those dictating that " '[v]isits *will* be conducted seven (7) days a week' " and that " '[a]n inmate *is* allowed three (3) separate visits * * * per week.' " Id. at 1915 (emphasis in the original).

2. Does the Court's discussion in *Thompson* of the genesis of state-created liberty interests comport with its conclusion in *Hewitt v. Helms* that certain Pennsylvania statutes and regulations gave prisoners a liberty interest in remaining in the general population unit of a prison?

3. Do you agree or disagree with the Supreme Court's view of the way in which liberty interests in the prison context are created?

4. The Supreme Court in *Hewitt* purported to apply the three-pronged balancing test previously applied by the Court in Mathews v. Eldridge, 424 U.S. 319, 96 S.Ct. 893 (1976). In *Mathews*, the Court described the factors to be balanced in the following way:

> First, the private interest that will be affected by the official action; second, the risk of an erroneous deprivation of such interest through the procedures used, and the probable value, if any, of additional or substitute procedural safeguards; and finally, the Government's interest, including the function involved and the fiscal and administrative burdens that the additional or substitute procedural requirement would entail.

Id. at 335, 96 S.Ct. at 903.

Did the Supreme Court in *Hewitt* apply the same balancing test as the one described in *Mathews*?

5. How specific must the notice of the reason for an inmate's transfer to administrative segregation be to pass constitutional muster? Compare Hanna v. Lane, No. 84–C–1635 (N.D.Ill.1985) (available on WESTLAW) (notice that inmate was being investigated for "a possible rule violation" was inadequate) with Shango v. Jurich, 608 F.Supp. 931 (N.D.Ill.1985) (notice that inmate was being investigated for "extortion, sexual assault and trafficking, etc." was sufficient even though the specific instances when the inmate was allegedly involved in such misconduct were not revealed.)

6. The Supreme Court in *Hewitt* said that "[o]rdinarily" inmates need only be afforded the opportunity to present a written statement to the prison officials considering their confinement in administrative segregation. When, if ever, would inmates have the right to personally appear before the prison officials to express their views on their administrative confinement?

7. By when must the basis for confining a prisoner in administrative segregation be reviewed to satisfy due process? In Sourbeer v. Robinson, 791 F.2d 1094 (3d Cir.1986), one court held that a 35–day delay before a

hearing was held where the inmate was permitted to present his views did not, under the circumstances, violate due process. Cf. Standard 2–4215 of the American Correctional Association's Standards for Adult Correctional Institutions (although an inmate can be immediately placed in segregation when "necessary to protect the inmate or others," a committee must then review, within three working days, the propriety of the inmate's confinement in segregation).

8. Apart from questions concerning the process due around the time of an inmate's confinement in administrative segregation, there are questions concerning the process due during the periodic review of an inmate's administrative confinement. One such question concerns the frequency with which the periodic reviews must take place. Compare Mims v. Shapp, 744 F.2d 946 (3d Cir.1984) (review every thirty days comports with due process) with Toussaint v. McCarthy, 801 F.2d 1080 (9th Cir.1986) (review once a year violates due process).

Another question concerns the extent to which, if at all, the reason or reasons for continuing an inmate's confinement in administrative segregation after a periodic review must be explained to the inmate. According to some of the lower courts, apparently assuming that some sort of explanation must be tendered to the inmate, not every statement of reasons for the continued confinement will satisfy the requirements of due process. See, e.g., U.S. ex rel. Hoss v. Cuyler, 452 F.Supp. 256, 295 (E.D.Pa.1978) (inmate has a right to "more than a periodical *ipse dixit* pronouncement that he is a 'security case'"). Some courts have found that the Constitution requires the taking of other steps to ensure that the protection afforded by the periodic review process is not illusory. For example, some courts have required the development of objective guidelines governing confinement in administrative segregation, guidelines against which the prisoner as well as others can assess the validity of the inmate's continued confinement in administrative segregation. See, e.g., *Cuyler,* id. But see Mims v. Shapp, 744 F.2d 946 (3d Cir.1984) (due process does not require that objective standards govern an inmate's retention in administrative segregation).

9. In most prison systems, classification decisions are made by classification committees comprised of correctional staff. The Model Sentencing and Corrections Act (1978) proposed the following procedures for classification committees:

§ 4–412. [Classification Committees; Hearing Procedures.]

(a) The director shall adopt rules establishing hearing procedures for classification committees. The rules must be consistent with the following:

(1) A confined person has, but may waive in writing, the right to,

(i) written notice at least 7 days before the hearing of the contemplated action and the facts on which it is based;

(ii) subject to the limitations of Section 4–122(c),[a] examine at least 3 days before the hearing all information in the committee's possession to be considered at the hearing;

(iii) legal assistance in preparing for the hearing and in contesting a material fact upon which classification is likely to be based other than a fact determined by a court at the trial of the offense or necessarily found as part of the conviction;

(iv) present relevant evidence and cross-examine persons giving adverse evidence.

(2) The classification committee must,

(i) preserve, in transcribable form, a record of the hearing, which must be retained until the time for appeal has expired or the appeal has been concluded; and

(ii) inform the confined person in writing of its decision and the reason therefor.

(b) This section does not require a person to appear or be examined or information to be disclosed if a classification committee makes a written factual finding that to do so would subject a person to a substantial risk of physical harm.

§ 4–413. [Classification Decisions; Appeal.]

(a) A confined person may appeal any decision of the committee to the chief executive officer, who shall decide the appeal within 7 days.

(b) The affected person may appeal to the director, who shall decide the appeal within 30 days.

(c) Failure by the appropriate officer to act within the time provided entitles the confined person to treat the failure as an adverse decision.

(d) A confined person is entitled to judicial review of a decision to reclassify him to a more restrictive classification, transfer him from his permanent facility assignment, or classify him as requiring a greater level of security than that generally provided in a maximum security facility.

§ 4–414. [Change in Status.]

(a) A confined person may not be reclassified to a more restrictive classification unless:

(1) he has committed a disciplinary infraction resulting in confinement in his own living quarters, placement in separate

[a. Section 4–122(c) exempts from disclosure information determined by a court in writing or the director to consist of:

(1) diagnostic opinion relating to physical or mental health problems the disclosure of which might affect adversely a course of on-going treatment;

(2) information obtained upon a promise of confidentiality if the promise was made before the effective date of this Act;

(3) information about a pending investigation of alleged disciplinary or criminal activity; or

(4) other information that, if disclosed, would create a substantial risk of physical harm to any person.]

housing for more than 10 days, loss of privileges for more than 40 days, or loss of good time;

(2) he is convicted of a new offense;

(3) his status changes from a pretrial detainee to an offender;

(4) new information becomes available that would have affected his initial classification and its relevance to his classification is not outweighed by his conduct in the facility since the initial classification; or

(5) he consents to the classification.

(b) A confined person may not be transferred to another facility unless:

(1) he is subject to reclassification pursuant to subsection (a);

(2) his transfer is necessary to allow him to receive special medical, psychological, psychiatric, or other similar treatment;

(3) his space in the facility would be more constructively utilized by another confined person and his transfer to another facility would not result in a substantially more onerous assignment;

(4) his transfer is necessary to allow him to return to a general population setting from protective confinement;

(5) the facility or part of a facility to which he is assigned is closed or its population is being reduced; or

(6) he consents to the transfer.

(c) Whenever a confined person is reclassified or transferred without his consent pursuant to this section, he is entitled to a hearing before a classification committee.

(d) Whenever a confined person is reclassified or transferred so as to affect adversely the conditions of his confinement, a classification committee shall review his classification and facility assignment within 6 months.

VITEK v. JONES

Supreme Court of the United States, 1980.
445 U.S. 480, 100 S.Ct. 1254, 63 L.Ed.2d 552.

[The plaintiff in this case, a prisoner incarcerated in Nebraska, brought a § 1983 suit claiming that he was deprived of liberty without due process of law when he was transferred to a state mental hospital. The plaintiff was transferred under a Nebraska statute, Neb.Rev.Stat. § 83–180(1), which provided in part as follows:

When a physician designated by the Director of Correctional Services finds that a person committed to the department suffers from a physical disease or defect, or when a physician or psychologist designated by the director finds that a person committed to the department suffers from a mental disease or defect, the chief executive officer may order such person to be segregated from other persons in the facility. If the physician or psychologist is of the opinion that the person cannot be given proper treatment in that facility, the director may arrange for his transfer for examination, study, and treatment to any medical-correctional facility, or to another institution in the Department of Public Institutions where proper treatment is available.

The Supreme Court discussed the plaintiff's due process claim in an opinion written by Justice White. Parts I, II, III, IV-A, and V of Justice White's opinion constituted the Court's opinion. Excerpts from Parts III, IV, and V of that opinion are set forth below.]

III

* * *

* * * Section 83–180(1) provides that if a designated physician finds that a prisoner "suffers from a mental disease or defect" that "cannot be given proper treatment" in prison, the Director of Correctional Services may transfer a prisoner to a mental hospital. The District Court also found that in practice prisoners are transferred to a mental hospital only if it is determined that they suffer from a mental disease or defect that cannot adequately be treated within the penal complex. This "objective expectation, firmly fixed in state law and official Penal Complex practice," that a prisoner would not be transferred unless he suffered from a mental disease or defect that could not be adequately treated in the prison, gave Jones a liberty interest that entitled him to the benefits of appropriate procedures in connection with determining the conditions that warranted his transfer to a mental hospital. * * *

Appellants maintain that any state-created liberty interest that Jones had was completely satisfied once a physician or psychologist designated by the director made the findings required by § 83–180(1) and that Jones was not entitled to any procedural protections. But if the State grants a prisoner a right or expectation that adverse action will not be taken against him except upon the occurrence of specified behavior, "the determination of whether such behavior has occurred becomes critical, and the minimum requirements of procedural due process appropriate for the circumstances must be observed." These minimum requirements being a matter of federal law, they are not diminished by the fact that the State may have specified its own procedures that it may deem adequate for determining the preconditions to adverse official action. In *Morrissey [v. Brewer*, 408 U.S. 471 (1972)], *Gagnon [v. Scarpelli*, 411 U.S. 778 (1973)], and *Wolff*, the States had adopted their own procedures for determining whether conditions warranting revocation of parole, probation, or good-time credits had occurred; yet we held that those procedures were constitutionally inadequate. In like manner, Nebraska's reliance on the opinion of a designated physician or psychologist for determining whether the conditions warranting a transfer exist neither removes the prisoner's interest from due process protection nor answers the question of what process is due under the Constitution.

The District Court was also correct in holding that independently of § 83–180(1), the transfer of a prisoner from a prison to a mental hospital must be accompanied by appropriate procedural protections. The issue is whether after a conviction for robbery, Jones retained a residuum of liberty that would be infringed by a transfer to a mental hospital without complying with minimum requirements of due process.

We have recognized that for the ordinary citizen, commitment to a mental hospital produces "a massive curtailment of liberty" and in consequence "requires due process protection." The loss of liberty produced by an involuntary commitment is more than a loss of freedom from confinement. It is indisputable that commitment to a mental hospital "can engender adverse social consequences to the individual" and that "[w]hether we label this phenomena 'stigma' or choose to call it something else . . . we recognize that it can occur and that it can have a very significant impact on the individual." Also, "[a]mong the historic liberties" protected by the Due Process Clause is the "right to be free from, and to obtain judicial relief for, unjustified intrusions on personal security." Compelled treatment in the form of mandatory behavior modification programs, to which the District Court found Jones was exposed in this case, was a proper factor to be weighed by the District Court.

*   *   *

Appellants maintain that the transfer of a prisoner to a mental hospital is within the range of confinement justified by imposition of a prison sentence, at least after certification by a qualified person that a prisoner suffers from a mental disease or defect. We cannot agree. None of our decisions holds that conviction for a crime entitles a State not only to confine the convicted person but also to determine that he has a mental illness and to subject him involuntarily to institutional care in a mental hospital. Such consequences visited on the prisoner are qualitatively different from the punishment characteristically suffered by a person convicted of crime. *   *   * [I]nvoluntary commitment to a mental hospital is not within the range of conditions of confinement to which a prison sentence subjects an individual. A criminal conviction and sentence of imprisonment extinguish an individual's right to freedom from confinement for the term of his sentence, but they do not authorize the State to classify him as mentally ill and to subject him to involuntary psychiatric treatment without affording him additional due process protections.

In light of the findings made by the District Court, Jones' involuntary transfer to the Lincoln Regional Center pursuant to § 83–180, for the purpose of psychiatric treatment, implicated a liberty interest protected by the Due Process Clause. Many of the restrictions on the prisoner's freedom of action at the Lincoln Regional Center by themselves might not constitute the deprivation of a liberty interest retained by a prisoner. But here, the stigmatizing consequences of a transfer to a mental hospital for involuntary psychiatric treatment, coupled with the subjection of the prisoner to mandatory behavior modification as a treatment for mental illness, constitute the kind of deprivations of liberty that requires procedural protections.

IV

The District Court held that to afford sufficient protection to the liberty interest it had identified, the State was required to observe the following minimum procedures before transferring a prisoner to a mental hospital:

"A. Written notice to the prisoner that a transfer to a mental hospital is being considered;

"B. A hearing, sufficiently after the notice to permit the prisoner to prepare, at which disclosure to the prisoner is made of the evidence being relied upon for the transfer and at which an opportunity to be heard in person and to present documentary evidence is given;

"C. An opportunity at the hearing to present testimony of witnesses by the defense and to confront and cross-examine witnesses called by the state, except upon a finding, not arbitrarily made, of good cause for not permitting such presentation, confrontation, or cross-examination;

"D. An independent decisionmaker;

"E. A written statement by the factfinder as to the evidence relied on and the reasons for transferring the inmate;

"F. Availability of legal counsel, furnished by the state, if the inmate is financially unable to furnish his own; and

"G. Effective and timely notice of all the foregoing rights."

A

We think the District Court properly identified and weighed the relevant factors in arriving at its judgment. Concededly the interest of the State in segregating and treating mentally ill patients is strong. The interest of the prisoner in not being arbitrarily classified as mentally ill and subjected to unwelcome treatment is also powerful, however; and as the District Court found, the risk of error in making the determinations required by § 83–180 is substantial enough to warrant appropriate procedural safeguards against error.

We recognize that the inquiry involved in determining whether or not to transfer an inmate to a mental hospital for treatment involves a question that is essentially medical. The question whether an individual is mentally ill and cannot be treated in prison "turns on the meaning of the facts which must be interpreted by expert psychiatrists and psychologists." The medical nature of the inquiry, however, does not justify dispensing with due process requirements. It is precisely "[t]he subtleties and nuances of psychiatric diagnoses" that justify the requirement of adversary hearings.

Because prisoners facing involuntary transfer to a mental hospital are threatened with immediate deprivation of liberty interests they are currently enjoying and because of the inherent risk of a mistaken transfer, the District Court properly determined that procedures similar to those required by the Court in *Morrissey v. Brewer,* 408 U.S. 471 (1972), were appropriate in the circumstances present here.

The notice requirement imposed by the District Court no more than recognizes that notice is essential to afford the prisoner an opportunity to challenge the contemplated action and to understand the nature of what is happening to him. Furthermore, in view of the nature of the determinations that must accompany the transfer to a mental hospital, we think each of the elements of the hearing specified by the District Court was appropriate. The interests of the State in avoiding disruption was recognized by limiting in appropriate circumstances the prisoner's right to call witnesses, to confront and cross examine. The District Court also avoided unnecessary intrusion into either medical or correctional judgments by providing that the independent decisionmaker conducting the transfer hearing need not come from outside the prison or hospital administration.

B *

The District Court did go beyond the requirements imposed by prior cases by holding that counsel must be made available to inmates facing transfer hearings if they are financially unable to furnish their own. We have not required the automatic appointment of counsel for indigent prisoners facing other deprivations of liberty, *Gagnon v. Scarpelli,* 411 U.S., at 790; *Wolff v. McDonnell,* [418 U.S.] at 569–570; but we have recognized that prisoners who are illiterate and uneducated have a greater need for assistance in exercising their rights. *Gagnon v. Scarpelli, supra,* at 786–787; *Wolff v. McDonnell, supra,* at 570. A prisoner thought to be suffering from a mental disease or defect requiring involuntary treatment probably has an even greater need for legal assistance, for such a prisoner is more likely to be unable to understand or exercise his rights. In these circumstances, it is appropriate that counsel be provided to indigent prisoners whom the State seeks to treat as mentally ill.

V

Because Mr. Justice Powell, while believing that Jones was entitled to competent help at the hearing, would not require the State to furnish a licensed attorney to aid him, the judgment below is affirmed as modified to conform with the separate opinion filed by Mr. Justice Powell.

* * *

Mr. Justice Powell, concurring in part.

* This part is joined only by Mr. Justice Brennan, Mr. Justice Marshall, and Mr. Justice Stevens.

I join the opinion of the Court except for Part IV–B. I agree with Part IV–B insofar as the Court holds that qualified and independent assistance must be provided to an inmate who is threatened with involuntary transfer to a state mental hospital. I do not agree, however, that the requirement of independent assistance demands that a licensed attorney be provided.

* * *

The essence of procedural due process is a fair hearing. I do not think that the fairness of an informal hearing designed to determine a medical issue requires participation by lawyers. Due process merely requires that the State provide an inmate with qualified and independent assistance. Such assistance may be provided by a licensed psychiatrist or other mental health professional. Indeed, in view of the nature of the issue involved in the transfer hearing, a person possessing such professional qualifications normally would be preferred. As the Court notes, "[t]he question whether an individual is mentally ill and cannot be treated in prison 'turns on the meaning of the facts which must be interpreted by expert psychiatrists and psychologists.'" I would not exclude, however, the possibility that the required assistance may be rendered by competent laymen in some cases. The essential requirements are that the person provided by the State be competent and independent, and that he be free to act solely in the inmate's best interest.

In sum, although the State is free to appoint a licensed attorney to represent an inmate, it is not constitutionally required to do so. Due process will be satisfied so long as an inmate facing involuntary transfer to a mental hospital is provided qualified and independent assistance.

[Justice Stewart, joined by Chief Justice Burger and Justice Rehnquist, dissented on the grounds that the case was mooted by the plaintiff's release on parole. Justice Blackmun also dissented on mootness grounds. The dissenting opinions are omitted here.]

Questions and Points for Discussion

1. Compare the procedural safeguards required by the Supreme Court in *Vitek v. Jones* with the procedural safeguards outlined in *Wolff v. McDonnell,* supra page 346. Can you reconcile the two cases?

2. In Washington v. Harper, 110 S.Ct. 1028 (1990), the Supreme Court addressed procedural due process issues stemming from the involuntary administration of psychotropic drugs to mentally ill prisoners. The pertinent facts of the case were described by Justice Kennedy in his opinion for the Court:

Policy 600.30 was developed in partial response to this Court's decision in Vitek v. Jones, 445 U.S. 480, 100 S.Ct. 1254 (1980). The Policy has several substantive and procedural components. First, if a psychiatrist determines that an inmate should be treated with antipsychotic drugs but the inmate does not consent, the inmate may be subjected to involuntary treatment with the drugs only if he (1) suffers from a "mental disorder" and (2) is "gravely disabled" or poses a "likelihood of serious harm" to himself, others, or their property. Only a psychiatrist may order or approve the medication. Second, an inmate who refuses to take the medication voluntarily is entitled to a hearing before a special committee consisting of a psychiatrist, psychologist, and the Associate Superintendent of the Center, none of whom may be, at the time of the hearing, involved in the inmate's treatment or diagnosis. If the committee determines by a majority vote that the inmate suffers from a mental disorder and is gravely disabled or dangerous, the inmate may be medicated against his will, provided the psychiatrist is in the majority.

Third, the inmate has certain procedural rights before, during, and after the hearing. He must be given at least 24 hours' notice of the Center's intent to convene an involuntary medication hearing, during which time he may not be medicated. In addition, he must receive notice of the tentative diagnosis, the factual basis for the diagnosis, and why the staff believes medication is necessary. At the hearing, the inmate has the right to attend; to present evidence, including witnesses; to cross-examine staff witnesses; and to the assistance of a lay advisor who has not been involved in his case and who understands the psychiatric issues involved. Minutes of the hearing must be kept, and a copy provided to the inmate. The inmate has the right to appeal the committee's decision to the Superintendent of the Center within 24 hours, and the Superintendent must decide the appeal within 24 hours after its receipt. The inmate may seek judicial review of a committee decision in state court by means of a personal restraint petition or extraordinary writ.

Fourth, after the initial hearing, involuntary medication can continue only with periodic review. When respondent first refused medication, a committee, again composed of a non-treating psychiatrist, a psychologist, and the Center's Associate Superintendent, was required to review an inmate's case after the first seven days of treatment. If the committee reapproved the treatment, the treating psychiatrist was required to review the case and prepare a report for the Department of Corrections medical director every 14 days while treatment continued.

In this case, respondent was absent when members of the Center staff met with the committee before the hearing. The committee then conducted the hearing in accordance with the Policy, with respondent being present and assisted by a nurse practitioner from another institution. The committee found that respondent was a danger to others as a result of a mental disease or disorder, and approved the involuntary administration of antipsychotic drugs. On appeal, the Superintendent upheld the committee's findings. Beginning on November 23, 1982, respondent was involuntarily medicated for about one year. Periodic review occurred in accordance with the Policy.

In November 1983, respondent was transferred from the Center to the Washington State Reformatory. While there, he took no medication, and as a result, his condition deteriorated. He was retransferred to the Center after only one month. Respondent was the subject of another committee hearing in accordance with Policy 600.30, and the committee again approved medication against his will. Respondent continued to receive antipsychotic drugs, subject to the required periodic reviews, until he was transferred to the Washington State Penitentiary in June 1986.

Id. at 1033–34.

In February of 1985, the respondent filed a § 1983 suit in which he claimed that the compulsory administration of antipsychotic drugs violated a number of his rights, including his right to procedural due process under the fourteenth amendment. In addressing this procedural due process claim, the Supreme Court first observed that when the respondent was given antipsychotic drug medication over his objection he was deprived of both a constitutionally derived and a state-created liberty interest. The latter interest found its source in the written prison policy dictating the circumstances under which inmates could be involuntarily treated with antipsychotic drugs.

The Court then rejected the respondent's argument that before being deprived of the liberty interest in not being involuntarily medicated with antipsychotic drugs, the decision had to be approved by a judge after a judicial hearing. Although the Court acknowledged that antipsychotic drugs can cause serious adverse side effects and even death, the Court opined that "an inmate's interests are adequately protected, and perhaps better served, by allowing the decision to medicate to be made by medical professionals rather than a judge," since medical professionals might be better able to assess the need for and the risks posed by certain medications. Id. at 1042–43. Due process was therefore satisfied as long as the decision to involuntarily medicate a prisoner was reviewed by "independent" medical professionals. Id. at 1043. In this particular case, this requirement was met, according to the Court, since the review panel was comprised of a psychiatrist, a psychologist, and an associate warden, none of whom at the time of the review were involved in the treatment of the respondent. Elsewhere in its opinion, however, the Court emphasized that under state law, an inmate could seek judicial review of a review panel's decision by filing a personal restraint petition or a petition for an extraordinary writ.

The Court also held that the respondent had no right to be represented by an attorney during the review process. Due process required no more than that the respondent be afforded assistance from "an independent lay advisor who understands the psychiatric issues involved." Id. at 1044.

Finally, the Court summarily rejected the respondent's argument that due process required the state to establish the need for the antipsychotic medication by "clear, cogent, and convincing evidence." The Court simply noted that "[t]his standard is neither required nor helpful when medical personnel are making the judgment required by the regulations here." Id.

Justice Stevens, joined by Justices Brennan and Marshall, dissented from the Court's resolution of the respondent's constitutional claims. While skirting the question whether antipsychotic drugs can ever be involuntarily administered to a mentally ill prisoner who has not been declared incompetent, Justice Stevens declared that, in any event, the compulsory treatment decision would have to be made by an "impartial professional." Id. at 1052. This requirement, according to Justice Stevens, was not met here, since there was too great a risk that the review panels, comprised of prison staff members, deferred to the recommendation of the treating physician or psychiatrist in return for similar deference to recommendations concerning their own patients. Justice Stevens was also unconvinced that the advisors appointed by prison officials to assist inmates contesting antipsychotic medication orders were sufficiently "qualified" and "independent" to satisfy the requirements of due process. Id. at 1055.

For a discussion of another claim asserted by the respondent in *Harper*—a substantive due process claim—see pages 473–478, infra.

B. EQUAL PROTECTION OF THE LAW

In the volatile confines of the nation's prisons, the threat of violence is ever-present. Most prisoners are bored, frustrated, resentful, and angry; deep down, many are also afraid—afraid of being sexually assaulted and afraid of being killed. Adding to the tension pervading the prisons is deep-seated animosity between prisoners of different races, animosity which is inflamed by the perception that the criminal justice system of which prisons are just a part is racist. See M. Mauer, Young Black Men and the Criminal Justice System 3 (1990) (one out of every four black men in the 20–29 age group and one out of every ten Hispanic males is in prison, in jail, on probation, or on parole as compared to one out of every sixteen white males; as a result, in 1989, over 55% of the nation's prisoners in this age group were black or Hispanic).

Some government officials have responded at times to the threat that racial tensions pose to security and order within the prisons by separating black prisoners from white prisoners. The constitutionality of such segregation policies has been considered by a number of courts, including the United States District Court for the Middle District of Alabama in Washington v. Lee, 263 F.Supp. 327 (M.D.Ala.1966).

The white and black prisoners who brought suit in *Washington v. Lee* challenged the segregation of prisoners by race in Alabama prisons and jails. The defendants defended this segregation by invoking institutional security. The district court, however, concluded that this broadbrush approach to the problem of racial violence in correctional facilities was unconstitutional:

> Although it is true that "[l]awful incarceration brings about the necessary withdrawal or limitation of many privileges and rights, a retraction justified by the considerations underlying our penal system," it is well established that prisoners do not lose all their constitutional rights and that the Due Process and Equal Protection Clauses of the Fourteenth Amendment follow them into prison and protect them there from unconstitutional action on the part of prison authorities carried out under color of state law. In this regard, this Court can

conceive of no consideration of prison security or discipline which will
sustain the constitutionality of state statutes that on their face require
complete and permanent segregation of the races in all the Alabama
penal facilities. We recognize that there is merit in the contention
that in some isolated instances prison security and discipline necessi-
tates segregation of the races for a limited period. However, recognition of such instances does nothing to bolster the statutes or the
general practice that requires or permits prison or jail officials to
separate the races arbitrarily. Such statutes and practices must be
declared unconstitutional in light of the clear principles controlling.

Id. at 331–32.

In a per curiam opinion, the Supreme Court affirmed the district
court's judgment. Lee v. Washington, 390 U.S. 333, 88 S.Ct. 994 (1968).
Responding to the correctional officials' argument that the district
court's orders failed to take into account institutional security needs,
the Court simply said, "[W]e do not so read the 'Order, Judgment and
Decree' of the District Court, which when read as a whole we find
unexceptionable." Id. at 334, 88 S.Ct. at 994. Justice Black, joined by
Justices Harlan and Stewart, wrote a separate concurring opinion more
explicitly addressing the correctional officials' concern:

In joining the opinion of the Court, we wish to make explicit
something that is left to be gathered only by implication from the
Court's opinion. This is that prison authorities have the right, acting
in good faith and in particularized circumstances, to take into account
racial tensions in maintaining security, discipline, and good order in
prisons and jails. We are unwilling to assume that state or local
prison authorities might mistakenly regard such an explicit pronouncement as evincing any dilution of this Court's firm commitment to the
Fourteenth Amendment's prohibition of racial discrimination.

Id. at 334, 88 S.Ct. at 994.

The lower courts have narrowly construed the exception to the
general rule propounded in *Washington v. Lee* and *Lee v. Washington*
that the segregation of prisoners by race is unconstitutional. It is clear
from these decisions that the general fear that the mixing of races will
spark violence is not enough to justify segregation. See, e.g., Stewart v.
Rhodes, 473 F.Supp. 1185, 1189 (S.D.Ohio 1979), affirmed, 785 F.2d 310
(6th Cir.1986); Mickens v. Winston, 462 F.Supp. 910, 912 (E.D.Va.1978),
affirmed 609 F.2d 508 (4th Cir.1979). Even when there is a specific
basis for fearing racial conflict, segregation is impermissible if there are
other means of maintaining institutional security. Blevins v. Brew,
593 F.Supp. 245, 248 (W.D.Wis.1984). Alternatives include closer supervision of the inmates, disciplining and removing troublemakers from
the general prison population, and decreasing the number of prisoners
in the prison. Id. See also McClelland v. Sigler, 456 F.2d 1266, 1267
(8th Cir.1972) ("We think it is incumbent upon the officials in charge to
make other provisions for housing those who would commit assaults or
aggravations on other inmates, white or black, and thus only penalize

those guilty of offending the personal and constitutional rights of others.")

Even limited segregation policies have been stricken down by the courts. For example, in Stewart v. Rhodes, 473 F.Supp. 1185 (S.D.Ohio 1979), affirmed, 785 F.2d 310 (6th Cir.1986), the court examined the constitutionality of a policy of double celling black inmates only with other black inmates and white inmates only with other white inmates in the reception center at one prison. Inmates were housed in the reception area for about eight weeks while being processed into the corrections system. The general housing units in the rest of the prison were integrated.

Prison officials defended the segregation in the reception area, pointing to the lack of information about a prisoner when he first enters the prison system. They argued that since prisoners may harbor prejudice against members of another race which may manifest itself through violence, black and white inmates should not be housed together in the same cell until more information is obtained about their biases and prejudices. The segregation policy, they contended, was based on their "common sense" understanding of race relations.

The district court responded, however, that "an equally 'common sense' attitude * * * would indicate that segregation of inmates rather than their integration tends to create racial misunderstandings and tensions." Id. at 1188. It then ordered cessation of the segregation of inmates by race in the reception center. See also Blevins v. Brew, 593 F.Supp. 245 (W.D.Wis.1984) (racial segregation in prison's admission and orientation unit violated the equal protection clause).

The courts have been no more hospitable to the claims of prison officials that segregation resulting from the "voluntary" choices of inmates as to where they want to live is constitutional. One such segregation scheme was before the Fifth Circuit Court of Appeals in Jones v. Diamond, 636 F.2d 1364 (5th Cir.1981). At the jail at issue in *Jones,* inmates could choose in which of two bullpens they would be confined. All of the whites chose one bullpen, and all of the blacks chose another.

The court of appeals held the resulting segregation to be unconstitutional:

> At least 48 prisoners—those in the two bull pens—were segregated by race with the explanation that this was the result of their choice. In prisons, where hostility of every kind is rampant, freedom of choice is but a gauze for discrimination. In the inherently coercive setting of a jail, the failure of officials properly to supervise their wards is an abdication of responsibility. A black person newly admitted to the crowded jail and ordered to choose between confinement in a cell crowded with white prisoners, some convicted of major felonies, could hardly find the "choice" to be aught but illusory. A white prisoner would be equally unlikely voluntarily to enter a cell full of black prisoners in preference to one occupied by whites. The defendants do

not suggest any justification for the policy. While it was disguised in terms of choice, the practice was racially discriminatory and, hence, unconstitutional.

Id. at 1373.

Questions and Points for Discussion

1. When, if ever, would making housing assignments in a prison or jail on the basis of race be constitutional?

2. Is the approach of the courts to questions concerning the constitutionality of racial segregation consistent with their analysis of other constitutional claims asserted by prisoners?

Chapter 13

SEARCHES, SEIZURES, AND PRIVACY RIGHTS

A. THE FOURTH AMENDMENT

The fourth amendment to the United States Constitution provides in part that "[t]he right of the people to be secure in their persons, houses, papers, and effects, against unreasonable searches and seizures, shall not be violated * * *." The language of the amendment raises two questions: (1) when has a search or seizure occurred, triggering the protections of the fourth amendment, and (2) when is a search or seizure prohibitively unreasonable? The Supreme Court discussed the first question in the case which follows.

HUDSON v. PALMER
Supreme Court of the United States, 1984.
468 U.S. 517, 104 S.Ct. 3194, 82 L.Ed.2d 393.

CHIEF JUSTICE BURGER delivered the opinion of the Court.

The facts underlying this dispute are relatively simple. Respondent Palmer is an inmate at the Bland Correctional Center in Bland, Va., serving sentences for forgery, uttering, grand larceny, and bank robbery convictions. On September 16, 1981, petitioner Hudson, an officer at the Correctional Center, with a fellow officer, conducted a "shakedown" search of respondent's prison locker and cell for contraband. During the "shakedown," the officers discovered a ripped pillowcase in a trash can near respondent's cell bunk. Charges against Palmer were instituted under the prison disciplinary procedures for destroying state property. After a hearing, Palmer was found guilty on the charge and was ordered to reimburse the State for the cost of the material destroyed; in addition, a reprimand was entered on his prison record.

[Palmer filed a § 1983 suit, contending that Hudson had violated his fourth amendment right not to be subjected to unreasonable searches and seizures; Palmer also alleged that Hudson had deprived him of his property without due process of law. The Supreme Court's disposition of this latter claim is discussed on page 459, infra.

The district court rejected Palmer's fourth amendment claim, granting Hudson's motion for summary judgment. On appeal, however, the Fourth Circuit Court of Appeals reversed. The court of appeals held that the fourth amendment accords inmates a "limited privacy right" to be protected from searches designed solely to harass them. To ensure that inmates are not subjected to such searches, a cell search, according to the court, had to be either based on the "reasonable belief" that a particular inmate possesses contraband or conducted pursuant to an "established program of random searches" that could reasonably be expected to detect or deter inmates' possession of contraband.

The Supreme Court then granted certiorari.]

The first question we address is whether respondent has a right of privacy in his prison cell entitling him to the protection of the Fourth Amendment against unreasonable searches. * * * Petitioner contends that the Court of Appeals erred in holding that respondent had even a limited privacy right in his cell, and urges that we adopt the "bright line" rule that prisoners have no legitimate expectation of privacy in their individual cells that would entitle them to Fourth Amendment protection.

* * *

* * * [W]hile persons imprisoned for crime enjoy many protections of the Constitution, it is also clear that imprisonment carries with it the circumscription or loss of many significant rights. * * * The curtailment of certain rights is necessary, as a practical matter, to accommodate a myriad of "institutional needs and objectives" of prison facilities, chief among which is internal security. Of course, these restrictions or retractions also serve, incidentally, as reminders that, under our system of justice, deterrence and retribution are factors in addition to correction.

We have not before been called upon to decide the specific question whether the Fourth Amendment applies within a prison cell, but the nature of our inquiry is well defined. We must determine here, as in other Fourth Amendment contexts, if a "justifiable" expectation of privacy is at stake. *Katz v. United States,* 389 U.S. 347 (1967). The applicability of the Fourth Amendment turns on whether "the person invoking its protection can claim a 'justifiable,' a 'reasonable,' or a 'legitimate expectation of privacy' that has been invaded by government action." We must decide, in Justice Harlan's words, whether a prisoner's expectation of privacy in his prison cell is the kind of expectation that "society is prepared to recognize as 'reasonable.'" *Katz, supra,* at 360, 361 (concurring opinion).

Notwithstanding our caution in approaching claims that the Fourth Amendment is inapplicable in a given context, we hold that society is not prepared to recognize as legitimate any subjective expectation of privacy that a prisoner might have in his prison cell and that, accordingly, the Fourth Amendment proscription against unreasonable searches does not apply within the confines of the prison cell. The recognition of privacy rights for prisoners in their individual cells simply cannot be reconciled with the concept of incarceration and the needs and objectives of penal institutions.

Prisons, by definition, are places of involuntary confinement of persons who have a demonstrated proclivity for antisocial criminal, and often violent, conduct. Inmates have necessarily shown a lapse in ability to control and conform their behavior to the legitimate standards of society by the normal impulses of self-restraint; they have shown an inability to regulate their conduct in a way that reflects either a respect for law or an appreciation of the rights of others. Even a partial survey of the statistics on violent crime in our Nation's prisons illustrates the magnitude of the problem. During 1981 and the first half of 1982, there were over 120 prisoners murdered by fellow inmates in state and federal prisons. A number of prison personnel were murdered by prisoners during this period. Over 29 riots or similar disturbances were reported in these facilities for the same time frame. And there were over 125 suicides in these institutions. Additionally, informal statistics from the United States Bureau of Prisons show that in the federal system during 1983, there were 11 inmate homicides, 359 inmate assaults on other inmates, 227 inmate assaults on prison staff, and 10 suicides. There were in the same system in 1981 and 1982 over 750 inmate assaults on other inmates and over 570 inmate assaults on prison personnel.

Within this volatile "community," prison administrators are to take all necessary steps to ensure the safety of not only the prison staffs and administrative personnel, but also visitors. They are under an obligation to take reasonable measures to guarantee the safety of the inmates themselves. They must be ever alert to attempts to introduce drugs and other contraband into the premises which, we can judicially notice, is one of the most perplexing problems of prisons today; they must prevent, so far as possible, the flow of illicit weapons into the prison; they must be vigilant to detect escape plots, in which drugs or weapons may be involved, before the schemes materialize. In addition to these monumental tasks, it is incumbent upon these officials at the same time to maintain as sanitary an environment for the inmates as feasible, given the difficulties of the circumstances.

The administration of a prison, we have said, is "at best an extraordinarily difficult undertaking." But it would be literally impossible to accomplish the prison objectives identified above if inmates retained a right of privacy in their cells. Virtually the only place inmates can conceal weapons, drugs, and other contraband is in their cells. Unfettered access to these cells by prison officials, thus, is imperative if drugs and contraband are to be ferreted out and sanitary surroundings are to be maintained.

Determining whether an expectation of privacy is "legitimate" or "reasonable" necessarily entails a balancing of interests. The two interests here are the interest of society in the security of its penal institutions and the interest of the prisoner in privacy within his cell. The latter interest, of course, is already limited by the exigencies of the circumstances: A prison "shares none of the attributes of privacy of a home, an automobile, an office, or a hotel room." We strike the balance in favor of institutional security, which we have noted is "central to all other corrections goals." A right of privacy in traditional Fourth Amendment terms is fundamentally incompatible with the close and continual surveillance of inmates and their cells required to ensure institutional security and internal order.[8] We are satisfied that society would insist that the prisoner's expectation of privacy always yield to what must be considered the paramount interest in institutional security. We believe that it is accepted by our society that "[l]oss of freedom of choice and privacy are inherent incidents of confinement."

The Court of Appeals was troubled by the possibility of searches conducted solely to harass inmates; it reasoned that a requirement that searches be conducted only pursuant to an established policy or upon reasonable suspicion would prevent such searches to the maximum extent possible. Of course, there is a risk of maliciously motivated searches, and of course, intentional harassment of even the most hardened criminals cannot be tolerated by a civilized society. However, we disagree with the court's proposed solution. The uncertainty that attends random searches of cells renders these searches perhaps the most effective weapon of the prison administrator in the constant fight against the proliferation of knives and guns, illicit drugs, and other contraband. * * *

A requirement that even random searches be conducted pursuant to an established plan would seriously undermine the effectiveness of this weapon. It is simply naive to believe that prisoners would not eventually decipher any plan officials might devise for "planned random searches," and thus be able routinely to anticipate searches. * * *

Respondent acknowledges that routine shakedowns of prison cells are essential to the effective administration of prisons. He contends, however, that he is constitutionally entitled not to be subjected to searches conducted only to harass. The crux of his claim is that

---

8. Respondent contends also that the destruction of his personal property constituted an unreasonable *seizure* of that property violative of the Fourth Amendment. Assuming that the Fourth Amendment protects against the destruction of property, in addition to its mere seizure, the same reasons that lead us to conclude that the Fourth Amendment's proscription against unreasonable searches is inapplicable in a prison cell, apply with controlling force to seizures. Prison officials must be free to seize from cells any articles which, in their view, disserve legitimate institutional interests.

That the Fourth Amendment does not protect against seizures in a prison cell does not mean that an inmate's property can be destroyed with impunity. We note, for example, that even apart from inmate grievance procedures, respondent has adequate state remedies for the alleged destruction of his property.

"because searches and seizures to harass are unreasonable, a prisoner has a reasonable expectation of privacy not to have his cell, locker, personal effects, [or] person invaded for such a purpose." This argument, which assumes the answer to the predicate question whether a prisoner has a legitimate expectation of privacy in his prison cell at all, is merely a challenge to the reasonableness of the particular search of respondent's cell. Because we conclude that prisoners have no legitimate expectation of privacy and that the Fourth Amendment's prohibition on unreasonable searches does not apply in prison cells, we need not address this issue.

Our holding that respondent does not have a reasonable expectation of privacy enabling him to invoke the protections of the Fourth Amendment does not mean that he is without a remedy for calculated harassment unrelated to prison needs. Nor does it mean that prison attendants can ride roughshod over inmates' property rights with impunity. The Eighth Amendment always stands as a protection against "cruel and unusual punishments." By the same token, there are adequate state tort and common-law remedies available to respondent to redress the alleged destruction of his personal property.

* * *

We hold that the Fourth Amendment has no applicability to a prison cell. * * *

Accordingly, the judgment of the Court of Appeals reversing and remanding the District Court's judgment on respondent's claim under the Fourth and Fourteenth Amendments is reversed. * * *

* * *

JUSTICE O'CONNOR, concurring. [Opinion omitted.]

JUSTICE STEVENS, with whom JUSTICE BRENNAN, JUSTICE MARSHALL, and JUSTICE BLACKMUN join, concurring in part and dissenting in part.

This case comes to us on the pleadings. We must take the allegations in Palmer's complaint as true. Liberally construing this *pro se* complaint as we must, it alleges that after examining it, prison guard Hudson maliciously took and destroyed a quantity of Palmer's property, including legal materials and letters, for no reason other than harassment.

* * *

Even if it is assumed that Palmer had no reasonable expectation of privacy in most of the property at issue in this case because it could be inspected at any time, that does not mean he was without Fourth Amendment protection.[5] For the Fourth Amendment protects Palm-

---

5. Though I am willing to assume that for purposes of this case * * * the Court's holding concerning most of Palmer's privacy interests is correct, that should not be taken as an endorsement of the Court's new "bright line" rule that a prisoner can have no expectation of privacy in his papers or effects. I cannot see any justification for applying this rule to minimum security facilities in which inmates who pose no realistic threat to security are housed. I also see no justification for reading the mail of a prisoner once it has cleared whatever censorship mechanism is employed by the prison and has been received by the prisoner.

er's possessory interests in this property entirely apart from whatever privacy interest he may have in it.

> "The first Clause of the Fourth Amendment provides that the 'right of the people to be secure in their persons, houses, papers, and effects, against unreasonable searches and seizures, shall not be violated . . . .' This text protects two kinds of expectations, one involving 'searches,' the other 'seizures.' A 'search' occurs when an expectation of privacy that society is prepared to consider reasonable is infringed. A 'seizure' of property occurs when there is some meaningful interference with an individual's possessory interests in that property." *United States v. Jacobsen*, 466 U.S. 109, 113 (1984).

There can be no doubt that the complaint adequately alleges a "seizure" within the meaning of the Fourth Amendment. * * *

The Court suggests that "the interest of society in the security of its penal institutions" precludes prisoners from having any legitimate possessory interests. That contention is fundamentally wrong for at least two reasons.

First, Palmer's possession of the material was entirely legitimate as a matter of state law. There is no contention that the material seized was contraband or that Palmer's possession of it was in any way inconsistent with applicable prison regulations. Hence, he had a legal right to possess it. * * *

Second, the most significant of Palmer's possessory interests are protected as a matter of substantive constitutional law, entirely apart from the legitimacy of those interests under state law or the Due Process Clause. The Eighth Amendment forbids "cruel and unusual punishments." Its proscriptions are measured by society's "evolving standards of decency." The Court's implication that prisoners have no possessory interests that by virtue of the Fourth Amendment are free from state interference cannot, in my view, be squared with the Eighth Amendment. To hold that a prisoner's possession of a letter from his wife, or a picture of his baby, has no protection against arbitrary or malicious perusal, seizure, or destruction would not, in my judgment, comport with any civilized standard of decency.

There are other substantive constitutional rights that also shed light on the legitimacy of Palmer's possessory interests. The complaint alleges that the material at issue includes letters and legal materials. This Court has held that the First Amendment entitles a prisoner to receive and send mail, subject only to the institution's right to censor letters or withhold delivery if necessary to protect institutional security, and if accompanied by appropriate procedural safeguards.[13] We have also held that the Fourteenth Amendment entitles a prisoner to reasonable access to legal materials as a corollary of the constitutional

---

13. See *Procunier v. Martinez*, 416 U.S. 396 (1974). A prisoner's possession of other types of personal property relating to religious observance, such as a Bible or a crucifix, is surely protected by the Free Exercise Clause of the First Amendment.

right of access to the courts.[14] Thus, these substantive constitutional rights affirmatively protect Palmer's right to possess the material in question free from state interference. It is therefore beyond me how the Court can question the legitimacy of Palmer's possessory interests which were so clearly infringed by Hudson's alleged conduct.

Once it is concluded that Palmer has adequately alleged a "seizure," the question becomes whether the seizure was "unreasonable." Questions of Fourth Amendment reasonableness can be resolved only by balancing the intrusion on constitutionally protected interests against the law enforcement interests justifying the challenged conduct.

* * * There can be no penological justification for the seizure alleged here. There is no contention that Palmer's property posed any threat to institutional security. Hudson had already examined the material before he took and destroyed it. The allegation is that Hudson did this for no reason save spite; there is no contention that under prison regulations the material was contraband * * *. When, as here, the material at issue is not contraband it simply makes no sense to say that its seizure and destruction serve "legitimate institutional interests." Such seizures are unreasonable.

The Court's holding is based on its belief that society would not recognize as reasonable the possessory interests of prisoners. Its perception of what society is prepared to recognize as reasonable is not based on any empirical data; rather it merely reflects the perception of the four Justices who have joined the opinion that The Chief Justice has authored. * * * The Court itself acknowledges that "intentional harassment of even the most hardened criminals cannot be tolerated by a civilized society." That being the case, I fail to see how a seizure that serves no purpose except harassment does not invade an interest that society considers reasonable, and that is protected by the Fourth Amendment.

The Court rests its view of "reasonableness" almost entirely upon its assessment of the security needs of prisons. Because deference to institutional needs is so critical to the Court's approach, it is worth inquiring as to the view prison administrators take toward conduct of the type at issue here. On that score the Court demonstrates a remarkable lack of awareness as to what penologists and correctional officials consider "legitimate institutional interests." I am unaware that any responsible prison administrator has ever contended that there is a need to take or destroy noncontraband property of prisoners; the Court certainly provides no evidence to support its conclusion that institutions require this sort of power. To the contrary, it appears to be the near-universal view of correctional officials that guards should neither seize nor destroy noncontraband property. * * *

Depriving inmates of any residuum of privacy or possessory rights is in fact plainly *contrary* to institutional goals. Sociologists recognize

14. See *Bounds v. Smith,* 430 U.S. 817 (1977).

that prisoners deprived of any sense of individuality devalue themselves and others and therefore are more prone to violence toward themselves or others. At the same time, such an approach undermines the rehabilitative function of the institution: "Without the privacy and dignity provided by fourth amendment coverage, an inmate's opportunity to reform, as small as it may be, will further be diminished. It is anomalous to provide a prisoner with rehabilitative programs and services in an effort to build self-respect while simultaneously subjecting him to unjustified and degrading searches and seizures." Gianelli & Gilligan, Prison Searches and Seizures: "Locking" the Fourth Amendment Out of Correctional Facilities, 62 Va.L.Rev. 1045, 1069 (1976).

To justify its conclusion, the Court recites statistics concerning the number of crimes that occur within prisons. For example, it notes that over an 18–month period approximately 120 prisoners were murdered in state and federal facilities. At the end of 1983 there were 438,830 inmates in state and federal prisons. The Court's homicide rate of 80 per year yields an annual prison homicide rate of 18.26 persons per 100,000 inmates. In 1982, the homicide rate in Miami was 51.98 per 100,000; in New York it was 23.50 per 100,000; in Dallas 31.53 per 100,000; and in the District of Columbia 30.70 per 100,000. Thus, the prison homicide rate, it turns out, is significantly lower than that in many of our major cities. I do not suggest this type of analysis provides a standard for measuring the reasonableness of a search or seizure within prisons, but I do suggest that the Court's use of statistics is less than persuasive.[30]

* * *

Questions and Points for Discussion

1. It is clear from *Hudson v. Palmer* and other Supreme Court cases that even when governmental officials have conducted a search from a layperson's perspective, a "search" within the meaning of the fourth amendment may not have occurred. See, e.g., California v. Greenwood, 486 U.S. 35, 108 S.Ct. 1625 (1988) (no "search" occurred when police officers examined the contents of garbage bags left at the curbside for pickup); Oliver v. United States, 466 U.S. 170, 104 S.Ct. 1735 (1984) (search of open field does not implicate the fourth amendment); Smith v. Maryland, 442

[30. I cannot help but think that the Court's holding is influenced by an unstated fear that if it recognizes that prisoners have any Fourth Amendment protection this will lead to a flood of frivolous lawsuits. Of course, this type of burden is not sufficient to justify a judicial modification of the requirements of law. "Frivolous cases should be treated as exactly that, and not as occasions for fundamental shifts in legal doctrine. Our legal system has developed procedures for speedily disposing of unfounded claims; if they are inadequate to protect [defendants] from vexatious litigation, then there is something wrong with those procedures, not with the [Fourth Amendment]." *Hoover* v. *Ronwin,* 466 U.S. 558, 601 (1984) (Stevens, J., dissenting). In fact, the lower courts have permitted such suits to be brought for some time now, without disastrous results. Moreover, costs can be awarded against the plaintiff when frivolous cases are brought. Even modest assessments against prisoners' accounts could provide an effective weapon for deterring truly groundless litigation.]

U.S. 735, 99 S.Ct. 2577 (1979) (use of pen register, a mechanical device placed on a phone line to record numbers dialed from the phone, not a "search"). Not unless there has been a governmental intrusion into an area in which an individual has a "legitimate" or "reasonable" expectation of privacy will a "search" have occurred falling within the rubric of the fourth amendment.

Although the Supreme Court in *Hudson* purported to explain why a cell shakedown is not a "search" as that word is used in the fourth amendment, did the Court fully explain why the confiscation of a prisoner's noncontraband property is not a "seizure" of the prisoner's "effects" and, in some cases, "papers"? Do you agree with this portion of the Court's decision? If not, what requirements would have to be met for the seizure of a prisoner's property to be reasonable under the fourth amendment?

2. After *Hudson,* cell searches, no matter how abusive and unwarranted, are apparently not actionable under the fourth amendment. A prisoner whose cell is searched ten times a day or even ten times a night has no cause for complaint as far as the fourth amendment is concerned. Even when the sole reason for searching the inmate's cell is to harass the inmate, no fourth amendment claim will lie.

Does a prisoner whose cell is searched or property taken have any potential claim under the Constitution? Did the prisoner in *Hudson*?

3. Searches of prisoners' cells have uncovered almost every type of contraband imaginable, including liquor, marijuana, heroin, cocaine, knives, and even guns. The photograph on the next page depicts some of the items confiscated from cells in prisons.

Measures have been taken by prison authorities to reduce the presence of weapons in prisons. For example, prisoners now generally use plastic eating utensils instead of metal ones, since the metal ones in the past were honed into knives. As the photograph demonstrates, however, the problem of disarming prisoners still persists.

4. In addition to not being able to contest cell searches and property seizures on fourth amendment grounds, prisoners have no constitutional right to observe a search of their cells to help ensure that their property is not wrongfully confiscated, stolen, or destroyed. The Supreme Court has indicated on two different occasions that even pretrial detainees have no such right. See Block v. Rutherford, 468 U.S. 576, 589–91, 104 S.Ct. 3227, 3235 (1984); Bell v. Wolfish, 441 U.S. 520, 555–57, 99 S.Ct. 1861, 1883–84 (1979).

In *Bell v. Wolfish,* the Court observed that even assuming that the fourth amendment provides protection to pretrial detainees, refusing to permit pretrial detainees to observe searches of their cells does not contravene the fourth amendment. Not allowing prisoners to be present during cell searches is "reasonable" and hence in conformance with the fourth amendment for at least two reasons. First, permitting detainees to observe a search of their cells might lead to friction between the detainees and the correctional officers conducting the search, friction which might even erupt into violence. Second, detainees in the cell search area might be able to

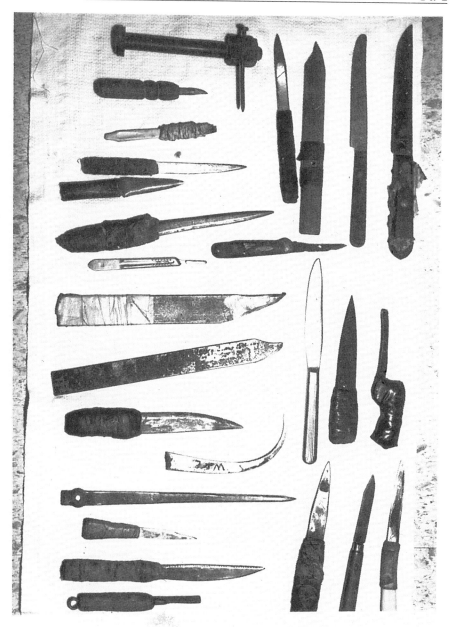

American Correctional Association

move contraband from one cell to another, frustrating the objectives of the search.

In the lower court proceedings in *Block v. Rutherford*, the district court had tried to allay the second concern by allowing jail officials to bring detainees one at a time from a holding room to watch the search of their cells. 468 U.S. at 582 n. 5, 104 S.Ct. at 3230 n. 5. Under this approach, the risk that the detainees would be wrongfully dispossessed of their property could be diminished without detainees undermining the purpose of cell searches through the passage of contraband from one cell to another.

The Supreme Court stood by its decision in *Bell v. Wolfish*, however, emphasizing that detainees have neither a fourth amendment nor a due process right to observe searches of their cells. To the argument that *Wolfish* was distinguishable since the detainees here, under the district court's order, could not pass contraband from cell to cell ahead of the searchers, the Court responded:

> This factual distinction is without legal significance. In effect, the order here merely attempts to impose on officials the least restrictive means available for accomplishment of their security objectives. We reaffirm that administrative officials are not obliged to adopt the least restrictive means to meet their legitimate objectives. Wolfish, 441 U.S. at 542, n. 25.

468 U.S. at 591 n. 11, 104 S.Ct. at 3235 n. 11.

Even if a least-restrictive-alternative requirement was applied when analyzing fourth amendment and due process claims of inmates and pretrial detainees, would a rule barring inmates or detainees from observing cell searches be unconstitutional?

———

Even when a search or seizure triggering the protections of the fourth amendment has occurred, the fourth amendment will not necessarily have been violated. The search or seizure must have been unreasonable to fall within the prohibitions of the fourth amendment. The question still remains as to when a search or seizure is prohibitively unreasonable, a question to which the Supreme Court turned in the case which follows.

BELL v. WOLFISH

Supreme Court of the United States, 1979.
441 U.S. 520, 99 S.Ct. 1861, 60 L.Ed.2d 447.

[This case arose as a class action suit filed by pretrial detainees and inmates housed at the Metropolitan Correctional Center (MCC) in New York City. The detainees and inmates raised a number of challenges to the conditions of their confinement, one of which is discussed below. The claim discussed is a fourth amendment challenge to visual body-cavity inspections conducted, after contact visits, on persons incarcerated at MCC.]

MR. JUSTICE REHNQUIST delivered the opinion of the Court.

* * *

Inmates at all Bureau of Prisons facilities, including the MCC, are required to expose their body cavities for visual inspection as a part of a strip search conducted after every contact visit with a person from outside the institution.[39] Corrections officials testified that visual cavity searches were necessary not only to discover but also to deter the smuggling of weapons, drugs, and other contraband into the institution. The District Court upheld the strip-search procedure but prohibited the body-cavity searches, absent probable cause to believe that the inmate is concealing contraband. Because petitioners proved only one instance in the MCC's short history where contraband was found during a body-cavity search, the Court of Appeals affirmed. In its view, the "gross violation of personal privacy inherent in such a search cannot be outweighed by the government's security interest in maintaining a practice of so little actual utility."

Admittedly, this practice instinctively gives us the most pause. However, assuming for present purposes that inmates, both convicted prisoners and pretrial detainees, retain some Fourth Amendment rights upon commitment to a corrections facility, we nonetheless conclude that these searches do not violate that Amendment. The Fourth Amendment prohibits only unreasonable searches, and under the circumstances, we do not believe that these searches are unreasonable.

The test of reasonableness under the Fourth Amendment is not capable of precise definition or mechanical application. In each case it requires a balancing of the need for the particular search against the invasion of personal rights that the search entails. Courts must consider the scope of the particular intrusion, the manner in which it is conducted, the justification for initiating it, and the place in which it is conducted. A detention facility is a unique place fraught with serious security dangers. Smuggling of money, drugs, weapons, and other contraband is all too common an occurrence. And inmate attempts to secrete these items into the facility by concealing them in body cavities are documented in this record and in other cases. That there has been only one instance where an MCC inmate was discovered attempting to smuggle contraband into the institution on his person may be more a testament to the effectiveness of this search technique as a deterrent than to any lack of interest on the part of the inmates to secrete and import such items when the opportunity arises.[40]

39. If the inmate is a male, he must lift his genitals and bend over to spread his buttocks for visual inspection. The vaginal and anal cavities of female inmates are also visually inspected. The inmate is not touched by security personnel at any time during the *visual* search procedure.

40. The District Court indicated that in its view the use of metal detection equipment represented a less intrusive and equally effective alternative to cavity inspections. We noted in *United States v. Martinez–Fuerte,* 428 U.S. 543, 556–557, n. 12 (1976), that "[t]he logic of such elaborate less-restrictive-alternative arguments could raise insuperable barriers to the exercise of virtually all search-and-seizure powers."

However, assuming that the existence of less intrusive alternatives is relevant to the determination of the reasonableness of the particular search method at issue, the alternative suggested by the District Court simply would not be as effective as the visual inspection procedure. Money, drugs, and other non-metallic contraband still could easily be smuggled into the institution. Another possible alternative, not mentioned by the lower courts, would be to closely observe inmate visits. But MCC officials have adopted the visual inspection procedure as an alternative to close and constant monitoring of contact visits to avoid the obvious disruption of the confidentiality and intimacy that these visits

We do not underestimate the degree to which these searches may invade the personal privacy of inmates. Nor do we doubt, as the District Court noted, that on occasion a security guard may conduct the search in an abusive fashion. Such abuse cannot be condoned. The searches must be conducted in a reasonable manner. But we deal here with the question whether visual body-cavity inspections as contemplated by the MCC rules can *ever* be conducted on less than probable cause. Balancing the significant and legitimate security interests of the institution against the privacy interests of the inmates, we conclude that they can.

[The Court also held that the visual body cavity searches of pretrial detainees did not constitute "punishment" proscribed by the due process clause, since the searches were reasonably related to the legitimate governmental interests in institutional security and order.]

* * *

MR. JUSTICE POWELL, concurring in part and dissenting in part.

I join the opinion of the Court except the discussion and holding with respect to body-cavity searches. In view of the serious intrusion on one's privacy occasioned by such a search, I think at least some level of cause, such as a reasonable suspicion, should be required to justify the anal and genital searches described in this case. I therefore dissent on this issue.

MR. JUSTICE MARSHALL, dissenting.

[Justice Marshall first observed that for a restriction on a pretrial detainee to be constitutional, the government must at least establish that the restriction is "substantially necessary to jail administration." If the restriction impinges on a fundamentally important interest or causes "significant" injury to a detainee, a higher standard is to be applied: the restriction must further a "compelling necessity" to pass constitutional scrutiny. Justice Marshall then applied the standards he had enunciated to the practice of conducting visual body-cavity searches in a correctional facility.]

In my view, the body-cavity searches of MCC inmates represent one of the most grievous offenses against personal dignity and common decency. After every contact visit with someone from outside the facility, including defense attorneys, an inmate must remove all of his or her clothing, bend over, spread the buttocks, and display the anal cavity for inspection by a correctional officer. Women inmates must assume a suitable posture for vaginal inspection, while men must raise their genitals. And, as the Court neglects to note, because of time

are intended to afford. That choice has not been shown to be irrational or unreasonable. Another alternative that might obviate the need for body-cavity inspections would be to abolish contact visits altogether. But the Court of Appeals, in a ruling that is not challenged in this Court and on which we, accordingly, express no opinion, held that pretrial detainees have a constitutional right to contact visits.[a]

[a. The Supreme Court later concluded in *Block v. Rutherford*, 468 U.S. 576, 104 S.Ct. 3227 (1984), that pretrial detainees have no constitutional right to contact visits.]

pressures, this humiliating spectacle is frequently conducted in the presence of other inmates.

The District Court found that the stripping was "unpleasant, embarrassing, and humiliating." A psychiatrist testified that the practice placed inmates in the most degrading position possible, a conclusion amply corroborated by the testimony of the inmates themselves. There was evidence, moreover, that these searches engendered among detainees fears of sexual assault, were the occasion for actual threats of physical abuse by guards, and caused some inmates to forgo personal visits.

Not surprisingly, the Government asserts a security justification for such inspections. These searches are necessary, it argues, to prevent inmates from smuggling contraband into the facility. In crediting this justification despite the contrary findings of the two courts below, the Court overlooks the critical facts. As respondents point out, inmates are required to wear one-piece jumpsuits with zippers in the front. To insert an object into the vaginal or anal cavity, an inmate would have to remove the jumpsuit, at least from the upper torso. Since contact visits occur in a glass-enclosed room and are continuously monitored by corrections officers,[18] such a feat would seem extraordinarily difficult. There was medical testimony, moreover, that inserting an object into the rectum is painful and "would require time and opportunity which is not available in the visiting areas," and that visual inspection would probably not detect an object once inserted. Additionally, before entering the visiting room, visitors and their packages are searched thoroughly by a metal detector, fluoroscope, and by hand. Correction officers may require that visitors leave packages or handbags with guards until the visit is over. Only by blinding itself to the facts presented on this record can the Court accept the Government's security rationale.

Without question, these searches are an imposition of sufficient gravity to invoke the compelling-necessity standard. It is equally indisputable that they cannot meet that standard. Indeed, the procedure is so unnecessarily degrading that it "shocks the conscience." *Rochin v. California*, 342 U.S. 165, 172 (1952). * * * Here, the searches are employed absent any suspicion of wrongdoing. It was this aspect of the MCC practice that the Court of Appeals redressed, requiring that searches be conducted only when there is probable cause to believe that the inmate is concealing contraband. The Due Process Clause, on any principled reading, dictates no less.

[The dissenting opinion of Justice Stevens, in which Justice Brennan joined, is omitted.]

18. To facilitate this monitoring, MCC officials limited to 25 the number of people in the visiting room at one time. Inmates were forbidden to use the locked lavatories, and visitors could use them only by requesting a key from a correctional officer. The lavatories, as well, contain a built-in window for observation.

Questions and Points for Discussion

1. In *Bell v. Wolfish*, the Supreme Court assumed without deciding that visual body-cavity examinations are "searches" within the meaning of the fourth amendment. After *Hudson v. Palmer*, how do you think the Supreme Court would and should resolve the question left open in *Bell*? What about strip searches of inmates or pretrial detainees not involving rectal or vaginal examinations? Would and should such searches be considered searches under the fourth amendment? Would pat-down frisks? Should they?

2. Most of the courts which have addressed the question have concluded or assumed that prisoners retain some residual fourth amendment rights after incarceration. The fourth amendment, according to these courts, places at least some constraints on searches of prisoners' bodies. See, e.g., Franklin v. Lockhart, 769 F.2d 509, 510–11 (8th Cir.1985) (entry of summary judgment for prison officials was inappropriate where prisoner claimed he was strip-searched twice a day while in punitive confinement even though he only had access to tissue and to his meals while in his cell); Batton v. North Carolina, 501 F.Supp. 1173, 1180 (E.D.N.C.1980) (claims that sterile procedures are not followed during vaginal searches of female inmates and that male guards watch such searches are actionable under the fourth amendment).

3. Assuming that searches of prisoners' bodies implicate the fourth amendment, the question is: What constraints does the fourth amendment place on such searches? In other words, what requirements must be met in order for such searches to be considered reasonable?

The Supreme Court has often held that searches must be based on probable cause to be reasonable. For example, the Court has required the presence of probable cause before police can search a home for evidence of a crime. In the prison context, imposition of a probable cause requirement would mean that before searching a prisoner's body, correctional officers would have to have probable cause to believe that the search would uncover contraband or some evidence of a crime or a violation of a prison regulation. Probable cause would exist if, looking at all of the circumstances, there was a "fair probability" that the search would yield contraband or inculpatory evidence. See Illinois v. Gates, 462 U.S. 213, 238, 103 S.Ct. 2317, 2332 (1983) (defining probable cause for a search).

In recent years, the Supreme Court has condoned more and more searches based on some degree of suspicion not rising to the level of probable cause. For example, the Court has held that a frisk of an unincarcerated person for weapons is constitutional as long as two requirements are met: one, that the search is grounded on reasonable and articulable suspicion that the person is armed and dangerous, and two, that the search is limited in scope to what is reasonably necessary to locate weapons. See Terry v. Ohio, 392 U.S. 1, 88 S.Ct. 1868 (1968).

In arriving at its conclusion that frisks for weapons are reasonable even though probable cause for the frisks may be absent, the Court applied a balancing test, like the one later applied by the Court in *Bell v. Wolfish*.

The Court said that when a police officer has a reasonable and articulable suspicion that an individual is armed and dangerous, the need to conduct a limited search for weapons outweighs the intrusion resulting from the search. The interest of the police officer in protecting himself or herself and the public from armed violence plus the societal interests in the prevention and detection of crimes warrant what the Court acknowledged to be a "serious intrusion upon the sanctity of the person," one which may involve the touching of genital areas.

In some cases, one of which is *Bell v. Wolfish,* the Supreme Court has upheld searches or seizures unsupported by any probable cause in the traditional sense or even reasonable and articulable suspicion. See, e.g., Skinner v. Railway Labor Executives' Ass'n, 489 U.S. 602, 109 S.Ct. 1402 (1989) (blood and urine tests of all railroad employees involved in a train accident administered whether or not there was any reason to believe an employee was under the influence of alcohol or drugs at the time of the accident); Colorado v. Bertine, 479 U.S. 367, 107 S.Ct. 738 (1987) (search of containers found in a car during an inventory search); Illinois v. Lafayette, 462 U.S. 640, 103 S.Ct. 2605 (1983) (inventory search of arrestee's shoulder bag before his placement in jail). The Court has often condoned such searches and seizures when the searches or seizures were "administrative" in nature. Although the line between administrative searches and seizures and searches and seizures to which traditional rules apply may be a bit obscure, administrative searches appear to be those whose principal purpose is to further some legitimate governmental objective other than the ones of capturing criminals or discovering evidence to be used in criminal prosecutions. The benign nature of an administrative search or seizure, in the Court's mind, diminishes the intrusiveness of the governmental action which in turn may tip the scales under the balancing test towards a finding of reasonableness and constitutionality.

In approving administrative searches and seizures not grounded on probable cause or even a reasonable and articulable suspicion, however, the Supreme Court has generally emphasized that the searches or seizures were conducted in accordance with standardized administrative or legislative procedures. See, e.g., Colorado v. Bertine, 479 U.S. at 374 n. 6, 107 S.Ct. at 742 n. 6 (1987) ("We emphasize that, in this case, the trial court found that the Police Department's procedures mandated the opening of closed containers and the listing of their contents. Our decisions have always adhered to the requirement that inventories be conducted according to standardized criteria."). Because of these standardized procedures, the discretion of government officials as to whether and how a search or seizure would be conducted was confined, thereby limiting the intrusiveness of the search or seizure.

In light of Supreme Court precedents, what fourth amendment limitations, if any, would or should be placed on pat-down frisks, strip searches, and visual body-cavity searches of prisoners? What about manual body-cavity searches, ones which entail an actual touching of the body cavities of an inmate?

4. According to the Supreme Court in *Bell v. Wolfish,* a search under the fourth amendment may be reasonable even though less intrusive means

of meeting the governmental objectives served by the search exist. Do you agree? Is the existence of less drastic means of accomplishing the governmental objectives at all relevant to the question of the reasonableness of the governmental intrusion?

5. The Court's refusal to find a least-restrictive-alternative requirement subsumed in the fourth amendment is due, at least in part, to a concern about "unrealistic second-guessing" by judges. United States v. Sharpe, 470 U.S. 675, 105 S.Ct. 1568 (1985). In *Sharpe*, the Court made some observations about judicial oversight of police conduct under the fourth amendment which the Court would presumably hold equally true in the prison context:

> A creative judge engaged in post-hoc evaluation of police conduct can almost always imagine some alternative means by which the objectives of the police might have been accomplished. But "[t]he fact that the protection of the public might, in the abstract, have been accomplished by 'less intrusive' means does not, by itself, render the search unreasonable." The question is not simply whether some other alternative was available, but whether the police acted unreasonably in failing to recognize or to pursue it.

Id. at 686–87, 105 S.Ct. at 1575–76.

6. Professional standards have urged correctional officials, as a matter of policy, to more carefully regulate searches than the case law requires. The Model Sentencing and Corrections Act (1978), for example, recommends the following:

§ 119. [Searches.]

(a) A confined person has a protected interest in freedom from unreasonable searches.

(b) Searches within facilities are subject to the following limitations:

(1) Searches must be conducted solely to detect contraband, prohibited material, or evidence of a crime;

(2) The frequency and scope of random or general searches of facilities or confined persons must conform to a plan approved in advance by the director as providing the least intrusive invasion of privacy necessary to the safety of the public and security and safety within the facility. The plan may include provisions for search of confined persons upon admittance to a facility, upon leaving and returning to a facility, and upon entering or leaving designated areas. The plan need not be published or adopted in compliance with the procedures governing the adoption of rules or other measures.

(c) Searches other than those authorized by the plan and directed at living quarters or a particular confined person must be conducted only upon obtaining reliable information that a search is necessary to detect contraband, prohibited material, or evidence of a crime. Except in an emergency, prior authorization to conduct such a search must be obtained from the chief executive officer or supervisory-level correctional employees to whom the chief executive officer has delegated the responsibility to authorize searches.

(d) A search requiring a confined person to remove his clothes must be conducted with due regard to the privacy and dignity of the confined person.

(e) A search requiring the examination of a body cavity other than visual observation of the mouth, nose, or ear must be conducted by medically trained personnel of the Division of Correctional Medical Services in the medical quarters of the facility, or, in the absence of medical quarters, in other quarters appropriate for conducting a private examination.

B. RIGHT OF PRIVACY

Nowhere in the Constitution is a right of privacy specifically set forth. But privacy interests are clearly protected and promoted by the fourth amendment which restricts governmental intrusions into our homes, seizures of our property, and searches and seizures of our bodies.

According to the Supreme Court, the constitutional protection of privacy interests is not confined to the fourth amendment. The Court has recognized a constitutional right of privacy which extends beyond the strictures of the fourth amendment; this right limits, for example, the extent to which the government can interfere with personal decisions involving such matters as marriage and contraception. See, e.g., Griswold v. Connecticut, 381 U.S. 479, 85 S.Ct. 1678 (1965) (striking down state statute barring use of contraceptive devices and prohibiting doctors from giving advice on use of such devices); Zablocki v. Redhail, 434 U.S. 374, 98 S.Ct. 673 (1978) (holding unconstitutional a law requiring a court's permission before a person, under court order to provide child support for a minor child, can marry).

The Supreme Court has variously described the source of this right to privacy. In *Griswold v. Connecticut,* for example, the Court found a right to privacy lurking within the combined "penumbras" of several constitutional guarantees—the first amendment right to freedom of association; the third amendment, which proscribes the quartering of soldiers in homes during times of peace; the fourth amendment; the fifth amendment privilege against self-incrimination; and the ninth amendment, which basically says that the rights enumerated in the Constitution are not the only rights with which people are vested. 381 U.S. at 484–85, 85 S.Ct. at 1681–82. In *Zablocki v. Redhail,* however, the approach of the Court was simpler; in that case, the Court simply found that a "fundamental right of privacy" was part of the "liberty" protected by the due process clause of the fourteenth amendment. 434 U.S. at 384, 98 S.Ct. at 679.

One question which presents itself is whether the right of privacy, whatever its source, extends to prisoners? And if so, to what extent must that right give way when it collides with other important governmental and private interests?

The courts have frequently encountered these questions in cases pitting inmates' asserted right to privacy against the equal employment rights of individuals of the opposite gender who are working or wish to work in prisons. In the case which follows, the United States District Court for the District of Nebraska confronted these questions.

BRAASCH v. GUNTER

United States District Court, District of Nebraska 1985.
Unpublished opinion (Case Nos. CV 83–L–459, CV 83–L–682) (available on WESTLAW).

United States Magistrate David L. Piester wrote the following opinion in this case:

* * *

In April 1983, Charles Benson, the former Director of the Department of Correctional Services, implemented a policy regarding the integration of women correctional personnel at the Nebraska State Penitentiary, an all-male prison population facility. This policy provides that:

1. Correctional officers may pat search offenders of the opposite sex.

2. Correctional officers may be assigned to posts where offenders of the opposite sex may be observed using shower or toilet facilities.

3. Correctional officers may work in housing units where offenders of the opposite sex reside.

4. Correctional officers may conduct room checks of offenders of the opposite sex.

5. Correctional officers employed by the Department at the time of the implementation of the policy who did not want to work in contact positions with offenders of the opposite sex would be retained but that such employees could not be promoted above the rank of corporal.

This policy also instructs that correctional officers should not be assigned positions where offenders of the opposite sex are routinely strip searched, nor should a correctional officer be permitted to strip search an offender of the opposite sex except in emergency circumstances. Additionally, the policy directs institution personnel to make use of "short" shower curtains or "other minor adjustments in shower and toilet areas to help ensure that offenders can secure minimal privacy without jeopardizing the security of the facility." This policy was apparently adopted in an effort to promote equal employment opportunities among women employees at the various penal institutions of the Department * * *. [A]fter the adoption of the policy female guards were assigned to the housing units at the Nebraska State

Penitentiary, including units where both plaintiffs reside or have resided. The implementation of the policy has created the present clash with the plaintiffs' claimed privacy rights in three respects: first, allowing female correctional personnel to view nude male inmates in the showers at the institution; second, to allow female correctional personnel to view male inmates in the nude or in various stages of undress in their respective cells or rooms while sleeping, using the toilet, or at any other times; and third, by permitting female correctional personnel to perform pat down searches of male inmates at any time such searches are necessary, wherever that may be within the institution.

There are four regular living units at the Nebraska State Penitentiary, each divided into two wings. Each wing has two levels of cells, which are more aptly described as rooms along a hall emanating from the center control area. Each wing has its own control room, from which the locks to the various doors or cells and other areas are operated, medications are dispensed, and the hallways of both the upper and lower levels of rooms are clearly visible. From the hallways security officers are able to peer into the inmates' rooms through the glass windows in the doors, which may not be covered at any time. During my visit to the institution it was demonstrated that while peering through the windows, the configuration of the room and the toilet is such that if an inmate is sitting on the toilet, his genital area would be visible to the guard from the hallway. In addition, there was testimony during the trial by inmates that some of them sleep in the nude due to personal habit or the temperature in the housing unit (there are windows in the units, but they are not permitted to be opened at any time, and in fact have been sealed closed for security reasons; the temperature of each housing unit is controlled by facility staff within the limitations of the building equipment). The beds of the inmates' rooms are clearly visible from the observation window to the hallway, and testimony before me revealed that when performing room checks, the guard is required to verify that an inmate is in fact in the room; if the room is checked during sleeping hours the guard must see the flesh of the inmate to assure his presence. (Observation of the genital area is not required; an arm, hand, foot, etc. will suffice.) There is no prohibition against inmates wearing pajamas or underwear as they sleep at night, nor is there any prohibition against an inmate placing a towel or other covering on his lap, during use of the toilet.

Each housing unit is staffed by three officers, a "first officer" and two others who are either beneath the first officer in rank or occupy the same rank. The "first officer" is the supervisor of the correctional staff in the housing unit. There are two security personnel in each control room at most times. The control room is, as noted, located at the end of the two hallways. The officers in the control room, therefore, have a clear line of view of the hallways and of anyone in them. Prior to the institution of the present policy regarding female personnel, inmates commonly walked to and from showers in the nude. That practice still continues with respect to some inmates; others attempt to cover themselves by wrapping a towel around them. The latter is not prohibited by institutional rules. Although it is possible that a bathrobe might be permitted an inmate who had been once outside the institution at another correctional facility, bathrobes are not regularly issued to inmates.

Both plaintiffs testified they had been observed in the showers by female officers, who, when observing plaintiffs, did so for periods of 10–15 seconds, and who were readily identifiable by plaintiffs while doing so. The shower rooms are located directly adjacent to the control room. During my visit to the penitentiary I visited housing unit 3 and observed the control rooms for both wings of that housing unit. I visited the showers in both "C" and "D" galleries, both of which are located on the upper floors of their respective wings, and looked into the shower area of "A" gallery from the control room window. From my observations of the facility it is clear that a security officer in the control room would have the ability to look at nude inmates in the shower areas in both the upper and lower galleries of the respective housing wings, by peering through the separate control room window which is approximately 11" × 17" in size, and thus to view the inmates' genital areas in an unobstructed fashion. The window's location (near the floor of the upper wing shower rooms, and near the ceiling of the lower wing shower rooms) would make some difference in the officer's viewing due to the accumulation of moisture and steam on the windows located near the ceiling of the shower area; this "fogging" would not, however, be sufficient to block the guard's view of the inmates' nude bodies in the shower from a distance of approximately 4'–10', depending upon the shower head being used.

Although there was considerable testimony regarding the security reasons for the requirement that inmates be visible in the showers, such as to prevent assaults, sexual activity, the passing of contraband, etc., the "vestibule" area located between the shower area itself and the hallway and consisting of an area approximately 4' × 9' in size, is not visible from the control room in any way. The purpose of the "vestibule" is to permit inmates to dry themselves before returning to their rooms to dress. There was no testimony to the effect that this area had been a site of any inmate assaults or other breaches of security.

In addition to the "regular" viewing of inmates in their rooms and in the shower areas, there are unscheduled or random "shakedowns" of the rooms performed by the housing unit officers for the purpose of finding any contraband located in the inmates' rooms. During the search of a room, an inmate is not permitted to be present, but must be subjected to a pat down search prior to being permitted to leave the immediate area. If the officer conducting the search is female, she also conducts the pat down search of the inmates. As noted, inmates are also subjected to pat down searches at random times when they are in the penitentiary's yard area, as well as when they travel between certain areas of the institution, such as to and from the "turn-key" area, law library, school area, and others. Again, these pat down searches may now be conducted by the women officers at the particular duty station requiring the pat down search. Such searches are common at the institution, and plaintiff Nielsen testified that he has been subjected to pat down searches as many as "a dozen or more" times in one day, although I do not find that number to be typical. It is safe to say, however, that the testimony supports the conclusion that pat down searches are a necessary part of prison security, and are conducted both regularly and at random on most inmates several times per day.

A pat down search is conducted by requiring the inmate to turn his back on the security officer and extend his arms and legs. His arms, legs, and torso, are patted or touched by the officer so as to detect any contraband located on the body. This is done while the inmate is fully clothed. There was differing testimony on the matter of whether a pat search, when conducted by a female officer, must omit the genital area. Defendant Gunter testified that although correctional officers receive initial and periodic training, there is no specific training regarding the conduct of pat down searches by women officers. Marilyn Ringer, the only female correctional sergeant at the institution, testified that in regard to conducting pat down searches of male inmates, she did not recall ever being told exactly how to treat the genital area. She said that in conducting the pat down searches, she made no specific effort to touch the area but that to avoid the genital area would compromise the search, as it was not uncommon to find contraband located in an inmate's genital area. Both plaintiffs testified that they had been subjected to pat down searches by female correctional officers, and Nielsen testified that in conducting the search, the female officers commonly touched his buttocks, penis, and testicles, through his clothing. There was no testimony that any policy exists at the institution, or ever existed, which would guide the female officers in conducting such searches, would prevent them from conducting such searches in the genital area, or would permit an inmate to request that at least that portion of the search be conducted by a male officer.

There was no testimony during the trial of this matter that the policy of using female correctional officers had any goal other than equal employment opportunity. That is, the placement of female officers in the housing units or in other positions to perform pat down searches of inmates was not shown to be related to penological objectives. Rather, the objective of the policy in question was to promote equal employment opportunity among women staff at the penitentiary.

* * *

* * *

It is true, as argued by the defendants in their brief, that the Supreme Court has never per se held that a convicted felon has a right to privacy such as would prevent his or her unclothed body from observation by correctional officers of the opposite sex, or being pat searched by correctional officers of the opposite sex. Nor, of course, has the Court declared precisely that such right does not exist. * * *

Outside the condition of confinement, the Supreme Court has recognized citizens' rights to privacy concerning a number of activities and subjects * * *. Although the Supreme Court has not specifically said that one has a protected privacy right to urinate, defecate, or bathe outside the viewing of a person of the opposite sex, or not to be touched in the genital area, even through clothing, by a member of the opposite sex, these things are so fundamental to personal dignity and self respect in this culture that I believe if presented with such issues, the Supreme Court would find one's own body and its personal functions protected by the recognized privacy rights of unincarcerated citizens. Other federal courts, in the context of employment rights, recognize the proposition that people enjoy a basic right to keep their bodies and personal functions and maintenance shielded from the uninvited view or touch of the opposite sex. See, e.g. Norwood v. Dale Maintenance System, Inc., 590 F.Supp. 1410 (N.D.Ill.1984) (privacy of tenants and patrons in business building washrooms from female attendants); Brooks v. ACF Industries, Inc., 537 F.Supp. 1122 (S.D.W.Va.1982) (privacy of male employees of plant in bath-toilet-locker-room facilities from female janitors); Ludke v. Klein, 461 F.Supp. 86 (S.D.N.Y.1978) (privacy of baseball players in locker room from women reporters); Fesel v. Masonic Hospital, 447 F.Supp. 1346 (D.Del.1978) (privacy of female residents of retirement home in intimate personal 'total care' by male nurse); Sutton v. National Distillers Products Co., 445 F.Supp. 1319 (S.D.Ohio 1978), aff'd 628 F.2d 936 (6th Cir.1980) (privacy of male distillery employees regarding search by female guard); Hodgson v. Robert Hall Clothes, Inc., 326 F.Supp. 1264 (D.Del.1971), aff'd in relevant part, 473 F.2d 589 (3d Cir.) (privacy of clothing store customers in service by same sex sales person).

It is clear that prisoners, by virtue of their confinement, do not lose all of the constitutional rights they hold as citizens of this country. The Supreme Court's most recent decision regarding prisoners' rights to privacy is noted by the plaintiff Braasch in his trial brief:

> (W)e have insisted that prisoners be accorded those rights not fundamentally inconsistent with imprisonment itself or incompatible with the objectives of incarceration.

Hudson v. Palmer. This is but an amplified restatement of the earlier standard set forth in Pell v. Procunier, 417 U.S. 817 (1974), whether challenged actions are "inconsistent with (the prisoner's) status as a prisoner or with the legitimate *penological* objectives of the correctional system." Id. at 822. (Emphasis added.) The inquiry here then becomes whether in the instances cited by the plaintiffs the conduct complained of runs afoul of this standard.

* * *

The prevention of employment discrimination on the basis of sex is one of the policies of [Title VII of the Civil Rights Act of 1964], 42

U.S.C. § 2000e.[b] It is without question a "legitimate" objective of every employer. In order to overcome the constitutional right to privacy of inmates, however, it must, in the prison setting, be consistent with legitimate penological objectives. Although the defendants argue that the security of the institution requires that inmates be observed while showering, using the toilet, [or are] otherwise in their rooms, and also that they be subjected to no-notice pat down searches in addition to regular pat down searches at specific locations, which argument I accept, it does not follow that the conducting of these activities by members of the opposite sex serves a legitimate penological interest.

The Supreme Court has proclaimed that "[I]nmates in jails, prisons, or mental institutions retain certain fundamental rights of privacy; they are not like animals in a zoo to be filmed and photographed at will by the public or by media reporters, however 'educational' the process may be for others." Houchins v. KQED, Inc., 438 U.S. at 5, n. 2.[c] The education of the public is not considered by the Court to be a legitimate penological objective of [an] incarcerating institution, no matter how beneficial unlimited access to the prison may be to others. Likewise, I

[b. Section 703(a) of Title VII, 42 U.S.C. § 2000e—2(a) provides as follows:

(a) It shall be an unlawful employment practice for an employer—

(1) to fail or refuse to hire or to discharge any individual, or otherwise to discriminate against any individual with respect to his compensation, terms, conditions, or privileges of employment, because of such individual's race, color, religion, sex, or national origin; or

(2) to limit, segregate, or classify his employees or applicants for employment in any way which would deprive or tend to deprive any individual of employment opportunities or otherwise adversely affect his status as an employee, because of such individual's race, color, religion, sex, or national origin.]

[c. Houchins involved a challenge by a television and radio broadcasting company to restrictions placed on media access to a county jail. The broadcasting company had sought permission to photograph parts of the jail after an inmate in the jail had committed suicide, but permission was denied. Instead, jail officials began conducting public tours of the jail, and members of the media could join in those tours. The tours, however, did not include all sections of the jail, including the area of the jail where the inmate had killed himself and which allegedly was the site of many rapes and beatings as well as poor physical conditions. Members of the tour group were also not allowed to take photo-

graphs, nor were they permitted to talk with inmates. In fact, jail inmates were rarely around when the tours were being conducted, since during the tours, the inmates were removed to sections of the jail not accessible to the public.

The United States District Court for the Northern District of California issued a preliminary injunction requiring the county sheriff, the person responsible for the jail's operation, to provide certain members of the media, "at reasonable times and hours," with access to all areas of the jail. Under the terms of this injunction, the sheriff could not preclude the broadcasting company and other media members from taking photographs and using sound equipment in the jail or from interviewing inmates. On appeal, the Ninth Circuit Court of Appeals affirmed. KQED v. Houchins, 546 F.2d 284 (9th Cir.1976).

In reversing the Court of Appeals, four of the seven Justices of the Supreme Court who participated in the decision concluded that members of the media generally have no greater right of access to jails than do members of the public. Former Chief Justice Warren Burger announced the Court's judgement in an opinion joined by Justices White and Rehnquist. In the course of this opinion, Chief Justice Burger mentioned that one reason given by the sheriff for the restrictions was to protect the privacy rights of inmates in the jail. Chief Justice Burger then dropped the telling footnote quoted above, acknowledging the retention by inmates of "certain fundamental rights of privacy."]

do not believe that the penitentiary exists as an institution to encourage laudable societal movement toward equality of sex roles.

Commentators suggest that using the societal norms and community standards of decency regarding opposite sex contact to justify an exception to the equal opportunity mandate is just a facade for perpetuating the differentiation of sex roles which has disadvantaged females in employment. It is argued that the sooner these notions surrounding bodily privacy dissipate or are ignored, the sooner complete equal employment can be realized, analogizing to the racial bigotry which had to be overridden by the courts to begin to establish equality for racial minorities. See, Bratt, Privacy and the Sex BFOQ: An Immodest Proposal, 48 Albany L.Rev. 923 (1984); Comment, Sex Discrimination in Prison Employment: The Bona Fide Occupational Qualification and Prisoner's Privacy Rights, 65 Iowa L.Rev. 428 (1980).

While that argument may have merit as a social catalyst, I do not believe the privacy of individuals in their person, which is currently a weighty enough societal concern to support recognition of the bfoq[d] defense in discrimination suits outside of the prison, should be disregarded as to prisoners in order to speed social change, especially when speeding social change is not a legitimate penological purpose. Just as inmates are not animals in the zoo for the public's indiscriminate gaze, neither are they a population whose standards of modesty may be forcibly lowered in order to achieve inroads on public attitudes toward women in sexually sensitive areas of employment.

* * *

The plaintiffs' testimony with respect to the bfoq matter is insufficient to establish that security guards at the Nebraska State Penitentiary must be male when working in the so-called "contact" positions. First, the testimony clearly established that many, if not a majority, of the inmates were not offended by the use of female correctional officers in such positions.[4] Second, there are, or appear to be, means available to the prison administration by which to accommodate both the privacy interests of the inmates and the equal employment interests of the female security personnel, such as would permit the coexistence of these interests, for the most part, without significant clashes. For these reasons, I do not find that the bfoq designation is appropriate so as to designate the contact positions at the penitentiary male only.

* * *

[d. "Bfoq" stands for "bona fide occupational qualification." Title VII provides for a bfoq defense under which gender-based discrimination is permissible "in those certain instances where * * * sex * * * is a bona fide occupational qualification reasonably necessary to the normal operation of that particular business or enterprise." 42 U.S.C. § 2000e–2(e).]

4. To the contrary the testimony indicated that at least in one housing unit, the trustee dormitory, which is not [at] issue in this case, the initial placement of female correctional officers at that facility had to be discontinued to permit the installation of screens or other remodeling, so as to prevent exhibitionism by the inmates. There was also testimony that some inmates requested the female guards to conduct searches of their rooms.

* * * [A]s is outlined in many of the cases involving these subjects, various institutions have taken various measures to reduce the conflict between privacy and equal employment opportunity, none of which has been taken at the Nebraska State Penitentiary. Such measures have included permitting windows to inmate's rooms to be covered for brief periods at designated times; removing opposite sex officers from shower areas altogether; prohibiting opposite sex officers from conducting pat searches of genital/anal areas; and requiring the announcement of [the] presence of opposite sex officers [or] personnel. The evidence before me does not support the necessity for taking the extreme measures in this case of excluding female officers [from] the housing units altogether.

With respect to inmate privacy in the rooms, the evidence is clear that there is no prohibition against the use of pajamas or other sleepwear by inmates to protect their privacy while sleeping and there is also no policy against an inmate covering himself while sitting on the toilet where he could be viewed by a correctional officer from the hallway. The inmate's back would be turned toward the window while he stood in front of the toilet to urinate. These measures are sufficient to allow the inmates to protect their own privacy, should they choose to do so, without any changes on the part of the defendants.

Similarly, the evidence before me indicates that if an inmate chooses to walk from his room to the shower of the housing unit in the nude, he may do so, and some still do even in the presence of female correctional officers, but that no policy of the defendants prohibits the inmates from covering themselves with a towel, or even wearing underwear or a swimming suit to and from the shower. Thus, again, no measures are necessary to be taken by the defendants to protect the plaintiffs' privacy interests.

The shower area involves a different matter altogether. Although it is true that the inmates are not prohibited from wearing bathing suits or underwear while showering, I find such a suggestion unreasonable; rather, the defendants must accommodate the inmates' privacy rights in this respect. Although I will not by this order require specific measures, I will require that sufficient measures be taken by the defendants to do so. It would seem from the evidence put forth during the trial, that such measures might include the following: erecting translucent screens or partial screens in the shower area; adjusting the shifts of officers in the control rooms so as to allow at least one full, eight-hour shift to be regularly and predictably staffed by only male correctional officers so as to accommodate showering by any inmates who wish to protect their privacy during that shift; adjusting the shifts of correctional officers in the control rooms so that during a portion of more than one shift the occupants of the control room would be male only; and/or closing off the window between the shower and the control room for a period of time every day, during which a male officer would be physically stationed in the shower area. There may be others, as well, and I leave it to the prison administration to decide exactly which measures will be taken in this respect, so long as those inmates who wish to protect their privacy are afforded an opportunity to do so, without negatively affecting their work assignments, accessibility to improvement programs, health care, or otherwise affecting their administrative status at the penitentiary.

The matter of pat down searches is more problematical, in that it, unlike the accommodations for showering, could require the expenditure of funds for extra personnel. Nevertheless, if necessary, such administrative expenses must be accepted in the observation of constitutional rights. Within the housing units, it appears possible that the staff of a particular housing unit could be arranged and flexible enough that, in the event an inmate who is subject to a pat search requests that such search be performed only by a male officer, that such a male officer should be available. The "first officer" of the housing unit staff was described in many ways as a "rover" who might or might not assist in room shakedowns and other incidents requiring pat down searches. In addition, if the "first officer" were female, it appears at least possible that one of the correctional officers assigned to the control room could be male, and available to perform such searches upon request, without compromising the security of the institution. At those posts where only one correctional officer is assigned, however, which require pat down searches either routinely or randomly, this ruling will require the availability of male officers to perform such searches, at least [as] to the genital areas of those male inmates who object to female officers searching such areas. This will require, it appears, either the assignment of guards to such positions in pairs, one male and one female, or the assignment of "roving" guards to assist female officers in conducting pat down searches when required by the circumstance of an inmate objecting to the female correctional officer performing at least that portion of the pat down search involving the genital area.

It should be made clear that these restrictions on the assignment of female correctional officers at the penitentiary do not apply in cases of emergencies which are of an immediate nature affecting the security of the institution. Although there was no evidence presented to me at the trial of this matter on the question of what might constitute an "emergency," common sense dictates that in situations where an unexpected upheaval arises or when the safety of inmates or prison personnel is threatened in such a manner as to require immediate action by officers in charge, such considerations override the inmates' interests in protecting their personal privacy, and during such situations inmates are clearly subject to being searched, viewed, and even strip searched, without regard to the sex of the officer performing those acts.

* * * Judgment will be entered accordingly.

Questions and Points for Discussion

1. The tension between protecting the privacy of inmates and affording equal employment opportunities to prison employees regardless of their gender becomes a non-issue from a constitutional perspective if inmates have no constitutionally protected privacy interests. The Supreme Court's decision in Turner v. Safley, 482 U.S. 78, 107 S.Ct. 2254 (1987), supra page 284, suggests that inmates do have a constitutionally based right to privacy. In *Turner,* the Court concluded that a rule restricting inmate marriages violated what the Court described as a fundamental right to marry. Although the Court did not allude to a constitutional right to privacy, the right to marry has commonly been recognized as one subsumed within the more general right to privacy. See, e.g., Zablocki v. Redhail, 434 U.S. 374, 385, 98 S.Ct. 673, 680 (1978).

Most of the lower courts have either assumed or decided that inmates enjoy some right to privacy under the Constitution. See, e.g., Michenfelder v. Sumner, 860 F.2d 328, 333 (9th Cir.1988); Hardin v. Stynchcomb, 691 F.2d 1364, 1373 (11th Cir.1982); Lee v. Downs, 641 F.2d 1117, 1119 (4th Cir. 1981). Often the courts have concluded that inmates have residual privacy rights without identifying the source of those rights. But see Smith v. Chrans, 629 F.Supp. 606, 610–11 (C.D.Ill.1986) (holding that inmates have residual privacy rights protected by the fourth amendment and the cruel and unusual punishment clause of the eighth amendment, but not by any constitutional penumbras).

2. As to the scope of the right to privacy, the courts have usually concluded, as did the court in *Braasch v. Gunter,* that inmates have the right to be protected from the unrestricted viewing of their genitals or bodily functions by members of the opposite sex. See, e.g., Lee v. Downs, 641 F.2d 1117, 1119 (4th Cir.1981); Bowling v. Enomoto, 514 F.Supp. 201, 204 (N.D.Cal.1981). But see Bagley v. Watson, 579 F.Supp. 1099 (D.Or. 1983). At the same time, however, inadvertent or infrequent viewings by a member of the opposite sex of an inmate who is naked or using the toilet have been treated by the courts as *de minimis* incursions on inmates' privacy interests, not rising to the level of a constitutional violation. See, e.g., Smith v. Chrans, 629 F.Supp. 606 (C.D.Ill.1986); Miles v. Bell, 621 F.Supp. 51 (D.Conn.1985). In addition, inmates' privacy interests are not unconstitutionally invaded when members of the opposite sex will only be in the inmates' living area a set, but short amount of time. The courts reason that if inmates are aware of the impending arrival at a specified time of someone of the other sex, they can take steps to avoid being seen naked or using the toilet. See, e.g., Avery v. Perrin, 473 F.Supp. 90, 92 (D.N.H.1979).

3. Another question concerning the scope of inmates' privacy rights, assuming they have such rights, is whether correctional officers of one gender can conduct pat-down searches of inmates of the opposite sex. The courts have generally condoned such searches when they do not include a touching of genital areas. See, e.g., Smith v. Fairman, 678 F.2d 52 (7th Cir. 1982) (approving frisks by female correctional officers of male inmates' necks, backs, chests, stomachs, waists, buttocks, and outer legs). More

troubling to the courts has been the question of the validity of pat-down searches of inmates' genital areas by correctional officers of the opposite sex. The courts disagree as to whether such searches unconstitutionally encroach on inmates' right to privacy when conducted in non-emergency situations. Compare *Braasch v. Gunter* with Bagley v. Watson, 579 F.Supp. 1099, 1103 (D.Or.1983) (pat-down searches of male inmates by female correctional officers which include the anal-genital area do not violate the fourth amendment or any constitutional right of privacy). With which viewpoint do you agree?

4. All of the courts agree that in emergency situations, correctional officers of the opposite sex can pat down inmates' genital areas and even view or conduct strip or body-cavity searches. See, e.g., Lee v. Downs, 641 F.2d 1117, 1120–21 (4th Cir.1981) (no invasion of female inmate's right to privacy when two male correctional officers restrained her arms and legs while a female nurse searched her vagina for matches after the inmate had set her paper dress on fire; although female correctional officers worked in the prison, there was a "reasonable necessity" for the male guards' presence during the body-cavity search since the female guards could not be removed from their posts within a "reasonable time" to restrain the inmate and since females would have had greater difficulty restraining the inmate, a big strong woman, increasing the risk that someone would get injured). Whether an emergency existed justifying the pat-down search of genital areas or an even greater intrusion by a member of the opposite sex will often be the subject of dispute.

5. Although the courts have generally recognized that inmates have certain privacy rights, they have not held that inmates' privacy interests always prevail over the equal employment rights of others. Instead, the courts have striven, as *Braasch v. Gunter* demonstrates, to accommodate both the prisoners and persons of the opposite sex who work or want to work in a prison.

Other cases where the courts have attempted to protect the privacy rights of inmates while limiting the impact on the equal employment rights of others include: Hardin v. Stynchcomb, 691 F.2d 1364 (11th Cir.1982) (male gender not a bfoq for deputy sheriff position; job responsibilities in county jail can be rearranged so female deputy sheriffs do not conduct strip searches of male inmates or watch them use the toilet or take showers); Gunther v. Iowa State Men's Reformatory, 612 F.2d 1079 (8th Cir.1980) (policy of refusing to promote women at men's prison violates Title VII; might be permissible to limit exclusively male positions to those where correctional officers mostly monitor toilets and showers and conduct strip searches; Forts v. Ward, 621 F.2d 1210 (2d Cir.1980) (requiring the provision of appropriate sleepwear to female inmates so that male correctional officers cannot see them scantily clad or nude while sleeping); Hudson v. Goodlander, 494 F.Supp. 890 (D.Md.1980) (noting with approval the assigning of only male correctional officers to certain tiers in men's prison where inmates could choose to be celled).

6. Accommodations which may be feasible in one prison may be infeasible in another. For example, while privacy curtains or covered windows in one prison might protect the privacy of inmates while avoiding

interferences with the employment opportunities of others, in another prison, where the inmates are more violent or unruly, privacy curtains or covered windows might pose a serious threat to the security of the prison. In addition, some accomodations may be impractical because of the way in which a prison has been built. For example, covering windows to protect inmates' privacy would not be a viable option where inmates are housed in cells with bars in the front of the cells rather than solid doors with windows.

7. *Braasch v. Gunter* focused on the tension between inmates' right to privacy and the equal employment rights of others. Other interests may also be implicated when correctional officials are deciding whether or not to hire members of the opposite sex to work in a particular prison or at certain stations in that prison. For example, some courts and commentators have argued that having correctional officers of the opposite sex work within a prison contributes to the rehabilitation of prisoners within that prison. This viewpoint was mentioned by the court in Bagley v. Watson, 579 F.Supp. 1099 (D.Or.1983):

> [W]omen clearly contribute to the normality of the prison. Prisoners are often people who have great difficulty dealing with women, especially when they do not have an intimate relationship with that woman. Their rehabilitation will not, therefore, be fostered by our creating artificial environments without women. To do this, is merely to ignore the problem during the time of incarceration. The period of incarceration would be a time for men to learn to relate to women in a nonaggressive and non-intimate way. Such a capacity could only serve to enhance their chances for a successful parole adjustment.

Id. at 1101 (quoting from a witness's affidavit).

Other courts have argued that having members of the opposite sex work in at least some positions in a prison is anti-rehabilitative. A case in point is Bowling v. Enomoto, 514 F.Supp. 201 (N.D.Cal.1981), where the court said:

> Defendants do not argue, and indeed they could not convincingly argue, that the practice of allowing female officers to view male inmates in the nude furthers the penological interest in rehabilitation. On the contrary, in the normal social setting which prison inmates are ostensibly being rehabilitated to function within, people do not undress, bathe, or defecate in the presence of strangers of the opposite sex.

Id. at 203–04. See also Hudson v. Goodlander, 494 F.Supp. 890, 893 (D.Md. 1980) ("While the Court defers to the Commissioner's judgment that normalization of the prison environment is a desirable policy, it finds that policy cannot be furthered rationally by subjecting male prisoners who are using the showers or toilet facilities to the scrutiny of female officers. Such a practice aggravates, rather than mitigates, the disparity between the prison environment and society at large."); Torres v. Wisconsin Dept. of Health and Social Services, 859 F.2d 1523 (7th Cir.1988) (presence of male correctional officers in a women's prison may be anti-rehabilitative since women prisoners, so many of whom have been physically and sexually abused by males, may need to be insulated from male authority figures to rehabilitate themselves).

8. Can a male prisoner assert an equal protection claim if male prisoners can be patted down by female correctional officers but male correctional officers cannot frisk female prisoners absent an emergency? The Seventh Circuit Court of Appeals in Madyun v. Franzen, 704 F.2d 954 (7th Cir.1983) answered this question in the negative. The court explained its decision as follows:

> Here the State of Illinois, in order to provide opportunities for women to serve as guards in its male prisons, has allowed women guards to frisk search male inmates, while male guards may not frisk search female inmates. This differentiation serves the important state interest of equal job opportunity for women, since women prison guards cannot be truly effective unless they can perform the full range of prison security tasks. Conversely, there is no indication that males have suffered a lack of opportunity to serve as prison guards because they are precluded from frisk searching female inmates. In the interest of being able to equalize opportunities for women to serve as guards in male prisons, therefore, the gender-based distinction that allows women guards to search male prisoners substantially advances an important state interest.

Id. at 962.

Do you agree with the court's reasoning and conclusion?

9. The courts have been much less hospitable to inmates' privacy claims not involving an objection to the presence of members of the opposite sex in the prison or parts of the prison. For example, in Michenfelder v. Sumner, 860 F.2d 328 (9th Cir.1988), the prisoner-plaintiff objected to routine strip searches of prisoners housed in the section of the prison reserved for the most dangerous prisoners and those most likely to escape; these strip searches occurred whenever the prisoners left their cells, even though they were handcuffed and manacled when outside their cells. After observing that the prisoner had failed to demonstrate that he would not have an opportunity to obtain contraband or a weapon while outside his cell, the court of appeals concluded that the strip search policy was reasonably related to a legitimate penological purpose.

The court in *Michenfelder* furthermore rejected the prisoner's argument that the searches were unconstitutional because they were conducted out on the tier where nine other inmates could observe the inmate as he stripped. Unlike the district court which had observed that "[t]his situation is no more offensive than the usual nudity found in a locker room in a school or YMCA," Michenfelder v. Sumner, 624 F.Supp. 457, 463 (D.Nev. 1985), the court of appeals found some merit in the prisoner's claim. The court ultimately concluded, however, that the practice of searching inmates in the hallway was constitutional because searching the inmates in their cells or moving them to be searched elsewhere posed dangers to the correctional officer or officers who were to conduct the search. See also Young v. Newton, No. 82–C–4327 (N.D.Ill.1985) (available on WESTLAW) (inmate has no right to have access to a toilet concealed from the view of others); Wagner v. Thomas, 608 F.Supp. 1095, 1103–04 (N.D.Tex.1985) (strip searches and body-cavity inspections conducted in front of other inmates and deputy sheriffs are constitutional; removing inmates one by one from large cell to be searched would make it easier for inmates to hide contraband and frustrate the objectives of the search).

While, as just discussed, the interest in rehabilitation has been asserted as a reason for assigning women to male prisons, the government's interest in maintaining prison security has been asserted as a reason for excluding women from certain prisons or positions within prisons. In the case which follows, the Supreme Court addressed such a bfoq defense grounded on the interest in institutional security.

DOTHARD v. RAWLINSON
Supreme Court of the United States, 1977.
433 U.S. 321, 97 S.Ct. 2720, 53 L.Ed.2d 786.

MR. JUSTICE STEWART delivered the opinion of the Court.

Appellee Dianne Rawlinson sought employment with the Alabama Board of Corrections as a prison guard, called in Alabama a "correctional counselor." After her application was rejected, she brought this class suit under Title VII of the Civil Rights Act of 1964 and under 42 U.S.C. § 1983, alleging that she had been denied employment because of her sex in violation of federal law. A three-judge Federal District Court for the Middle District of Alabama decided in her favor. We noted probable jurisdiction of this appeal from the District Court's judgment.

I

At the time she applied for a position as correctional counselor trainee, Rawlinson was a 22-year-old college graduate whose major course of study had been correctional psychology. She was refused employment because she failed to meet the minimum 120–pound weight requirement established by an Alabama statute. The statute also establishes a height minimum of 5 feet 2 inches.

After her application was rejected because of her weight, Rawlinson filed a charge with the Equal Employment Opportunity Commission, and ultimately received a right-to-sue letter. She then filed a complaint in the District Court on behalf of herself and other similarly situated women, challenging the statutory height and weight minima as violative of Title VII and the Equal Protection Clause of the Fourteenth Amendment. A three-judge court was convened. While the suit was pending, the Alabama Board of Corrections adopted Administrative Regulation 204, establishing gender criteria for assigning correctional counselors to maximum-security institutions for "contact positions," that is, positions requiring continual close physical proximity to inmates of the institution. Rawlinson amended her class-action complaint by adding a challenge to Regulation 204 as also violative of Title VII and the Fourteenth Amendment.

Like most correctional facilities in the United States, Alabama's prisons are segregated on the basis of sex. Currently the Alabama Board of Corrections operates four major all-male penitentiaries—Holman Prison, Kilby Corrections Facility, G.K. Fountain Correction Center, and Draper Correctional Center. The Board also operates the Julia Tutwiler Prison for Women, the Frank Lee Youth Center, the Number Four Honor Camp, the State Cattle Ranch, and nine Work Release Centers, one of which is for women. The Julia Tutwiler Prison for Women and the four male penitentiaries are maximum-security institutions. Their inmate living quarters are for the most part large dormitories, with communal showers and toilets that are open to the domitories and hallways. The Draper and Fountain penitentiaries carry on extensive farming operations, making necessary a large number of strip searches for contraband when prisoners re-enter the prison buildings.

* * *

At the time this litigation was in the District Court, the Board of Corrections employed a total of 435 people in various correctional counselor positions, 56 of whom were women. Of those 56 women, 21 were employed at the Julia Tutwiler Prison for Women, 13 were employed in noncontact positions at the four male maximum-security institutions, and the remaining 22 were employed at the other institutions operated by the Alabama Board of Corrections. Because most of Alabama's prisoners are held at the four maximum-security male penitentiaries, 336 of the 435 correctional counselor jobs were in those institutions, a majority of them concededly in the "contact" classification. Thus, even though meeting the statutory height and weight requirements, women applicants could under Regulation 204 compete equally with men for only about 25% of the correctional counselor jobs available in the Alabama prison system.

II

In enacting Title VII, Congress required "the removal of artificial, arbitrary, and unnecessary barriers to employment when the barriers operate invidiously to discriminate on the basis of racial or other impermissible classification." The District Court found that the minimum statutory height and weight requirements that applicants for employment as correctional counselors must meet constitute the sort of arbitrary barrier to equal employment opportunity that Title VII forbids. The appellants assert that the District Court erred both in finding that the height and weight standards discriminate against women, and in its refusal to find that, even if they do, these standards are justified as "job related."

A

* * *

Although women 14 years of age or older compose 52.75% of the Alabama population and 36.89% of its total labor force, they hold only 12.9% of its correctional counselor positions. * * * When the height and weight restrictions are combined, Alabama's statutory standards would exclude 41.13% of the female population while excluding less than 1% of the male population. Accordingly, the District Court found that Rawlinson had made out a prima facie case of unlawful sex discrimination.

* * *

* * * [W]e cannot say that the District Court was wrong in holding that the statutory height and weight standards had a discriminatory impact on women applicants.

B

We turn, therefore, to the appellants' argument that they have rebutted the prima facie case of discrimination by showing that the height and weight requirements are job related. These requirements, they say, have a relationship to strength, a sufficient but unspecified amount of which is essential to effective job performance as a correctional counselor. In the District Court, however, the appellants produced no evidence correlating the height and weight requirements with the requisite amount of strength thought essential to good job performance. Indeed, they failed to offer evidence of any kind in specific justification of the statutory standards.

If the job-related quality that the appellants identify is bona fide, their purpose could be achieved by adopting and validating a test for applicants that measures strength directly. Such a test, fairly administered, would fully satisfy the standards of Title VII because it would be one that "measure[s] the person for the job and not the person in the abstract." But nothing in the present record even approaches such a measurement.

For the reasons we have discussed, the District Court was not in error in holding that Title VII of the Civil Rights Act of 1964, as amended, prohibits application of the statutory height and weight requirements to Rawlinson and the class she represents.

III

Unlike the statutory height and weight requirements, Regulation 204 explicitly discriminates against women on the basis of their sex. In defense of this overt discrimination, the appellants rely on § 703(e) of Title VII, 42 U.S.C. § 2000e–2(e), which permits sex-based discrimination "in those certain instances where . . . sex . . . is a bona fide occupational qualification reasonably necessary to the normal operation of that particular business or enterprise."

The District Court rejected the bona-fide-occupational-qualification (bfoq) defense, relying on the virtually uniform view of the federal courts that § 703(e) provides only the narrowest of exceptions to the general rule requiring equality of employment opportunities. * * * [T]he federal courts have agreed that it is impermissible under Title VII to refuse to hire an individual woman or man on the basis of stereotyped characterizations of the sexes, and the District Court in the present case held in effect that Regulation 204 is based on just such stereotypical assumptions.

We are persuaded—by the restrictive language of § 703(e), the relevant legislative history, and the consistent interpretation of the Equal Employment Opportunity Commission—that the bfoq exception was in fact meant to be an extremely narrow exception to the general prohibition of discrimination on the basis of sex.[20] In the particular factual circumstances of this case, however, we conclude that the District Court erred in rejecting the State's contention that Regulation 204 falls within the narrow ambit of the bfoq exception.

The environment in Alabama's penitentiaries is a peculiarly inhospitable one for human beings of whatever sex. Indeed, a Federal District Court has held that the conditions of confinement in the prisons of the State, characterized by "rampant violence" and a "jungle atmosphere," are constitutionally intolerable. *Pugh v. Locke,* 406 F.Supp. 318, 325 (M.D.Ala.). The record in the present case shows that because of inadequate staff and facilities, no attempt is made in the four maximum-security male penitentiaries to classify or segregate inmates according to their offense or level of dangerousness—a procedure that, according to expert testimony, is essential to effective penological administration. Consequently, the estimated 20% of the male prisoners who are sex offenders are scattered throughout the penitentiaries' dormitory facilities.

In this environment of violence and disorganization, it would be an oversimplification to characterize Regulation 204 as an exercise in "romantic paternalism." In the usual case, the argument that a particular job is too dangerous for women may appropriately be met by the rejoinder that it is the purpose of Title VII to allow the individual woman to make that choice for herself. More is at stake in this case, however, than an individual woman's decision to weigh and accept the risks of employment in a "contact" position in a maximum-security male prison.

The essence of a correctional counselor's job is to maintain prison security. A woman's relative ability to maintain order in a male, maximum-security, unclassified penitentiary of the type Alabama now runs could be directly reduced by her womanhood. There is a basis in fact for expecting that sex offenders who have criminally assaulted women in the past would be moved to do so again if access to women were established within the prison. There would also be a real risk that other inmates, deprived of a normal heterosexual environment, would assault women guards because they were women. In a prison

20. In the case of a state employer, the bfoq exception would have to be interpreted at the very least so as to conform to the Equal Protection Clause of the Fourteenth Amendment. The parties do not suggest, however, that the Equal Protection Clause requires more rigorous scrutiny of a State's sexually discriminatory employment policy than does Title VII. There is thus no occasion to give independent consideration to the District Court's ruling that Regulation 204 violates the Fourteenth Amendment as well as Title VII.

system where violence is the order of the day, where inmate access to guards is facilitated by dormitory living arrangements, where every institution is understaffed, and where a substantial portion of the inmate population is composed of sex offenders mixed at random with other prisoners, there are few visible deterrents to inmate assaults on women custodians.

Appellee Rawlinson's own expert testified that dormitory housing for aggressive inmates poses a greater security problem than single-cell lockups, and further testified that it would be unwise to use women as guards in a prison where even 10% of the inmates had been convicted of sex crimes and were not segregated from the other prisoners.[23] The likelihood that inmates would assault a woman because she was a woman would pose a real threat not only to the victim of the assault but also to the basic control of the penitentiary and protection of its inmates and the other security personnel. The employee's very womanhood would thus directly undermine her capacity to provide the security that is the essence of a correctional counselor's responsibility.

There was substantial testimony from experts on both sides of this litigation that the use of women as guards in "contact" positions under the existing conditions in Alabama maximum-security male penitentiaries would pose a substantial security problem, directly linked to the sex of the prison guard. On the basis of that evidence, we conclude that the District Court was in error in ruling that being male is not a bona fide occupational qualification for the job of correctional counselor in a "contact" position in an Alabama male maximum-security penitentiary.[24]

The judgment is accordingly affirmed in part and reversed in part, and the case is remanded to the District Court for further proceedings consistent with this opinion.

* * *

MR. JUSTICE REHNQUIST, with whom THE CHIEF JUSTICE and MR. JUSTICE BLACKMUN join, concurring in the result and concurring in part.

I agree with, and join, Parts I and III of the Court's opinion in this case and with its judgment. While I also agree with the Court's conclusion in Part II of its opinion, holding that the District Court was "not in error" in holding the statutory height and weight requirements in this case to be invalidated by Title VII, the issues with which that

23. Alabama's penitentiaries are evidently not typical. Appellee Rawlinson's two experts testified that in a normal, relatively stable maximum-security prison—characterized by control over the inmates, reasonable living conditions, and segregation of dangerous offenders—women guards could be used effectively and beneficially. Similarly, an *amicus* brief filed by the State of California attests to that State's success in using women guards in all-male penitentiaries.

24. The record shows, by contrast, that Alabama's minimum-security facilities, such as work-release centers, are recognized by their inmates as privileged confinement situations not to be lightly jeopardized by disobeying applicable rules of conduct. Inmates assigned to these institutions are thought to be the "cream of the crop" of the Alabama prison population.

Part deals are bound to arise so frequently that I feel obliged to separately state the reasons for my agreement with its result. I view affirmance of the District Court in this respect as essentially dictated by the peculiarly limited factual and legal justifications offered below by appellants on behalf of the statutory requirements. For that reason, I do not believe—and do not read the Court's opinion as holding—that all or even many of the height and weight requirements imposed by States on applicants for a multitude of law enforcement agency jobs are pretermitted by today's decision.

I agree that the statistics relied upon in this case are sufficient, absent rebuttal, to sustain a finding of a prima facie violation of § 703(a)(2), in that they reveal a significant discrepancy between the numbers of men, as opposed to women, who are automatically disqualified by reason of the height and weight requirements. * * *

* * *

Appellants, in order to rebut the prima facie case under the statute, had the burden placed on them to advance job-related reasons for the qualification. This burden could be shouldered by offering evidence or by making legal arguments not dependent on any new evidence. The District Court was confronted, however, with only one suggested job-related reason for the qualification—that of strength. Appellants argued only the job-relatedness of actual physical strength; they did not urge that an equally job-related qualification for prison guards is the *appearance* of strength. As the Court notes, the primary job of correctional counselor in Alabama prisons "is to maintain security and control of the inmates . . .," a function that I at least would imagine is aided by the psychological impact on prisoners of the presence of tall and heavy guards. If the appearance of strength had been urged upon the District Court here as a reason for the height and weight minima, I think that the District Court would surely have been entitled to reach a different result than it did. For, even if not perfectly correlated, I would think that Title VII would not preclude a State from saying that anyone under 5′2″ or 120 pounds, no matter how strong in fact, does not have a sufficient appearance of strength to be a prison guard.

* * *

MR. JUSTICE MARSHALL, with whom MR. JUSTICE BRENNAN joins, concurring in part and dissenting in part.

I agree entirely with the Court's analysis of Alabama's height and weight requirements for prison guards, and with its finding that these restrictions discriminate on the basis of sex in violation of Title VII. Accordingly, I join Parts I and II of the Court's opinion. I also agree with much of the Court's general discussion in Part III of the bona-fide-occupational-qualification exception contained in § 703(e) of Title VII. The Court is unquestionably correct when it holds "that the bfoq exception was in fact meant to be an extremely narrow exception to the general prohibition of discrimination on the basis of sex." I must, however, respectfully disagree with the Court's application of the bfoq exception in this case.

The Court properly rejects two proffered justifications for denying women jobs as prison guards. It is simply irrelevant here that a guard's occupation is dangerous and that some women might be unable to protect themselves adequately. Those themes permeate the testimony of the state officials below, but as the Court holds, "the argument that a particular job is too dangerous for women" is refuted by the "purpose of Title VII to allow the individual woman to make that choice for herself." Some women, like some men, undoubtedly are not qualified and do not wish to serve as prison guards, but that does not justify the exclusion of all women from this employment opportunity. Thus, "[i]n the usual case," the Court's interpretation of the bfoq exception would mandate hiring qualified women for guard jobs in maximum-security institutions. The highly successful experiences of other States allowing such job opportunities confirm that absolute disqualification of women is not, in the words of Title VII, "reasonably necessary to the normal operation" of a maximum-security prison.

What would otherwise be considered unlawful discrimination against women is justified by the Court, however, on the basis of the "barbaric and inhumane" conditions in Alabama prisons, conditions so bad that state officials have conceded that they violate the Constitution. To me, this analysis sounds distressingly like saying two wrongs make a right. It is refuted by the plain words of § 703(e). The statute requires that a bfoq be "reasonably necessary to the normal operation of that particular business or enterprise." But no governmental "business" may operate "normally" in violation of the Constitution. Every action of government is constrained by constitutional limitations. While those limits may be violated more frequently than we would wish, no one disputes that the "normal operation" of all government functions takes place within them. A prison system operating in blatant violation of the Eighth Amendment is an exception that should be remedied with all possible speed, as Judge Johnson's comprehensive order in *Pugh v. Locke* is designed to do. In the meantime, the existence of such violations should not be legitimatized by calling them "normal." Nor should the Court accept them as justifying conduct that would otherwise violate a statute intended to remedy age-old discrimination.

The Court's error in statutory construction is less objectionable, however, than the attitude it displays toward women. Though the Court recognizes that possible harm to women guards is an unacceptable reason for disqualifying women, it relies instead on an equally speculative threat to prison discipline supposedly generated by the sexuality of female guards. There is simply no evidence in the record to show that women guards would create any danger to security in Alabama prisons significantly greater than that which already exists. All of the dangers—with one exception discussed below—are inherent in a prison setting, whatever the gender of the guards.

The Court first sees women guards as a threat to security because "there are few visible deterrents to inmate assaults on women custodians." In fact, any prison guard is constantly subject to the threat of attack by inmates, and "invisible" deterrents are the guard's only real protection. No prison guard relies primarily on his or her ability to ward off an inmate attack to maintain order. Guards are typically unarmed and sheer numbers of inmates could overcome the normal complement. Rather, like all other law enforcement officers, prison guards must rely primarily on the moral authority of their office and the threat of future punishment for miscreants. As one expert testified below, common sense, fairness, and mental and emotional stability are the qualities a guard needs to cope with the dangers of the job. Well qualified and properly trained women, no less than men, have these psychological weapons at their disposal.

The particular severity of discipline problems in the Alabama maximum-security prisons is also no justification for the discrimination sanctioned by the Court. The District Court found in *Pugh v. Locke* that guards "must spend all their time attempting to maintain control or to protect themselves." If male guards face an impossible situation, it is difficult to see how women could make the problem worse, unless one relies on precisely the type of generalized bias against women that the Court agrees Title VII was intended to outlaw. For example, much of the testimony of appellants' witnesses ignores individual differences among members of each sex and reads like "ancient canards about the proper role of women." The witnesses claimed that women guards are not strict disciplinarians; that they are physically less capable of protecting themselves and subduing unruly inmates; that inmates take advantage of them as they did their mothers, while male guards are strong father figures who easily maintain discipline, and so on. Yet the record shows that the presence of women guards has not led to a single incident amounting to a serious breach of security in any Alabama institution. And, in any event, "[g]uards rarely enter the cell blocks and dormitories," *Pugh v. Locke*, 406 F.Supp., at 325, where the danger of inmate attacks is the greatest.

It appears that the real disqualifying factor in the Court's view is "[t]he employee's very womanhood." The Court refers to the large number of sex offenders in Alabama prisons, and to "[t]he likelihood that inmates would assault a woman because she was a woman." In short, the fundamental justification for the decision is that women as guards will generate sexual assaults. With all respect, this rationale regrettably perpetuates one of the most insidious of the old myths about women—that women, wittingly or not, are seductive sexual objects. The effect of the decision, made I am sure with the best of intentions, is to punish women because their very presence might provoke sexual assaults. It is women who are made to pay the price in lost job opportunities for the threat of depraved conduct by prison inmates. Once again, "[t]he pedestal upon which women have been placed has . . ., upon closer inspection, been revealed as a cage." *Sail'er Inn,*

Inc. v. Kirby, 5 Cal.3d 1, 20, 485 P.2d 529, 541 (1971). It is particularly ironic that the cage is erected here in response to feared misbehavior by imprisoned criminals.

The Court points to no evidence in the record to support the asserted "likelihood that inmates would assault a woman because she was a woman." Perhaps the Court relies upon common sense, or "innate recognition." But the danger in this emotionally laden context is that common sense will be used to mask the " 'romantic paternalism' " and persisting discriminatory attitudes that the Court properly eschews. To me, the only matter of innate recognition is that the incidence of sexually motivated attacks on guards will be minute compared to the "likelihood that inmates will assault" a *guard* because he or she is a *guard.*

The proper response to inevitable attacks on both female and male guards is not to limit the employment opportunities of law-abiding women who wish to contribute to their community, but to take swift and sure punitive action against the inmate offenders. Presumably, one of the goals of the Alabama prison system is the eradication of inmates' anti-social behavior patterns so that prisoners will be able to live one day in free society. Sex offenders can begin this process by learning to relate to women guards in a socially acceptable manner. To deprive women of job opportunities because of the threatened behavior of convicted criminals is to turn our social priorities upside down.[5]

Although I do not countenance the sex discrimination condoned by the majority, it is fortunate that the Court's decision is carefully limited to the facts before it. I trust the lower courts will recognize that the decision was impelled by the shockingly inhuman conditions in Alabama prisons, and thus that the "extremely narrow [bfoq] exception" recognized here will not be allowed "to swallow the rule" against sex discrimination. Expansion of today's decision beyond its narrow factual basis would erect a serious roadblock to economic equality for women.

Mr. Justice White, dissenting [Opinion omitted.]

5. The appellants argue that restrictions on employment of women are also justified by consideration of inmates' privacy. It is strange indeed to hear state officials who have for years been violating the most basic principles of human decency in the operation of their prisons suddenly become concerned about inmate privacy. It is stranger still that these same officials allow women guards in contact positions in a number of nonmaximum-security institutions, but strive to protect inmates' privacy in the prisons where personal freedom is most severely restricted. I have no doubt on this record that appellants' professed concern is nothing but a feeble excuse for discrimination.

As the District Court suggested, it may well be possible, once a constitutionally adequate staff is available, to rearrange work assignments so that legitimate inmate privacy concerns are respected without denying jobs to women. Finally, if women guards behave in a professional manner at all times, they will engender reciprocal respect from inmates, who will recognize that their privacy is being invaded no more than if a woman doctor examines them. The suggestion implicit in the privacy argument that such behavior is unlikely on either side is an insult to the professionalism of guards and the dignity of inmates.

Questions and Points for Discussion

1. Several courts have distinguished *Dothard v. Rawlinson*, rejecting the contentions of correctional officials that for security reasons, maleness is a bona fide occupational qualification to work in certain men's prisons. See, e.g., Griffin v. Michigan Dept. of Corrections, 654 F.Supp. 690, 700–01 (E.D.Mich.1982) (probability of sexual assaults on female correctional officers less than in the "jungle-like" conditions in Alabama prisons at issue in *Dothard*); Hardin v. Stynchcomb, No. 77–35974A, (N.D.Ga., Oct. 21, 1980), reversed on other grounds, 691 F.2d 1364 (11th Cir.1982) (the jail at issue housed substantially fewer sex offenders than did the maximum-security prisons in Alabama at issue in *Dothard*).

2. *Class Exercise*: Discuss and debate the following three questions:

1. What limitations, if any, should be placed on the employment of female correctional officers in men's prisons?

2. What limitations, if any, should be placed on the employment of male correctional officers in women's prisons?

3. What restrictions, if any, does the Constitution place on the audiotaping of inmates' conversations, whether with other inmates or with visitors, and the videotaping of their activities while in their cells?

Chapter 14

DUE PROCESS CLAIMS FOR PERSONAL INJURIES AND PROPERTY DEPRIVATIONS

As discussed in earlier chapters, the due process clause of the fourteenth amendment prohibits any state from depriving a person of life, liberty, or property without due process of law. A similar prohibition, applicable to the federal government, can be found in the fifth amendment. To prevail on a due process claim asserted against a governmental official, an individual must have lost his or her life, liberty, or property; the loss must constitute a governmental deprivation within the meaning of the due process clause; and the deprivation must have occurred without due process of law.

The question of when a person has been deprived of a "liberty" interest falling within the rubric of the due process clause was discussed in chapter 12. This chapter will focus on two questions: (1) what constitutes a deprivation within the meaning of the due process clause, and (2) when has a prisoner whose property has been lost, damaged, or destroyed or who has suffered personal injuries because of a prison official's actions or inaction been afforded due process?

Both of these questions were addressed by the Supreme Court in Parratt v. Taylor, 451 U.S. 527, 101 S.Ct. 1908 (1981), infra page 456. In *Parratt*, a prisoner brought a § 1983 suit to recover damages for the loss of a hobby kit worth $23.50 caused by the alleged negligence of several prison officials. The Supreme Court held that the negligence of a governmental official could effect a deprivation of property within the meaning of the due process clause, although the Court ultimately concluded that the prisoner in that case had been afforded due process of law. Five years later, the Court in *Daniels v. Williams,* the case below, reexamined the question whether negligence will suffice to trigger the requirements of due process.

DANIELS v. WILLIAMS

Supreme Court of the United States, 1986.
474 U.S. 327, 106 S.Ct. 662, 88 L.Ed.2d 662.

JUSTICE REHNQUIST delivered the opinion of the Court.

* * *

In this § 1983 action, petitioner seeks to recover damages for back and ankle injuries allegedly sustained when he fell on a prison stairway. He claims that, while an inmate at the city jail in Richmond, Virginia, he slipped on a pillow negligently left on the stairs by respondent, a correctional deputy stationed at the jail. Respondent's negligence, the argument runs, "deprived" petitioner of his "liberty" interest in freedom from bodily injury; because respondent maintains that he is entitled to the defense of sovereign immunity in a state tort suit, petitioner is without an "adequate" state remedy. Accordingly, the deprivation of liberty was without "due process of law."

The District Court granted respondent's motion for summary judgment. * * * [On appeal, the Fourth Circuit Court of Appeals affirmed.]

* * *

In *Parratt*, before concluding that Nebraska's tort remedy provided all the process that was due, we said that the loss of the prisoner's hobby kit, "even though negligently caused, amounted to a deprivation [under the Due Process Clause]." Justice Powell, concurring in the result, criticized the majority for "pass[ing] over" this important question of the state of mind required to constitute a "deprivation" of property. He argued that negligent acts by state officials, though causing loss of property, are not actionable under the Due Process Clause. To Justice Powell, mere negligence could not "wor[k] a deprivation in the *constitutional sense*." Not only does the word "deprive" in the Due Process Clause connote more than a negligent act, but we should not "open the federal courts to lawsuits where there has been no affirmative abuse of power." * * * Upon reflection, we agree and overrule *Parratt* to the extent that it states that mere lack of due care by a state official may "deprive" an individual of life, liberty, or property under the Fourteenth Amendment.

The Due Process Clause of the Fourteenth Amendment provides: "[N]or shall any State deprive any person of life, liberty, or property, without due process of law." Historically, this guarantee of due process has been applied to *deliberate* decisions of government officials to deprive a person of life, liberty, or property. *E.g., Davidson v. New Orleans,* 96 U.S. 97 (1878) (assessment of real estate); *Rochin v. California,* 342 U.S. 165 (1952) (stomach pumping); *Bell v. Burson,* 402 U.S. 535 (1971) (suspension of driver's license); *Ingraham v. Wright,* 430 U.S. 651 (1977) (paddling student); *Hudson v. Palmer,* 468 U.S. 517 (1984) (intentional destruction of inmate's property). No decision of this Court before *Parratt* supported the view that negligent conduct by a state official, even though causing injury, constitutes a deprivation under the Due Process Clause. This history reflects the traditional and common-sense notion that the Due Process Clause, like its forebear in the Magna Carta was "'intended to secure the individual from the arbitrary exercise of the powers of government.'" By requiring the government to follow appropriate procedures when its agents decide to "deprive any person of life, liberty, or property," the Due Process Clause promotes fairness in such decisions. And by barring certain government actions regardless of the fairness of the procedures used to implement them, it serves to prevent governmental power from being "used for purposes of oppression."

We think that the actions of prison custodians in leaving a pillow on the prison stairs, or mislaying an inmate's property, are quite remote from the concerns just discussed. Far from an abuse of power, lack of due care suggests no more than a failure to measure up to the conduct of a reasonable person. To hold that injury caused by such conduct is a deprivation within the meaning of the Fourteenth Amendment would trivialize the centuries-old principle of due process of law.

The Fourteenth Amendment is a part of a Constitution generally designed to allocate governing authority among the Branches of the Federal Government and between that Government and the States, and to secure certain individual rights against both State and Federal Government. When dealing with a claim that such a document creates a right in prisoners to sue a government official because he negligently created an unsafe condition in the prison, we bear in mind Chief Justice Marshall's admonition that "we must never forget, that it is *a constitution* we are expounding," *McCulloch v. Maryland,* 4 Wheat. 316, 407 (1819) (emphasis in original). Our Constitution deals with the large concerns of the governors and the governed, but it does not purport to supplant traditional tort law in laying down rules of conduct to regulate liability for injuries that attend living together in society. We have previously rejected reasoning that "'would make of the Fourteenth Amendment a font of tort law to be superimposed upon whatever systems may already be administered by the States,'" *Paul v. Davis,* 424 U.S. 693, 701 (1976).

*   *   *

That injuries inflicted by governmental negligence are not addressed by the United States Constitution is not to say that they may not raise significant legal concerns and lead to the creation of protectible legal interests. *   *   * It is no reflection on either the breadth of the United States Constitution or the importance of traditional tort law to say that they do not address the same concerns.

In support of his claim that negligent conduct can give rise to a due process "deprivation," petitioner makes several arguments, none of which we find persuasive. He states, for example, that "it is almost certain that *some* negligence claims are within § 1983," and cites as an example the failure of a State to comply with the procedural requirements of *Wolff v. McDonnell* before depriving an inmate of good-time credit. We think the relevant action of the prison officials in that situation is their deliberate decision to deprive the inmate of good-time credit, not their hypothetically negligent failure to accord him the procedural protections of the Due Process Clause. But we need not rule out the possibility that there are other constitutional provisions that would be violated by mere lack of care in order to hold, as we do, that such conduct does not implicate the Due Process Clause of the Fourteenth Amendment.

Petitioner also suggests that artful litigants, undeterred by a requirement that they plead more than mere negligence, will often be able to allege sufficient facts to support a claim of intentional deprivation. In the instant case, for example, petitioner notes that he could have alleged that the pillow was left on the stairs with the intention of harming him. This invitation to "artful" pleading, petitioner contends, would engender sticky (and needless) disputes over what is fairly pleaded. What's more, requiring complainants to allege something more than negligence would raise serious questions about what "more" than negligence—intent, recklessness, or "gross negligence"—is required,[3] and indeed about what these elusive terms mean. But even if accurate, petitioner's observations do not carry the day. In the first place, many branches of the law abound in nice distinctions that may be troublesome but have been thought nonetheless necessary:

> "I do not think we need trouble ourselves with the thought that my view depends upon differences of degree. The whole law does so as soon as it is civilized." *LeRoy Fibre Co. v. Chicago, M. & St. P.R. Co.*, 232 U.S. 340, 354 (1914) (Holmes, J., partially concurring).

More important, the difference between one end of the spectrum—negligence—and the other—intent—is abundantly clear. In any event, we decline to trivialize the Due Process Clause in an effort to simplify constitutional litigation.

Finally, petitioner argues that respondent's conduct, even if merely negligent, breached a sheriff's "special duty of care" for those in his custody. * * *

* * * Jailers may owe a special duty of care to those in their custody under state tort law, see Restatement (Second) of Torts § 314A(4) (1965), but for the reasons previously stated we reject the contention that the Due Process Clause of the Fourteenth Amendment embraces such a tort law concept. Petitioner alleges that he was injured by the negligence of respondent, a custodial official at the city jail. Whatever other provisions of state law or general jurisprudence

---

3. Despite his claim about what he might have pleaded, petitioner concedes that respondent was at most negligent. Accordingly, this case affords us no occasion to consider whether something less than intentional conduct, such as recklessness or "gross negligence," is enough to trigger the protections of the Due Process Clause.

he may rightly invoke, the Fourteenth Amendment to the United States Constitution does not afford him a remedy.

Affirmed.

[Justices Marshall, Blackmun, and Stevens concurred in the Court's judgment. Excerpts from Justice Stevens' opinion, in which he concurred in the judgments in both *Daniels v. Williams* and *Davidson v. Cannon,* 474 U.S. 344, 106 S.Ct. 668 (1986) can be found in note 1 below and note 2, *infra* page 460.]

Questions and Points for Discussion

1. In a companion case to *Daniels v. Williams, Davidson v. Cannon,* id., the Supreme Court reiterated that negligence cannot effect a deprivation within the meaning of the due process clause. In *Davidson,* the plaintiff, a prisoner, had warned prison officials that he had been threatened by another inmate. The prison officials took no steps to protect the plaintiff, who was housed in the same unit with the inmate who had threatened him, and the plaintiff was subsequently attacked by that inmate and seriously injured.

In reaffirming its holding in *Daniels,* the Court, in an opinion written by Justice Rehnquist, emphasized that the plaintiff did not contend that the prison officials had been anything other than negligent in their failure to protect him. A claim of negligence, said the Court, "is quite different from one involving injuries caused by an unjustified attack by prison guards themselves or by another prisoner where officials simply stood by and permitted the attack to proceed." Id. at 348, 106 S.Ct. at 670–71.

Justice Stevens wrote a separate opinion, concurring in the judgments in both *Davidson* and *Daniels.* In his opinion, he stated:

> I would not reject these claims, as the Court does, by attempting to fashion a new definition of the term "deprivation" and excluding negligence from its scope. * * * "Deprivation," it seems to me, identifies, not the actor's state of mind, but the victim's infringement or loss. The harm to a prisoner is the same whether a pillow is left on a stair negligently, recklessly, or intentionally; so too, the harm resulting to a prisoner from an attack is the same whether his request for protection is ignored negligently, recklessly, or deliberately. In each instance, the prisoner is losing—being "deprived" of—an aspect of liberty as the result, in part, of a form of state action.

Id. at 340–41, 106 S.Ct. at 679–80 (Stevens, J., concurring). Justice Stevens, however, concurred in the Court's judgment because he believed that *Daniels* and *Davidson* had been afforded due process. See note 2, infra page 460.

Justice Blackmun, joined by Justice Marshall, dissented in *Davidson,* making the following observations:

> When the State of New Jersey put Robert Davidson in its prison, it stripped him of all means of self-protection. It forbade his access to a weapon. N.J. Dept. of Corrections Standards 251.4.a.201 and .202. It forbade his fighting back. Standards 251.4.a.002, .003, and .004. It

blocked all avenues of escape. The State forced Davidson to rely solely on its own agents for protection. When threatened with violence by a fellow inmate, Davidson turned to the prison officials for protection, but they ignored his plea for help. As a result, Davidson was assaulted by another inmate. He suffered stab wounds on his face and body as well as a broken nose that required surgery.

* * *

The Court appears to recognize that the injuries to Davidson (as well as that to Daniels in the companion case) implicates the "liberty" protected by the Fourteenth Amendment. It is well established that this liberty includes freedom from unjustified intrusions on personal security. In particular, it includes a prisoner's right to safe conditions and to security from attack by other inmates. * * *

Although Daniels' and Davidson's liberty interests were infringed, the Court holds that they were not "deprived" of liberty in the constitutional sense. * * * I agree that mere negligent activity *ordinarily* will not amount to an abuse of state power. Where the Court today errs, in my view, is in elevating this sensible rule of thumb to the status of inflexible constitutional dogma. The Court declares that negligent activity can *never* implicate the concerns of the Due Process Clause. I see no justification for this rigid view. In some cases, by any reasonable standard, governmental negligence is an abuse of power. This is one of those cases.

It seems to me that when a State assumes sole responsibility for one's physical security and then ignores his call for help, the State cannot claim that it did not know a subsequent injury was likely to occur. Under such circumstances, the State should not automatically be excused from responsibility. In the context of prisons, this means that once the State has taken away an inmate's means of protecting himself from attack by other inmates, a prison official's negligence in providing protection can amount to a deprivation of the inmate's liberty, at least absent extenuating circumstances. Such conduct by state officials seems to me to be the "arbitrary action" against which the Due Process Clause protects. The officials' actions in such cases thus are not remote from the purpose of the Due Process Clause and § 1983.

Moreover, this case does not raise the concern noted in *Daniels* that "[t]he only tie between the facts . . . and anything governmental in nature" is the identity of the parties. In *Daniels,* the negligence was only coincidentally connected to an inmate-guard relationship; the same incident could have occurred on any staircase. Daniels in jail was as able as he would have been anywhere else to protect himself against a pillow on the stairs. The State did not prohibit him from looking where he was going or from taking care to avoid the pillow.

In contrast, where the State renders a person vulnerable and strips him of his ability to defend himself, an injury that results from a state official's negligence in performing his duty is peculiarly related to the governmental function. Negligence in such a case implicates the " '[m]isuse of power, possessed by virtue of state law and made possible only because the wrongdoer is clothed with the authority of state law.'" Monroe v. Pape, 365 U.S. 167, 184, 81 S.Ct. 473, 482 (1961), quoting United States v. Classic, 313 U.S. 299, 326, 61 S.Ct. 1031, 1043 (1941).

Justice Blackmun also dissented in *Davidson* because he felt that a due process deprivation could, in any event, occur through the recklessness or deliberate indifference of government officials. In this case, he believed that there was sufficient evidence of recklessness for this question to be considered on remand.

Justice Brennan wrote a dissenting opinion in *Davidson* because he too felt that the prison officials had probably been reckless, thereby depriving Davidson of a liberty interest. Justice Brennan, however, agreed with the majority that negligence alone would not support the finding of a due process violation.

2. How would you resolve the question left open in *Daniels* and *Davidson*—whether recklessness or gross negligence will suffice for there to be a deprivation within the meaning of the due process clause? How would you define these terms? See the definitions propounded by Judge Posner in Duckworth v. Franzen, 780 F.2d 645, 652–53 (7th Cir.1985), which can be found in note 4, infra page 470.

Since the Supreme Court concluded in *Daniels* and *Davidson* that the plaintiffs had not suffered any deprivation of their liberty when they were injured, it did not have to address the question whether or not the plaintiffs had been afforded due process. In *Parratt v. Taylor*, however, pertinent excerpts of which are set forth below, the Court discussed how the requirements of due process can be satisfied.

PARRATT v. TAYLOR
Supreme Court of the United States, 1981.
451 U.S. 527, 101 S.Ct. 1908, 68 L.Ed.2d 420.

JUSTICE REHNQUIST delivered the opinion of the Court.

[The plaintiff in this case, a prisoner at the Nebraska Penal and Correctional Complex, brought a § 1983 suit to recover damages for a hobby kit worth $23.50, which was lost because of the alleged negligence of several prison officials. As was discussed earlier, *supra* page 450, the Supreme Court held that a deprivation of property within the meaning of the due process clause could occur through the negligence of government officials. This portion of the Court's opinion in *Parratt* was subsequently overruled by the Court in *Daniels v. Williams, supra* page 451. The Court then turned to the question whether the deprivation of the plaintiff's property had occurred without due process of law.]

This Court has never directly addressed the question of what process is due a person when an employee of a State negligently takes his property. In some cases this Court has held that due process requires a predeprivation hearing before the State interferes with any liberty or property interest enjoyed by its citizens. In most of these cases, however, the deprivation of property was pursuant to some established state procedure and "process" could be offered before any actual deprivation took place. For example, * * * in *Bell v. Burson,* 402 U.S. 535 (1971), we reviewed a state statute which provided for the taking of the driver's license and registration of an uninsured motorist who had been involved in an accident. We recognized that a driver's license is often involved in the livelihood of a person and as such could not be summarily taken without a prior hearing. * * *

We have, however, recognized that postdeprivation remedies made available by the State can satisfy the Due Process Clause. In such cases, the normal predeprivation notice and opportunity to be heard is pretermitted if the State provides a postdeprivation remedy. In *North American Cold Storage Co. v. Chicago,* 211 U.S. 306 (1908), we upheld the right of a State to seize and destroy unwholesome food without a preseizure hearing. The possibility of erroneous destruction of property was outweighed by the fact that the public health emergency justified immediate action and the owner of the property could recover his damages in an action at law after the incident. * * * Similarly, in *Fahey v. Mallonee,* 332 U.S. 245 (1947), we recognized that the protection of the public interest against economic harm can justify the immediate seizure of property without a prior hearing when substantial questions are raised about the competence of a bank's management. * * * These cases recognize that either the necessity of quick action by the State or the impracticality of providing any meaningful predeprivation process, when coupled with the availability of some meaningful means by which to assess the propriety of the State's action at some time after the initial taking, can satisfy the requirements of procedural due process. * * *

Our past cases mandate that some kind of hearing is required at some time before a State finally deprives a person of his property interests. The fundamental requirement of due process is the opportunity to be heard and it is an "opportunity which must be granted at a meaningful time and in a meaningful manner." *Armstrong v. Manzo,* 380 U.S. 545, 552 (1965). However, as many of the above cases recognize, we have rejected the proposition that "at a meaningful time and in a meaningful manner" *always* requires the State to provide a hearing prior to the initial deprivation of property. * * *

The justifications which we have found sufficient to uphold takings of property without any predeprivation process are applicable to a situation such as the present one involving a tortious loss of a prisoner's property as a result of a random and unauthorized act by a state employee. In such a case, the loss is not a result of some established state procedure and the State cannot predict precisely when the loss will occur. It is difficult to conceive of how the State could provide a meaningful hearing before the deprivation takes place. The loss of property, although attributable to the State as action under "color of law," is in almost all cases beyond the control of the State. Indeed, in most cases it is not only impracticable, but impossible, to provide a meaningful hearing before the deprivation. That does not mean, of course, that the State can take property without providing a meaningful postdeprivation hearing. The prior cases which have excused the prior-hearing requirement have rested in part on the availability of some meaningful opportunity subsequent to the initial taking for a determination of rights and liabilities.

* * *

Application of the principles recited above to this case leads us to conclude the respondent has not alleged a violation of the Due Process Clause of the Fourteenth Amendment. Although he has been deprived of property under color of state law, the deprivation did not occur as a result of some established state procedure. Indeed, the deprivation occurred as a result of the unauthorized failure of agents of the State to follow established state procedure. There is no contention that the procedures themselves are inadequate nor is there any contention that it was practicable for the State to provide a predeprivation hearing. Moreover, the State of Nebraska has provided respondent with the means by which he can receive redress for the deprivation. The State provides a remedy to persons who believe they have suffered a tortious loss at the hands of the State. See Neb.Rev.Stat. § 81–8,209 et seq. (1976). Through this tort claims procedure the State hears and pays claims of prisoners housed in its penal institutions. This procedure was in existence at the time of the loss here in question but respondent did not use it. It is argued that the State does not adequately protect the respondent's interests because it provides only for an action against the State as opposed to its individual employees, it contains no provisions for punitive damages, and there is no right to a trial by jury. Although the state remedies may not provide the respondent with all the relief which may have been available if he could have proceeded under § 1983, that does not mean that the state remedies are not adequate to satisfy the requirements of due process. The remedies provided could have fully compensated the respondent for the property loss he suffered, and we hold that they are sufficient to satisfy the requirements of due process.

Our decision today is fully consistent with our prior cases. To accept respondent's argument that the conduct of the state officials in this case constituted a violation of the Fourteenth Amendment would almost necessarily result in turning every alleged injury which may have been inflicted by a state official acting under "color of law" into a violation of the Fourteenth Amendment cognizable under § 1983. It is hard to perceive any logical stopping place to such a line of reasoning. Presumably, under this rationale any party who is involved in nothing more than an automobile accident with a state official could allege a constitutional violation under § 1983. Such reasoning "would make of the Fourteenth Amendment a font of tort law to be superimposed upon whatever systems may already be administered by the States." *Paul v. Davis,* 424 U.S. 693, 701 (1976). We do not think that the drafters of the Fourteenth Amendment intended the Amendment to play such a role in our society.

Accordingly, the judgment of the Court of Appeals is

Reversed.

[Justices Stewart, White, and Blackmun, while joining the Court's opinion, also wrote separate concurring opinions. Justice Powell concurred in the result. These concurring opinions are omitted, as is Justice Marshall's opinion in which he concurred in part and dissented in part.]

Questions and Points for Discussion

1. In Hudson v. Palmer, 468 U.S. 517, 104 S.Ct. 3194 (1984), the Supreme Court extended its holding in *Parratt* to intentional property deprivations. The plaintiff in that case, a prisoner, sued the defendant, a correctional officer, after the defendant allegedly searched the plaintiff's cell and destroyed some of his personal property just to harass him. The plaintiff contended that the defendant's actions violated his rights under the fourth amendment and the due process clause of the fourteenth amendment.

The Supreme Court rejected the plaintiff's fourth amendment claim. See supra page 409. Turning to the plaintiff's due process claim, the Court stated as follows:

> While *Parratt* is necessarily limited by its facts to negligent deprivations of property, it is evident, as the Court of Appeals recognized, that its reasoning applies as well to intentional deprivations of property. The underlying rationale of *Parratt* is that when deprivations of property are effected through random and unauthorized conduct of a state employee, predeprivation procedures are simply "impracticable" since the state cannot know when such deprivations will occur. We can discern no logical distinction between negligent and intentional deprivations of property insofar as the "practicability" of affording predeprivation process is concerned. The state can no more anticipate and control in advance the random and unauthorized intentional conduct of its employees than it can anticipate similar negligent conduct. Arguably, intentional acts are even more difficult to anticipate because one bent on intentionally depriving a person of his property might well take affirmative steps to avoid signalling his intent.

> * * *

> Respondent * * * contends that, because an agent of the state who intends to deprive a person of his property "*can* provide predeprivation process, then as a matter of due process he must do so." This argument reflects a fundamental misunderstanding of *Parratt*. There we held that postdeprivation procedures satisfy due process because the *state* cannot possibly know in advance of a negligent deprivation of property. Whether an individual employee himself is able to foresee a deprivation is simply of no consequence. The control-

ling inquiry is solely whether the state is in a position to provide for predeprivation process.

Id. at 533–34, 104 S.Ct. at 3203–04. The Court then concluded by holding that when a state employee has in a random fashion intentionally, though without authorization, destroyed someone's property, the requirements of due process are met as long as the state affords the aggrieved individual a "meaningful postdeprivation remedy." Id. at 533, 104 S.Ct. at 3203.

While Justice Stevens, in an opinion joined by Justices Brennan, Marshall, and Blackmun, concurred in the Court's disposition of the plaintiff's due process claim, he emphasized that he did not construe the Court's decision to extend either to violations of substantive constitutional rights— those which occur regardless of the procedures employed by the government—or to deprivations effected through "established prison procedures." Id. at 541 n. 4, 104 S.Ct. at 3208 n. 4. (Stevens, J., concurring and dissenting). A majority of the Court concurred with this view in Zinermon v. Burch, 110 S.Ct. 975 (1990), which involved a claimed deprivation of due process when the plaintiff was "voluntarily" admitted into a mental hospital at a time when he was allegedly incapable of giving informed consent. In addition, the Court in that case narrowly construed *Parratt v. Taylor* and *Hudson v. Palmer,* concluding that those cases only stand for the proposition that postdeprivation remedies will satisfy due process when predeprivation procedures could not avert the deprivation complained of.

2. You will recall that Justice Stevens did not join the majority's opinion in Davidson v. Cannon, 474 U.S. 344, 106 S.Ct. 668 (1986), supra page 454, because he believed, unlike the majority, that the negligence of a governmental employee could deprive someone of an interest protected by the due process clause. Justice Stevens still concurred in the judgment in that case, however, because he believed that the state had afforded Davidson with the requisite due process. He arrived at this conclusion despite the fact that a statute accorded immunity to state employees sued by prisoners for personal injuries inflicted by other prisoners. He explained his reasoning as follows:

> *Davidson* puts the question whether a state policy of noncompensability for certain types of harm, in which state action may play a role, renders a state procedure constitutionally defective. In my judgment, a state policy that defeats recovery does not, in itself, carry that consequence. Those aspects of a State's tort regime that defeat recovery are not constitutionally invalid, so long as there is no fundamental unfairness in their operation. Thus, defenses such as contributory negligence or statutes of limitations may defeat recovery in particular cases without raising any question about the constitutionality of a State's procedures for disposing of tort litigation. Similarly, in my judgment, the mere fact that a State elects to provide some of its agents with a sovereign immunity defense in certain cases does not justify the conclusion that its remedial system is constitutionally inadequate. There is no reason to believe that the Due Process Clause of the Fourteenth Amendment and the legislation enacted pursuant to § 5 of that Amendment should be construed to suggest that the doctrine of sovereign immunity renders a state procedure fundamental-

ly unfair. Davidson's challenge has been only to the fact of sovereign immunity; he has not challenged the difference in treatment of a prisoner assaulted by a prisoner and a non-prisoner assaulted by a prisoner, and I express no comment on the fairness of that differentiation.

Id. at 342–43, 106 S.Ct. at 680–81. (Stevens, J., concurring).

In a dissenting opinion in which he was joined by Justice Marshall, Justice Blackmun spurned the notion that Davidson had a meaningful postdeprivation remedy available to him even though any claim that he filed in state court would immediately be defeated by the assertion of a state immunity defense. Because the majority of the Court concluded that Davidson had not suffered a deprivation in the constitutional sense, it left to another day and another case the resolution of the question of whether an individual is afforded due process when an immunity defense will preclude the recovery of damages.

How do you believe this issue should be resolved?

3.   Federal and state statutes and regulations often define what personal property an inmate will be permitted to retain while in prison. Draft a model regulation outlining what personal property prisoners can have in general population units, administrative segregation units, and disciplinary segregation units.

Chapter 15

CRUEL AND UNUSUAL PUNISHMENT

The eighth amendment to the United States Constitution proscribes the infliction of "cruel and unusual punishments." This amendment extends its protection to individuals who have been convicted of crimes. If pretrial detainees contend that they are being treated cruelly and unusually, their claims will be assessed under another constitutional provision, usually the due process clause.

Cruel and unusual punishment claims have arisen in a number of different contexts. For example, prisoners have challenged, as cruel and unusual punishment, inadequacies in the medical care with which they were afforded, correctional officers' use of force against them, the failure to protect them from attacks by other inmates, and the conditions of their confinement.

In the sections below, these types of cruel and unusual punishment claims are discussed. In addition, cases discussing eight amendment challenges to the sentences imposed in criminal cases can be found in Chapters 6 and 7.

A. MEDICAL, DENTAL, AND PSYCHIATRIC CARE

1. THE RIGHTS TO BE TREATED AND NOT TO BE TREATED

CARE AND PUNISHMENT: MEDICINE BEHIND BARS

Olive Talley, The Dallas Morning News, June 25 and June 30, 1989.

Ronnie Holley was a healthy 32–year–old carpenter from South Texas when he was sentenced to federal prison for falsifying gun records. He was released early—disfigured and impotent—because of what officials called the "devastating effects" of surgery he underwent at the U.S. Medical Center for Federal Prisoners.

Ben Firth, a 56–year–old former truck driver convicted of hauling cocaine, died of a heart attack at the same prison medical center in

462

Springfield, Mo. He had suffered chest pains for several hours without examination by a doctor. A prison doctor later concluded that Mr. Firth's death likely could have been prevented.

Danny Ranieri, sentenced to seven years in federal prison on a tax conviction, was blinded by an overdose of drugs prescribed by a Kentucky prison doctor whose practice behind bars ultimately cost him his medical license.

Isabella Suarez, in a federal lockup in Chicago on charges of stealing mail, lapsed into a coma and died after prison officials withheld her medication for epilepsy, according to inmates who were incarcerated with her. Charges against the 41–year–old mother had been dropped shortly before her death.

Criminologists and penal experts long have regarded the U.S. Bureau of Prisons—and its health care for inmates—as the Cadillac of the nation's network of state and federal prisons. But an investigation by *The Dallas Morning News* reveals a medical system plagued by severe overcrowding, critical shortages of doctors, nurses and physician's assistants, and life-threatening delays in transfers of inmate patients to major prison hospitals.

*   *   *

*   *   * "When the court sentenced me, I was sentenced to the CARE and custody of the Bureau of Prisons.

"Well, I've been in your custody, but far from in your care. . . . Please release me to an outside hospital. Please."

(written by an inmate who weighed 210 pounds when first incarcerated, but who, six years later, weighed 141 pounds, was partially paralyzed, and had chronic breathing problems).

ESTELLE v. GAMBLE

Supreme Court of the United States, 1976.
429 U.S. 97, 97 S.Ct. 285, 50 L.Ed.2d 251.

Mr. Justice Marshall delivered the opinion of the Court.

Respondent J.W. Gamble, an inmate of the Texas Department of Corrections, was injured on November 9, 1973, while performing a prison work assignment. On February 11, 1974, he instituted this civil rights action under 42 U.S.C. § 1983, complaining of the treatment he received after the injury. Named as defendants were the petitioners, W.J. Estelle, Jr., Director of the Department of Corrections, H.H. Husbands, warden of the prison, and Dr. Ralph Gray, medical director of the Department and chief medical officer of the prison hospital. The District Court, *sua sponte,* dismissed the complaint for failure to state a claim upon which relief could be granted. The Court of Appeals reversed and remanded with instructions to reinstate the complaint. We granted certiorari.

I

Because the complaint was dismissed for failure to state a claim, we must take as true its handwritten, *pro se* allegations. According to the complaint, Gamble was injured on November 9, 1973, when a bale of cotton fell on him while he was unloading a truck. He continued to work but after four hours he became stiff and was granted a pass to the unit hospital. At the hospital a medical assistant, "Captain" Blunt, checked him for a hernia and sent him back to his cell. Within two hours the pain became so intense that Gamble returned to the hospital where he was given pain pills by an inmate nurse and then was examined by a doctor. The following day, Gamble saw a Dr. Astone who diagnosed the injury as a lower back strain, prescribed Zactirin (a pain reliever) and Robaxin (a muscle relaxant), and placed respondent on "cell-pass, cell-feed" status for two days, allowing him to remain in his cell at all times except for showers. On November 12, Gamble again saw Dr. Astone who continued the medication and cell-pass, cell-feed for another seven days. He also ordered that respondent be moved from an upper to a lower bunk for one week, but the prison authorities did not comply with that directive. The following week, Gamble returned to Dr. Astone. The doctor continued the muscle relaxant but prescribed a new pain reliever, Febridyne, and placed respondent on cell-pass for seven days, permitting him to remain in his cell except for meals and showers. On November 26, respondent again saw Dr. Astone, who put respondent back on the original pain reliever for five days and continued the cell-pass for another week.

On December 3, despite Gamble's statement that his back hurt as much as it had the first day, Dr. Astone took him off cell-pass, thereby certifying him to be capable of light work. At the same time, Dr. Astone prescribed Febridyne for seven days. Gamble then went to a Major Muddox and told him that he was in too much pain to work. Muddox had respondent moved to "administrative segregation." On December 5, Gamble was taken before the prison disciplinary committee, apparently because of his refusal to work. When the committee heard his complaint of back pain and high blood pressure, it directed that he be seen by another doctor.

On December 6, respondent saw petitioner Gray, who performed a urinalysis, blood test, and blood pressure measurement. Dr. Gray prescribed the drug Ser–Ap–Es for the high blood pressure and more Febridyne for the back pain. The following week respondent again saw Dr. Gray, who continued the Ser–Ap–Es for an additional 30 days. The prescription was not filled for four days, however, because the staff lost it. Respondent went to the unit hospital twice more in December; both times he was seen by Captain Blunt, who prescribed Tiognolos (described as a muscle relaxant). For all of December, respondent remained in administrative segregation.

In early January, Gamble was told on two occasions that he would be sent to the "farm" if he did not return to work. He refused, nonetheless, claiming to be in too much pain. On January 7, 1974, he requested to go on sick call for his back pain and migraine headaches. After an initial refusal, he saw Captain Blunt who prescribed sodium salicylate (a pain reliever) for seven days and Ser–Ap–Es for 30 days. Respondent returned to Captain Blunt on January 17 and January 25, and received renewals of the pain reliever prescription both times. Throughout the month, respondent was kept in administrative segregation.

On January 31, Gamble was brought before the prison disciplinary committee for his refusal to work in early January. He told the committee that he could not work because of his severe back pain and his high blood pressure. Captain Blunt testified that Gamble was in "first class" medical condition. The committee, with no further medical examination or testimony, placed respondent in solitary confinement.

Four days later, on February 4, at 8 a.m., respondent asked to see a doctor for chest pains and "blank outs." It was not until 7:30 that night that a medical assistant examined him and ordered him hospitalized. The following day a Dr. Heaton performed an electrocardiogram; one day later respondent was placed on Quinidine for treatment of irregular cardiac rhythm and moved to administrative segregation. On February 7, respondent again experienced pain in his chest, left arm, and back and asked to see a doctor. The guards refused. He asked again the next day. The guards again refused. Finally, on February 9, he was allowed to see Dr. Heaton, who ordered the Quinidine continued for three more days. On February 11, he swore out his complaint.

II

The gravamen of respondent's § 1983 complaint is that petitioners have subjected him to cruel and unusual punishment in violation of the Eighth Amendment, made applicable to the States by the Fourteenth. We therefore base our evaluation of respondent's complaint on those Amendments and our decisions interpreting them.

The history of the constitutional prohibition of "cruel and unusual punishments" has been recounted at length in prior opinions of the Court and need not be repeated here. See, *e.g., Gregg v. Georgia,* 428 U.S. 153, 169–173 (1976) (joint opinion of Stewart, Powell, and Stevens, JJ. It suffices to note that the primary concern of the drafters was to proscribe "torture[s]" and other "barbar[ous]" methods of punishment.

*　*　*

Our more recent cases, however, have held that the Amendment proscribes more than physically barbarous punishments. The Amendment embodies "broad and idealistic concepts of dignity, civilized standards, humanity, and decency . . .," *Jackson v. Bishop,* 404 F.2d 571, 579 (CA8 1968), against which we must evaluate penal measures. Thus, we have held repugnant to the Eighth Amendment punishments which are incompatible with "the evolving standards of decency that mark the progress of a maturing society," or which "involve the unnecessary and wanton infliction of pain."

These elementary principles establish the government's obligation to provide medical care for those whom it is punishing by incarceration. An inmate must rely on prison authorities to treat his medical needs; if the authorities fail to do so, those needs will not be met. In the worst cases, such a failure may actually produce physical "torture or a lingering death," the evils of most immediate concern to the drafters of the Amendment. In less serious cases, denial of medical care may result in pain and suffering which no one suggests would serve any penological purpose. The infliction of such unnecessary suffering is inconsistent with contemporary standards of decency as manifested in modern legislation codifying the common-law view that "it is but just that the public be required to care for the prisoner, who cannot by reason of the deprivation of his liberty, care for himself."

We therefore conclude that deliberate indifference to serious medical needs of prisoners constitutes the "unnecessary and wanton infliction of pain" proscribed by the Eighth Amendment. This is true whether the indifference is manifested by prison doctors in their response to the prisoner's needs [10] or by prison guards in intentionally denying or delaying access to medical care or intentionally interfering with the treatment once prescribed. Regardless of how evidenced, deliberate indifference to a prisoner's serious illness or injury states a cause of action under § 1983.

This conclusion does not mean, however, that every claim by a prisoner that he has not received adequate medical treatment states a violation of the Eighth Amendment. An accident, although it may produce added anguish, is not on that basis alone to be characterized as wanton infliction of unnecessary pain. * * *

Similarly, in the medical context, an inadvertent failure to provide adequate medical care cannot be said to constitute "an unnecessary and wanton infliction of pain" or to be "repugnant to the conscience of mankind." Thus, a complaint that a physician has been negligent in diagnosing or treating a medical condition does not state a valid claim of medical mistreatment under the Eighth Amendment. Medical malpractice does not become a constitutional violation merely because the victim is a prisoner. In order to state a cognizable claim, a prisoner must allege acts or omissions sufficiently harmful to evidence deliberate indifference to serious medical needs. It is only such indifference

10. See, *e.g., Williams v. Vincent,* 508 F.2d 541 (CA2 1974) (doctor's choosing the "easier and less efficacious treatment" of throwing away the prisoner's ear and stitching the stump may be attributable to "deliberate indifference . . . rather than an exercise of professional judgment"); *Thomas v. Pate,* 493 F.2d 151, 158 (CA7) (injection of penicillin with knowledge that prisoner was allergic, and refusal of doctor to treat allergic reaction); *Jones v. Lockhart,* 484 F.2d 1192 (CA8 1973) (refusal of paramedic to provide treatment); *Martinez v. Mancusi,* 443 F.2d 921 (CA2 1970) (prison physician refuses to administer the prescribed pain killer and renders leg surgery unsuccessful by requiring prisoner to stand despite contrary instructions of surgeon).

that can offend "evolving standards of decency" in violation of the Eighth Amendment.

III

Against this backdrop, we now consider whether respondent's complaint states a cognizable § 1983 claim. The handwritten *pro se* document is to be liberally construed. As the Court unanimously held in *Haines v. Kerner,* 404 U.S. 519 (1972), a *pro se* complaint, "however inartfully pleaded," must be held to "less stringent standards than formal pleadings drafted by lawyers" and can only be dismissed for failure to state a claim if it appears " 'beyond doubt that the plaintiff can prove no set of facts in support of his claim which would entitle him to relief.' " *Id.,* at 520–521, quoting *Conley v. Gibson,* 355 U.S. 41, 45–46 (1957).

Even applying these liberal standards, however, Gamble's claims against Dr. Gray, both in his capacity as treating physician and as medical director of the Corrections Department, are not cognizable under § 1983. Gamble was seen by medical personnel on 17 occasions spanning a three-month period: by Dr. Astone five times; by Dr. Gray twice; by Dr. Heaton three times; by an unidentified doctor and inmate nurse on the day of the injury; and by medical assistant Blunt six times. They treated his back injury, high blood pressure, and heart problems. Gamble has disclaimed any objection to the treatment provided for his high blood pressure and his heart problem; his complaint is "based solely on the lack of diagnosis and inadequate treatment of his back injury." The doctors diagnosed his injury as a lower back strain and treated it with bed rest, muscle relaxants, and pain relievers. Respondent contends that more should have been done by way of diagnosis and treatment, and suggests a number of options that were not pursued. The Court of Appeals agreed, stating: "Certainly an X-ray of [Gamble's] lower back might have been in order and other tests conducted that would have led to appropriate diagnosis and treatment for the daily pain and suffering he was experiencing." But the question whether an X-ray—or additional diagnostic techniques or forms of treatment—is indicated is a classic example of a matter for medical judgment. A medical decision not to order an X-ray, or like measures, does not represent cruel and unusual punishment. At most it is medical malpractice, and as such the proper forum is the state court under the Texas Tort Claims Act. * * *

The Court of Appeals focused primarily on the alleged actions of the doctors, and did not separately consider whether the allegations against the Director of the Department of Corrections, Estelle, and the warden of the prison, Husbands, stated a cause of action. Although we reverse the judgment as to the medical director, we remand the case to the Court of Appeals to allow it an opportunity to consider, in conformity with this opinion, whether a cause of action has been stated against the other prison officials.

* * *

MR. JUSTICE BLACKMUN concurs in the judgment of the Court.

MR. JUSTICE STEVENS, dissenting.

* * *

On the basis of Gamble's handwritten complaint it is impossible to assess the quality of the medical attention he received. As the Court points out, even if what he alleges is true, the doctors may be guilty of nothing more than negligence or malpractice. On the other hand, it is surely not inconceivable that an overworked, undermanned medical staff in a crowded prison [2] is following the expedient course of routinely prescribing nothing more than pain killers when a thorough diagnosis would disclose an obvious need for remedial treatment. Three fine judges sitting on the United States Court of Appeals for the Fifth Circuit thought that enough had been alleged to require some inquiry into the actual facts. If this Court meant what it said in *Haines v. Kerner,* 404 U.S. 519, these judges were clearly right.

* * *

* * * [B]y its repeated references to "deliberate indifference" and the "intentional" denial of adequate medical care, I believe the Court improperly attaches significance to the subjective motivation of the defendant as a criterion for determining whether cruel and unusual punishment has been inflicted. Subjective motivation may well determine what, if any, remedy is appropriate against a particular defendant. However, whether the constitutional standard has been violated should turn on the character of the punishment rather than the motivation of the individual who inflicted it.[13] Whether the conditions in Andersonville were the product of design, negligence, or mere poverty, they were cruel and inhuman.

* * *

Questions and Points for Discussion

1. The Supreme Court in *Estelle v. Gamble* did not define what constitutes a "serious medical need." Some lower court cases have defined a medical need as "serious" if a physician has diagnosed the condition as

2. According to a state legislative report quoted by the Court of Appeals, the Texas Department of Corrections has had at various times one to three doctors to care for 17,000 inmates with occasional part-time help.

13. * * * If a State elects to impose imprisonment as a punishment for crime, I believe it has an obligation to provide the persons in its custody with a health care system which meets minimal standards of adequacy. As a part of that basic obligation, the State and its agents have an affirmative duty to provide reasonable access to medical care, to provide competent, diligent medical personnel, and to ensure that prescribed care is in fact delivered. For denial of medical care is surely not part of

the punishment which civilized nations may impose for crime.

Of course, not every instance of improper health care violates the Eighth Amendment. Like the rest of us, prisoners must take the risk that a competent, diligent physician will make an error. Such an error may give rise to a tort claim but not necessarily to a constitutional claim. But when the State adds to this risk, as by providing a physician who does not meet minimum standards of competence or diligence or who cannot give adequate care because of an excessive caseload or inadequate facilities, then the prisoner may suffer from a breach of the State's constitutional duty.

one requiring medical treatment or if the need for medical treatment would be "obvious," even to a layperson. See, e.g., Hampton v. Holmesburg Prison Officials, 546 F.2d 1077, 1081 (3d Cir.1976). Whether the need for medical treatment is "obvious" may depend on a number of factors, including the following: the nature of the medical problem, the likelihood that pain or injury will result if medical treatment is delayed or denied, the severity of the pain or injury which might result from the delay or denial of medical services, and the extent to which pain or other harm attributable to the delay or denial of medical care has actually occurred.

Even if a prisoner would suffer no physical injury from a delay in providing medical treatment, a "serious medical need" might be implicated if the prisoner was experiencing pain which could be alleviated through prompt medical attention. For example, in one lower court case, a prisoner who was bruised and lacerated after falling down some stairs brought a § 1983 suit because of a six-day delay in providing him with medical care. Although the prisoner suffered no permanent physical impairment from the delay, the court held that the prisoner's claim for the pain endured during the six days before a doctor prescribed painkillers was actionable. Isaac v. Jones, 529 F.Supp. 175, 180 (N.D.Ill.1981).

2. Although prisoners may not normally have a "serious medical need" for certain elective operations, such as tonsillectomies, at least one court has found that a prisoner had a constitutional right to two elective operations—a tonsillectomy and a resectioning of his nasal septum. Derrickson v. Keve, 390 F.Supp. 905 (D.Del.1975). The two operations would apparently have relieved the prisoner from the discomfort suffered from headaches, congestion, and a sore throat. Emphasizing that the prisoner was serving a life sentence, the court noted that the prisoner, unlike most other prisoners, could not opt to have the operations when later released from prison. His need for the operations, according to the court, was consequently much greater. See also Monmouth County Correctional Institutional Inmates v. Lanzaro, 834 F.2d 326, 351 (3d Cir.1987) (in the absence of alternative means of funding elective, nontherapeutic abortions for inmates, county must pay for them).

3. According to the courts, "serious" medical needs are not confined to physical ailments; a prisoner may also have a "serious" medical need because of psychiatric or psychological problems. See, e.g., the cases cited in Meriwether v. Faulkner, 821 F.2d 408, 413 (7th Cir.1987). It is felt that such problems, if left unattended, may cause pain and suffering as unendurable as that experienced from physical injuries.

The question arises as to when a mental or emotional affliction will give rise to a constitutional duty to provide care. An inmate's complaint that he feels depressed will not suffice. Partee v. Lane, 528 F.Supp. 1254, 1261 (N.D.Ill.1981). As the court pointed out in *Partee,* if such a complaint could give rise to a constitutional claim, almost all prisoners would be entitled to psychological or psychiatric treatment since almost all prisoners are depressed some or even all of the time because of their incarceration.

In Bowring v. Godwin, 551 F.2d 44 (4th Cir.1977), the Fourth Circuit Court of Appeals set forth a three-part test to be applied when determining whether a prisoner is constitutionally entitled to psychological or psychiat-

ric care. A prisoner is entitled to such care under this test "if a physician
or other health care provider, exercising ordinary skill and care at the time
of observation, concludes with reasonable medical certainty (1) that the
prisoner's symptoms evidence a serious disease or injury; (2) that such
disease or injury is curable or may be substantially alleviated; and (3) that
the potential for harm to the prisoner by reason of delay or the denial of
care would be substantial." Id. at 47. The court added the caveat,
however, that even when these conditions are met, the right to treatment is
not an unlimited one; the right only extends to treatment which can be
provided on a "reasonable cost and time basis." Nor is there a right to
treatment which is "merely desirable;" the governing test is one of "medical necessity." Id. at 48.

4. As noted by the Supreme Court in *Estelle v. Gamble,* the failure to
attend to a prisoner's "serious medical needs" will not alone contravene the
eighth amendment. For a violation of the eighth amendment to occur, the
prison officials must have acted more than negligently; their actions or
inaction must have risen to the level of "deliberate indifference."

Perhaps the most considered discussion of what constitutes the "deliberate indifference" that will trigger an eighth amendment inquiry can be
found in Judge Richard Posner's opinion for the Seventh Circuit Court of
Appeals in Duckworth v. Franzen, 780 F.2d 645 (7th Cir.1985), portions of
which are set forth below:

> The infliction of punishment is a deliberate act intended to chas-
> tise or deter. This is what the word means today; it is what it meant
> in the eighteenth century; Samuel Johnson's Dictionary of the English
> Language (1755) defines "punishment" as "Any infliction or pain
> imposed in vengeance of a crime." If a guard decided to supplement a
> prisoner's official punishment by beating him, this would be punish-
> ment, and "cruel and unusual" because the Supreme Court has inter-
> preted the term to forbid unauthorized and disproportionate, as well as
> barbarous, punishments. But if the guard accidentally stepped on the
> prisoner's toe and broke it, this would not be punishment in anything
> remotely like the accepted meaning of the word, whether we consult
> the usage of 1791, or 1868, or 1985. Again, if a prisoner has a serious
> illness and the prison staff, though fully aware of the gravity of the
> illness, refuses to treat it and the prisoner dies, this could well be
> deemed, and under current case law would be deemed, the infliction of
> punishment. But if the staff merely misdiagnoses the illness and
> thinking it trivial does not treat it, and the prisoner dies, this would
> not be punishment in any accepted meaning of the word even if the
> diagnosis was negligent.

> These are the easy cases; the hard ones are where the behavior of
> the prison's staff is somewhere in between careless and deliberate
> infliction of suffering; and we must consider where the line is drawn.
> The reigning formula of course is "deliberate indifference," but the
> term is not self-defining. Indeed, like other famous oxymorons in
> law—"all deliberate speed" for example or "substantive due process"—
> it evades rather than expresses precise meaning.

The usual intermediate category in law between negligence and deliberateness is recklessness; and reflection on the commonest legal meanings of "reckless" may point us to a solution of our conundrum. One usage, common in tort law, essentially equates recklessness to gross negligence. See Prosser and Keeton on the Law of Torts 214 (5th ed. 1984). If negligence under Judge Learned Hand's formula in United States v. Carroll Towing Co., 159 F.2d 169, 173 (2d Cir.1947), and in later cases such as United States Fidelity & Guaranty Co. v. Jadranska Slobodna Plovidba, 683 F.2d 1022, 1026 (7th Cir.1982), means that the cost of averting an accident is less, even if just a hair's breadth less, than the expected cost of the accident that would be averted, recklessness in the sense of gross negligence means that the disparity between the cost of prevention and the expected accident cost is great. A quite different sense of recklessness, familiar from criminal law, is the sense in which for example a wrongful, deliberate, and very dangerous act which results in death though death was not intended may be downgraded to second-degree murder, with first-degree murder being reserved for deliberate homicide. A classic example is where the defendant chokes his victim, intending to injure him seriously but not to kill him, but death results. The defendant has deliberately committed an act that is at once socially costless to avoid (by not choking his victim in the first place) and highly dangerous. So he is severely punished, for an act that was deliberate and wrongful as well as for a consequence that was lethal though unintended. As this example suggests, recklessness in criminal law implies an act so dangerous that the defendant's knowledge of the risk can be inferred.

If the word "punishment" in cases of prisoner mistreatment is to retain a link with normal usage, the infliction of suffering on prisoners can be found to violate the Eighth Amendment only if that infliction is either deliberate, or reckless in the criminal law sense. Gross negligence is not enough. Unlike criminal recklessness it does not import danger so great that knowledge of the danger can be inferred; and we remind that the "indifference" to the prisoner's welfare must be "deliberate," implying such knowledge. * * *

The cases where a prisoner complaining of mistreatment has been allowed to recover damages under the Eighth Amendment in fact involve recklessness in the strong sense. For example, if a prisoner tells the prison doctor that he is allergic to penicillin, but the doctor injects him with penicillin anyway and the prisoner has a severe reaction, the doctor is guilty of having inflicted a cruel and unusual punishment. But if before injecting him the doctor merely fails to tell the prisoner what is in the syringe, and thus gives the prisoner no chance to alert him to a possible (and quite common) allergy, the doctor is not guilty of violating the Eighth Amendment even if it is a palpable act of medical malpractice to inject someone with penicillin without first asking him whether he is allergic. In the first case the doctor knows there is a great danger, could avert it at trivial cost (though greater than in the case of reckless murder that we gave earlier), but instead ignores it. In the second case the doctor should know there is some danger, but he is inadvertent. Although it is conceivable if improbable that his inadvertence would be deemed unreasonable enough—given the trivial burden of inquiry—to make his conduct reckless in a tort sense, punishment cannot be inadvertent. Punishment implies at a minimum actual knowledge of impending harm easily preventable, so that a conscious, culpable refusal to prevent the harm can be inferred from the defendant's failure to prevent it. Such facts "as a history of accidents or a previous request for repairs that had fallen on deaf ears" are therefore important.

Id. at 652–53.

Do you agree with Judge Posner's definition of "deliberate indifference?"

5. "Deliberate indifference" is manifested in a number of different ways. The refusal of correctional or medical personnel to provide medical treatment to a prisoner or their delay in providing such treatment, for example, may be attributable to their "deliberate indifference." See, e.g., Toombs v. Bell, 798 F.2d 297 (8th Cir.1986) (prisoner, whose complaints of abdominal pain were ignored for three weeks and whose gallbladder ultimately had to be removed because of the delay in treatment, sufficiently alleged deliberate indifference).

A number of the lower courts have also suggested that "deliberate indifference" may become apparent through a series of incidents which, if viewed in isolation, appear to involve only negligence. See, e.g., Wellman v. Faulkner, 715 F.2d 269, 272 (7th Cir.1983); Ramos v. Lamm, 639 F.2d 559, 575 (10th Cir.1980). They have also recognized that general systemic problems in staffing, facilities, equipment, and procedures may be so egregious that the inability to render adequate medical care is evident; the failure to redress these problems, according to the courts, is then tantamount to "deliberate indifference." See, e.g., Bass v. Wallenstein, 769 F.2d 1173 (7th Cir.1985) (sick call procedures which failed to ensure prompt access to medical care; medical personnel not qualified to use cardiac life support equipment); Ramos v. Lamm, 639 F.2d 559 (10th Cir.1980) (primary physician worked at the prison only ten hours a week, instead of the forty hours considered necessary by all of the expert witnesses; inmates used as x-ray technicians, laboratory technicians, and other medical assistants; no on-site psychiatrist or psychologist, although experts agreed prison needed one full-time psychiatrist; delay of two to five weeks before receiving mental health treatment); Wellman v. Faulkner, 715 F.2d 269 (7th Cir. 1983) (two of three doctors at the prison could barely speak English; no onsite psychiatrist; failure to stock necessary medical supplies, such as colostomy bags); and Williams v. Edwards, 547 F.2d 1206 (5th Cir.1977) (about half of the inmate-nurses had a fifth grade education or less; pharmacist had neither a pharmacological license or schooling; "filthy" emergency equipment; live fish kept in the whirlpool bath in the physical therapy department).

6. The courts thus far have held that as long as the medical care afforded a prisoner is "adequate," which does not mean "perfect, the best obtainable, or even very good," Brown v. Beck, 481 F.Supp. 723, 726 (S.D. Ga.1980), the prisoner generally has no right to be treated by a private physician. See, e.g., Hawley v. Evans, 716 F.Supp. 601, 603–04 (N.D.Ga.

1989); Gahagan v. Pennsylvania Board of Probation and Parole, 444 F.Supp. 1326, 1330 (E.D.Pa.1978). This is true even when the inmate is willing and able to pay the costs of obtaining private medical assistance.

7. The claims of pretrial detainees that they have been unconstitutionally deprived of needed medical treatment have been analyzed under the due process clauses of the fifth and fourteenth amendments rather than under the eighth amendment. The courts have agreed that due process affords pretrial detainees with at least the protection afforded convicted prisoners under the cruel and unusual punishment clause; in other words correctional officials cannot be "deliberately indifferent" to the "serious medical needs" of pretrial detainees. See, e.g., City of Revere v. Massachusetts General Hospital, 463 U.S. 239, 244, 103 S.Ct. 2979, 2983 (1983). One question which remains is whether the constitutional standard which must be met when providing pretrial detainees with medical care exceeds the eighth amendment standard. Compare Cupit v. Jones, 835 F.2d 82, 85 (5th Cir.1987) (pretrial detainees are entitled to "reasonable medical care unless the failure to supply it is reasonably related to a legitimate governmental objective") with Boring v. Kozakiewicz, 833 F.2d 468, 472 (3d Cir.1987) (standards for pretrial detainees are the same as those for convicted inmates).

8. While *Estelle v. Gamble* dealt with the question of the right of inmates to medical treatment, the Supreme Court in Washington v. Harper, 110 S.Ct. 1028 (1990) discussed the opposite question—when do inmates have the right to refuse medical treatment? The plaintiff in *Harper* was a mentally ill prisoner who was forced, over his objection, to take antipsychotic medication which he claimed had caused serious adverse side effects. The prison policy under which the plaintiff was involuntarily medicated permitted such compulsory administration of antipsychotic drugs when an inmate "suffers from a mental disorder and as a result of that disorder constitutes a likelihood of serious harm to himself or others and/or is gravely disabled."

The substantive due process issue before the Court concerned the circumstances under which the involuntary administration of antipsychotic drugs to an inmate is constitutional. Portions of the Court's opinion, written by Justice Kennedy, addressing this issue follow:

Respondent contends that the State, under the mandate of the Due Process Clause, may not override his choice to refuse antipsychotic drugs unless he has been found to be incompetent, and then only if the factfinder makes a substituted judgment that he, if competent, would consent to drug treatment. We disagree. The extent of a prisoner's right under the Clause to avoid the unwanted administration of antipsychotic drugs must be defined in the context of the inmate's confinement. The Policy under review requires the State to establish, by a medical finding, that a mental disorder exists which is likely to cause harm if not treated. Moreover, the fact that the medication must first be prescribed by a psychiatrist, and then approved by a reviewing psychiatrist, ensures that the treatment in question will be ordered only if it is in the prisoner's medical interests, given the legitimate needs of his institutional confinement.[8] These standards, which recognize both the prisoner's medical interests and the State's interests, meet the demands of the Due Process Clause.

The legitimacy, and the necessity, of considering the State's interests in prison safety and security are well established by our cases. In Turner v. Safley, 482 U.S. 78, 107 S.Ct. 2254 (1987), and O'Lone v. Estate of Shabazz, 482 U.S. 342, 107 S.Ct. 2400 (1987), we held that the proper standard for determining the validity of a prison regulation claimed to infringe on an inmate's constitutional rights is to ask whether the regulation is "reasonably related to legitimate penological interests." This is true even when the constitutional right claimed to have been infringed is fundamental, and the State under other circumstances would have been required to satisfy a more rigorous standard of review. * * *

* * *

In *Turner*, we considered various factors to determine the reasonableness of a challenged prison regulation. Three are relevant here. "First, there must be a 'valid, rational connection' between the prison regulation and the legitimate governmental interest put forward to justify it." Second, a court must consider "the impact accommodation of the asserted constitutional right will have on guards and other inmates, and on the allocation of prison resources generally." Third, "the absence of ready alternatives is evidence of the reasonableness of a prison regulation," but this does not mean that prison officials "have to set up and then shoot down every conceivable alternative method of accommodating the claimant's constitutional complaint."

Applying these factors to the regulation before us, we conclude that the Policy comports with constitutional requirements. There can be little doubt as to both the legitimacy and the importance of the governmental interest presented here. There are few cases in which the State's interest in combating the danger posed by a person to both himself and others is greater than in a prison environment, which, "by definition," is made up of persons with "a demonstrated proclivity for antisocial criminal, and often violent, conduct." We confront here the State's obligations, not just its interests. The State has undertaken the obligation to provide prisoners with medical treatment consistent not only with their own medical interests, but also with the needs of the institution. Prison administrators have not only an interest in ensuring the safety of prison staffs and administrative personnel, but the duty to take reasonable measures for the prisoners' own safety. These concerns have added weight when a penal institution, like the Special Offender Center, is restricted to inmates with mental illnesses. Where an inmate's mental disability is the root cause of the threat he poses to the inmate population, the State's interest in decreasing the danger to

8. * * * Unlike the dissent, we will not assume that physicians will prescribe these drugs for reasons unrelated to the medical needs of the patients; indeed, the ethics of the medical profession are to the contrary. See Hippocratic Oath; American Psychiatric Association, Principles of Medical Ethics With Annotations Especially Applicable to Psychiatry, in Codes of Professional Responsibility 129–135 (R. Gorlin ed. 1986). * * *

others necessarily encompasses an interest in providing him with medical treatment for his illness.

Special Offender Center Policy 600.30 is a rational means of furthering the State's legitimate objectives. Its exclusive application is to inmates who are mentally ill and who, as a result of their illness, are gravely disabled or represent a significant danger to themselves or others. The drugs may be administered for no purpose other than treatment, and only under the direction of a licensed psychiatrist. There is considerable debate over the potential side effects of antipsychotic medications, but there is little dispute in the psychiatric profession that proper use of the drugs is one of the most effective means of treating and controlling a mental illness likely to cause violent behavior.

The alternative means proffered by respondent for accommodating his interest in rejecting the forced administration of antipsychotic drugs do not demonstrate the invalidity of the State's policy. Respondent's main contention is that, as a precondition to antipsychotic drug treatment, the State must find him incompetent, and then obtain court approval of the treatment using a "substituted judgment" standard. The suggested rule takes no account of the legitimate governmental interest in treating him where medically appropriate for the purpose of reducing the danger he poses. A rule that is in no way responsive to the State's legitimate interests is not a proper accommodation, and can be rejected out of hand. Nor are physical restraints or seclusion "alternative[s] that fully accommodat[e] the prisoner's rights at *de minimis* cost to valid penological interests." Physical restraints are effective only in the short term, and can have serious physical side effects when used on a resisting inmate, as well as leaving the staff at risk of injury while putting the restraints on or tending to the inmate who is in them. Furthermore, respondent has failed to demonstrate that physical restraints or seclusion are acceptable substitutes for antipsychotic drugs, in terms of either their medical effectiveness or their toll on limited prison resources.

We hold that, given the requirements of the prison environment, the Due Process Clause permits the State to treat a prison inmate who has a serious mental illness with antipsychotic drugs against his will, if the inmate is dangerous to himself or others and the treatment is in the inmate's medical interest. Policy 600.30 comports with these requirements; we therefore reject respondent's contention that its substantive standards are deficient under the Constitution.

110 S.Ct. at 1037–40.

Justice Stevens, joined by Justices Brennan and Marshall, dissented from the Court's resolution of the substantive due process issue in *Harper*. Excerpts from the dissenting opinion are set forth below:

The Court acknowledges that under the Fourteenth Amendment "respondent possesses a significant liberty interest in avoiding the unwanted administration of antipsychotic drugs," but then virtually ignores the several dimensions of that liberty. They are both physical and intellectual. Every violation of a person's bodily integrity is an invasion of his or her liberty. The invasion is particularly intrusive if it creates a substantial risk of permanent injury and premature death. Moreover, any such action is degrading if it overrides a competent person's choice to reject a specific form of medical treatment. And when the purpose or effect of forced drugging is to alter the will and the mind of the subject, it constitutes a deprivation of liberty in the most literal and fundamental sense.

* * *

The record of one of Walter Harper's involuntary medication hearings at the Special Offense Center (SOC) notes: "Inmate Harper stated he would rather die th[a]n take medication."[4] That Harper would be so opposed to taking psychotropic drugs is not surprising: as the Court acknowledges, these drugs both "alter the chemical balance in a patient's brain" and can cause irreversible and fatal side effects. The prolixin injections that Harper was receiving at the time of his statement exemplify the intrusiveness of psychotropic drugs on a person's body and mind. Prolixin acts "at all levels of the central nervous system as well as on multiple organ systems." It can induce catatonic-like states, alter electroencephalographic tracings, and cause swelling of the brain. Adverse reactions include drowsiness, excitement, restlessness, bizarre dreams, hypertension, nausea, vomiting, loss of appetite, salivation, dry mouth, perspiration, headache, constipation, blurred vision, impotency, eczema, jaundice, tremors, and muscle spasms. As with all psychotropic drugs, prolixin may cause tardive dyskinesia, an often irreversible syndrome of uncontrollable movements that can prevent a person from exercising basic functions such as driving an automobile, and neuroleptic malignant syndrome, which is 30% fatal for those who suffer from it. The risk of side effects increases over time.

* * *

The Court does not suggest that psychotropic drugs, any more than transfer for medical treatment, may be forced on prisoners as a necessary condition of their incarceration or as a disciplinary measure. Rather, it holds:

"[G]iven the requirements of the prison environment, the Due Process Clause permits the State to treat a prison inmate who has a serious mental illness with antipsychotic drugs against his will, if the inmate is dangerous to himself or others *and the treatment is in the inmate's medical interest.* * * *

* * * Whether or not the State's alleged interest in providing medically beneficial treatment to those in its custody who are mentally ill may alone override the refusal of psychotropic drugs by a presumptively competent person, a plain reading of Policy 600.30 reveals that it does not meet the substantive standard set forth by the Court. Even on the Court's terms, the Policy is constitutionally insufficient.

* * *

4. Record, Book 8, Jan. 5, 1984, Hearing (Harper testified: "Well all you want to do is medicate me and you've been medicating me . . . . Haldol paral[y]zed my right side of my body. . . . you are burning me out of my life . . . you are burning me out of my freedom").

Although any application of Policy 600.30 requires a medical judgment as to a prisoner's mental condition and the cause of his behavior, the Policy does not require a determination that forced medication would advance his medical interest. Use of psychotropic drugs, the State readily admits, serves to ease the institutional and administrative burdens of maintaining prison security and provides a means of managing an unruly prison population and preventing property damage. By focusing on the risk that the inmate's mental condition poses to other people and property, the Policy allows the State to exercise either *parens patriae* authority or police authority to override a prisoner's liberty interest in refusing psychotropic drugs. Thus, most unfortunately, there is simply no basis for the Court's assertion that medication under the Policy must be to advance the prisoner's medical interest.

Policy 600.30 sweepingly sacrifices the inmate's substantive liberty interest to refuse psychotropic drugs, regardless of his medical interests, to institutional and administrative concerns. The State clearly has a legitimate interest in prison security and administrative convenience that encompasses responding to potential risks to persons and property. However, to the extent that the Court recognizes "both the prisoner's medical interests and the State's interests" as potentially *independent* justifications for involuntary medication of inmates, it seriously misapplies the standard announced in Turner v. Safley, 482 U.S. 78, 107 S.Ct. 2254 (1987). * * *

* * *

In *Turner* we concluded on the record before us that the marriage "regulation, as written, [was] not reasonably related to . . . penological interests," and that there were "obvious, easy alternatives" that the State failed to rebut by reference to the record. Today the Court concludes that alternatives to psychotropic drugs would impose more than *de minimis* costs on the State. However, the record before us does not establish that a more narrowly drawn policy withdrawing psychotropics from only those inmates who actually refuse consent [15] and who do not pose an imminent threat of serious harm [16] would increase the marginal costs of SOC administration. Harper's own

15. There is no evidence that more than a small fraction of inmates would refuse drugs under a voluntary policy. Harper himself voluntarily took psychotropics for six years, and intermittantly consented to them after 1982. See e.g., Rogers v. Okin, 478 F.Supp. 1342, 1369 (Mass.1979) (only 12 of 1,000 institutionalized patients refused psychotropic drugs for prolonged periods during the two years that judicial restraining order was in effect. The efficacy of forced drugging is also marginal; involuntary patients have a poorer prognosis than cooperative patients. See Rogers & Webster, Assessing Treatability in Mentally Disordered Offenders, 13 Law and Human Behavior 19, 20–21 (1989).

16. As the Court notes, properly used, these drugs are "one of the most effective means of treating and controlling" certain incurable mental illnesses, but they are not a panacea for long-term care of all patients.

"[T]he maintenance treatment literature . . . shows that many patients (approximately 30%) relapse despite receiving neuroleptic medication, while neuroleptics can be withdrawn from other patients for many months and in some cases for years without relapse. Standard maintenance medication treatment strategies, though they are indisputably effective in group comparisons, may be quite inefficient in addressing the treatment requirements of the individual pa-

record reveals that administrative segregation and standard disciplinary sanctions were frequently imposed on him over and above forced medication and thus would add no new costs. Similarly, intramuscular injections of psychotropics, such as those frequently forced on Harper, entail no greater risk than administration of less dangerous drugs such as tranquilizers. Use of psychotropic drugs simply to suppress an inmate's potential violence, rather than to achieve therapeutic results, may also undermine the efficacy of other available treatment programs that would better address his illness.

The Court's careful differentiation in *Turner* between the State's articulated goals of security and rehabilitation should be emulated in this case. The flaw in Washington's Policy 600.30—and the basic error in the Court's opinion today—is the failure to divorce from each other the two justifications for forced medication and to consider the extent to which the Policy is reasonably related to either interest. The State, and arguably the Court, allows the SOC to blend the state interests in responding to emergencies and in convenient prison administration with the individual's interest in receiving beneficial medical treatment. The result is a muddled rationale that allows the "exaggerated response" of forced psychotropic medication on the basis of purely institutional concerns. So serving institutional convenience eviscerates the inmate's substantive liberty interest in the integrity of his body and mind.

110 S.Ct. at 1046, 1048, 1050–51 (Stevens, J., concurring and dissenting).

The Supreme Court in *Harper* also addressed some procedural due process issues, one of which was whether a judge must approve a recommendation to administer antipsychotic drugs to an inmate before the inmate is involuntarily medicated with such drugs. The Court's resolution of these procedural due process issues is discussed on pages 402–405, supra.

2. AIDS AND HIV INFECTION

In recent years, prison administrators, already confronted with the difficult task of operating prisons, have had to contend with a new set of problems arising from having inmates who are infected with the HIV, the virus that causes AIDS. Set forth below are some excerpts from an article providing some basic information about what was

tient." Lieberman et al., Reply to Ethics of Drug Discontinuation Studies in Schizophrenia, 46 Archives of General Psychiatry 387, 387 (1989).

Indeed, the drugs appear to have produced at most minor "savings" in Harper's case. Dr. Petrich reported that "medications are not satisfactory in containing the worst excesses of his labile and irritable behavior. He is uncooperative when on medication," and a therapy supervisor reported before Harper's involuntary medication began: "during the time in which he assaulted the nurse at Cabrini he was on neuroleptic medication yet there is indication that he was psychotic. However, during his stay at SOC he has been off of all neuroleptic medications and at times has shown some preoccupation and appearance of psychosis but has not become assaultive. His problems on medication, such as the paradoxical effect from the neuroleptic medications, may be precipitated by increased doses of neuroleptic medications and may cause an exacerbation of his psychosis. Though Mr. Harper is focused on psychosomatic problems from neuroleptic medications as per the side effects, the real problem may be that the psychosis is exacerbated by neuroleptic medications."

known about AIDS and the HIV at the time this book was published. Consider this information as you then contemplate the appropriate response to the HIV and AIDS in the prison context.

LYNN S. BRANHAM, OUT OF SIGHT, OUT OF DANGER?: PROCEDURAL DUE PROCESS AND THE SEGREGATION OF HIV–POSITIVE INMATES

17 Hastings Constitutional Law Quarterly 293, 293–98, 332, 340–42 (1990). Reprinted with the permission of the Hastings Constitutional Law Quarterly.

Are they not excluded from public assemblies and feastdays like murderers, parricides, fated to be perpetual exiles, and even more unhappy than these! For murderers are at least permitted to live with other men; these are driven away like enemies. They are denied the same roof, the same table, the same utensils with others. Moreover they are barred from the cleansing waters for public usage, and there is fear that even the rivers may be infected with their malady. If a dog should lap water with a wounded tongue, we should not consider the water to have been contaminated by the brute; but let one of these afflicted ones approach it and we believe the water is rendered impure by this human being.[1]

Although the scourge of leprosy has disappeared from most parts of the world, what many view as the modern equivalent of leprosy, AIDS, continues to rampage from person to person, city to city, and country to country. AIDS was not even identified in this country until 1981,[2] but by August of 1989, according to government figures, it had claimed the lives of at least 61,655 Americans.[3]

The statistics on AIDS fatalities in the United States, however, actually mask the enormous dimensions of the health threats posed by AIDS. Public health officials have estimated that up to one and one-half million Americans may be infected with human immunodeficiency virus (HIV), the virus that causes AIDS.[4] Although officials are unsure how many of these seropositive individuals will develop AIDS, present estimates range from sixty-five to one hundred percent. In addition, even if some seropositive individuals do not become ill themselves, they may continue to spread the virus if they do not refrain from what is referred to as "the exchange of bodily fluids" with others.

* * *

1. S. Brody, The Disease of the Soul: Leprosy in Medieval Literature 80 (1974) (quoting St. Gregory of Nysse) (description of lepers in the Middle Ages).

2. U.S. Dep't of Health and Human Services, Surgeon General's Report on Acquired Immune Deficiency Syndrome 5 (1986) [hereinafter Surgeon General's Rep.].

3. Centers for Disease Control, Public Health Service, U.S. Dep't of Health and Human Services, HIV/AIDS Surveillance Report 12 (Sept. 1989).

4. Centers for Disease Control, Public Health Service, U.S. Dep't of Health and Human Services, *Human Immunodeficiency Virus Infection in the United States: A Review of Current Knowledge,* 36 Morbidity and Mortality Weekly Rep. 14–15 (1987). At least five million people worldwide may already be infected with HIV. 3 AIDS Pol'y & Law (Buraff Pubs.) No. 11, at 3 (1988).

AIDS is caused by a virus known as human immunodeficiency virus (HIV). This virus weakens the body's immune system, the system through which the body combats disease. As a result, people with AIDS are susceptible to and contract diseases that they would not normally contract and from which they eventually die.

Fortunately, the modes of transmission of HIV are limited. Documented cases of transmission have been confined to instances in which an infected person exchanged blood, semen, or vaginal secretions with an uninfected person. Medical authorities also suspect that HIV may be transmitted through breast milk.

Although only certain bodily fluids have been implicated in the spread of HIV, the virus has been found in other bodily fluids, including saliva, tears, and urine. Still, public health officials and the vast majority of doctors emphatically insist that HIV is not transmitted through the types of nonsexual, casual contacts that occur between people in their daily lives.[18] These views are grounded on the results of a number of studies of persons living with individuals who have AIDS. None of these studies revealed any uninfected person becoming infected because of having had casual contacts with an infected person. The absence of any evidence of the AIDS virus being transmitted through casual contact is believed by medical authorities to be particularly significant since many of the uninfected participants in the studies shared eating utensils, toilets, and even toothbrushes with infected household members.

A person may become infected with HIV by engaging in certain high-risk behaviors. Sexual activity involving the exchange of semen, blood, or vaginal secretions with an infected partner is one form of high-risk behavior that may lead to the transmission of the virus. The sharing of needles by intravenous drug abusers is also a common mode of transmission, since infected blood may remain in an unsterilized needle, permitting the virus to be transmitted to an uninfected drug abuser who subsequently uses the needle to inject himself or herself with drugs. The virus is also transmitted through transfusions of infected blood or blood products, and perinatally from a mother to a fetus.

Infected persons can spread the virus even though they may not have any symptoms. For this reason, the control of the spread of AIDS has proven particularly difficult. Many asymptomatic HIV carriers are totally unaware that they are spreading the virus; the Centers for Disease Control (CDC), the federal agency responsible for disease control, estimated in August of 1987 that most of the one to one-and-a-half

18. *See, e.g.,* Centers for Disease Control, Public Health Service, U.S. Dep't of Health and Human Services, *Public Health Service Guidelines for Counseling and Antibody Testing to Prevent HIV Infection and AIDS,* 36 Morbidity and Mortality Weekly Rep. 514 (1987) [hereinafter *CDC HIV–Antibody Testing Guidelines*]; Am. Hospital Ass'n, AIDS/HIV Infection Policy: Ensuring a Safe Hospital Environment 4 (1987) [hereinafter Hospital Environment Rep.]; Surgeon General's Rep., *supra* note 2, at 13.

million Americans infected with HIV were unaware of their HIV positivity and might unwittingly be transmitting the virus to others. Even when HIV carriers are aware of their positive status, some persist in engaging in activities that pose a high risk of transmitting the virus.[27] Their potential victims, duped by the healthy appearance of their sexual or needle-sharing partners, often fail to take the necessary steps to protect themselves. As a result, more people become infected with the virus, more people develop AIDS, and more people die.

At present, tests developed to determine HIV status do not detect the presence of the virus itself in a person. The tests instead are antibody tests, ones that detect whether a person's body has produced certain antibodies in an attempt to thwart the infiltrating HIV.[29] Experts presume that persons who test positive for HIV antibodies are infected with the virus and capable of transmitting it.

One problem with antibody tests is that there is a lapse of time between infection with the AIDS virus and the body's discernible production of HIV antibodies. Although most people produce antibodies within six to twelve weeks after contracting the virus, experts have reported much longer time lapses, ranging up to fourteen months between the date of infection and the time when seropositivity becomes evident.[32] A person may therefore be an HIV carrier and capable of spreading the virus, but test negative on an antibody test.

In addition to the possibility of false-negative test results, some persons who are not infected with the virus have tested positive for HIV antibodies. Under "optimal laboratory conditions," repeat antibody testing, which is recommended by the CDC if a person tests positive on an initial antibody test, can be at least 99% accurate in identifying persons who are actually seropositive.[33] But in practice, the percentage of persons falsely identified as seropositive is quite high.

Not only is there a lapse of time between infection with HIV and when a person tests positive for antibodies, but there is also a lapse of time between the infection and the development of AIDS. The CDC estimates that an average of over seven years will elapse between the time of HIV infection and the advent of AIDS.[35] All persons who are HIV carriers, however, may not necessarily develop AIDS. Although

---

27. *See* R. Shilts, And the Band Played On, 198 *passim* (1987) (recounting the sexual behavior of one seropositive man who, immediately after having sex one time with another man, showed his partner some purple lesions on his chest and announced, "Gay cancer. Maybe you'll get it too."); *see also* 3 AIDS Pol'y & Law (Buraff Pubs.) No. 15, at 2 (1988) (reporting court martial of a soldier who was seropositive, had unprotected sex with three other soldiers, and did not tell any of them about his HIV status).

29. Tests for the virus itself are, however, in the process of being developed.

32. *Quality AIDS Testing: Hearings before the Subcomm. on Regulation and Business Opportunities of the House Comm. on Small Business*, 100th Cong., 1st Sess. 4 (1987) (statement of Dr. Lawrence Miike) [hereinafter *Hearing on AIDS Testing*].

33. *CDC HIV–Antibody Testing Guidelines*, *supra* note 18, at 510.

35. Centers for Disease Control, Public Health Service, U.S. Dep't of Health and Human Services, *Human Immunodeficiency Virus Infection in the United States*, 36 Morbidity and Mortality Weekly Rep. 801 (1987). Researchers at the San Francisco Department of Public Health

the CDC presently estimates that at least 99% of the persons who are HIV–positive will develop AIDS, these estimates may prove to be high.

Some HIV-positive persons who do not have AIDS are still not healthy. Some develop AIDS–Related Complex (ARC), suffering such symptoms as fever, weight loss, diarrhea, and swollen lymph nodes. Many, but possibly not all persons with ARC eventually develop AIDS. With AIDS comes the potpourri of "opportunistic diseases," such as Kaposi's sarcoma, a form of skin cancer, and *pneumocystis carinii* pneumonia, from which persons with AIDS may eventually succumb.[39]

* * *

Although a few health-care workers have apparently contracted the AIDS virus through exposure of their broken skin or mucous membranes to HIV-infected blood, the risk that they will become infected from their patients is considered quite low. In studies conducted by the CDC, the National Institute of Health, and the University of California, of 435 health-care workers who had open wounds or mucous membranes exposed to HIV–infected blood, none became infected.[226] Even when health-care workers had been exposed to HIV–infected blood through needlestick or other puncture wounds, which would heighten their risk of contracting the virus, only a small number later tested positive. Of the 812 health-care workers in the CDC, NIH, and California studies who were exposed to HIV through needlestick or other puncture wounds, only four seroconverted.

* * *

Two types of errors can occur in the interpretation of HIV-antibody test results. First, the laboratory personnel might fail to identify as seropositive someone who is actually a carrier of the AIDS virus. The resulting error is known as a false negative, a positive blood sample mistakenly reported to be negative for HIV antibodies. The other type of error occurs when the laboratory personnel report that a person is HIV-positive when in fact the person is not. This type of error is known as a false positive, the incorrect description of a person as HIV-positive.

The more sensitive an HIV-antibody test is, the fewer false negatives there will be. In other words, the sensitivity rate measures the ability of a test to accurately identify who is HIV-negative. The specificity rate, on the other hand, refers to the extent to which persons identified as seropositive are in fact seropositive. The higher the

have estimated that the incubation period between the time of HIV infection and the onset of AIDS may range anywhere from one to thirty-five years. 3 AIDS Pol'y & Law (Buraff Pubs.) No. 11, at 5 (1988).

39. Surgeon General's Rep., *supra* note 2, at 10. AIDS is presently considered a fatal disease. Of the persons diagnosed with AIDS in 1981, at least 90% have died. The fatality rate for those diagnosed with AIDS in 1984 is 80 percent.

226. Nat'l Inst. of Justice, U.S. Dep't of Justice, Risk of Infection With the AIDS Virus Through Exposures to Blood 2 (1987) [hereinafter Risk of Infection]; *see also* 4 AIDS Pol'y & Law (Buraff Pubs.) No. 12, at 6–7 (1989) (reporting findings of Centers for Disease Control's Cooperative Needlestick Surveillance Group that of 1,449 health-care workers exposed to HIV-infected blood, none of those with mucous membrane exposures became seropositive).

specificity rate of the antibody tests, the fewer the number of uninfected persons incorrectly identified as HIV-positive.

HIV antibody tests can in theory be quite reliable. When performed under "optimal laboratory conditions," the ELISA test is at least 99% accurate in terms of both its sensitivity and its specificity. Under ideal circumstances, the accuracy of the Western blot test is also quite high, with sensitivity and specificity rates both exceeding 99%.

In practice, however, the accuracy rates of the tests are often lower.[282] Whether there is a problem with false positives or false negatives will depend in large part on the prevalence of HIV in the population being tested. With high-risk populations, persons who are actually HIV carriers will be more likely to be misidentified as HIV-negative. It has been estimated that when high-risk populations are tested for HIV, at least one out of ten people tested may be falsely described as HIV–negative.

With low-risk populations, the recurrent problem is with false positives. It has been estimated that even if every effort is made to ensure that an HIV-antibody test is performed and interpreted accurately, for every fifteen persons in a low-risk population identified as seropositive, five will be misidentified. In other words, five people will actually not be infected with HIV.

The rate of error in HIV testing has been aggravated by the deficient performance of testing laboratories. This deficient performance was highlighted by a string of witnesses who testified before a congressional subcommittee in October of 1987. One of these witnesses, Colonel Donald S. Burke, the Director of the Army's HIV screening program, described the performance of a large number of the laboratories conducting HIV-antibody tests as "grossly unacceptable" and "disconcertingly substandard." He stated that ten out of nineteen laboratories that had submitted bids to do antibody testing for the Army had at some point failed to meet the government's proficiency standards. What was truly alarming was that these proficiency standards were relatively lax since they permitted one misidentified sample for every twenty tested.

Another witness disclosed that seven of eleven laboratories analyzed a blood sample from a person diagnosed as having AIDS and failed to correctly interpret the test results as positive. Other witnesses testified about how the inept performance of laboratories exacerbates the problem with false positives when a low-risk population is tested. According to Dr. Lawrence Miike, an AIDS laboratory testing analyst from the Office of Technology Assessment, the actual performance of HIV-antibody tests by laboratories has yielded a false positive rate of about 90% when low-risk populations are tested.

* * *

282. *Hearing on AIDS Testing, supra* note 32, at 6, 7, 11.

Questions and Points for Discussion

1. In light of what is presently known about AIDS and HIV infection, how would you resolve the following questions?

a. Is the mandatory HIV-antibody testing of all inmates in a correctional facility constitutional? For conflicting views on this question, see Branham, Opening the Bloodgates: The Blood Testing of Prisoners for the AIDS Virus, 20 Conn.L.Rev. 763 (1988) and Hanssens and Jacobi, Blood Testing of Prisoners for the AIDS Virus: A Brief Reply, id. at 813. See also Dunn v. White, 880 F.2d 1188 (10th Cir. 1989).

b. Do inmates who wish to be tested for evidence of HIV infection have the right to such tests? In answering this question, consider the relevance of recent studies revealing that the administration of the drug AZT to asymptomatic HIV-positive persons can delay the onset of AIDS or ARC by at least a year. [1989] Aids Policy & Law Vol. 4, No. 16, at 1.

c. As a policy matter, when should HIV-antibody tests be administered to inmates?

d. When, if ever, is the segregation of HIV-positive inmates constitutional? When is it advisable?

e. Does the Constitution require the segregation of HIV-positive inmates? See Glick v. Henderson, 855 F.2d 536 (8th Cir.1988); Jarrett v. Faulkner, 662 F.Supp. 928 (S.D.Ind.1987).

f. What procedural safeguards, if any, would have to attend the segregation of inmates solely because they were believed to be seropositive? See Branham, Out of Sight, Out of Danger?: Procedural Due Process and the Segregation of HIV–Positive Inmates, 17 Hastings Constitutional Law Quarterly 293 (1990).

g. Who can be informed of an inmate's HIV status? See Woods v. White, 689 F.Supp. 874 (W.D.Wis.1988), affirmed 899 F.2d 17 (7th Cir. 1990). Who should be so informed? See American Bar Association Policy on AIDS and the Criminal Justice System 2 (1989).

h. To what extent, if at all, should inmates' HIV status affect decisions concerning their release on parole or on furlough and other forms of community release? Id. at 2–3.

i. Can and should inmates be required to disclose their HIV status to spouses or lovers as a condition of their release on parole, on a furlough, or into some other community release program? Id. at 3.

B. USE OF FORCE AND THE PROTECTION OF INMATES

JACKSON v. BISHOP

Court of Appeals, Eighth Circuit, 1968.
404 F.2d 571.

BLACKMUN, CIRCUIT JUDGE.

The three plaintiffs-appellants, inmates of the Arkansas penitentiary, in separate actions call upon us to direct the entry of an injunction barring the use of the strap as a disciplinary measure in Arkansas' penal institutions. The claim is that the district court

> erred in refusing to hold that corporal punishment of prisoners is cruel and unusual punishment within the meaning of the Eighth Amendment to the United States Constitution, and in holding that the whipping of prisoners was not unconstitutional per se.

* * *

The facts, at this stage of the litigation, are in no real dispute. * * * We regard the following history and facts as particularly pertinent for our review:

1. The Arkansas penal institutions are under the general supervision of a five-man "honorary" commission known as the State Penitentiary Board. Actual day-to-day supervision is delegated by the Board to a full-time compensated superintendent. * * *

* * *

3. The Board has the duty to publish and appropriately post all rules and regulations it promulgates with respect to prisoner conduct. The Superintendent has "general supervision and control of" and is "solely responsible for, the discipline, management, and control" of all inmates.

* * *

6. The Board, by statute, § 46–158, has the duty to prescribe the mode and extent of punishments for violation of prison rules. One who inflicts, or causes to be inflicted, punishment more severe than is prescribed by the Board is guilty of a felony. Section 46–158, however, does not itself specify the type of punishment which may be imposed.

7. Corporal punishment in the Arkansas system was authorized formally only in 1962 but evidently it had been employed for many years. At that time the Board, by resolution, authorized such punishment whenever, in the Superintendent's judgment, its infliction was necessary in order to maintain discipline. The resolution did not prescribe form or limit of punishment.

8. In [*Talley v. Stephens*, 247 F.Supp. 683 (E.D.Ark.1965)], the three petitioning inmates sought injunctive relief with respect to certain prison practices including the infliction of corporal punishment. * * * Chief Judge Henley found that, at that time, there were no

written rules as to whipping; that such punishment was administered in the sole discretion of the one inflicting it, subject to an informal requirement that the blows not exceed ten for a single offense; and that two of those three petitioners had been whipped and one beaten by a field-line supervisor-trusty. The judge noted that the Supreme Court of Arkansas, over 80 years ago, deplored the whipping of convicts, and that the Arkansas statutes do not themselves specifically prescribe whipping even as a punishment for crime. He observed, however, that corporal punishment had not been viewed historically as a constitutionally forbidden cruel and unusual punishment. The court concluded that it was not prepared to say that such punishment was unconstitutional per se. Nevertheless, Judge Henley said, this conclusion presupposes that the infliction of such punishment is surrounded by appropriate safeguards, that is, it must not be excessive, it must be inflicted dispassionately and by responsible people, and it must be applied under recognizable standards so that the convict knows what conduct will cause him to be whipped and how much punishment his conduct will produce. The court found that those safeguards did not exist in the Arkansas system and enjoined further corporal punishment of the petitioners until they were established.

9. The *Talley* opinion was filed on November 15, 1965. As a result, the Board issued written rules and regulations on January 10, 1966. These were in effect until the district court decision in the present case was rendered June 3, 1967. In addition to a number of other provisions, the rules state that certain "major offenses will warrant corporal punishment." The ones listed are homosexuality, agitation, insubordination, making or concealing weapons, refusal to work when medically certified able to work, and participating in or inciting a riot. They further state:

> No inmate shall ever be authorized to inflict any corporal punishment under color of prison authority on another inmate.

> Punishment shall not, in any case, exceed Ten lashes with the strap, the number of lashes to be administered shall be determined by a Board of inquiry, consisting of at least two officials of the Arkansas State Penitentiary, The Superintendent or Assistant Superintendent, and the head Warden or an associate Warden. The Board of Inquiry will request that the accused inmate appear before the Board and speak in his own behalf. No Punishment will be administered in the field.

10. The straps used in Arkansas vary somewhat but all are similar. Each is of leather and from 3½ to 5½ feet in length, about 4 inches wide, and ¼ inch thick. Each has a wooden handle 8 to 12 inches long.

11. Since *Talley*, whippings are administered by wardens. The prisoner lies face down and the blows are to his buttocks. Supposedly, they are administered while the prisoner is fully clothed. Petitioners Ernst and Mask, however, testified without contradiction that they

were required to lower their trousers and that they received lashes on the bare buttocks. There is corroborating and other evidence to the same effect with respect to other inmates and there was proof, some offered through the State Police, of deep bruises and bleeding.

12. Whipping is the primary disciplinary measure used in the Arkansas system. Prisoners there have few privileges which can be withheld from them as punishment. Facilities for segregation and solitary confinement are limited.

13. There is testimony that the strap hurts the inmate's pride, that it has been needed in order to preserve discipline, and that the work level improves after its administration. Contrarily, there is testimony that the whipping generates hate in the inmate who is whipped and that this hate flows toward the whipper, the institution and the system.

14. * * * The testimony of James V. Bennett, former Director of the Federal Bureau of Prisons, and that of Fred T. Wilkinson, Director of the Department of Corrections of the State of Missouri (and former Deputy Director of the Federal Bureau of Prisons) are summarized in the district court's opinion. This testimony is to the effect that, among other things, corporal punishment has not been used for disciplinary purposes in federal prisons for years and that only Mississippi, in addition to Arkansas, uses it officially. Testifying as a penologist, it was Mr. Bennett's opinion that the whippings administered to the three plaintiffs were "cruel, degrading and certainly they were unusual in this day and age." Mr. Wilkinson testified that use of the strap "is cruel and unusual and unnecessary."

15. On July 20, 1966, six months after the issuance of the January 1966 regulations, plaintiff Ernst received two whippings of ten lashes each to the bare buttocks within a period of 45 minutes.

* * *

17. The district judges concluded that the post-*Talley* rules and regulations of January 1966 still did not provide adequate safeguards. The use of the strap was therefore enjoined until further safeguards were provided. * * *.[5]

* * *

5. At oral argument we were advised that since the entry of the district court's decree other new rules and regulations have been adopted. * * * Before punishment is imposed, a full hearing before a Board of Inquiry is required. The accusing warden may not sit on the Board of Inquiry or take part in carrying out the punishment. Punishment may include solitary confinement, reduction of rations, corporal punishment, loss of mail, recreation and other privileges, loss of future good time, and recording the offense for parole purposes. Corporal punishment shall not exceed ten lashes with the strap and a period in solitary confinement. In no case may the strap be applied to the bare buttocks. An accuser or other inmate shall not administer the strap. The strap shall not be used in the fields. No inmate shall be whipped within 24 hours of any preceding whipping. Each inmate sentenced to corporal punishment has the right of appeal to the superintendent or the assistant superintendent and this official or his designee may change the sentence. * * *

* * *

Imposed by inmates holding

* * * [W]e have no difficulty in reaching the conclusion that the use of the strap in the penitentiaries of Arkansas is punishment which, in this last third of the 20th century, runs afoul of the Eighth Amendment; that the strap's use, irrespective of any precautionary conditions which may be imposed, offends contemporary concepts of decency and human dignity and precepts of civilization which we profess to possess * * *.

Our reasons for this conclusion include the following: (1) We are not convinced that any rule or regulation as to the use of the strap, however seriously or sincerely conceived and drawn, will successfully prevent abuse. The present record discloses misinterpretation and obvious overnarrow interpretation even of the newly adopted January 1966 rules. (2) Rules in this area seem often to go unobserved. Despite the January 1966 requirement that no inmate was to inflict punishment on another, the record is replete with instances where this very thing took place. (3) Regulations are easily circumvented. Although it was a long-standing requirement that a whipping was to be administered only when the prisoner was fully clothed, this record discloses instances of whippings upon the bare buttocks, and with consequent injury. (4) Corporal punishment is easily subject to abuse in the hands of the sadistic and the unscrupulous. (5) Where power to punish is granted to persons in lower levels of administrative authority, there is an inherent and natural difficulty in enforcing the limitations of that power. (6) There can be no argument that excessive whipping or an inappropriate manner of whipping or too great frequency of whipping or the use of studded or overlong straps all constitute cruel and unusual punishment. But if whipping were to be authorized, how does one, or any court, ascertain the point which would distinguish the permissible from that which is cruel and unusual? (7) Corporal punishment generates hate toward the keepers who punish and toward the system which permits it. It is degrading to the punisher and to the punished alike. It frustrates correctional and rehabilitative goals. This record cries out with testimony to this effect from the expert penologists, from the inmates and from their keepers. (8) Whipping creates other penological problems and makes adjustment to society more difficult. (9) Public opinion is obviously adverse. Counsel concede that only two states still permit the use of the strap. Thus almost uniformly has it been abolished. It has been expressly outlawed by statute in a number of states. And 48 states, including Arkansas, have constitutional provisions against cruel or unusual punishment.

We are not convinced contrarily by any suggestion that the State needs this tool for disciplinary purposes and is too poor to provide other accepted means of prisoner regulation. Humane considerations and constitutional requirements are not, in this day, to be measured or limited by dollar considerations or by the thickness of the prisoner's clothing.

* * *

We choose to draw no significant distinction between the word "cruel" and the word "unusual" in the Eighth Amendment. We would not wish to place ourselves in the position of condoning punishment which is shown to be only "cruel" but not "unusual" or vice versa. In any event, the testimony of the two expert penologists clearly demonstrates that the use of the strap in this day is unusual and we encounter no difficulty in holding that its use is cruel.

Neither do we wish to draw, in this context, any meaningful distinction between punishment by way of sentence statutorily prescribed and punishment imposed for prison disciplinary purposes. It seems to us that the Eighth Amendment's proscription has application to both.

The district court's decree is vacated and the case is remanded with directions to enter a new decree embracing the injunctive relief heretofore granted but, in addition, restraining the Superintendent of the Arkansas State Penitentiary and all personnel of the penitentiary system from inflicting corporal punishment, including the use of the strap, as a disciplinary measure.

Questions and Points for Discussion

1. As was discussed in Chapter 6, the Supreme Court has condoned imposition of the death penalty in some circumstances. If it is not cruel and unusual punishment to sometimes kill a prisoner, why is it cruel and unusual punishment to whip the prisoner?

2. In Ingraham v. Wright, 430 U.S. 651, 97 S.Ct. 1401 (1977), the Supreme Court addressed the constitutionality of paddling students as a form of discipline. Such paddling, the Court observed, does not inflict cruel and unusual punishment, since the eighth amendment generally only protects those convicted of crimes. Nor does the paddling of students violate their due process rights unless the amount of force used under the circumstances is excessive.

If paddling children can be constitutional, why isn't it constitutional to whip or at least paddle convicted criminals?

3. If the majority of states authorized the corporal punishment of prisoners who had committed certain disciplinary infractions, would such punishment contravene the eighth amendment? Why or why not? For one view on the significance of there being a consensus amongst a majority of the states as to the propriety of a particular punishment, see Stanford v. Kentucky, 109 S.Ct. 2969 (1989), supra page 234.

* * *

WHITLEY v. ALBERS

Supreme Court of the United States, 1986.
475 U.S. 312, 106 S.Ct. 1078, 89 L.Ed.2d 251.

JUSTICE O'CONNOR delivered the opinion of the Court.

This case requires us to decide what standard governs a prison inmate's claim that prison officials subjected him to cruel and unusual punishment by shooting him during the course of their attempt to quell a prison riot.

I

At the time he was injured, respondent Gerald Albers was confined in cellblock "A" of the Oregon State Penitentiary. Cellblock "A" consists of two tiers of barred cells housing some 200 inmates. The two tiers are connected by a stairway that offers the only practical way to move from one tier to another.

At about 8:30 on the evening of June 27, 1980, several inmates were found intoxicated at the prison annex. Prison guards attempted to move the intoxicated prisoners, some of whom resisted, to the penitentiary's isolation and segregation facility. This incident could be seen from the cell windows in cellblock "A," and some of the onlookers became agitated because they thought that the guards were using unnecessary force. Acting on instructions from their superiors, Officers Kemper and Fitts, who were on duty in cellblock "A," ordered the prisoners to return to their cells. The order was not obeyed. Several inmates confronted the two officers, who were standing in the open area of the lower tier. One inmate, Richard Klenk, jumped from the second tier and assaulted Officer Kemper. Kemper escaped but Officer Fitts was taken hostage. Klenk and other inmates then began breaking furniture and milling about.

Upon being informed of the disturbance, petitioner Harol Whitley, the prison security manager, entered cellblock "A" and spoke with Klenk. Captain Whitley agreed to permit four residents of cellblock "A" to view the inmates who had been taken to segregation earlier. These emissaries reported back that the prisoners in segregation were intoxicated but unharmed. Nonetheless, the disturbance in cellblock "A" continued.

Whitley returned to the cellblock and confirmed that Fitts was not harmed. Shortly thereafter, Fitts was moved from an office on the lower tier to cell 201 on the upper tier, and Klenk demanded that media representatives be brought into the cellblock. In the course of the negotiations, Klenk, who was armed with a homemade knife, informed Whitley that one inmate had already been killed and other deaths would follow. In fact, an inmate had been beaten but not killed by other prisoners.

Captain Whitley left the cellblock to organize an assault squad. When Whitley returned to cellblock "A," he was taken to see Fitts in cell 201. Several inmates assured Whitley that they would protect Fitts from harm, but Klenk threatened to kill the hostage if an attempt was made to lead an assault. Klenk and at least some other inmates were aware that guards had assembled outside the cellblock and that shotguns had been issued. Meanwhile, respondent had left his cell on the upper tier to see if elderly prisoners housed on the lower tier could be moved out of harm's way in the event that tear gas was used.

Respondent testified that he asked Whitley for the key to the row of cells housing the elderly prisoners, and Whitley indicated that he would return with the key. Whitley denied that he spoke to respondent at any time during the disturbance.

Whitley next consulted with his superiors, petitioners Cupp, the prison Superintendent, and Kenney, the Assistant Superintendent. They agreed that forceful intervention was necessary to protect the life of the hostage and the safety of the inmates who were not rioting, and ruled out tear gas as an unworkable alternative. Cupp ordered Whitley to take a squad armed with shotguns into cellblock "A."

Whitley gave the final orders to the assault team, which was assembled in the area outside cellblock "A." Petitioner Kennicott and two other officers armed with shotguns were to follow Whitley, who was unarmed, over the barricade the inmates had constructed at the cellblock entrance. A second group of officers, without firearms, would be behind them. Whitley ordered Kennicott to fire a warning shot as he crossed the barricade. He also ordered Kennicott to shoot low at any prisoners climbing the stairs toward cell 201, since they could pose a threat to the safety of the hostage or to Whitley himself, who would be climbing the stairs in an attempt to free the hostage in cell 201.

At about 10:30 p.m., Whitley reappeared just outside the barricade. By this time, about a half hour had elapsed since the earlier breaking of furniture, and the noise level in the cellblock had noticeably diminished. Respondent, who was standing at the bottom of the stairway, asked about the key. Whitley replied "No," clambered over the barricade, yelled "shoot the bastards," and ran toward the stairs after Klenk, who had been standing in the open areaway along with a number of other inmates. Kennicott fired a warning shot into the wall opposite the cellblock entrance as he followed Whitley over the barricade. He then fired a second shot that struck a post near the stairway. Meanwhile, Whitley chased Klenk up the stairs, and shortly thereafter respondent started up the stairs. Kennicott fired a third shot that struck respondent in the left knee. Another inmate was shot on the stairs and several others on the lower tier were wounded by gunshot. The inmates in cell 201 prevented Klenk from entering, and Whitley subdued Klenk at the cell door, freeing the hostage.

As a result of the incident, respondent sustained severe damage to his left leg and mental and emotional distress. He subsequently commenced this action pursuant to 42 U.S.C. § 1983, alleging that petitioners deprived him of his rights under the Eighth and Fourteenth Amendments * * *. Many of the facts were stipulated, but both sides also presented testimony from witnesses to the disturbance and the rescue attempt, as well as from expert witnesses with backgrounds in prison discipline and security. At the conclusion of trial, the District Judge directed a verdict for petitioners. * * *

A panel of the Court of Appeals for the Ninth Circuit reversed in part and affirmed in part, with one judge dissenting. The court held that an Eighth Amendment violation would be established "if a prison official deliberately shot Albers under circumstances where the official, with due allowance for the exigency, knew or should have known that it was unnecessary," or "if the emergency plan was adopted or carried out with 'deliberate indifference' to the right of Albers to be free of cruel [and] unusual punishment." The Court of Appeals pointed to evidence that the general disturbance in cellblock "A" was subsiding and to respondent's experts' testimony that the use of deadly force was excessive under the circumstances and should have been preceded by a verbal warning, and concluded that the jury could have found an Eighth Amendment violation.

* * *

II

* * * The Cruel and Unusual Punishments Clause "was designed to protect those convicted of crimes," and consequently the Clause applies "only after the State has complied with the constitutional guarantees traditionally associated with criminal prosecutions." An express intent to inflict unnecessary pain is not required, *Estelle v. Gamble*, 429 U.S. 97, 104 (1976) ("deliberate indifference" to a prisoner's serious medical needs is cruel and unusual punishment), and harsh "conditions of confinement" may constitute cruel and unusual punishment unless such conditions "are part of the penalty that criminal offenders pay for their offenses against society."

Not every governmental action affecting the interests or well-being of a prisoner is subject to Eighth Amendment scrutiny, however. "After incarceration, only the ' "unnecessary and wanton infliction of pain" ' . . . constitutes cruel and unusual punishment forbidden by the Eighth Amendment." To be cruel and unusual punishment, conduct that does not purport to be punishment at all must involve more than ordinary lack of due care for the prisoner's interests or safety. This reading of the Clause underlies our decision in *Estelle v. Gamble*, which held that a prison physician's "negligen[ce] in diagnosing or treating a medical condition" did not suffice to make out a claim of cruel and unusual punishment. It is obduracy and wantonness, not inadvertence or error in good faith, that characterize the conduct prohibited by the Cruel and Unusual Punishments Clause, whether that conduct occurs in connection with establishing conditions of confinement, supplying medical needs, or restoring official control over a tumultuous cellblock. The infliction of pain in the course of a prison security measure, therefore, does not amount to cruel and unusual punishment simply because it may appear in retrospect that the degree of force authorized or applied for security purposes was unreasonable, and hence unnecessary in the strict sense.

The general requirement that an Eighth Amendment claimant allege and prove the unnecessary and wanton infliction of pain should also be applied with due regard for differences in the kind of conduct against which an Eighth Amendment objection is lodged. The deliberate indifference standard articulated in *Estelle* was appropriate in the context presented in that case because the State's responsibility to attend to the medical needs of prisoners does not ordinarily clash with other equally important governmental responsibilities. Consequently, "deliberate indifference to a prisoner's serious illness or injury" can typically be established or disproved without the necessity of balancing competing institutional concerns for the safety of prison staff or other inmates. But, in making and carrying out decisions involving the use of force to restore order in the face of a prison disturbance, prison officials undoubtedly must take into account the very real threats the unrest presents to inmates and prison officials alike, in addition to the possible harms to inmates against whom force might be used. As we said in *Hudson v. Palmer*, 468 U.S. 517, 526–527 (1984), prison administrators are charged with the responsibility of ensuring the safety of the prison staff, administrative personnel, and visitors, as well as the "obligation to take reasonable measures to guarantee the safety of the inmates themselves." In this setting, a deliberate indifference standard does not adequately capture the importance of such competing obligations, or convey the appropriate hesitancy to critique in hindsight decisions necessarily made in haste, under pressure, and frequently without the luxury of a second chance.

Where a prison security measure is undertaken to resolve a disturbance, such as occurred in this case, that indisputably poses significant risks to the safety of inmates and prison staff, we think the question whether the measure taken inflicted unnecessary and wanton pain and suffering ultimately turns on "whether force was applied in a good faith effort to maintain or restore discipline or maliciously and sadistically for the very purpose of causing harm." *Johnson v. Glick*, 481 F.2d 1028, 1033 (CA2) (Friendly, J.) As the District Judge correctly perceived, "such factors as the need for the application of force, the relationship between the need and the amount of force that was used, [and] the extent of injury inflicted" are relevant to that ultimate determination. From such considerations inferences may be drawn as to whether the use of force could plausibly have been thought necessary, or instead evinced such wantonness with respect to the unjustified infliction of harm as is tantamount to a knowing willingness that it occur. See *Duckworth v. Franzen*, 780 F.2d 645, 652 (CA7 1985) (equating "deliberate indifference," in an Eighth Amendment case involving security risks, with "recklessness in criminal law," which "implies an act so dangerous that the defendant's knowledge of the risk can be inferred"); cf. *Block v. Rutherford*, 468 U.S. 576, 584 (1984) (requiring pretrial detainees claiming that they were subjected to "punishment" without due process to prove intent to punish or show that the challenged conduct " 'is not reasonably related to a legitimate goal,' " from which an intent to punish may be inferred). But equally relevant are such factors as the extent of the threat to the safety of staff and inmates, as reasonably perceived by the responsible officials on the basis of the facts known to them, and any efforts made to temper the severity of a forceful response.

When the "ever-present potential for violent confrontation and conflagration," ripens into *actual* unrest and conflict, the admonition that "a prison's internal security is peculiarly a matter normally left to the discretion of prison administrators" carries special weight. "Prison administrators . . . should be accorded wide-ranging deference in the adoption and execution of policies and practices that in their judgment are needed to preserve internal order and discipline and to maintain institutional security." That deference extends to a prison security measure taken in response to an actual confrontation with riotous inmates, just as it does to prophylactic or preventive measures intended to reduce the incidence of these or any other breaches of prison discipline. It does not insulate from review actions taken in bad faith and for no legitimate purpose, but it requires that neither judge nor jury freely substitute their judgment for that of officials who have made a considered choice. Accordingly, in ruling on a motion for a directed verdict in a case such as this, courts must determine whether the evidence goes beyond a mere dispute over the reasonableness of a particular use of force or the existence of arguably superior alternatives. Unless it appears that the evidence, viewed in the light most favorable to the plaintiff, will support a reliable inference of wantonness in the infliction of pain under the standard we have described, the case should not go to the jury.

III

Since this case comes to us from a decision of the Court of Appeals reversing the District Court's directed verdict for petitioners, we evaluate the facts in the light most favorable to respondent. The Court of Appeals believed that testimony that the disturbance was subsiding at the time the assault was made, and the conflicting expert testimony as to whether the force used was excessive, were enough to allow a jury to find that respondent's Eighth Amendment rights were violated. We think the Court of Appeals effectively collapsed the distinction between mere negligence and wanton conduct that we find implicit in the Eighth Amendment. Only if ordinary errors of judgment could make out an Eighth Amendment claim would this evidence create a jury question.

To begin with, although the evidence could be taken to show that the general disturbance had quieted down, a guard was still held hostage, Klenk was armed and threatening, several other inmates were armed with homemade clubs, numerous inmates remained outside their cells, and the cellblock remained in the control of the inmates. The situation remained dangerous and volatile. * * * Prison officials had no way of knowing what direction matters would take if they continued to negotiate or did nothing, but they had ample reason to believe that these options presented unacceptable risks.

Respondent's expert testimony is likewise unavailing. One of respondent's experts opined that petitioners gave inadequate consideration to less forceful means of intervention, and that the use of deadly force under the circumstances was not necessary to "prevent imminent danger" to the hostage guard or other inmates. Respondent's second expert testified that prison officials were "possibly a little hasty in using the firepower" on the inmates. At most, this evidence, which was controverted by petitioners' experts, establishes that prison officials arguably erred in judgment when they decided on a plan that employed potentially deadly force. It falls far short of a showing that there was no plausible basis for the officials' belief that this degree of force was necessary. Indeed, any such conclusion would run counter to common sense, in light of the risks to the life of the hostage and the safety of inmates that demonstrably persisted notwithstanding repeated attempts to defuse the situation. An expert's after-the-fact opinion that danger was not "imminent" in no way establishes that there was no danger, or that a conclusion by the officers that it *was* imminent would have been wholly unreasonable.

Once the basic design of the plan was in place, moreover, it is apparent why any inmate running up the stairs after Captain Whitley, or interfering with his progress towards the hostage, could reasonably be thought to present a threat to the success of the rescue attempt and to Whitley—particularly after a warning shot was fired. A sizable group of inmates, in defiance of the cell-in order and in apparent support of Klenk, continued to stand in the open area on the lower tier. Respondent testified that this was not "an organized group", and that he saw no inmates armed with clubs in that area. But the fact remains that the officials had no way of knowing which members of that group of inmates had joined with Klenk in destroying furniture, breaking glass, seizing the hostage, and setting up the barricade, and they certainly had reason to believe that some members of this group might intervene in support of Klenk. It was perhaps also foreseeable that one or more of these inmates would run up the stairs after the shooting started in order to return to their cells. But there would be neither means nor time to inquire into the reasons why each inmate acted as he did. Consequently, the order to shoot, qualified as it was by an instruction to shoot low, falls short of commanding the infliction of pain in a wanton and unnecessary fashion.

As petitioners' own experts conceded, a verbal warning would have been desirable, in addition to a warning shot, if circumstances permitted it to be given without undue risk. While a jury might conclude that this omission was unreasonable, we think that an inference of wantonness could not properly be drawn. First, some warning was given in the form of the first shot fired by Officer Kennicott. Second, the prison officials could have believed in good faith that such a warning might endanger the success of the security measure because of the risk that it would have allowed one or more inmates to climb the stairs before they could be stopped. The failure to provide for verbal warnings is thus not so insupportable as to be wanton. Accordingly, a jury could not properly find that this omission, coupled with the order to shoot, offended the Eighth Amendment.

To be sure, the plan was not adapted to take into account the appearance of respondent on the scene, and, on the facts as we must take them, Whitley was aware that respondent was present on the first tier for benign reasons. Conceivably, Whitley could have added a proviso exempting respondent from his order to shoot any prisoner climbing the stairs. But such an oversight simply does not rise to the level of an Eighth Amendment violation. Officials cannot realistically be expected to consider every contingency or minimize every risk, and it was far from inevitable that respondent would react as he did. Whitley was about to risk his life in an effort to rescue the hostage, and he was understandably focusing on the orders essential to the success of the plan. His failure to make special provision for respondent may have been unfortunate, but is hardly behavior from which a wanton willingness to inflict unjustified suffering on respondent can be inferred.

Once it is established that the order to shoot low at anyone climbing the stairs after a warning shot was not wanton, respondent's burden in showing that the actual shooting constituted the wanton and unnecessary infliction of pain is an extremely heavy one. Accepting that respondent could not have sought safety in a cell on the lower tier, the fact remains that had respondent thrown himself to the floor he would not have been shot at. Instead, after the warning shot was fired, he attempted to return to his cell by running up the stairs behind Whitley. That is equivocal conduct. While respondent had not been actively involved in the riot and indeed had attempted to help matters, there is no indication that Officer Kennicott knew this, nor any claim that he acted vindictively or in retaliation. Respondent testified that as he started to run up the stairs he "froze" when he looked to his left and saw Kennicott, and that "we locked eyes." Kennicott testified that he saw several inmates running up the stairs, that he thought they were pursuing Whitley, and that he fired at their legs. To the extent that this testimony is conflicting, we resolve the conflict in respondent's favor by assuming that Kennicott shot at respondent rather than at the inmates as a group. But this does not establish that Kennicott shot respondent knowing it was unnecessary to do so. Kennicott had some basis for believing that respondent constituted a threat to the hostage and to Whitley, and had at most a few seconds in which to react. He was also under orders to respond to such a perceived threat in precisely the manner he did. Under these circumstances, the actual shooting was part and parcel of a good-faith effort to restore prison security. As such, it did not violate respondent's Eighth Amendment right to be free from cruel and unusual punishments.

IV

As an alternative ground for affirmance, respondent contends that, independently of the Eighth Amendment, the shooting deprived him of a protected liberty interest without due process of law, in violation of the Fourteenth Amendment. ＊ ＊ ＊

The District Court was correct in ruling that respondent did not assert a *procedural* due process claim that the State was obliged to afford him some kind of hearing either before or after he was shot. But we believe respondent did raise a claim that his "substantive rights under the Due Process Clause of the Fourteenth Amendment" were infringed by prison officials when he was shot. ＊ ＊ ＊

We need say little on this score. We think the Eighth Amendment, which is specifically concerned with the unnecessary and wanton infliction of pain in penal institutions, serves as the primary source of substantive protection to convicted prisoners in cases such as this one, where the deliberate use of force is challenged as excessive and unjustified. It would indeed be surprising if, in the context of forceful prison security measures, "conduct that shocks the conscience" or "afford[s] brutality the cloak of law," and so violates the Fourteenth Amendment, *Rochin v. California,* 342 U.S. 165, 172, 173 (1952), were not also punishment "inconsistent with contemporary standards of decency" and " 'repugnant to the conscience of mankind,' " *Estelle v. Gamble,* 429 U.S., at 103, 106, in violation of the Eighth. We only recently reserved the general question "whether something less than intentional conduct, such as recklessness or 'gross negligence,' is enough to trigger the protections of the Due Process Clause." *Daniels v. Williams,* 474 U.S. 327, 334, n. 3 (1986). Because this case involves prison inmates rather than pretrial detainees or persons enjoying unrestricted liberty we imply nothing as to the proper answer to that question outside the prison security context by holding, as we do, that in these circumstances the Due Process Clause affords respondent no greater protection than does the Cruel and Unusual Punishments Clause.

＊ ＊ ＊

The judgment of the Court of Appeals is

Reversed.

JUSTICE MARSHALL, with whom JUSTICE BRENNAN, JUSTICE BLACKMUN, and JUSTICE STEVENS join, dissenting.

＊ ＊ ＊

The Court properly begins by acknowledging that, for a prisoner attempting to prove a violation of the Eighth Amendment, "[a]n express intent to inflict unnecessary pain is not required." Rather, our cases have established that the "unnecessary and wanton" infliction of pain on prisoners constitutes cruel and unusual punishment prohibited by the Eighth Amendment, even in the absence of intent to harm. [*Estelle v. Gamble,* 429 U.S. 97, 104 (1976)]. Having correctly articulated the teaching of our cases on this issue, however, the majority inexplicably arrives at the conclusion that a constitutional violation in the context of a prison uprising can be established only if force was used "maliciously and sadistically for the very purpose of causing harm," thus requiring the very "express intent to inflict unnecessary pain" that it had properly disavowed.

The Court imposes its heightened version of the "unnecessary and wanton" standard only when the injury occurred in the course of a "disturbance" that "poses significant risks". But those very questions—whether a disturbance existed and whether it posed a risk—are likely to be hotly contested. It is inappropriate, to say the least, to condition the choice of a legal standard, the purpose of which is to determine whether to send a constitutional claim to the jury, upon the court's resolution of factual disputes that in many cases should themselves be resolved by the jury.

The correct standard for identifying a violation of the Eighth Amendment under our cases is clearly the "unnecessary and wanton" standard, which establishes a high hurdle to be overcome by a prisoner seeking relief for a constitutional violation. The full circumstances of the plaintiff's injury, including whether it was inflicted during an attempt to quell a riot and whether there was a reasonable apprehension of danger, should be considered by the factfinder in determining whether that standard is satisfied in a particular case. There is simply no justification for creating a distinct and more onerous burden for the plaintiff to meet merely because the judge believes that the injury at issue was caused during a disturbance that "pose[d] significant risks to the safety of inmates and prison staff." Determination of whether there was such a disturbance or risk, when disputed, should be made by the jury when it resolves disputed facts, not by the court in its role as arbiter of law.

[Justice Marshall then discussed the facts of the case, concluding that there was enough evidence of unnecessary and wanton infliction of pain for the question to be submitted to and decided by a jury. He also observed, in the course of his opinion, that recklessness could give rise to a substantive due process violation.]

Questions and Points for Discussion

1. Should the *Whitley* standard apply only when there is a prison riot or disturbance involving a number of inmates? The lower courts which have addressed this question have generally not confined *Whitley* to its facts. To establish an eighth amendment violation, they have, for example, required proof that force was employed "maliciously and sadistically for the very purpose of causing harm" when a correctional officer tried to control an allegedly unruly inmate. See, e.g., Corselli v. Coughlin, 842 F.2d 23 (2d Cir.1988); Brown v. Smith, 813 F.2d 1187 (11th Cir.1987).

2. Excessive force claims have arisen outside the prison context. For example, in Tennessee v. Garner, 471 U.S. 1, 105 S.Ct. 1694 (1985), a § 1983 suit was brought after the decedent was shot in the head and killed by a

police officer when fleeing the scene of a burglary. The Supreme Court concluded that the use of deadly force under the circumstances subjected the decedent to an "unreasonable seizure" in violation of the fourth amendment. The Court outlined three of the requirements that must be met before deadly force can be employed to effect an arrest: first, the force must be necessary to avert an escape; second, the officer must have "probable cause to believe that the suspect poses a significant threat of death or serious bodily injury to the officer or others;" and third, if it is possible, the police officer must provide the person against whom deadly force is about to be employed with some type of warning before using the force.

If an escaping prisoner has managed to scale the wall or a fence surrounding a prison, under what circumstances can deadly force constitutionally be used to apprehend the prisoner? What standard or standards will be applied when assessing the constitutionality of the force employed? See, e.g., Newby v. Serviss, 590 F.Supp. 591 (W.D.Mich.1984).

3. It is clear that a pretrial detainee against whom excessive force has been used cannot assert an eighth amendment claim, since the eighth amendment only applies to individuals following a criminal conviction and sentencing. Graham v. Connor, 109 S.Ct. 1865 (1989). When excessive force used against a pretrial detainee is tantamount to punishment of that detainee, however, the Court has said that a violation of due process results. Id. at 1871 n. 10. Left unresolved by the Court is the question whether pretrial detainees, as well as convicted prisoners, can, like free citizens, assert a fourth amendment claim when challenging the excessive use of force. Id.

4. The courts have generally concurred that the eighth amendment not only protects inmates from certain assaults by correctional officials, but also sometimes from the failure of correctional officials to protect them from assaults by other inmates. See, e.g., Morgan v. District of Columbia, 824 F.2d 1049 (D.C.Cir.1987); Pressly v. Hutto, 816 F.2d 977 (4th Cir.1987). They have also generally agreed that to be liable under the eighth amendment, correctional officials must have been more than just negligent in failing to protect one inmate from another; the correctional officials must have been deliberately indifferent to the inmate's need for protection for liability to ensue. See, e.g., Santiago v. Lane, 894 F.2d 218, 221 (7th Cir. 1990); Ruefly v. Landon, 825 F.2d 792, 793 (4th Cir.1987). Where the courts have had some trouble is in defining what exactly constitutes "deliberate indifference." The difficulty in answering this question was acknowledged by the Seventh Circuit Court of Appeals in the excerpt from Duckworth v. Franzen, 780 F.2d 645 (7th Cir.1985) found in note 4, supra page 470.

In addition to struggling with the formulation of a test for "deliberate indifference," the courts have differed as to the significance of certain facts to the "deliberate indifference" determination. Compare, e.g., Morgan v. District of Columbia, 824 F.2d 1049, 1061 (D.C.Cir.1987) (persistent jail crowding, which precluded appropriate housing assignments, cited as evidence of deliberate indifference to threat of serious violence) with Wheeler v. Sullivan, 599 F.Supp. 630, 645 (D.Del.1984) (crowding, which limited prison officials' flexibility in making housing assignments, cited as evidence indicating a lack of deliberate indifference to the risk of homosexual rape).

5. According to the Supreme Court in Davidson v. Cannon, 474 U.S. 344, 348, 106 S.Ct. 668, 671 (1986), supra page 454, the failure to protect an inmate from an attack by another inmate may also give rise to a due process claim. Assume that the plaintiff in that case had contended that the failure to protect him constituted deliberate indifference to his safety needs in contravention of his eighth amendment and due process rights. Should the plaintiff have prevailed on that claim? What if a prisoner was attacked by twenty inmates and two officers in a control room failed to intervene? Would their inaction constitute cruel and unusual punishment or a violation of due process? See Stubbs v. Dudley, 849 F.2d 83, 87 (2d Cir. 1988).

6. The courts have generally agreed that the eighth amendment, and in the case of pretrial detainees, the due process clause, can be violated not only if correctional officials are deliberately indifferent to the risk that an inmate will be injured or killed by others, but also if they are deliberately indifferent to the risk that the inmate will commit suicide. See, e.g., Partridge v. Two Unknown Police Officers, 751 F.2d 1448, 1453 (5th Cir. 1985); Roberts v. City of Troy, 773 F.2d 720, 725 (6th Cir.1985). The rationale of the courts is that an inmate with suicidal tendencies has mental problems which constitute a "serious medical need" to which, under Estelle v. Gamble, 429 U.S. 97, 97 S.Ct. 285 (1976), correctional officials cannot be deliberately indifferent. See Partridge v. Two Unknown Police Officers, 751 F.2d at 1452; Guglielmoni v. Alexander, 583 F.Supp. 821, 827 (D.Conn.1984).

Just because an inmate kills himself or herself, however, does not mean that correctional officials have manifested the requisite deliberate indifference. The courts have recognized that correctional facilities cannot guarantee the safety of the persons confined within them and that inmates bent on killing themselves will most likely eventually succeed in doing so. See, e.g., Freedman v. City of Allentown, 853 F.2d 1111, 1115 (3d Cir.1988). At the same time, however, most of the courts have held that deliberate indifference will exist and liability may ensue "when action is not taken in the face of 'a strong likelihood, rather than a mere possibility' that failure to provide care would result in harm to the prisoner." Matje v. Leis, 571 F.Supp. 918, 930 (S.D.Ohio 1983) (quoting State Bank of St. Charles v. Camic, 712 F.2d 1140, 1146 (7th Cir.1983)).

Some cases in which the courts found there to be sufficient evidence of deliberate indifference, at least to withstand a motion to dismiss or for summary judgment include: Colburn v. Upper Darby Township, 838 F.2d 663 (3d Cir.1988) (complaint should not have been dismissed where decedent shot herself with a gun undiscovered during a search preceding her confinement in jail, police knew she had jumped out of a window the day before, and she had "obvious" scars on her wrist from a previous suicide attempt); Partridge v. Two Unknown Police Officers, 751 F.2d 1448 (5th Cir.1985) (complaint alleging that decedent was kicking and otherwise violent at the time of his arrest, that decedent's father informed the arresting officers that the decedent had had a nervous breakdown, and that jail records revealed a previous suicide attempt by the decedent when he was confined in the past should not have been dismissed even though the jailor was unaware of the information in the jail records about the previous suicide attempt); Guglielmoni v. Alexander, 583 F.Supp. 821 (D.Conn.1984) (defendants' motion for summary judgment denied in case where decedent had earlier tried unsuccessfully to hang himself in the prison); and Matje v. Leis, 571 F.Supp. 918 (S.D.Ohio 1983) (defendants' motion for summary judgment denied where authorities were aware that the decedent had threatened to kill herself with drugs that she would smuggle into the prison behind her diaphragm, but she was not subjected to a body-cavity search upon entry into the prison). Cases in which the courts have found insufficient allegations or evidence of deliberate indifference include: Freedman v. City of Allentown, 853 F.2d 1111 (3d Cir.1988) (complaint properly dismissed where police officers did not realize that scars on decedent's wrists and neck were from a previous suicide attempt); State Bank v. Camic, 712 F.2d 1140 (7th Cir.1983) (fact that decedent was intoxicated, unruly, and violent at time of his arrest not enough to show that he posed a sufficiently high risk of suicide); and Boyd v. Harper, 702 F.Supp. 578 (E.D.Va.1988) (no "strong likelihood" of suicide just because decedent was crying in his cell before he committed suicide).

Other than focusing on evidence suggesting that a particular decedent had suicidal tendencies, is there any other way to establish that correctional officials were deliberately indifferent to the risk of suicide? See Partridge v. Two Unknown Police Officers, 751 F.2d at 1454; Boyd v. Harper, 702 F.Supp. at 580.

C. CONDITIONS OF CONFINEMENT

If only one word could be used to describe the state of the nation's prisons and jails, that word would be "crowded." At the end of 1989, the nation's prisons held 710,054 inmates, an increase of about 115% since 1980. Bureau of Justice Statistics, U.S. Dep't of Justice, Prisoners in 1989 1 (1990). While in 1980, 139 of every 100,000 residents in the United States were confined in prison, by 1989, this number had increased to 274 per every 100,000 residents, an increase of more than 97%. Id.

The number of persons confined in the nation's jails burgeoned as well. Between 1978 and 1986, the size of the nation's jail population increased by 73% so that during 1986 a total of about 8 million people were admitted to jails. Bureau of Justice Statistics, U.S. Dep't of Justice, Our Crowded Jails: A National Plight 1 (1988). During the same time period, the jails' rated capacity, which measures the space available for inmates, increased by only 16%. Id.

With so many prisons and jails operating above capacity, correctional officials have had to scramble to simply find a place where each inmate can sleep. Inmates have been housed in gymnasiums, television rooms, libraries, hallways, and in other nooks and crannies throughout correctional institutions. Tents have been erected to hold prisoners, and authorities have even contemplated placing prisoners on barges—

"floating prisons"—to stem their overcrowding problems. N.Y. Times, May 12, 1989, at B4.

At great cost, the states and federal government have also embarked on a prison and jail construction frenzy in an attempt to find room for the increasing numbers of persons sentenced to prison and jail. This construction effort has proven to be quite costly. Experts estimated that in 1987, it cost an average of at least $66,000 in construction costs to add one bed to a prison system. Prison Projections: Can the United States Keep Pace?: Hearing before the Subcomm. on Federal Spending, Budget, and Accounting of the Sen. Comm. on Governmental Affairs, 100th Cong., 1st Sess. 49 (statement of William J. Anderson). See also Corrections Compendium 10 (Sept.– Oct., 1989) (reporting that states and federal government planned to spend $6.7 billion on new prison construction during 1989 and 1990). In addition, an average of at least $16,315 had to be spent per prisoner in 1988 to pay for the food, staff, medical care, and other operating costs associated with the running of a correctional institution. G. Camp and C. Camp, The Corrections Yearbook 28 (1989). But while adding to the capacity of the nation's prisons has been enormously expensive, it has failed to eliminate the crowding problem. While somewhere between 40,000 and 60,000 beds were added in the nation's prisons between 1988 and 1989, for example, the number of prisoners housed in these prisons during this time period increased by almost 82,466. Bureau of Justice Statistics, U.S. Dept. of Justice, Prisoners in 1989 1, 7 (1990).

In part because of the pervasive crowding in the nation's correctional facilities and the insufficient funds made available to operate prisons, correctional officials have had difficulty in operating their facilities in conformance with the Constitution. As a result, as of January 1, 1990, forty-one of the states and the District of Columbia had some or all of their prisons operating under court order because of unconstitutional conditions of confinement. The National Prison Project, Status Report: The Courts and the Prisons (1990). The cases and materials set forth below discuss questions concerning when conditions of confinement transgress constitutional boundaries.

RHODES v. CHAPMAN

Supreme Court of the United States, 1981.
452 U.S. 337, 101 S.Ct. 2392, 69 L.Ed.2d 59.

JUSTICE POWELL delivered the opinion of the Court.

The question presented is whether the housing of two inmates in a single cell at the Southern Ohio Correctional Facility is cruel and unusual punishment prohibited by the Eighth and Fourteenth Amendments.

I

Respondents Kelly Chapman and Richard Jaworski are inmates at the Southern Ohio Correctional Facility (SOCF), a maximum-security state prison in Lucasville, Ohio. They were housed in the same cell when they brought this action in the District Court for the Southern District of Ohio on behalf of themselves and all inmates similarly situated at SOCF. Asserting a cause of action under 42 U.S.C. § 1983, they contended that "double celling" at SOCF violated the Constitution. The gravamen of their complaint was that double celling confined cellmates too closely. It also was blamed for overcrowding at SOCF, said to have overwhelmed the prison's facilities and staff. As relief, respondents sought an injunction barring petitioners, who are Ohio officials responsible for the administration of SOCF, from housing more than one inmate in a cell, except as a temporary measure.

*   *   *

SOCF was built in the early 1970's. In addition to 1,620 cells, it has gymnasiums, workshops, schoolrooms, "dayrooms," two chapels, a hospital ward, commissary, barbershop, and library. Outdoors, SOCF has a recreation field, visitation area, and garden. The District Court described this physical plant as "unquestionably a top-flight, first-class facility."

Each cell at SOCF measures approximately 63 square feet. Each contains a bed measuring 36 by 80 inches, a cabinet-type night stand, a wall-mounted sink with hot and cold running water, and a toilet that the inmate can flush from inside the cell. Cells housing two inmates have a two-tiered bunk bed. Every cell has a heating and air circulation vent near the ceiling, and 960 of the cells have a window that inmates can open and close. All of the cells have a cabinet, shelf, and radio built into one of the walls, and in all of the cells one wall consists of bars through which the inmates can be seen.

The "dayrooms" are located adjacent to the cellblocks and are open to inmates between 6:30 a.m. and 9:30 p.m. According to the District Court, "[t]he day rooms are in a sense part of the cells and they are designed to furnish that type of recreation or occupation which an ordinary citizen would seek in his living room or den." Each dayroom contains a wall-mounted television, card tables, and chairs. Inmates can pass between their cells and the dayrooms during a 10–minute period each hour, on the hour, when the doors to the dayrooms and cells are opened.

As to the inmate population, the District Court found that SOCF began receiving inmates in late 1972 and double celling them in 1975 because of an increase in Ohio's statewide prison population. At the time of trial, SOCF housed 2,300 inmates, 67% of whom were serving life or other long-term sentences for first-degree felonies. Approximately 1,400 inmates were double celled. Of these, about 75% had the choice of spending much of their waking hours outside their cells, in the dayrooms, school, workshops, library, visits, meals, or showers. The other double-celled inmates spent more time locked in their cells because of a restrictive classification.[3]

The remaining findings by the District Court addressed respondents' allegation that overcrowding created by double celling overwhelmed SOCF's facilities and staff. The food was "adequate in every respect," and respondents adduced no evidence "whatsoever that prisoners have been underfed or that the food facilities have been taxed by the prison population." The air ventilation system was adequate, the cells were substantially free of offensive odor, the temperature in the cellblocks was well controlled, and the noise in the cellblocks was not excessive. Double celling had not reduced significantly the availability of space in the dayrooms or visitation facilities, nor had it rendered inadequate the resources of the library or schoolrooms.[5] Although there were isolated incidents of failure to provide medical or dental care, there was no evidence of indifference by the SOCF staff to inmates' medical or dental needs. As to violence, the court found that the number of acts of violence at SOCF had increased with the prison population, but only in proportion to the increase in population. Respondents failed to produce evidence establishing that double celling itself caused greater violence, and the ratio of guards to inmates at SOCF satisfied the standard of acceptability offered by respondents' expert witness. Finally, the court did find that the SOCF administration, faced with more inmates than jobs, had "water[ed] down" jobs by assigning more inmates to each job than necessary and by reducing the number of hours that each inmate worked; it also found that SOCF had not increased its staff of psychiatrists and social workers since double celling had begun.

Despite these generally favorable findings, the District Court concluded that double celling at SOCF was cruel and unusual punishment. The court rested its conclusion on five considerations. One, inmates at SOCF are serving long terms of imprisonment. In the court's view, that fact "can only accent[uate] the problems of close confinement and overcrowding." Two, SOCF housed 38% more inmates at the time of trial than its "design capacity." In reference to this the court asserted: "Overcrowding necessarily involves excess limitation of general movement as well as physical and mental injury from long exposure." Three, the court accepted as contemporary standards of decency several studies recommending that each person in an institution have at least 50–55 square feet of living quarters.[7] In contrast, double-celled inmates

3. Inmates who requested protective custody but could not substantiate their fears were classified as "limited activity" and were locked in their cells all but six hours a week. Inmates classified as "voluntarily idle" and newly arrived inmates awaiting classification had only four hours a week outside their cells. Inmates housed in administrative isolation for disciplinary reasons were allowed out of their cells for

two hours a week to attend religious services, a movie, or the commissary.

5. * * * [N]o inmate who was "ready, able, and willing to receive schooling has been denied the opportunity," although there was some delay before an inmate received the opportunity to attend.

7. The District Court cited, *e.g.*, American Correctional Assn., Manual of Stan-at SOCF share 63 square feet. Four, the court asserted that "[a]t the best a prisoner who is double celled will spend most of his time in the cell with his cellmate."[8] Five, SOCF has made double celling a practice; it is not a temporary condition.

On appeal, [the Sixth Circuit Court of Appeals affirmed.]

We granted the petition for certiorari because of the importance of the question to prison administration. We now reverse.

II

* * *

No static "test" can exist by which courts determine whether conditions of confinement are cruel and unusual, for the Eighth Amendment "must draw its meaning from the evolving standards of decency that mark the progress of a maturing society." The Court has held, however, that "Eighth Amendment judgments should neither be nor appear to be merely the subjective views" of judges. To be sure, "the Constitution contemplates that in the end [a court's] own judgment will be brought to bear on the question of the acceptability" of a given punishment. But such " 'judgment[s] should be informed by objective factors to the maximum possible extent.' " For example, when the question was whether capital punishment for certain crimes violated contemporary values, the Court looked for "objective indicia" derived from history, the action of state legislatures, and the sentencing by juries. *Gregg v. Georgia,* [428 U.S.] at 176–187. * * *

These principles apply when the conditions of confinement compose the punishment at issue. Conditions must not involve the wanton and unnecessary infliction of pain, nor may they be grossly disproportionate to the severity of the crime warranting imprisonment. In *Estelle v. Gamble,* we held that the denial of medical care is cruel and unusual because, in the worst case, it can result in physical torture, and, even in less serious cases, it can result in pain without any penological purpose. In *Hutto v. Finney,* the conditions of confinement in two Arkansas prisons constituted cruel and unusual punishment because they resulted in unquestioned and serious deprivations of basic human needs. Conditions other than those in *Gamble* and *Hutto,* alone or in combination, may deprive inmates of the minimal civilized measure of life's necessities. Such conditions could be cruel and unusual under the contemporary standard of decency that we recognized in *Gamble.* But conditions that cannot be said to be cruel and unusual under contemporary standards are not unconstitutional. To the extent that such

dards for Adult Correctional Institutions, Standard No. 4142, p. 27 (1977) (60–80 square feet); National Sheriffs' Assn., A Handbook on Jail Architecture 63 (1975) (70–80 square feet); National Council on Crime and Delinquency, Model Act for the Protection of Rights of Prisoners, § 1, 18 Crime & Delinquency 4, 10 (1972) (50 square feet).

8. The basis of the District Court's assertion as to the amount of time that inmates spend in their cells does not appear in the court's opinion. Elsewhere in its opinion, the court found that 75% of the double-celled inmates at SOCF are free to be out of their cells from 6:30 a.m. to 9 p.m. * * *

conditions are restrictive and even harsh, they are part of the penalty that criminal offenders pay for their offenses against society.

In view of the District Court's findings of fact, its conclusion that double celling at SOCF constitutes cruel and unusual punishment is insupportable. Virtually every one of the court's findings tends to *refute* respondents' claim. The double celling made necessary by the unanticipated increase in prison population did not lead to deprivations of essential food, medical care, or sanitation. Nor did it increase violence among inmates or create other conditions intolerable for prison confinement. Although job and educational opportunities diminished marginally as a result of double celling, limited work hours and delay before receiving education do not inflict pain, much less unnecessary and wanton pain; deprivations of this kind simply are not punishments. We would have to wrench the Eighth Amendment from its language and history to hold that delay of these desirable aids to rehabilitation violates the Constitution.

The five considerations on which the District Court relied also are insufficient to support its constitutional conclusion. The court relied on the long terms of imprisonment served by inmates at SOCF; the fact that SOCF housed 38% more inmates than its "design capacity"; the recommendation of several studies that each inmate have at least 50–55 square feet of living quarters; the suggestion that double-celled inmates spend most of their time in their cells with their cellmates; and the fact that double celling at SOCF was not a temporary condition. These general considerations fall far short in themselves of proving cruel and unusual punishment, for there is no evidence that double celling under these circumstances either inflicts unnecessary or wanton pain or is grossly disproportionate to the severity of crimes warranting imprisonment.[13] At most, these considerations amount to a theory that double celling inflicts pain. Perhaps they reflect an aspiration toward an ideal environment for long-term confinement. But the Constitution does not mandate comfortable prisons, and prisons of SOCF's type, which house persons convicted of serious crimes, cannot be free of discomfort. Thus, these considerations properly are weighed by the legislature and prison administration rather than a court. There being no constitutional violation,[15] the District Court had no authority to consider whether

---

13. Respondents and the District Court erred in assuming that opinions of experts as to desirable prison conditions suffice to establish contemporary standards of decency. As we noted in *Bell v. Wolfish*, 441 U.S., at 543–544, n. 27, such opinions may be helpful and relevant with respect to some questions, but "they simply do not establish the constitutional minima; rather, they establish goals recommended by the organization in question." Indeed, generalized opinions of experts cannot weigh as heavily in determining contemporary standards of decency as "the public attitude toward a given sanction." We

could agree that double celling is not desirable, especially in view of the size of these cells. But there is no evidence in this case that double celling is viewed generally as violating decency. Moreover, though small, the cells in SOCF are exceptionally modern and functional; they are heated and ventilated and have hot and cold running water and a sanitary toilet. Each cell also has a radio.

15. * * * The dissent * * * makes much of the fact that SOCF was housing 38% more inmates at the time of trial than its "rated capacity." According to the

double celling in light of these considerations was the best response to the increase in Ohio's statewide prison population.

* * *

In this case, the question before us is whether the conditions of confinement at SOCF are cruel and unusual. As we find that they are not, the judgment of the Court of Appeals is reversed.

* * *

Justice Brennan, with whom Justice Blackmun and Justice Stevens join, concurring in the judgment.

Today's decision reaffirms that "[c]ourts certainly have a responsibility to scrutinize claims of cruel and unusual confinement." With that I agree. I also agree that the District Court's findings in this case do not support a judgment that the practice of double celling in the Southern Ohio Correctional Facility is in violation of the Eighth Amendment. I write separately, however, to emphasize that today's decision should in no way be construed as a retreat from careful judicial scrutiny of prison conditions, and to discuss the factors courts should consider in undertaking such scrutiny.

* * *

* * * [T]his Court and the lower courts have been especially deferential to prison authorities "in the adoption and execution of policies and practices that in their judgment are needed to preserve internal order and discipline and to maintain institutional security." Many conditions of confinement, however, including overcrowding, poor sanitation, and inadequate safety precautions, arise from neglect rather than policy. There is no reason of comity, judicial restraint, or recognition of expertise for courts to defer to negligent omissions of officials who lack the resources or motivation to operate prisons within limits of decency. Courts must and do recognize the primacy of the legislative and executive authorities in the administration of prisons; however, if the prison authorities do not conform to constitutional minima, the courts are under an obligation to take steps to remedy the violations.

The first aspect of judicial decisionmaking in this area is scrutiny of the actual conditions under challenge. It is important to recognize that various deficiencies in prison conditions "must be considered together." *Holt v. Sarver*, 309 F.Supp., at 373. The individual conditions "exist in combination; each affects the other; and taken together they [may] have a cumulative impact on the inmates." *Ibid.* Thus, a court considering an Eighth Amendment challenge to conditions of confinement must examine the totality of the circumstances.[10] Even if

United States Bureau of Prisons, at least three factors influence prison population: the number of arrests, prosecution policies, and sentencing and parole decisions. Because these factors can change rapidly, while prisons require years to plan and build, it is extremely difficult to calibrate a prison's "rated" or "design capacity" with predictions of prison population. The

question before us is not whether the designer of SOCF guessed incorrectly about future prison population, but whether the actual conditions of confinement at SOCF are cruel and unusual.

10. The Court today adopts the totality-of-the-circumstances test. (Prison conditions *"alone or in combination,* may de-

no single condition of confinement would be unconstitutional in itself, "exposure to the cumulative effect of prison conditions may subject inmates to cruel and unusual punishment." *Laaman v. Helgemoe,* 437 F.Supp. 269, 322–323 (N.H.1977).

* * *

In determining when prison conditions pass beyond legitimate punishment and become cruel and unusual, the "touchstone is the effect upon the imprisoned." *Laaman v. Helgemoe,* 437 F.Supp., at 323. The court must examine the effect upon inmates of the condition of the physical plant (lighting, heat, plumbing, ventilation, living space, noise levels, recreation space); sanitation (control of vermin and insects, food preparation, medical facilities, lavatories and showers, clean places for eating, sleeping, and working); safety (protection from violent, deranged, or diseased inmates, fire protection, emergency evacuation); inmate needs and services (clothing, nutrition, bedding, medical, dental, and mental health care, visitation time, exercise and recreation, educational and rehabilitative programming); and staffing (trained and adequate guards and other staff, avoidance of placing inmates in positions of authority over other inmates). When "the cumulative impact of the conditions of incarceration threatens the physical, mental, and emotional health and well-being of the inmates and/or creates a probability of recidivism and future incarceration," the court must conclude that the conditions violate the Constitution. [*Id.*]

* * *

I have not the slightest doubt that 63 square feet of cell space is not enough for two men. I understand that every major study of living space in prisons has so concluded. That prisoners are housed under such conditions is an unmistakable signal to the legislators and officials of Ohio: either more prison facilities should be built or expanded, or fewer persons should be incarcerated in prisons. Even so, the findings of the District Court do not support a conclusion that the conditions at the Southern Ohio Correctional Facility—cramped though they are—constitute cruel and unusual punishment.

The "touchstone" of the Eighth Amendment inquiry is " 'the effect upon the imprisoned.' " The findings of the District Court leave no doubt that the prisoners are adequately sheltered, fed, and protected, and that opportunities for education, work, and rehabilitative assistance are available. One need only compare the District Court's description of conditions at the Southern Ohio Correctional Facility with descriptions of other major state and federal facilities to realize that this prison, crowded though it is, is one of the better, more humane large prisons in the Nation.[15]

* * *

prive inmates of the minimal civilized measure of life's necessities") (emphasis added).

15. If it were true that any prison providing less than 63 square feet of cell space per inmate were a *per se* violation of the Eighth Amendment, then approximately two-thirds of all federal, state, and local inmates today would be unconstitutionally confined.

The District Court may well be correct *in the abstract* that prison overcrowding and double celling such as existed at the Southern Ohio Correctional Facility generally results in serious harm to the inmates. But cases are not decided in the abstract. A court is under the obligation to examine the *actual effect* of challenged conditions upon the well-being of the prisoners.[16] The District Court in this case was unable to identify any actual signs that the double celling at the Southern Ohio Correctional Facility has seriously harmed the inmates there; indeed, the court's findings of fact suggest that crowding at the prison has not reached the point of causing serious injury. Since I cannot conclude that the totality of conditions at the facility offends constitutional norms, and am of the view that double celling in itself is not *per se* impermissible, I concur in the judgment of the Court.

JUSTICE BLACKMUN, concurring in the judgment. [Opinion omitted.]

JUSTICE MARSHALL, dissenting.

From reading the Court's opinion in this case, one would surely conclude that the Southern Ohio Correctional Facility (SOCF) is a safe, spacious prison that happens to include many two-inmate cells because the State has determined that that is the best way to run the prison. But the facility described by the majority is not the one involved in this case. SOCF is overcrowded, unhealthful, and dangerous. * * *

* * *

In a doubled cell, each inmate has only some 30–35 square feet of floor space.[3] Most of the windows in the Supreme Court building are larger than that. The conclusion of every expert who testified at trial and of every serious study of which I am aware is that a long-term inmate must have to himself, at the very least, 50 square feet of floor space—an area smaller than that occupied by a good-sized automobile—in order to avoid serious mental, emotional, and physical deterioration.[4] The District Court found that as a fact. * * *

16. This is not to say that injury to the inmates from challenged prison conditions must be "demonstrate[d] with a high degree of specificity and certainty." *Ruiz v. Estelle,* 503 F.Supp., at 1286. Courts may, as usual, employ common sense, observation, expert testimony, and other practical modes of proof.

3. The bed alone, which is bunk-style in the doubled cells, takes up approximately 20 square feet. Thus the actual amount of floor space per inmate, without making allowance for any other furniture in the room, is some 20–24 square feet, an area about the size of a typical door.

4. See, *e.g.,* American Public Health Assn., Standard for Health Services in Correctional Institutions 62 (1976) ("a minimum of 60 sq. ft."); Commission on Accreditation for Corrections, Manual of Standards for Adult Correctional Institutions 27 (1977) ("a floor area of at least 60 square feet"; "[i]n no case should the present use of the facility exceed designed use standards"); 3 National Institute of Justice, American Prisons and Jails 85, n. 6 (1980) ("80 square feet of floor space in long-term institutions"); National Sheriffs' Assn., A Handbook on Jail Architecture 63 (1975) ("[s]ingle occupancy detention rooms should average 70 to 80 square feet in area"); U.S. Dept. of Justice, Federal Standards for Prisons and Jails 17 (1980) ("at least 60 square feet of floor space"); National Council on Crime and Delinquency, Model Act for the Protection of Rights of Prisoners, 18 Crime & Delinquency 4, 10 (1972) ("not less than fifty square feet of floor space in any confined sleeping area"). Most of these studies recommend even more space for inmates who must spend more than 10 hours per day in their cells. * * *

* * * [T]he State cannot impose punishment that violates "the evolving standards of decency that mark the progress of a maturing society." For me, the legislative judgment and the consistent conclusions by those who have studied the problem provide considerable evidence that those standards condemn imprisonment in conditions so crowded that serious harm will result. The record amply demonstrates that those conditions are present here. It is surely not disputed that SOCF is severely overcrowded. The prison is operating at 38% above its design capacity.[5] It is also significant that some two-thirds of the inmates at SOCF are serving lengthy or life sentences, for, as we have said elsewhere, "the length of confinement cannot be ignored in deciding whether the confinement meets constitutional standards." *Hutto v. Finney,* 437 U.S. 678, 686 (1978). Nor is double celling a short-term response to a temporary problem. The trial court found, and it is not contested, that double celling, if not enjoined, will continue for the foreseeable future. The trial court also found that most of the double-celled inmates spend most of their time in their cells.[6]

It is simply not true, as the majority asserts, that "there is no evidence that double celling under these circumstances either inflicts unnecessary or wanton pain or is grossly disproportionate to the severity of crimes warranting imprisonment." The District Court concluded from the record before it that long exposure to these conditions will "*necessarily*" involve "excess limitation of general movement as well as physical and mental injury . . . ."[7] And of course, of all the judges who have been involved in this case, the trial judge is the only one who has actually visited the prison. That is simply an additional reason to give in this case the deference we have always accorded to the careful conclusions of the finder of fact. * * * I see no reason to set aside

5. * * * Rated capacity, the majority argues, is irrelevant because of the numerous factors that influence prison population. Actually, it is the factors that influence prison population that are irrelevant. By definition, rated capacity represents "the number of inmates that a confinement unit, facility, or entire correctional agency can hold." 3 National Institute of Justice, American Prisons and Jails 41–42 (1980). If prison population, for whatever reason, exceeds rated capacity, then the prison must accommodate more people than it is designed to hold—in short, it is overcrowded. And the greater the proportion by which prison population exceeds rated capacity, the more severe the overcrowding. I certainly do not suggest that rated capacity is the only factor to be considered in determining whether a prison is unconstitutionally overcrowded, but I fail to understand why the majority feels free to dismiss it entirely.

6. * * * I read the District Court's opinion as finding that although most in-

mates are permitted to be out of their cells up to 14 hours each day, conditions in the prison are such that many choose not to do so.

        * * *

7. In its findings, the District Court credited expert testimony that "close quarters" would likely increase the incidence of schizophrenia and other mental disorders and that the double celling imposed in this case had led to increases in tension and in "aggressive and anti-social characteristics." There is no dispute that the prison was violent even before it became overcrowded, and that it has become more so. I do not assert that violence has increased due to *double celling.* I accept the finding of the District Court that violence has increased due to *overcrowding.* Plainly, this case involves much more than just the constitutionality of double celling *per se.* * * *

the concurrent conclusions of two courts that the overcrowding and double celling here in issue are sufficiently severe that they will, if left unchecked, cause deterioration in respondents' mental and physical health. These conditions in my view go well beyond contemporary standards of decency and therefore violate the Eighth and Fourteenth Amendments. I would affirm the judgment of the Court of Appeals.

* * *

Questions and Points for Discussion

1. In Bell v. Wolfish, 441 U.S. 520, 99 S.Ct. 1861 (1979), the Supreme Court also rejected a constitutional challenge to double-celling. In that case, the plaintiffs were pretrial detainees incarcerated in a federal correctional center. The rooms in that facility, which had about seventy-five square feet of floor space, were designed to house one person, but when the facility became crowded, the correctional authorities instituted double-celling. The plaintiffs contended in their § 1983 suit that this double-celling inflicted punishment on them in violation of their due process rights. Although the lower courts agreed with this contention, the Supreme Court, in a decision written by Justice (now Chief Justice) Rehnquist, did not:

> We disagree with both the District Court and the Court of Appeals that there is some sort of "one man, one cell" principle lurking in the Due Process Clause of the Fifth Amendment. While confining a given number of people in a given amount of space in such a manner as to cause them to endure genuine privations and hardship over an extended period of time might raise serious questions under the Due Process Clause as to whether those conditions amounted to punishment, nothing even approaching such hardship is shown by this record.

> Detainees are required to spend only seven or eight hours each day in their rooms, during most or all of which they presumably are sleeping. The rooms provide more than adequate space for sleeping. During the remainder of the time, the detainees are free to move between their rooms and the common area. While "double-bunking" may have taxed some of the equipment or particular facilities in certain of the common areas, this does not mean that the conditions at the MCC failed to meet the standards required by the Constitution. Our conclusion in this regard is further buttressed by the detainees' length of stay at the MCC. Nearly all of the detainees are released within 60 days. We simply do not believe that requiring a detainee to share toilet facilities and this admittedly rather small sleeping place with another person for generally a maximum period of 60 days violates the Constitution.

Id. at 542–43, 99 S.Ct. at 1875–76.

2. The conditions of confinement at the correctional facilities discussed in *Rhodes v. Chapman* and *Bell v. Wolfish* are to be contrasted with the conditions in the Arkansas prisons described by the Supreme Court in the course of its opinion in Hutto v. Finney, 437 U.S. 678, 98 S.Ct. 2565 (1978).

The routine conditions that the ordinary Arkansas convict had to endure were characterized by the District Court as "a dark and evil world completely alien to the free world." That characterization was amply supported by the evidence.[3] The punishments for misconduct not serious enough to result in punitive isolation were cruel, unusual, and unpredictable. It is the discipline known as "punitive isolation" that is most relevant for present purposes.

Confinement in punitive isolation was for an indeterminate period of time. An average of 4, and sometimes as many as 10 or 11, prisoners were crowded into windowless 8'x10' cells containing no furniture other than a source of water and a toilet that could only be flushed from outside the cell. At night the prisoners were given mattresses to spread on the floor. Although some prisoners suffered from infectious diseases such as hepatitis and venereal disease, mattresses were removed and jumbled together each morning, then returned to the cells at random in the evening. Prisoners in isolation received fewer than 1,000 calories a day;[7] their meals consisted primarily of 4-inch squares of "grue," a substance created by mashing meat, potatoes, oleo, syrup, vegetables, eggs, and seasoning into a paste and baking the mixture in a pan.

Id. at 681–83, 98 S.Ct. at 2568–70.

The Supreme Court observed in *Hutto* that the district court was correct in concluding that the above conditions inflicted cruel and unusual punishment on Arkansas prisoners. The Court also approved the district court's order directing that inmates be confined in punitive isolation for no more than thirty days. The Court observed as follows:

It is perfectly obvious that every decision to remove a particular inmate from the general prison population for an indeterminate period could not be characterized as cruel and unusual. If new conditions of confinement are not materially different from those affecting other prisoners, a transfer for the duration of a prisoner's sentence might be completely unobjectionable and well within the authority of the prison administrator. It is equally plain, however, that the length of confine-

3. The administrators of Arkansas' prison system evidently tried to operate their prisons at a profit. Cummins Farm, the institution at the center of this litigation, required its 1,000 inmates to work in the fields 10 hours a day, six days a week, using mule-drawn tools and tending crops by hand. The inmates were sometimes required to run to and from the fields, with a guard in an automobile or on horseback driving them on. They worked in all sorts of weather, so long as the temperature was above freezing, sometimes in unsuitably light clothing or without shoes.

The inmates slept together in large, 100-man barracks, and some convicts, known as "creepers," would slip from their beds to crawl along the floor, stalking their sleeping enemies. In one 18-month period, there were 17 stabbings, all but 1 occurring in the barracks. Homosexual rape was so common and uncontrolled that some potential victims dared not sleep; instead they would leave their beds and spend the night clinging to the bars nearest the guards' station.

7. A daily allowance of 2,700 calories is recommended for the average male between 23 and 50. National Academy of Sciences, Recommended Dietary Allowances, Appendix (8th rev. ed. 1974). Prisoners in punitive isolation are less active than the average person; but a mature man who spends 12 hours a day lying down and 12 hours a day simply sitting or standing consumes approximately 2,000 calories a day. Id., at 27.

ment cannot be ignored in deciding whether the confinement meets constitutional standards. A filthy, overcrowded cell and a diet of "grue" might be tolerable for a few days and intolerably cruel for weeks or months.

*   *   *

The order is supported by the interdependence of the conditions producing the violation. The vandalized cells and the atmosphere of violence were attributable, in part, to overcrowding and to deep-seated enmities growing out of months of constant daily friction. The 30–day limit will help to correct these conditions.

Id. at 686–88, 98 S.Ct. at 2571–72.

Other cases discussing the types of onerous conditions that have prevailed in many of the nation's correctional facilities include: Howard v. Adkison, 887 F.2d 134 (8th Cir.1989) (inmate's cell, food slot, and mattress covered with "human waste;" no cleaning supplies provided; laundry not cleaned for five months); Ramos v. Lamm, 639 F.2d 559 (10th Cir.1980) (cells with 31.5 to 49 square feet of living space; poor ventilation; sewage accumulating in cells because of leaking pipes; rodent and insect infestation; trash and decaying food on the floors in inmate living areas; soiled bedding; rotten food, dirt, and rodent droppings on the kitchen floors); Gates v. Collier, 501 F.2d 1291 (5th Cir.1974) (water supply contaminated with sewage; exposed electrical wiring; lack of sufficient fire fighting equipment; broken windows; cells known as the "dark holes," which were devoid of lights, a sink, a toilet, or furniture and which had a hole in the floor for bodily wastes; inmates placed in the dark hole without clothes or bedding; brutal methods of discipline employed, including the forced administration of milk of magnesia to inmates and turning fans on wet and naked inmates); Anderson v. Redman, 429 F.Supp. 1105 (D.Del.1977) (because of crowding, inmates housed in the prison hospital, staff dining room, libraries, and TV rooms; receiving cells designed for eight men housing sixty during the day and twenty-four at night; inmates having to stand on mattresses while using the toilet and sometimes urinating on them; inmates having to share beds and sleep under bunk beds; homosexual rape "the norm" in the receiving rooms); Pugh v. Locke, 406 F.Supp. 318 (M.D. Ala.1976) (mattresses in hallways and next to urinals; one toilet for over two hundred men in one part of the prison; broken and unscreened windows; food infested with insects; inmates in wheelchairs left unsupervised in areas only accessible by stairway; up to six inmates housed in each "isolation cell" with thirty-two square feet of living space, no beds, no lights, no running water, and a hole in the floor for a toilet, fed only once a day and often given no utensils, and permitted to shower only every eleven days); and Costello v. Wainwright, 397 F.Supp. 20 (M.D.Fla.1975), affirmed, 525 F.2d 1239 (5th Cir.1976) (Florida prison system had a "normal capacity" of 7000 and an "emergency capacity" of 8300 inmates, but housed 10,300 inmates; as a result, four inmates were sometimes housed in one-person cells. See the photograph on the next page which was included in the appendix to the court's opinion, id. at 40.).

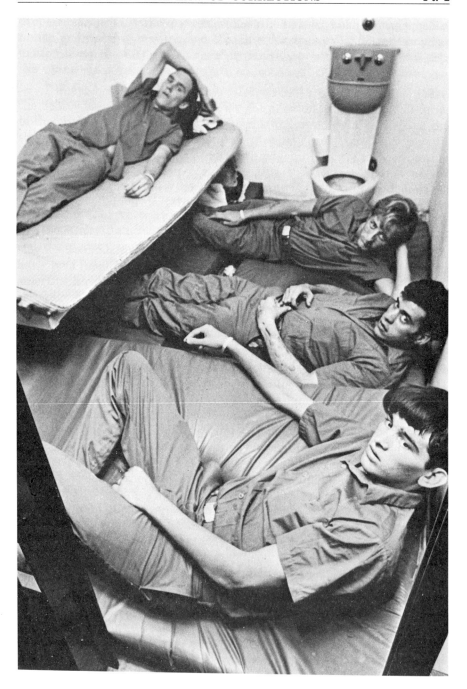

3. The lower courts have generally held that prisoners have no constitutional right to be rehabilitated while they are in prison. See, e.g., Rizzo v. Dawson, 778 F.2d 527, 531 (9th Cir.1985); Lovell v. Brennan, 566 F.Supp. 672, 689 (D.Me.1983), affirmed, 728 F.2d 560 (1st Cir.1984). In other words, the government is not obligated to take affirmative steps to

reform prisoners and make them better persons. Thus, it has been held that correctional officials need not make educational, vocational, and other rehabilitative programs available to inmates. See, e.g., Hoptowit v. Ray, 682 F.2d 1237, 1254–55 (9th Cir.1982); Spencer v. Snell, 626 F.Supp. 1096, 1096–97 (E.D.Mo.1986), affirmed, 786 F.2d 1171 (8th Cir.1986).

On the other hand, some courts have concurred with Justice Brennan's observation in *Rhodes v. Chapman* that correctional officials do have a constitutional duty to prevent inmates from becoming much worse and more criminally inclined because of the conditions of their confinement. See, e.g., Doe v. District of Columbia, 697 F.2d 1115, 1124 n. 23 (D.C.Cir. 1983) (while inmates have no constitutional right to rehabilitation, they do have the right "not to be subjected to conditions (apart from the reasonable incidents of incarceration itself) that reduce their ability to earn a living and otherwise to conduct themselves in the world following their release"). Compare the remarks of Justice (now Chief Justice) Rehnquist in his order staying, pending appellate review, an injunction issued to alleviate prison crowding: "[N]obody promised them a rose garden; and I know nothing in the Eighth Amendment which requires that they be housed in a manner most pleasing to them, or considered even by most knowledgeable penal authorities to be likely to avoid confrontation, psychological depression, and the like." Atiyeh v. Capps, 449 U.S. 1312, 1315–16, 101 S.Ct. 829, 831– 32 (1981) (Rehnquist, Circuit Justice). See also Newman v. Alabama, 559 F.2d 283, 291 (5th Cir.1977) ("We decline to enter this uncharted bog. If the state furnishes its prisoners with reasonably adequate food, clothing, shelter, sanitation, medical care, and personal safety, so as to avoid the imposition of cruel and unusual punishment, that ends its obligations under Amendment Eight. The Constitution does not require that prisoners, as individuals or as a group, be provided with any and every amenity which some person may think is needed to avoid mental, physical, and emotional deterioration.").

4. *Class Exercise:* Divide the class in two. Half of the class will represent the prisoners who are contesting the constitutionality of the conditions of confinement in the prison described below. The other half of the class will represent the prison officials, who are defending the constitutionality of the prison conditions.

The prison in question is a maximum-security penitentiary, which was built in 1871. Designed to hold up to 1200 inmates, the prison now houses 1918 inmates. The majority of these inmates are serving lengthy sentences for serious and violent offenses—murder, rape, and armed robbery.

Fifty-six per cent of the inmates in the prison are double-celled; the rest are mostly confined in segregation or protective-custody units. A study introduced at the time of the hearing on the prisoners' motion for injunctive relief in 1981 revealed that there was single-celling in 80% of the cells in state prisons and 90% of the cells in federal prisons.

The inmates who are double-celled in the prison are housed in the west and south cellhouses. The trial judge visited the prison and measured the cells in each cellhouse. The dimensions of the cells in the west cellhouse are about 75 inches by 124 inches, which means that there is about 64.5 square feet of living space. The cells in the south cellhouse are smaller—

64 inches by 125 inches—with about 55.5 square feet of living space. A state statute requires that new or renovated state institutions provide at least 50 square feet of cell space per person.

Each cell contains a bunkbed, a sink, a toilet, and a chest of drawers or cardboard boxes used for storage. Each inmate is permitted to keep twenty-five books, twelve records, a tape player, a radio, and a television set in the cell. Because of the accoutrements in each cell, inmates are often left with only nine square feet or less of room in which to stand or walk in their cells. Consequently, an inmate generally has to climb onto the bunkbed to avoid being touched when his cellmate is moving within or attempting to leave the cell.

The lighting in each cell is dim, since each cell only has one fluorescent bulb in the ceiling. Although each cell is fairly clean, a "borderline stench" pervades the cellhouses because of the number of people confined in such a small area. Problems with ventilation are exacerbated by the inmates, who cover the air vents in their cells to keep out roaches and dust.

The amount of time that each inmate spends in his cell varies, depending on whether the inmate has a work or school assignment. On average, inmates housed in the south cellhouse spend a minimum of about twenty hours in their cells, while those in the west cellhouse are confined in their cells eighteen to twenty hours a day.

Only about half of the prisoners have work or school assignments. Even when an inmate is assigned a job, the job is often a makeweight one, created just to give the inmate something to do. For example, one inmate testified that he is assigned to do lawnwork in a small area of the prison grounds. His job only takes about fifteen minutes to complete, and for the rest of the four-hour shift, he just pushes dirt into a pile and then rakes down the pile.

A licensed physician can be found at the prison seven days a week, twenty-four hours a day. In addition, the prison employs a full-time dentist, dental assistants, an x-ray technician, and a full-time pharmacist. The kitchen and dining rooms are clean, and the food fed the inmates is nutritious and edible.

A number of inmates testified about the problems caused by double-celling, problems which were compounded by the lack of a classification program to ensure the proper placement of inmates in double cells. Some of the problems alluded to include the following: (1) the fear of homosexual attack by a cellmate; (2) violence or threats of violence directed against a cellmate because of a cellmate's refusal to share personal property, his failure to keep the cell clean and neat, or for other reasons; (3) an inability to study, both because of a lack of desks and because, with so many inmates housed in the cellhouse, there is a great deal of noise; (4) interference with religious practices, such as inmates turning on the television while their cellmates are praying; and (5) tension, frustration, and anger caused by the loss of privacy, particularly in the use of the toilet, and in the housing together of people with different religious beliefs, moral standards, gang affiliations, ages, and idiosyncrasies. One fifty-three-year-old inmate, for example, talked about his irritation with his sixteen-year-old cellmate, who frequently sat in the corner masturbating before the picture of a nude woman.

A number of experts testified at trial for the prisoners and the prison officials as did a court-appointed expert witness. Many of the experts testified that crowding increases death and illness rates, the percentage of psychiatric commitments, and institutional violence. The warden of the prison, however, testified that during his three years as warden, the number of violent incidents had decreased by fifty percent.

Chapter 16

PAROLE RELEASE AND PROBATION AND PAROLE REVOCATION

Parole boards determine inmates' suitability for release from prison so that they can serve the remainder of their sentences outside prison walls. In recent years, public demands to "get tough on criminals" have led many legislatures to abolish their parole systems, adopting mandatory and determinate sentencing statutes in their stead. Under these statutes, the amount of time that a criminal offender will be incarcerated for a crime is determined either exclusively by the legislature or by the legislature and the sentencing judge. See Chapter 5, pages 151–158, supra. Since discretion as to when inmates will be released from prison is eliminated once their sentences are imposed, parole boards are unnecessary.

Despite the current trend towards abolishing parole, some jurisdictions have still retained their parole systems. In the sections which follow, the constitutional standards which must be adhered to when deciding whether or not to release inmates on parole and whether or not to revoke their parole are discussed. Because the Supreme Court's decision in Morrissey v. Brewer, 408 U.S. 471, 92 S.Ct. 2593 (1972), which concerned parole revocation proceedings, informed its later decisions concerning parole release hearings, we will begin with a discussion of the subject of parole revocation.

A. PROBATION AND PAROLE REVOCATION

MORRISSEY v. BREWER

Supreme Court of the United States, 1972.
408 U.S. 471, 92 S.Ct. 2593, 33 L.Ed.2d 484.

MR. CHIEF JUSTICE BURGER delivered the opinion of the Court.

We granted certiorari in this case to determine whether the Due Process Clause of the Fourteenth Amendment requires that a State afford an individual some opportunity to be heard prior to revoking his parole.

Petitioner Morrissey was convicted of false drawing or uttering of checks in 1967 pursuant to his guilty plea, and was sentenced to not more than seven years' confinement. He was paroled from the Iowa State Penitentiary in June 1968. Seven months later, at the direction of his parole officer, he was arrested in his home town as a parole violator and incarcerated in the county jail. One week later, after review of the parole officer's written report, the Iowa Board of Parole revoked Morrissey's parole, and he was returned to the penitentiary located about 100 miles from his home. Petitioner asserts he received no hearing prior to revocation of his parole.

The parole officer's report on which the Board of Parole acted shows that petitioner's parole was revoked on the basis of information that he had violated the conditions of parole by buying a car under an assumed name and operating it without permission, giving false statements to police concerning his address and insurance company after a minor accident, obtaining credit under an assumed name, and failing to report his place of residence to his parole officer. The report states that the officer interviewed Morrissey, and that he could not explain why he did not contact his parole officer despite his effort to excuse this on the ground that he had been sick. Further, the report asserts that Morrissey admitted buying the car and obtaining credit under an assumed name, and also admitted being involved in the accident. The parole officer recommended that his parole be revoked because of "his continual violating of his parole rules."

[The Court then discussed the claim of petitioner Booher, who also contended that his parole had been revoked without a hearing.]

After exhausting state remedies, both petitioners filed habeas corpus petitions in the United States District Court for the Southern District of Iowa alleging that they had been denied due process because their paroles had been revoked without a hearing. The State responded by arguing that no hearing was required. The District Court held on the basis of controlling authority that the State's failure to accord a hearing prior to parole revocation did not violate due process. On appeal, the two cases were consolidated.

The Court of Appeals, dividing 4 to 3, held that due process does not require a hearing. * * *

* * *

I

Before reaching the issue of whether due process applies to the parole system, it is important to recall the function of parole in the correctional process.

During the past 60 years, the practice of releasing prisoners on parole before the end of their sentences has become an integral part of the penological system. Rather than being an *ad hoc* exercise of

clemency, parole is an established variation on imprisonment of convicted criminals. Its purpose is to help individuals reintegrate into society as constructive individuals as soon as they are able, without being confined for the full term of the sentence imposed. It also serves to alleviate the costs to society of keeping an individual in prison.
* * *

To accomplish the purpose of parole, those who are allowed to leave prison early are subjected to specified conditions for the duration of their terms. These conditions restrict their activities substantially beyond the ordinary restrictions imposed by law on an individual citizen. Typically, parolees are forbidden to use liquor or to have associations or correspondence with certain categories of undesirable persons. Typically, also they must seek permission from their parole officers before engaging in specified activities, such as changing employment or living quarters, marrying, acquiring or operating a motor vehicle, traveling outside the community, and incurring substantial indebtedness. Additionally, parolees must regularly report to the parole officer to whom they are assigned and sometimes they must make periodic written reports of their activities.

* * *

The enforcement leverage that supports the parole conditions derives from the authority to return the parolee to prison to serve out the balance of his sentence if he fails to abide by the rules. In practice, not every violation of parole conditions automatically leads to revocation. Typically, a parolee will be counseled to abide by the conditions of parole, and the parole officer ordinarily does not take steps to have parole revoked unless he thinks that the violations are serious and continuing so as to indicate that the parolee is not adjusting properly and cannot be counted on to avoid antisocial activity. * * *

Implicit in the system's concern with parole violations is the notion that the parolee is entitled to retain his liberty as long as he substantially abides by the conditions of his parole. The first step in a revocation decision thus involves a wholly retrospective factual question: whether the parolee has in fact acted in violation of one or more conditions of his parole. Only if it is determined that the parolee did violate the conditions does the second question arise: should the parolee be recommitted to prison or should other steps be taken to protect society and improve chances of rehabilitation? The first step is relatively simple; the second is more complex. The second question involves the application of expertise by the parole authority in making a prediction as to the ability of the individual to live in society without committing antisocial acts. This part of the decision, too, depends on facts, and therefore it is important for the board to know not only that some violation was committed but also to know accurately how many and how serious the violations were. Yet this second step, deciding what to do about the violation once it is identified, is not purely factual but also predictive and discretionary.

If a parolee is returned to prison, he usually receives no credit for the time "served" on parole. Thus, the returnee may face a potential of substantial imprisonment.

II

We begin with the proposition that the revocation of parole is not part of a criminal prosecution and thus the full panoply of rights due a defendant in such a proceeding does not apply to parole revocations. Parole arises after the end of the criminal prosecution, including imposition of sentence. * * * Revocation deprives an individual, not of the absolute liberty to which every citizen is entitled, but only of the conditional liberty properly dependent on observance of special parole restrictions.

We turn, therefore, to the question whether the requirements of due process in general apply to parole revocations. * * * Whether any procedural protections are due depends on the extent to which an individual will be "condemned to suffer grievous loss." The question is not merely the "weight" of the individual's interest, but whether the nature of the interest is one within the contemplation of the "liberty or property" language of the Fourteenth Amendment. * * *

We turn to an examination of the nature of the interest of the parolee in his continued liberty. The liberty of a parolee enables him to do a wide range of things open to persons who have never been convicted of any crime. The parolee has been released from prison based on an evaluation that he shows reasonable promise of being able to return to society and function as a responsible, self-reliant person. Subject to the conditions of his parole, he can be gainfully employed and is free to be with family and friends and to form the other enduring attachments of normal life. Though the State properly subjects him to many restrictions not applicable to other citizens, his condition is very different from that of confinement in a prison. He may have been on parole for a number of years and may be living a relatively normal life at the time he is faced with revocation.[9] The parolee has relied on at least an implicit promise that parole will be revoked only if he fails to live up to the parole conditions. In many cases, the parolee faces lengthy incarceration if his parole is revoked.

We see, therefore, that the liberty of a parolee, although indeterminate, includes many of the core values of unqualified liberty and its termination inflicts a "grievous loss" on the parolee and often on others. It is hardly useful any longer to try to deal with this problem in terms of whether the parolee's liberty is a "right" or a "privilege." By whatever name, the liberty is valuable and must be seen as within the protection of the Fourteenth Amendment. Its termination calls for some orderly process, however informal.

9. See, *e.g., Murray v. Page,* 429 F.2d 1359 (CA10 1970) (parole revoked after eight years; 15 years remaining on original term).

Turning to the question what process is due, we find that the State's interests are several. The State has found the parolee guilty of a crime against the people. That finding justifies imposing extensive restrictions on the individual's liberty. Release of the parolee before the end of his prison sentence is made with the recognition that with many prisoners there is a risk that they will not be able to live in society without committing additional antisocial acts. Given the previous conviction and the proper imposition of conditions, the State has an overwhelming interest in being able to return the individual to imprisonment without the burden of a new adversary criminal trial if in fact he has failed to abide by the conditions of his parole.

Yet, the State has no interest in revoking parole without some informal procedural guarantees. Although the parolee is often formally described as being "in custody," the argument cannot even be made here that summary treatment is necessary as it may be with respect to controlling a large group of potentially disruptive prisoners in actual custody. Nor are we persuaded by the argument that revocation is so totally a discretionary matter that some form of hearing would be administratively intolerable. A simple factual hearing will not interfere with the exercise of discretion. * * *

* * * The parolee is not the only one who has a stake in his conditional liberty. Society has a stake in whatever may be the chance of restoring him to normal and useful life within the law. Society thus has an interest in not having parole revoked because of erroneous information or because of an erroneous evaluation of the need to revoke parole, given the breach of parole conditions. And society has a further interest in treating the parolee with basic fairness: fair treatment in parole revocations will enhance the chance of rehabilitation by avoiding reactions to arbitrariness.

Given these factors, most States have recognized that there is no interest on the part of the State in revoking parole without any procedural guarantees at all. What is needed is an informal hearing structured to assure that the finding of a parole violation will be based on verified facts and that the exercise of discretion will be informed by an accurate knowledge of the parolee's behavior.

III

We now turn to the nature of the process that is due, bearing in mind that the interest of both State and parolee will be furthered by an effective but informal hearing. In analyzing what is due, we see two important stages in the typical process of parole revocation.

(a) Arrest of Parolee and Preliminary Hearing. The first stage occurs when the parolee is arrested and detained, usually at the direction of his parole officer. The second occurs when parole is formally revoked. There is typically a substantial time lag between the arrest and the eventual determination by the parole board whether parole should be revoked. Additionally, it may be that the parolee is

arrested at a place distant from the state institution, to which he may
be returned before the final decision is made concerning revocation.
Given these factors, due process would seem to require that some
minimal inquiry be conducted at or reasonably near the place of the
alleged parole violation or arrest and as promptly as convenient after
arrest while information is fresh and sources are available. Such an
inquiry should be seen as in the nature of a "preliminary hearing" to
determine whether there is probable cause or reasonable ground to
believe that the arrested parolee has committed acts that would constitute a violation of parole conditions.

In our view, due process requires that after the arrest, the determination that reasonable ground exists for revocation of parole should be
made by someone not directly involved in the case. It would be unfair
to assume that the supervising parole officer does not conduct an
interview with the parolee to confront him with the reasons for revocation before he recommends an arrest. It would also be unfair to
assume that the parole officer bears hostility against the parolee that
destroys his neutrality; realistically the failure of the parolee is in a
sense a failure for his supervising officer. However, we need make no
assumptions one way or the other to conclude that there should be an
uninvolved person to make this preliminary evaluation of the basis for
believing the conditions of parole have been violated. The officer
directly involved in making recommendations cannot always have
complete objectivity in evaluating them.[14] * * *

This independent officer need not be a judicial officer. The granting and revocation of parole are matters traditionally handled by
administrative officers. * * * It will be sufficient, therefore, in the
parole revocation context, if an evaluation of whether reasonable cause
exists to believe that conditions of parole have been violated is made by
someone such as a parole officer other than the one who has made the
report of parole violations or has recommended revocation. A State
could certainly choose some other independent decisionmaker to perform this preliminary function.

With respect to the preliminary hearing before this officer, the
parolee should be given notice that the hearing will take place and that
its purpose is to determine whether there is probable cause to believe
he has committed a parole violation. The notice should state what
parole violations have been alleged. At the hearing the parolee may
appear and speak in his own behalf; he may bring letters, documents,
or individuals who can give relevant information to the hearing officer.
On request of the parolee, a person who has given adverse information
on which parole revocation is to be based is to be made available for
questioning in his presence. However, if the hearing officer determines
that an informant would be subjected to risk of harm if his identity

14. This is not an issue limited to bad
motivation. "Parole agents are human,
and it is possible that friction between the
agent and parolee may have influenced the
agent's judgment." 4 Attorney General's
Survey on Release Procedures: Parole 246
(1939).

were disclosed, he need not be subjected to confrontation and cross-examination.

The hearing officer shall have the duty of making a summary, or digest, of what occurs at the hearing in terms of the responses of the parolee and the substance of the documents or evidence given in support of parole revocation and of the parolee's position. Based on the information before him, the officer should determine whether there is probable cause to hold the parolee for the final decision of the parole board on revocation. Such a determination would be sufficient to warrant the parolee's continued detention and return to the state correctional institution pending the final decision. * * * "[T]he decision maker should state the reasons for his determination and indicate the evidence he relied on . . . ." but it should be remembered that this is not a final determination calling for "formal findings of fact and conclusions of law." No interest would be served by formalism in this process; informality will not lessen the utility of this inquiry in reducing the risk of error.

(b) The Revocation Hearing. There must also be an opportunity for a hearing, if it is desired by the parolee, prior to the final decision on revocation by the parole authority. This hearing must be the basis for more than determining probable cause; it must lead to a final evaluation of any contested relevant facts and consideration of whether the facts as determined warrant revocation. The parolee must have an opportunity to be heard and to show, if he can, that he did not violate the conditions, or, if he did, that circumstances in mitigation suggest that the violation does not warrant revocation. The revocation hearing must be tendered within a reasonable time after the parolee is taken into custody. A lapse of two months, as respondents suggest occurs in some cases, would not appear to be unreasonable.

We cannot write a code of procedure; that is the responsibility of each State. Most States have done so by legislation, others by judicial decision usually on due process grounds. Our task is limited to deciding the minimum requirements of due process. They include (a) written notice of the claimed violations of parole; (b) disclosure to the parolee of evidence against him; (c) opportunity to be heard in person and to present witnesses and documentary evidence; (d) the right to confront and cross-examine adverse witnesses (unless the hearing officer specifically finds good cause for not allowing confrontation); (e) a "neutral and detached" hearing body such as a traditional parole board, members of which need not be judicial officers or lawyers; and (f) a written statement by the factfinders as to the evidence relied on and reasons for revoking parole. We emphasize there is no thought to equate this second stage of parole revocation to a criminal prosecution in any sense. It is a narrow inquiry; the process should be flexible enough to consider evidence including letters, affidavits, and other material that would not be admissible in an adversary criminal trial.

We do not reach or decide the question whether the parolee is entitled to the assistance of retained counsel or to appointed counsel if he is indigent.

We have no thought to create an inflexible structure for parole revocation procedures. The few basic requirements set out above, which are applicable to future revocations of parole, should not impose a great burden on any State's parole system. Control over the required proceedings by the hearing officers can assure that delaying tactics and other abuses sometimes present in the traditional adversary trial situation do not occur. Obviously a parolee cannot relitigate issues determined against him in other forums, as in the situation presented when the revocation is based on conviction of another crime.

* * *

We reverse and remand to the Court of Appeals for further proceedings consistent with this opinion.

* * *

MR. JUSTICE BRENNAN, with whom MR. JUSTICE MARSHALL joins, concurring in the result.

I agree that a parole may not be revoked, consistently with the Due Process Clause, unless the parolee is afforded, first, a preliminary hearing at the time of arrest to determine whether there is probable cause to believe that he has violated his parole conditions and, second, a final hearing within a reasonable time to determine whether he has, in fact, violated those conditions and whether his parole should be revoked. * * *

The Court, however, states that it does not now decide whether the parolee is also entitled at each hearing to the assistance of retained counsel or of appointed counsel if he is indigent. *Goldberg v. Kelly,* 397 U.S. 254 (1970),[a] nonetheless plainly dictates that he at least "must be allowed to retain an attorney if he so desires." As the Court said there, "Counsel can help delineate the issues, present the factual contentions in an orderly manner, conduct cross-examination, and generally safeguard the interests of" his client. The only question open under our precedents is whether counsel must be furnished the parolee if he is indigent.

MR. JUSTICE DOUGLAS, dissenting in part.

* * *

If a violation of a condition of parole is involved, rather than the commission of a new offense, there should not be an arrest of the parolee and his return to the prison or to a local jail.[8] Rather, notice of

[a. *Goldberg v. Kelly* dealt with the procedural safeguards which must attend the termination of welfare benefits.]

8. As Judge Skelly Wright said in *Hyser v. Reed,* 115 U.S.App.D.C. 254, 291, 318 F.2d 225, 262 (1963) (concurring in part and dissenting in part):

"Where serious violations of parole have been committed, the parolee will have been arrested by local or federal authorities on charges stemming from those violations. Where the violation of parole is not serious, no reason appears why he should be incarcerated before hearing. If, of course, the parolee willfully fails to

the alleged violation should be given to the parolee and a time set for a hearing. The hearing should not be before the parole officer, as he is the one who is making the charge and "there is inherent danger in combining the functions of judge and advocate." Moreover, the parolee should be entitled to counsel. As the Supreme Court of Oregon said in *Perry v. Williard* [247 Ore. 145, 427 P.2d 1020 (Or.1967)], "A hearing in which counsel is absent or is present only on behalf of one side is inherently unsatisfactory if not unfair. Counsel can see that relevant facts are brought out, vague and insubstantial allegations discounted, and irrelevancies eliminated."

[Justice Douglas then stated that at the parole revocation hearing, the parolee should have the right to make arguments on his own behalf, to present evidence, and to confront his accusers.]

Questions and Points for Discussion

1. In Gagnon v. Scarpelli, 411 U.S. 778, 93 S.Ct. 1756 (1973), the Supreme Court concluded that before individuals on probation can have their probation revoked, they must be afforded the procedural protections outlined in *Morrissey v. Brewer*. The Court in *Gagnon* also addressed a question left unanswered by the Court in *Morrissey*—whether indigent individuals have the right to be represented by appointed counsel during parole or probation revocation hearings. Pertinent portions of the Court's discussion of this issue are set forth below:

> [W]e think that the Court of Appeals erred in accepting respondent's contention that the State is under a constitutional duty to provide counsel for indigents in all probation or parole revocation cases. While such a rule has the appeal of simplicity, it would impose direct costs and serious collateral disadvantages without regard to the need or the likelihood in a particular case for a constructive contribution by counsel. In most cases, the probationer or parolee has been convicted of committing another crime or has admitted the charges against him. And while in some cases he may have a justifiable excuse for the violation or a convincing reason why revocation is not the appropriate disposition, mitigating evidence of this kind is often not susceptible of proof or is so simple as not to require either investigation or exposition by counsel.

> The introduction of counsel into a revocation proceeding will alter significantly the nature of the proceeding. If counsel is provided for the probationer or parolee, the State in turn will normally provide its own counsel; lawyers, by training and disposition, are advocates and bound by professional duty to present all available evidence and arguments in support of their clients' positions and to contest with vigor all adverse evidence and views. The role of the hearing body itself, aptly described in *Morrissey* as being "predictive and discretionary" as well as factfinding, may become more akin to that of a judge at a trial, and less attuned to the rehabilitative needs of the individual

appear for his hearing, this in itself would justify issuance of the warrant."

probationer or parolee. In the greater self-consciousness of its quasi-judicial role, the hearing body may be less tolerant of marginal deviant behavior and feel more pressure to reincarcerate than to continue nonpunitive rehabilitation. Certainly, the decisionmaking process will be prolonged, and the financial cost to the State—for appointed counsel, counsel for the State, a longer record, and the possibility of judicial review—will not be insubstantial.

* * *

We thus find no justification for a new inflexible constitutional rule with respect to the requirement of counsel. We think, rather, that the decision as to the need for counsel must be made on a case-by-case basis in the exercise of a sound discretion by the state authority charged with responsibility for administering the probation and parole system. Although the presence and participation of counsel will probably be both undesirable and constitutionally unnecessary in most revocation hearings, there will remain certain cases in which fundamental fairness—the touchstone of due process—will require that the State provide at its expense counsel for indigent probationers or parolees.

It is neither possible nor prudent to attempt to formulate a precise and detailed set of guidelines to be followed in determining when the providing of counsel is necessary to meet the applicable due process requirements. The facts and circumstances in preliminary and final hearings are susceptible of almost infinite variation, and a considerable discretion must be allowed the responsible agency in making the decision. Presumptively, it may be said that counsel should be provided in cases where, after being informed of his right to request counsel, the probationer or parolee makes such a request, based on a timely and colorable claim (i) that he has not committed the alleged violation of the conditions upon which he is at liberty; or (ii) that, even if the violation is a matter of public record or is uncontested, there are substantial reasons which justified or mitigated the violation and make revocation inappropriate, and that the reasons are complex or otherwise difficult to develop or present. In passing on a request for the appointment of counsel, the responsible agency also should consider, especially in doubtful cases, whether the probationer appears to be capable of speaking effectively for himself. In every case in which a request for counsel at a preliminary or final hearing is refused, the grounds for refusal should be stated succinctly in the record.

Id. at 787–88, 790–91, 93 S.Ct. at 1762–63, 1763–64.

After *Gagnon,* the question still remains whether probationers or parolees have the right to be represented by a retained attorney in probation and parole revocation hearings where an indigent would have no right to appointed counsel. Id. at 783 n. 6, 93 S.Ct. at 1760 n. 6. How would you resolve this question?

2. Since *Morrissey,* the Supreme Court has concluded that parolees have no right to an initial preliminary hearing before being transferred back to prison for a suspected parole violation when they have already been convicted of the crime upon which the parole revocation is based. The

conviction itself provides the requisite probable cause to believe the parolees have violated the terms and conditions of their parole. Moody v. Daggett, 429 U.S. 78, 86 n. 7, 97 S.Ct. 274, 278 n. 7 (1976).

The Court in *Moody* also clarified the meaning of its observation in *Morrissey* that the opportunity for a final revocation hearing must be afforded a parolee "within a reasonable time after the parolee is taken into custody." 408 U.S. at 488, 92 S.Ct. at 2603. The parolee in *Moody* had pled guilty to two crimes—manslaughter and second-degree murder—committed while he was on parole for rape. For these two homicides, he was sentenced to ten years in prison. Following his convictions, the United States Board of Parole issued, but did not execute, a parole violator warrant. The issuance of the warrant simply held the parolee's rape sentence and parole term in abeyance while he served his other sentences.

Hoping that he could serve any imprisonment resulting from the revocation of his parole at the same time that he was serving the prison sentences for the homicides, the parolee asked the parole board to immediately execute the parole violator warrant and decide whether or not to revoke his parole. The parole board refused. The parolee then filed a habeas corpus action contending that any revocation of his parole was barred by the board's failure to afford him the prompt parole revocation hearing guaranteed by *Morrissey*.

The Supreme Court, however, disagreed, holding that a parolee has no right to a parole revocation hearing unless and until he is taken into custody as a parole violator. The Court also opined that delaying the parole revocation hearing made sense in a case such as this one, since the parolee's conduct while in prison might be revealing to a parole board later deciding whether parole revocation was warranted.

3.   Many states only require that a parole violation be established by a preponderance of the evidence. See, e.g., Baker v. Pennsylvania Board of Probation and Parole, 108 Pa.Cmwlth. 409, 411, 529 A.2d 1164, 1165 (1987). Most courts therefore agree that a parolee's acquittal on criminal charges will generally not bar the revocation of parole for the crime of which the parolee was acquitted. See, e.g., Martin v. Pennsylvania Board of Probation and Parole, 96 Pa.Cmwlth. 321, 325–26, 507 A.2d 907, 909–10 (1986); People ex rel. Matthews by Greenberg v. New York State Division of Parole, 58 N.Y.2d 196, 203, 460 N.Y.S.2d 746, 447 N.E.2d 689, 692 (1983). The courts reason that even if the government is unable to prove the parolee's guilt beyond a reasonable doubt, the government may be able to meet the lesser burden of proof applicable in parole revocation proceedings.

One might think that if the government decides to proceed first with a parole revocation hearing and is unable to meet its burden of proof at that hearing, collateral estoppel principles would bar a subsequent criminal prosecution based on the same alleged underlying conduct. Some of the courts which have addressed this issue, however, have concluded that for somewhat undefined public policy reasons, the outcome of a parole revocation hearing should not dictate whether or not a criminal prosecution will go forward. See, e.g., People v. Fagan, 66 N.Y.2d 815, 498 N.Y.S.2d 335, 489 N.E.2d 222 (1985); Washington v. Dupard, 93 Wash.2d 268, 276–77, 609 P.2d 961, 965 (1980). The courts have defended this conclusion in a general fashion, simply mentioning that different procedures and different purposes characterize the two proceedings.

4. A parole revocation hearing may raise several issues, including the following: (1) Did the parolee violate a condition of his or her parole? See, e.g., Arciniega v. Freeman, 404 U.S. 4, 92 S.Ct. 22 (1971) (per curiam) (construing a condition that the parolee not associate with other ex-convicts as not encompassing contacts with ex-convicts employed at the same restaurant). (2) Is the condition violated constitutional? (3) Does the violation of the condition warrant the revocation of the parolee's parole and his or her return to prison? Similar questions will also be addressed during probation revocation proceedings except that a judge, rather than a parole board, will decide whether the probationer's sentence must be altered because of the violation of a condition of probation.

The Federal Probation Act, the pertinent portion of which—18 U.S.C. § 3563—can be found on page 123, supra, exemplifies the types of conditions that can be imposed as conditions of probation or parole. Judges have traditionally been accorded broad discretion when imposing probation conditions as have parole boards when imposing parole conditions. As long as the conditions are reasonably related to the penological goals served by probation or parole, the conditions have generally been upheld. See, e.g., United States v. Stine, 675 F.2d 69 (3d Cir.1982) (condition of probation that defendant undergo psychological counseling not an unconstitutional impingement on his right to privacy); People v. Roth, 154 Mich.App. 257, 397 N.W.2d 196 (1986) (subjecting probationer convicted of obtaining a controlled substance by fraud to unannounced urinalysis tests as a condition of probation was lawful); People v. Mills, 81 Cal.App.3d 171, 182, 146 Cal. Rptr. 411, 417 (1978) (probation condition prohibiting defendant, who had been convicted of a sex offense involving a child, from being in the company of any young people under the age of 18 unless a responsible adult was present did not unconstitutionally infringe on his freedom of association). At times, however, probation or parole conditions have been deemed unconstitutional. See, e.g., State v. Mosburg, 13 Kan.App.2d 257, 768 P.2d 313 (1989) and the cases cited therein (requiring that defendants convicted of child abuse or neglect not become pregnant while on probation or parole violated their constitutional right to privacy); Wiggins v. State, 386 So.2d 46 (Fla.App.1980) (probation condition prohibiting defendants, who claimed they had committed forgeries and burglary so they could feed their illegitimate children, from having sexual intercourse with anyone with whom they were not married was invalid); Inman v. State, 124 Ga.App. 190, 183 S.E.2d 413 (1971) (unconstitutional to require defendant, who was convicted of marijuana possession, to keep his hair short as a condition of probation).

Where the courts have sometimes had different views is on the question of the constitutionality of a condition prohibiting the defendant from entering or remaining in a particular geographical area during the probation or parole period. Compare Edwards v. State, 173 Ga.App. 589, 327 S.E.2d 559 (1985) (condition banning defendant from seven counties for 10–year probation period upheld) with People v. Beach, 147 Cal.App.3d 612, 621–23, 195 Cal.Rptr. 381, 386–87 (1983) (probation condition requiring defendant, who had been found guilty of involuntary manslaughter, to leave the community where she had lived for 24 years unconstitutionally impinged on her right to intrastate travel and to possess and enjoy her personal property). In your opinion, would a probation or parole condition prohibiting a defendant who had been convicted of prostitution from entering portions of the city where prostitution was prevalent be constitutional? Compare State v. Morgan, 389 So.2d 364 (La.1980) with In re White, 97 Cal.App.3d 141, 158 Cal.Rptr. 562 (1979).

5. Not only are the rights of probationers and parolees limited because of the restrictions placed on them as conditions of probation or parole, but they are also limited because the Constitution affords them less protection than that extended to individuals not subject to probation or parole supervision. That the Constitution may apply differently to probationers, for example, is evident from Griffin v. Wisconsin, 483 U.S. 868, 107 S.Ct. 3164 (1987). In that case, a probationer's apartment was searched by probation officers after they received a call from a police detective informing them that the probationer might have guns in his apartment. Several police officers were present during the search. During the search, a gun was found which led to the probationer's conviction of the crime of possession of a firearm by a convicted felon.

The probation officers did not first procure a warrant before conducting their search, nor could they have obtained such a warrant since they lacked probable cause. Nonetheless, the Supreme Court held that the search did not violate any fourth amendment rights of the probationer. In arriving at this conclusion, the Court, in an opinion written by Justice Scalia, balanced the need for warrantless searches and searches without probable cause in this context against the intrusiveness of such searches. The Court's balancing analysis is set forth below:

> A warrant requirement would interfere to an appreciable degree with the probation system, setting up a magistrate rather than the probation officer as the judge of how close a supervision the probationer requires. Moreover, the delay inherent in obtaining a warrant would make it more difficult for probation officials to respond quickly to evidence of misconduct and would reduce the deterrent effect that the possibility of expeditious searches would otherwise create. By way of analogy, one might contemplate how parental custodial authority would be impaired by requiring judicial approval for search of a minor child's room. And on the other side of the equation—the effect of dispensing with a warrant upon the probationer: Although a probation officer is not an impartial magistrate, neither is he the police officer who normally conducts searches against the ordinary citizen. He is an employee of the State Department of Health and Social Services who, while assuredly charged with protecting the public interest, is also supposed to have in mind the welfare of the probationer. * * *

> * * *

> We think that the probation regime would also be unduly disrupted by a requirement of probable cause. To take the facts of the present case, it is most unlikely that the unauthenticated tip of a police officer—bearing, as far as the record shows, no indication whether its basis was firsthand knowledge or, if not, whether the firsthand source

was reliable, and merely stating that Griffin "had or might have" guns in his residence, not that he certainly had them—would meet the ordinary requirement of probable cause. But this is different from the ordinary case in two related respects: First, even more than the requirement of a warrant, a probable-cause requirement would reduce the deterrent effect of the supervisory arrangement. The probationer would be assured that so long as his illegal (and perhaps socially dangerous) activities were sufficiently concealed as to give rise to no more than reasonable suspicion, they would go undetected and uncorrected. The second difference is * * * we deal with a situation in which there is an ongoing supervisory relationship—and one that is not, or at least not entirely, adversarial—between the object of the search and the decisionmaker.

In such circumstances it is both unrealistic and destructive of the whole object of the continuing probation relationship to insist upon the same degree of demonstrable reliability of particular items of supporting data, and upon the same degree of certainty of violation, as is required in other contexts. In some cases—especially those involving drugs or illegal weapons—the probation agency must be able to act based upon a lesser degree of certainty than the Fourth Amendment would otherwise require in order to intervene before a probationer does damage to himself or society.

Id. at 876–879, 107 S.Ct. at 3169–71.

In *Griffin,* the Court emphasized that the search by the probation officers had been conducted under a state regulation authorizing probation officers to search a probationer's home whenever there were "reasonable grounds" to believe contraband was in the home. What if Wisconsin had not had a regulation authorizing the warrantless search of a probationer's home as long as there were "reasonable grounds" to believe there was contraband in the home? See United States v. Giannetta, 711 F.Supp. 1144, 1147–48 (D.Me.1989) (such a search constitutional where, as a condition of probation, the defendant was required to permit searches of his home). What if such warrantless searches were neither authorized by a state statute or regulation, nor mentioned as a condition of probation in the court order placing the defendant on probation? Would the warrantless search be constitutional under these circumstances if the probation officer had reasonable and articulable suspicion that there was contraband in the probationer's home? What if the probation officer had no particular reason to believe that there was contraband in the probationer's home, but wanted to make sure and searched the home without a warrant? Would the search violate the fourth amendment rights of the probationer?

B. PAROLE RELEASE

In the case which follows, the Supreme Court considered the implications of Morrissey v. Brewer, 408 U.S. 471, 92 S.Ct. 2593 (1972), supra page 518, to parole release decisions. The Court addressed two questions: does due process require that certain procedures be followed when determining whether or not an inmate should be released on parole, and if so, what procedural safeguards are constitutionally mandated?

GREENHOLTZ v. INMATES OF NEBRASKA PENAL AND CORRECTIONAL COMPLEX

Supreme Court of the United States, 1979.
442 U.S. 1, 99 S.Ct. 2100, 60 L.Ed.2d 668.

MR. CHIEF JUSTICE BURGER delivered the opinion of the Court.

* * *

I

Inmates of the Nebraska Penal and Correctional Complex brought a class action under 42 U.S.C. § 1983 claiming that they had been unconstitutionally denied parole by the Board of Parole. The suit was filed against the individual members of the Board. One of the claims of the inmates was that the statutes and the Board's procedures denied them procedural due process.

* * *

The procedures used by the Board to determine whether to grant or deny discretionary parole arise partly from statutory provisions and partly from the Board's practices. Two types of hearings are conducted: initial parole review hearings and final parole hearings. At least once each year initial review hearings must be held for every inmate, regardless of parole eligibility. At the initial review hearing, the Board examines the inmate's entire preconfinement and postconfinement record. Following that examination it provides an informal hearing; no evidence as such is introduced, but the Board interviews the inmate and considers any letters or statements that he wishes to present in support of a claim for release.

If the Board determines from its examination of the entire record and the personal interview that he is not yet a good risk for release, it denies parole, informs the inmate why release was deferred and makes recommendations designed to help correct any deficiencies observed. It also schedules another initial review hearing to take place within one year.

If the Board determines from the file and the initial review hearing that the inmate is a likely candidate for release, a final hearing is scheduled. The Board then notifies the inmate of the month in which the final hearing will be held; the exact day and time is posted on a bulletin board that is accessible to all inmates on the day of the hearing. At the final parole hearing, the inmate may present evidence, call witnesses and be represented by private counsel of his choice. It is not a traditional adversary hearing since the inmate is not permitted to hear adverse testimony or to cross-examine witnesses who present such evidence. However, a complete tape recording of the hearing is preserved. If parole is denied, the Board furnishes a written statement of the reasons for the denial within 30 days.

II

The District Court held that the procedures used by the Parole Board did not satisfy due process. It concluded that the inmate had the same kind of constitutionally protected "conditional liberty" interest, recognized by this Court in *Morrissey v. Brewer,* 408 U.S. 471 (1972), held that some of the procedures used by the Parole Board fell short of constitutional guarantees, and prescribed several specific requirements.

On appeal, the Court of Appeals for the Eighth Circuit agreed with the District Court that the inmate had a *Morrissey*-type, conditional liberty interest at stake and also found a statutorily defined, protectible interest in Neb.Rev.Stat. § 83–1,114 (1976). The Court of Appeals, however, modified the procedures required by the District Court as follows:

(a) When eligible for parole each inmate must receive a full formal hearing;

(b) the inmate is to receive written notice of the precise time of the hearing reasonably in advance of the hearing, setting forth the factors which may be considered by the Board in reaching its decision;

(c) subject only to security considerations, the inmate may appear in person before the Board and present documentary evidence in his own behalf. Except in unusual circumstances, however, the inmate has no right to call witnesses in his own behalf;

(d) A record of the proceedings, capable of being reduced to writing, must be maintained; and

(e) within a reasonable time after the hearing, the Board must submit a full explanation, in writing, of the facts relied upon and reasons for the Board's action denying parole.

* * *

III

* * *

There is no constitutional or inherent right of a convicted person to be conditionally released before the expiration of a valid sentence. The natural desire of an individual to be released is indistinguishable from the initial resistance to being confined. But the conviction, with all its procedural safeguards, has extinguished that liberty right: "[G]iven a valid conviction, the criminal defendant has been constitutionally deprived of his liberty."

Decisions of the Executive Branch, however serious their impact, do not automatically invoke due process protection; there simply is no constitutional guarantee that all executive decisionmaking must comply with standards that assure error-free determinations. This is especially true with respect to the sensitive choices presented by the administrative decision to grant parole release.

* * *

IV

Respondents suggest two theories to support their view that they have a constitutionally protected interest in a parole determination which calls for the process mandated by the Court of Appeals. First, they claim that a reasonable entitlement is created whenever a state provides for the *possibility* of parole. Alternatively, they claim that the language in Nebraska's statute, Neb.Rev.Stat. § 83–1,114(1) (1976), creates a legitimate expectation of parole, invoking due process protections.

A

In support of their first theory, respondents rely heavily on *Morrissey v. Brewer,* 408 U.S. 471 (1972), where we held that a parole-revocation determination must meet certain due process standards. See also *Gagnon v. Scarpelli,* 411 U.S. 778 (1973). They argue that the ultimate interest at stake both in a parole-revocation decision and in a parole determination is conditional liberty and that since the underlying interest is the same the two situations should be accorded the same constitutional protection.

The fallacy in respondents' position is that parole *release* and parole *revocation* are quite different. There is a crucial distinction between being deprived of a liberty one has, as in parole, and being denied a conditional liberty that one desires. The parolees in *Morrissey* (and probationers in *Gagnon*) were at liberty and as such could "be gainfully employed and [were] free to be with family and friends and to form the other enduring attachments of normal life." The inmates here, on the other hand, are confined and thus subject to all of the necessary restraints that inhere in a prison.

A second important difference between discretionary parole *release* from confinement and *termination* of parole lies in the nature of the decision that must be made in each case. As we recognized in *Morrissey,* the parole-revocation determination actually requires two decisions: whether the parolee in fact acted in violation of one or more conditions of parole and whether the parolee should be recommitted either for his or society's benefit. "The first step in a revocation decision thus involves a wholly retrospective factual question."

The parole-release decision, however, is more subtle and depends on an amalgam of elements, some of which are factual but many of which are purely subjective appraisals by the Board members based upon their experience with the difficult and sensitive task of evaluating the advisability of parole release. Unlike the revocation decision, there is no set of facts which, if shown, mandate a decision favorable to the individual. The parole determination, like a prisoner-transfer decision, may be made

> "for a variety of reasons and often involve[s] no more than informed predictions as to what would best serve [correctional purposes] or the safety and welfare of the inmate."

The decision turns on a "discretionary assessment of a multiplicity of imponderables, entailing primarily what a man is and what he may become rather than simply what he has done."

* * *

That the state holds out the *possibility* of parole provides no more than a mere hope that the benefit will be obtained. To that extent the general interest asserted here is no more substantial than the inmate's hope that he will not be transferred to another prison, a hope which is not protected by due process. *Meachum v. Fano,* 427 U.S., at 225.

B

Respondents' second argument is that the Nebraska statutory language itself creates a protectible expectation of parole. They rely on the section which provides in part:

"Whenever the Board of Parole considers the release of a committed offender who is eligible for release on parole, it shall order his release unless it is of the opinion that his release should be deferred because:

"(a) There is a substantial risk that he will not conform to the conditions of parole;

"(b) His release would depreciate the seriousness of his crime or promote disrespect for law;

"(c) His release would have a substantially adverse effect on institutional discipline; or

"(d) His continued correctional treatment, medical care, or vocational or other training in the facility will substantially enhance his capacity to lead a law-abiding life when released at a later date." Neb.Rev.Stat. § 83–1,114(1) (1976).[5]

Respondents emphasize that the structure of the provision together with the use of the word "shall" binds the Board of Parole to release an inmate unless any one of the four specifically designated reasons are found. In their view, the statute creates a presumption that parole release will be granted, and that this in turn creates a legitimate expectation of release absent the requisite finding that one of the justifications for deferral exists.

* * *

* * * We can accept respondents' view that the expectancy of release provided in this statute is entitled to some measure of constitutional protection. However, we emphasize that this statute has unique structure and language and thus whether any other state statute provides a protectible entitlement must be decided on a case-by-case basis. We therefore turn to an examination of the statutory procedures to determine whether they provide the process that is due in these circumstances.

5. The statute also provides a list of 14 explicit factors and one catchall factor that the Board is obligated to consider in reaching a decision. Neb.Rev.Stat. §§ 83–1,114(2)(a)–(n) (1976). See Appendix to this opinion.

* * * The function of legal process, as that concept is embodied in the Constitution, and in the realm of factfinding, is to minimize the risk of erroneous decisions. Because of the broad spectrum of concerns to which the term must apply, flexibility is necessary to gear the process to the particular need; the quantum and quality of the process due in a particular situation depend upon the need to serve the purpose of minimizing the risk of error.

* * *

It is important that we not overlook the ultimate purpose of parole which is a component of the long-range objective of rehabilitation. The fact that anticipations and hopes for rehabilitation programs have fallen far short of expectations of a generation ago need not lead states to abandon hopes for those objectives; states may adopt a balanced approach in making parole determinations, as in all problems of administering the correctional systems. The objective of rehabilitating convicted persons to be useful, law-abiding members of society can remain a goal no matter how disappointing the progress. But it will not contribute to these desirable objectives to invite or encourage a continuing state of adversary relations between society and the inmate.

Procedures designed to elicit specific facts, such as those required in *Morrissey, Gagnon,* and *Wolff,* are not necessarily appropriate to a Nebraska parole determination. Merely because a statutory expectation exists cannot mean that in addition to the full panoply of due process required to convict and confine there must also be repeated, adversary hearings in order to continue the confinement. However, since the Nebraska Parole Board provides at least one and often two hearings every year to each eligible inmate, we need only consider whether the additional procedures mandated by the Court of Appeals are required * * *.

Two procedures mandated by the Court of Appeals are particularly challenged by the Board: [6] the requirement that a formal hearing be held for every inmate, and the requirement that every adverse parole decision include a statement of the evidence relied upon by the Board.

The requirement of a hearing as prescribed by the Court of Appeals in all cases would provide at best a negligible decrease in the risk of error. When the Board defers parole after the initial review hearing, it does so because examination of the inmate's file and the personal interview satisfies it that the inmate is not yet ready for conditional release. * * * At the Board's initial interview hearing, the inmate is permitted to appear before the Board and present letters and statements on his own behalf. He is thereby provided with an effective

---

6. The Board also objects to the Court of Appeals' order that it provide written notice reasonably in advance of the hearing together with a list of factors that might be considered. At present the Board informs the inmate in advance of the month during which the hearing will be held, thereby allowing time to secure letters or statements; on the day of the hearing it posts notice of the exact time. There is no claim that either the timing of the notice or its substance seriously prejudices the inmate's ability to prepare adequately for the hearing. The present notice is constitutionally adequate.

opportunity first, to insure that the records before the Board are in fact the records relating to his case; and second, to present any special considerations demonstrating why he is an appropriate candidate for parole. Since the decision is one that must be made largely on the basis of the inmate's files, this procedure adequately safeguards against serious risks of error and thus satisfies due process.[7]

Next, we find nothing in the due process concepts as they have thus far evolved that requires the Parole Board to specify the particular "evidence" in the inmate's file or at his interview on which it rests the discretionary determination that an inmate is not ready for conditional release. The Board communicates the reason for its denial as a guide to the inmate for his future behavior. To require the parole authority to provide a summary of the evidence would tend to convert the process into an adversary proceeding and to equate the Board's parole-release determination with a guilt determination. The Nebraska statute contemplates, and experience has shown, that the parole-release decision is, as we noted earlier, essentially an experienced prediction based on a host of variables. The Board's decision is much like a sentencing judge's choice—provided by many states—to grant or deny probation following a judgment of guilt, a choice never thought to require more than what Nebraska now provides for the parole-release determination. The Nebraska procedure affords an opportunity to be heard, and when parole is denied it informs the inmate in what respects he falls short of qualifying for parole; this affords the process that is due under these circumstances. The Constitution does not require more.

Accordingly, the judgment of the Court of Appeals is reversed and the case is remanded for further proceedings consistent with this opinion.[8]

* * *

APPENDIX TO OPINION OF THE COURT

The statutory factors that the Board is required to take into account in deciding whether or not to grant parole are the following:

(a) The offender's personality, including his maturity, stability, sense of responsibility and any apparent development in his personality which may promote or hinder his conformity to law;

7. The only other possible risk of error is that relevant adverse factual information in the inmate's file is wholly inaccurate. But the Board has discretion to make available to the inmate any information "[w]henever the board determines that it will facilitate the parole hearing." Neb. Rev.Stat. § 83–1,112(1) (1976). Apparently the inmates are satisfied with the way this provision is administered since there is no issue before us regarding access to their files.

8. The Court of Appeals in its order required the Board to permit all inmates to appear and present documentary support for parole. Since both of these requirements were being complied with prior to this litigation, the Board did not seek review of those parts of the court's order and the validity of those requirements is not before us. The Court of Appeals also held that due process did not provide a right to cross-examine adverse witnesses or a right to present favorable witnesses. The practice of taping the hearings also was declared adequate. Those issues are not before us and we express no opinion on them.

(b) The adequacy of the offender's parole plan;

(c) The offender's ability and readiness to assume obligations and undertake responsibilities;

(d) The offender's intelligence and training;

(e) The offender's family status and whether he has relatives who display an interest in him or whether he has other close and constructive associations in the community;

(f) The offender's employment history, his occupational skills, and the stability of his past employment;

(g) The type of residence, neighborhood or community in which the offender plans to live;

(h) The offender's past use of narcotics, or past habitual and excessive use of alcohol;

(i) The offender's mental or physical makeup, including any disability or handicap which may affect his conformity to law;

(j) The offender's prior criminal record, including the nature and circumstances, recency and frequency of previous offenses;

(k) The offender's attitude toward law and authority;

(l) The offender's conduct in the facility, including particularly whether he has taken advantage of the opportunities for self-improvement, whether he has been punished for misconduct within six months prior to his hearing or reconsideration for parole release, whether any reductions of term have been forfeited, and whether such reductions have been restored at the time of hearing or reconsideration;

(m) The offender's behavior and attitude during any previous experience of probation or parole and the recency of such experience; and

(n) Any other factors the board determines to be relevant. Neb. Rev.Stat. § 83–1,114(2) (1976).

MR. JUSTICE POWELL, concurring in part and dissenting in part.

[For the reasons set forth in Justice Marshall's dissenting opinion, Justice Powell observed that when a state sets up a system of parole, it creates a liberty interest in parole release protected by the due process clause, regardless of the language of the parole release statute. In addition, Justice Powell concluded that the notice provided Nebraska inmates of their impending parole release hearings did not comport with due process.]

MR. JUSTICE MARSHALL, with whom MR. JUSTICE BRENNAN and MR. JUSTICE STEVENS join, dissenting in part.

My disagreement with the Court's opinion extends to both its analysis of respondents' liberty interest and its delineation of the procedures constitutionally required in parole release proceedings.
* * *

* * *

I

A

It is self-evident that all individuals possess a liberty interest in being free from physical restraint. Upon conviction for a crime, of course, an individual may be deprived of this liberty to the extent authorized by penal statutes. But when a State enacts a parole system, and creates the possibility of release from incarceration upon satisfaction of certain conditions, it necessarily qualifies that initial deprivation. In my judgment, it is the existence of this system which allows prison inmates to retain their protected interest in securing freedoms available outside prison. Because parole release proceedings clearly implicate this retained liberty interest, the Fourteenth Amendment requires that due process be observed, irrespective of the specific provisions in the applicable parole statute.

* * *

* * * [T]he Court discerns two distinctions between "parole *release* and parole *revocation*" * * *.

First, the Court finds a difference of constitutional dimension between a deprivation of liberty one has and a denial of liberty one desires. While there is obviously some difference, it is not one relevant to the established constitutional inquiry. Whether an individual currently enjoys a particular freedom has no bearing on whether he possesses a protected interest in securing and maintaining that liberty. The Court acknowledged as much in *Wolff v. McDonnell* when it held that the loss of good-time credits implicates a liberty interest even though the forfeiture only deprived the prisoner of freedom he expected to obtain sometime hence. * * *

The Court's distinction is equally unrelated to the nature or gravity of the interest affected in parole release proceedings. The nature of a criminal offender's interest depends on the range of freedoms available by virtue of the parole system's existence. On that basis, *Morrissey* afforded constitutional recognition to a parolee's interest because his freedom on parole includes "many of the core values of unqualified liberty." This proposition is true regardless of whether the inmate is presently on parole or seeking parole release. As the Court of Appeals for the Second Circuit has recognized, "[w]hether the immediate issue be release or revocation, the stakes are the same: conditional freedom versus incarceration." *United States ex rel. Johnson* v. *Chairman of New York State Board of Parole*, 500 F.2d 925, 928 (1974).

The Court's second justification for distinguishing between parole release and parole revocation is based on the "nature of the decision that must be made in each case." The majority apparently believes that the interest affected by parole release proceedings is somehow diminished if the administrative decision may turn on "subjective evaluations." Yet the Court nowhere explains why the *nature of the decisional process* has even the slightest bearing in assessing the *nature* *of the interest* that this process may terminate. Indeed, the Court's reasoning here is flatly inconsistent with its subsequent holding that respondents do have a protected liberty interest under Nebraska's parole statutes, which require a decision that is "subjective in part and predictive in part." * * *

But even assuming the subjective nature of the decision-making process were relevant to due process analysis in general, this consideration does not adequately distinguish the processes of granting and revoking parole. Contrary to the Court's assertion that the decision to revoke parole is predominantly a " 'retrospective factual question,' " *Morrissey* recognized that only the first step in the revocation decision can be so characterized. And once it is

> "determined that the parolee did violate the conditions [of parole, a] second question arise[s]: should the parolee be recommitted to prison or should other steps be taken to protect society and improve chances of rehabilitation? The first step is relatively simple; the second is more complex. The second question involves the application of expertise by the parole authority in making a prediction as to the ability of the individual to live in society without committing antisocial acts. . . . [T]his second step, deciding what to do about the violation once it is identified, *is not purely factual but also predictive and discretionary.*"

Morrissey thus makes clear that the parole revocation decision includes a decisive subjective component. Moreover, to the extent parole release proceedings hinge on predictive determinations, those assessments are necessarily predicated on findings of fact.[8] Accordingly, the presence of subjective considerations is a completely untenable basis for distinguishing the interests at stake here from the liberty interest recognized in *Morrissey.*

* * *

II

A

I also cannot subscribe to the Court's assessment of the procedures necessary to safeguard respondents' liberty interest. Although the majority purports to rely on *Morrissey v. Brewer* and the test enunciated in *Mathews v. Eldridge,* 424 U.S. 319 (1976), its application of these standards is fundamentally deficient in several respects.

To begin with, the Court focuses almost exclusively on the likelihood that a particular procedure will significantly reduce the risk of error in parole release proceedings. Yet *Mathews* advances *three* factors to be considered in determining the specific dictates of due process:

---

8. The Nebraska statutes, in particular, demonstrate the factual nature of the parole release inquiry. One provision enumerates factual considerations such as the inmate's intelligence, family status, and employment history, which bear upon the four predictive determinations underlying the ultimate parole decision.

"First, the private interest that will be affected by the official action; second, the risk of an erroneous deprivation of such interest through the procedures used, and the probable value, if any, of additional or substitute procedural safeguards; and finally, the Government's interest, including the function involved and the fiscal and administrative burdens that the additional or substitute procedural requirement would entail."

By ignoring the other two factors set forth in *Mathews*, the Court skews the inquiry in favor of the Board. For example, the Court does not identify any justification for the Parole Board's refusal to provide inmates with specific advance notice of the hearing date or with a list of factors that may be considered. Nor does the Board demonstrate that it would be unduly burdensome to provide a brief summary of the evidence justifying the denial of parole. To be sure, these measures may cause some inconvenience, but "the Constitution recognizes higher values than speed and efficiency." Similarly lacking in the Court's analysis is any recognition of the private interest affected by the Board's action. Certainly the interest in being released from incarceration is of sufficient magnitude to have some bearing on the process due.

The second fundamental flaw in the Court's analysis is that it incorrectly evaluates the only factor actually discussed. The contribution that additional safeguards will make to reaching an accurate decision necessarily depends on the risk of error inherent in existing procedures. Here, the Court finds supplemental procedures to be inappropriate because it assumes existing procedures adequately reduce the likelihood that an inmate's files will contain incorrect information which could lead to an erroneous decision. No support is cited for this assumption, and the record affords none. In fact, researchers and courts have discovered many substantial inaccuracies in inmate files, and evidence in the instant case revealed similar errors.[15] Both the District Court and the Court of Appeals found additional procedures necessary to decrease the margin of error in Nebraska's parole release proceedings. Particularly since the Nebraska statutes tie the parole decision to a number of highly specific factual inquiries, I see no basis in the record for rejecting the lower courts' conclusion.

Finally, apart from avoiding the risk of actual error, this Court has stressed the importance of adopting procedures that preserve the appearance of fairness and the confidence of inmates in the decisionmaking process. The Chief Justice recognized in *Morrissey* that "fair

---

15. In this case, for example, the form notifying one inmate that parole had been denied indicated that the Board believed he should enlist in a self-improvement program at the prison. But in fact, the inmate was already participating in all such programs available. Such errors in parole files are not unusual. *E.g., Kohlman v. Norton*, 380 F.Supp. 1073 (Conn.1974) (parole denied because file erroneously indicated that applicant had used gun in committing robbery); *State v. Pohlabel*, 61 N.J. Super. 242, 160 A.2d 647 (1960) (files erroneously showed that prisoner was under a life sentence in another jurisdiction); Hearings on H.R. 13118 et al. before Subcommittee No. 3 of the House Judiciary Committee, 92d Cong., 2d Sess., pt. VII–A, p. 451 (1972) (testimony of Dr. Willard Gaylin: "I have seen black men listed as white and Harvard graduates listed with borderline IQ's").

treatment in parole revocations will enhance the chance of rehabilitation by avoiding reactions to arbitrariness," a view shared by legislators, courts, the American Bar Association, and other commentators. This consideration is equally significant whether liberty interests are extinguished in parole release or parole revocation proceedings. * * *

B

Applying the analysis of *Morrissey* and *Mathews*, I believe substantially more procedural protection is necessary in parole release proceedings than the Court requires. The types of safeguards that should be addressed here, however, are limited by the posture of this case.[17] Thus, only three specific issues need be considered.

While the question is close, I agree with the majority that a formal hearing is not always required when an inmate first becomes eligible for discretionary parole. The Parole Board conducts an initial parole review hearing once a year for every inmate, even before the inmate is eligible for release. Although the scope of this hearing is limited, inmates are allowed to appear and present letters or statements supporting their case. If the Board concludes that an eligible inmate is a good candidate for release, it schedules a final and substantially more formal hearing.

The Court of Appeals directed the Parole Board to conduct such a formal hearing as soon as an inmate becomes eligible for parole, even where the likelihood of a favorable decision is negligible * * *. From a practical standpoint, this relief offers no appreciable advantage to the inmates. If the Board would not have conducted a final hearing under current procedures, inmates gain little from a requirement that such a hearing be held, since the evidence almost certainly would be insufficient to justify granting release. * * * The inmates' interest in this modification of the Board's procedures is thus relatively slight.[18]   Yet

17. In accordance with the majority opinion, I do not address whether the Court of Appeals was correct in holding that the Nebraska Parole Board may not abandon the procedures it already provides. These safeguards include permitting inmates to appear and present documentary support at hearings, and providing a statement of reasons when parole is denied or deferred. Because the inmates failed to seek review of the Court of Appeals' decision, I also express no view on whether it correctly held that the Board's practice of allowing inmates to present witnesses and retain counsel for final parole hearings was not constitutionally compelled. Finally, it would be inappropriate to consider the suggestion advanced here for the first time that inmates should be allowed access to their files in order to correct factual inaccuracies.

Nevertheless, the range of protections currently afforded does affect whether additional procedures are constitutionally compelled. The specific dictates of due process, of course, depend on what a particular situation demands. Nebraska's use of formal hearings when the possibility of granting parole is substantial and informal hearings in other cases, for example, combined with provision of a statement of reasons for adverse decisions, obviously reduces the need for supplemental procedures.

18. Although a formal hearing at the point of initial eligibility would reduce the risk of error and enhance the appearance of fairness, providing a summary of essential evidence and reasons, together with allowing inmates to appear at informal hearings, decreases the justification for re-

the burden imposed on the Parole Board by the additional formal hearings would be substantial. Accordingly, I believe the Board's current practice of combining both formal and informal hearings is constitutionally sufficient.

However, a different conclusion is warranted with respect to the hearing notices given inmates. The Board currently informs inmates only that it will conduct an initial review or final parole hearing during a particular month within the next year. The notice does not specify the day or hour of the hearing. Instead, inmates must check a designated bulletin board each morning to see if their hearing is scheduled for that day. In addition, the Board refuses to advise inmates of the criteria relevant in parole release proceedings, despite a state statute expressly listing 14 factors the Board must consider and 4 permissible reasons for denying parole.

Finding these procedures insufficient, the District Court and the Court of Appeals ordered that each inmate receive written advance notice of the time set for his hearing, along with a list of factors the Board may consider.[19] Although the Board has proffered no justification for refusing to institute these procedures, the Court sets aside the relief ordered below on the ground that "[t]here is no claim that either the timing of the notice or its substance seriously prejudices the inmate's ability to prepare adequately for the hearing." But respondents plainly have contended throughout this litigation that reasonable advance notice is necessary to enable them to organize their evidence, call the witnesses permitted by the Board, and notify private counsel allowed to participate in the hearing, and the courts below obviously agreed. Given the significant private interests at stake, and the importance of reasonable notice in preserving the appearance of fairness, I see no reason to depart here from this Court's longstanding recognition that adequate notice is a fundamental requirement of due process * * *.

Finally, I would require the Board to provide a statement of the crucial evidence on which it relies in denying parole. At present, the Parole Board merely uses a form letter noting the general reasons for its decision. In ordering the Board to furnish as well a summary of the essential facts underlying the denial, the Court of Appeals made clear that " 'detailed findings of fact are not required.' " The majority here, however, believes even this relief to be unwarranted, because it might render parole proceedings more adversary and equate unfavorable decisions with a determination of guilt.

The Court nowhere explains how these particular considerations are relevant to the inquiry required by *Morrissey* and *Mathews*. More-

quiring the Board to conduct formal hearings in every case.

19. The courts below found that 72 hours' advance notice ordinarily would enable prisoners to prepare for their appearances. The Court of Appeals further determined that the statutory criteria were sufficiently specific that the Board need only include a list of those criteria with the hearing notices or post such a list in public areas throughout the institution.

over, it is difficult to believe that subsequently disclosing the factual justification for a decision will render the proceeding more adversary, especially when the Board already provides a general statement of reasons. And to the extent unfavorable parole decisions resemble a determination of guilt, the Board has no legitimate interest in concealing from an inmate the conduct or failings of which he purportedly is guilty.

While requiring a summation of the essential evidence might entail some administrative inconvenience, in neither *Morrissey v. Brewer, Gagnon v. Scarpelli,* nor *Wolff v. McDonnell* did the Court find that this factor justified denying a written statement of the essential evidence and the reasons underlying a decision. It simply is not unduly

> "burdensome to give reasons when reasons exist. Whenever an application . . . is denied . . . there should be some reason for the decision. It can scarcely be argued that government would be crippled by a requirement that the reason be communicated to the person most directly affected by the government's action." *Board of Regents v. Roth,* 408 U.S. 564, 591 (1972) (MARSHALL, J., dissenting).

And an inability to provide any reasons suggests that the decision is, in fact, arbitrary.

Moreover, considerations identified in *Morrissey* and *Mathews* militate in favor of requiring a statement of the essential evidence. Such a requirement would direct the Board's focus to the relevant statutory criteria and promote more careful consideration of the evidence. It would also enable inmates to detect and correct inaccuracies that could have a decisive impact.[23] And the obligation to justify a decision publicly would provide the assurance, critical to the appearance of fairness, that the Board's decision is not capricious. Finally, imposition of this obligation would afford inmates instruction on the measures needed to improve their prison behavior and prospects for parole, a consequence surely consistent with rehabilitative goals. Balancing these considerations against the Board's minimal interest in avoiding this procedure, I am convinced that the Fourteenth Amendment requires the Parole Board to provide inmates a statement of the essential evidence as well as a meaningful explanation of the reasons for denying parole release.[25]

23. The preprinted list of reasons for denying parole is unlikely to disclose these types of factual errors. Out of 375 inmates denied parole during a 6–month period, the only reason given 285 of them was: "Your continued correctional treatment, vocational, educational, or job assignment in the facility will substantially enhance your capacity to lead a law-abiding life when released at a later date." Although the denial forms also include a list of six "[r]ecommendations for correcting deficien-

cies," such as "[e]xhibit some responsibility and maturity," the evidence at trial showed that all six items were checked on 370 of the 375 forms, regardless of the facts of the particular case.

25. This statement of reasons and the summary of essential evidence should be provided to all inmates actually eligible for parole, whether the adverse decision is rendered following an initial review or a final parole hearing.

Because the Court's opinion both depreciates inmates fundamental liberty interest in securing parole release and sanctions denial of the most rudimentary due process protection, I respectfully dissent.

Questions and Points for Discussion

1. In Board of Pardons v. Allen, 482 U.S. 369, 107 S.Ct. 2415 (1987), the Supreme Court held that the following parole statute in Montana created a liberty interest in parole of which a prisoner could not be divested without due process of law:

> Prisoners eligible for parole. (1) Subject to the following restrictions, the board shall release on parole * * * any person confined in the Montana state prison or the women's correctional center * * * when in its opinion there is reasonable probability that the prisoner can be released without detriment to the prisoner or to the community[.]
>
> * * *
>
> (2) A parole shall be ordered only for the best interests of society and not as an award of clemency or reduction of sentence or pardon. A prisoner shall be placed on parole only when the board believes that he is able and willing to fulfill the obligations of a law-abiding citizen.

The Court refused to distinguish between parole statutes like Nebraska's that mandated parole release "unless" certain conditions were met and other parole statutes like Montana's that required release "if" or "when" certain conditions were met. The Court conceded that the standards governing parole release in Montana, which focused on whether release on parole would be detrimental to the prisoner or the community and in "the best interests of society," were more general than the Nebraska standards which were before the Court in *Greenholtz*. The Court, however, rejected the arguments of the three dissenting Justices—O'Connor, Rehnquist, and Scalia—that Montana prisoners would have no more than a hope of being released on parole, rather than a protected liberty interest in such release, when the discretion of the Montana parole board was not specifically and meaningfully circumscribed by statute.

2. Would the following parole statute create a liberty interest falling within the rubric of the due process clause?

> No person shall be placed on parole until and unless the commission shall find that there is reasonable probability that, if he is placed on parole, he will live and conduct himself as a respectable and law-abiding person and that his release will be compatible with his own welfare and the welfare of society. No person shall be placed on parole unless and until the commission is satisfied that he will be suitably employed in self-sustaining employment, or that he will not become a public charge.

See, Staton v. Wainwright, 665 F.2d 686 (5th Cir.1982). Would a liberty interest be created by a statute like the following?

> A parole shall be ordered only for the best interest of society, not as an award of clemency; it shall not be considered to be a reduction of sentence or pardon. A prisoner shall be placed on parole only when arrangements have been made for his proper employment, or for his

maintenance and care, and only when the Indiana parole board believes that he is able and willing to fulfill the obligations of a law-abiding citizen.

See Averhart v. Tutsie, 618 F.2d 479 (7th Cir.1980).

3. *Greenholtz and Board of Pardons v. Allen* should be contrasted with Connecticut Board of Pardons v. Dumschat, 452 U.S. 458, 101 S.Ct. 2460 (1981). In *Dumschat,* a prisoner who was serving a life sentence for murder contended that he was deprived of a liberty interest without due process of law when the Connecticut Board of Pardons denied his application for a commutation of his sentence. He argued that certain procedures should have been followed by the board when reviewing his commutation application.

Under the applicable Connecticut statute, the board was vested with unconfined discretion to commute sentences or grant pardons. The prisoner nonetheless contended that he had a legitimate expectation that his life sentence would be commuted, since the board commuted the vast majority—eighty-five to ninety per cent—of the sentences of inmates serving life sentences. The Supreme Court, however, rejected this argument:

> In terms of the Due Process Clause, a Connecticut felon's expectation that a lawfully imposed sentence will be commuted or that he will be pardoned is no more substantial than an inmate's expectation, for example, that he will not be transferred to another prison; it is simply a unilateral hope. A constitutional entitlement cannot "be created—as if by estoppel—merely because a wholly and *expressly* discretionary state privilege has been granted generously in the past." No matter how frequently a particular form of clemency has been granted, the statistical probabilities standing alone generate no constitutional protections; a contrary conclusion would trivialize the Constitution. The ground for a constitutional claim, if any, must be found in statutes or other rules defining the obligations of the authority charged with exercising clemency.

Id. at 465, 101 S.Ct. at 2464. See also Jago v. Van Curen, 454 U.S. 14, 102 S.Ct. 31 (1981) (rescission of parole release decision which occurred before inmate's actual release and which was prompted by the discovery that the inmate had provided false information to the parole board did not implicate a liberty interest; inmate's understanding that he would be released on parole did not give rise to a liberty interest).

4. One of the questions left open in *Greenholtz* was whether inmates have a right of access to information in their prison files reviewed by parole boards. Such files may include a presentence report; reports of disciplinary infractions; medical and psychiatric information; the prisoner's criminal record; reports about the inmate's adjustment while in prison; letters from the sentencing judge, police officers, victims, family members, and friends; and other materials.

The lower courts have divided on the question of whether inmates have a right of access to their prison files when they are being considered for possible release on parole. Some courts have held that inmates simply have no such right. See, e.g., Schuemann v. Colorado State Board of Adult

Parole, 624 F.2d 172, 175 (10th Cir.1980); Franklin v. Shields, 569 F.2d 784, 800 (4th Cir.1977). Others have analyzed inmates' access demands on a case-by-case basis. See, e.g., Williams v. Ward, 556 F.2d 1143, 1160–61 (2d Cir.1977) (inmate had no right of access when he knew in advance of his parole hearing that the board might rely on allegedly false information, but took no steps to refute that information); Coralluzzo v. New York State Parole Board, 566 F.2d 375, 380 (2d Cir.1977) (where parole board's statement of reasons for ordered minimum period of imprisonment revealed that board had relied on information ordered stricken from the inmate's file by a state court, prisoner had a right of access to the file to confirm whether or not the information was still in his file). Still other courts have crafted more general rules providing for access to files under certain circumstances. See, e.g., Walker v. Prisoner Review Board, 694 F.2d 499, 503 (7th Cir.1982) (inmates have right of access to documents considered by the parole board); Williams v. Missouri Board of Probation and Parole, 585 F.2d 922, 925–26 (8th Cir.1978) (inmates up for parole have a general right to be apprised of adverse information in their files).

When, if ever, do you believe that inmates being considered for parole release have a constitutional right of access to their institutional files?

5. Because of the many procedural safeguards already afforded prisoners being considered for parole in Nebraska, the Supreme Court in *Greenholtz* did not have to decide whether those procedures were constitutionally mandated. Which of the procedures which follow, if any, does due process require in a state where the denial of parole implicates a liberty interest? The right to appear before the parole board? The right to present documentary evidence? The right to call witnesses to testify on the inmate's behalf? The right to cross-examine adverse witnesses? The right to be represented by an attorney or to receive some other form of assistance? The right to receive a statement of the reason or reasons for a parole denial? The right to a "neutral and detached" decisionmaker?

6. Assuming that inmates have the right to a written statement outlining the reason or reasons why parole was denied, would a statement that release would deprecate the seriousness of the offense of which the inmate had been found guilty and engender disrespect for the law suffice? What would prevent a parole board from routinely reciting such reasons? How much more specific could the parole board be in relating its reasons for the parole denial? Compare Walker v. Prisoner Review Board, 694 F.2d 499, 502 (7th Cir.1982) with United States ex rel. Scott v. Illinois Parole and Pardon Board, 669 F.2d 1185, 1190–91 (7th Cir.1982).

Chapter 17

RIGHTS UPON RELEASE

A. RESTRICTED OPPORTUNITIES AND RIGHTS OF RELEASED PRISONERS

Each year, over 200,000 people are released from prison into the community. Bureau of Justice Statistics, U.S. Dep't of Justice, Probation and Parole 1987 4 (1988). Bereft of resources and money, the prisoners, upon release, are usually given a new change of clothing and a small amount of money, like $50, and then sent on their way. P. Rossi, R. Berk, & K. Lenihan, Money, Work, and Crime 9 (1980). The prospects of finding a job with which to support themselves are dim. On average, the academic skills of released prisoners are at the sixth-grade level, and most have little or no work experience. Id. at 8. Few have been groomed on such basics as how to fill out a job application form, how to dress for an interview, or even on the need to be punctual for an interview or job. And for those who are unable to procure a job, there is no unemployment compensation and often no welfare assistance upon which to temporarily fall back. Id. at 9.

The prisoners who are lucky enough to secure a job upon their release from prison generally find that the jobs are low-paying and often accompanied by poor working conditions. It is little wonder then that the impulse to return to a life of crime, where the financial remuneration is often quite high, frequently proves irresistible to a released prisoner. Studies have revealed that prisoners who, upon release, are unemployed or underemployed are four times more likely to be reincarcerated than other prisoners. Finn & Fontaine, The Association Between Selected Characteristics and Perceived Employability of Offenders, 12 Crim.Just. & Behavior 353, 354 (1985). Ex-offender unemployment therefore explains at least in part the very high recidivism rates which presently prevail in this country. As was mentioned earlier in Chapter 8, one study conducted by the Bureau of Justice Statistics revealed that 61% of the inmates sentenced to prison in the study had been previously incarcerated. Bureau of Justice Statistics, U.S. Dep't of Justice, Examining Recidivism 1 (1985). See also Bureau of Justice Statistics, U.S. Dep't of Justice, Recidivism of Young Parolees 1 (1987) (69% of young parolees studied were rearrested for a serious crime within six years after being released from prison, 53% were convicted, and 49% were sent back to prison). These studies on recidivism have found, not surprisingly, that recidivism rates are highest during the first few years after a prisoner's release from prison.

In addition to the practical obstacles which impede released prisoners' successful reintegration into the community, there are legal obstacles which stand in their way. There are a number of federal and state statutes for example, which forbid ex-felons from holding certain jobs. Some statutes exclude individuals convicted of certain types of official misconduct from many government jobs. See, e.g., Colo. Const. art. XII, § 4; Nev.Rev.Stat. § 197.230. Others bar certain ex-felons from serving as union officers. See, e.g., 29 U.S.C. § 405; N.D.Cent.Code § 34–01–16. See also De Veau v. Braisted, 363 U.S. 144, 80 S.Ct. 1146 (1960) (upholding the constitutionality of a state law which had the effect of disqualifying ex-felons as officers of any waterfront labor union unless they had been pardoned or received a certificate of good conduct from the parole board). And convicted felons are barred from serving in the United States Army, Navy, Air Force, Marine Corps, or Coast Guard, although exceptions can be made in "meritorious cases." 10 U.S.C. § 504. There are still other legal impediments which make it difficult for ex-offenders to put their criminal past behind them. One of the most common forms of restrictions involves curtailed voting rights, which were the subject of the Supreme Court case which follows.

RICHARDSON v. RAMIREZ

Supreme Court of the United States, 1974.
418 U.S. 24, 94 S.Ct. 2655, 41 L.Ed.2d 551.

MR. JUSTICE REHNQUIST delivered the opinion of the Court.

The three individual respondents in this case were convicted of felonies and have completed the service of their respective sentences and paroles. They filed a petition for a writ of mandate in the Supreme Court of California to compel California county election officials to register them as voters.[9] * * *

[9]. Respondent Ramirez was convicted in Texas of the felony of "robbery by assault" in 1952. He served three months in jail and successfully terminated his parole in 1962. In February 1972 the San Luis Obispo County Clerk refused to allow Ramirez to register to vote on the ground that he had been convicted of a felony and spent time in incarceration. Respondent Lee was convicted of the felony of heroin possession in California in 1955, served two years in prison, and successfully terminated his parole in 1959. In March 1972 the Monterey County Clerk refused to allow Lee to register to vote on the sole ground that he had been convicted of a felony and had not been pardoned by the Governor. Respondent Gill was convicted in 1952 and 1967 of second-degree burglary in California, and in 1957 of forgery. He served some time in prison on each conviction, followed by a successful parole. In April 1972 the Stanislaus County Registrar of Voters refused to allow Gill to register to vote on the sole ground of his prior felony convictions.

Article XX, § 11, of the California Constitution has provided since its adoption in 1879 that "[l]aws shall be made" to exclude from voting persons convicted of bribery, perjury, forgery, malfeasance in office, "or other high crimes." At the time respondents were refused registration, former Art. II, § 1, of the California Constitution provided in part that "no alien ineligible to citizenship, no idiot, no insane person, no person convicted of any infamous crime, no person hereafter convicted of the embezzlement or misappropriation of public money, and no person who shall not be able to read the Constitution in the English language and write his or her name, shall ever exercise the privileges of an elector in this State." Sections 310 and 321 of the California Elections Code provide that an affidavit of registration shall show whether the affiant has been convicted of "a felony which disqualifies [him] from voting." Sections 383, 389, and 390 direct the county clerk to cancel the registration of all voters who have been convicted of "any infamous crime or of the embezzlement or misappropriation of any public money." Sections 14240 and 14246 permit a voter's qualifications to be challenged on the ground that he has been convicted of "a felony" or of "the embezzlement or misappropriation of public money." California provides by statute for restoration of the right to vote to persons convicted of crime either by court order after the completion of probation, or, if a prison term was served, by executive pardon after completion of rehabilitation proceedings. California also provides a procedure by which a person refused registration may obtain judicial review of his disqualification.[8]

* * *

* * * The petition for a writ of mandate challenged the constitutionality of respondents' exclusion from the voting rolls on two grounds. First, it was contended that California's denial of the franchise to the class of ex-felons could no longer withstand scrutiny under the Equal Protection Clause of the Fourteenth Amendment. Relying on the Court's recent voting-rights cases, respondents argued that a compelling state interest must be found to justify exclusion of a class from the franchise, and that California could assert no such interest with respect to ex-felons. Second, respondents contended that application of the challenged California constitutional and statutory provisions by election officials of the State's 58 counties was so lacking in uniformity as to deny them due process and "geographical . . . equal protection." They appended a report by respondent California Secretary of State, and the questionnaires returned by county election officials on which it was based. The report concluded that there was wide variation in the county election officials' interpretation of the challenged voting exclusions.[12] The Supreme Court of California upheld the first contention and therefore did not reach the second one.

* * *

8. Respondents contended that pardon was not an effective device for obtaining the franchise, noting that during 1968–1971, 34,262 persons were released from state prisons but only 282 pardons were granted.

* * *

12. * * * The report concluded:

"2. Although the policy within most counties may be consistent, the fact that some counties have adopted different policies has created a situation in which there

* * *

Unlike most claims under the Equal Protection Clause, for the decision of which we have only the language of the Clause itself as it is embodied in the Fourteenth Amendment, respondents' claim implicates not merely the language of the Equal Protection Clause of § 1 of the Fourteenth Amendment, but also the provisions of the less familiar § 2 of the Amendment:

> "Representatives shall be apportioned among the several States according to their respective numbers, counting the whole number of persons in each State, excluding Indians not taxed. But when the right to vote at any election for the choice of electors for President and Vice President of the United States, Representatives in Congress, the Executive and Judicial officers of a State, or the members of the Legislature thereof, is denied to any of the male inhabitants of such State, being twenty-one years of age, and citizens of the United States, or in any way abridged, *except for participation in rebellion, or other crime*, the basis of representation therein shall be reduced in the proportion which the number of such male citizens shall bear to the whole number of male citizens twenty-one years of age in such State." (Emphasis supplied.)

Petitioner contends that the italicized language of § 2 expressly exempts from the sanction of that section disenfranchisement grounded on prior conviction of a felony. She goes on to argue that those who framed and adopted the Fourteenth Amendment could not have intended to prohibit outright in § 1 of that Amendment that which was expressly exempted from the lesser sanction of reduced representation imposed by § 2 of the Amendment. This argument seems to us a persuasive one unless it can be shown that the language of § 2, "except for participation in rebellion, or other crime," was intended to have a different meaning than would appear from its face.

* * * The legislative history bearing on the meaning of the relevant language of § 2 is scant indeed; the framers of the Amendment were primarily concerned with the effect of reduced representation upon the States, rather than with the two forms of disenfranchisement which were exempted from that consequence by the language with which we are concerned here. Nonetheless, what legislative history there is indicates that this language was intended by Congress to mean what it says.

* * *

Further light is shed on the understanding of those who framed and ratified the Fourteenth Amendment, and thus on the meaning of § 2, by the fact that at the time of the adoption of the Amendment, 29 States had provisions in their constitutions which prohibited, or authorized the legislature to prohibit, exercise of the franchise by persons convicted of felonies or infamous crimes.

---

is a lack of uniformity across the state. It appears from the survey that a person convicted of almost any given felony would find that he is eligible to vote in some California counties and ineligible to vote in others.

More impressive than the mere existence of the state constitutional provisions disenfranchising felons at the time of the adoption of the Fourteenth Amendment is the congressional treatment of States readmitted to the Union following the Civil War. For every State thus readmitted, affirmative congressional action in the form of an enabling act was taken, and as a part of the readmission process the State seeking readmission was required to submit for the approval of the Congress its proposed state constitution. * * *

A series of enabling acts in 1868 and 1870 admitted those States to representation in Congress. The Act admitting Arkansas, the first State to be so admitted, attached a condition to its admission. That Act provided: * * *

> "*Be it enacted* . . . That the State of Arkansas is entitled and admitted to representation in Congress as one of the States of the Union upon the following fundamental condition: That the constitution of Arkansas shall never be so amended or changed as to deprive any citizen or class of citizens of the United States of the right to vote who are entitled to vote by the constitution herein recognized, except as a punishment for such crimes as are now felonies at common law, whereof they shall have been duly convicted, under laws equally applicable to all the inhabitants of said State: *Provided,* That any alteration of said constitution prospective in its effect may be made in regard to the time and place of residence of voters." * * *

The same "fundamental condition" as was imposed by the act readmitting Arkansas was also, with only slight variations in language, imposed by the Act readmitting North Carolina, South Carolina, Louisiana, Georgia, Alabama, and Florida, enacted three days later. That condition was again imposed by the Acts readmitting Virginia, Mississippi, Texas, and Georgia early in 1870.

* * *

Despite this settled historical and judicial understanding of the Fourteenth Amendment's effect on state laws disenfranchising convicted felons, respondents argue that our recent decisions invalidating other state-imposed restrictions on the franchise as violative of the Equal Protection Clause require us to invalidate the disenfranchisement of felons as well. They rely on such cases as *Dunn v. Blumstein,* 405 U.S. 330 (1972), *Bullock v. Carter,* 405 U.S. 134 (1972), *Kramer v. Union Free School District,* 395 U.S. 621 (1969), and *Cipriano v. City of Houma,* 395 U.S. 701 (1969), to support the conclusions of the Supreme Court of California that a State must show a "compelling state interest" to justify exclusion of ex-felons from the franchise and that California has not done so here.

As we have seen, however, the exclusion of felons from the vote has an affirmative sanction in § 2 of the Fourteenth Amendment, a sanction which was not present in the case of the other restrictions on the franchise which were invalidated in the cases on which respondents rely. We hold that the understanding of those who adopted the

Fourteenth Amendment, as reflected in the express language of § 2 and in the historical and judicial interpretation of the Amendment's applicability to state laws disenfranchising felons, is of controlling significance in distinguishing such laws from those other state limitations on the franchise which have been held invalid under the Equal Protection Clause by this Court. * * *

Pressed upon us by the respondents, and by *amici curiae,* are contentions that these notions are outmoded, and that the more modern view is that it is essential to the process of rehabilitating the ex-felon that he be returned to his role in society as a fully participating citizen when he has completed the serving of his term. We would by no means discount these arguments if addressed to the legislative forum which may properly weigh and balance them against those advanced in support of California's present constitutional provisions. But it is not for us to choose one set of values over the other. If respondents are correct, and the view which they advocate is indeed the more enlightened and sensible one, presumably the people of the State of California will ultimately come around to that view. And if they do not do so, their failure is some evidence, at least, of the fact that there are two sides to the argument.

We therefore hold that the Supreme Court of California erred in concluding that California may no longer, consistent with the Equal Protection Clause of the Fourteenth Amendment, exclude from the franchise convicted felons who have completed their sentences and paroles. The California court did not reach respondents' alternative contention that there was such a total lack of uniformity in county election officials' enforcement of the challenged state laws as to work a separate denial of equal protection, and we believe that it should have an opportunity to consider the claim before we address ourselves to it. Accordingly, we reverse and remand for further proceedings not inconsistent with this opinion.

* * *

MR. JUSTICE MARSHALL, with whom MR. JUSTICE BRENNAN joins, dissenting.

* * *

* * * The Court construes § 2 of the Fourteenth Amendment as an express authorization for the States to disenfranchise former felons. Section 2 does except disenfranchisement for "participation in rebellion, or other crime" from the operation of its penalty provision. As the Court notes, however, there is little independent legislative history as to the crucial words "or other crime"; the proposed § 2 went to a joint committee containing only the phrase "participation in rebellion" and emerged with "or other crime" inexplicably tacked on. * * *

* * *

It is clear that § 2 was not intended and should not be construed to be a limitation on the other sections of the Fourteenth Amendment. Section 2 provides a special remedy—reduced representation—to cure a particular form of electoral abuse—the disenfranchisement of Negroes. There is no indication that the framers of the provisions intended that special penalty to be the exclusive remedy for all forms of electoral discrimination. * * *

* * *

The Court's references to congressional enactments contemporaneous to the adoption of the Fourteenth Amendment, such as the Reconstruction Act and the readmission statutes, are inapposite. They do not explain the purpose for the adoption of § 2 of the Fourteenth Amendment. They merely indicate that disenfranchisement for participation in crime was not uncommon in the States at the time of the adoption of the Amendment. Hence, not surprisingly, that form of disenfranchisement was excepted from the application of the special penalty provision of § 2. But because Congress chose to exempt one form of electoral discrimination from the reduction-of-representation remedy provided by § 2 does not necessarily imply congressional approval of this disenfranchisement.[24] By providing a special remedy for disenfranchisement of a particular class of voters in § 2, Congress did not approve all election discriminations to which the § 2 remedy was inapplicable, and such discriminations thus are not forever immunized from evolving standards of equal protection scrutiny. There is no basis for concluding that Congress intended by § 2 to freeze the meaning of other clauses of the Fourteenth Amendment to the conception of voting rights prevalent at the time of the adoption of the Amendment. In fact, one form of disenfranchisement—one-year durational residence requirements—specifically authorized by the Reconstruction Act, one of the contemporaneous enactments upon which the Court relies to show the intendment of the framers of the Fourteenth Amendment, has already been declared unconstitutional by this Court in *Dunn v. Blumstein,* 405 U.S. 330 (1972).

* * *

In my view, the disenfranchisement of ex-felons must be measured against the requirements of the Equal Protection Clause of § 1 of the Fourteenth Amendment. That analysis properly begins with the observation that because the right to vote "is of the essence of a democratic society, and any restrictions on that right strike at the heart of representative government," voting is a "fundamental" right. * * * "[I]f a challenged statute grants the right to vote to some citizens and

---

24. To say that § 2 of the Fourteenth Amendment is a direct limitation on the protection afforded voting rights by § 1 leads to absurd results. If one accepts the premise that § 2 authorizes disenfranchisement for any crime, the challenged California provision could, as the California Supreme Court has observed, require disenfranchisement for seduction under promise of marriage, or conspiracy to operate a motor vehicle without a muffler. Disenfranchisement extends to convictions for vagrancy in Alabama or breaking a water pipe in North Dakota, to note but two examples. Note, Disenfranchisement of Ex-felons: A Reassessment, 25 Stan.L. Rev. 845, 846 (1973). Even a jaywalking or traffic conviction could conceivably lead to disenfranchisement, since § 2 does not differentiate between felonies and misdemeanors

denies the franchise to others, 'the Court must determine whether the exclusions are *necessary* to promote a *compelling* state interest.' "

To determine that the compelling-state-interest test applies to the challenged classification is, however, to settle only a threshold question. "Compelling state interest" is merely a shorthand description of the difficult process of balancing individual and state interests that the Court must embark upon when faced with a classification touching on fundamental rights. Our other equal protection cases give content to the nature of that balance. The State has the heavy burden of showing, first, that the challenged disenfranchisement is necessary to a legitimate and substantial state interest; second, that the classification is drawn with precision—that it does not exclude too many people who should not and need not be excluded; and, third, that there are no other reasonable ways to achieve the State's goal with a lesser burden on the constitutionally protected interest.

I think it clear that the State has not met its burden of justifying the blanket disenfranchisement of former felons presented by this case. There is certainly no basis for asserting that ex-felons have any less interest in the democratic process than any other citizen. Like everyone else, their daily lives are deeply affected and changed by the decisions of government. As the Secretary of State of California observed in his memorandum to the Court in support of respondents in this case:

> "It is doubtful . . . whether the state can demonstrate either a compelling or rational policy interest in denying former felons the right to vote. The individuals involved in the present case are persons who have fully paid their debt to society. They are as much affected by the actions of government as any other citizens, and have as much of a right to participate in governmental decision-making. Furthermore, the denial of the right to vote to such persons is a hindrance to the efforts of society to rehabilitate former felons and convert them into law-abiding and productive citizens."

It is argued that disenfranchisement is necessary to prevent vote frauds. Although the State has a legitimate and, in fact, compelling interest in preventing election fraud, the challenged provision is not sustainable on that ground. First, the disenfranchisement provisions are patently both overinclusive and underinclusive. The provision is not limited to those who have demonstrated a marked propensity for abusing the ballot by violating election laws. Rather, it encompasses all former felons and there has been no showing that ex-felons generally are any more likely to abuse the ballot than the remainder of the population. In contrast, many of those convicted of violating election laws are treated as misdemeanants and are not barred from voting at all. It seems clear that the classification here is not tailored to achieve its articulated goal, since it crudely excludes large numbers of otherwise qualified voters.

Moreover, there are means available for the State to prevent voting fraud which are far less burdensome on the constitutionally protected right to vote. * * * [T]he State "has at its disposal a variety of criminal laws that are more than adequate to detect and deter whatever fraud may be feared." * * *

Another asserted purpose is to keep former felons from voting because their likely voting pattern might be subversive of the interests of an orderly society. * * *

Although, in the last century, this Court may have justified the exclusion of voters from the electoral process for fear that they would vote to change laws considered important by a temporal majority, I have little doubt that we would not countenance such a purpose today. The process of democracy is one of change. Our laws are not frozen into immutable form, they are constantly in the process of revision in response to the needs of a changing society. The public interest, as conceived by a majority of the voting public, is constantly undergoing re-examination. * * * Voters who opposed the repeal of prohibition could have disenfranchised those who advocated repeal "to prevent persons from being enabled by their votes to defeat the criminal laws of the country." Today, presumably those who support the legalization of marihuana could be barred from the ballot box for much the same reason. The ballot is the democratic system's coin of the realm. To condition its exercise on support of the established order is to debase that currency beyond recognition. * * *

* * *

The disenfranchisement of ex-felons had "its origin in the fogs and fictions of feudal jurisprudence and doubtless has been brought forward into modern statutes without fully realizing either the effect of its literal significance or the extent of its infringement upon the spirit of our system of government." I think it clear that measured against the standards of this Court's modern equal protection jurisprudence, the blanket disenfranchisement of ex-felons cannot stand.

I respectfully dissent.

* * *

Questions and Points for Discussion

1. The Supreme Court distinguished *Richardson v. Ramirez* when holding unconstitutional a voting restriction in Hunter v. Underwood, 471 U.S. 222, 105 S.Ct. 1916 (1985). The restriction at issue in that case, a portion of the Alabama Constitution, precluded persons convicted of "any crime * * * involving moral turpitude" from voting. The Alabama Constitutional Convention of 1901 adopted this provision in order to disenfranchise blacks whom it was felt were convicted of these types of crimes with greater frequency than white people. Because of the discriminatory intent which prompted the enactment of the disenfranchisement provision and because it continued to have a disproportionately adverse effect on blacks, the Supreme Court, in a unanimous opinion written by Justice

Rehnquist, struck down the provision on equal protection grounds. The Court, however, left open the question whether the provision would have passed constitutional muster if it had been enacted without a discriminatory intent.

2. Under what circumstances, if any, do you believe that the conviction of a person of a crime should lead to his or her disenfranchisement?

3. In addition to maybe losing the right to vote, released prisoners and other ex-felons may find that they are barred from serving on juries. See, e.g., Alaska Stat. § 09.20.020(2) (unless civil rights have been restored); Colo.Rev.Stat. § 13–71–109(2)(d).

B. RESTORATION OF RIGHTS

There are a number of ways in which the adverse collateral effects of criminal convictions can be dissipated—through pardons, restoration-of-rights procedures, the expungement or sealing of criminal records, and statutes barring discrimination against ex-offenders. Each one of these mechanisms is briefly discussed below.

1. PARDONS

All of the states and the federal government have procedures in place for issuing pardons to criminal offenders. Burton, Travis, & Cullen, Reducing the Legal Consequences of a Felony Conviction: A National Survey of State Statutes, 12 Int'l J. of Comp. & Applied Crim. Just. 101, 104–05 (1988). In some states, the governor makes the pardoning decision, while in others, the decision is made by the parole board or a board of pardons. Id. at 103, 105. And in the federal system, the power to grant pardons is vested in the President. U.S. Const. art. II, § 2, cl. 1.

If the pardoning authority grants a pardon and the offender accepts the pardon, the offender will generally be relieved from most of the legal disabilities which attend a criminal conviction. The offender, for example, will be able to vote and hold public office. In some jurisdictions, however, there may be some limitations on the ability of a pardon to fully restore the rights of individuals convicted of crimes. In accepting a pardon, convicted offenders are implicitly acknowledging their guilt of the crimes for which they are being pardoned. Burdick v. United States, 236 U.S. 79, 94, 35 S.Ct. 267, 270 (1915). Consequently, in some jurisdictions, those crimes can appropriately be considered when the ex-convicts apply for some positions that require that applicants meet certain character requirements. For example, a prior conviction may lead to a determination that an ex-convict is unfit to practice law even though the offender has been officially pardoned for his or her crime.

2. AUTOMATIC RESTORATION OF RIGHTS

Automatic restoration statutes restore some or all of criminal offenders' civil rights after they have successfully served their sentences.   See, e.g., N.H.Rev.Stat.Ann. § 607–A:5(I); Wis.Stat.Ann § 57.078.   More and more states are opting to remove the vestiges of criminal convictions through the automatic restoration of rights. While in 1973 there were only thirteen states with automatic restoration statutes, by 1988 there were forty-two.   Burton, Travis, and Cullen, Reducing the Legal Consequences of a Felony Conviction: A National Survey of State Statutes, 12 Int'l J. of Comp. & Applied Crim. Just. 101, 108 (1988).

Automatic restoration statutes are like pardons in the sense that even offenders whose rights have been fully restored may be denied professional or occupational licenses because of their criminal convictions.   American Bar Association, Removing Offender Employment Restrictions 5 (2d ed. 1973).   In addition, ex-convicts whose rights have been restored, like pardoned offenders, may still be obliged to reveal their criminal records on job application forms.   Id.   The difference between pardons and automatic restoration statutes is that the former are discretionary while the latter are triggered automatically by the occurrence of a certain event.

3. EXPUNGEMENT AND SEALING OF CRIMINAL RECORDS

The expungement or sealing of criminal records is another way of reducing or eliminating the adverse effects of a criminal conviction.   If the criminal records are expunged, they are totally destroyed.   If they are sealed, access to the records is limited, but the records themselves are preserved.   The advantage, from the offenders' perspective, of having criminal records expunged or sealed is that they may be entitled to refrain from mentioning their criminal records on job application forms.   See, e.g., Ark.Code Ann. § 16–93–303(b)(3).

A study conducted in 1988 revealed that twenty-eight states provided some mechanism for expunging or sealing criminal records.   Burton, Travis, & Cullen, Reducing the Legal Consequences of a Felony Conviction: A National Survey of State Statutes, 12 Int'l J. of Comp. & Applied Crim. Just. 101, 106 (1988).   State statutes vary, however, as to when expungement or sealing of criminal records is appropriate. Some, for example, apply only to individuals placed on probation.   See, e.g., Ark.Code Ann. § 16–93–303(b)(1); Okla.Stat.Ann. tit. 22, § 991c. Others only apply to non-violent offenders.   See, e.g., R.I.Gen.Laws § 12–1.3–2(A).   Still others permit only first-time felony offenders to get records of their convictions expunged.   See, e.g., Okla.Stat.Ann. tit. 22 § 991c; R.I.Gen.Laws § 12–1.3–2(A).   Under what circumstances, if any, do you believe the expungement or sealing of criminal records is appropriate?

4. DISCRIMINATION BANS

A final way of mitigating the adverse effects of a criminal conviction is through statutes and case law forbidding discrimination against ex-offenders.   The ABA Standards Relating to the Legal Status of

Prisoners (1981) contain standards which can be incorporated in statutes to limit the collateral consequences of a criminal conviction. Some of those standards are set forth below:

Standard 23–8.1. Repeal of mandatory civil disabilities

Laws or regulations which require that convicted persons be subjected to collateral disabilities or penalties, or be deprived of civil rights, should be repealed except for those specifically preserved in part VIII of these standards.

Standard 23–8.3. Procedure for imposing authorized disabilities

(a) When the imposition of collateral disabilities or penalties, or the deprivation of civil rights, is authorized as a consequence of a conviction, a procedure should be established to assure that there is a determination in each individual case that the disability or penalty is necessary to advance an important governmental or public interest.

(b) The procedure established should be comparable to that provided for agency adjudications in the Model State Administrative Procedure Act.

(c) A disability should be imposed for a stated period, after which the person subject to the disability should be entitled to have the appropriateness of the disability reconsidered. Within the stated period of the disability, if a person can present evidence that the disability imposed no longer effectuates an important governmental interest, the person should be entitled to a reconsideration.

(d) The burden of proving the appropriateness of the disability should be on those seeking to impose it, except a convicted person should bear the burden of proving an allegation that the fact of conviction has unfairly affected his or her application for or status in private employment.

Standard 23–8.4. Voting rights

Persons convicted of any offense should not be deprived of the right to vote either by law or by the action or inaction of government officials. Prisoners should be authorized to vote at their last place of residence prior to confinement unless they can establish some other residence in accordance with rules applicable to the general public. They should not, however, be authorized to establish voting residence or domicile in the jurisdiction where they are incarcerated solely because of that incarceration.

Standard 23–8.5. Judicial rights

Persons convicted of any offense should be entitled to:

(a) initiate and defend suit in any court in their own names under procedures applicable to the general public;

(b) serve on juries except while actually confined or while on probation or parole;

(c) execute judicially enforceable documents and agreements; and

(d) serve as court-appointed fiduciaries except during actual confinement.

Standard 23–8.6. Domestic rights

(a) The domestic relationships of convicted persons should be governed by rules applicable to the general public. Conviction or confinement alone should be insufficient to deprive a person of any of the following domestic rights:

(i) the right to contract or dissolve a marriage;

(ii) parental rights, including the right to direct the rearing of children;

(iii) the right to grant or withhold consent to the adoption of children; and

(iv) the right to adopt children.

(b) Conviction or confinement alone should not constitute neglect or abandonment of a spouse or child, and persons convicted or confined should be assisted in making appropriate arrangements for their spouse or children during periods of confinement.

Standard 23–8.7. Property and financial rights

(a) Persons convicted of any offense should not be deprived of the right to acquire, inherit, sell, or otherwise dispose of real or personal property consistent with the rule that a person should not profit from his or her own wrong. Persons unable to manage or preserve their property by reason of confinement should be entitled to appoint someone of their own choosing to act on their behalf.

(b) Persons convicted of any offense or confined as a result of a conviction should not, for that reason alone, lose any otherwise vested pension rights or become ineligible to participate in any governmental program providing relief, medical care, and old age pensions.

(c) State departments of insurance should require companies to offer insurance of all kinds to persons who have been convicted of any offense and should ensure that any rate differential based solely on a conviction is justified.

(d) Agencies that compile and report information used to determine a person's suitability for credit or employment should be prohibited from disclosing criminal convictions that from the date of parole or release antedate the report by more than [five] years.

Standard 23–8.8.　Employment and licensing

(a) Barriers to employment of convicted persons based solely on a past conviction should be prohibited unless the offense committed bears a substantial relationship to the functions and responsibilities of the employment. Among the factors that should be considered in evaluating the relationship between the offense and the employment are the following:

(i) the likelihood the employment will enhance the opportunity for commission of similar offenses;

(ii) the time elapsed since conviction;

(iii) the person's conduct subsequent to conviction; and

(iv) the circumstances of the offense and of the person that led to the crime and the likelihood that such circumstances will recur.

(b) Each jurisdiction should enact legislation protecting persons convicted of criminal offenses from unreasonable barriers in private employment. Such legislation should govern:

(i) denying employment;

(ii) discharging persons from employment;

(iii) denying fair employment conditions, remuneration, or promotion;

(iv) denying membership in a labor union or other organization affecting employability; and

(v) denying or revoking a license necessary to engage in any occupation, profession, or employment.

Jurisdictions should adopt appropriate mechanisms for the enforcement of prohibitions against barriers to private employment applicable to convicted persons.

(c) Past convictions should not bar a person from running for elected office, although jurisdictions may provide that conviction of specified offenses will result in the automatic forfeiture of elective office held at the time of conviction. A conviction should not bar a person from holding appointive public office, although the appointing entity may require forfeiture of an office held at the time of conviction.

(d) Public employment should be governed by the same standards proposed for private employment.

(e) For purposes of this standard, "appointive public office" includes policy-making positions. "Public employment" includes positions that generally are governed by civil service or personnel systems, or are considered career appointments.

(f) Licensing or other governmental regulations should not automatically exclude persons convicted of any offense from participation in regulated activities. Persons should not be barred from regulated activity on the basis of a conviction unless the offense committed bears a substantial relationship to participation in the activity. In determinations of whether such a relationship exists, the factors listed in paragraph (a) should be considered.

See also Uniform Law Commissioners' Model Sentencing and Corrections Act, § 4–1005 (employment discrimination against convicted offenders is unlawful unless "the underlying offense directly relates to the particular occupation, profession, or educational endeavor involved"); Wis.Stat. §§ 111.321, 111.335 (generally barring employment discrimination because of prior arrests or convictions).

In addition to statutory restrictions, the Constitution may sometimes constrain governments from denying government employment to individuals simply because of their criminal records. Supreme Court decisions have generally observed that due process requires at least a rational connection between the type of job for which the applicant applied and the criterion which led to the applicant's rejection. See, e.g., Schware v. Board of Bar Examiners, 353 U.S. 232, 239, 77 S.Ct. 752, 756 (1957). This rational relationship test simply may not be met in certain circumstances when an applicant's criminal conviction serves as the basis for denial of a job.

Question for Discussion

What steps do you believe can and should be taken, both while prisoners are incarcerated and after their release, to facilitate their successful reentry back into society, to reduce the adverse effects of criminal convictions on all ex-offenders, and to reduce recidivism rates?

Part Three

PRISONERS' RIGHTS LITIGATION

Chapter 18

THE MECHANICS OF LITIGATING INMATES' § 1983 SUITS

A. THE COMPLAINT

1. ELEMENTS OF A CAUSE OF ACTION UNDER § 1983

The statute under which inmates customarily challenge their treatment while in a prison or jail or the conditions of their confinement, 42 U.S.C. § 1983, provides in part as follows:

> Every person who, under color of any statute, ordinance, regulation, custom, or usage, of any State or Territory or the District of Columbia, subjects, or causes to be subjected, any citizen of the United States or other person within the jurisdiction thereof to the deprivation of any rights, privileges, or immunities secured by the Constitution and laws, shall be liable to the party injured in an action at law, suit in equity, or other proper proceeding for redress * * *.

The elements which must be established by an inmate asserting a § 1983 cause of action are outlined below.

1. *Person* —According to the Supreme Court, the word "person" in § 1983 is not confined to human beings. At the time that Congress enacted § 1 of the Civil Rights Act of 1871, 17 Stat. 13, which was the predecessor to § 1983, another statute, known as the Dictionary Act, provided that "in all acts hereafter passed * * * the word "person" may extend and be applied to bodies politic and corporate * * * unless the context shows that such words were intended to be used in a more limited sense." Act of Feb. 25, 1871, § 2, 16 Stat. 431. Relying on the terms of the Dictionary Act as well as the legislative history of § 1983, the Supreme Court in Monell v. Department of Social Services, 436 U.S. 658, 98 S.Ct. 2018 (1978), concluded that municipalities as well as other local governing bodies are "persons" within the meaning of § 1983.

In Will v. Michigan Department of State Police, 109 S.Ct. 2304 (1989), the Court, however, held, in a 5–4 decision, that states are not "persons" who can be sued in a § 1983 suit. The Court grounded its decision on the eleventh amendment immunity of states when they are sued in federal court. See pages 582–583, infra. The Court reasoned that Congress, when it enacted § 1983, would have been aware of this immunity and could not have intended that a state be amenable to a § 1983 suit brought in a state court while it was insulated from § 1983 liability in a lawsuit filed in federal court.

The Supreme Court in *Will* also addressed the question whether a state official sued in his or her official capacity is a "person" against whom a § 1983 suit can be brought. The Court answered this question in the negative:

> Obviously, state officials literally are persons. But a suit against a state official in his or her official capacity is not a suit against the official but rather is a suit against the official's office. As such, it is not different from a suit against the State itself.

Id. at 2311.

In an interesting footnote, however, the Court added: "Of course a State official in his or her official capacity, when sued for injunctive relief, would be a person under § 1983 because 'official-capacity actions for prospective relief are not treated as actions against the State.'" Id. at 2311 n. 10 (quoting Kentucky v. Graham, 473 U.S. 159, 167 n. 14, 105 S.Ct. 3099, 3106 n. 14 (1985)). It therefore appears as though state officials, when sued in their official capacity, are sometimes "persons" within the meaning of § 1983 and other times not.

2. *"Under Color of" State Law* —To be liable under § 1983, a person must have acted "under color of" a "statute, ordinance, regulation, custom, or usage" of a state, United States territory, or the District of Columbia. This requirement is known as the under-color-of-state-law requirement.

In Monroe v. Pape, 365 U.S. 167, 81 S.Ct. 473 (1961), which was discussed in Chapter 8 on page 268, the Supreme Court elaborated on the meaning of "under color of" state law. In that case, some of the defendants who were sued under § 1983 were Chicago police officers who had allegedly entered the plaintiffs' home without a warrant and forced the plaintiffs to stand nude while their home was searched. Portions of the Illinois Constitution and certain state statutes proscribed such conduct by police officers. Nonetheless, the Court concluded that the officers had acted "under color of" state law because of their alleged " '[m]isuse of power, possessed by virtue of state law and made possible only because the wrongdoer is clothed with the authority of state law.' " Id. at 184, 81 S.Ct. at 482 (quoting United States v. Classic, 313 U.S. 299, 326, 61 S.Ct. 1031, 1043 (1941)). To the Court it did not matter that the police officers' actions were unlawful under state law, since § 1983 was enacted in large part because of Congress's concern about the failure of southern states after the Civil War to enforce their own laws against the Ku Klux Klan. The need for and existence of a federal remedy under § 1983 when federal rights were violated therefore did not hinge on the existence of state law provisions which might or might not be enforced.

One of the more salient questions which has arisen in recent years concerning § 1983's under-color-of-state-law requirement is whether a private contractor who provides services, such as medical care or food preparation, to a correctional facility acts "under color of" state law. In West v. Atkins, 487 U.S. 42, 108 S.Ct. 2250 (1988), the Supreme Court addressed this question. The defendant in that case was a private physician who had contracted with the state of North Carolina to provide medical services to inmates two days a week. The doctor was sued under § 1983 by a prisoner who claimed that the doctor had been deliberately indifferent to his serious medical needs in violation of the eighth amendment.

The Supreme Court, in a unanimous decision, held that the defendant had acted "under color of" state law. Writing for the Court, Justice Blackmun explained its conclusion:

It is the physician's function within the state system, not the precise terms of his employment, that determines whether his actions can fairly be attributed to the State. Whether a physician is on the state payroll or is paid by contract, the dispositive issue concerns the relationship among the State, the physician, and the prisoner. Contracting out prison medical care does not relieve the State of its constitutional duty to provide adequate medical treatment to those in its custody, and it does not deprive the State's prisoners of the means to vindicate their Eighth Amendment rights. The State bore an affirmative obligation to provide adequate medical care to West; the State delegated that function to respondent Atkins; and respondent voluntarily assumed that obligation by contract.

Nor does the fact that Doctor Atkins' employment contract did not require him to work exclusively for the prison make him any less a state actor than if he performed those duties as a full-time, permanent member of the state prison medical staff. It is the physician's function while working for the State, not the amount of time he spends in performance of those duties or the fact that he may be employed by others to perform similar duties, that determines whether he is acting under color of state law.

Id. at 55–56, 108 S.Ct. at 2259.

The Supreme Court's decision in *West* is of particular significance because jurisdictions are, with increasing frequency, turning to private contractors, not only to provide selected services to correctional facilities, but to operate entire correctional facilities. For very different perspectives on the advisability of "privatizing" prisons and jails and on the issues raised by such privatization, see C. Logan, Private Prisons:

Cons and Pros (1990) and I. Robbins, The Legal Dimensions of Private Incarceration (1988).

3. *Causation*—Liability under § 1983 is extended only to a "person" who "subjects" an individual to a violation of federal rights or "causes" the individual "to be subjected" to such a violation. In the past, the Court has said that § 1983 "should be read against the background of tort liability that makes a man responsible for the natural consequences of his actions." Monroe v. Pape, 365 U.S. 167, 187, 81 S.Ct. 473, 484 (1961). Consequently, § 1983 liability may ensue even though the person sued had no intent to deprive the plaintiff of a federal right. Id. In fact, the Court has specifically observed that § 1983 contains no state-of-mind requirement whatsoever. Daniels v. Williams, 474 U.S. 327, 329–30, 106 S.Ct. 662, 664 (1986). For there to be a violation of the federal right underlying the § 1983 action, the defendant may need to have acted with a certain state of mind, see, e.g., Estelle v. Gamble, 429 U.S. 97, 97 S.Ct. 285 (1976), but § 1983 itself imposes no such requirement.

The Supreme Court's pronouncements in *Monroe v. Pape* and *Daniels v. Williams* might seem to suggest that ordinary tort principles concerning causation should be applied in a § 1983 action. A classic example of such a principle is the doctrine of *respondeat superior*. Under this doctrine, a "master" or employer can generally be held liable for torts committed by the "servant" or employee that fall within the scope of the servant's employment. W. Keeton, D. Dobbs, R. Keeton, and D. Owen, Prosser and Keeton on the Law of Torts 500 (5th ed.1984). The employer is considered a cause of the injury for which suit is brought simply because the employer employed a tortfeasor.

The Supreme Court has, however, thus far rejected application of this doctrine in § 1983 suits. In Monell v. Department of Social Services, 436 U.S. 658, 98 S.Ct. 2018 (1978), the Supreme Court held that a municipality cannot be held liable under § 1983 simply because of the unconstitutional conduct of one of its employees. The Court said that the original language of § 1983, which referred to "any person who * * * shall subject, or cause to be subjected," as well as § 1983's legislative history supported its conclusion.

Deciding that an employer-employee relationship will not suffice for § 1983 liability has proven easier for the Court than deciding what will suffice for municipal liability under § 1983. In *Monell* itself, the Court described in general terms when municipal liability under § 1983 would ensue:

> Local governing bodies, therefore, can be sued directly under § 1983 for monetary, declaratory, or injunctive relief where, as here, the action that is alleged to be unconstitutional implements or executes a policy statement, ordinance, regulation, or decision officially adopted and promulgated by that body's officers. Moreover, although the touchstone of the § 1983 action against a government body is an allegation that official policy is responsible for a deprivation of rights

protected by the Constitution, local governments, like every other § 1983 "person," by the very terms of the statute, may be sued for constitutional deprivations visited pursuant to governmental "custom" even though such a custom has not received formal approval through the body's official decisionmaking channels.

Id. at 690–91, 98 S.Ct. at 2035–36. Elsewhere in its opinion, the Court seemed to suggest that the official policy or custom had to be the "moving force" behind a constitutional violation for the municipality to be liable under § 1983. Id. at 694, 98 S.Ct. at 2037.

Particularly troubling to the Supreme Court since *Monell* was decided has been the question of what constitutes a municipal "policy" to which a constitutional violation is attributable. The Supreme Court's opinions discussing municipal policies are generally a morass of plurality, concurring, and dissenting opinions. See St. Louis v. Praprotnik, 485 U.S. 112, 108 S.Ct. 915 (1988); Pembaur v. Cincinnati, 475 U.S. 469, 106 S.Ct. 1292 (1986); Oklahoma City v. Tuttle, 471 U.S. 808, 105 S.Ct. 2427 (1985). The Court did, however, reach a consensus in Canton v. Harris, 489 U.S. 378, 109 S.Ct. 1197 (1989) as to when a municipality's failure to properly train its employees can lead to municipal liability under § 1983.

In *Canton*, the plaintiff brought a § 1983 suit against the city of Canton, Ohio in which she claimed that she had been denied needed medical treatment after her arrest. Her claim against the city rested on her belief that, with proper training, the municipal employees would have recognized her need for treatment. In an opinion written by Justice White, the Court observed as follows:

> We hold today that the inadequacy of police training may serve as the basis for § 1983 liability only where the failure to train amounts to deliberate indifference to the rights of persons with whom the police come into contact. This rule is most consistent with our admonition in *Monell,* and Polk County v. Dodson, 454 U.S. 312, 326 (1981), that a municipality can be liable under § 1983 only where its policies are the "moving force [behind] the constitutional violation." Only where a municipality's failure to train its employees in a relevant respect evidences a "deliberate indifference" to the rights of its inhabitants can such a shortcoming be properly thought of as a city "policy or custom" that is actionable under § 1983. As Justice Brennan's opinion in Pembaur v. Cincinnati, 475 U.S. 469, 483–484 (1986) (plurality) put it: "[M]unicipal liability under § 1983 attaches where—and only where—a deliberate choice to follow a course of action is made from among various alternatives" by city policy makers. Only where a failure to train reflects a "deliberate" or "conscious" choice by a municipality—a "policy" as defined by our prior cases—can a city be liable for such a failure under § 1983.

> * * * It may seem contrary to common sense to assert that a municipality will actually have a policy of not taking reasonable steps to train its employees. But it may happen that in light of the duties assigned to specific officers or employees the need for more or different

training is so obvious, and the inadequacy so likely to result in the violation of constitutional rights, that the policymakers of the city can reasonably be said to have been deliberately indifferent to the need.[10] In that event, the failure to provide proper training may fairly be said to represent a policy for which the city is responsible, and for which the city may be held liable if it actually causes injury.

In resolving the issue of a city's liability, the focus must be on adequacy of the training program in relation to the tasks the particular officers must perform. That a particular officer may be unsatisfactorily trained will not alone suffice to fasten liability on the city, for the officer's shortcomings may have resulted from factors other than a faulty training program. It may be, for example, that an otherwise sound program has occasionally been negligently administered. Neither will it suffice to prove that an injury or accident could have been avoided if an officer had had better or more training, sufficient to equip him to avoid the particular injury-causing conduct. Such a claim could be made about almost any encounter resulting in injury, yet not condemn the adequacy of the program to enable officers to respond properly to the usual and recurring situations with which they must deal. And plainly, adequately trained officers occasionally make mistakes; the fact that they do says little about the training program or the legal basis for holding the city liable.

Moreover, for liability to attach in this circumstance the identified deficiency in a city's training program must be closely related to the ultimate injury. Thus in the case at hand, respondent must still prove that the deficiency in training actually caused the police officers' indifference to her medical needs. Would the injury have been avoided had the employee been trained under a program that was not deficient in the identified respect? Predicting how a hypothetically well-trained officer would have acted under the circumstances may not be an easy task for the factfinder, particularly since matters of judgment may be involved, and since officers who are well trained are not free from error and perhaps might react very much like the untrained officer in similar circumstances. But judge and jury, doing their respective jobs, will be adequate to the task.

109 S.Ct. at 1204–06. See also Oklahoma City v. Tuttle, 471 U.S. 808, 105 S.Ct. 2427 (1985) (cannot infer simply from one unconstitutional act of a police officer, who is a lower-level municipal employee rather than a municipal policymaker, that the city had a policy of inadequate training which caused the constitutional violation).

Is *Canton v. Harris* consistent with the Supreme Court's pronouncement in Daniels v. Williams, 474 U.S. 327, 329–30, 106 S.Ct. 662, 664 (1986) that § 1983 contains no state-of-mind requirement? Would the test for municipal liability set forth in *Canton* apply when the claim against the municipality is based, not on the municipality's alleged

* * *

10. It could also be that the police, in exercising their discretion, so often violate constitutional rights that the need for fur- ther training must have been plainly obvious to the city policy makers, who, nevertheless, are "deliberately indifferent" to the need.

failure to adequately train its employees, but on its alleged failure to properly supervise its employees? What if the failure-to-train claim or failure-to-supervise claim is asserted against one of the upper-echelon officials in a department of corrections, such as the director of the department or a warden? What standard would have to be met for liability to be imposed? See, e.g., Sample v. Diecks, 885 F.2d 1099, 1118 (3d Cir.1989).

4. *Violation of Federal Rights*—To be liable under § 1983, the "person" sued must have caused the violation of another's federal rights—either rights under the United States Constitution or rights under federal laws. Many of the constitutional rights sought to be vindicated in § 1983 suits were discussed in previous chapters in this book.

2. *BIVENS* ACTIONS

Section 1983 only extends liability to persons who, while acting under the color of state law, violated the federal rights of others. No similar statute extends liability to federal officials who, for example, violate others' constitutional rights. Does the absence of such a statute mean that inmates confined in federal prisons are remediless if their constitutional rights are violated?

The answer to that question, according to the Supreme Court, is no. In Bivens v. Six Unknown Federal Narcotics Agents, 403 U.S. 388, 91 S.Ct. 1999 (1971), the Court concluded that an individual could sue FBI agents for damages incurred as a result of an allegedly unlawful arrest and search of his home. According to the Court, this damages remedy was implicitly conferred by the fourth amendment itself. In subsequent cases, the Court has specifically upheld the bringing of a *"Bivens* suit" for violations of the fifth amendment's due process clause, see Davis v. Passman, 442 U.S. 228, 99 S.Ct. 2264 (1979), as well as the eighth amendment's prohibition of cruel and unusual punishment. See Carlson v. Green, 446 U.S. 14, 100 S.Ct. 1468 (1980).

3. JURISDICTION

When a complaint is filed in a federal court, the complaint must identify the source of the court's jurisdiction over the case. Fed.R.Civ. P. 8(a). Federal district courts have jurisdiction over § 1983 suits under 28 U.S.C. § 1331 and sometimes under 28 U.S.C. § 1343(3). These statutory provisions are set forth below:

28 U.S.C. § 1331

The district courts shall have original jurisdiction of all civil actions arising under the Constitution, laws, or treaties of the United States.

28 U.S.C. § 1343(3)

The district courts shall have original jurisdiction of any civil action authorized by law to be commenced by any person:

*   *   *

(3) To redress the deprivation, under color of any State law, statute, ordinance, regulation, custom or usage, of any right, privilege or immunity secured by the Constitution of the United States or by any Act of Congress providing for equal rights of citizens or of all persons within the jurisdiction of the United States.

Section 1331 used to contain a requirement that the amount in controversy be over $10,000 before the district court could assume jurisdiction. Consequently, plaintiffs bringing civil rights suits under § 1983 tried to invoke the courts' jurisdiction under § 1343. With the abolition in 1980 of § 1331's jurisdictional-amount requirement, § 1983 suits can be and generally are filed in federal district courts under 28 U.S.C. § 1331.

Since the jurisdiction of the federal courts under both § 1331 and 1343(3) is not exclusive, § 1983 suits can be filed in a state court. Whether suit should be filed in a federal or state court will depend on a number of factors, including the procedural rules, particularly the discovery rules, governing civil litigation in the state and federal courts; the speed with which the case can be processed through the courts because of their docket loads; the location of the courts; and the perceived receptivity of the state court to federal-law-based claims. For an in-depth discussion of the factors to be considered when deciding whether to file a § 1983 suit in a state or federal court, see S. Steinglass, Section 1983 Litigation in State Courts, ch. 8, Tactical Choice of Forum Considerations (1989).

4. SUFFICIENCY OF THE COMPLAINT

HAINES v. KERNER

Supreme Court of the United States, 1972.
404 U.S. 519, 92 S.Ct. 594, 30 L.Ed.2d 652.

Per Curiam.

Petitioner, an inmate at the Illinois State Penitentiary, Menard, Illinois, commenced this action against the Governor of Illinois and other state officers and prison officials under the Civil Rights Act of 1871, 17 Stat. 13, 42 U.S.C. § 1983, and 28 U.S.C. § 1343(3), seeking to recover damages for claimed injuries and deprivation of rights while incarcerated under a judgment not challenged here. Petitioner's *pro se* complaint was premised on alleged action of prison officials placing him in solitary confinement as a disciplinary measure after he had struck another inmate on the head with a shovel following a verbal altercation. The assault by petitioner on another inmate is not denied. Petitioner's *pro se* complaint included general allegations of physical injuries suffered while in disciplinary confinement and denial of due process in the steps leading to that confinement. The claimed physical suffering was aggravation of a preexisting foot injury and a circulatory ailment caused by forcing him to sleep on the floor of his cell with only blankets.

The District Court granted respondents' motion under Rule 12(b)(6) of the Federal Rules of Civil Procedure to dismiss the complaint for failure to state a claim upon which relief could be granted, suggesting that only under exceptional circumstances should courts inquire into the internal operations of state penitentiaries and concluding that petitioner had failed to show a deprivation of federally protected rights. The Court of Appeals affirmed, emphasizing that prison officials are vested with "wide discretion" in disciplinary matters. We granted certiorari and appointed counsel to represent petitioner. The only issue now before us is petitioner's contention that the District Court erred in dismissing his *pro se* complaint without allowing him to present evidence on his claims.

[margin handwriting: Inspect proceedings]

Whatever may be the limits on the scope of inquiry of courts into the internal administration of prisons, allegations such as those asserted by petitioner, however inartfully pleaded, are sufficient to call for the opportunity to offer supporting evidence. We cannot say with assurance that under the allegations of the *pro se* complaint, which we hold to less stringent standards than formal pleadings drafted by lawyers, it appears "beyond doubt that the plaintiff can prove no set of facts in support of his claim which would entitle him to relief." *Conley v. Gibson,* 355 U.S. 41, 45–46 (1957).

Accordingly, although we intimate no view whatever on the merits of petitioner's allegations, we conclude that he is entitled to an opportunity to offer proof. The judgment is reversed and the case is remanded for further proceedings consistent herewith.

* * *

Questions and Points for Discussion

1. An indigent inmate will often not have the money to pay the filing fee required when filing a lawsuit in a federal court. The inmate can then file a petition with the court under 28 U.S.C. § 1915(a) seeking leave to proceed *in forma pauperis.* Section 1915(a) provides as follows:

[margin handwriting: privilege given to prosecute an appeal]

(a) Any court of the United States may authorize the commencement, prosecution or defense of any suit, action or proceeding, civil or criminal, or appeal therein, without prepayment of fees and costs or security therefor, by a person who makes affidavit that he is unable to pay such costs or give security therefor. Such affidavit shall state the nature of the action, defense or appeal and affiant's belief that he is entitled to redress.

An appeal may not be taken in forma pauperis if the trial court certifies in writing that it is not taken in good faith.

If the court determines that the inmate actually could prepay the necessary fees and costs or that the inmate's claim is "frivolous" or "malicious," the court "may" dismiss the case. 28 U.S.C. § 1915(d). According to the Supreme Court, however, a complaint will be considered "frivolous" only if it has no "arguable basis either in law or in fact." *Neitzke v. Williams,* 490 U.S. 319, 109 S.Ct. 1827, 1831 (1989). This standard for testing the sufficiency of a complaint is a more liberal standard than the standard applied when a Rule 12(b)(6) motion is filed to dismiss a complaint for failure to state a claim upon which relief can be granted, since the liberal pleading test set forth in *Haines v. Kerner* applies only to the factual allegations in the complaint. Id. at 1834 n. 9. As the Court explained in *Neitzke,* "[w]hen a complaint raises an arguable question of law which the district court ultimately finds is correctly resolved against the plaintiff, dismissal on Rule 12(b)(6) grounds is appropriate, but dismissal on the basis of frivolousness is not." Id. at 1833. There will therefore be some times when a complaint fails to state a claim upon which relief could be granted and yet the complaint is not "frivolous" within the meaning of § 1915(d).

One reason given by the Supreme Court for applying a more lenient standard when testing the sufficiency of a complaint under § 1915(d) is that a plaintiff faced with a Rule 12(b)(6) motion will receive notice, through the motion, of deficiencies in the complaint; the plaintiff can then often amend the complaint, avoiding a dismissal. By contrast, since *sua sponte* dismissals—dismissals on the court's own motion—are contemplated by and generally occur under § 1915(d), an indigent litigant's suit can be dismissed under § 1915(d) without the plaintiff ever having had any real opportunity to rectify deficiencies in the complaint before it was dismissed. Consequently, under the test set forth in *Neitzke,* courts must be especially careful to ensure that a complaint is baseless before dismissing it at the *in forma pauperis* stage of the litigation.

2. Section 1915(d) also provides that a federal court "may request" an attorney to represent a party in a federal lawsuit who cannot afford to hire an attorney. Whether or not to appoint counsel under § 1915(d) falls within the court's discretion, and the court's decision not to appoint an attorney will be reversed only if it abused its discretion. Jackson v. Cain, 864 F.2d 1235, 1242 (5th Cir.1989); McNeil v. Lowney, 831 F.2d 1368, 1371 (7th Cir.1987).

Although a federal court can ask an attorney to represent an indigent litigant in a civil suit without payment, the Supreme Court has held that the court has no power under § 1915(d) to require the attorney to provide such representation. Mallard v. United States District Court, 490 U.S. 296, 109 S.Ct. 1814 (1989). Left unresolved by the Court in *Mallard* were the questions whether courts have inherent authority to make such compulsory assignments and whether such compulsory assignments would be constitutional.

3. Set forth below is an example of a complaint filed in a prisoners' rights suit. The complaint was filed in the case of *Inmates of Occoquan v. Barry* by the National Prison Project of the American Civil Liberties Union.

Attorneys for Plaintiffs

IN THE UNITED STATES DISTRICT COURT FOR THE
DISTRICT OF COLUMBIA

INMATES OF OCCOQUAN, WILLIAM ALSTON-EL, MICHAEL CLAY, JAMES DAVIS, ALLEN GLAZER, RONNIE GOODMAN, JAMES HARRINGTON, JOHN HARRIS, CARL HENDERSON, JEFFREY HOWARD, MICHAEL IVEY, THOMAS OLIVER, FRED OWENS, AHMED PASHA, WALTER ROBINSON, CALVIN ROOKARD, CARL WILLIAMS AND ROBERT LEON WILSON, individually and on behalf of all other persons similarly situated, Plaintiffs, v. MARION BARRY, MAYOR, AND JAMES F. PALMER, DIRECTOR, DEPARTMENT OF CORRECTIONS, in their official capacities, Defendants.	Civ. No.

COMPLAINT

On behalf of themselves and the class alleged herein, plaintiffs state the following for their complaint against defendants:

I. PRELIMINARY STATEMENT

1. This is a class action brought by plaintiffs on behalf of all inmates who are or will be confined at the District of Columbia Department of Corrections Occoquan Facilities I, II and III in Lorton, Virginia (hereinafter Occoquan). Plaintiffs seek declaratory and injunctive relief for deprivations under color of state law of the rights, privileges and immunities secured by the Constitution of the United States and, in particular, those secured by the Fifth and Eighth Amendments thereof.

2. Plaintiffs specifically seek relief from conditions at Occoquan which fall below standards of human decency, inflict needless suffering on prisoners and create an environment which threaten prisoners' physical and mental well-being and results in the unnecessary deterioration of prisoners confined there.

3.   Occoquan I and II are administered separately from Occoquan III. All three are medium security facilities.   ~~Occoquan I houses sentenced felons.~~   ~~Occoquan II houses primarily misdemeanants as well as felons awaiting sentencing.~~   ~~Occoquan III also houses sentenced felons.~~   On July 9, 1986, the combined population of the facilities was approximately 1750, with a rated capacity of 1366.   On July 10, 1986, a major disturbance occurred at Occoquan I and II.   On July 11, 1986, the combined population was reduced to 1034, but has steadily increased since that date to approximately 1242 as of July 28, 1986.

II.   JURISDICTION

4.   This action is filed under 42 U.S.C. § 1983 to redress injuries suffered by plaintiffs and the class they represent for deprivation under color of state law of rights secured by the Fifth and Eighth Amendments to the United States Constitution.   Plaintiffs' claims also arise directly under the Fifth and Eighth Amendments.   The Court has jurisdiction pursuant to 28 U.S.C. § 1331 and 28 U.S.C. § 1343(a)(3).

5.   Venue in the District Court for the District of Columbia is proper. Defendants Marion S. Barry and James E. Palmer reside in the District of Columbia and each of the claims for relief arose in this district.

III.   PARTIES

6.   Each of the named plaintiffs is currently an inmate confined by the District of Columbia Department of Corrections at, or subject to return to, Occoquan I, II or III.

7.   Plaintiff William Alston–El has been confined at Occoquan III for at least six months.

8.   Plaintiff Michael Clay has been confined at Occoquan I and II for at least seven months as a protective custody inmate in the cellblock and in at least six dorms.

9.   Plaintiff James Davis has been confined at Occoquan I and II for at least one year, including the J–2 dorm for approximately two months.

10.   Plaintiff Allen Glazer has been confined intermittently at Occoquan I and II and at Central Facility, Lorton Reformatory for at least one year and continuously at Occoquan I and II since approximately July 30, 1986.

11.   Plaintiff Ronnie Goodman has been confined at Occoquan I and II for at least fifteen months.

12.   Plaintiff James Harrington is currently confined at the Central Detention Facility, but was recently confined at Occoquan I and II in the cellblock and is subject to return.

13.   Plaintiff John Harris has been confined at Occoquan III, Dorm 5 since June 13, 1986.

14.   Plaintiff Carl Henderson is currently confined at the Central Detention Facility, but was recently confined at Occoquan I and II and is subject to return.

15. Plaintiff Jeffrey Howard has been confined at Occoquan I and II for approximately three weeks.

16. Plaintiff Michael Ivey has been confined at Occoquan III, Dorm 5 since June 13, 1986.

17. Plaintiff Thomas Oliver is currently confined at Maximum Security, Lorton Reformatory, but was recently confined at Occoquan I and II and Occoquan III and is subject to return.

18. Plaintiff Fred Owens has been confined by the D.C. Department of Corrections for at least seventeen months, including Occoquan I and II, Occoquan III and the Central Detention Facility, and is currently at Occoquan III.

19. Plaintiff Ahmed Pasha has been confined at Occoquan I and II for at least three months.

20. Plaintiff Walter Robinson is currently confined at the Central Detention Facility, but was recently confined at Occoquan I and II and is subject to return.

21. Plaintiff Calvin Rookard has been confined at Occoquan I and II for at least twenty-two months.

22. Plaintiff Carl Williams has been confined at Occoquan I and II for at least two years.

23. Plaintiff Robert Leon Wilson is currently confined at Maximum Security, Lorton Reformatory, but was recently confined at Occoquan I and II and is subject to return.

24. Defendant Marion S. Barry is the Mayor of the District of Columbia. As chief executive officer of the District, he has ultimate administrative and fiscal control of and responsibility for, among other District agencies, the District of Columbia Department of Corrections. He has the overall control and supervision of D.C. correctional institutions, including Occoquan I, II and III.

25. Defendant James F. Palmer is the Director of the District of Columbia Department of Corrections. He has the overall control and supervision of D.C. correctional institutions, including Occoquan I, II and III.

IV. CLASS ACTION ALLEGATIONS

26. This is a class action under Rules 23(a) and 23(b)(1) and (2) of the Federal Rules of Civil Procedure.

27. Plaintiffs are representative parties of a class of all persons who are under the control of the District of Columbia Department of Corrections and who are confined at Occoquan or who may be so confined in the future.

28. Plaintiffs are members of the class and their claims are typical of all class members. Plaintiffs are represented by competent counsel and will fairly and adequately protect the interests of the class.

29. The class is so numerous that joinder of the numbers is impracticable. Current members of the class number over 1200.

30. The lawsuit challenges various conditions of confinement at the prisons and there are questions of law and fact common to the class.

31. The defendants have acted and refused to act on grounds generally applicable to the class, thereby making appropriate final injunctive and declaratory relief with respect to the class.

V. FACTUAL ALLEGATIONS

A. *Living Conditions*

32. The Department of Corrections has been enjoined from exceeding certain population limits at the Central Detention Facility (hereinafter Jail); Lorton Reformatory, Central Facility (hereinafter Central); and Lorton Reformatory, Maximum Security (hereinafter Maximum). Because of these court-ordered limits, and the absence of adequate alternatives to incarceration, such as work release programs, halfway houses, supervised furloughs and third party custody programs, Occoquan, which is not under any court-ordered limits, has been forced to receive prisoners beyond any reasonable capacity.

33. Plaintiffs are subject to frequent transfers within the D.C. Department of Corrections because, in the absence of adequate alternatives to incarceration, defendants constantly shuffle inmates from one facility to another in an effort to comply with these population limits. Each of the named plaintiffs has been or is subject to such transfers.

34. The principal living units at Occoquan are dormitories. According to American Correctional Association (hereinafter ACA) minimum standards, only minimum security inmates should be housed in dormitories with a maximum of 50 prisoners per dorm in order to protect inmates from unnecessary risk of harm. Nevertheless, these dorms are being used to house medium security prisoners.

35. There is one cellblock for the three Occoquan facilities which mainly houses prisoners confined to protective custody, administrative segregation and disciplinary segregation.

36. Prior to the July 10 disturbance, Occoquan was severely overcrowded. The population exceeded the maximum rated capacity which itself is substantially above standards used for other medium security dormitories within the Department of Corrections.

37. After July 10, 1986, many prisoners were temporarily moved to other facilities during the repair work at Occoquan I and II, but the influx of new prisoners has already increased the population to more than 25% over what it was following the disturbance. Severe overcrowding at Occoquan III has persisted throughout this period. At present, even with the temporary reduction at Occoquan I and II, the population at each of the three facilities exceeds standards employed by the Department of Corrections for medium security dormitories.

38. Substantially all of the dormitories house more than the ACA standard of 50 minimum security men per dorm. In several dorms, more than double that number of prisoners must sleep together in a single room. The beds are placed so close together that they nearly touch and there is no reasonable assurance of physical integrity while prisoners are sleeping or

otherwise occupying their beds. Double-bunking is commonplace, particularly in Occoquan III, including 5 Dorm, and J Dorm and the Youth dorm (M) at Occoquan I and II.

39. Prisoners lack adequate storage lockers for their clothes, cosmetics, books, papers and other possessions. Many use paper boxes or bags to store these items. Where cabinets or lockers have been provided, locks are frequently missing or broken.

40. There are not enough toilets or showers in many dorms; mattresses are not cleaned between use by prisoners and there is a lack of adequate clothing. These conditions, exacerbated by the overcrowding, increase the risk of the spread of communicable diseases.

41. Because of the overcrowding, noise levels in the dormitories are high, exceeding reasonable limits in some dorms to the point where it is necessary to almost shout to be heard.

42. There is no ventilation system. In order to ventilate the dorms, it is necessary to open the windows and doors, which draws in dust and fumes. Screens are frequently torn or missing causing serious infestations of flies and other insects. In one dorm, hot water or steam pipes run to it from the kitchen and other living units. The back part of this unit is exceedingly hot. The fans that are mounted in that part of the dorm only aggravate the situation by blowing hot air into the rest of the dorm.

43. Loose plaster over the T.V. area of one dorm is falling and at least one inmate has been hit in the head and injured.

B. *Fire Hazards*

44. Occoquan was a fire hazard, presenting a grave risk of injuries and death to those who lived there before July 10. Fires set during the July 10 disturbance spread quickly inside the dorms and from roof line to roof line. There were no automatic sprinklers installed under the wooden rafters or on the ceilings of the dorms at the time, nor have any been installed since then.

45. Occoquan is still a fire hazard. Almost all the dorms are deficient in crucial ways. Minimally adequate fire standards require two exits from each living area but some dorms and anterooms have only one exit. In some dorms, exits are blocked by beds or cabinets or boxes. Many electric smoke detectors are disconnected and very few, if any, dorms contain battery-powered smoke detectors. Mattresses are not flame-retardant which enables any fire to spread quickly. This problem is exacerbated by the general clutter of books, papers and clothing often stashed in paper bags and boxes which provide ready fuel for a fire. In the winter, this condition is made more hazardous by beds pushed up against radiators and books, papers and clothes piled on top. The anterooms in back of some of the dorms provide no egress for residents housed there, and in one dorm, the only exit into the main dorm is blocked by a large floor fan. Until approximately July 28, some inmates in Dorm J–1 were housed on a balcony above other beds with a pipe blocking the only exit from that area. Inmates housed beneath the balcony have hung extremely flammable

plastic garbage bags to keep dirt from falling on their beds, causing a potential "death trap" for those bunked above.

C. *Personal Safety*

46. Overcrowding has led to scarcity of resources, tension and stress which in turn encourage inmate confrontations and violence. Other conditions also create an unsafe environment for inmates. The defendants' indifference to and failure to provide reasonable personal safety to inmates is evident.

47. On May 23, 1986, inmates rebelled and threw beds out of dormitories and set mattresses afire when corrections officials attempted to place additional beds in the already overcrowded dormitories.

48. The major disturbance at Occoquan I and II on July 10 was a reaction to severe overcrowding. Many inmates were shot and injured by correctional officers as inmates were escorted to buses out of Occoquan the next day.

49. The atmosphere at Occoquan is tense and dangerous. Idleness is pervasive. There simply are not enough jobs, vocational and educational programs and recreational opportunities to engage the vast majority of residents. Population pressures have led at times to the opening of makeshift dorms. For example, such a dorm was opened recently in the visiting hall that served Occoquan I and II. Visiting took place in the gym, further reducing the amount of exercise time available for inmates. Idleness has led to tension and frustration and aggressive acts by prisoners. The lack of programming also adversely affects parole opportunities which in turn further exacerbates the overcrowding and tension.

50. The provision of one telephone per dorm for prisoners' use is insufficient. A telephone is the main lifeline to families, friends and community. With so many men vying for its use, violence among inmates often begins with conflicts over telephone use.

51. The failure to provide secure lockers for inmates' personal property allows inmates to steal from others, leading to further tension and violence among inmates.

52. The configuration and layout of some of the dorms, including pillars and anterooms, and crowded conditions and double-bunking prevent correctional officers from observing activities in certain areas. This makes it impossible for defendants to reasonably ensure the physical integrity of the prisoners. On hot days the lights are turned off in an attempt to reduce discomfort but this results in further reduction of officers' ability to supervise prisoners.

53. Defendants fail to adequately classify inmates. Because inmates' assignments to dormitories are based primarily on the availability of bed space, aggressive and predatory inmates are housed with vulnerable inmates whose personal safety is jeopardized.

54. Defendants' housing of aggressive and predatory inmates in dormitory style housing fails to comply with the ACA standard that no more than 50 minimum security inmates be housed in dormitory style housing.

55. Inmates who require protective custody because of violent conditions at Occoquan are housed in a cellblock known as Q Building which is temporarily closed. Protective custody inmates were housed there with inmates confined for disciplinary or administrative reasons. Other protective custody inmates are housed in the J dorms. Defendants' failure to protect inmates is shown by housing protective custody inmates in the cellblock and in dorms together with more aggressive inmates.

D. *Medical and Dental Services*

56. Medical care and treatment at Occoquan is grossly inadequate and constitutes deliberate indifference to prisoners' serious medical needs.

57. The overcrowding has exacerbated deficiencies in staff and services and increases the likelihood of the transmission of communicable diseases and creates other health risks.

58. Delays in receiving medical care as a result of overcrowding cause needless pain and suffering for inmates.

59. The medical team is understaffed, particularly after 4 p.m. when there is one physician's assistant for all of Occoquan and after midnight there is no coverage at all.

60. The medical services at Occoquan III are particularly inadequate. There is no medical staffing after 4 p.m. or on weekends. Emergencies are handled through Occoquan I and II. Clinical care is routinely delayed because appointments must be made through Occoquan I and II which are backed up with their own prisoners' needs. With the addition of dorm 5 to an already overcrowded situation, medical care at Occoquan III is grossly inadequate.

61. Frequently, inmates transferred from other facilities to Occoquan are deprived of adequate or appropriate medical treatment because of delays in getting their medical records transferred. In one dorm, two inmates were not known to have AIDS by the medical officer in charge until they reported to sick call.

62. Dental treatment falls far short of minimum standards set forth by the American Dental Association and the ACA. Dental care is routinely delayed because medical records are unavailable to the dental staff.

63. Inmates in urgent need of dental care are forced to endure pain and suffering because of long delays in receiving dental care.

64. Those inmates identified as having mental health problems are held inappropriately in the cellblock to await available space at the Jail because Occoquan does not provide mental health facilities or treatment.

VI. CLAIMS FOR RELIEF

65. Plaintiffs reallege and incorporate by reference paragraphs 32 through 64.

66. Defendants fail to provide plaintiffs with the basic necessities of life, including adequate shelter, sanitation, personal safety, and medical and dental health care, especially because the ill effects of such deprivation are exacerbated or caused by related conditions including overcrowding. The resulting conditions at Occoquan, which are incompatible with contem-

porary standards of decency, cause unnecessary and wanton infliction of pain as well as genuine privation, and are not reasonably related to any legitimate governmental objectives. Inmates are thereby subjected to cruel and unusual punishment in violation of the Fifth and Eighth Amendments to the United States Constitution.

VII. NO ADEQUATE REMEDY AT LAW

67. As a proximate result of the defendants' policies, practices, procedures, acts and omissions, plaintiffs have suffered, do suffer, and will continue to suffer immediate and irreparable injury, including physical, psychological and emotional injury. Plaintiffs' physical and psychological health and well-being will continue to deteriorate during the course of their confinement under the conditions described in this complaint. Plaintiffs have no plain, adequate or complete remedy at law to redress the wrongs described herein. Plaintiffs will continue to be irreparably injured by the policies, practices, procedures, acts and omissions of the defendants unless this Court grants the injunctive relief that plaintiffs seek.

VIII. PRAYER FOR RELIEF

WHEREFORE, plaintiffs and the class they represent pray this Court:

1. Determine by order pursuant to Rule 23, Federal Rules of Civil Procedure, that this action may be maintained as a class action;

2. Issue a declaratory judgment stating the defendants' policies, practices, acts and omissions described in this complaint violate plaintiffs' rights, guaranteed to them by the Fifth and Eighth Amendments to the United States Constitution;

3. Permanently enjoin defendants, their officers, agents, employees and successors in office, as well as those acting in concert and participating with them, from engaging in the unlawful practices described in this complaint;

4. Retain jurisdiction of this matter until this Court's order has been carried out;

5. Award plaintiffs their reasonable costs and attorneys' fees pursuant to 42 U.S.C. § 1988; and

6. Grant such other relief as may be just and equitable.

This 4th day of August, 1986.

Edward I. Koren

Alexa P. Freeman

Steven Ney

National Prison Project of the
American Civil Liberties Union
Foundation
1616 P Street N.W., Suite 340
Washington, D.C. 20036

Attorneys for Plaintiffs

* * *

The plaintiffs in the case in which the complaint just set forth was filed, incidentally, prevailed in the district court, with the court finding that the conditions of the inmates' confinement violated their right not to be subjected to cruel and unusual punishment. Inmates of Occoquan v. Barry, 717 F.Supp. 854 (D.D.C.1989).

B. AFFIRMATIVE DEFENSES

To avoid liability in a § 1983 suit, a defendant can assert a number of defenses. An attorney handling a § 1983 suit should be fully conversant with the procedural rules governing litigation in the court where suit was filed so that the attorney knows by when an affirmative defense must be asserted and whether the defense must be asserted in the answer, in a motion to dismiss or for summary judgment, or in either the answer or a motion. Set forth below is a discussion of a few of the defenses upon which § 1983 litigation has more frequently focused.

1. IMMUNITY

a. *Eleventh Amendment*

The eleventh amendment to the United States Constitution provides that "[t]he Judicial power of the United States shall not be construed to extend to any suit in law or equity, commenced or prosecuted against one of the United States by Citizens of another State, or by Citizens or Subjects of any Foreign State." Despite the literal language of the amendment, the Supreme Court has held that a state also cannot be sued in federal court by one of its own citizens. Hans v. Louisiana, 134 U.S. 1, 10 S.Ct. 504 (1890).

At the same time, however, the Supreme Court has recognized several exceptions or limitations to the general rule that a state is immune from suit in federal court. First, the Court has observed that a state can consent to be sued, waiving its eleventh amendment immunity. Alabama v. Pugh, 438 U.S. 781, 782, 98 S.Ct. 3057, 3057 (1978). That a state can consent to be sued, however, will not help a § 1983 plaintiff who wishes to sue a state, since the Court has now held that a state cannot be sued in any event under § 1983 because it is not a "person" within the meaning of the statute. See Will v. Michigan Department of State Police, 109 S.Ct. 2304 (1989), discussed supra on page 565.

Second, the Supreme Court has held that Congress has the power under § 5 of the fourteenth amendment to abrogate states' eleventh amendment immunity in order to effectuate the provisions of the fourteenth amendment. Fitzpatrick v. Bitzer, 427 U.S. 445, 456, 96 S.Ct. 2666, 2671 (1976). According to the Court, however, when Congress enacted § 1983, it did not intend to exercise this power. Quern v. Jordan, 440 U.S. 332, 341, 99 S.Ct. 1139, 1145 (1979). The significance of the Court's holding in *Fitzpatrick* is that Congress, if it wishes to, can amend § 1983 to include states as suable defendants who cannot raise a sovereign immunity defense.

While the Court has held that states sued under § 1983 in federal court retain their eleventh amendment immunity, the Court has also held that states may nonetheless have to sometimes pay for the plaintiff's attorney's fees incurred in the course of litigating a § 1983 suit. In Hutto v. Finney, 437 U.S. 678, 98 S.Ct. 2565 (1978), the Court held that the Civil Rights Attorney's Fees Awards Act of 1976, 42 U.S.C. § 1988, overrides the eleventh amendment immunity of states. That Act provides that "[i]n any action or proceeding" to enforce certain civil rights statutes, including 42 U.S.C. § 1983, "the court, in its discretion, may allow the prevailing party, other than the United States, a reasonable attorney's fee as part of the costs." Although the Act on its face does not mention the liability of states for attorney's fees awards, the Court in *Hutto* emphasized that the Senate and House Reports discussing the Act made it clear that Congress contemplated that such awards would be leveled against states.

When will a state have to pay a prevailing plaintiff's attorney's fees even though the state was not, and according to the Supreme Court, could not be a defendant in a § 1983 action? As was mentioned earlier, in a footnote in Will v. Michigan Department of State Police, 109 S.Ct. 2304 (1989) the Court mentioned that while state officials sued in their official capacities are not "persons" within the meaning of § 1983 when damages are sought as relief, they are amenable to suit when the plaintiff seeks injunctive relief. Id. at 2311 n. 10. And in *Hutto v. Finney,* the Court observed that when state officials sued in their official capacities have litigated a § 1983 suit in good faith but lost, Congress intended that the state bear the financial burden of paying the plaintiff's attorney's fees. Consequently, in § 1983 suits seeking injunctive relief against state officials sued in their official capacities, the states may end up being liable for a prevailing plaintiff's attorney's fees.

b. Sovereign Immunity—The United States

It is now well-established that the United States cannot be sued without its consent. United States v. Mitchell, 463 U.S. 206, 212, 103 S.Ct. 2961, 2965 (1983). Congress, however, has consented to the bringing of constitutional claims against the government. See 28 U.S.C. § 1346(a)(2). Under the Federal Tort Claims Act, the United

States can also be liable for the negligent acts of its employees. See 28 U.S.C. §§ 1346(b), 1402(b), 1504, 2110, 2401, 2411–12, and 2671–80. There are many exceptions to this Act, however, with which an attorney contemplating or litigating a claim under the FTCA should become familiar.

c. Official Immunity—Absolute and Qualified
CLEAVINGER v. SAXNER
Supreme Court of the United States, 1985.
474 U.S. 193, 106 S.Ct. 496, 88 L.Ed.2d 507.

MR. JUSTICE BLACKMUN delivered the opinion of the Court.

[The plaintiffs in this case, two inmates incarcerated at the Federal Correctional Institution in Terre Haute, Indiana, filed a *Bivens* action against three members of a prison disciplinary committee that had found them guilty of disciplinary infractions. A jury found that the defendants had violated the plaintiffs' due process rights under the fifth amendment and awarded each plaintiff $1,500 in compensatory damages from each of the three defendants. The defendants moved for a judgment notwithstanding the verdict, arguing that they were absolutely immune from damages liability. The trial court rejected this argument as did the Seventh Circuit Court of Appeals on appeal. The Supreme Court then granted certiorari.]

A. This Court has observed: "Few doctrines were more solidly established at common law than the immunity of judges from liability for damages for acts committed within their judicial jurisdiction." *Pierson v. Ray,* 386 U.S. 547, 553–554 (1967). * * * In *Pierson v. Ray,* the Court held that absolute immunity shielded a municipal judge who was sued for damages under 42 U.S.C. § 1983 by clergymen who alleged that he had convicted them unconstitutionally for a peaceful protest against racial segregation. The Court stressed that such immunity was essential to protect the integrity of the judicial process. * * *

With this judicial immunity firmly established, the Court has extended absolute immunity to certain others who perform functions closely associated with the judicial process. The federal hearing examiner and administrative law judge have been afforded absolute immunity. "There can be little doubt that the role of the modern federal hearing examiner or administrative law judge . . . is 'functionally comparable' to that of a judge." *Butz v. Economou,* 438 U.S. 478, 513 (1978). * * *

* * *

B. The Court has extended absolute immunity to the President when damages liability is predicated on his official act. *Nixon v. Fitzgerald,* 457 U.S. 731, 744–758 (1982). See *Harlow v. Fitzgerald,* 457 U.S. 800, 807 (1982). "For executive officials in general, however, our cases make plain that qualified immunity represents the norm." See *Scheuer v. Rhodes,* 416 U.S. 232 (1974) (State Governor and his aides);

Harlow v. Fitzgerald (Presidential aides); *Butz v. Economou* (Cabinet member * * *); *Procunier v. Navarette*, 434 U.S. 555 (1978) (state prison officials); *Wood v. Strickland*, 420 U.S. 308 (1975) (school board members); *Pierson v. Ray* (police officers). * * * In any event, "federal officials who seek absolute exemption from personal liability for unconstitutional conduct must bear the burden of showing that public policy requires an exemption of that scope."

C. * * * "[O]ur cases clearly indicate that immunity analysis rests on functional categories, not on the status of the defendant." Absolute immunity flows not from rank or title or "location within the Government," but from the nature of the responsibilities of the individual official. And in *Butz* the Court mentioned the following factors, among others, as characteristic of the judicial process and to be considered in determining absolute as contrasted with qualified immunity: (a) the need to assure that the individual can perform his functions without harassment or intimidation; (b) the presence of safeguards that reduce the need for private damages actions as a means of controlling unconstitutional conduct; (c) insulation from political influence; (d) the importance of precedent; (e) the adversary nature of the process; and (f) the correctability of error on appeal.

* * *

Petitioners, seemingly in order to negate the significance of certain of the specified factors, point out that grand jury proceedings possess few procedural safeguards that are associated with court proceedings, and are largely immune from any type of judicial review. Petitioners also observe that prosecutorial decisionmaking is not subject to the formalities of trials; instead, the prosecutor exercises broad and generally unreviewable discretion. Yet grand jurors and prosecutors enjoy absolute immunity. Petitioners finally argue that the Court's cases teach that absolute immunity shields an official if (a) the official performs an adjudicatory function comparable to that of a judge, (b) the function is of sufficient public importance, and (c) the proper performance of that function would be subverted if the official were subjected to individual suit for damages.

* * * The committee members, in a sense, do perform an adjudicatory function in that they determine whether the accused inmate is guilty or innocent of the charge leveled against him; in that they hear testimony and receive documentary evidence; in that they evaluate credibility and weigh evidence; and in that they render a decision. We recognize, too, the presence of some societal importance in this dispute-resolution function. The administration of a prison is a difficult undertaking at best, for it concerns persons many of whom have demonstrated a proclivity for antisocial, criminal, and violent conduct. We also acknowledge that many inmates do not refrain from harassment and intimidation. The number of nonmeritorious prisoners' cases that come to this Court's notice is evidence of this. * * * And we do not underestimate the fact, stressed by petitioners, that committee

members usually are persons of modest means and, if they are suable and unprotected, perhaps would be disinclined to serve on a discipline committee.

We conclude, nonetheless, that these concerns, to the extent they are well grounded, are overstated in the context of constitutional violations. We do not perceive the discipline committee's function as a "classic" adjudicatory one, as petitioners would describe it. Surely, the members of the committee, unlike a federal or state judge, are not "independent"; to say that they are is to ignore reality. They are not professional hearing officers, as are administrative law judges. They are, instead, prison officials, albeit no longer of the rank and file, temporarily diverted from their usual duties. They are employees of the Bureau of Prisons and they are the direct subordinates of the warden who reviews their decision. They work with the fellow employee who lodges the charge against the inmate upon whom they sit in judgment. The credibility determination they make often is one between a co-worker and an inmate. They thus are under obvious pressure to resolve a disciplinary dispute in favor of the institution and their fellow employee. * * *

* * *

We relate this committee membership * * * to the school board service the Court had under consideration in *Wood v. Strickland*, 420 U.S. 308 (1975). The school board members were to function as "adjudicators in the school disciplinary process," and they were to "judge whether there have been violations of school regulations and, if so, the appropriate sanctions for the violations." Despite the board's adjudicative function of that extent, the Court concluded that the board members were to be protected by only qualified immunity. After noting the suggestion of the presence of a deterrence-from-service factor, the Court concluded that "absolute immunity would not be justified since it would not sufficiently increase the ability of school officials to exercise their discretion in a forthright manner to warrant the absence of a remedy for students subjected to intentional or otherwise inexcusable deprivations."

That observation and conclusion are equally applicable here. * * * If qualified immunity is sufficient for the schoolroom, it should be more than sufficient for the jailhouse where the door is closed, not open, and where there is little, if any, protection by way of community observation.

Petitioners assert with some vigor that procedural formality is not a prerequisite for absolute immunity. They refer to well-known summary and *ex parte* proceedings, such as the issuance of search warrants and temporary restraining orders, and the setting of bail. * * * In any event, it is asserted, committee proceedings contain ample safeguards to ensure the avoidance or correction of constitutional errors. Among these are the qualifications for committee service; prior notice to the inmate; representation by a staff member; the right to present certain evidence at the hearing; the right to be present; the requirement for a detailed record; the availability of administrative review at three levels * * *; and the availability of ultimate review in federal court under 28 U.S.C. § 2241. Finally, it is said that qualified immunity would provide insufficient protection for committee members.

We are not persuaded. To be sure, the line between absolute immunity and qualified immunity often is not an easy one to perceive and structure. That determination in this case, however, is not difficult, and we readily conclude that these committee members fall on the qualified-immunity side of the line.

Under the Bureau's disciplinary policy in effect at the time of respondents' hearings, few of the procedural safeguards contained in the Administrative Procedure Act under consideration in *Butz* were present. The prisoner was to be afforded neither a lawyer nor an independent nonstaff representative. There was no right to compel the attendance of witnesses or to cross-examine. There was no right to discovery. There was no cognizable burden of proof. No verbatim transcript was afforded. Information presented often was hearsay or self-serving. The committee members were not truly independent. In sum, the members had no identification with the judicial process of the kind and depth that has occasioned absolute immunity.

Qualified immunity, however, is available to these committee members. That, we conclude, is the proper point at which to effect the balance between the opposing considerations. This less-than-absolute protection is not of small consequence. As the Court noted in *Butz*, insubstantial lawsuits can be recognized and be quickly disposed of, and firm application of the Federal Rules of Civil Procedure "will ensure that federal officials are not harassed by frivolous lawsuits." All the committee members need to do is to follow the clear and simple constitutional requirements of *Wolff v. McDonnell*; they then should have no reason to fear substantial harassment and liability. Qualified immunity has been widely imposed on executive officials who possess greater responsibilities. "[I]t is not unfair to hold liable the official who knows or should know he is acting outside the law, and . . . insisting on an awareness of clearly established constitutional limits will not unduly interfere with the exercise of official judgment."

* * *

* * *

We likewise are not impressed with the argument that anything less than absolute immunity will result in a flood of litigation and in substantial procedural burdens and expense for committee members. This argument, too, has been made before. But this Court's pronouncements in *Harlow v. Fitzgerald*, 457 U.S., at 813–820, place the argument in appropriate perspective, for many cases may be disposed of without the necessity of pretrial discovery proceedings. Our experience teaches us that the vast majority of prisoner cases are resolved on the complaint alone. Of those prisoners whose complaints survive initial dismissal, few attempt discovery and fewer still actually obtain it. See Turner, When Prisoners Sue: A Study of Prisoner Section 1983 Suits in the Federal Courts, 92 Harv.L.Rev. 610 (1979). And any expense of litigation largely is alleviated by the fact that a Government official who finds himself as a defendant in litigation of this kind is often represented, as in this case, by Government counsel. If the problem becomes acute, the Government has alternatives available to it: it might decide to indemnify the defendant official; Congress could make the claim a subject for the Federal Tort Claims Act; and Congress could even consider putting in place administrative law judges to preside at prison committee hearings.

The judgment of the Court of Appeals is affirmed.

JUSTICE REHNQUIST, with whom THE CHIEF JUSTICE and JUSTICE WHITE join, dissenting. [Opinion omitted.]

Questions and Points for Discussion

1. When looking at the language of § 1983, one might wonder, not whether officials sued in their individual capacity under § 1983 should enjoy absolute or qualified immunity from damages liability, but whether the officials should be afforded any immunity whatsoever. On its face, § 1983 does not exempt any culpable officials from liability; it says that "*[e]very* person" who violates another's constitutional rights when acting under the color of state law "*shall* be liable."

The Supreme Court, however, has repeatedly observed that § 1983 must be read in light of the immunities afforded by the common law at the time of § 1983's enactment. See, e.g., the cases cited in Newport v. Fact Concerts, Inc., 453 U.S. 247, 258 & n. 18, 101 S.Ct. 2748, 2755 & n. 18 (1981). Since, according to the Court, there is no indication, other than of course the plain language of § 1983, that Congress intended to abolish these longstanding common-law immunities when officials were sued under § 1983, § 1983 defendants enjoy the same immunities which they enjoyed at common law unless recognition of the immunity defense would conflict with the policies underlying § 1983. Id. at 258–59, 101 S.Ct. at 2755–56.

2. In Procunier v. Navarette, 434 U.S. 555, 98 S.Ct. 855 (1978), the Supreme Court concluded that state prison officials sued under § 1983 for alleged unconstitutional interference with a prisoner's mail could assert the defense of qualified immunity. Prison officials can prevail on such a defense unless they violated "clearly established statutory or constitutional rights of which a reasonable person would have known." Harlow v. Fitzgerald, 457 U.S. 800, 818, 102 S.Ct. 2727, 2738 (1982).

Harlow left open the question of when a right is "clearly established" so as to expose a defendant who violates the right to liability. In the subsequent case of Anderson v. Creighton, 483 U.S. 635, 107 S.Ct. 3034 (1987), the Court addressed this question. The plaintiffs in *Anderson* had filed a *Bivens* action against some federal law enforcement officials, as well as others who had participated in a warrantless search of the plaintiffs' home. The plaintiffs contended that the defendants could not invoke the defense of qualified immunity, since the right not to have one's home searched without a warrant unless there are exigent circumstances or consent to the warrantless search was "clearly established" at the time of the search. The Supreme Court responded as follows:

> The operation of this [the *Harlow*] standard, however, depends substantially upon the level of generality at which the relevant "legal rule" is to be identified. For example, the right to due process of law is quite clearly established by the Due Process Clause, and thus there is a sense in which any action that violates that Clause (no matter how unclear it may be that the particular action is a violation) violates a clearly established right. Much the same could be said of any other constitutional or statutory violation. But if the test of "clearly established law" were to be applied at this level of generality, it would bear no relationship to the "objective legal reasonableness" that is the touchstone of *Harlow*. Plaintiffs would be able to convert the rule of qualified immunity that our cases plainly establish into a rule of virtually unqualified liability simply by alleging violation of extremely abstract rights. *Harlow* would be transformed from a guarantee of immunity into a rule of pleading. Such an approach, in sum, would destroy "the balance that our cases strike between the interests in vindication of citizens' constitutional rights and in public officials' effective performance of their duties," by making it impossible for officials "reasonably [to] anticipate when their conduct may give rise to liability for damages." It should not be surprising, therefore, that our cases establish that the right the official is alleged to have violated must have been "clearly established" in a more particularized, and hence more relevant, sense: The contours of the right must be sufficiently clear that a reasonable official would understand that what he is doing violates that right. This is not to say that an official action is protected by qualified immunity unless the very action in question has previously been held unlawful, but it is to say that in the light of pre-existing law the unlawfulness must be apparent.

Id. at 639–40, 107 S.Ct. at 3038–39. The Court concluded by saying that "[t]he relevant question in this case * * * is the objective (albeit fact-specific) question whether a reasonable officer could have believed Anderson's warrantless search to be lawful, in light of clearly established law and the information the searching officers possessed. Anderson's subjective beliefs about the search are irrelevant." Id. at 641, 107 S.Ct. at 3039.

Do you agree with the qualified immunity test adopted by the Supreme Court? When, if ever, do you believe that prison officials who have violated a prisoner's constitutional rights should be immune from damages liability? What about members of parole boards? See Johnson v. Rhode Island Parole Board Members, 815 F.2d 5 (1st Cir.1987). If damages liability is limited to when an official has violated a "clearly established" right, what effect will that limitation have on an individual's willingness to bring suit to redress the violation of a right not yet "clearly established"? See Owen v. City of Independence, 445 U.S. 622, 651 n. 33, 100 S.Ct. 1398, 1415 n. 33 (1980).

3. Municipalities are not protected by the sovereign immunity reflected in the eleventh amendment. Will v. Michigan Department of State Police, 109 S.Ct. 2304, 2311 (1989). In addition, the Supreme Court has held that municipalities sued under § 1983 cannot invoke, as a defense, the

good faith of their officials and employees. Owen v. City of Independence, 445 U.S. 622, 100 S.Ct. 1398 (1980). According to the Court, this type of municipal immunity was not "firmly rooted" in the common law at the time of § 1983's passage. Id. at 637–50, 100 S.Ct. at 1408–15. In addition, refusing to insulate municipalities from § 1983 liability through an immunity defense furthers the compensatory and deterrent aims of § 1983. Id. at 650–56, 100 S.Ct. at 1415–18.

The Supreme Court has, however, construed § 1983 to preclude an award of punitive damages against a municipality. Newport v. Fact Concerts, Inc., 453 U.S. 247, 101 S.Ct. 2748 (1981). According to the Court, municipalities were immune from punitive damages awards under the common law. Id. at 259–60, 101 S.Ct. at 2755–56. In addition, the Court felt that while it was fair to spread the loss suffered by an individual whose constitutional rights were violated across the community, it was unfair to go beyond that and penalize innocent taxpayers, through a punitive damages award, for the wrongdoing of others. Id. at 267, 101 S.Ct. at 2759.

4. The burden rests upon a defendant sued under § 1983 to plead good faith as an affirmative defense. Gomez v. Toledo, 446 U.S. 635, 100 S.Ct. 1920 (1980). In other words, a plaintiff need not allege in the complaint that the defendant acted in bad faith. The lower courts are, however, divided on the question of who has the burden of proof, as opposed to the burden of pleading, on the qualified immunity issue. Compare Bennett v. City of Grand Prairie, 883 F.2d 400, 408 (5th Cir.1989) (plaintiff has burden of proof) with Garvie v. Jackson, 845 F.2d 647, 652 (6th Cir. 1988) and Kovats v. Rutgers, 822 F.2d 1303, 1312–13 (3d Cir.1987) (defendants have the burden of proof).

5. Since an immunity defense is designed to protect government officials not only from the burdens of paying damages but also from the costs and hassles of litigation, the question of an official's entitlement to immunity should normally be resolved before discovery in a case commences. Harlow v. Fitzgerald, 457 U.S. 800, 818, 102 S.Ct. 2727, 2738 (1982). For the same reason, if a judge denies a defendant's motion to dismiss on immunity grounds, the defendant can immediately appeal that order. Mitchell v. Forsyth, 472 U.S. 511, 530, 105 S.Ct. 2806, 2817 (1985).

2. STATUTE OF LIMITATIONS

Section 1983 itself does not specify by when a § 1983 suit must be brought, nor does any other federal statute outline the limitations period for § 1983 suits. In the absence of a controlling federal statute of limitations, 42 U.S.C. § 1988 directs courts to apply the statute of limitations in effect in the state where the suit is brought unless application of the statute would conflict with the Constitution or federal law. The Supreme Court has held that the state statute of limitations to be applied in a § 1983 suit is the one governing personal injury actions. Wilson v. Garcia, 471 U.S. 261, 105 S.Ct. 1938 (1985). If the state has two statutes of limitations, one governing certain intentional torts and the other covering all other personal injury actions, the more general personal injury statute of limitations is to be applied. Owens v. Okure, 488 U.S. 235, 109 S.Ct. 573 (1989).

In Hardin v. Straub, 109 S.Ct. 1998 (1989), the Supreme Court considered whether a tolling provision for prisoners in a state statute of limitations conflicted with the Constitution. Because of the tolling provision, Michigan prisoners did not always have to bring suit within three years after their cause of action accrued, as was generally required by the state's statute of limitations; the tolling provision permitted the prisoners to defer filing suit until up to a year after their release from prison.

In a unanimous decision announced in an opinion written by Justice Stevens, the Court concluded that this tolling provision comported with the Constitution. The Court noted that the tolling provision was not only consistent with, but furthered § 1983's goal of compensating those whose constitutional rights have been violated. Nor did the Court believe that the tolling provision would undermine another purpose of § 1983—that of deterring constitutional violations. Prisoners, who as plaintiffs have the burden of proof in § 1983 suits, would still have an incentive to promptly file § 1983 suits because evidence which might sustain their claims could be lost if their suits were unduly delayed. In addition, prison officials might be more inclined to refrain from violating the civil rights of prisoners if they knew that prisoners could wait to file a § 1983 suit until after they were released from prison and free from the practical impediments which hinder the litigation of a lawsuit while in prison.

3. MOOTNESS

Even if a civil rights suit is filed within the time allotted under the applicable statute of limitations, the case can and must be dismissed at any stage of the litigation, including on appeal, if the court concludes that the case is now moot. Mootness questions arise with some frequency when a prisoner who is challenging the conditions of confinement or treatment at a particular prison is transferred to another prison or released on parole. See, e.g., Hewitt v. Helms, 482 U.S. 755, 107 S.Ct. 2672 (1987); Board of Pardons v. Allen, 482 U.S. 369, 107 S.Ct. 2415 (1987); Vitek v. Jones, 445 U.S. 480, 100 S.Ct. 1254 (1980). To avoid a dismissal for mootness, therefore, an attorney bringing a civil rights suit on behalf of a prisoner should consider what can and should be done to avoid potential mootness problems.

A prisoner's transfer or release will not normally moot the case if the prisoner has sought damages relief. Boag v. MacDougall, 454 U.S. 364, 102 S.Ct. 700 (1982) (per curiam). Nor will the case be mooted if the prisoner has filed a class action suit, and the class has been certified. Sosna v. Iowa, 419 U.S. 393, 95 S.Ct. 553 (1975). Even when a court has refused to certify a class and the prisoner bringing the civil rights suit is then released from prison, the prisoner's claim on appeal that a class should have been certified is not mooted. United States Parole Commission v. Geraghty, 445 U.S. 388, 100 S.Ct. 1202 (1980).

4. EXHAUSTION OF REMEDIES

The Supreme Court has repeatedly held that a plaintiff bringing suit under § 1983 need not first exhaust available state judicial or administrative remedies. See the cases cited in Patsy v. Florida Board of Regents, 457 U.S. 496, 500, 102 S.Ct. 2557, 2559 (1982). Congress has now enacted a limited statutory exception to this general no-exhaustion-requirement rule. That exception is outlined in 42 U.S.C. § 1997e, whose provisions are outlined below:

(a)(1) Subject to the provisions of paragraph (2), in any action brought pursuant to section 1983 of this title by an adult convicted of a crime confined in any jail, prison, or other correctional facility, the court shall, if the court believes that such a requirement would be appropriate and in the interests of justice, continue such case for a period of not to exceed ninety days in order to require exhaustion of such plain, speedy, and effective administrative remedies as are available.

(2) The exhaustion of administrative remedies under paragraph (1) may not be required unless the Attorney General has certified or the court has determined that such administrative remedies are in substantial compliance with the minimum acceptable standards promulgated under subsection (b) of this section.

(b)(1) No later than one hundred eighty days after May 23, 1980, the Attorney General shall, after consultation with persons, State and local agencies, and organizations with background and expertise in the area of corrections, promulgate minimum standards for the development and implementation of a plain, speedy, and effective system for the resolution of grievances of adults confined in any jail, prison, or other correctional facility. The Attorney General shall submit such proposed standards for publication in the Federal Register in accordance with section 553 of Title 5. Such standards shall take effect thirty legislative days after publication unless, within such period, either House of Congress adopts a resolution of disapproval of such standards.

(2) The minimum standards shall provide—

(A) for an advisory role for employees and inmates of any jail, prison, or other correctional institution (at the most decentralized level as is reasonably possible), in the formulation, implementation, and operation of the system;

(B) specific maximum time limits for written replies to grievances with reasons thereto at each decision level within the system;

(C) for priority processing of grievances which are of an emergency nature, including matters in which delay would subject the grievant to substantial risk of personal injury or other damages;

(D) for safeguards to avoid reprisals against any grievant or participant in the resolution of a grievance; and

(E) for independent review of the disposition of grievances, including alleged reprisals, by a person or other entity not under the direct supervision or direct control of the institution.

(c)(1) The Attorney General shall develop a procedure for the prompt review and certification of systems for the resolution of grievances of adults confined in any jail, prison, or other correctional facility, or pretrial detention facility, to determine if such systems, as voluntarily submitted by the various States and political subdivisions, are in substantial compliance with the minimum standards promulgated under subsection (b) of this section.

(2) The Attorney General may suspend or withdraw the certification under paragraph (1) at any time that he has reasonable cause to believe that the grievance procedure is no longer in substantial compliance with the minimum standards promulgated under subsection (b) of this section.

(d) The failure of a State to adopt or adhere to an administrative grievance procedure consistent with this section shall not constitute the basis for an action under section 1997a or 1997c of this title.

Proposals have been made to further expand this statutory exhaustion requirement. See e.g., Report of the Federal Courts Study Committee 48–49 (1990) (urging that 42 U.S.C. § 1997e be amended to require prisoners who have filed § 1983 suits to exhaust state institutional remedies for up to 120 days before any action is taken on their § 1983 claims, as long as the court or the U.S. Attorney General considers the remedies "fair and effective").

Chapter 19

REMEDIES

A. § 1983 ACTIONS

1. DAMAGES

CAREY v. PIPHUS

Supreme Court of the United States, 1978.
435 U.S. 247, 98 S.Ct. 1042, 55 L.Ed.2d 252.

MR. JUSTICE POWELL delivered the opinion of the Court.

[After two students, Jarius Piphus and Silas Brisco, were summarily suspended from school for misconduct—one for allegedly smoking marijuana and the other for wearing an earring while at school—they and their mothers filed § 1983 suits against various school officials contending that their suspensions violated their procedural due process rights. The federal district court agreed that their constitutional rights had been violated, but refused to award the plaintiffs any damages since they had failed to present any evidence demonstrating that they were harmed by the suspensions.

On appeal, the Seventh Circuit Court of Appeals reversed. The court held that if the suspensions were justified, though effected without due process of law, the plaintiffs could not recover damages for the value of the time which they missed in school because of their suspensions. The court held, however, that they could still recover "substantial non-punitive damages" just for having been deprived of their procedural due process rights. The Supreme Court then granted certiorari.]

Title 42 U.S.C. § 1983, Rev.Stat. § 1979, derived from § 1 of the Civil Rights Act of 1871, 17 Stat. 13, provides:

"Every person who, under color of any statute, ordinance, regulation, custom, or usage, of any State or Territory, subjects, or causes to be subjected, any citizen of the United States or other person within the jurisdiction thereof to the deprivation of any rights, privileges, or immunities secured by the Constitution and laws, shall be liable to the

594

party injured in an action at law, suit in equity, or other proper proceeding for redress."

The legislative history of § 1983 * * * demonstrates that it was intended to "[create] a species of tort liability" in favor of persons who are deprived of "rights, privileges, or immunities secured" to them by the Constitution.

Petitioners contend that the elements and prerequisites for recovery of damages under this "species of tort liability" should parallel those for recovery of damages under the common law of torts. In particular, they urge that the purpose of an award of damages under § 1983 should be to compensate persons for injuries that are caused by the deprivation of constitutional rights; and, further, that plaintiffs should be required to prove not only that their rights were violated, but also that injury was caused by the violation, in order to recover substantial damages. Unless respondents prove that they actually were injured by the deprivation of procedural due process, petitioners argue, they are entitled at most to nominal damages.

Respondents seem to make two different arguments in support of the holding below. First, they contend that substantial damages should be awarded under § 1983 for the deprivation of a constitutional right *whether or not* any injury was caused by the deprivation. This, they say, is appropriate both because constitutional rights are valuable in and of themselves, and because of the need to deter violations of constitutional rights. Respondents believe that this view reflects accurately that of the Congress that enacted § 1983. Second, respondents argue that even if the purpose of a § 1983 damages award is, as petitioners contend, primarily to compensate persons for injuries that are caused by the deprivation of constitutional rights, every deprivation of procedural due process may be *presumed* to cause some injury. This presumption, they say, should relieve them from the necessity of proving that injury actually was caused.

Insofar as petitioners contend that the basic purpose of a § 1983 damages award should be to compensate persons for injuries caused by the deprivation of constitutional rights, they have the better of the argument. Rights, constitutional and otherwise, do not exist in a vacuum. Their purpose is to protect persons from injuries to particular interests, and their contours are shaped by the interests they protect.

Our legal system's concept of damages reflects this view of legal rights. "The cardinal principle of damages in Anglo–American law is that of *compensation* for the injury caused to plaintiff by defendant's breach of duty." 2 F. Harper & F. James, Law of Torts § 25.1, p. 1299 (1956) (emphasis in original). * * *

The Members of the Congress that enacted § 1983 did not address directly the question of damages, but the principle that damages are designed to compensate persons for injuries caused by the deprivation of rights hardly could have been foreign to the many lawyers in Congress in 1871. * * * To the extent that Congress intended that awards under § 1983 should deter the deprivation of constitutional rights, there is no evidence that it meant to establish a deterrent more formidable than that inherent in the award of compensatory damages.

It is less difficult to conclude that damages awards under § 1983 should be governed by the principle of compensation than it is to apply this principle to concrete cases. But over the centuries the common law of torts has developed a set of rules to implement the principle that a person should be compensated fairly for injuries caused by the violation of his legal rights. These rules, defining the elements of damages and the prerequisites for their recovery, provide the appropriate starting point for the inquiry under § 1983 as well.

It is not clear, however, that common-law tort rules of damages will provide a complete solution to the damages issue in every § 1983 case. In some cases, the interests protected by a particular branch of the common law of torts may parallel closely the interests protected by a particular constitutional right. In such cases, it may be appropriate to apply the tort rules of damages directly to the § 1983 action. In other cases, the interests protected by a particular constitutional right may not also be protected by an analogous branch of the common law of torts. In those cases, the task will be the more difficult one of adapting common-law rules of damages to provide fair compensation for injuries caused by the deprivation of a constitutional right.

Although this task of adaptation will be one of some delicacy—as this case demonstrates—it must be undertaken. The purpose of § 1983 would be defeated if injuries caused by the deprivation of constitutional rights went uncompensated simply because the common law does not recognize an analogous cause of action. In order to further the purpose of § 1983, the rules governing compensation for injuries caused by the deprivation of constitutional rights should be tailored to the interests protected by the particular right in question—just as the common-law rules of damages themselves were defined by the interests protected in the various branches of tort law. * * * With these principles in mind, we now turn to the problem of compensation in the case at hand.

The Due Process Clause of the Fourteenth Amendment provides:

"[N]or shall any State deprive any person of life, liberty, or property, without due process of law . . . ."

This Clause "raises no impenetrable barrier to the taking of a person's possessions," or liberty, or life. Procedural due process rules are meant to protect persons not from the deprivation, but from the mistaken or unjustified deprivation of life, liberty, or property. * * *

In this case, the Court of Appeals held that if petitioners can prove on remand that "[respondents] would have been suspended even if a proper hearing had been held," then respondents will not be entitled to recover damages to compensate them for injuries caused by the suspensions. The court thought that in such a case, the failure to accord procedural due process could not properly be viewed as the cause of the suspensions. The court suggested that in such circumstances, an award of damages for injuries caused by the suspensions would constitute a windfall, rather than compensation, to respondents. We do not understand the parties to disagree with this conclusion. Nor do we.

The parties do disagree as to the further holding of the Court of Appeals that respondents are entitled to recover substantial—although unspecified—damages to compensate them for "the injury which is 'inherent in the nature of the wrong,'" even if their suspensions were justified and even if they fail to prove that the denial of procedural due process actually caused them some real, if intangible, injury. Respondents, elaborating on this theme, submit that the holding is correct because injury fairly may be "presumed" to flow from every denial of procedural due process. Their argument is that in addition to protecting against unjustified deprivations, the Due Process Clause also guarantees the "feeling of just treatment" by the government. They contend that the deprivation of protected interests without procedural due process, even where the premise for the deprivation is not erroneous, inevitably arouses strong feelings of mental and emotional distress in the individual who is denied this "feeling of just treatment." They analogize their case to that of defamation *per se,* in which "the plaintiff is relieved from the necessity of producing any proof whatsoever that he has been injured" in order to recover substantial compensatory damages.

Petitioners do not deny that a purpose of procedural due process is to convey to the individual a feeling that the government has dealt with him fairly, as well as to minimize the risk of mistaken deprivations of protected interests. They go so far as to concede that, in a proper case, persons in respondents' position might well recover damages for mental and emotional distress caused by the denial of procedural due process. Petitioners' argument is the more limited one that such injury cannot be presumed to occur, and that plaintiffs at least should be put to their proof on the issue, as plaintiffs are in most tort actions.

We agree with petitioners in this respect. * * *

First, it is not reasonable to assume that every departure from procedural due process, no matter what the circumstances or how minor, inherently is as likely to cause distress as the publication of defamation *per se* is to cause injury to reputation and distress. Where the deprivation of a protected interest is substantively justified but procedures are deficient in some respect, there may well be those who suffer no distress over the procedural irregularities. Indeed, in contrast to the immediately distressing effect of defamation *per se,* a person may not even know that procedures *were* deficient until he enlists the aid of counsel to challenge a perceived substantive deprivation.

Moreover, where a deprivation is justified but procedures are deficient, whatever distress a person feels may be attributable to the justified deprivation rather than to deficiencies in procedure. But as the Court of Appeals held, the injury caused by a justified deprivation, including distress, is not properly compensable under § 1983. This ambiguity in causation, which is absent in the case of defamation *per se,* provides additional need for requiring the plaintiff to convince the trier of fact that he actually suffered distress because of the denial of procedural due process itself.

Finally, we foresee no particular difficulty in producing evidence that mental and emotional distress actually was caused by the denial of procedural due process itself. Distress is a personal injury familiar to the law, customarily proved by showing the nature and circumstances of the wrong and its effect on the plaintiff.[20] In sum, then, although mental and emotional distress caused by the denial of procedural due process itself is compensable under § 1983, we hold that neither the likelihood of such injury nor the difficulty of proving it is so great as to justify awarding compensatory damages without proof that such injury actually was caused.

* * *

Even if respondents' suspensions were justified, and even if they did not suffer any other actual injury, the fact remains that they were deprived of their right to procedural due process. * * *

Common-law courts traditionally have vindicated deprivations of certain "absolute" rights that are not shown to have caused actual injury through the award of a nominal sum of money. By making the deprivation of such rights actionable for nominal damages without proof of actual injury, the law recognizes the importance to organized society that those rights be scrupulously observed; but at the same time, it remains true to the principle that substantial damages should be awarded only to compensate actual injury or, in the case of exemplary or punitive damages, to deter or punish malicious deprivations of rights.

Because the right to procedural due process is "absolute" in the sense that it does not depend upon the merits of a claimant's substantive assertions, and because of the importance to organized society that procedural due process be observed, we believe that the denial of procedural due process should be actionable for nominal damages without proof of actual injury. We therefore hold that if, upon remand, the District Court determines that respondents' suspensions were justified, respondents nevertheless will be entitled to recover nominal damages not to exceed one dollar from petitioners.

The judgment of the Court of Appeals is reversed, and the case is remanded for further proceedings consistent with this opinion.

* * *

MR. JUSTICE MARSHALL concurs in the result.

---

20. We use the term "distress" to include mental suffering or emotional anguish. Although essentially subjective, genuine injury in this respect may be evidenced by one's conduct and observed by others. * * *

Questions and Points for Discussion

1. Consider the implications of *Carey v. Piphus* to prisoners' § 1983 suits. See, e.g., Madison County Jail Inmates v. Thompson, 773 F.2d 834 (7th Cir.1985); Redding v. Fairman, 717 F.2d 1105 (7th Cir.1983). When could a prisoner recover compensatory damages for a violation of procedural due process rights during a disciplinary hearing?

2. Most of the lower courts have held that a § 1983 plaintiff who is awarded only nominal damages can still recover punitive damages. See, e.g., Erwin v. County of Manitowoc, 872 F.2d 1292, 1299 (7th Cir.1989); Piver v. Pender County Board of Education, 835 F.2d 1076, 1082 (4th Cir. 1987).

3. In Smith v. Wade, 461 U.S. 30, 103 S.Ct. 1625 (1983), the Supreme Court described when an award of punitive damages in a § 1983 action would be appropriate. To be liable for punitive damages, a defendant need not have acted with a malicious intent to harm the plaintiff. "[R]eckless or callous indifference to the federally protected rights of others" as well as an "evil motive or intent" will suffice to justify a punitive damages award. Id. at 56, 103 S.Ct. at 1640.

2. EQUITABLE RELIEF

In § 1983 suits, plaintiffs frequently seek declaratory or injunctive relief. When entering a declaratory judgment, a court may, for example, declare a state statute or regulation unconstitutional. Through injunctive relief, a court goes further in providing redress to plaintiffs—prohibiting the defendants from engaging in certain unconstitutional conduct in the future or mandating that they take certain steps to avoid further violations of the Constitution.

Injunctive relief may be afforded in the form of a temporary restraining order, a preliminary injunction, or a permanent injunction. Standards governing the issuance of these types of injunctive orders are described in D. Dobbs, Remedies 106–111 (1973).

Courts can issue a broad array of injunctive orders in § 1983 suits. To limit any unnecessary intrusion by the federal courts into states' operations of their prisons or jails though, many courts, after finding conditions at a prison or jail unconstitutional because of excessive crowding, simply order state and/or local officials to develop a plan to eliminate the crowding. See, e.g., Williams v. Edwards, 547 F.2d 1206, 1218 (5th Cir.1977); Palmigiano v. DiPrete, 700 F.Supp. 1180, 1199 (D.R.I.1988). The officials' failure to develop or implement such a plan may then lead the court to take more drastic steps, including ordering the closing of the institution or even the release of inmates, to rectify unconstitutional conditions. See, e.g., Inmates of Allegheny County Jail v. Wecht, 874 F.2d 147, 153–55 (3d Cir.1989) (affirming jail closing order); Duran v. Elrod, 713 F.2d 292, 298 (7th Cir.1983) (affirming order directing the release of pretrial detainees incarcerated simply because they could not pay low bonds).

The Supreme Court's decision in Missouri v. Jenkins, 110 S.Ct. 1651 (1990) suggests that a court may go even further to ensure that government officials take the steps necessary to remedy unconstitutional conditions of confinement in a correctional facility. In that case, a federal district court had concluded that the Kansas City, Missouri, School District (KCMSD) had unconstitutionally maintained a segregated school system. To remedy this constitutional violation, the district court approved a magnet school program proposed by the school district that would cost over $380 million to implement. The district court, however, recognized that the school district lacked the resources to pay for its share of the costs of this plan and that the state constitution placed limits on its ability to raise property taxes to pay for the desegregation plan. The court therefore ordered that property taxes be raised to cover the costs of desegregation.

The State of Missouri, which the district court had held jointly and severally liable for the costs of the plan, on appeal challenged this desegregation remedy, contending that the district court had exceeded its equitable powers by raising taxes. The Supreme Court agreed, but at the same time, confirmed that the equitable powers of the court to remedy a constitutional violation are quite broad:

> We turn to the tax increase imposed by the District Court. The State urges us to hold that the tax increase violated Article III, the Tenth Amendment, and principles of federal/state comity. We find it unnecessary to reach the difficult constitutional issues, for we agree with the State that the tax increase contravened the principles of comity that must govern the exercise of the District Court's equitable discretion in this area.

> It is accepted by all the parties, as it was by the courts below, that the imposition of a tax increase by a federal court was an extraordinary event. In assuming for itself the fundamental and delicate power of taxation the District Court not only intruded on local authority but circumvented it altogether. Before taking such a drastic step the District Court was obliged to assure itself that no permissible alternative would have accomplished the required task. We have emphasized that although the "remedial powers of an equity court must be adequate to the task, . . . they are not unlimited," and one of the most important considerations governing the exercise of equitable power is a proper respect for the integrity and function of local government institutions. Especially is this true where, as here, those institutions are ready, willing, and—but for the operation of state law curtailing their powers—able to remedy the deprivation of constitutional rights themselves.

> The District Court believed that it had no alternative to imposing a tax increase. But there was an alternative, the very one outlined by the Court of Appeals: it could have authorized or required KCMSD to levy property taxes at a rate adequate to fund the desegregation remedy and could have enjoined the operation of state laws that would have prevented KCMSD from exercising this power. The difference

between the two approaches is far more than a matter of form. Authorizing and directing local government institutions to devise and implement remedies not only protects the function of those institutions but, to the extent possible, also places the responsibility for solutions to the problems of segregation upon those who have themselves created the problems.

* * *

* * *[T]he State argues that an order to increase taxes cannot be sustained under the judicial power of Article III. Whatever the merits of this argument when applied to the District Court's own order increasing taxes, a point we have not reached, a court order directing a local government body to levy its own taxes is plainly a judicial act within the power of a federal court. We held as much in Griffin v. Prince Edward County School Bd., 377 U.S., at 233, 84 S.Ct., at 1234, where we stated that a District Court, faced with a county's attempt to avoid desegregation of the public schools by refusing to operate those schools, could "require the [County] Supervisors to exercise the power that is theirs to levy taxes to raise funds adequate to reopen, operate, and maintain without racial discrimination a public school system . . . ." *Griffin* followed a long and venerable line of cases in which this Court held that federal courts could issue the writ of mandamus to compel local governmental bodies to levy taxes adequate to satisfy their debt obligations. * * *

The State maintains, however, that even under these cases, the federal judicial power can go no further than to require local governments to levy taxes *as authorized under state law.* In other words, the State argues that federal courts cannot set aside state-imposed limitations on local taxing authority because to do so is to do more than to require the local government "to exercise the power *that is theirs.*" We disagree. * * *

* * * Here the KCMSD may be ordered to levy taxes despite the statutory limitations on its authority in order to compel the discharge of an obligation imposed on KCMSD by the Fourteenth Amendment. To hold otherwise would fail to take account of the obligations of local governments, under the Supremacy Clause, to fulfill the requirements that the Constitution imposes on them. However wide the discretion of local authorities in fashioning desegregation remedies may be, "if a state-imposed limitation on a school authority's discretion operates to inhibit or obstruct the operation of a unitary school system or impede the disestablishing of a dual school system, it must fall; state policy must give way when it operates to hinder vindication of federal constitutional guarantees." Even though a particular remedy may not be required in every case to vindicate constitutional guarantees, where (as here) it has been found that a particular remedy is required, the State cannot hinder the process by preventing a local government from implementing that remedy.

110 S.Ct. at 1662–63, 1665–66. What is the potential significance of this decision in the correctional context?

As was mentioned earlier, some courts have ordered the release of prisoners from a prison to redress unconstitutional crowding. Ordering prisoners released from prison as a remedy in a suit challenging unconstitutional crowding, however, must be distinguished from the situation where a prisoner is challenging, not the conditions of confinement, but the fact or duration of the prisoner's confinement and as a remedy, is seeking earlier or an immediate release from confinement. In Preiser v. Rodriguez, 411 U.S. 475, 93 S.Ct. 1827 (1973), the plaintiffs, prisoners confined in a New York prison, brought suit under § 1983 claiming that they lost good-time credits as a result of disciplinary proceedings that did not meet due process requirements. For relief, the plaintiffs sought an injunction directing that their good-time credits be restored. The restoration of these credits would have led to the plaintiffs' immediate release from prison.

The Supreme Court concluded in *Preiser* that when state prisoners, such as the plaintiffs, are challenging the fact or duration of their confinement and seeking immediate or an earlier release from confinement, they must assert their claims in a habeas corpus action brought under 28 U.S.C. § 2254. See page 609, infra. That statute generally requires that individuals exhaust available state court remedies before seeking a writ of habeas corpus from a federal court directing their release from unconstitutional custody. The purpose of this exhaustion requirement is to avoid, whenever possible, the conflict that would result between federal and state courts if a federal court, rather than a state court, set aside a state court conviction.

The Court in *Preiser* observed that to permit prisoners in § 1983 actions to seek injunctions directing their release from prison would undermine the comity considerations underlying § 2254(c)'s exhaustion requirement. Do you agree? Does the Court's conclusion in *Preiser* comport with the no-exhaustion rule that it has propounded in § 1983 suits? See page 592, supra.

In Wolff v. McDonnell, 418 U.S. 539, 554–55, 94 S.Ct. 2963 (1974), the Court held that prisoners alleging an unconstitutional deprivation of good-time credits can still seek damages relief in a § 1983 suit without first exhausting available state remedies. The Court acknowledged that prisoners might then be litigating two suits at once—one in the state courts to gain restoration of the revoked good-time credits and one in the federal courts for damages. Interestingly, the Court noted in a footnote that "[o]ne would anticipate that normal principles of *res judicata* would apply in such circumstances." Id. at 554 n. 12, 94 S.Ct. at 2974 n. 12. The Court seemed to be suggesting in this footnote that if the federal § 1983 suit was resolved before the state lawsuit, the state court would then be required to enter a judgment consonant with the federal court judgment. In other words, if a prisoner prevailed in the § 1983 suit, for example, the prisoner would be entitled to the restoration of good-time credits by the state court. Would this application of *res judicata* principles comport with the comity considerations which underlay the Court's decision in *Preiser v. Rodriguez?*

3. ATTORNEY'S FEES

The Civil Rights Attorney's Fees Awards Act of 1976, which is found in 42 U.S.C. § 1988, provides that in § 1983 suits, as well as certain other suits to enforce some other federal statutes, "the court, in its discretion, may allow the prevailing party, other than the United States, a reasonable attorney's fee as part of the costs." It should be noted that § 1988 does not require an award of attorney's fees to the prevailing party. Whether or not to award fees falls within the court's discretion. Absent "special circumstances" which would make an award of fees "unjust," however, a prevailing plaintiff should normally be awarded attorney's fees. Hensley v. Eckerhart, 461 U.S. 424, 429, 103 S.Ct. 1933, 1937 (1983).

Despite § 1988's reference to prevailing parties, rather than prevailing plaintiffs, the Supreme Court has held that prevailing defendants sued under § 1983 should not normally recover attorney's fees from the plaintiff. Hughes v. Rowe, 449 U.S. 5, 14–15, 101 S.Ct. 173, 178–79 (1980) (per curiam). To permit fee awards against plaintiffs who bring suit under § 1983 would discourage the bringing of those suits and undermine the intent of § 1988 to encourage private enforcement of the civil rights laws. Consequently, fees should be assessed against the plaintiff only when the plaintiff's case was " 'frivolous, unreasonable, or without foundation, even though not brought in subjective bad faith.' " Id. at 14, 101 S.Ct. at 178 (quoting Christiansburg Garment Co. v. EEOC, 434 U.S. 412, 421, 98 S.Ct. 694, 700 (1978)). Just because the plaintiff lost the case is not reason enough to award the defendant attorney's fees. And the Court has counseled special hesitancy before attorney's fees are assessed against prisoners who filed *pro se* civil rights actions, since prisoners will often have particular difficulty in understanding the factual and legal nuances of litigation. 449 U.S. at 15, 101 S.Ct. at 178.

Proper application of § 1988 requires that the terms "prevailing party" and "reasonable attorney's fee" be further defined. The Supreme Court in Texas State Teachers Association v. Garland Independent School District, 489 U.S. 782, 109 S.Ct. 1486 (1989) concluded that a plaintiff should be considered a prevailing party if the plaintiff succeeded on " 'any significant issue in litigation which achieve[d] some of the benefit the parties sought in bringing suit.' " Id. at 1493 (quoting Nadeau v. Helgemoe, 581 F.2d 275, 278–79 (1st Cir.1978)). The Court rejected the notion that the plaintiff must have prevailed on the "central issue" in the case in order to be considered the prevailing party.

Nor is it necessary for there to be a trial in the case for the plaintiff to be considered a prevailing party. In Maher v. Gagne, 448 U.S. 122, 100 S.Ct. 2570 (1980), the Supreme Court concluded that the plaintiffs were entitled to attorney's fees even though the case was settled through the entry of a consent decree, which is a court order reflecting the parties' agreement as to how a legal dispute should be settled. This holding is of especial significance to prisoners and their attorneys who litigate § 1983 suits, since many of the prisoners' rights suits challenging the conditions of confinement in particular prisons or prison systems culminate in the entry of consent decrees.

In calculating what constitutes a "reasonable attorney's fee" within the meaning of § 1988, the Supreme Court has said that what is known as the lodestar figure must first be computed. Hensley v. Eckerhart, 461 U.S. 424, 433, 103 S.Ct. 1933, 1939 (1983). This figure is arrived at by multiplying the hours "reasonably expended" on the litigation times a "reasonable" hourly rate. Id. If the parties cannot agree on the amount of fees to be paid the prevailing party, then the party seeking fees has the burden of establishing the reasonableness of the hours expended on the case and the reasonableness of the hourly rate. Id. at 437, 103 S.Ct. at 1941.

Having calculated the lodestar figure, a court can then shift the fee award either upwards or downwards, depending on a number of factors. The Supreme Court, for example, has held that the plaintiff's degree of success or lack of success in a case may warrant an increase or decrease in the fee award. Id. The amount of attorney's fees awarded, however, does not necessarily have to be proportionate to the amount of damages recovered by the plaintiff. See, City of Riverside v. Rivera, 477 U.S. 561, 106 S.Ct. 2686 (1986) (approving $245,456.25 fee award in a case where the plaintiffs recovered $33,350 in damages).

In Missouri v. Jenkins, 109 S.Ct. 2463 (1989), the Supreme Court held that in calculating a fee award under § 1988, a court can properly adjust the fee award to compensate the plaintiff's attorneys for any delay in receiving payment. In that case, the trial court had made this adjustment by using current market rates when calculating the lodestar figure rather than the hourly rates which had prevailed when the attorneys had performed the work for their clients. Five of the Justices on the Supreme Court have also said that the risk of nonpayment that an attorney assumes when taking on a lawsuit may justify an upwards adjustment in the fee award. Pennsylvania v. Delaware Valley Citizens' Council for Clean Air, 483 U.S. 711, 107 S.Ct. 3078 (1987) (O'Connor, J., concurring and Blackmun, Brennan, Marshall, and Stevens, JJ., dissenting). Recovery of attorney's fees under § 1988 is not, however, limited by the amount that an attorney can recover under a contingent-fee agreement with a client. Blanchard v. Bergeron, 489 U.S. 87, 109 S.Ct. 939 (1989). What is a "reasonable" fee within the meaning of § 1988 might be more than, less than, or the same as the amount the attorney can recover under a contingent-fee agreement with a client. At the same time, however, a prevailing plaintiff in a § 1983 suit may, because of the terms of a contingent fee agreement with the attorney who represented the plaintiff during the litigation, have to pay the attorney more in attorney's fees than the plaintiff recovered under § 1988. *Venegas v. Mitchell,* 110 S.Ct. 1679 (1990) (plaintiff, who obtained a $2.08 million judgment and who was awarded $117,000 in attorney's fees under § 1988, was bound by contingent-fee contract under which he had agreed to pay his attorney 40% of the gross amount of any money judgment awarded in his favor).

For more information on the award of attorney's fees under § 1988, see S. Steinglass, Section 1983 Litigation in State Courts, ch. 22, Attorney Fees in § 1983 Litigation (1989).

B. ENFORCING COURT ORDERS THROUGH CONTEMPT PROCEEDINGS AND OTHER MEANS

BADGLEY v. SANTACROCE
Court of Appeals, Second Circuit, 1986.
800 F.2d 33.

JON O. NEWMAN, CIRCUIT JUDGE:

More than two years ago, this Court characterized as a "disaster" the persistent violation by the Nassau County Sheriff and the Warden of the Nassau County Correctional Center ("NCCC") of a consent judgment limiting inmate population at the NCCC. *Badgley v. Varelas,* 729 F.2d 894, 902 (2d Cir.1984) ("*Badgley I* "). We now confront a situation of continuing violation of an amended consent judgment and discover that, since we last saw this case, little if any meaningful action has been taken to alleviate the overcrowding at the NCCC. * * *

* * *

The amended consent judgment slightly increases the inmate population limit and also incorporates an enforcing mechanism. Paragraph 4 provides that "the actual maximum in-house population of the NCCC shall not exceed 710 [the maximum allowable in cells] plus the number of inmates actually housed in [newly constructed] dormitories." Paragraph 3 establishes the maximum capacity of the new dormitory housing as 157. Thus, the judgment contemplates a maximum in-house population of 867. Paragraph 31 incorporates, with appropriate numerical adjustments, the remedial provisions ordered by the District Court in March 1984 in conformity with *Badgley I:* The Sheriff of Nassau County must not deliver any person to the NCCC until the in-cell population is no more than 710 and must not deliver any person who would increase the population above 710, the Warden of the NCCC must not accept any person until the in-cell population is no more than 710, and the Warden must notify all courts and agencies that send prisoners to the NCCC for confinement any time the in-cell population equals or exceeds 685 for five consecutive days. Paragraph 32 allows the defendants to accept, "without regard to the in-house population cap," persons charged with class A or B felonies and persons held without bail or with bail of $100,000 or more.

Beginning on October 7, 1985, the county defendants began housing inmates at the NCCC above the in-cell limit of 710. Since that time, the defendants' record of compliance with the amended consent judgment has been abysmal. Paragraph 28 of the judgment requires the defendants to provide plaintiffs with weekly inmate population statistics. A review of the statistics for weekday population between October 7, 1985, and March 28, 1986, reveals that the in-cell maximum was met on only fifteen days. The average daily in-cell population at the NCCC was 732 for November, 712 for December, 746 for January, 739 for February, and 751 for March. On March 17, 1986, the in-cell population rose to a high of 781; that same day, the total in-house population (including inmates in dormitories) was 961. Overcrowding in violation of the amended consent judgment has been the rule and compliance the rare exception.

On October 17, 1985, the plaintiffs moved for an order holding the county defendants in contempt of court for violation of paragraph 31 of the amended consent judgment. After a series of hearings, the District Court on January 6, 1986, concluded that the county defendants had not willfully violated the judgment, that they had made every reasonable effort to comply with the population limit, and that it was impossible for them to comply with the judgment without the assistance of state officials. The Court therefore denied the contempt motion, and the inmates appealed. We now reverse.

The purpose of civil contempt, broadly stated, is to compel a reluctant party to do what a court requires of him. Because compliance with a court's directive is the goal, an order of civil contempt is appropriate "only when it appears that obedience is within the power of the party being coerced by the order." *Maggio v. Zeitz,* 333 U.S. 56, 69, (1948). A court's power to impose coercive civil contempt is limited by an individual's ability to comply with the court's coercive order. A party may defend against a contempt by showing that his compliance is "factually impossible." In raising this defense, the defendant has a burden of production that may be difficult to meet, particularly in cases such as this where the defendants have a long history of delay and the plaintiffs' needs are urgent.

A classic application of the factual impossibility defense arises when a court orders an individual to produce documents that are not in his possession or control. Similarly, a witness who refuses to answer a grand jury's questions cannot be held in contempt after the term of the grand jury expires, since it is no longer possible for the witness to purge himself of the contempt by testifying. And an inability to comply with an order requiring the payment of money because of poverty or insolvency will generally be a defense to contempt. In all these situations, the contempt is excused because compliance is literally impossible and, as a result, any attempts at coercion are pointless.

By contrast, on the undisputed facts of this case, nothing makes it factually impossible for the Sheriff to cease delivering persons to the

NCCC or for the Warden to refuse to accept such persons until the population requirements of the amended consent judgment are met. As we noted in *Badgley I,* if a natural disaster such as fire or disease required the NCCC to be closed, the county defendants would place the inmates elsewhere and would not deliver or accept new prisoners until the crisis ended. The continued violation of the amended consent judgment is a legal crisis of equal gravity, and it is obvious that the defendants are just as able to decline to deliver and accept new prisoners until this crisis is ended. The terms of the amended consent judgment automatically operate, whenever the population limit is exceeded, to close the jail's doors as tightly as would fire or disease.

* * *

The defendants also suggested to the District Court that compliance might place them in contempt of the state courts that send them prisoners. Justice Arthur D. Spatt, Administrative Judge for Nassau County, told the District Court that, if the Sheriff refused to accept prisoners committed to his custody by local criminal courts, he would be in contempt of those courts. Significantly, however, he added that state judges do not commit prisoners to specific facilities and would not direct the Sheriff to take prisoners to the NCCC in light of the federal court's order barring delivery and acceptance of additional inmates. Compliance with the amended consent judgment has not been shown to pose a risk of contempt of state courts.

Even if a state court would hold the defendants in contempt for refusing to house inmates at the NCCC, or if compliance would otherwise violate state law, Supremacy Clause considerations require that the judgment of the federal court be respected. In any attempt by a state court to hold defendants in contempt for taking actions required by the judgment of the District Court, that judgment would provide a complete defense.

The respect due the federal judgment is not lessened because the judgment was entered by consent. The plaintiffs' suit alleged a denial of their constitutional rights. When the defendants chose to consent to a judgment, rather than have the District Court adjudicate the merits of the plaintiffs' claims, the result was a fully enforceable federal judgment that overrides any conflicting state law or state court order. The strong policy encouraging settlement of cases requires that the terms of a consent judgment, once approved by a federal court, be respected as fully as a judgment entered after trial.

* * *

CONCLUSION

Compliance with the amended consent judgment must now occur, and the remedial provisions of that judgment must be put into effect. We will allow a delay of thirty days only to permit necessary notification to the appropriate court, agency, and police officials.

The judgment of the District Court is reversed, and the cause is remanded with directions to enter forthwith an order (1) declaring paragraph 31 of the amended consent judgment to be operative thirty days after the date of this Court's decision and (2) requiring the county defendants promptly to give notice to all courts, police departments, and other federal, state, and local governmental agencies that send persons for confinement at the NCCC that, thirty days after the date of this Court's decision, the NCCC will be unavailable to house additional persons, except to the extent permitted by paragraph 32. The District Court is also directed to hold the county defendants in civil contempt in the event of any subsequent failure to implement paragraph 31 of the amended consent judgment and, in that event, to assess compensatory damages in favor of the plaintiffs of not less than $5,000 for each person admitted to the NCCC in violation of the amended consent judgment and to order any additional remedies that may be appropriate. * * *

Questions and Points for Discussion

1. Failure to comply with a court order may result in the institution of either civil or criminal contempt proceedings against the defendant. As was discussed in *Badgley v. Santacroce,* the purpose of the sanction imposed if a defendant is found in civil contempt is remedial—to induce the defendant to provide the plaintiff with the relief to which the plaintiff is entitled under a previously entered court order. Thus, if a defendant found in civil contempt is sentenced to jail, the defendant can avoid the jail sentence or obtain release from the jail by simply complying with the court order. If the defendant is ordered to pay a fine for not complying with the court's order, the fine is payable to the plaintiff.

The purpose of criminal contempt, by contrast, is punishment—to punish the defendant for disobeying a court order. If a defendant is held in criminal contempt and, as a result, sentenced to jail, the defendant cannot avoid the penalty by complying with the court's order. And any fine leveled against the defendant is payable to the court, since the purpose of the finding of contempt is to vindicate the court's authority.

The reason why it is important to discern whether the contempt proceedings instituted against a defendant are civil or criminal is that if they are criminal, the defendant is entitled to the constitutional protections afforded individuals charged with a crime, including the requirement that guilt be established beyond a reasonable doubt. Hicks on Behalf of Feiock v. Feiock, 485 U.S. 624, 632, 108 S.Ct. 1423, 1430 (1988). If ability to comply with the court's order is an element of the offense of contempt, the plaintiff then has the burden of proof on this question. By contrast, in civil contempt proceedings, courts often place the burden on the defendant of demonstrating that compliance with the court's order is not possible. See, e.g., O'Leary v. Moyer's Landfill, Inc., 536 F.Supp. 218, 219 (E.D.Pa.1982). But see Combs v. Ryan's Coal Company, Inc., 785 F.2d 970, 984 (11th Cir. 1986) (party seeking the contempt citation has the ultimate burden of proof on the issue of ability to comply).

2. To assist in the enforcement of a court's order entered in a prisoner's suit brought under § 1983, a court will sometimes exercise its

authority under Rule 53 of the Federal Rules of Civil Procedure and appoint what is called a "master." The master is generally charged with reporting to the court at periodic intervals about the defendant's compliance with the court's decree. The master may also be responsible for assisting in the implementation of the court's decree. For a discussion of the use of masters in prisoners' rights litigation, see Brakel, Special Masters in Institutional Litigation, 3 Am. B. Foundation Research J. 543 (1979); Note "Mastering" Intervention in Prisons, 88 Yale L.J. 1062 (1979).

C. OTHER REMEDIES

1. HABEAS CORPUS

As was mentioned in the earlier discussion in this chapter of Preiser v. Rodriguez, 411 U.S. 475, 93 S.Ct. 1827 (1973), see page 602, supra, the Supreme Court has held that inmates challenging the constitutionality of their confinement and seeking their release or early release from confinement must seek redress, not in a § 1983 suit, but by petitioning a court for a writ of habeas corpus. Pertinent sections of one of the principal federal statutes governing habeas corpus actions brought by state prisoners are set forth below:

28 U.S.C. § 2254

(a) The Supreme Court, a Justice thereof, a circuit judge, or a district court shall entertain an application for a writ of habeas corpus in behalf of a person in custody pursuant to the judgment of a State court only on the ground that he is in custody in violation of the Constitution or laws or treaties of the United States.

(b) An application for a writ of habeas corpus in behalf of a person in custody pursuant to the judgment of a State court shall not be granted unless it appears that the applicant has exhausted the remedies available in the courts of the State, or that there is either an absence of available State corrective process or the existence of circumstances rendering such process ineffective to protect the rights of the prisoner.

(c) An applicant shall not be deemed to have exhausted the remedies available in the courts of the State, within the meaning of this section, if he has the right under the law of the State to raise, by any available procedure, the question presented.

(d) In any proceeding instituted in a Federal court by an application for a writ of habeas corpus by a person in custody pursuant to the judgment of a State court, a determination after a hearing on the merits of a factual issue, made by a State court of competent jurisdiction in a proceeding to which the applicant for the writ and the State or an officer or agent thereof were parties, evidenced by a written finding, written opinion, or other reliable and adequate written indicia, shall be presumed to be correct, unless the applicant shall establish or it shall otherwise appear, or the respondent shall admit—

(1) that the merits of the factual dispute were not resolved in the State court hearing;

(2) that the factfinding procedure employed by the State court was not adequate to afford a full and fair hearing;

(3) that the material facts were not adequately developed at the State court hearing;

(4) that the State court lacked jurisdiction of the subject matter or over the person of the applicant in the State court proceeding;

(5) that the applicant was an indigent and the State court, in deprivation of his constitutional right, failed to appoint counsel to represent him in the State court proceeding;

(6) that the applicant did not receive a full, fair, and adequate hearing in the State court proceeding; or

(7) that the applicant was otherwise denied due process of law in the State court proceeding;

(8) or unless that part of the record of the State court proceeding in which the determination of such factual issue was made, pertinent to a determination of the sufficiency of the evidence to support such factual determination, is produced as provided for hereinafter, and the Federal court on a consideration of such part of the record as a whole concludes that such factual determination is not fairly supported by the record:

And in an evidentiary hearing in the proceeding in the Federal court, when due proof of such factual determination has been made, unless the existence of one or more of the circumstances respectively set forth in paragraphs numbered (1) to (7), inclusive, is shown by the applicant, otherwise appears, or is admitted by the respondent, or unless the court concludes pursuant to the provisions of paragraph numbered (8) that the record in the State court proceeding, considered as a whole, does not fairly support such factual determination, the burden shall rest upon the applicant to establish by convincing evidence that the factual determination by the State court was erroneous.

(e) If the applicant challenges the sufficiency of the evidence adduced in such State court proceeding to support the State court's determination of a factual issue made therein, the applicant, if able, shall produce that part of the record pertinent to a determination of the sufficiency of the evidence to support such determination. If the applicant, because of indigency or other reason is unable to produce such part of the record, then the State shall produce such part of the record and the Federal court shall direct the State to do so by order directed to an appropriate State official.

If the State cannot provide such pertinent part of the record, then the court shall determine under the existing facts and circumstances what weight shall be given to the State court's factual determination.

(f) A copy of the official records of the State court, duly certified by the clerk of such court to be a true and correct copy of a finding, judicial opinion, or other reliable written indicia showing such a factual determination by the State court shall be admissible in the Federal court proceeding.

See also 28 U.S.C. § 2241, a statute under which federal prisoners may seek post-conviction relief.

The rules and law governing habeas corpus actions are quite complex and beyond the scope of this book. For further information on habeas corpus actions, see 3 J. Cook, Constitutional Rights of the Accused, ch. 24 (2d ed. & Supp.1989) and J. Liebman, Federal Habeas Corpus Practice and Procedure (1988 & Supp.1989).

2. OTHER REMEDIES

A state prisoner's treatment while in prison or the conditions of confinement at a correctional facility may give rise to state common-law claims for such torts as assault, battery, and negligence. Inmates may also be able to assert state statutory claims or claims under the state's constitution. These claims may be asserted in a lawsuit filed in state court or possibly as pendent claims in a § 1983 suit filed in federal court. But one of the impediments to a prisoner's prevailing on a state-law claim is the existence, in a number of states, of immunity statutes limiting the liability of correctional officials against whom prisoners have asserted state-law based claims. See, e.g., Ill.Rev.Stat. ch. 85, § 4–103 ("Neither a local public entity nor a public employee is liable for failure to provide a jail, detention, or correctional facility, or if such facility is provided, for failure to provide sufficient equipment, personnel, supervision or facilities therein. Nothing in this Section requires the periodic inspection of prisoners.")

A number of states as well as the Federal Bureau of Prisons have also set up administrative procedures through which a prisoner may prosecute a grievance against correctional officials. The United States Department of Justice has promulgated standards for inmate grievance procedures. 40 C.F.R. § 40 (1988). If the Attorney General certifies that a state's grievance procedures meet these standards, then inmates in that state generally have to first seek redress under these grievance procedures before seeking redress in a § 1983 action. See pages 592–593, supra.

*

Index

References are to Pages

613

†